INTRODUCING THE NEW TESTAMENT

INTRODUCING THE NEW TESTAMENT

A HISTORICAL, LITERARY, AND THEOLOGICAL SURVEY

SECOND EDITION

Mark Allan Powell

Baker Academic

a division of Baker Publishing Group
Grand Rapids, Michigan

© 2009, 2018 by Mark Allan Powell

Published by Baker Academic
a division of Baker Publishing Group
P.O. Box 6287, Grand Rapids, MI 49516-6287
www.bakeracademic.com

Printed in the United States of America

Library of Congress Cataloging-in-Publication Data
Names: Powell, Mark Allan, 1953– author.
Title: Introducing the New Testament : a historical, literary, and theological survey / Mark Allan Powell.
Description: Second Edition. | Grand Rapids : Baker Academic, 2018. | Includes bibliographical references and index.
Identifiers: LCCN 2017046791 | ISBN 9780801099601 (cloth : alk. paper)
Subjects: LCSH: Bible. New Testament—Introductions.
Classification: LCC BS2330.3 .P67 2018 | DDC 225.6/1—dc23
LC record available at https://lccn.loc.gov/2017046791

All maps are based upon originals created by International Mapping.

Interior design by Brian Brunsting, Baker Publishing Group

21   22   23   24   7   6   5   4

For Missy Baby

I love you

Contents

Maps

Preface

Welcome to the New Testament! You probably are a student at a college, university, or seminary. Perhaps you are taking this course because you are really interested in learning more about these Christian writings, or perhaps you just need the class to meet a requirement. Either way, my intent in writing this book is to help you have an interesting, enjoyable, and intellectually rewarding experience.

The New Testament is a fascinating book. And, whatever your experience with it has been up to now, an academic encounter in an educational setting is sure to open your eyes to ideas and concepts that you have not considered previously. Some will be provocative, some might be inspiring, a few could be exasperating, but not many will be boring. Bottom line: this should be a good class.

Let's take a quick overview of this book. A few chapters deal with general topics (e.g., the world of the New Testament, the life and thought of Paul), but most of the book deals directly with the New Testament writings themselves. A typical chapter takes one of the New Testament books and offers you three things:

- a brief overview of the book's contents
- a discussion of historical background questions: Who wrote the book? Where? When? Why?
- a presentation of major themes: What is the message of the book? What topics in this book have interested people the most over the years?

Now let me note a few things that are distinctive about this particular New Testament introduction, things that might set it apart from other textbooks that you have used (and from other New Testament introductions).

The Chapters Can Be Read in Almost Any Order

I think that the book works quite nicely if it is simply read in the manner in which it was written, taking up each part of the New Testament in its canonical order (i.e., the order in which the writings appear in modern editions of the New Testament). But many professors will want to introduce the chapters in a different order, and they may have good reasons for doing so. Here are a few ideas:

- Some may want to read the chapter on Mark before the chapter on Matthew because they think that Mark was the first Gospel to be written. It is also the shortest of the four Gospels and, for that reason, can make a good "starter Gospel" for beginning students.
- Some may want to read the chapters on Luke and Acts back to back because those two New Testament books were probably written by the same person.
- Some may want to read the chapters on Ephesians and Colossians or on Jude and 2 Peter back to back. In both of these pairs the two books appear to be related to each other and often are treated as "literary siblings."
- Some may want to read the chapters on Paul's letters before reading the chapters on the Gospels because, chronologically, Paul's letters were written before any of the Gospels.

There are other possible variations. The point is, don't freak out if your professor scrambles the book and directs you to read chapters out of order. The book was designed to work that way, and your professor (probably) knows what she or he is doing.

The Book Urges Engagement of Ideas but Does Not Attempt to Resolve Disputes

The book is somewhat unique in its approach. The standard practice for a New Testament textbook is for the author to (1) present questions and controversies that have arisen concerning the New Testament documents, (2) describe various positions that have been taken regarding these issues, and (3) tell the student which ideas and positions ought to be accepted (i.e., which views are correct in the mind of the author). I have omitted this third step, not because I have no opinions about such matters but because as a teacher I don't usually find it helpful for a textbook to make such determinations for me (or for my students). I assume that your professor will offer you some guidance with regard to evaluating the different ideas and will do so in a manner appropriate to the particular academic environment in which you are using this book. Such assessments are made differently in different contexts (a Protestant Bible college, a

Roman Catholic seminary, a state university): different principles, priorities, and presuppositions come into play, and what counts as convincing evidence in one setting might commend less attention in another. In any case, the goal of this book is engagement, not indoctrination. However, if we should ever meet, I will be happy to tell you what I think you should believe about all sorts of things!

The Book Draws on the Rich Resources of Christian Art

You probably have already noticed this book's extensive use of artwork—assuming you were not so intrigued by this preface that you took to reading it before looking at anything else. This book contains the usual maps and historical photos that characterize conventional New Testament introductions, but it also offers about 150 reproductions of artwork from many lands and many centuries. Why?

- I hope that these illustrations have aesthetic appeal and make your use of the textbook more pleasant. Life should be pleasant—or at least as pleasant as it can be—and studying is not always the most pleasurable of pursuits. Perhaps the art will help. There's not much in the art that you will have to learn for tests at any rate, so be grateful for that.
- The individual works illustrate key themes or points that are made in the book or in the New Testament writings themselves. They have not been chosen haphazardly; each work corresponds to a motif or concept or illustrates some particular point that is discussed. Sometimes this is obvious; other times you might not get it at first ("What's this in here for?"). Think about it, ask someone else, let the art inspire reflection and conversation.
- I hope that the art will convey something of the *influence* of these writings—the importance of the New Testament to history and to culture. Much of the art looks very old; some looks very new. Some pieces are representational; others are abstract. Some are Western; others Eastern. Some you may like; others not so much. Taken together, they illustrate the range of the New Testament's spatial, temporal, cultural, and aesthetic impact on our world. They depict its appeal, which helps to explain why we are studying such a book in the first place.

The Book Has a Companion Website That Features Numerous Additional Resources

The website (www.IntroducingNT.com) accompanying this book is filled with materials that you may find useful in this course and beyond. If you like, you can print and reproduce many of these materials for use in teaching the New Testament to others, should you find yourself in a position to do that.

A few of these items are indicated by ⊙ EXPLORE references printed in the margin of the text—those references alert you that something is available at the website that pertains to the topic under discussion. But you really want to go to the website to see everything that is available.

⊙ EXPLORE
Sample

The materials there are of different sorts:

- All the various boxes in the book itself are also on the website. Thus if you want to use one of those items as a handout in some context, you may simply print the item from the website (rather than trying to photocopy from the book).
- Many additional items that could have been boxes in the book are also on the website. I had too many to put in the book itself, and I thought that readers might like to have some of these materials as extras.
- Several long pieces presenting short essays or in-depth discussion of matters are included on the website. These provide further content regarding matters that are touched on only briefly in the book.
- Bibliographies for the various books of the New Testament and related topics discussed in the text are on the website. These will help the student who wants to do advanced study or write a term paper.
- The website's multimedia resources, including videos, maps, and interactive learning tools, illustrate and reinforce key material from the book.
- And, although most of the ⊙ EXPLORE materials are educational (this *is* a textbook), I have also included quite a few items that I think are just interesting or fun.

The website also features

- study aids, such as chapter summaries, chapter objectives, study questions, flash cards, and self-quizzes;
- instructor resources, including PowerPoint chapter outlines, discussion prompts, pedagogical suggestions, and a test/quiz bank.

Acknowledgments and an Exciting Announcement

Those who appreciate this book and find it of value in their study of the New Testament owe a debt of gratitude to Trinity Lutheran Seminary, the fine institution where I teach. Community leaders at Trinity provided me with time and resources to complete this project, and they did so for no other reason than that they are committed to furthering theological and biblical education. Likewise, those who appreciate this book should be grateful to many good people associated with Baker Academic: James Kinney and James Ernest had the vision for this project that culminated in the highly successful first edition of the work; Brian Bolger served as project manager; Rachel Klompmaker secured rights for most of the artwork; and Jeremy Wells developed the website. Kinney, Bolger, and Wells continued their service for this new edition, and they were joined by textbook specialist Christina Jasko, who had primary responsibility for the greatly expanded website, and acquisitions assistant Brandy Scritchfield, who obtained rights for the artwork and other wonderful images. Join me in offering thanks to all these people.

Exciting announcement: Baker Academic is preparing a Spanish version of this book, and when it becomes available, los que pueden leer un poco de español deben obtenerlo y leer todo de nuevo para practicar.

I think that's it for now. Why are you reading a preface? Shouldn't you be studying?

1

New Testament Background

The Roman World

The world of the New Testament can be a strange place for the uninitiated. People beat their breasts (Luke 18:13; 23:48), tear their clothing (Mark 14:63), speak in tongues (Acts 2:4–13; 1 Cor. 14), and wash one another's feet (John 13:3–15). Some people wear phylacteries, which Jesus thinks should be narrow, not broad (Matt. 23:5). When people eat, they don't sit at a table; they lie on the floor (John 13:23, 25). When they want to elect an important leader, they don't take a vote; they cast lots (Acts 1:26).

This world is often a harsh one by our standards. When a woman wants to make a request of a man, she kneels in the dirt and waits for him to call on her (Matt. 20:20); when a man defaults on a debt, his wife and children are sold into slavery (Matt. 18:25). It is a brutal world, one in which thieves can be nailed naked to wooden poles and hung up in public where people can watch them slowly die (Mark 15:27). It is a world in which some people think that a woman who commits adultery should be hauled out into the street and pelted with rocks until she is dead (John 8:2–5).

It is also a world filled with surprising tenderness and dignity. People speak freely and affectionately of how deeply they love one another (Phil. 1:3–8; 4:1). Families are valued, friendships are treasured, and hospitality to strangers can almost be taken for granted. It is a world where faith, hope, and love are primary values (1 Cor. 13:13) and where the retention or attainment of honor trumps all other goals in life. This is also a world with a finely tuned moral compass, with some widely accepted notions of what constitutes virtue and what constitutes vice (see, e.g., Rom. 1:29–31; 13:13; 1 Cor. 5:10–11; 6:9–10; 2 Cor. 6:6–7; Gal. 5:19–23).

phylactery: a small case containing texts of Scripture worn on the forehead or left arm by pious Jews in obedience to Exodus 13:9, 16; Deuteronomy 6:8; 11:18.

casting lots: a practice akin to "drawing straws," used to select a person for a given task; "lots" were marked stones similar to dice (see Acts 1:26).

All the books of the New Testament were written by people whom we would call Christians, so in order to understand them, we have to know a few things about what these Christians believed: what they valued, what they feared, how they lived. But, to be a bit more specific, all the books of the New Testament were written by Roman Christians—that is, Christians who lived in the Roman Empire. Furthermore, even though all these books were written *by* Christians, not all were written *about* Christians. Jesus, John the Baptist, the Virgin Mary, and many other celebrated New Testament personalities were not Christians, but Jews. To be more specific, they were Roman Jews—that is, Jews who lived in the Roman Empire.

To understand the New Testament, then, we must know about three different worlds: the Christian world, the Jewish world, and the Roman world. In all of the New Testament writings, these three worlds overlap.

Map 1.1. The
Roman Empire.

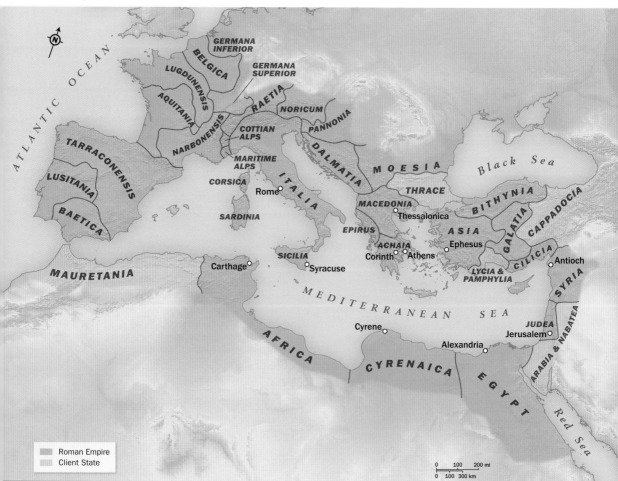

Roman Rule during the Christian Era

BCE: an abbreviation meaning "before the common era"; in academic studies BCE is typically used for dates in place of BC ("before Christ").

CE: an abbreviation meaning "common era"; in academic studies CE is typically used for dates in place of AD (*anno Domini*, "in the year of our Lord").

Jesus was born during the reign of the first great Roman emperor, Caesar Augustus (27 BCE–14 CE), and he conducted his ministry during the reign of the next emperor, Tiberius (14–37 CE). Rome is a long way from Jerusalem, but the emperor's presence was always felt. Later, as Christianity moved out into the world around the Mediterranean Sea, the new faith came to the attention of the emperors in ways that invited direct engagement. For example, the Roman historian Suetonius reports that the emperor Claudius expelled Jews from Rome around 49 CE due to a disturbance over someone known as "Chrestus" (probably a mangled reference to Christ). Claudius's successor, Nero, violently persecuted Christians, murdering them in sadistic ways that generally repulsed the Roman public.

For Jesus and his followers in Palestine, however, the local Roman rulers had more immediate relevance than the emperors in faraway Rome. When the Romans conquered a country, they typically set up a king, governor, or some other ruler in the land, but they also tried to preserve some institutions of native rule. Thus, according to the New Testament, a council of Jewish leaders, the Sanhedrin, had authority in Jerusalem in some matters (Mark 14:55–64; Acts 5:21–40), but the Roman authorities always had the final say (cf. John 18:31). Some knowledge of these Roman authorities is important for understanding the New Testament, so here we look briefly at some of these rulers.

Herod the Great

Herod the Great ruled all of Palestine from 37 to 4 BCE. He was first appointed king by Marc Antony but was later confirmed in that position by Antony's arch-rival, Caesar Augustus. The fact that he attained support from both of these rival leaders indicates that he was adept at political maneuvering (switching sides at exactly the right time). Herod would also become known as a master builder; his projects included a harbor at Caesarea and a number of fortresses (including Masada, Machaerus, and the Herodium). He rebuilt the ancient city of Samaria into the Greek metropolis Sebaste and, perhaps most important, was responsible for expanding and refurbishing the Jewish temple in Jerusalem. At the time of Jesus, this "Herodian temple" was regarded as one of the seven wonders of the ancient world; its pinnacle was the highest architectural point in the world.

> **Box 1.1**
>
> ### *Herod and the Temple*
>
> The Jewish Roman historian Josephus reports, "In the fifteenth year of his reign, (Herod) restored the temple and, by erecting new foundation-walls, enlarged the surrounding area to double its former extent. The expenditure devoted to this work was incalculable, its magnificence never surpassed" (*Jewish War* 1.401).
>
> Josephus, *Jewish War: Books 1–2*, trans. H. St. J. Thackeray, Loeb Classical Library (Cambridge, MA: Harvard University Press, 1927), §1.401.

Map 1.2. Palestine in the time of Jesus.

Fig. 1.1. Herod the baby-killer. Herod the Great will always be remembered for "the massacre of the innocents" described in Matthew 2:1–18 and portrayed in this fifth-century fresco from Verona (northern Italy). The story is not mentioned in any other ancient record, but historians agree that it seems in keeping with the sort of atrocities for which the otherwise capable ruler was renowned. (Bridgeman Images)

Ethnically an Idumean, Herod was considered to be "half-Jewish," but he was viewed by the Jewish people as a foreigner and a Roman collaborator. Though Herod the Great appears to have been a competent ruler in many respects, he was famously paranoid to the point that he actually inspired a Roman proverb attributed to Caesar Augustus: "Better to be a pig than a son in the house of Herod" (the Romans found it humorous that Herod did not eat pork but did kill three of his children when he suspected them of wanting to usurp his throne). Herod also murdered his Jewish wife, Mariamne, when he suspected her of plotting against him, and this incident inspired numerous legends (e.g., tales of how he remained hopelessly in love with her and/or was haunted by her ghost). Herod was ruler of Palestine at the time Jesus was born (Matt. 2:1), and he remains known to Christians for the biblical story in which he confronts the magi and orders a massacre of babies in Bethlehem (Matt. 2:1–18).

magi: astrologers or sorcerers associated with Persian religion.

⊙ EXPLORE 1.3
Roman Emperors of the New Testament Period

⊙ EXPLORE 1.4
Roman Rulers in Palestine: New Testament References

Herod Antipas

Herod Antipas ruled Perea and Galilee from 4 BCE to 39 CE. In Roman literature he is often referred to simply as "Antipas," but the New Testament Gospels consistently call him "Herod," and this can lead to some confusion, since Herod the Great is also called "Herod" in the New Testament. In any

Fig. 1.2. Death of a prophet. Mark 6:14–29 tells the story of a gruesome banquet in which Herod Antipas provides his stepdaughter with "the head of John the Baptist on a platter" after her mother, Herodias, prompts her to request this as a reward for pleasing the drunken ruler with her dancing. (Bridgeman Images)

tetrarch: a ruler of a quarter of a province or region.

case, Herod Antipas ruled less territory than did Herod the Great (whose lands were divided when he died), and he was only a tetrarch, not a king. Still, his tenure was a long one, and it included the entire time of Jesus's life and ministry in Galilee.

About the time Jesus began his public ministry, John the Baptist criticized Antipas for marrying his niece Herodias, who was already married to a different uncle. Antipas had John arrested and, later, beheaded at Herodias's request (Mark 6:14–29). Luke's Gospel reports that Antipas also took an ominous interest in Jesus, who refers to the ruler as a "fox" (13:31–33)—probably a reference to his penchant for violence (the Jews considered foxes to be rapacious animals that would kill not only for food but also for sport). According to Luke, Antipas heard speculation that Jesus might be John the Baptist raised from the dead (9:7–9), and he examined Jesus briefly when he was arrested in Jerusalem, hoping to see Jesus perform a miracle (23:6–12).

Pontius Pilate

Pontius Pilate ruled Judea as a prefect or procurator from 26 to 36 CE. He was, in essence, a governor who served as the representative of Caesar. Pilate is portrayed in some literature (notably the writings of Philo of Alexandria) as a cruel ruler who hated the Jews and did not understand their religion. Some scholars think that this vilification is perhaps exaggerated, but many reports do indicate that Pilate's term in office was marred by episodes of conflict and violence. During his first week in power he sought to install imperial banners in Jerusalem, which precipitated a crisis among Jews, who saw the banners as idolatrous. Embarrassed, Pilate removed the banners in response to virulent protest and threats of riot. He later used temple funds to finance an aqueduct, and this precipitated more protests, but this time he did not back down; he sent soldiers (disguised as civilians) into the crowd of protesters and, at a pre-arranged signal, had them beat and kill people at random. The New Testament reports that Pilate was the governor who sentenced Jesus to be crucified while also declaring him to be innocent (Matt. 27:1–26; Mark 15:1–15; Luke 23; John 18:28–19:26). Some years later, Pilate was recalled after using extreme force to suppress a religious revival led by a Samaritan prophet. Two more procurators of Judea figure in later New Testament stories: Felix (53–60 CE) and Festus (60–62 CE), both of whom kept Paul imprisoned in Caesarea and presided over his hearings there (Acts 23–25).

Herod Agrippa I

Herod Agrippa I ruled Galilee (like Herod Antipas) from 37 to 41 CE and then became king over all of Palestine (like his grandfather Herod the Great) from 41 to 44 CE. He is also simply called "Herod" in the New Testament, which can be confusing for readers who do not realize there are three different people who bear that name; also, the person

prefect: in the Roman Empire, a magistrate or high official whose duties and level of authority varied in different contexts.

procurator: a governor appointed by the Roman emperor to administer a province for an indefinite period of time.

⊙ EXPLORE 1.12
Pontius Pilate in History and Ancient Literature

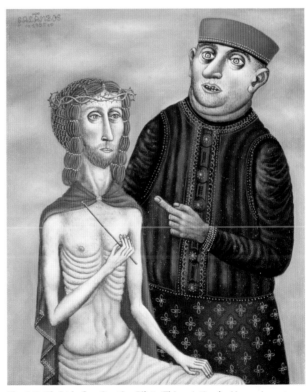

Fig. 1.3. *Christ before Pontius Pilate.* This painting by Hungarian artist Tamas Galambos tries to capture the contrast between the tranquil power of an ascetic Jesus (wasted away from a life of self-denial) and the pomposity of Roman rule, evident in Pontius Pilate. (Bridgeman Images)

Fig. 1.4. *The Triumph of Truth.* This work, by nineteenth-century Italian artist Luigi Mussini, celebrates the victory of philosophy and science over superstition and ignorance—a viewpoint that would sometimes be used to justify colonialism (anticipated here in the submission of the African). The empires of Greece and Rome justified their conquests in a similar manner, as they brought Hellenistic enlightenment to cultures regarded as primitive and undeveloped. (Mondadori Portfolio / Art Resource, NY)

called "Agrippa" in Acts 25:13–26:32 is not Herod Agrippa I but is a later ruler of Galilee whom historians call "Herod Agrippa II." Herod Agrippa I was a politically popular and successful ruler, but he persecuted the fledgling Christian movement in Jerusalem, putting Jesus's disciple James to death and imprisoning Peter (Acts 12:1–3). He ultimately met with a somewhat gruesome death, which the New Testament attributes to divine wrath (Acts 12:20–23).

Philosophy and Religion in the Roman World

Everyone who lived in the world that produced the New Testament was influenced directly or indirectly by different patterns of thought that the Greeks and Romans brought to the lands that they subdued and occupied. The people of this era were heirs to the three greatest Greek philosophers—Socrates (ca. 470–ca. 399 BCE), Plato (ca. 428–ca. 348 BCE), and Aristotle (384–322 BCE)—and to some extent the thinking of most people was shaped by what these masters had

⊙ EXPLORE 1.7
Major Philosophical
Schools

taught. Indeed, the case could be made that the thinking of most people today is still shaped by the ideas expounded and explored by these influential thinkers.

New Testament scholars focus more attention, however, on certain philosophical movements that were popular during the period in which the New Testament documents were written. These include the following:

- Cynicism—a philosophical orientation that emphasized radical authenticity, repudiation of shame, simplicity of lifestyle, and a desire to possess only what is obtained naturally and freely
- Epicureanism—a philosophical orientation that emphasized free will, questioned fate, and encouraged the attainment of true pleasure through avoidance of anxiety, concentration on the present, and enjoyment of all things in moderation
- Platonism—a philosophical orientation that emphasized the reality of a transcendent world of "ideals" standing behind everything physical or earthly
- Pythagoreanism—a philosophical orientation that emphasized the value of intelligent reasoning, memory, and radical honesty, all in service of a quest to attain harmony of ideas and of body and soul
- Stoicism—a philosophical orientation that emphasized the attainment of virtue through acceptance of fate, based on the notion that all things are predetermined and that there is logic to all that transpires

New Testament scholars detect the influence of these philosophical schools in various ways. Paul is depicted as interacting with Epicurean and Stoic philosophers in Acts 17:16–34, but the impact of Greek and Roman philosophy can be detected even when there is no reason to suspect direct contact. Josephus, a first-century Jewish Roman historian, thought that the Essenes (who produced the Dead Sea Scrolls) were analogous to Pythagoreans and that the Pharisees had much in common with Stoics. Likewise, many modern scholars have noted similarities between the first followers of Jesus and Cynic philosophers (e.g., in their renunciation of materialism and worldly status). Several letters in the New Testament (including 1 Corinthians, Galatians, and James) make use of the "diatribe" and other forms of rhetorical argument that were popular among Cynic and Stoic philosophers. The Letter to the Hebrews is often read as an engagement with Platonic philosophy, and the concept of the "Logos" in John 1:1–18 also owes much to that school of thought. The "banquet talks" that Jesus gives in Luke's Gospel (7:44–46; 14:7–14) and the lengthy discourses that he offers in the Gospel of John (5:19–47; 6:25–70; 7:14–52; 8:12–59; 10:1–18, 22–39; 12:23–36; 14:1–16:33) are similar in style and content to writings of various philosophical schools.

Essenes: ascetic, separatist Jews who lived in private communities.

Dead Sea Scrolls: a collection of Jewish documents copied and preserved between 250 BCE and 70 CE.

diatribe: a rhetorical device derived from Greek philosophy in which an author argues with an imaginary opponent by proposing objections and then responding to them.

Of course, not everyone in the Roman world would have identified as a follower of one of these particular schools. Jewish peasants in Palestine may not have known one system from another. Still, these philosophies represent the sort of thinking that was "in the air" at the time. They represent efforts to answer questions that virtually everyone wondered about: What is the purpose or goal or highest good in life? Is everything predetermined, or can people make choices that affect how their lives turn out? Is there life beyond death? What is the secret of happiness? Even uneducated people in far-flung corners of the empire (e.g., Galilean fishermen or shepherds or carpenters) tended to think about things like this and to orient themselves in a manner more compatible with one philosophical system than with others. Naturally, people then (as now) could also be eclectic and inconsistent, simultaneously holding to notions derived from schools that the philosophers themselves might not have considered compatible.

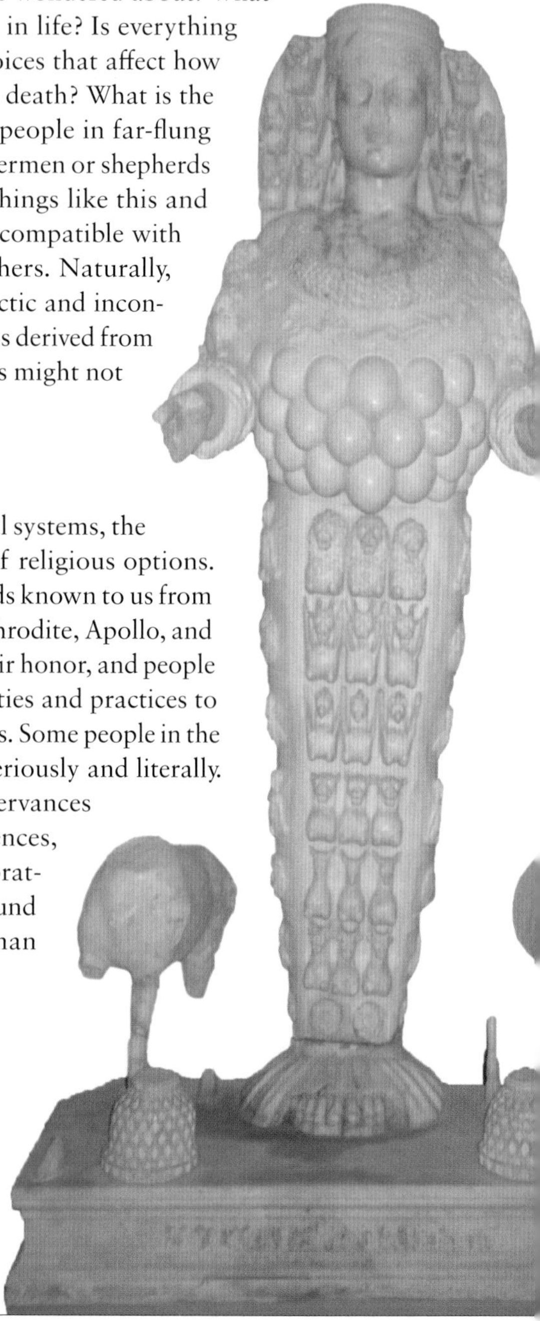

Roman Religion

In addition to the major philosophical systems, the Roman world offered a smorgasbord of religious options. There were, first of all, the numerous gods known to us from Greek and Roman mythology (Zeus, Aphrodite, Apollo, and others). Most of these had temples in their honor, and people were invited to engage in various festivities and practices to earn the gods' favor or celebrate their gifts. Some people in the empire appear to have taken this very seriously and literally. For others, the ostensibly religious observances were more social and symbolic experiences, something akin to modern people celebrating Christmas with rituals designed around the Santa Claus story. Thus when Roman

Fig. 1.5. Artemis. One of the more popular deities of the ancient world, the goddess Artemis was especially revered in Ephesus. A mother goddess, Artemis is easily recognizable by the numerous globes on her chest. These are usually thought to be breasts, although an alternative theory holds that they could be eggs. Either way, Artemis was regarded as a provider of fertility and as an overseer of children. See also fig. 17.2. (Craig Koester)

⊙ EXPLORE 1.8
Artemis of the
Ephesians

pagans converted to Christianity, there was some question as to whether purely social observances connected with pagan mythology were incompatible with their new faith. Some Roman Christians saw nothing wrong with celebrating traditional festivals inspired by stories of mythical gods, whom they knew to be unreal. Other Christians (like most Jews) saw this as a dire compromise.

Something similar probably applied to emperor worship. The Roman emperors often were identified as divine figures to whom appropriate homage was due. In popular piety, various miracles and divine benefits were attributed to the emperors. Beyond this, however, no real "religion" developed around the emperors: what Jews and Christians regarded as "worship" of emperors, most Romans saw as simple acts of patriotism (analogous to pledging allegiance to a flag). The Romans rarely understood why Christians refused to pay such homage to Caesar.

The Roman world also featured a wide variety of cults that modern scholars identify as "mystery religions." The mystery religions were organized around gods and goddesses from various mythologies: Demeter, Dionysius, Orpheus, Cybele, Astarte (Ishtar), and Artemis (Diana) were particularly popular. They differed from one another but always involved participation in secret rites, such as ritual washings, common meals, and sometimes sexual rites related to concerns for fertility (of crops or of humans). The secret knowledge that was obtained allowed the devotees to bond with the god or goddess in this life and to establish an intimate connection that would continue in the world beyond death. We know that these religions were popular, but we know little about them because their practitioners deliberately kept their ideas and practices secret. What reports we do have might be hyperbolic accounts based on speculation and rumor. After all, Christianity was regarded as a mystery religion by some Romans when it first appeared, and early reports concerning Christian worship included allegations of orgies and cannibalism—probably because the Christians called their eucharistic meal a "love feast" and talked about "eating the body of Christ."

Finally, it might be helpful to mention a few other areas of spiritual interest that were so widespread in the New Testament world that they need not be connected with any one particular religion.

Animism

There was widespread belief in the existence of spirits, good and bad, and in the possibility that these spirits could possess people and animals. They could also dwell in rocks, trees, streams, and other phenomena. The common perception was that such spirits interacted with the world of nature—for example, storms at sea were caused by water sprites; diseases were caused by demonic possession. As a result of these beliefs, protective amulets often were

pagans: nonconverted gentiles, often associated by Jews and Christians with idolatry, polytheism, erratic religious beliefs, and an immoral lifestyle.

fertility: the ability to produce offspring; used of humans able to conceive children, or of fields able to produce crops.

eucharistic meal or Eucharist: from a Greek word meaning "thanksgiving"; the Christian rite or sacrament also known as the "Lord's Supper" or "Holy Communion."

Fig. 1.6. Animism. In the Roman world it was commonly believed that trees, rocks, rivers, and other natural phenomena were inhabited by spirits. (Bridgeman Images)

worn by people from all social classes, and magical potions and spells were used to influence or manipulate the spirits into doing one's bidding. The city of Ephesus appears to have been a center for these magical arts (see Acts 19:11–21). Along these same lines, we should note that virtually everyone in the New Testament world believed in ghosts (spirits of the departed); some tried to contact them.

Augury and Divination

There was great interest in knowing the future: dreams, visions, and other portents could reveal the future, but an interpreter might be needed to know their meaning. Priests known as augurs tried to determine the will of the gods by observing flight patterns or eating habits of birds (the "auspices"). Professional oracles, usually women, claimed to have the ability to predict the future for those who sought them out (and performed required services). The most famous of these was at Delphi in Greece. Astrology was also practiced, offering predictions of the future (and attendant advice for the present) based on the observation of stars, which were believed to be deities affecting earthly events.

divination: any practice used to discern the will of divine beings and/or to predict the future.

oracle: a person, usually female, capable of receiving messages from the gods in response to particular queries, including questions about the future.

Supernaturalism

There was common acknowledgment among most people in the Roman world that what we might regard as supernatural events could and did occur: what we deem impossible, they considered extraordinary. Miracles often were attributed to individuals who seemed to have an especially close link to the spiritual realm; a person believed to have such a link was called a *theios anēr* ("divine man"). Examples of such "divine men" include Honi the Circle Drawer (a Jewish teacher from the first century BCE) and Apollonius of Tyana (a Greek philosopher from the first century CE). Jesus, who lived in between the lifetimes of these two individuals, no doubt would have been regarded as a *theios anēr* by Romans who heard the miracle stories reported in the New Testament.

Interestingly, while women were more likely to be regarded as oracles who could predict the future, most miracle-workers were men.

On the Horizon: Gnosticism

One of the more significant developments for Christianity in the second century was the emergence of gnosticism, a religious movement or perspective that appealed to many Christians and became the bane of many prominent church leaders who sought to defend the orthodox faith from what they called the "gnostic heresy." Gnosticism is difficult to define because as a religious and ideological phenomenon it took many forms and had many different expressions (think, for instance, of how difficult it would be to define exactly what is meant by "new age" religion or thinking today). Gnosticism also demonstrated a remarkable capacity for integration with different religions and philosophies: there were gnostic Jews, gnostic Christians, and gnostic pagans. Ultimately, however, the marriage of gnosticism and Christianity proved especially effective, and throughout the second, third, and fourth centuries gnostic versions of Christianity constituted the primary alternatives to what we usually think of as "mainstream" Christianity. There were hundreds of gnostic Christian churches, complete with their own clergy, bishops, liturgies, and all the other accoutrements of any organized religious system. The gnostics also wrote their own gospels, telling stories about Jesus in ways that reflected their particular interests and then backdating the books by falsely attributing them to Jesus's disciples or close acquaintances. A library of gnostic writings was discovered in Egypt at Nag Hammadi in 1945, and the availability of that literature has greatly enhanced our understanding of Christian diversity.

All the various expressions of gnostic thought derive from a radically dualistic attitude that regards "spirit" as fundamentally good and "matter" as fundamentally evil. Thus the physical world in general and individual human bodies in particular are understood to be material prisons in which divine souls or spirits have been trapped. The most prevalent form of gnosticism known to us held that the world was created by an evil or at least inferior god known as the Demiurge. Human beings are basically eternal spirits that were captured by the Demiurge and are now being confined in bodies of flesh and in a world of matter. Gnostic Christians believed that Christ had come as a spiritual redeemer (disguised as a human being) to impart secret knowledge (Greek, *gnōsis*). This knowledge enables the enlightened to be liberated from their material existence and to realize their true identities as spiritual beings. The implications of such a belief system for life in this world varied dramatically. Many (probably most) gnostics held that liberation from the flesh involved renunciation of bodily pleasures and material concerns: they encouraged virginity, celibacy, fasting, strict

heresy: false teaching, or teaching that does not conform to the official standards of a religious community.

dualistic: exhibiting the tendency to separate phenomena into sharply opposed categories.

Fig. 1.7. Roman cities. These images portray reconstructions of Roman cities in New Testament times. *Above*, the city of Rome, capital of the empire; *below*, Caesarea, a coastal city in Judea. See also figs. 10.4; 13.1; 14.1; 17.2; 18.1. (Balage Balogh / www.archaeologyillustrated.com)

diets, and other aspects of an ascetic and austere lifestyle that would enable them to become more spiritual. But other gnostics drew the opposite conclusion: they engaged freely in all manner of wanton excesses on the grounds that since the spirit is all that matters, what one does with the flesh is completely irrelevant.

ascetic: religiously strict or severe, especially with regard to self-denial or renunciation of worldly pleasures.

We need to emphasize that gnosticism appears to be a development of the second, third, and fourth centuries; there is no evidence that the movement as such had any traction at the time when events reported in the New Testament were occurring or when the books of the New Testament were being written. Nevertheless, historical scholars do not think that a movement such as this one simply appeared fully formed in the middle of the second century; the assumption is that the ideas and tendencies that would later define gnosticism must have been present earlier. Thus it has become common for New Testament scholars to speak of an almost invisible and largely unidentified "proto-gnosticism" as part of the milieu that made up the New Testament world. The apostle Paul writes about the distinction between "what is of the flesh" and "what is of the spirit" (Rom. 8:4–13; Gal. 5:16–26; 6:8). The Gospel of John and the Johannine Letters emphasize that Jesus was not just a spiritual being but rather a man with a body of actual flesh (John 1:14; 1 John 4:2). Texts such as these (there are many more) seem to indicate that gnosticism was "on the horizon": people were already thinking about the kinds of things that gnosticism would seek to address, sometimes in ways that were compatible with the New Testament documents and sometimes in ways that were radically distinct from those writings.

Social Systems and Cultural Values

Understanding the New Testament world also involves getting to know the mind-set of the people for whom these documents were first written. In recent years New Testament scholarship has become more attentive to identifying the unwritten social codes for this world—matters that may have been so pervasive they could simply be taken for granted. Some of these topics will be discussed more thoroughly in the chapters that follow. A few deserve mention here.

Wealth and Poverty

The Roman Empire was characterized by grotesque economic inequality. There was nothing comparable to what we would call a "middle class"; for the most part, people were either extremely rich (about 3 percent of the population) or extremely poor (about 90 percent). Most of those who belonged to the latter group lived at or near a subsistence level, making just enough to survive, with little hope of saving anything that would allow them to improve

⊙ EXPLORE 2.8
Commerce in the New Testament Period

their position or provide them with a hedge against calamity. The more fortunate of these impoverished persons might at least learn a trade (as was apparently the case with Jesus, his disciples, and the apostle Paul), but for many people in rural areas "subsistence" meant living off the land, and so life was subject to the vicissitudes of agriculture. Thus for the least fortunate—beggars, widows, orphans, prisoners, unskilled day laborers—survival itself may frequently have been in question. Modern estimates suggest that about 28 percent of the population of the Roman Empire during New Testament times lived below subsistence level, meaning that such people did not know from day to day whether they would be able to obtain those things necessary to sustain life.

Given the extremes of such a situation, attitudes toward wealth and poverty were a significant part of the social world. Some religious people at the time of Jesus believed that wealth could be viewed as a sign of God's blessing and that poverty could be understood as a consequence of divine displeasure. It is difficult, however, to know how widespread this notion was. What seems more certain is that virtually everyone in this time period held to what is now called a theory of "limited good." People believed that money and the things that money can buy were in short (or at least finite) supply; the common perception—in stark contrast to modern capitalism—was that acquisition of wealth or resources by some necessitated depletion of wealth or resources for others. Simply put, virtually everyone in New Testament times believed that there was only so much "stuff" to go around and that some people had less than they needed because other people had more than they needed.

Patronage and Loyalty

Roman society (in Palestine and everywhere else) functioned in accord with strong expectations regarding benefaction and obligation. At the simplest level, the exchange of favors was virtually definitive of friendship. "Friends" were people who did things for one another, and even though no one was supposed to keep score, the assistance and support would have to be mutual over the long term or else the friendship would break down. At another level, however, almost all people were involved in patron-client relationships with people who were not their social equals. Very few people had money or power, but those who did were expected to serve as benefactors for those who did not. The wealthy might, for instance, allow peasants to live on their land or provide them with food or grain or employment. In sociological terms, such benefactors are called "patrons," and the recipients of the benefits are called "clients." In such a relationship the exchange of favors could not be mutual, but the clients were expected to offer their patron what they could: gratitude and, above all, loyalty.

patron-client relationship: a social system according to which people with power serve as benefactors to those lacking power.

They were expected to praise their patron, to speak well of their patron, and to enhance his or her social reputation. They were expected to trust their patron to continue providing for them. And, as necessary, they were expected to perform various services that the patron might request of them. Such relationships were not constituted legally, but at a basic level they represented how most people thought the world was supposed to work and, indeed, how it usually did work.

Patron-client relationships would form a significant backdrop for the development of Christian theology. The term most often used for the patron's bestowal of benefits is *charis* (typically translated as "grace" in the New Testament), and the term that is often used for the client's expected attitude of loyalty toward his or her patron is *pistis* (often translated as "faith" in the New Testament). Thus the phenomenon of patron-client relationships seems to have served as a rough analogy for divine-human encounters in which the constitutive elements are grace and faith: God gives to people freely and generously (grace), and this arouses within people an appropriate response of trust, devotion, and willingness to serve (faith).

Honor and Shame

The pivotal social value in the New Testament world (among Greeks, Romans, Jews, and everyone else) was honor—that is, the status that one has in the eyes of those whose opinions one considers to be significant. To some extent, honor was ascribed through factors beyond an individual's control: age, gender, nationality, ethnicity, height, physical health, economic class, and the like could set certain parameters that defined the limits of how much honor one could hope to attain. Given such limitations, however, many things might increase one's honor (religious piety, courage, virtuous behavior, a congenial or charitable disposition, etc.), and many things might precipitate a loss of honor or even bring its opposite, shame.

Such a value system may not seem strange to us because even in modern Western society everyone likes to receive honor and nobody wants to be put to shame. The difference, however, could be one of magnitude: the New Testament world was one in which honor was to be prized above all else and shame was to be avoided at all costs. For example, people wanted to be wealthy not primarily because wealth would enable them to live in luxury but because almost everyone believed that it was honorable to have money to spare. Likewise, it was shameful to be needy; Ben Sira, a prominent Jewish teacher of the Second Temple period taught that "it is better to die than to beg" (Sir. 40:28). He said this not because begging was immoral or sinful but because it was disgraceful, and life without honor is not worth living. Everyone in Jesus's day (including beggars) probably believed this.

Fig. 1.8. Shame. In the New Testament world shame was not just a temporary emotional response (like embarrassment) but rather an overriding psychological status according to which one lived in disgrace and was considered to be unworthy of divine or human attention (or even of life itself). Cowards, failures, and fools lived in shame, as did tax collectors, lepers, beggars, and prostitutes. Compare the use of nakedness to display shame here with the nineteenth-century depiction of Truth in fig. 1.4. (Bridgeman Images)

The language of honor and shame is found throughout the New Testament. Some voices in the New Testament seize on the language to present faithfulness as a path to achieving honor and avoiding shame (1 Pet. 1:7; 2:6). Other voices seek to overturn the conventional wisdom regarding how those values are applied, claiming, for instance, that it is more honorable to behave like a servant than to lord over others as a person of power and privilege (Mark 10:42–43; cf. Luke 14:7–11). And some New Testament documents repudiate the fixation with honor altogether, calling on readers to develop a new value system defined by Christ, who did not seek honor or fame or glory but instead bore the shame of the cross (Heb. 12:2).

Life under Roman Rule

What was life like under Roman rule? On the one hand, the Romans were very good at administration, and many things probably ran more smoothly under their control than they would have otherwise. They cleared the sea of pirates, built aqueducts and roads, kept crime to a minimum, and provided many opportunities for employment. The extent of the Roman Empire, and its basic stability, brought an unprecedented unity to the world, a phenomenon sometimes referred to as the *Pax Romana*. Trade flowed more freely than ever before, and both travel and communication (e.g., the sending of letters) became relatively easy—a factor essential to the rapid spread of Christianity.

In Palestine, however, these benefits came at a very high price. First, the tax burden appears to have been incredibly oppressive, forcing most people into poverty and keeping them there. Indeed, it has been estimated that in the New Testament era between one-fourth and one-third of all people in the Roman Empire were slaves (see box 23.2). Some people actually became slaves voluntarily in hopes of improving their lot (at least then one would be

⊙ EXPLORE 1.16
Josephus on the Destruction of Jerusalem

fed). Second, the Jewish people (even those who were not literally slaves) knew that they were not free, and this knowledge was an affront to their national honor and religious sensibilities. There were soldiers everywhere, reminding them that they were a conquered people. The Jews were officially allowed to practice their religion, but Israel had a long-standing tradition of prophets who railed against injustice and exposed the shenanigans of the powerful, and the Romans did not go for that sort of thing (as John the Baptist discovered). What was allowed was an innocuous sort of religion that did not upset or challenge the powers that be.

Several ancient sources indicate that Palestine became increasingly unstable in the latter half of the first century (after the time of Herod Agrippa I). Passionate Jewish rebels known as Zealots eventually led an all-out war against Rome (66–73 CE) that had disastrous consequences for the Jewish people. The city of Jerusalem was conquered and the temple destroyed in 70 CE. About sixty years later, a second Jewish revolt, led by Simon ben Kosiba, popularly known as Bar Kokhba, was also ruthlessly repressed. After that, on pain of death, no Jew was permitted to enter what had once been Jerusalem.

We do not know for certain what happened to the Christian church in Palestine, but the focal point for the growing Christian movement shifted from Jerusalem to places like Ephesus, Antioch, and Rome. This was primarily due to the success of missionaries such as Paul in bringing the gospel to large numbers of gentiles. In those areas the Christians sometimes encountered hostility from Jewish neighbors who had come to see the new faith as an aberration or false religion (see 1 Thess. 2:14). The Romans were always the biggest threat, however, and their hostility came to a head under the emperor Nero, who initiated the first overt, government-sponsored persecution of Christians in Rome in the 60s, a horrifying purge in which Peter, Paul, and numerous others were martyred.

⊙ EXPLORE 1.17
Pliny the Younger
on Persecution
of Christians

⊙ EXPLORE 1.18,
1.19, and 1.20

By the start of the second century, almost all the books of the New Testament had been written, including the Gospels and all of Paul's letters. By this time the Romans had come to regard Christianity and Judaism as separate religions, and the former was now regarded as an unauthorized innovation and was officially outlawed. We get a good picture of what this meant in practice from a set of letters sent by the Roman governor Pliny to the emperor Trajan in about the year 112. The overall policy was something of a "Don't ask, don't tell" approach: Christians were not sought out, but when they came to a ruler's attention, they were to be tortured and killed unless they renounced their faith and made sacrifices to Roman gods (see box 26.6).

> ### Box 1.2
>
> ### *Whose Pax?*
>
> The *Pax Romana* was established through conquest. Calgacus, a Caledonian leader of one of the nations defeated to this end, remarked bitterly, "They create desolation and call it peace" (Tacitus, *Agricola* 30).
>
> Tacitus, *Agricola*, trans. Harold Mattingly (New York: Penguin, 2009).

Conclusion

The documents of the New Testament are value-laden writings that critique the cultural standards of the world in which they were produced. Both Roman and Jewish social systems are evaluated, sometimes positively, sometimes negatively. For instance, as we make our way through these writings, we will find a fairly sustained critique of Roman imperialism. The perspective is not completely negative—there were benefits to the Roman system. Still, though it is not always stated outright, one does not have to look hard to see that most New Testament authors are at least suspicious of the *Pax Romana*: World peace is nice, but at what cost has it been attained, and at what cost is it maintained?

liberation theology: a movement in Christian theology, developed mainly by twentieth-century Latin American Roman Catholics, that emphasizes liberation from oppression.

It should come as no surprise to discover that modern theologians have sought to apply these critiques to the world in which we now live. Feminists challenge the status quo of male supremacy, and liberation theologians critique the process of "colonialism" through which European powers impose their political and religious systems on developing nations. In the twenty-first century some theologians would speak critically of the *Pax Americana* or even of the *Pax Christiana*, according to which relative peace may be preserved through the dominance of one political, cultural, and/or religious system—and, of course, the New Testament writings are referenced in such discussions. As we will see, however, those documents do not speak unilaterally, and people with different sociopolitical ideas often are able to find support for their preferred position in comments offered in one or another of the New Testament books. But even when there is lack of clarity regarding application of New Testament values to our modern world, the questions are invariably brought to the fore: At what cost have the benefits of modern society been attained? And at what cost are they maintained?

FOR FURTHER READING: **The Roman World**

Bell, Albert A. *Exploring the New Testament World: An Illustrated Guide to the World of Jesus and the First Christians.* Nashville: Nelson, 1998.

Carter, Warren. *Seven Events That Shaped the New Testament World.* Grand Rapids: Baker Academic, 2013.

Esler, Philip F. *The First Christians in Their Social World.* London: Routledge, 1994.

Green, Joel, and Lee Martin McDonald, eds. *The World of the New Testament: Cultural, Social, and Historical Contexts.* Grand Rapids: Baker Academic, 2013.

Jeffers, James S. *The Greco-Roman World of the New Testament Era: Exploring the Background of Early Christianity.* Downers Grove, IL: InterVarsity, 1999.

Malina, Bruce J. *The New Testament World: Insights from Cultural Anthropology.* 3rd ed. Louisville: Westminster John Knox, 2001.

Roetzel, Calvin J., and David L. Tiede. *The World That Shaped the New Testament.* Rev. ed. Louisville: Westminster John Knox, 2002.

Smith, David Lynwood. *Into the World of the New Testament: Greco-Roman and Jewish Texts and Contexts.* London: Bloomsbury, 2015.

Stegemann, Ekkehard W., and Wolfgang Stegemann. *The Jesus Movement: A Social History of Its First Century.* Minneapolis: Fortress, 1995.

⊙ Go to www
.IntroducingNT.com
for summaries,
videos, and other
study tools.

2

New Testament Background

The Jewish World

The New Testament relates a story already in progress. It assumes that its readers know the material that constitutes what Christians call the "Old Testament," and they are also expected to know what happened to the Jewish people in the intervening years since those books were written.

Let's try a quick exercise. Look at the list of words below and try to guess what they all have in common—two things actually:

baptism	exorcism	parable	Samaritan
centurion	gentile	Pharisee	synagogue
crucifixion	hell	rabbi	tax collector
denarius	Jew	Roman	
devil	messiah	Sadducee	

What do these words have in common?

- First, they all designate common phenomena that are mentioned frequently in the New Testament.
- Second, they designate rare phenomena, mentioned infrequently (if at all) in the Old Testament.

Clearly, a lot has changed in what might broadly be called "the biblical world." The Israelites of the Old Testament have become the Jews of the New Testament, and much has happened to them and to the world in which they live.

The Story Thus Far

The Old Testament relates the story of a people who identified themselves as God's chosen ones. Their history as a people began with God's selection of Abraham and Sarah and with God's decision to have a special relationship with all of their descendants. Those descendants were organized into twelve tribes but were known collectively as the children of Israel. They had to endure hard years of slavery in Egypt, but God called Moses to deliver them, give them the Torah (instruction in how God's people ought to live), and lead them to the promised land (a region the Romans would later call Palestine). There they became a significant nation that reached its high point under King David around 1000 BCE. They built a magnificent temple, but subsequent centuries were marked by division and decline.

In 587 BCE the Babylonians conquered the capital city of Jerusalem, destroyed the temple, and took the population into exile. Fifty years later Cyrus of Persia allowed the people (now called Jews) to return and build a new temple, which was dedicated in 515 BCE and much later destroyed by the Romans in 70 CE. Thus the span of Jewish history from 515 BCE to 70 CE is often referred to as the Second Temple period. It is further subdivided into four periods.

The Persian Period (ca. 537–332 BCE)

Throughout this period the Jewish nation was ruled by high priests with minimal interference from the Persian kings. It was at this time that synagogues emerged as significant sites for teaching and worship. The Jews became increasingly focused on faithfulness to Torah as the hallmark of their religion.

Hellenistic: affected by Hellenism—that is, the influence of Greek and Roman culture, customs, philosophy, and modes of thought.

The Hellenistic Period (ca. 332–167 BCE)

With the conquests of Alexander the Great, Palestine came under Greek control; after Alexander's death Palestine came first to be part of the empire of the Ptolemies, whose power was centered in Egypt (320–198 BCE). Then it became part of the empire of the Seleucids, whose power was centered in Syria (198–167 BCE). One of the Seleucid rulers, Antiochus IV Epiphanes (175–164 BCE), sought to exterminate the Jewish religion by inflicting horrible atrocities on anyone who professed or practiced the faith.

The Hasmonean Period (167–63 BCE)

⊙ **EXPLORE 2.13**
Tales of Heroism and Martyrdom from the Time of Antiochus IV Epiphanes

Jewish rebels nicknamed "Maccabees" ("hammers") led a revolt against Antiochus and won independence. The temple (defiled by Antiochus) was rededicated in an event that would come to be commemorated through the Festival of

Hanukkah. The Maccabees established a Jewish state ruled by the Hasmonean dynasty ("Hasmonean" being the official family name for the leaders of the Maccabees). Jewish sects, including those that would eventually be known as "Pharisees" and "Sadducees," emerged at this time.

The Roman Period (63 BCE–70 CE)

Civil war among the Hasmoneans left the Jewish state ripe for conquest by the growing Roman Empire. The Roman general Pompey annexed the territory without much of a struggle in 63 BCE, and Palestine would remain under Roman rule to the end of the Second Temple period—and beyond.

The People of Palestine at the Time of Jesus

During the lifetime of Jesus the population of Palestine was incredibly diverse. Even among Jewish people there was no single, unified system of beliefs or practices. Still, there were certain things that almost all Jewish people believed: there is only one God, and this God had chosen them to be an elect and holy people, distinct from all other peoples or nations on earth; also, God had made a covenant with them and given them the Torah. Accordingly, they lived in ways that set them apart from those who were not God's people: they practiced circumcision, kept the Sabbath, observed dietary restrictions, and committed themselves to certain standards of morality (e.g., the Ten Commandments).

Box 2.1

Basic New Testament Chronology

63 BCE	Pompey conquers Jerusalem for Rome
ca. 6–4 BCE	birth of Jesus
ca. 30–33 CE	crucifixion of Jesus
ca. 32–36 CE	Paul becomes a follower of Christ
ca. 46–65 CE	Paul's missionary journeys and imprisonment (as recorded in Acts); Paul's letters written during this period
ca. 62–65 CE	martyrdom of Peter and Paul in Rome
ca. 65–73 CE	Gospel of Mark written
66 CE	outbreak of Jewish war with Rome
70 CE	destruction of the Jerusalem temple
73 CE	fall of Masada—definitive end of the Jewish war
ca. 80–100 CE	other New Testament books written: Matthew, Luke, John, Acts, and "second-generation" letters by followers of the original apostles

Fig. 2.1. Galilee today. The land where Jesus lived remains a lush and largely rural environment. The octagonal building near the center of this photo is a church built over the house that is said to have belonged to Peter, one of Jesus's disciples (Matt. 8:14). Just to the right of the structure are the remains of a synagogue on the site where Jesus taught and performed an exorcism (Mark 1:21–27). (Todd Bolen / BiblePlaces.com)

Beyond these basics, however, the Jewish people in the time of Jesus were quite diverse. And, of course, not everyone in Palestine was Jewish (see Matt. 15:21–28; Luke 3:14; John 4:5–9).

Let's take a quick survey of some people we will meet in the New Testament world of Palestine.

Pharisees

The Pharisees may be the best known of the Jewish sects to readers of the New Testament. In many Gospel stories they are the opponents of Jesus, and often they are portrayed as narrow-minded legalists (Matt. 23:23–24) or even as hypocrites who don't follow their own teaching (Matt. 23:3). Such an understanding, however, would be incomplete (at best), representing a hostile assessment of how Christians (who became their religious competitors) believed some Pharisees behaved some of the time. In a broader sense, the Pharisees were noted for emphasizing faithfulness to Torah, including the study of Scripture and obedience to God's demands. They were the Jews who founded synagogues throughout the land and encouraged every Jewish person to participate in prayer, Bible study, and regular worship.

The Pharisees also assigned authoritative status to an oral body of material known as "the tradition of the elders" (see Matt. 15:2), which eventually became codified within Judaism as the Mishnah (part of the Talmud).

Mishnah: a collection of rabbinic discussions regarding interpretation of the law of Moses.

Talmud: a collection of sixty-three books (including the Mishnah) that contain Jewish civil and canonical law based on interpretations of Scripture.

Their interpretations of the law seem to have been driven by a conviction that all of God's people should live with the utmost sanctity. They urged laypeople to follow the same purity regulations in their daily lives that were expected of priests serving in the temple, the idea being that (in some sense) every house was a temple, every table was an altar, and every man was a priest. For example, the Pharisees and their followers practiced handwashings originally designated for temple service before eating any meal (see Matt. 15:2; cf. Mark 7:3–4).

Many Pharisees appear to have been scribes, and it is possible that some New Testament references to "the scribes" refer to scribes who were Pharisees (cf. Mark 2:16; Luke 5:30; Acts 23:9). The same is probably true of the "lawyers" whom we hear about now and then (cf. Matt. 22:35; Luke 11:45); they were experts in the law (i.e., Torah) and thus probably were Pharisees. Many Pharisees were synagogue leaders, and some are referred to as "rabbis"—that is, teachers (cf. Matt. 23:6–8). Jesus (who also is called "rabbi") probably had more in common with the Pharisees than with any other Jewish group of his day, which could explain why most of his arguments were with them: they had enough in common to make debate possible. The apostle Paul was raised a Pharisee and continued to regard himself as a Pharisee even after he became a missionary for Christ (see Phil. 3:5).

the law: "the law of Moses" or any regulations that the Jewish people understood as delineating faithfulness to God in terms of the covenant that God had made with Israel.

priests: in Second Temple Judaism, people authorized to oversee the sacrificial system in the Jerusalem temple.

scribes: Jewish professionals skilled in teaching, copying, and interpreting Jewish law; closely associated with the Pharisees.

rabbis: Jewish teachers, many of whom had disciples or followers.

Sadducees

The Sadducees probably were the most powerful Jewish group of the day. They figure less prominently in our Gospel stories because they appear to have been centered in Jerusalem, and Jesus spends most of his time in Galilee (but see Mark 12:18–23). They seem to have controlled the temple system and often dominated the Sanhedrin, the Jewish ruling body. The high priest and the chief priests whom we hear about in the New Testament probably were Sadducees. Pharisees and Sadducees were able to cooperate with one another on matters of common interest, but they were divided over a number of theological and political issues. For example, it is said that the Sadducees did not believe in life after death and that they were skeptical of nonbiblical stories regarding angels and demons. They regarded only the Pentateuch (the first five books of our Old Testament) as sacred Scripture and viewed the other books that Jews and Christians now consider to be Scripture simply as religious writings. Whereas

Pharisees were teachers who emphasized Torah and synagogues, the Sadducees were priests who focused on sacrifices and temple worship. On the crucial matter of interaction with Rome, the Sadducees appear to have been more willing than the Pharisees to compromise on political matters as long as the temple and sacrificial system could continue unabated. (For a side-by-side comparison of Pharisees and Sadducees, see box 2.3; see also the story in Acts 23:6–9).

Essenes

The Essenes were ascetic separatists who lived in private communities. They probably are to be connected with the group that lived in the desert at Qumran and preserved the library now known as the Dead Sea Scrolls. The Essenes advocated strict dietary laws and other rigorous paths to holiness, including, for some of their members, a commitment to celibacy; they also practiced ritual baths and sacred meals similar to the Christian sacraments of baptism and Eucharist. They espoused messianic beliefs and harbored apocalyptic ideas

Box 2.3

Pharisees and Sadducees

Pharisees	Sadducees
generally middle class	mainly upper class
power base outside Jerusalem	power base in Jerusalem
closely associated with synagogues	closely associated with the temple
primarily teachers and scholars	primarily priests
theologically committed to maintaining Israel's relationship with God through obedience to the law	theologically committed to maintaining Israel's relationship with God through the sacrificial system
accepted as Scripture most of what Christians call the "Old Testament"	accepted only the Torah (Pentateuch) as Scripture
believed in resurrection of humans to a life beyond death	did not believe in resurrection to a life beyond death
recognized existence of spiritual beings, including angels and demons	skeptical of beliefs regarding different spiritual beings
regarded as social moderates who objected to imposition of Roman authority but did not advocate armed revolt against the Roman powers	regarded as social conservatives who sought collaboration with Roman authorities in ways that would ensure their own place in the status quo
prominent Pharisees: Shammai (strict interpretations of law), Hillel (more lenient interpretations of law)	prominent Sadducees: Caiaphas and Annas, identified as high priests during the lifetime of Jesus
in the New Testament they argue with Jesus over matters of law but are only peripherally connected to the plot to have Jesus put to death	in the New Testament they are the primary architects of the plot to have Jesus put to death
the primary forebears of modern Judaism	disappear from history after the disastrous Jewish war with Rome in 66–73 CE

Fig. 2.2. Jewish cities. These images portray reconstructions of Jewish cities in New Testament times. *Above*, the crowded metropolis of Jerusalem; *below*, the village of Nazareth, where Jesus grew up. See also fig. 4.1. (Balage Balogh / www .archaeologyillustrated.com)

about imminent judgment and divine deliverance. The Essenes are never mentioned in the New Testament, and there is no sure indication that any New Testament figure knew about them or had any contact with them. Nevertheless, scholars like to compare and contrast Essene beliefs and practices with those of Christianity. In particular, John the Baptist has been evaluated in this light: like the Essenes, he lived in the wilderness, called for radical repentance, and baptized people. It is impossible to know for sure, but most scholars today find no direct evidence to suggest that John was an Essene (or had ever been one), but he may have been influenced by some of their ideas.

Zealots

The Zealots were radical anti-Roman Jews who advocated armed rebellion against the Roman forces. Their numbers included the *sicarii*, knife-wielding assassins who mingled in with crowds and stabbed Jews suspected of collaborating with the Romans. Ultimately, the Zealots and their sympathizers would be responsible for leading the Jews into a disastrous war against Rome in 66–73 CE. They probably are not mentioned in the New Testament itself, though one of Jesus's disciples was called "Simon the Zealot" (the term could simply mean "Simon the zealous one"). The Zealots may not have appeared as an organized force in Palestine until a few years after the time of Jesus.

Herodians

The Herodians were a political coalition of Jews who supported the family and dynasty of Herod, which included many Roman leaders who ruled various areas of Palestine at various times. In the New Testament they are mentioned as collaborating with Pharisees to trip up Jesus politically and to establish grounds for having him banished or destroyed (see Mark 3:6; 12:13).

Samaritans

The Samaritans lived primarily in Samaria, the region situated between Judea (where Jerusalem was) and Galilee (where Jesus lived and conducted most of his ministry; see map 1.2). They claimed that they were the true Israel (descendants of the "lost" tribes taken into Assyrian captivity around 722 BCE) and that the

⊙ **EXPLORE 2.5**
Dead Sea Scrolls

Jews represented a heretical splinter group that had gotten its start when Eli set up a rival sanctuary in Shiloh (see 1 Sam. 1:3). The Samaritans had their own temple on Mount Gerizim and claimed that it was the original sanctuary; they regarded the temple in Jerusalem as a secondary sanctuary built by heretics (see John 4:19–22). They did not accept anything as Scripture but the Pentateuch (the first five books of the Bible), and they had their own version of the Pentateuch, which differed at key points from that of the Jews (e.g., one of the Ten Commandments states that the Lord is to be worshiped only on Mount Gerizim). The Samaritans claimed that their version of the Pentateuch was the original and that the Jews had a falsified text produced by Ezra during the Babylonian exile.

According to the Jews, the Samaritans were not children of Israel at all; rather, they were either descendants of foreign colonists whom the Assyrians

Fig. 2.3. The Jerusalem temple. The temple was the center of worship and religious life for Jewish people. This model displays the building and its outer courts as they looked at the time of Jesus. The outer plaza was open to all people, but the walled compound in the center of the plaza could be entered only by Jews. The tall building in the center is the inner part of the sanctuary, or "holy of holies," which could be entered only by designated priests on specific occasions. (Craig Koester)

Fig. 2.4. Women's work. The world in which Jesus lived had fairly fixed ideas about gender roles, but women were active in most aspects of life, including jobs that required hard physical labor. They worked in the fields at all stages of agriculture, from seedtime to harvest. Other tasks might include spinning and weaving cloth (Matt. 6:28), making or patching clothing (Mark 2:21; Acts 9:39), grinding meal (Matt. 24:41), making bread (Matt. 13:33), sweeping the house (Luke 15:8), going to a well for water (John 4:7), and waiting on houseguests (Mark 1:31; Luke 10:40). Women had primary responsibility for childrearing and were expected to please their husbands (1 Cor. 7:34). They often were in charge of the family finances. Women often were more educated than men, and many were successful in business and were able to provide charitable support for others out of their resources (Luke 8:3). We also hear of women who are guards (John 18:16), prophets (Luke 2:36), merchants (Acts 16:14), tentmakers (Acts 18:3), and missionaries (Phil. 4:3). (John Swanson)

had brought into the land after the conquest in 722 BCE or, at best, the offspring of Israelites who had forsaken their traditions and intermarried with foreigners. Both Jewish and Samaritan religious leaders taught that it was wrong to have any contact with the opposite group. Ideally, Jews and Samaritans were not to enter each other's territories or even to speak to one another. During the New Testament period, however, Samaria was under Roman rule, and the Romans did not recognize Samaria and Judea as separate countries; they simply grouped them together (along with Idumea) as one realm with a single ruler. The Jewish Roman historian Josephus reports numerous violent confrontations between Jews and Samaritans throughout the first half of the first century.

In the New Testament Jesus often is represented as having a compassionate, if not friendly, attitude toward Samaritans: he surprises a Samaritan woman by engaging her in conversation (John 4:3–26), and he even points to individual Samaritans as good examples for his Jewish followers to emulate (Luke 10:30–37; 17:11–19). The book of Acts indicates that some Samaritans became Christians (Acts 8:5–17).

Gentiles

Gentiles were also prominent in Palestine at this time. Large numbers of Romans, Greeks, and Persians had moved into the area and settled there, contributing to the urbanization of traditionally rural areas. Indeed, the two largest cities in Galilee at the time of Jesus were Tiberias and Sepphoris, but Jesus is never said to visit either one of them. As he travels about the countryside, he demonstrates an obvious preference for villages, completely avoiding the large urban centers, where most of the gentiles lived. Jewish attitudes toward gentiles varied: among the Pharisees, Rabbi Shammai is reported to have espoused intolerance of gentiles, whereas Rabbi Hillel is said to have been more conciliatory. The evidence on Jesus is mixed (for a negative attitude toward gentiles, see Matt. 6:7; 10:5; 18:17; 20:25–26; for a positive attitude, see Matt. 8:5–13). Even Paul, who devoted the latter part of his life to bringing salvation to the gentiles, does not always seem to have thought highly of them (see, e.g., Rom. 1:18–32).

The attitude of gentiles toward Jews was also somewhat varied. Anti-Semitism was high, with many gentiles (including those who lived in Palestine) openly hating Jews and despising their culture, customs, and religion. But there were also a good number of gentiles who were attracted to the Jewish religion. Of particular interest to New Testament study are those gentiles who were called "God-fearers." The God-fearers were half-converts—gentiles who embraced Jewish theology, worship, and morality but did not follow ritual purity laws, which they regarded as specific for ethnic Jews. They were allowed to attend

gentiles: people who are not Jewish.

God-fearers: gentiles who were sympathetic to Jewish theology and morality.

⊙ EXPLORE 6.25
The Bias against Gentiles in the Gospel of Matthew

synagogues, but typically they were not circumcised (which would have constituted a full conversion and made them "Jews"). Eventually, these God-fearers became prime candidates for conversion to Christianity (see Acts 10:1–2).

The Effects of Hellenism on the New Testament World

"Hellenism" refers broadly to the influence of Greek culture, which was prominent in the Roman Empire (or in what is sometimes referred to as the Greco-Roman world). During the New Testament period Jewish people throughout the world were said to be "Hellenized" because they had been influenced to a greater or lesser degree by the culture of Greece and Rome.

Hellenistic influences included simple cultural matters. For example, many Jewish people of the time, including Jesus and his disciples, had adopted the Greek practice of reclining at table to eat (i.e., they ate lying down, on floor cushions). Of course, the degree of Hellenism varied; in some instances it was embraced, while in others it was resisted. One extreme example of Hellenistic influence is recounted by the Jewish Roman historian Josephus, who says that in some cities young Jewish men paid to have surgical operations performed on their penises so that when seen exercising naked at the gymnasium, they would appear to be uncircumcised—apparently, circumcision was unfashionable, and the Jewish males did not want to be ridiculed by the gentiles. At the opposite extreme, some Jews virulently resisted anything that smacked of Hellenism and sought to isolate themselves from the secular world, denouncing seemingly innocent social practices as instances of pagan infection.

pagan: Greco-Roman religion and culture as viewed from the perspective of Jews and Christians, who tended to associate what was "pagan" with erratic religious beliefs and an immoral lifestyle.

Hellenistic influences were evident in Palestine, but they were even more prominent in the "Diaspora." This term (meaning "dispersion") refers to Jews living outside the traditional homeland of Palestine. Some Diaspora Jews were descendants of Jewish people who had not returned from the Babylonian exile. Many others were Jews who discovered that the *Pax Romana* allowed them to emigrate and live freely elsewhere. They did so, and for a variety of reasons: business opportunities, education, or a simple desire to see more of the world. But because Diaspora Jews often were far from Jerusalem (indeed, many never saw the city), the temple system lost some of its relevance and meaning for them. Diaspora Jews tended to look to synagogues rather than to the temple for their religious needs, with the result that, over time, rabbis became more important than priests and obedience to Torah took precedence over the offering of sacrifices (which was allowed only in Jerusalem).

The effects of Hellenism were also felt in another very practical way: Hebrew ceased to be the primary language of the Jewish people. It was all but forgotten in the Diaspora, and it tended to be used only in religious services in Palestine itself. The common language for Jesus and other Palestinian Jews was

Fig. 2.5. Jewish teachers. This illustration, *Christ the Student*, based on a story in Luke 2:41–51, recognizes the training that Jesus received from the Jewish teachers of his day, a legacy of *torah* ("teaching") that had been passed down for centuries. Jesus himself was thoroughly Jewish, the New Testament is steeped in Jewish tradition, and the religion of Christianity to this day retains a strong Jewish matrix. (Michael O'Neill McGrath)

Fig. 2.6. Torah. Hellenistic culture prized beauty, honor, strength, and acceptance of fate, but in the traditional Jewish mind-set there was nothing more precious than Torah—the revelation of God's will that was sweeter than honey and to be desired more than gold (Ps. 19:10). (Randy Zucker)

Aramaic. Thus in Palestine Aramaic paraphrases of Scripture called "Targums" were widely used. Outside of Palestine the common language for Diaspora Jews was Greek, the language in which all books of the New Testament would be written. Indeed, long before the time of Jesus, during the third century BCE, the Jewish Scriptures had been translated into Greek. This Greek translation of the Jewish Bible is called the "Septuagint" (the word means "seventy," and a common abbreviation for the Septuagint is "LXX," the Roman numeral for seventy). Why this name? According to legend, the translation was done by seventy (or seventy-two) scholars who, working independently, produced seventy (or seventy-two) identical translations. The Septuagint was widely used throughout the Diaspora and also appears to have been used in many parts of Palestine. Notably, most New Testament authors quote from the Septuagint rather than translating from the Hebrew Bible when they make reference to something said in Scripture.

The Septuagint contained fifteen additional books written in Greek in the years after the writing of the Hebrew Scriptures (what Christians generally call the "Old Testament"). These extra books are often called the "Apocrypha" by Protestant Christians, though eleven of them are classed as "deuterocanonical writings" by Roman Catholics. Their status as Scripture was disputed among Jews at the time of Jesus, as it is among Christians today. In the New Testament

⊙ EXPLORE 2.7
Aramaic Expressions in the New Testament

⊙ EXPLORE 2.6
The Septuagint

⊙ EXPLORE 2.15
Christians and the Apocrypha

the Apocrypha is never cited *as Scripture*, but Paul and other authors do appear to have read some of these books and to regard their teaching favorably.

Hellenism also brought a pervasive increase of religious syncretism. As populations mixed, religious ideas were exchanged. For example, some Jewish people came to believe in immortality of the soul, the idea from Greek philosophy that each person has a soul that continues to live after his or her body dies. There is material in the Jewish Scriptures that could be read in support of such a view, though it had not been understood that way previously.

Other tendencies in Jewish religion were amplified and modified through religious syncretism. Here we take a brief look at three.

Wisdom Theology

Wisdom theology became more popular than ever before. The wisdom tradition of Israel focused less on divinely revealed truth (prophets declaring a word of the Lord that often went contrary to human thinking) and more on common sense (truth that is gained through general insight into life and the human condition). There is a good deal of wisdom material in the Jewish Scriptures (in books such as Proverbs, Job, and Ecclesiastes), and the Hellenistic Jews may have found a theology based on this material consonant with life in a secular, more philosophically oriented world. In the New Testament the influence of wisdom theology is evident in the teachings of Jesus (see Matt. 5–7) and in the writings of some of his followers (see especially the Letter of James).

Dualism

Dualism came to the fore as a more prominent aspect of religious perspective. Dualism reflects the tendency to separate phenomena into sharply opposed categories, with little room for anything in between. For instance, a dualistic perspective tends to objectify "good" and "evil" as realities within nature. The Jewish religion had originally resisted extreme dualism, emphasizing that all people and nations have both good and evil tendencies. In the New Testament world, however, we find that it has become common to think that there are "good people" and "evil people" in the world (cf. Matt. 5:45; 13:38), and that there are also good spirits (angels) and evil spirits (demons). Furthermore, traditional Jewish religion had attributed virtually all power to what was good, to what derived from the all-powerful and righteous God, who ruled over all. The dualistic impulse granted far more power to Satan. Thus in the New Testament we discover that Christians influenced by Hellenistic Judaism have become so dualistic that they actually refer to Satan as "the god of this world" (2 Cor. 4:4; cf. Luke 4:6; John 14:30; 1 John 5:19).

syncretism: the combination or fusion of different religious or cultural beliefs and perspectives.

Apocalypticism

Apocalypticism combined a radical dualistic outlook (clear distinction between good and evil) with a deterministic view of history (the idea that everything is proceeding according to a divine plan). The apocalyptic perspective typically was twofold: (1) a pessimistic forecast for the world at large—things will go from bad to worse; and (2) an optimistic outlook for a favored remnant, those who would be rescued out of the evil world through some act of divine intervention (which was always believed to be imminent). Thus a limit was placed on the power of evil, but it was primarily a temporal limit: Satan may rule the world for now, but not for long! Apocalypticism as a dimension of Jewish religion emerged during the Babylonian exile (see the book of Zechariah) and may have been influenced by Persian religion, which was extremely dualistic. In any case, it came to full expression during the Hellenistic period (see the book of Daniel) and flourished during the Roman period. In Jesus's day apocalypticism tended to be embraced by Jews as a reaction against Roman imperialism and its cultural by-product, Hellenism. In the New Testament apocalypticism is most conspicuous in the book of Revelation, but it underscores many other writings as well (e.g., Matt. 24–25; Mark 13; Luke 21:5–36; 1 Thess. 4:13–5:11; 2 Thess. 2:1–12; 2 Pet. 3:1–18).

Preservation of Jewish Identity

The influence of Hellenism may have been far-reaching in the world of Second Temple Judaism, but few Jews wanted to lose their national and cultural identity completely. Certain traditions—circumcision, Sabbath observance, holidays and festivals—became markers that would remind the people who they were and inhibit total immersion into Greco-Roman society. On a day-to-day basis the key markers of such identity may have been the various "purity codes" that the Jewish people had developed. Such codes were typically derived from Torah, and they often articulated public, observable ways in which Jewish people would live differently than most of the population.

purity codes: regulations derived from Torah that specified what was "clean" or "unclean" for the Jewish people.

Of course, all societies have culturally determined values regarding what they deem "clean" and "unclean." In the modern Western world most people shampoo their hair on a regular basis, not to prevent disease but because they think that oily hair is gross or dirty. But globally and historically, there have been many people (including all those we read about in the Bible) who have thought oily hair is simply natural, the way hair is supposed to be. Such ideas reflect the standards of particular societies, values that might be deeply held (and vigorously defended) but that are not universal. Likewise, the Jewish people at the time of Jesus (like many Jewish people today) had strong ideas about what was clean or unclean, but, as identity markers, these ideas had become integral to their religion. Eating pork or lobster was not just gross or disgusting; it was something that God had directed them not to do. Furthermore, the primary reason why God had directed them not to eat pork or lobster was not because doing so would be immoral or intrinsically evil; rather, abstention from such foods set them apart from other peoples of the world.

In a positive vein, the Jewish concept declared certain things to be holy or sacred: Jerusalem was a holy city (see Matt. 27:53), the temple was a holy building, and the Sabbath was a holy day. Negatively, there were many things that could render a person unclean, such as contact with a corpse or with various bodily fluids. Lepers were unclean, as were women during menstruation and men who had recently had a sexual discharge (including nocturnal emissions). It is important to note that being unclean or encountering uncleanness was not

Fig. 2.7. Jewish *mikveh*. Jewish purity laws required those who had become ritually unclean to purify themselves by taking a ritual bath in a *mikveh*, a type of cistern or tub filled with water. Ancient *mikvot* (plural of *mikveh*) from the time of Jesus can be found throughout the land of Israel. This one is in Jerusalem, just south of the Temple Mount. (Todd Bolen / BiblePlaces.com)

necessarily a bad or shameful thing; often the point was simply to notice what made one unclean and to perform certain purification rituals in recognition of this. For a modern (though flawed) analogy, we might consider the act of changing a baby's diaper: no one in our modern world would think that this is a bad or shameful thing to do, but most people probably would wash their hands after doing it.

One thing that we do not know is how seriously everyone took the purity codes. Some Jews might have ignored them or observed them selectively and sporadically, but many (often the ones we hear about) took ritual purity very seriously and found the codes to be not the least bit oppressive. The Jews of the New Testament era did not go through life with a paranoid aversion to avoiding pollution at all costs, nor did they suffer from perpetually low self-esteem due to an inability to remain ritually clean at all times. They simply avoided what was avoidable, noted what was not, and performed purification rites as part of their regular spiritual discipline. This was a deeply meaningful part of religious life for many Jewish people in both Palestine and the Diaspora.

Conclusion

The world of the New Testament is actually many worlds. The Gospels are set in Palestine, but Paul's letters are addressed to cities such as Corinth, Philippi, and Rome, far from the homeland of Jesus. Furthermore, even though the Gospels relate events that happened in places such as Bethlehem, Nazareth, and Jerusalem, they were written by and for people who lived elsewhere—Antioch, or Ephesus, or Rome. The stories are told with a dual focus: they report what happened *there* and why it is important *here*, what happened *then* and why it is important *now*.

One thing to remember, however, is that in every New Testament writing the Christian, Jewish, and Roman contexts overlap: Christian concerns, Jewish concerns, and Roman concerns are superimposed. The Christian claim in these writings is that Jews and Romans alike find a new identity in Jesus Christ (see Gal. 3:28). The God of Israel is the hope of the gentiles and, indeed, is the God of the entire universe (cf. Rom. 1:20; 15:4–12).

FOR FURTHER READING: **The Jewish World**

Bauckham, Richard. *The Jewish World around the New Testament*. Grand Rapids: Baker Academic, 2010.

Bell, Albert A. *Exploring the New Testament World: An Illustrated Guide to the World of Jesus and the First Christians*. Nashville: Nelson, 1998.

Carter, Warren. *Seven Events That Shaped the New Testament World*. Grand Rapids: Baker Academic, 2013.

Green, Joel, and Lee Martin McDonald, eds. *The World of the New Testament: Cultural, Social, and Historical Contexts*. Grand Rapids: Baker Academic, 2013.

Malina, Bruce J. *The New Testament World: Insights from Cultural Anthropology*. 3rd ed. Louisville: Westminster John Knox, 2001.

Murphy, Frederick, Jr. *The Religious World of Jesus: An Introduction to Second Temple Palestinian Judaism*. Nashville: Abingdon, 1991.

Roetzel, Calvin J., and David L. Tiede. *The World That Shaped the New Testament*. Rev. ed. Louisville: Westminster John Knox, 2002.

Scott, J. Julius, Jr. *Jewish Backgrounds of the New Testament*. Grand Rapids: Baker, 1995.

Smith, David Lynwood. *Into the World of the New Testament: Greco-Roman and Jewish Texts and Contexts*. London: Bloomsbury, 2015.

⊙ Go to www
.IntroducingNT.com
for summaries,
videos, and other
study tools.

3

The New Testament Writings

One of the most prominent Christians of the second century was a man now known to us as Justin Martyr (i.e., Justin the Martyr). Justin produced a number of theological writings, but he is perhaps best known today for a single paragraph in which he provides an early description of a Christian worship service (see box 3.1). Most of the elements of contemporary liturgies already appear to be in place: preaching, prayers, eucharistic meal, even an offering.

We want to pay special attention to one line of Justin's remarks: "The memoirs of the apostles or the writings of the prophets are read, as long as time permits." What does he mean by "the memoirs of the apostles"? He is referring to writings now found in the Christian New Testament (specifically, the four Gospels). These writings are being read publicly in worship alongside "the writings of the prophets"—that is, the Jewish Scriptures contained in what Christians now call the "Old Testament."

The early Christians believed the Jewish Scriptures provided a record of God's covenant (or testament) with Israel. But Christians also believed God had done something new in Jesus Christ, and they found language to describe this in Jeremiah 31:31–34, where the prophet speaks of God making a "new covenant" (see also Matt. 26:28; Mark 14:24; Luke 22:20; 1 Cor. 11:25). Christians eventually decided that the apostolic writings testifying to this new covenant should also be counted as Scripture, and it seemed natural to call these works the "new covenant writings" or, simply, the "New Testament."

apostle: "one who is sent" (*apostolos*); used for certain leaders among the earliest followers of Jesus, especially the twelve disciples and Paul.

covenant: an agreement or pact between God and human beings that establishes the terms of their ongoing relationship.

testament: here, a written account of a covenant; it is in this sense that parts of the Bible are called the Old Testament and New Testament.

Box 3.1

Christian Worship in the Second Century

In chapter 67 of his *First Apology*, the Christian theologian Justin Martyr (110–65) provides us with our earliest account of Christian worship outside the New Testament itself:

> On the day called Sunday, all who live in cities or in the country gather together to one place, and the memoirs of the apostles or the writings of the prophets are read, as long as time permits; then, when the reader has ceased, the president verbally instructs, and exhorts to the imitation of these good things. Then we all rise together and pray, and . . . when our prayer is ended, bread and wine and water are brought, and the president in like manner offers prayers and thanksgivings, according to his ability, and the people assent, saying Amen; and there is a distribution to each, and a participation of that over which thanks have been given, and to those who are absent a portion is sent by the deacons. And they who are well to do, and willing, give what each thinks fit; and what is collected is deposited with the president, who succors the orphans and widows and those who, through sickness or any other cause, are in want, and those who are in bonds and the strangers sojourning among us, and in a word takes care of all who are in need. But Sunday is the day on which we all hold our common assembly, because it is the first day on which God, having wrought a change in the darkness and matter, made the world; and Jesus Christ our Savior on the same day rose from the dead.

Ante-Nicene Fathers, ed. A. Roberts and J. Donaldson, 10 vols. (1885–96; repr., Grand Rapids: Eerdmans, 1986–89), 1:186.

An Overview of the New Testament

We should begin by looking at a basic "table of contents" for the New Testament. There are twenty-seven books, ranging in length from the Gospel of Luke (the longest) to 3 John (the shortest). The books are arranged into seven categories:

1. *The Gospels.* There are four of these (Matthew, Mark, Luke, John), and they are named for the individuals who traditionally have been identified as their authors. All four report on the life, ministry, death, and resurrection of Jesus; thus they provide four different versions of the same basic story, and there is a good deal of overlap in their content.

2. *The book of Acts.* This book is actually "part two" of the Gospel of Luke, but it has been put in its own section in the New Testament (following the four Gospels) because it is the only book that relates the history of the early church—that is, what happened after the events reported in the Gospels.

3. *Letters from Paul to churches.* There are nine of these (Romans, 1 Corinthians, 2 Corinthians, Galatians, Ephesians, Philippians, Colossians, 1 Thessalonians, 2 Thessalonians). If you are unfamiliar with the New Testament, the names of these books may strike you as odd or difficult to pronounce; they are geographical references to the people in various

cities or regions to which the letters were sent (e.g., the "Ephesians" were people who lived in the city of Ephesus). The designated author of all nine letters is Paul, an important Christian missionary. These letters are presented in the New Testament in order of length, from Romans (the longest) to 2 Thessalonians (the shortest).

4. *Letters from Paul to individuals.* There are four of these (1 Timothy, 2 Timothy, Titus, Philemon), and they are named for the individuals to whom they were sent. Again, they are presented in order of length. The designated author is the same Paul who is associated with the nine letters to churches, making, all told, thirteen letters from Paul.

5. *The letter to the Hebrews.* This one is in a class of its own. It is an anonymous work, and we do not know who wrote it or to whom it was sent, but since it appears to have been written for Jewish Christians (i.e., Hebrew Christians), it is traditionally called "The Letter to the Hebrews."

6. *Letters by other people.* There are seven of these (James, 1 Peter, 2 Peter, 1 John, 2 John, 3 John, Jude). Unlike the letters from Paul, these are named not for the people to whom they were sent but rather for the individuals who traditionally have been identified as their authors. They are often called "The General Letters (Epistles)" or "The Catholic Letters (Epistles)." The word *catholic* in the latter designation has nothing to do with the Roman Catholic Church but simply means "universal" or "general."

7. *The book of Revelation.* This one too is in a class of its own. It offers an account of a visionary experience as recounted by someone whose name was John. It is sometimes called "The Apocalypse of John" (the word *apocalypse* means "revelation").

General or Catholic Letters (Epistles): the seven letters traditionally thought to have been written to the church "at large" rather than to specific individual congregations: James, 1 Peter, 2 Peter, 1 John, 2 John, 3 John, Jude.

Two warnings or caveats may be sounded regarding first impressions of these New Testament books. First, the books are not arranged in chronological order. To take just one example, the Gospels come first in the New Testament, but they were not the first books to be written; all four of them probably were written after the death of Paul, and thus they must be later chronologically than any letters that Paul wrote. Second, the titles that these books now bear reflect ancient church traditions that often do not hold up to scrutiny. The first book in the New Testament is titled "The Gospel according to Matthew" (or just "Matthew" for short), but the Bible itself does not say that Matthew wrote this book, and very few modern scholars think that he did. Likewise, we have books in our New Testament called "The First Letter of John," "The Second Letter of John," and "The Third Letter of John," but the books themselves are anonymous and could have been written in any order (they are numbered in our Bibles from longest to shortest).

Development of the Canon

canon: literally, "rule" or "standard"; used by religious groups to refer to an authoritative list of books that are officially accepted as Scripture.

The authors of our New Testament books did not know that they were writing Scripture—our current books of the Bible. They did not know that a New Testament would ever exist, much less that their writings would be a part of it. Nevertheless, these writings owe their prominence and influence to the fact that they came to be included in that corpus.

To understand this significant point, let us imagine for a moment that Paul's letter to the Romans had simply come down to us as an independent writing, a document from antiquity presenting the thoughts of a Christian missionary at the height of his career. Who would read it, and why? In all likelihood, it would be an interesting work to scholars who wanted to reconstruct the early

Fig. 3.1. Preservation of manuscripts. We do not possess any original copies of New Testament documents as produced by their authors. For centuries, monasteries and other institutions copied the manuscripts by hand. In some cases, the work was done hastily and produced copies filled with errors. But the reproduction of Scripture could also be regarded as a high calling, undertaken with painstaking seriousness that produced amazingly accurate results. (Bridgeman Images)

history of one of the world's major religions. But elderly men and women would not be reading it in nursing homes, business professionals would not gather weekly to read it at prayer breakfasts, and teenagers would not memorize passages from it at summer camps. It would no doubt be regarded as a classic of ancient epistolary literature (like the letters of Cicero), and it might get quoted now and then, but it probably would not have inspired hundreds of paintings, thousands of hymns, and millions of sermons. The impact and significance of all New Testament writings is owed in large part to their inclusion in the Christian canon.

The word *canon* literally means "rule" or "standard," but it is used by religious groups to refer to a list of books that are officially accepted as Scripture. In the early years Christians simply gathered together writings that they found to be helpful and shared them with one another. Paul encouraged the churches to which he wrote letters to exchange those letters with one another so that they could read what he had written to other congregations as well as to their own community (see Col. 4:16). Likewise, we are reasonably sure that multiple copies of Mark's Gospel were produced and distributed to different parts of the Roman Empire a few years after it was written (both Matthew and Luke appear to have had copies). Since there were no printing presses at that time, the production of manuscripts was a costly and time-consuming process; nevertheless, Christians throughout the world wanted copies of these documents, and they seem to have done a remarkable job of making and sharing copies with one another.

At first there was no need for official agreement as to which books were to be read; for the most part, the works that circulated were the writings produced by people who had founded or led the earliest churches, people such as Paul and the original disciples of Jesus, or at least people who had known Paul or those original disciples. This chain of connection to Jesus and/or to Paul would come to be known as the "apostolic tradition," and as long as churches were copying and sharing writings that stood within this tradition, there was little need to decide which of those writings was worthy of being labeled "Scripture."

Almost from the start, however, there were voices within Christianity that were in tension with that developing tradition. From many of Paul's letters, we learn that there were people arguing for versions of the Christian faith that Paul himself rejected; these people were preaching a message that they thought was "the gospel" but that Paul claimed was a perversion of the gospel (see Gal. 1:6–9). Some of these alternative voices in the Christian movement probably produced writings as well (see 2 Thess. 2:2), but their works do not appear to have been preserved or included in the New Testament. In one sense, then, the New Testament is not just a *collection* of early Christian writings; rather, it is a *selection* of those writings. The New Testament contains those works

apostolic tradition: oral or written materials that are believed to bear a close connection to Jesus, his original disciples, or the missionary Paul, or believed to be congruent with what those people taught.

Scripture: the sacred writings of a religion, believed to be inspired by God and viewed as authoritative for faith and practice.

that were considered to be most representative of what became mainstream and orthodox.

The process through which such selections were made was complex, and there is controversy among modern scholars as to how the judgments were made. By the second century, however, two developments made the question of canon a pressing one for Christians.

First, there were now Christians who wanted to exclude writings with ties to the apostolic tradition that were not to their liking. The most prominent figure in this regard was the Christian scholar and evangelist Marcion (ca. 110–60), who came to prominence in the first half of the second century. Marcion appears to have been influenced by a movement called "gnosticism," which valued what was spiritual but despised anything material or physical (see "On the Horizon: Gnosticism" in chap. 1). He also wanted to purge Christianity of Jewish influences and make it into a more purely gentile religion. Marcion urged his followers to reject writings that taught a version of the faith different from what he was promoting. Eventually he came up with an approved list of writings that

Box 3.2

From Jesus to Us: Six Stages in the Transmission of the Gospel Tradition

Stage One: Historical Jesus

Jesus says and does things that are considered remarkable.

Stage Two: Early Tradition

Oral		Written
People remember what Jesus said and did and share these memories with others.	**and/or**	People write down brief accounts of things that Jesus said and did.

Stage Three: Composition of the Gospels

The Gospel writers compile their books, drawing on both oral tradition and early written sources to form narratives of Jesus's life and work.

Stage Four: Preservation of Manuscripts

People make copies of the Gospel narratives and distribute them.

Stage Five: Translation

Scholars translate copies of the Gospel narratives into other languages, including, eventually, our own.

Stage Six: Reception

In modern editions of the Gospels we hear or read about what Jesus said and did.

he thought should be considered Scripture for Christians: ten letters of Paul (all but 1 Timothy, 2 Timothy, and Titus) and a copy of the Gospel of Luke. He also edited these eleven books to remove positive references to the Jewish God, or to the Jewish Scriptures, or to other matters that did not fit with his anti-Jewish, hyperspiritual version of the faith (he claimed that the writings had been previously modified by heretics and that by editing them he was merely restoring them to their original form). In any case, many writings currently in our New Testament were rejected by Marcion and his followers not because they were considered to be out of step with the apostolic tradition but rather because that tradition itself was considered to be corrupt (steeped in Jewishness and overly concerned with physical life in a material world).

Second, there were Christians in the second century who began producing new writings and attributing these to people who had belonged to the original circle of apostolic witnesses. In virtually every case these new writings were copycat versions of books that had been written in the first century: someone would write a letter promoting gnostic ideas and claim that it was a newly discovered letter of Paul; someone else would write a gospel portraying Jesus as a major supporter of gnosticism and claim that it was a newly discovered work by one of his twelve disciples. These books continued to be produced well into the fourth century. Their anachronisms and idiosyncrasies make the fictional attributions of authorship readily apparent today, but the production of such writings did cause confusion among Christians in the first few centuries.

Thus the twofold problem: on the one hand, most Christian churches wanted to use only those writings that could be reasonably connected to the apostolic tradition; on the other hand, they wanted to use all the writings that were connected with that tradition, not just ones that fit with some particular teacher's ideological preferences. Thus by the end of the second century lists began to appear specifying which writings were thought to meet these criteria. From these lists it becomes apparent that most of the writings now found in our New Testament were universally accepted as reliable witnesses to the apostolic tradition. Seven books, however, had a more difficult time gaining such acceptance: Hebrews, James, 2 Peter, 2 John, 3 John, Jude, and Revelation. We have no indication that these books were ever denounced or rejected outright, but the more cautious church leaders seem to have been reluctant to regard them as being on a par with the others (i.e., as being works that should be regarded as Scripture). Eventually, however, a consensus emerged, and by the beginning of the fifth century our current New Testament canon of twenty-seven books was well established.

Two conclusions regarding the canon of New Testament writings would be accepted by most scholars today. On the one hand, all the books in our current New Testament are ones that were deemed compatible with what came to be

⊙ EXPLORE 3.6
New Testament
Canon: The Early Lists

regarded as "apostolic Christianity": there are certain, basic matters of faith on which they seem to speak with unanimity. On the other hand, the selection of canonical writings was not a narrow one that eliminated diversity of opinion: the twenty-seven New Testament writings present a wide variety of viewpoints, including positions that sometimes are difficult to reconcile. Indeed, if all the authors of these writings had been gathered into a single room at a given place and time, they almost certainly would have argued with one another over many matters that have continued to be of interest to Christians throughout the centuries. In short, the New Testament writings evince a basic unity but also remarkable diversity.

How Scholars Study the New Testament

The academic field of New Testament study has developed into a discipline that encompasses different approaches and employs a variety of methods.

Text Criticism

variant: in text criticism, an alternative reading of a text, supported by some manuscripts.

Text critics analyze the various manuscripts of the New Testament that have been preserved over the centuries, comparing them, dating them, and employing various techniques to determine which are the most reliable. Their goal is to reconstruct what the original manuscripts probably said, noting also "variant readings" when one or more of the copies that have been made over the years say something different. Significant variant readings are sometimes noted in footnotes in English Bibles (e.g., see the footnote to Matt. 10:3 in the NRSV, which notes that the disciple of Jesus called "Thaddaeus" is referred to as "Lebbaeus" in some manuscripts).

Archaeology

Archaeologists excavate ancient cities and other sites important to the New Testament world, and they have uncovered an enormous amount of physical evidence that supplies background information for interpreting these texts. They have also discovered ancient documents from this period, the most important finds being the library of the Dead Sea Scrolls, which tells us a good deal about the diversity of first-century Jewish religion, and the Nag Hammadi gnostic library, which tells us a good deal about the diversity of early Christianity.

Sociological Criticism

⊙ **EXPLORE 3.9**
Text Criticism: Determining the Original Reading of the Text

Scholars examine the New Testament with perspectives and tools derived from the social sciences, including the field of sociology. They are attentive to a number of matters that characterized the social world of the Roman Empire during the New Testament era: the phenomenon of the *Pax Romana*; the Diaspora migrations of Jewish people; the military occupation of Palestine; and an economic system that virtually eliminated the middle class, leaving a few people rich and almost everyone else poor. New Testament scholars who are trained in sociology examine the New Testament writings to see how the effects of these social phenomena are addressed.

Cultural Anthropology

Derived from the social sciences, cultural anthropology seeks to understand what happens in a given culture by way of comparison with what is known about other cultures. Cultural anthropologists study matters such as kinship relations, power structures, gender roles, economic systems, and strategies for education. With regard to the New Testament, they have analyzed the purity codes that defined what most people considered to be "clean" and "unclean" and the social value system that led people to prize acquisition of honor above all else.

Historical Criticism

"Historical criticism" sometimes has been used in New Testament studies as an umbrella term for those approaches that focus on the circumstances of a text's composition (e.g., source criticism, form criticism, redaction criticism [all discussed below]) as distinct from "literary criticism," which encompasses approaches that focus on interpretation of the text that is now before us (e.g., narrative criticism, rhetorical criticism, reader-response criticism, ideological criticism [also discussed below]). In a strict sense, however, "historical criticism" refers to the ways in which a historian might use the New Testament to learn about history. Historians (whether they are Christian or not) view Jesus, Paul, and other figures of the New Testament as important and interesting people, and they understand the emergence of Christianity to be one of the most significant developments in human history. Thus they use the New Testament as a resource for understanding the lives and circumstances of these people and for reconstructing the events that transpired concerning them.

Source Criticism

The discipline of source criticism attempts to move behind the New Testament texts to posit hypotheses regarding materials that the biblical authors might have used in composing their documents. Paul quotes from an early Christian liturgy in 1 Corinthians 11:23–26, and he appears to incorporate a

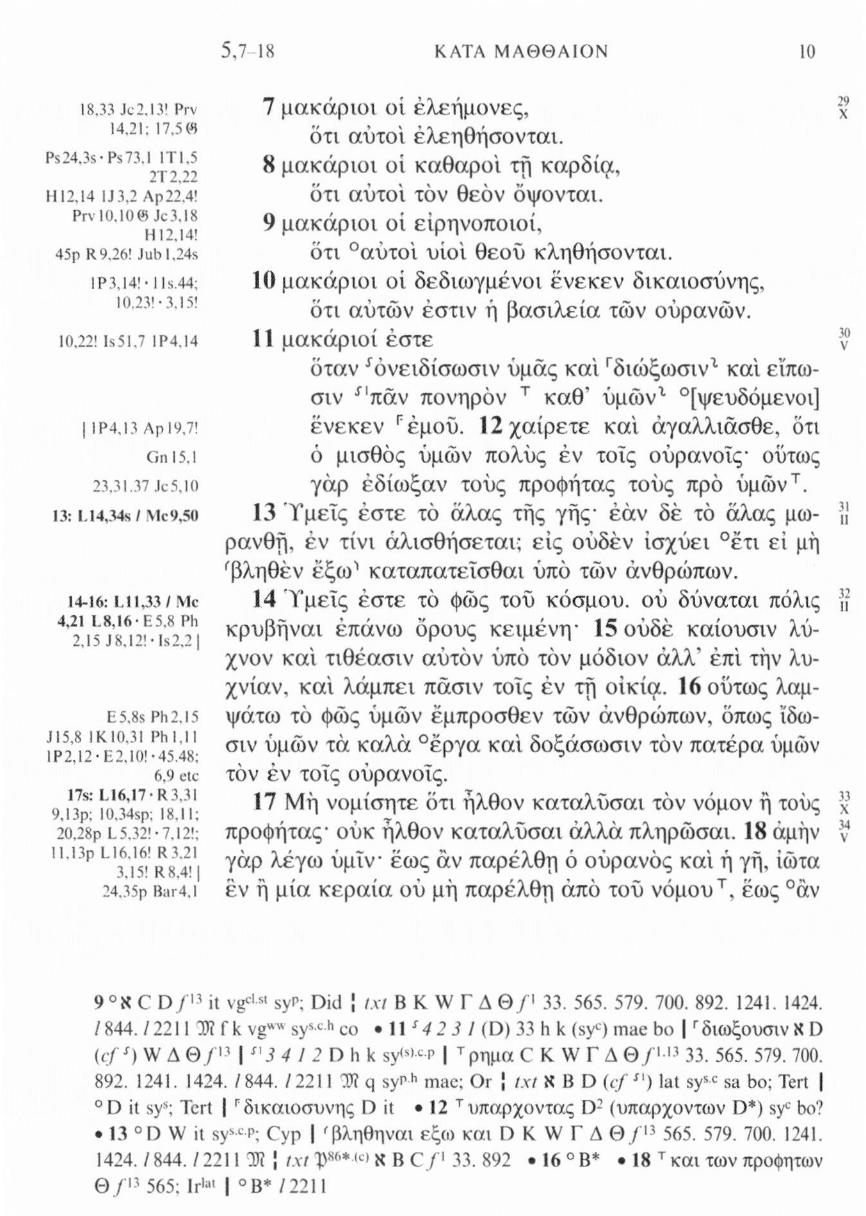

7 μακάριοι οἱ ἐλεήμονες,
ὅτι αὐτοὶ ἐλεηθήσονται.   ^{29 X}

8 μακάριοι οἱ καθαροὶ τῇ καρδίᾳ,
ὅτι αὐτοὶ τὸν θεὸν ὄψονται.

9 μακάριοι οἱ εἰρηνοποιοί,
ὅτι °αὐτοὶ υἱοὶ θεοῦ κληθήσονται.

10 μακάριοι οἱ δεδιωγμένοι ἕνεκεν δικαιοσύνης,
ὅτι αὐτῶν ἐστιν ἡ βασιλεία τῶν οὐρανῶν.

11 μακάριοί ἐστε   ^{30 V}
ὅταν ⸆ὀνειδίσωσιν ὑμᾶς καὶ ⸀διώξωσιν⸃ καὶ εἴπω-
σιν ⸂¹πᾶν πονηρὸν ᵀ καθ' ὑμῶν⸃ °[ψευδόμενοι]
ἕνεκεν ⸀ἐμοῦ. **12** χαίρετε καὶ ἀγαλλιᾶσθε, ὅτι
ὁ μισθὸς ὑμῶν πολὺς ἐν τοῖς οὐρανοῖς· οὕτως
γὰρ ἐδίωξαν τοὺς προφήτας τοὺς πρὸ ὑμῶνᵀ.

13 Ὑμεῖς ἐστε τὸ ἅλας τῆς γῆς· ἐὰν δὲ τὸ ἅλας μω-   ^{31 II}
ρανθῇ, ἐν τίνι ἁλισθήσεται; εἰς οὐδὲν ἰσχύει °ἔτι εἰ μὴ
⸀βληθὲν ἔξω⸃ καταπατεῖσθαι ὑπὸ τῶν ἀνθρώπων.

14 Ὑμεῖς ἐστε τὸ φῶς τοῦ κόσμου. οὐ δύναται πόλις   ^{32 II}
κρυβῆναι ἐπάνω ὄρους κειμένη· **15** οὐδὲ καίουσιν λύ-
χνον καὶ τιθέασιν αὐτὸν ὑπὸ τὸν μόδιον ἀλλ' ἐπὶ τὴν λυ-
χνίαν, καὶ λάμπει πᾶσιν τοῖς ἐν τῇ οἰκίᾳ. **16** οὕτως λαμ-
ψάτω τὸ φῶς ὑμῶν ἔμπροσθεν τῶν ἀνθρώπων, ὅπως ἴδω-
σιν ὑμῶν τὰ καλὰ °ἔργα καὶ δοξάσωσιν τὸν πατέρα ὑμῶν
τὸν ἐν τοῖς οὐρανοῖς.

17 Μὴ νομίσητε ὅτι ἦλθον καταλῦσαι τὸν νόμον ἢ τοὺς   ^{33 X} ^{34 V}
προφήτας· οὐκ ἦλθον καταλῦσαι ἀλλὰ πληρῶσαι. **18** ἀμὴν
γὰρ λέγω ὑμῖν· ἕως ἂν παρέλθῃ ὁ οὐρανὸς καὶ ἡ γῆ, ἰῶτα
ἓν ἢ μία κεραία οὐ μὴ παρέλθῃ ἀπὸ τοῦ νόμουᵀ, ἕως °ἂν

Left margin references:

18,33 Jc 2,13! Prv
14,21; 17,5 𝔊

Ps 24,3s · Ps 73,1 1T 1,5
2T 2,22
H 12,14 1J 3,2 Ap 22,4!
Prv 10,10 𝔊 Jc 3,18
H 12,14!
45p R 9,26! Jub 1,24s

1P 3,14! · 11s.44;
10,23! · 3,15!

10,22! Is 51,7 1P 4,14

| 1P 4,13 Ap 19,7!

Gn 15,1

23,31.37 Jc 5,10

13: L 14,34s / Mc 9,50

14-16: L 11,33 / Mc
4,21 L 8,16 · E 5,8 Ph
2,15 J 8,12! · Is 2,2 |

E 5,8s Ph 2,15
J 15,8 1K 10,31 Ph 1,11
1P 2,12 · E 2,10! · 45.48;
6,9 etc

17s: L 16,17 · R 3,31
9,13p; 10,34sp; 18,11;
20,28p L 5,32! · 7,12!;
11,13p L 16,16! R 3,21
3,15! R 8,4! |
24,35p Bar 4,1

---

9 °ℵ C D ƒ¹³ it vg^{cl.st} sy^p; Did ¦ *txt* B K W Γ Δ Θ ƒ¹ 33. 565. 579. 700. 892. 1241. 1424.
l 844. *l* 2211 𝔐 f k vg^{ww} sy^{s.c.h} co • **11** ⸃4 2 3 1 (D) 33 h k (sy^c) mae bo ⸀διωξουσιν ℵ D
(*cf* ⸂) W Δ Θ ƒ¹³ | ⸂¹3 4 1 2 D h k sy^{(s).c.p} | ᵀρημα C K W Γ Δ Θ ƒ¹.¹³ 33. 565. 579.
892. 1241. 1424. *l* 844. *l* 2211 𝔐 q sy^{p.h} mae; Or ¦ *txt* ℵ B D (*cf* ⸂¹) lat sy^{s.c} sa bo; Tert |
°D it sy^s; Tert ⸀δικαιοσυνης D it • **12** ᵀυπαρχοντας D² (υπαρχοντων D*) sy^c bo?
• **13** °D W it sy^{s.c.p}; Cyp | ⸀βληθηναι εξω και D K W Γ Δ Θ ƒ¹³ 565. 579. 700. 1241.
1424. *l* 844. *l* 2211 𝔐 ¦ *txt* 𝔓^{86*.(c)} ℵ B C ƒ¹ 33. 892 • **16** °B* • **18** ᵀκαι των προφητων
Θ ƒ¹³ 565; Ir^{lat} | °B* *l* 2211

Fig. 3.2. The Greek New Testament. This typical page from the Nestle-Aland Greek New Testament
(28th ed.) shows the text of Matthew 5:7–18. The narrow column on the right side of the page lists
parallel passages found elsewhere in the Gospels. The column on the left side shows related passages in the Old Testament, the New Testament, and other ancient literature. The bottom part of
the page indicates variant readings, using an elaborate system of codes developed by text critics.
The codes indicate, for each verse, many of the different readings found in extant manuscripts,
along with a list of which manuscripts contain those divergent readings. (German Bible Society)

Christian hymn into his letter to the Philippians (see Phil. 2:6–11). The authors of our four Gospels also appear to have possessed some written materials about Jesus that they drew on when writing their books (see Luke 1:1). Source critics try to identify these materials, and sometimes they even attempt to reconstruct them.

Form Criticism

The discipline of form criticism seeks to classify different materials found in the New Testament according to literary genre or type ("form") and to draw conclusions relevant to interpretation based on these classifications. Different types of material can be discerned: genealogies, parables, miracle stories, speeches, hymns, creeds, proverbs, and many more. The fruit of such investigations will become apparent in this book when we consider "Types of Material in the Gospels" (in chap. 5) and the "Typical Structure or Format for a Letter" (in chap. 11). Form critics usually are interested in identifying the *Sitz im Leben* ("setting in life") that each of these types of literature would have served, which implies certain assumptions about purpose: a joke might be employed for the purpose of entertainment, while a prayer might be employed for the purpose of worship. Form critics often have practiced their discipline in tandem with source criticism but with a view to discerning oral sources that stand behind the New Testament texts.

Redaction Criticism

Used mainly in Gospel studies, redaction criticism tries to determine the particular intentions of New Testament authors by analyzing how they arranged and edited their source materials. The discipline typically involves two methods: (1) *composition analysis* looks at how various units are arranged within the particular book—the order or placement of individual units, the sequence of material, and the overall organization of the book; and (2) *emendation analysis* looks at alterations that the Gospel author probably made in the source material—additions, omissions, and other changes that reveal the author's priorities and preferences. For summaries of redaction-critical analyses of the Gospels of Matthew and Luke, see box 6.2 and box 8.2.

Narrative Criticism

Also used primarily with the Gospels (and the book of Acts), narrative criticism draws on the insights of modern literary analysis to determine the particular effects that the biblical stories are expected to have on their readers.

Like redaction criticism, narrative criticism is interested in treating each book on its own and discerning what is distinctive about it, but whereas redaction

⊙ **EXPLORE 3.10**
Source Criticism of the Gospels and Acts

⊙ **EXPLORE 3.11**
Form Criticism of the Gospels and Acts

⊙ **EXPLORE 3.12**
Redaction Criticism of the Gospels

criticism focuses on composition (how the author organized and edited the material), narrative criticism focuses on reception (how readers are expected to be impacted or affected by the work). Narrative critics often analyze a Gospel the way literary critics interpret a short story: they pay attention to how the plot is advanced, how characters are developed, how conflict is introduced or resolved, and how rhetorical features such as symbolism and irony affect the reader's perception of what is happening.

Rhetorical Criticism

The focus of rhetorical criticism is on the strategies employed by biblical authors to achieve particular purposes. Rhetorical critics are interested not only in the point that a work wishes to make but also in the basis on which that point is established (the types of arguments or proofs that are used): sometimes external evidence or documentation is cited; sometimes the trustworthy character of the writer is invoked; at other times an appeal is made to the readers' emotions or sense of logic.

Reader-Response Criticism

The approach to New Testament texts known as reader-response criticism focuses on how texts have been understood and might be understood by readers who engage them in different ways and in various contexts. Reader-response critics are typically interested in "polyvalence"—that is, the capacity for any text to mean different things to different people. Most reader-response critics are interested in exploring how readers contribute to the process of interpretation, bringing their own perspectives and presuppositions to texts and reading them in light of these. For example, they analyze how factors of social location (age, gender, nationality, economic status, etc.) inevitably affect the ways readers engage texts and help to determine what they think those texts mean. One type of reader-response criticism known as *Wirkungsgeschichte* ("history of influence") seeks to document and explain how given texts have been read throughout history—how they have been used in theological discussions, liturgy, preaching, art, and other modes of both scholarly and popular reception.

⊙ **EXPLORE 3.13**
Narrative Criticism of the Gospels and Acts

⊙ **EXPLORE 3.14**
Rhetorical Criticism

⊙ **EXPLORE 3.15**
Reader-Response Criticism

Ideological Criticism

Somewhat related to reader-response criticism are a number of approaches to the New Testament that seek to explore how these writings might be interpreted when they are read from particular ideological perspectives. Varieties of feminist criticism expound what different books or passages mean when read from a feminist point of view. A related field called "womanist criticism"

Fig. 3.3. Students of Scripture 1. The Christian penchant for studying Scripture in an academic and serious manner derives from Judaism. Jewish rabbis first established standards for the interpretation of Scripture, many of which are still respected today. In Jewish households instruction in the Scriptures may begin in childhood; indeed, many Jewish children learn Hebrew in order to understand the Bible better. (Bridgeman Images)

interprets texts from the specific perspective of African American women, and a developing field called "mujerista criticism" does the same from the perspective of Latin American women. "Postcolonial criticism" brings to the fore interpretations from the perspectives of marginalized and oppressed peoples of the world, especially those in Asia, Africa, or Latin America. These approaches and others like them (Marxist, Jungian, etc.) seek to put forward interpretations that other scholars may have missed due to the limitations of their own, usually unacknowledged, ideological perspectives. They also ask questions about the ideological perspectives of the biblical authors themselves, and they seek to expose ideological assumptions that may be inherent in texts produced in particular cultures and contexts.

Deconstruction

postmodern philosophy: a relativistic approach to life and thought that denies absolutes and objectivity.

The approach to texts called "deconstruction" is a rather extreme mode of interpretation that arose in the late twentieth century and became popular with scholars influenced by postmodern philosophy. It attempts to demonstrate that all proposed interpretations are ideological constructs that have no objective claim to legitimacy. The process of interpretation inevitably privileges certain possibilities at the expense of others. Thus postmodern scholars often claim that interpretation reveals more about the interpreter than it does about the text, and they employ the method of deconstruction to demonstrate that proposed interpretations of any given text depend on subjective criteria: they may be correct interpretations from a particular point of view, but any number of other interpretations would have to be considered equally valid. From the postmodern perspective, meaning in any absolute sense is unobtainable. Still, interpreters can "play" with texts, and this might be worthwhile if they learn things about themselves and about other interpreters in the process. Positively, deconstruction often brings to the fore neglected possibilities for biblical meaning and raises questions regarding why those avenues have not been more thoroughly explored.

Exegesis and Hermeneutics

Biblical scholars sometimes make a distinction between exegesis and hermeneutics. The first term, *exegesis*, refers to scholarly study of the Bible with an emphasis on the actual explication of texts; the academic approaches described above involve the use of exegetical methods. The second term, *hermeneutics*, refers more broadly to philosophical reflection on the process of interpretation, including consideration of questions regarding what the goal of interpretation should be, and of the various ways in which biblical passages might be regarded as meaningful or authoritative. Should the New Testament be studied as a collection of historical documents to determine what they reveal about the origins of Christian religion? Should it be analyzed and evaluated for its aesthetic and artistic qualities? Should it be approached as a resource for the development of religious dogma? Should it be studied (academically) as Scripture, as a book that reveals the very thoughts of God, and if so, what does that mean? One person might believe that the New Testament is the inerrant word of God;

Fig. 3.4. Students of Scripture 2. Bible study has always been an essential part of the Christian church. Even before there was a New Testament believers gathered regularly to attend to "the teachings of the apostles" (Acts 2:42), and congregations passed letters of Paul from one church to another to be read (Col. 4:16) and struggled to understand them (2 Pet. 3:15–16). Much later, after the printing press was invented and the Scriptures had been translated into multiple languages, Bible study groups sprang up everywhere Christians were to be found. (Trustees of the Wallace Collection, London / Art Resource, NY)

another might regard it as containing books that retain the marks of both divine inspiration and human fallibility. Clearly, interpretation of the New Testament can be affected by the different hermeneutical assumptions that interpreters make regarding these writings.

One of the most common mistakes that students make when they are new to the field of academic biblical studies is to associate particular exegetical methods with specific hermeneutical stances. Here are some examples: (1) a student reads a book by an archaeologist who claims to provide evidence that certain biblical stories are factual and correct, so the student concludes that archaeology typically is used by scholars who want to prove the accuracy of biblical narratives; (2) a student reads a book by a redaction critic who claims that the Gospel authors edited their source material in ways that reveal they had inconsistent and competing agendas, so the student concludes that redaction criticism typically is used by scholars who want to emphasize contradictory points in Scripture; (3) a student reads a book by a rhetorical critic who maintains that Paul's argument in a particular letter is so persuasive it should be accepted by everyone today, so the student concludes that rhetorical criticism typically is used by scholars who want to encourage readers to accept what the biblical authors taught as being valid for our time; and (4) a student reads a book by a narrative critic who regards the Gospels as fictional tales, so the student concludes that narrative criticism typically is used by scholars who do not think that the Gospels offer historically accurate accounts of first-century events.

All of these conclusions are false. All the exegetical methods and academic disciplines described above are used by people who operate with different hermeneutical assumptions and interests. The methods themselves are simply tools that are employed for very different purposes by people with different attitudes and goals. The beginning student must be careful not to evaluate the legitimacy or value of a method based on limited exposure to its employment. Furthermore, most scholars use these methods in combination with one another; they examine a text with one approach to answer one set of questions and with another approach to answer a different set of questions. They use one method one day and another method the next day.

Conclusion

The writings of the New Testament are not simply read; they are studied. In fact, it probably is safe to say that these books have been more carefully investigated and more closely scrutinized than any other writings in history. The academic field of New Testament studies has developed into a discipline that encompasses many different approaches and employs a variety of methods. Some scholars are most interested in historical questions; they rely on archaeology to reconstruct the settings in which the New Testament books were written, and they draw on the insights of sociology, cultural anthropology, and other disciplines to understand what is reported within the context of the ancient world. Other scholars tend to be more interested in understanding the messages that the books convey or the effects that the books seek to have on their readers, so they rely more heavily on methods that analyze the rhetorical and literary features of the texts. And, of course, many New Testament scholars are interested in theological issues, and so they study these writings in light of specific ideological and doctrinal concerns. In a general sense, the different methodological approaches to the New Testament may be likened to keys on a ring: different keys open different doors and grant access to different types of insight. It is difficult to know at the outset which doors one will want to open. Accordingly, the best advice for budding Bible interpreters is usually this: try to obtain as full a set of keys as possible.

FOR FURTHER READING: **The New Testament Writings**

Bock, Darrell L., and Buist M. Fanning, eds. *Interpreting the New Testament Text: Introduction to the Art and Science of Exegesis*. Wheaton: Crossway, 2006.

Brown, Jeannine K. *Scripture as Communication: Introducing Biblical Hermeneutics*. Grand Rapids: Baker Academic, 2007.

Carter, Warren, and Amy-Jill Levine. *The New Testament: Methods and Meanings*. Nashville: Abingdon, 2013.

Croy, N. Clayton. *Prima Scriptura: An Introduction to New Testament Interpretation*. Grand Rapids: Baker Academic, 2011.

Erickson, Richard J. *A Beginner's Guide to New Testament Exegesis: Taking the Fear Out of Critical Method*. Downers Grove, IL: InterVarsity, 2005.

Fee, Gordon D. *New Testament Exegesis: A Handbook for Students and Pastors*. 3rd ed. Louisville: Westminster John Knox, 2002.

Green, Joel B., ed. *Hearing the New Testament: Strategies for Interpretation*. Rev. ed. Grand Rapids: Eerdmans, 2008.

Kruger, Michael J. *Canon Revisited: Establishing the Origins and Authority of the New Testament Books*. Wheaton: Crossway, 2012.

⊙ Go to www
.IntroducingNT.com
for summaries,
videos, and other
study tools.

4

Jesus

Get up on a Sunday morning and drive around your town. If you live in America, you will find churches, just as you would in many other countries. They are of all sorts: historic denominations and recent innovations, major "name brands" and generic community fellowships. You will find people meeting in towering cathedrals and in rented-out storefronts, in spacious auditoriums and in ranch-style sanctuaries. You'll see vestments and paraments, stained glass and video screens, expensive commissioned artwork and tacky homemade banners. And the people are as diverse as their furnishings.

Now here is an amazing fact: all these people have gotten out of bed and gathered with others on Sunday morning because of one person—a Jewish man who was born on the other side of the world over two thousand years ago.

Listen!

You will hear people singing:

> Jesus shall reign where'er the sun
> Does its successive journeys run . . .
>
>   . . .
> What a friend we have in Jesus
> All our sins and griefs to bear . . .
>
>   . . .
> All hail the power of Jesus' name
> Let angels prostrate fall . . .

You will hear congregations confessing a creed:

> We believe in one Lord, Jesus Christ
> the only Son of God,

Historical Significance of Jesus

On a spring morning in about the year 30 CE, three men were executed by the Roman authorities in Judea. Two were "brigands." . . . The third was executed as another type of political criminal. He had not robbed, pillaged, murdered or even stored arms. He was convicted, however, of having claimed to be "king of the Jews"—a political title. Those who looked on . . . doubtless thought that the world would little note what happened that spring morning. . . . It turned out, of course, that this third man, Jesus of Nazareth, would become one of the most important figures in human history.

—E. P. Sanders*

Regardless of what anyone may personally think or believe about him, Jesus of Nazareth has been the dominant figure in the history of Western culture for almost twenty centuries. If it were possible, with some sort of super-magnet, to pull up out of that history every scrap of metal bearing at least a trace of his name, how much would be left?

—Jaroslav Pelikan[†]

*E. P. Sanders, The Historical Figure of Jesus (London: Penguin, 1993), 1.
†Jaroslav Pelikan, Jesus through the Centuries (New Haven: Yale University Press, 1985), 1.

eternally begotten of the Father,
God from God, Light from Light,
true God from true God,
begotten not made,
of one Being with the Father.

You will hear an evangelist exhorting individuals to accept Jesus as their personal Lord and Savior, inviting them to ask him into their hearts to cleanse them from sin. You will hear inspired worshipers claiming that Jesus has spoken to them this very morning and given them a word of direction for others who are present. You will hear a priest intoning Latin or Greek and promising those who have gathered that they are about to eat the flesh of Jesus and consume his blood.

If you are not one of these people—if you are not a Christian—all of this might seem bizarre. Even if you are a Christian, some of this might seem bizarre, for you probably have some ideas about which groups of Christians have this stuff about Jesus right, and which have it wrong.

Jesus in the New Testament: Earthly and Exalted

Jesus is the central figure of the New Testament; every book is written because of him and, in some sense, about him. Still, the Jesus whom we read about in the New Testament may be spoken of in two different ways. First, the New Testament tells us about a man named "Jesus" who lived in Galilee and who said and did many remarkable things before eventually being crucified. Second, the New Testament also speaks of Jesus as an exalted, eternal figure who

Fig. 4.1. Where Jesus lived. These reconstructions portray the village of Capernaum at the time of Jesus, showing houses typical of those in which Jesus and his disciples would have lived. Capernaum appears to have been "home base" for Jesus during the time of his ministry in Galilee, perhaps because Peter owned a house there where Jesus and the others could stay. See also figs. 2.1, 2.2. (Balage Balogh / www.archaeologyillustrated.com)

existed prior to creation and who now continues to reign from heaven, seated at the right hand of God and dwelling in the hearts of those who believe in him.

Christian faith and doctrine affirm the unity of these two figures: they are the same Jesus, not two different Jesuses. Still, Christian scholars often find it helpful to distinguish between the two, especially when they are interpreting the New Testament. For example, there is one passage in the Gospel of Matthew in which Jesus says to his disciples, "You always have the poor with you, but you will not always have me" (26:11). Then, later in Matthew's Gospel, Jesus says to these same disciples, "I will be with you always" (28:20). The first passage refers to what scholars call the earthly, historical figure of Jesus (or, sometimes, "the pre-Easter Jesus")—the man who lived in Galilee and who told his disciples he would not remain present with them on earth forever. But then, in the second passage, when Jesus says, "I will be with you always," he must be referring to something else. Christian theologians would say that the eternal exalted Jesus ("the post-Easter Jesus") remains present in a way that the earthly, historical figure does not.

The Earthly Figure of Jesus in the New Testament: An Overview

The New Testament Gospels consistently refer to Jesus as being a Jew from Nazareth, a small village in the province of Galilee. He is the son of Joseph and Mary, and he has several brothers and sisters. He is a Jewish peasant who works as a *tektōn*, some sort of carpenter or builder or construction worker. Almost nothing is said about his early life, though some process of education is implied by the fact that, as an adult, he is able to read (Luke 4:16–20) and is knowledgeable of the Scriptures. Nothing is said of his marital status, which probably means that he is to be regarded as a single adult, committed (for religious reasons?) to a life of celibacy (cf. Matt. 19:12).

The New Testament focuses primarily on the last year or years of Jesus's life. He is baptized by John the Baptist, a fiery preacher of repentance who appears to have modeled his ministry after prophets such as Elijah from the Old Testament. Then Jesus begins a public ministry of his own, traveling throughout the villages of Galilee, teaching, preaching, and healing. He calls disciples to follow him and chooses twelve of those disciples to constitute an inner circle of followers patterned after the twelve tribes of Israel. Certain facets of his ministry are especially noteworthy:

⊙ EXPLORE 10.17
The Twelve Disciples

- It is an *itinerant* ministry. Whereas John the Baptist preached in the wilderness, expecting the crowds to come out to hear him, Jesus preaches on the road, taking his message to different groups as he and his disciples move from place to place (see Matt. 8:20).

- It is a *rural* ministry. Although there were large cities in Palestine (Caesarea, Sepphoris, Tiberias), Jesus is never said to visit any of them except for Jerusalem; the focus of his ministry is villages and market towns, places such as Bethsaida and Capernaum. He often is pictured as ministering to people in outdoor settings (e.g., beside the Sea of Galilee).
- It is a *Jewish* ministry. Despite occasional encounters with gentiles or Samaritans, the ministry of Jesus is directed primarily to Jews and conducted in terms meaningful to Jewish people. He frequently teaches in synagogues, he quotes from the Jewish Scriptures, and he discusses topics such as how the Jewish law might be best observed and how the writings of Jewish prophets are fulfilled.

gentiles: people who are not Jewish.

Samaritans: Semitic people who lived in Samaria at the time of Jesus and claimed to be the true Israel.

Thus the New Testament presents Jesus as a Jewish peasant who assumes the roles of rabbi and prophet on behalf of other Jewish peasants in Galilee during the rule of Herod Antipas; the most prominent phase of his ministry, furthermore, occurs just after Herod has John the Baptist arrested (see Mark 1:14).

In terms of content, the most prominent topic addressed by Jesus in the New Testament is the imminence and certainty of God's rule. Jesus often uses the phrase "kingdom of God" (or sometimes "kingdom of heaven") to describe the sphere of God's influence and power, a phenomenon that cannot be restricted by time and space. According to Jesus, the "kingdom of God" (a phrase that also can be translated "rule of God" or "reign of God") is not just in heaven or in the future but is a reality to be experienced here and now. When Jesus says, "The kingdom of God has come near" (Mark 1:15), he means something like, "God is ready and willing to rule our lives—right here, right now." But that is not all there is to it; the kingdom also has a future dimension, and the New Testament presents Jesus as speaking of this as well. There will be a final judgment at which Jesus himself will preside and human beings will either be granted access to eternal bliss or be condemned to everlasting punishment, depending on their status relative to God and to Jesus himself. Jesus indicates that the blessings of the future kingdom are for those who believe in him and who are faithful to him in word and deed.

kingdom of God / kingdom of heaven: phrases used to describe the phenomenon of God ruling, wherever and whenever that might be.

The overall emphasis on God's presence and power has numerous implications. Other prominent themes in Jesus's teaching and preaching include: (1) a call to uncompromising allegiance to God and absolute trust in God; (2) a promise of forgiveness that leads to the reconciliation of sinners and a new inclusion of outcasts among God's people; (3) a reassessment of certain legal interpretations, particularly those that are deemed burdensome or viewed as fostering spiritual elitism; (4) a radical "love ethic" that declares love for God and neighbor to be a synopsis of all of God's demands and that urges people to love everyone, even their enemies; and (5) a reversal of value judgments that insists that God favors the poor over the rich and the meek over the powerful, with the obvious corollary that those who wish to please God should humble themselves through voluntary poverty and service.

The New Testament also presents Jesus as teaching about himself—that is, about his identity as one who has a unique relationship with God—and

The Kingdom of God in the Teaching of Jesus

Jesus often teaches about "the kingdom of God." Sometimes he appears to be talking about the present reign of God in human lives; other times he appears to be talking about a future realm where people will live forever with God in heaven. Frequently his references to "the kingdom of God" appear to entail both meanings. The kingdom of God is a phenomenon that cannot be limited by time or space; it is both present reign and future realm.

- "Strive first for the kingdom of God and [God's] righteousness" (Matt. 6:33; cf. Luke 12:31).
- "If it is by the Spirit of God that I cast out demons, then the kingdom of God has come to you" (Matt. 12:28; cf. Luke 11:20).
- "The time is fulfilled, and the kingdom of God has come near; repent, and believe in the good news" (Mark 1:15; cf. Matt. 4:17).
- "The kingdom of God is as if someone would scatter seed on the ground, and would sleep and rise night and day, and the seed would sprout and grow, he does not know how" (Mark 4:26–27).
- "There are some standing here who will not taste death until they see that the kingdom of God has come with power" (Mark 9:1; cf. Matt. 16:28; Luke 9:27).
- "It is better for you to enter the kingdom of God with one eye than to have two eyes and be thrown into hell" (Mark 9:47).
- "Let the little children come to me; do not stop them; for it is to such as these that the

kingdom of God belongs" (Mark 10:14; cf. Matt. 19:14; Luke 18:16).
- "Whoever does not receive the kingdom of God as a little child will never enter it" (Mark 10:15; cf. Matt. 18:3).
- "How hard it will be for those who have wealth to enter the kingdom of God" (Mark 10:23; cf. Matt. 19:23; Luke 18:24).
- "I will never again drink of the fruit of the vine until that day when I drink it new in the kingdom of God" (Mark 14:25).
- "Blessed are you who are poor, for yours is the kingdom of God" (Luke 6:20).
- "There will be weeping and gnashing of teeth when you see Abraham and Isaac and Jacob and all the prophets in the kingdom of God, and you yourselves thrown out" (Luke 13:28).
- "The kingdom of God is not coming with things that can be observed; nor will they say, 'Look, here it is!' or 'There it is!' For, in fact, the kingdom of God is among you" (Luke 17:20–21).
- "No one can see the kingdom of God without being born from above" (John 3:3).

Compare These References from the Letters of Paul:

- "The kingdom of God is not food and drink but righteousness and peace and joy in the Holy Spirit" (Rom. 14:17).
- "The kingdom of God depends not on talk but on power" (1 Cor. 4:20).
- "Flesh and blood cannot inherit the kingdom of God" (1 Cor. 15:50).

as speaking proleptically—that is, in a manner that anticipates matters of concern to Christians in the life of the early church (see, e.g., Matt. 18:15–18). He often refers to himself in the third person as "the Son of Man," and he also wants to be identified (at least privately) as the Messiah and as the Son of God. In general, he seems to indicate that the possibility and necessity of living under God's rule is a new reality, one that is now available because of him: he is the mediator through whom people experience the power and presence of God's rule.

Fig. 4.2. Children in the marketplace. Jesus compared himself and John the Baptist to children playing music in a marketplace. No matter what type of music they play—funeral dirges or festive dances—most people pay no attention. So Jesus and John had very different styles of ministry, but both were dismissed by many (see Matt. 11:16–19; Luke 7:31–35). (Lalo Garcia)

The style or conduct of Jesus's ministry is also noteworthy. He is especially fond of telling parables, although he also uses proverbs, aphorisms, and other memorable forms of speech associated with the Jewish wisdom tradition. In addition, he is depicted as performing what might be called "prophetic acts" (unconventional public displays intended to make a particular point). The Old Testament narrates that Isaiah walked about naked for three years to illustrate the shame that would come upon Israel when the nation was taken into exile (Isa. 20:3), and that Jeremiah wore a yoke (Jer. 27:1–7) and broke a pot (Jer. 19:1–11). Prophetic acts attributed to Jesus include dining with tax collectors (Mark 2:15–17), riding into Jerusalem on a donkey (Mark 11:1–10), and overturning tables of money changers in the temple court (Mark 11:15–17).

Another prominent aspect of Jesus's ministry in the New Testament is his regular practice of healing the sick. He cleanses lepers; he makes the mute to speak, the deaf to hear, and the blind to see; he enables the lame or paralyzed

parables: figurative stories or sayings that convey spiritual truth through reference to mundane and earthly phenomena.

⊙ EXPLORE 4.3
Some Sayings of Jesus

⊙ EXPLORE 4.4
Parables in the Gospels

exorcism: the act of
casting a demon out
of a person or thing.

demon: an evil (or
"unclean") spirit ca-
pable of possessing
people and inca-
pacitating them with
some form of illness
or disability.

to walk. Often these healings are performed through acts of exorcism. People suffer various afflictions because they are possessed by demons, but when Jesus forces the unclean spirits to leave, the people are instantly cured. Jesus says that he is able to do this because the kingdom of God has come (Matt. 12:28); thus his healings and exorcisms also become prophetic acts, illustrating his central message about the presence and power of God's rule. In a few cases he even restores dead people to life. He also works what are sometimes called "nature miracles," doing things that ordinarily are impossible for a human being: he walks on water, he multiplies a limited quantity of food, he changes water into wine, he controls the weather, he withers a fig tree. To the extent that these miracles are prophetic acts, they serve to illustrate the power of faith in God (see Matt. 14:28–31; Mark 11:21–24); sometimes they also seem to carry symbolic meaning—for example, water being changed into wine symbolizes a transformation from mundane life to abundant life (see John 2:1–11).

In any case, Jesus's ministry brings him into conflict with the religious leaders of Israel. They disagree with him over many matters regarding interpretation of the law (e.g., Sabbath regulations, criteria for divorce) and the appropriate practice of piety (e.g., fasting, ritual handwashings, almsgiving, the wearing of phylacteries). According to the New Testament, these leaders are jealous of Jesus's popularity with the people, and they are scandalized by his public fellowship with sinners; they are also offended by his claim to speak with a divine authority that trumps their own judgments. But Jesus finds them offensive as well: he regards them as pedantic fools, as insincere hypocrites, and as pompous paragons of self-righteousness, and he denounces them publicly in precisely those terms.

The career of the earthly Jesus comes to a climax when he is arrested in Jerusalem on what the New Testament presents as trumped-up charges. He seeks to prepare his disciples for this trauma by displaying foreknowledge of what will occur, predicting exactly what will happen, and observing a final meal with his followers replete with last words and advice for them to follow in the days to come. His death is presented in the New Testament as a result of collaborative evil: high-ranking Jewish opponents want him out of the way, and they manipulate a predictably unjust Roman ruler (Pontius Pilate) into commanding the torture and execution of a man he knows to be innocent. Even Jesus's own disciples contribute to his disgraceful demise, as one of them betrays him, all of them desert him, and his right-hand man (Peter) denies that he even knows who Jesus is. Nailed to a cross, Jesus suffers and dies; his body is placed in a tomb donated by a sympathetic member of the Jewish elite. Then, just as he predicted, he rises from the dead and appears to a number of his followers.

⊙ EXPLORE 4.5
Miracles of Jesus Re-
ported in the Four
Gospels

Fig. 4.3. The universal Jesus. Throughout history, people in different cultures often have conceived of Jesus (and sometimes of the Virgin Mary) in terms appropriate for their particular context. The artists behind these three paintings are trying to portray Mary and Jesus not the way they "actually looked" in first-century Palestine but rather the way they might appear to devotees through the eyes of faith. Compare fig. 4.4. (*left*, Rose Walton; *center*, Bridgeman Images; *right*, National Trust Photo Library / Art Resource, NY)

The Earthly Jesus as Understood by Individual New Testament Authors

The foregoing sketch of the earthly Jesus resembles what is often taught and believed about Jesus in Christian churches and Sunday school classes. Academic study of the New Testament, however, takes a somewhat different approach to the subject: the primary goal of such study is not to understand what Christians believe about Jesus but rather to understand the writings of the New Testament itself. This is not an entirely different subject; obviously there is a lot of overlap between "the writings of the New Testament" and "what Christians believe about Jesus," since Christian beliefs are based on those writings. Still, the topics are not exactly the same, and we are now going to look at one of the most important ways in which they typically differ.

Christian beliefs about Jesus usually seek to encompass everything that the New Testament teaches concerning him—all the points made in different books combined. In order to understand any particular writing of the New Testament, however, it is necessary to focus on what that one book or author says apart from consideration of what is said in other books. Thus in New Testament studies it is customary to speak about "Matthew's Jesus" or "the Matthean Jesus," "John's Jesus" or "the Johannine Jesus," "Paul's Jesus" or "the Pauline Jesus," and so forth. This can be somewhat confusing or daunting for a beginning student, so a few examples will illustrate the matter.

In the Gospel of Matthew, Jesus does not ask for information from his disciples or other people. In Mark's Gospel, Jesus asks his disciples questions such as "How many loaves have you?" (6:38) and "What are you arguing about?" (9:16). The stories in which these questions occur are found in Matthew's Gospel also, but in Matthew the stories are told in such a way that no questions are asked (see 14:16–18; 17:14–16). There are several more examples of this. What are we to make of such a phenomenon? Certainly Jesus did ask people for information—the New Testament makes that clear. But the Matthean Jesus does not ask people for information. Recognizing this fact may not help us to know anything about Jesus (a goal of Christian theology and faith), but it does help us to understand Matthew's Gospel (a goal of New Testament study). In order to get a firm grasp of the Gospel of Matthew we need to ask, "Why doesn't this book portray Jesus as asking for information? Is it just a coincidence that it doesn't do this? Or is the author trying to make a point?"

Let's take another example. In the Gospel of John, Jesus performs no exorcisms and tells no parables. We know from the other Gospels that Jesus did perform exorcisms and tell parables. So the Jesus of the Synoptic Gospels does these things, but the Johannine Jesus does not. Again, knowing this probably does not enhance our understanding of the life and mission of the earthly Jesus, but it may contribute significantly to our understanding of one particular book of the New Testament: scholars who study the Gospel of John want to know why this Gospel does not include exorcisms or parables.

Students of the New Testament need to become accustomed to hearing statements such as the following:

- The Matthean Jesus insists that all the commandments of the law will remain valid until the end of time (Matt. 5:18).
- The Markan Jesus is unable to work miracles for those who lack faith (Mark 6:5; cf. Matt. 13:58).
- The Lukan Jesus promises that God will give the Holy Spirit to those who ask (Luke 11:13; cf. Matt. 7:11).
- The Johannine Jesus often uses metaphors to describe himself (John 6:35; 8:12; 10:7, 11; 11:25; 14:6; 15:1).

⊙ EXPLORE 4.6
Four Pictures of Jesus

⊙ EXPLORE 4.15
Quests for the Historical Jesus: Highlights in the History of the Discipline

⊙ EXPLORE 4.17
Modern Biographies of Jesus

More troubling to some students, particularly those steeped in Christian faith and tradition, are statements that seem to indicate that a book contradicts the beliefs or values of Christianity. For instance, New Testament scholars will say, "The Markan Jesus was not born of a virgin." To the uninitiated, this might sound like a denial of the Christian doctrine of the virgin birth, but the scholars are simply stating a fact: there are no references to the virgin birth of Jesus in the Gospel of Mark. The author of Mark's Gospel either did not know the story of the virgin birth or deliberately chose to omit it. Either way, if we want to understand what the author of Mark's Gospel intended to communicate through the book that he wrote, we must focus on interpreting that book as it was written rather than on supplementing it with information from other sources. At an introductory level, the goal of New Testament studies is always to understand each book on its own terms; the later integration of themes and ideas from all the New Testament writings is usually associated with an advanced field of study called "New Testament theology."

The Earthly Jesus as Understood by Modern Historians

Historians are also interested in studying the earthly Jesus portrayed in the New Testament, and they use the New Testament writings the same way they use any other writings from antiquity. They view these writings as primary sources to be analyzed in order to extract information pertinent to a credible reconstruction of who Jesus was and what happened in the world because of him. In using the New Testament for this purpose, we should note, historians do not use it the same way theologians do when they seek to explicate

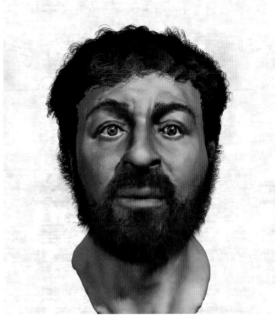

Fig. 4.4. The historical Jesus? This "reconstructed head of Christ" was produced by Richard Neave, a forensic scientist and medical artist at the University of Manchester. Dr. Neave worked with three skulls of Semitic Galilean men from the first century CE to compose a reasonable facsimile of what Jesus actually looked like. Neave further suggests that Jesus would have been about five feet one and weighed about 110 pounds. He likely had a beard because this was customary for teachers, but he would have worn his curly hair roughly cropped because shoulder-length hair on men was considered disgraceful (1 Cor. 11:14). (BBC Photo Library)

what Christians should believe about Jesus, nor do they use it in the same way as scholars whose goal is to understand the messages of individual books. The object of the historian's quest is not "the New Testament Jesus," who is important to Christian faith, nor is it "the Matthean Jesus" or "the Johannine Jesus" or any other such figure who is often the focus of New Testament study. They seek "the historical Jesus"—that is, the person who emerges from an analysis of sources in accord with generally accepted principles of historical science. In this sense, the historical study of Jesus is a decidedly different field from New Testament studies: it is a field that uses the New Testament to understand history rather than a field that views interpretation of the New Testament as an end in itself. Still, the overlap of interest between these two fields is considerable, such that some discussion of what is called "historical Jesus studies" may be appropriate.

The first thing to say is that "the historical Jesus" should not be equated with the actual man Jesus who lived in Galilee. Historians recognize that Jesus,

Box 4.3

A Historian's Biography of Jesus: An Excerpt

He comes as yet unknown into a hamlet of Lower Galilee. He is watched by the cold, hard eyes of peasants living long enough at subsistence level to know exactly where the line is drawn between poverty and destitution. He looks like a beggar, yet his eyes lack the proper cringe, his voice the proper whine, his walk the proper shuffle. He speaks about the rule of God, and they listen as much from curiosity as anything else. They know all about rule and power, about kingdom and empire, but they know it in terms of tax and debt, malnutrition and sickness, agrarian oppression and demonic possession. What, they really want to know, can this kingdom of God do for a lame child, a blind parent, a demented soul screaming its tortured isolation among the graves that mark the edges of the village? Jesus walks with them to the tombs, and, in the silence after the exorcism, the villagers listen once more, but now with curiosity giving way to cupidity, fear, and embarrassment. He is invited, as honor demands, to the home of the village leader. He goes, instead, to stay in the home of a dispossessed woman. Not quite proper, to be sure, but it would be unwise to censure an exorcist, to criticize a magician.

John Dominic Crossan, *The Historical Jesus* (San Francisco: Harper San Francisco, 1991), xi.

the actual person, said and did many things that are unknown to us. They also allow that he may have said and done things reported in the New Testament that cannot be regarded as historical, simply because there is insufficient evidence to verify or confirm what is reported there. Historical science is skeptical by nature. For example, historians usually are unwilling to accept allegations that people performed miracles or other supernatural feats that defy known laws of science. They do not necessarily deny that such things occurred, but they usually maintain that such claims cannot be confirmed in ways that allow them to be regarded as historical facts. They are not matters that can be verified on the basis of what counts as historical evidence.

Historians are also cautious about accepting unsubstantiated reports from authors who are reporting things that they would have wanted to be true or that would have helped to promote their particular cause. Thus, from a historian's perspective, the New Testament documents must be classified as "religious propaganda"; they were written for the express purpose of promoting the Christian faith and persuading people to believe certain things about Jesus. For example, the Gospels of Matthew and Luke report that Jesus (who usually was said to be from Nazareth) was actually born in Bethlehem. But this is something that Christians would have wanted people to believe about Jesus; a birth in Bethlehem would help to boost his credentials as the Jewish Messiah, who was expected to be born there (see Matt. 2:4–6; cf. Mic. 5:2). Accordingly, historians are cautious about accepting such a report as historical fact.

This skeptical use of the New Testament is a far cry from the theological appreciation accorded to the writings by people who believe that they are inspired Scripture. Still, students should not assume that "historical Jesus scholars" are necessarily irreligious. Many may be devout Christians who are simply committed to honesty with regard to the practice of their discipline (historical

⊙ **EXPLORE 4.13**
The Enlightenment: Historical Skepticism and Religious Faith

⊙ **EXPLORE 4.16**
Criteria for Historical Criticism

⊙ **EXPLORE 4.20**
Historical Jesus Studies and Christian Apologetics

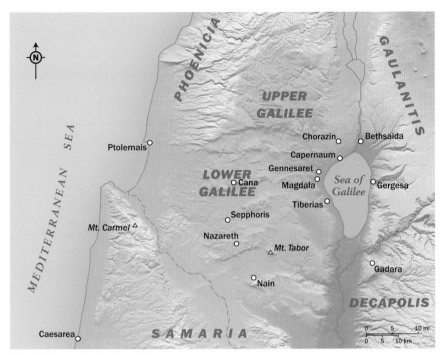

Map 4.1. Galilee in the time of Jesus.

science); they realize that even if they personally believe in Jesus (in a spiritual or theological or religious sense), they should not fudge the evidence or treat the historical materials concerning him differently than they would if they were studying any other individual from the ancient world.

Students sometimes find it awkward to think of biblical assertions about Jesus in these terms. It may seem sacrilegious to admit that some things they believe about Jesus, things clearly presented in the New Testament, do not pass muster in terms of historical science. But there may be a sense in which we already know this to be the case. In the United States certain things can be taught about Jesus in public schools: a history teacher may tell students that Jesus was Jewish, that he taught the Golden Rule, that he called disciples, that he was crucified—these are regarded as "historical facts" about Jesus that can be presented without any suspicion that the teacher is promoting the Christian religion. Yet most people in America realize that it would be inappropriate for a public school teacher to tell students that Jesus was born to a virgin, that he was the Messiah, or that he died for people's sins. A teacher who said such things would probably get in trouble for teaching religious beliefs rather than simply presenting historical information. Of course, the categories of "historical facts" and "religious assertions" get fuzzy, but most of us probably have some degree of awareness that certain things about Jesus are verifiable apart from faith while other things are not. The search for "the historical Jesus" is basically a quest for "the historically verifiable Jesus."

Golden Rule: a traditional name given to the words of Jesus in Matthew 7:12: "In everything do to others as you would have them do to you."

Box 4.4

Images and Titles for Jesus in the New Testament

Advocate	1 John 2:1	High Priest	Heb. 3:1	Prophet	Luke 13:33
Alpha and Omega	Rev. 21:6	Holy One of God	Mark 1:24	Rabbi	John 3:2
Apostle	Heb. 3:1	Image of God	Col. 1:15	The Resurrection	John 11:25
Author of Life	Acts 3:15	Judge	Acts 10:42	Root of David	Rev. 5:5
Bread of Life	John 6:35	King	Matt. 25:40	Root of Jesse	Rom. 15:12
Bridegroom	Mark 2:19–20	King of Kings	Rev. 19:16	Sanctifier	Heb. 2:11
Brother	Matt. 25:40	Lamb of God	John 1:29	Savior	Luke 2:11
Chief Cornerstone	Eph. 2:20	The Life	John 14:6	Savior of the World	John 4:42
Chief Shepherd	1 Pet. 5:4	Light of the World	John 9:5	Second Adam	Rom. 12:5–19
Christ (Messiah)	Mark 8:29	Lion of Judah	Rev. 5:5	Servant	Mark 10:45
Emmanuel	Matt. 1:23	Lord	Rom. 10:9	Son of Abraham	Matt. 1:1
Firstborn from the Dead	Col. 1:18	Lord of Glory	1 Cor. 2:8	Son of David	Matt. 9:27
Firstborn of Creation	Col. 1:15	Lord of Lords	Rev. 19:16	Son of God	John 20:31
Friend	John 15:13–15	Master	Luke 17:13	Son of Man	Matt. 20:28
The Gate	John 10:7	Mediator	1 Tim. 2:5	Spirit	Acts 16:7
God	Titus 2:13	Minister	Heb. 8:2	Teacher	John 13:13
Good Shepherd	John 10:11	Morning Star	Rev. 22:16	The Truth	John 14:6
Guarantee	Heb. 7:22	Our Peace	Eph. 2:14	The Vine	John 15:5
Head of the Body	Col. 1:18	Perfecter of Faith	Heb. 12:2	The Way	John 14:6
Heir	Heb. 1:2	Pioneer	Heb. 12:2	The Word	John 1:1

The Exalted Figure of Jesus in the New Testament

So far we have focused all of our attention on the earthly figure of Jesus, the man who lived in Galilee (and who thus is subject to historical investigation). But, as indicated above, the New Testament also pays a good deal of attention to Jesus as an exalted figure who continues to be active in human lives even though he is no longer physically present on earth. In fact, the New Testament generally presents "being a Christian" as a matter of being in a living relationship with Jesus Christ, a relationship that must be construed differently from that which human beings once had with the earthly Jesus. Sometimes Jesus is envisioned as dwelling within the individual believer (Gal. 2:19–20). More often the metaphor is reversed such that the believer is found in Christ (Phil. 3:9)—that is, as one part of the corporate entity that now makes up Christ's body on earth (1 Cor. 12:27). In any event, the relationship is mutual: believers abide in Jesus Christ, and Jesus Christ abides in them (John 15:5).

There is considerable variation in such imagery. The exalted Jesus can be identified as the bridegroom of the church (Mark 2:19) or as a great high priest who serves God in a heavenly sanctuary (Heb. 4:14). Indeed, the exalted Jesus is often located in heaven (Col. 3:1), though he remains active on earth, especially through the words and deeds of those who speak and act in his name (Acts 4:30).

He sometimes is identified as a spirit who continues to inspire and direct affairs on earth (Acts 16:7). He communicates with people through visions (2 Cor. 12:1) and prophecies (1 Cor. 14:29–31). His presence sometimes is experienced by way of interaction with other people, especially the disadvantaged (Matt. 25:40) or vulnerable (Mark 9:37) or persecuted (Acts 9:5). The realization or manifestation of his presence sometimes is linked to baptism (Gal. 3:27) or to participation in a ritual reenactment of his last supper (1 Cor. 11:23–26). He answers prayers (John 14:14) and also offers prayers for his followers (Rom. 8:34). Furthermore, the New Testament provides absolute assurance that this exalted Jesus is coming again: he will return to the earth in a tangible way at the end of time, coming

Fig. 4.5. Christ in glory. A sixth-century image from Saqqara, Egypt. (Bridgeman Images)

on the clouds of heaven to preside at the final judgment (Matt. 24:30; 25:31–32).

Until then, Jesus remains an object of devotion: Christians can almost be defined as people "who call on the name of the Lord Jesus Christ" (1 Cor. 1:2), or as people who believe in Jesus without physical evidence of his existence (John 20:29), or as people who love Jesus even though they have not seen him (1 Pet. 1:8). Indeed, they are people who regard him as worthy of worship and praise (Rev. 5:6–14).

This general overview of how the New Testament presents the figure of the exalted Jesus is important for Christian theology and faith. But, as with the earthly figure of Jesus, the field of New Testament studies wants to get more specific and focus on how individual books or authors understand the exalted Christ. Some writers exhibit what is called a "high Christology," according to which the exalted Jesus is virtually equated with God (see box 4.5); others strive to maintain some distinction between Jesus (exalted though he might be) and God the Father, to whom he remains subordinate (see Mark 10:18;

Christ: "anointed one" or Messiah; the man known as "Jesus the Christ" eventually came to be called simply "Jesus Christ."

Christology: a branch of theology that focuses on the person and work of Jesus Christ, often understood as an eternal divine figure.

Jesus as God: New Testament References

The following verses often are cited as examples of instances in which the New Testament refers to Jesus as God:

- "the Word was God" (John 1:1)
- "God, the only Son" (John 1:18)
- "My Lord and my God" (John 20:28)
- "the Messiah, who is over all, God blessed forever" (Rom. 9:5)
- "our great God and Savior, Jesus Christ" (Titus 2:13)
- "of the Son, he says, 'Your throne, O God'" (Heb. 1:8)
- "our God and Savior, Jesus Christ" (2 Pet. 1:1)
- "Jesus Christ . . . is the true God" (1 John 5:20)

See Murray J. Harris, *Jesus as God: The New Testament Use of* Theos *in Reference to Jesus* (Grand Rapids: Baker Academic, 1992).

John 14:28). Some books or writers emphasize certain aspects of the exalted Jesus's identity or ministry and pay little attention to others. For example, the Letter to the Hebrews is largely constructed around an exposition of the exalted Jesus as high priest, an image given little (if any) attention in most of the other New Testament books. The image of the exalted Jesus being manifest in a body of believers on earth is especially prominent in the letters of Paul. New Testament scholars do not just assume that every author operated with the full range of understanding regarding the exalted Jesus found in the New Testament as a whole; rather, they try to discern which aspects of New Testament imagery are operative for each book, so as to understand each book on its own terms.

Conclusion

So how many Jesuses are there? Have you been keeping track?

Let's see. We have "the New Testament Jesus" (also called "the canonical Jesus"). We have "the earthly Jesus" (sometimes called "the pre-Easter Jesus" or "the Jesus of history"). We have "the exalted Jesus" (also called "the post-Easter Jesus" or "the Christ of faith"). And then there is "the historical Jesus" (also called "the historically verifiable Jesus"). And we have all the different Jesuses associated with the various writings or authors of the New Testament: the Pauline Jesus, the Johannine Jesus, the Petrine Jesus (i.e., the Jesus of 1 Peter), and so forth. Ultimately we might also speak of the "Jesus of Christian theology," or indeed we might speak of "the Baptist Jesus," "the Calvinist Jesus," "the Catholic Jesus," "the Lutheran Jesus," "the Wesleyan Jesus," and so on. We might (and scholars definitely do) speak of "the American Jesus," "the Asian Jesus," "the African Jesus," "the Latin American Jesus," and on and on.

It is daunting, and eventually it probably does get a little bit silly. But the complexity of classifications is a measure of the stature and significance of the man himself. No other person in history or in literature has ever been accorded this much attention; no one else attracts this level or this variety of interest. According to the New Testament, that is nothing new; almost from the very start, Jesus is said to have prompted consideration of the questions that people continue to ask today:

"What is this? A new teaching?" (Mark 1:27)

"Why does this fellow speak in this way?" (Mark 2:7)

"Who then is this?" (Mark 4:41)

"Where did this man get all this?" (Mark 6:2)

All of those verses come from just one book, the Gospel of Mark. Then, as that story continues (in Mark 8:27–28), Jesus asks his disciples to respond to this question: "Who do people say that I am?" And then he asks them to respond to another question: "Who do *you* say that I am?" The academic task may be to learn about how various New Testament authors, historians, and theologians identify the person and significance of Jesus. But most students eventually end up wanting to answer the question for themselves.

FOR FURTHER READING: **Jesus**

Borg, Marcus J. *Jesus: Uncovering the Life, Teachings, and Relevance of a Religious Revolutionary*. New York: HarperCollins, 2006.

Burridge, Richard A., and Graham Gould. *Jesus Now and Then*. Grand Rapids: Eerdmans, 2004.

Ehrman, Bart D. *How Jesus Became God: The Exaltation of a Jewish Preacher from Galilee*. San Francisco: HarperCollins, 2014.

Gowler, David B. *What Are They Saying about the Historical Jesus?* Mahwah, NJ: Paulist Press, 2007.

O'Collins, Gerald. *Christology: A Biblical, Historical, and Systematic Study of Jesus*. 2nd ed. Oxford: Oxford University Press, 2009.

Powell, Mark Allan. *Jesus as a Figure in History: How Modern Historians View the Man from Galilee*. 2nd ed. Louisville: Westminster John Knox, 2013.

Tuckett, Christopher M. *Christology and the New Testament: Jesus and His Earliest Followers*. Louisville: Westminster John Knox, 2001.

Wright, N. T. *The Challenge of Jesus: Rediscovering Who Jesus Was and Is*. Downers Grove, IL: InterVarsity, 2015.

⊙ Go to www .IntroducingNT.com for summaries, videos, and other study tools.

ὉΆΓΙΟΣ ἌΓΓΕΛΟΣ

ὉΆΓΙΟΣ ΛΕΏΝ

ὉΆΓΙΟΣ ΜΌΣΧΟΣ

ὉΆΓΙΟΣ ἈΕΤῸΣ

⳨ ΤΥΠΟΙ ΙΕΡΟΥΡΓΙΑΣ ΑΓΓΕΛΟΣ ΜΟΣΧΟΣ ΛΕΩΝ ΚΑΙ ΑΕΤΟΣ ✝ ΕΙΚΩΝ ΤΟΥ ΕΤΟΥΣ 1997 ΟΚΤΩΒΡΙΟΥ 15 ΕΝ ΜΟΝΕΜΒΑΣΙΑ ΜΑΝΩΛΗ Γ Ο ΠΟΝΟΣ ✝ ✕ ⳨

5

The Gospels

Think about drawings, paintings, and other pictures of Jesus that you have seen. How do they portray him? What appeals to you? Are there pictures that you really like or dislike? Why?

You do not have to look far for examples! This book contains quite a variety. For example, in the last chapter there is a portrayal of Jesus that strives for realism, attempting to depict the man as he actually may have looked (fig. 4.4). And then there are examples of artwork that go another route, intentionally portraying Jesus in ways that will help contemporary people relate to him (fig. 4.3). These artists are not trying to be literal; they want to paint Jesus "as we see him today."

As we begin our study of the four New Testament Gospels, it may be helpful to think of the books as providing "portraits of Jesus," and you may want to give some thought to the question of what sort of portrait is provided. Did the Gospel authors strive to describe the person and work of Jesus with precise, literal, historical accuracy, or were they more interested in presenting Jesus in a manner that would make him relevant to an intended audience? You will not be surprised to hear that scholars disagree on this point, but the discord can be overstated. Very few scholars would maintain that the Gospel writers had no interest in historically accurate representation, and virtually no one would deny that they shaped their accounts of Jesus in ways that would highlight his significance for their readers. The question is whether one concern dominated the other.

We can go further with this analogy because "historical reconstruction versus contemporary relevance" is only one issue to be considered. Look at pictures of Jesus and you will find works that show Jesus in very spiritual terms, gazing heavenward, with a halo about his head; other times he looks just like any other man, like "one of us." Some artists portray him as gentle and tender, cradling a little lamb in his bosom or holding children on his lap. But that does not look very much like the Jesus who screamed at Pharisees ("You brood of vipers!") or drove money changers out of the temple. The questions that artists inevitably face are these: "Which Jesus do I want to present? Which aspects of this multifaceted person do I want to emphasize?"

Likewise, each of the four Gospels presents a portrait of Jesus that is distinctive from those of the other three. Near the end of the second century (about a hundred years after the Gospels were written), Irenaeus, bishop of Lyons, suggested that the Gospels could be symbolized by the four "living creatures" mentioned in both Ezekiel 1:4–14 and Revelation 4:6–8. This became standard practice in Christian art throughout the centuries. Matthew is portrayed as a man, Mark as a lion, Luke as an ox, and John as an eagle. Thus the church recognized from the start that each Gospel was unique.

The temptation for Bible readers is to combine all four portraits in order to obtain as complete a picture of Jesus as possible. But doing that causes us to miss the particular image that each Gospel writer wanted to present. The goal of Gospel study should first be to recognize the four separate portraits that these individual books offer (see box 5.1). When we focus on any one Gospel, and on that Gospel alone, what is the image of Jesus that emerges? This is the image that the author (a literary artist) wanted to show us. Once we see *that* Jesus, we may go on to another Gospel and obtain a second image, and then a third, and a fourth.

Genre

What is a "Gospel" anyway? Most modern readers are familiar with many different types of literature—a walk through a modern bookstore reveals sections

---

Box 5.1

Four Pictures of Jesus

- The Gospel of Matthew presents Jesus as the one who abides with his people always until the end of time. Jesus founds the church, in which sins are forgiven, prayers are answered, and the power of death is overcome (Matt. 16:18–19; 18:18–20).
- The Gospel of Mark presents Jesus as the one who announces the advent of God's reign, in which the humble are exalted and the proud brought low. Obedient to this rule, he dies on a cross, giving his life as a ransom for many (Mark 10:45).
- The Gospel of Luke presents Jesus as the one whose words and deeds liberate those who are oppressed. Jesus comes to seek and to save the lost and to bring release to all those whom he describes as "captives" (Luke 4:18; 19:10).
- The Gospel of John presents Jesus as the one who reveals what God is truly like. Jesus is the Word of God made flesh, and he reveals through his words and deeds all that can be known of God (John 1:14; 14:8).

devoted to history, fiction, travel, and so forth. We might wonder: If there had been bookstores like this in the ancient world, where would they have shelved the Gospel of Matthew? Or Mark, or Luke, or John?

The word *gospel* was first used to describe not a type of book but rather the content of Christian preaching. The word literally means "good news" (Greek, *euangelion*), and for this reason the authors of the four New Testament Gospels have often been called "the four evangelists" because they wrote good news (essentially the same good news that other "evangelists" were preaching). In a sense, then, our written Gospels are only a short step removed from preaching, but they don't really read like sermons. What are they?

Many modern scholars think that the Gospels can be placed loosely into the genre of "ancient biography." Books belonging to that genre were especially popular in the Roman world, and many of them have survived to the present day. The Greek historian Plutarch (45–125 CE) wrote more than fifty biographies of prominent Greeks and Romans. Around the same time as Plutarch, Suetonius and Tacitus recounted the lives of the Roman emperors. There were biographies of generals and military heroes and also of philosophers and religious leaders. A Roman bookstore or library probably would have put our New Testament Gospels on the same shelf as *Lives of Eminent Philosophers* by Diogenes Laertius and *Life of Apollonius of Tyana* by Philostratus.

Understanding the Gospels as ancient biographies is helpful, but at least five more things need to be said in this regard.

1. *They are compilations.* Although the Gospels as finished products might be identified as ancient biographies, they include other genres of literature within their pages: genealogies, hymns, parables, miracle stories, speeches, pronouncement stories, and more.

2. *They are influenced by Jewish literature.* All four New Testament Gospels are written in Greek, the language of the Greco-Roman world, but they were written by persons well versed in the Scriptures of Israel. Those Scriptures also contain semibiographical narratives of people such as Abraham, Moses, and Elijah. Even though our Gospels were written for the Greco-Roman world, their authors knew these Old Testament stories and were influenced by them.

3. *They are ancient biographies, not modern ones.* The Gospels make no pretense of offering objective or balanced perspectives on Jesus's life. They do not reveal their sources or offer any way for readers to check the reliability of what they report. Their treatment is far from comprehensive: they offer little insight into Jesus's personality or motivation; they provide almost no information about his early life; they do not even bother to describe his physical appearance. They also lack the sort of

evangelist: in New Testament studies, an author of any one of the four Gospels; Matthew, Mark, Luke, and John are the four evangelists.

⊙ **EXPLORE 5.22**
The Gospel: Four Stages

Box 5.2

Characteristics of Ancient Biographies

- no pretense of detached objectivity
- no concern for establishing facts (e.g., by citing evidence or sources)
- little attention to historical data (names, dates, places)
- little attention to chronology of events or development of the subject's thought
- no psychological interest in the subject's inner motivations
- anecdotal style of narration
- emphasis on the subject's character and defining traits
- consistent focus on the subject's philosophy of life
- strong interest in the subject's death, as consistent with philosophy of life
- presentation of the subject as a model worthy of emulation
- depiction of the subject as superior to competitors or rivals
- overall concern with the subject's legacy, evident in followers who carry on the tradition

data—references to names, dates, and places—that would be standard for any modern biography: the Gospel of Mark tells us that Jesus healed a man in a synagogue (3:1–6), but it does not give us the man's name or tell us when this happened or what happened next (Was the healing permanent? Did the man become a follower of Jesus? Did he continue to attend the synagogue?). Though it may seem strange to us, audiences in the ancient world did not expect such questions to be addressed in biographies. The point of ancient biographies was to relate accounts that portrayed the essential character of the person who was the subject of the work. Indeed, the purpose of the biography was to define that person's character in a manner that would invite emulation. The anecdotal style of ancient biographies, furthermore, allowed events to be related without much concern for chronology. Events were not necessarily reported in the order in which they occurred; rather, they were recounted in a sequence likely to have a desired rhetorical effect on the book's readers. This characteristic may explain why our four Gospels often relate events in different sequences (e.g., the account of Jesus overturning tables in the Jerusalem temple is found near the beginning of John's Gospel but comes near the end of the Gospel of Mark). See box 5.2.

4. *They employ a fictive ("fiction-like") style of narration.* In many ways the literary style of the New Testament Gospels is closer to that of modern fiction than it is to modern historical reporting. To say this is not to cast any aspersions on the accuracy of what is reported: scholars who regard the content of the Gospels as historically reliable can still recognize that the style of writing is quite similar to that of works that we now classify as historical fiction. The Gospel authors knew the art of storytelling, and they employ literary devices such as irony, symbolism, and foreshadowing. They solicit our empathy so that, as their stories unfold, we feel

⊙ EXPLORE 5.16
Plutarch on the Purpose of Writing a Biography

drawn into the drama. Thus scholars who employ "narrative criticism" (see "Narrative Criticism" in chap. 3) often talk about the "plot" of a particular Gospel or about how its rhetorical features bring the story to a climax in a way intended to generate specific effects on the readers. The genre of ancient biography allows for such analysis because biographies in the ancient world tended to treat history as a story and to relate events with a flair that modern readers associate with fiction.

5. *They are overtly evangelistic.* Most biographies written in the ancient world were evangelistic in a broad sense. They did not simply pass on information about interesting individuals; rather, they reported on extraordinary lives with an obvious hope that readers would be inspired by what was presented and would be motivated to change their values or behaviors accordingly. Our New Testament Gospels exhibit this tendency to an extreme. Their authors tell the story of Jesus in a way that may inspire people to accept his teaching or practice his way of life. But there is more: the claim of the Gospels is that what has happened in and through Jesus has altered the very course of history and the nature of human existence. These authors are telling a story of ultimate significance, recounting things that they claim will affect the lives of all people, whether they believe in Jesus or not.

Types of Material in the Gospels

As noted earlier, the Gospels are best viewed as compilations. Their authors composed them to serve as biographies of Jesus, but in so doing they incorporated many different types of material into the overall "biography" framework. Some of these are specific to particular Gospels: fulfillment citations are especially popular in Matthew; hymns are found only in Luke and John; genealogies are found only in Matthew and Luke. But other types of material are found in most or all of the Gospels. We will survey here some types of material that are particularly pervasive.

fulfillment citation: a form-critical category for a declaration that something has happened in order to fulfill what was prophesied in the Scriptures (e.g., Matt. 2:15).

Parables

Jesus is famous for telling parables. More than forty parables of Jesus are included in the Gospels of Matthew, Mark, and Luke (see box 5.3). There are no parables in John's Gospel, but even there we see instances of figurative speech not far removed from the parable genre (4:35–37; 8:35; 10:1–5; 12:24; 16:21).

What, exactly, is a parable? The stories and sayings that get classed as parables in the Gospels are of many different types. A couple of Jesus's better-known parables are explicitly presented as allegories: he explains the parable

allegory: a type of figurative speech in which the elements or characters that make up a story signify concepts or other entities in the real world.

Box 5.3

Parables in the Gospels

Parable	Matthew	Mark	Luke
New patch on an old cloak	9:16	2:21	5:36
New wine in old wineskins	9:17	2:22	5:37–38
The sower	13:3–8	4:3–8	8:5–8
Lamp under a bowl	5:14–16	4:21–22	8:16; 11:33
Seed growing secretly		4:26–29	
Mustard seed	13:31–32	4:30–32	13:18–19
Wicked tenants	21:33–44	12:1–11	20:9–18
Fig tree	24:32–33	13:28–29	21:29–31
Watchful slaves		13:33–37	12:35–38
Wise and foolish builders	7:24–27		6:47–49
Yeast leavens flour	13:33		13:20–21
Lost sheep	18:12–14		15:4–7
Thief in the night	24:42–44		12:39–40
Faithful and wise slave	24:45–51		12:42–48
The talents (or the pounds)	25:14–30		19:12–27
Weeds among the wheat	13:24–30		
Treasure hidden in a field	13:44		
Pearl of great value	13:45–46		
Net full of good and bad fish	13:47–50		
Treasure new and old	13:52		
Unmerciful servant	18:23–34		
Workers in the vineyard	20:1–16		
Two sons	21:28–32		
Wedding banquet	22:2–14		
Ten bridesmaids	25:1–13		
The two debtors			7:41–43
The good Samaritan			10:30–37
Friend at midnight			11:5–8
Rich fool			12:16–21
Severe and light beatings			12:47–48
Barren tree			13:6–9
Lowest seat at a banquet			14:7–14
Excuses for not attending a banquet			14:16–24
Building a tower			14:28–30
Waging war			14:31–32
Lost coin			15:8–10
Prodigal son			15:11–32
Shrewd manager			16:1–9
Rich man and Lazarus			16:19–31
Slave serves the master			17:7–10
Widow and judge			18:2–5
Pharisee and tax collector			18:10–14

Summary

9 parables from Mark (all but one of which are also in Matthew and/or Luke)

6 parables from material that is often ascribed to Q (found in Matthew and Luke but not in Mark)

10 parables unique to Matthew

17 parables unique to Luke

42 parables in all

of the sower (Mark 4:3–8; cf. 4:13–20) and the parable of the weeds (Matt. 13:24–30; cf. 13:36–43) by indicating that every element of these stories stands for something else (the seed is the word, the birds are the devil, etc.). Most of the parables, however, are not allegories. A few are simply one-liners that seem more like "ideas for parables" than parables proper (see Matt. 15:13; cf. 15:15). Jesus compares heavenly or spiritual things to mundane realities: the kingdom of God is like a mustard seed (Mark 4:30–32) or a pearl (Matt. 13:45–46) or a treasure hidden in a field (Matt. 13:44). Many parables are short anecdotes that function like sermon illustrations: the parable of the rich fool in Luke 12:16–21 illustrates the folly of equating quality of life with the acquisition of possessions. But in other cases the parables do not help to clarify a difficult point; they do exactly the opposite, introducing an element of complication with regard to what would otherwise be clear. God prefers those who keep Torah to those who do not, right? Well, not in the case of a particular Pharisee and a particular tax collector (Luke 18:10–14). Indeed, in some instances the parables pose riddles for people to figure out (Mark 3:23), and in certain cases they function as a sort of code language for speaking of divine matters in terms that the unenlightened will not comprehend (see Mark 4:11–12, 33–34; 7:17). C. H. Dodd, a parable expert, said a parable often has the tendency to "leave the mind in sufficient doubt about its precise application to tease it into active thought" (*Parables of the Kingdom* [London: Collins, 1961], 16).

In general, scholars seek to discern the basic point that each parable was expected to make and warn against reading too much into the stories. Jesus tells a parable about prayer, using the example of a persistent widow who seeks justice from a corrupt and uncaring judge (Luke 18:2–5). The basic point is that persistence is important with regard to spiritual quests; we would be amiss to think that Jesus wanted people to view God as corrupt and uncaring. He tells another parable about laborers all being paid the same wage even though they worked different amounts of hours (Matt. 20:1–16). The basic point seems to be that God can be surprisingly generous in a way that offends those who see themselves as more deserving; it is less likely that Matthew preserved this parable in his Gospel because he wanted to propose some new pay scale for day laborers. That said, interpreters do sometimes try to go beyond the "basic point" of the parables to ask why Jesus would make these points in these particular ways: Do the stories above offer any hints as to his view of judges or labor relations?

⊙ EXPLORE 5.20
Parables as Allegories

⊙ EXPLORE 5.23
Literary Characteristics of Parables

Box 5.4

A Jewish Perspective on Parables

The parable should not be lightly esteemed in your eyes, since by means of the parable one arrives at the true meaning of the words of the Torah.

—Midrash, *Song of Songs Rabbah* 1.8

Harry Freedman and Maurice Smith, eds., *Midrash Rabbah* (London: Soncino, 1939).

Miracle Stories

Jesus is also famous for working miracles, and all four Gospels contain numerous accounts of him doing so (see box 5.5). The preferred Greek term for "miracle" in the Synoptic Gospels (Matthew, Mark, Luke) is *dynamis*, which means "power" or "deed of power" (e.g., Matt. 11:20–23; Mark 6:2, 5). In John's Gospel the miracles often are called *sēmeia*, or "signs," because they point beyond themselves to the truth about God that Jesus has come to reveal (e.g., 2:11; 12:37).

The most common miracle stories are accounts of Jesus healing those who are sick or physically disabled; in a few cases he is even said to restore dead people to life. Many of these stories exhibit a focus on faith, either that of the afflicted person (Mark 5:34; 10:52; Luke 17:19) or that of others (Mark 2:5;

Fig. 5.1. Jesus casts out a demon. (The Bridgeman Art Library International)

⊙ **EXPLORE 5.25**
Miracles and the
Modern Mind

Miracles of Jesus Reported in the Four Gospels

	Matthew	Mark	Luke	John
Healings and Exorcisms				
Demoniac in synagogue		1:23–26	4:33–35	
Peter's mother-in-law	8:14–15	1:30–31	4:38–39	
Man with leprosy	8:2–4	1:40–42	5:12–13	
Paralytic	9:2–7	2:3–12	5:18–25	
Man with withered hand	12:10–13	3:1–5	6:6–10	
Gadarene demoniac(s)	8:28–34	5:1–15	8:27–35	
Woman with hemorrhage	9:20–22	5:25–34	8:43–48	
Gentile woman's daughter	15:21–28	7:24–30		
Deaf mute		7:31–37		
Blind man at Bethsaida		8:22–26		
Demon-possessed boy	17:14–18	9:17–29		
Blind Bartimaeus (and companion?)	20:29–34?	10:46–52		
Centurion's servant	8:5–13		7:1–10	4:46–54
(Blind) mute demoniac	12:22		11:14	
Two blind men	9:27–31			
Mute demoniac	9:32–33			
Crippled woman			13:11–13	
Man with dropsy			14:1–4	
Ten lepers			17:11–19	
High priest's servant			22:50–51	
Invalid at Pool of Bethesda				5:1–9
Man born blind				9:1–7
Resuscitation (dead brought back to life)				
Jairus's daughter	9:18–25	5:22–42	8:41–56	
Widow's son			7:11–15	
Lazarus				11:1–44
Provision				
Five thousand people fed	14:15–21	6:35–44	9:12–17	6:5–13
Four thousand people fed	15:32–38	8:1–9		
Catch of fish			5:1–11	
Changing water into wine				2:1–11
Post-Easter catch of fish				21:1–11
Miscellaneous				
Calming a storm at sea	8:23–27	4:37–41	8:22–25	
Walking on water	14:25	6:48–51		6:19–21
Transfiguration	17:1–8	9:2–8	9:28–36	
Withering a fig tree	21:18–22	11:12–25		
Predicting coin in fish's mouth	17:24–27			
Vanishing at Emmaus			24:31	
Appearing in Jerusalem				20:19, 26

7:29; 9:23). Sometimes the healing stories are intended to be read with a degree of symbolic interpretation. For example, the story of Jesus healing a blind man leads to commentary on Jesus's ability to grant spiritual insight (John 9:39).

Healing stories overlap considerably with accounts of exorcism. In the Bible, possession by an unclean spirit does not cause a person to become sinful or immoral; rather, it causes the person to become blind or deaf, to have seizures or be crippled, or to experience some other sort of physical or emotional distress. The exorcism stories in the New Testament usually focus on the interaction of Jesus and the unclean spirit; the afflicted person apparently is incapable of independent action or response, which may explain why no such person in the New Testament ever requests an exorcism (note how the father requests help for his demon-possessed son in Mark 9:18, 22).

There are also a handful of miracle stories in the Gospels in which Jesus rescues people from danger (stilling storms at sea) or provides for people's physical needs (multiplying loaves, changing water into wine, effecting a large catch of fish). And, finally, there are a couple instances of what are sometimes called "epiphany miracles" because they serve to manifest Jesus's divine presence (walking on water, transfiguration).

In our modern world, miracle stories often seem to present Jesus as violating known laws of nature or in some other way doing what scientists regard as impossible. Such an attitude would be anachronistic for the New Testament world, in which almost everyone believed that there were spiritual and magical powers that might enable people to do what they could not have done on their own. Thus the most common response to miracles in the New Testament is not disbelief but astonishment (see, e.g., Matt. 9:33–34). The onlookers recognize

unclean spirit: a demon; a spiritual being that inhabits people and causes them to become sick or disabled.

epiphany: a manifestation of divine truth or presence.

Box 5.6

Pronouncement Stories in the Gospels: Some Examples

Correction Stories

- let the dead bury the dead (Matt. 8:21–22)
- forgive seventy-seven times (Matt. 18:21–22)
- whoever wants to be first (Mark 9:33–35)
- whoever is not against us (Mark 9:38–40)
- who is truly blessed (Luke 11:27–28)

Commendation Stories

- the confession by Peter (Matt. 16:13–20)
- the generous widow (Mark 12:21–44)
- the woman who anoints Jesus (Mark 14:3–9)

Controversy Stories

- eating with sinners (Mark 2:15–17)
- Jesus's disciples don't fast (Mark 2:18–22)
- picking grain on the Sabbath (Mark 2:23–28)
- eating with defiled hands (Mark 7:1–15)
- by what authority? (Mark 11:27–33)
- paying taxes to Caesar (Mark 12:13–17)
- whose wife will she be? (Mark 12:18–27)

See Robert C. Tannehill, "The Gospels and Narrative Literature," in *The New Interpreters Bible: New Testament Survey* (Nashville: Abingdon, 2005), 1–16.

that some extraordinary power is at work; the question involves *what* power, and *to what end*.

Pronouncement Stories

All four canonical Gospels contain numerous examples of what scholars call "pronouncement stories," anecdotes that preserve the memory of something Jesus said (see box 5.6). In such a story everything leads up to a climactic and provocative pronouncement: the saying, which usually comes at the end, is the whole point of the anecdote (just as a "punch line" is the whole point of a joke). Such stories were popular in the ancient world, and we possess numerous books filled with pronouncement stories preserved for other ancient figures. Here is one example from an educational textbook called the *Progymnasmata* by Theon:

> Some people came up to Alexander the Great and asked him, "Where have you hidden your treasure?" He pointed to his friends and said, "In them."

Fig. 5.2. Jesus speaks with authority. (The Bridgeman Art Library International)

Sayings of Jesus: Some Examples

Wisdom sayings provide insight into how life really works:

- "Where your treasure is, there your heart will be also" (Luke 12:34).
- "If a kingdom is divided against itself, that kingdom cannot stand" (Mark 3:24).

Prophetic sayings proclaim the activity or judgment of God:

- "The kingdom of God has come near; repent, and believe in the good news" (Mark 1:15).

Eschatological sayings reflect the view that the future is of primary importance:

- "The Son of Man is to come with his angels in the glory of his Father, and then he will repay everyone for what has been done" (Matt. 16:27).

Legal sayings interpret God's will:

- "In everything do to others as you would have them do to you; for this is the law and the prophets" (Matt. 7:12).

"I" sayings are autobiographical:

- "I have come to call not the righteous but sinners" (Mark 2:17).
- "I came that they may have life, and have it abundantly" (John 10:10).

Our Gospels recount dozens of stories about Jesus that are stylistically similar to these secular anecdotes. Sometimes the climactic saying of Jesus constitutes a correction: Peter offers to forgive his sibling seven times; Jesus says, "Not seven times, but seventy-seven times" (Matt. 18:21–22). In other cases it offers a commendation: a widow gives a penny to the temple, and Jesus says, "This poor widow has put in more than all who are contributing . . . , for she put in everything she had" (Mark 12:41–44). In our Gospels, furthermore, pronouncement stories often occur within a context of controversy. Many of Jesus's most memorable sayings are prompted by objections that are raised to his ministry or by other challenges to his authority. In response to a conflict with the scribes and Pharisees, Jesus declares, "The sabbath was made for humankind, and not humankind for the sabbath" (Mark 2:23–27); in response to an attempt to lure him into self-incrimination, he exhorts people, "Give to the emperor the things that are the emperor's, and to God the things that are God's" (Mark 12:13–17).

Individual Sayings

The Gospels also contain numerous sayings of Jesus that lack narrative context. Sometimes these sayings are strung together to make what appear to be speeches of Jesus given on some particular occasion. Scholars sometimes

Fig. 5.3. Jesus crucified. (photo © Boltin Picture Library / The Bridgeman Art Library International)

group sayings together into different types or categories for ease of reference and discussion (see box 5.7).

Passion and Resurrection Narratives

All four Gospels conclude with an extended account of Jesus's passion (arrest, trial, crucifixion, burial) and resurrection. In each Gospel this portion of the story is treated with more intense detail than any other portion of the narrative, and the pace of the narrative slows to the point that the reader receives an almost hour-by-hour account of what is happening. Scholars have noted similarities between these accounts and death scenes of other famous men in

passion: in Christian theology, a term for the suffering and death of Jesus Christ.

⊙ **EXPLORE 5.13**
What Happens When
Jesus Dies

ancient Greco-Roman biographies. These accounts also show an especially strong degree of interaction with Old Testament Scripture: they appear to be written by people who have already thought deeply about the meaning of Jesus's death and resurrection and to have reflected on those events in light of passages from the psalms, the prophets, and other passages of Scripture. Thus the death and resurrection of Jesus is not just one more episode in a series of remarkable occurrences; for each of the four Gospels, it is treated as the climax of the story, the point to which everything has been moving all along. Indeed, each of the Gospels prepares its readers for this capstone event by having Jesus predict exactly what will occur (e.g., Mark 8:31–32; 9:31; 10:33–34) and/or offer vague allusions that the readers are expected to understand in a manner that characters in the story do not (see Mark 2:20; John 2:19–22; 3:14; 8:28; 12:32–34). More to the point, each Gospel tells the story of Jesus's death and resurrection in a distinctive way that pulls together certain threads and fulfills important themes of that particular work. For example, in Matthew, Jesus dies as the Messiah of Israel, fulfilling prophecies that indicated he would be the one to save his people from their sin (see 1:21); in Mark, he gives his life as a ransom for many, demonstrating the sacrificial way of self-denial that is to mark all of his followers (8:34–35; 10:43–45); in Luke, he dies as a noble martyr, a victim of injustice, who will overcome death in a way that promises an end to oppression (4:18); in John, he dies triumphantly, as one who is glorified and exalted in an ultimate expression of God's love (12:23; 15:13). In these and many other ways, each of the passion and resurrection stories serves as the narrative and theological climax of the Gospel in which it appears.

Box 5.8

The Dying Words of Jesus

Jesus speaks seven times from the cross, but not seven times in any one Gospel. The Gospels relate three very different stories regarding Jesus's dying words. In one story, Jesus speaks only once; in a second, he speaks three times; and in a third, he speaks another three times. However, there are no parallels between what is said in any one of these three stories and what is said in the other two stories.

Story A	Story B	Story C
Matthew and Mark	**Luke**	**John**
"My God, my God, why have you forsaken me" (Matt. 27:46; Mark 15:34)?	"Father, forgive them; for they do not know what they are doing" (Luke 23:34).	"Woman, here is your son. . . . Here is your mother" (John 19:26–27).
	"Truly, I tell you, today you will be with me in Paradise" (Luke 23:43).	"I am thirsty." (John 19:28)
	"Father, into your hands, I commend my spirit" (Luke 23:46).	"It is finished" (John 19:30).

Composition of the Gospels: The Synoptic Puzzle

Christian piety sometimes has imagined that the Gospel authors were secretaries for God. Medieval paintings often show one of the Gospel authors seated at a desk with an angel standing behind him and whispering in his ear. According to this view, the composition of the Gospels was a simple process of taking dictation, writing word for word what a heavenly messenger said to write. Academic scholarship assumes that the matter was a bit more complicated. The Gospel writers do not claim to have received any special guidance of this sort (cf. Rev. 1:10–11); indeed, the author of the Gospel of Luke says that he has done some

Fig. 5.4. Divine inspiration. Matthew gets some help from an angel.

Box 5.9

The Gospels and Apostolic Authorship

A popular misconception holds that the four New Testament Gospels were written by apostles—earthly followers of Jesus who were among his twelve disciples. But the church has always maintained that this was not the case for two of the Gospels (Mark and Luke), and Augustine thought that this was theologically significant:

> The Holy Spirit willed to choose for the writing of the Gospels two who were not even from those who made up the Twelve, so that it might not be thought that the grace of evangelization had come only to the apostles and that in them the fountain of grace had dried up. (*Sermon* 239.1)*

The great majority of scholars today would want to apply Augustine's thinking to all four Gospels, since Matthew and John were also probably not composed by members of the Twelve, at least in the finished editions that we now possess.

*Alexander Roberts, James Donaldson, and Henry Wace eds., *The Early Church Fathers* (1867; repr., Peabody, MA: Hendrickson, 1994), 38:244.

research and that his intent is to provide an orderly account of what has been handed on "from the beginning" (1:1–4). As this comment implies, the Gospel authors did not have to start from scratch. They had what scholars call "oral sources" (nuggets of material that had been told from memory), and they probably also had written sources (materials that people had put into writing a generation before the Gospels themselves were produced).

A potentially complicating factor with regard to composition of the Gospels concerns the question of whether the evangelists operated independently of one another. Did each of the Gospel authors produce his biography of Jesus without any clue that others were doing (or had done) the same thing? Or did they consult with one another? More to the point, did the ones who wrote last have copies of the Gospel or Gospels that were written first? Three of the four Gospels—Matthew, Mark, and Luke—are called the "Synoptic Gospels" because they appear to be related to one another in a way that the fourth one (John) is not. The word *synoptic* literally means "seeing together," and it came to be applied to the first three Gospels because their contents could be set in parallel columns that allowed them to be read and interpreted side by side. The amount of overlapping material is remarkable, as are the similarities in structure, style, perspective, and overall tone. The question of exactly how these three Gospels should be related to one another may be called the "Synoptic Puzzle" (or, more commonly, the "Synoptic Problem").

To get an inkling of what this involves, let's consider just one piece of the puzzle. Scholars have long noted that the Gospel of Matthew is twice as long as the Gospel of Mark and that about 90 percent of the material found in Mark is found in Matthew also. Why would this be? Augustine (fourth century) thought that Mark perhaps had a copy of Matthew's Gospel and produced a "condensed version" of it. But most modern scholars think that Augustine got it backward: Matthew had a copy of Mark's Gospel and produced an expanded version of it. Why do they think this? For one thing, it's a little hard to imagine Mark deciding that some of Matthew's material wasn't worthy of inclusion. For example, by Augustine's reckoning, passages such as the Beatitudes and the Lord's Prayer ended up on Mark's cutting-room floor, as did Matthew's account of the virgin birth and reports of Jesus's resurrection appearances. Furthermore, Mark's Gospel is written in a rather rustic and casual style, while Matthew's work follows more conventional rules of grammar and is more polished. Are we to imagine that Mark copied from a sophisticated work, changing passages that were grammatically correct to read in ways that are grammatically questionable? Most interpreters think that we should assume the opposite: Matthew altered Mark's material, editing it for grammar and style in order to produce a Gospel that would appeal to people who cared about such things. If this is correct, then the Gospel of Matthew is almost a "second edition" of the Gospel of Mark, a rewritten and greatly expanded version of that book presented in a different style for a different audience.

As indicated, the theory that Matthew had a copy of Mark's Gospel and expanded it is only one piece of what scholars ultimately mean when they talk about the Synoptic Puzzle. The full picture that emerges when all the pieces are in place is shown in the first of the two illustrations provided in box 5.10. In a nutshell, the proposal is as follows: (1) Mark's Gospel was written first, and Matthew and Luke both had copies of Mark's Gospel; (2) another early source, called "Q," was also produced in the early church, and Matthew and Luke had copies of Q as well; (3) Matthew had some additional material that Luke did not have, which we call the "M" material; and (4) Luke had some additional material that Matthew did not have, which we call the "L" material. This construal is called the "Two-Source Hypothesis" (or, sometimes, the "Four-Source Hypothesis") because Matthew and Luke each used two major sources (Mark and Q) in addition to other materials (M and L).

According to this widely accepted theory, there was a period in early church history (ca. 70–85) when Christians had two writings about Jesus: the Gospel of Mark and what we now call the "Q" source. Churches made copies of these two works and passed them around. It wasn't long, however, before people began to think, "Why not combine them?" And Matthew and Luke did exactly that, each in his own way. Each of them did this independently, without knowing what the other was doing, and, according to this theory, they also wove other traditions about Jesus into the mix (the M material for Matthew, the L material for Luke). As gifted writers with some time on their hands, they edited everything to produce books that worked on their own terms. As a result, the Gospels of Matthew and Luke turned out to be much more than just "expanded versions of Mark" or even "Mark-Q hybrids." They turned out to be truly distinctive biographies of Jesus that tell the story of Jesus from particular perspectives,

ማቴዎስ፡   ማርቆስ፡

Fig. 5.5. Evangelical collaboration. This illustration from a seventeenth-century "synopsis of the Gospels" shows Luke and John collaborating on what to write in their respective books. Modern scholars, however, do not believe that the authors of our four Gospels had any direct contact with one another. Similarities between the works may be explained through the use of common sources (including oral traditions), and the differences may be explained in light of the evangelists' individual interests and tendencies. (© British Library Board / Bridgeman Images)

works that would prove to be effective in different ways for different people. This, of course, is why the Christian church chose to keep all three Synoptic Gospels in spite of the overlap in content.

If this theory is correct—and it is *only* a theory—then we might consider the different ways in which Matthew and Luke expanded Mark by adding new material. Those who follow this theory surmise that Matthew chose to insert the material from Q and M at five key points in Mark's narrative: Matthew

Suggested Solutions to the Synoptic Puzzle

Two-Source Hypothesis

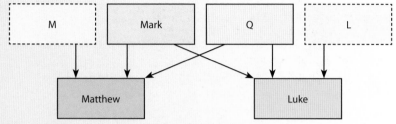

Farrer Theory

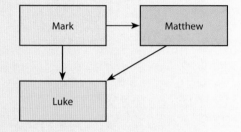

Two-Gospel Hypothesis

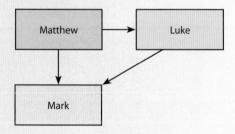

decided that Jesus could give speeches at those points in the story, and the material from Q and M gets organized topically and presented as the content of those five speeches. Likewise, those who follow this theory think that Luke took material from Q and L and created a ten-chapter insertion into Mark's narrative according to which Jesus takes his disciples on a journey, teaching them as they travel to Jerusalem. The result is that, in Matthew, discipleship has an academic, classroom feel to it—Jesus the rabbi instructs his students with thematic lessons—but in Luke's Gospel discipleship seems more like an immersion experience of learning on the job.

We should say a bit more about the hypothetical Q source, which has attracted a lot of attention in New Testament studies. No one remembers

Contents of Q: Material in Matthew and Luke but Not in Mark

Preaching of John the Baptist	Luke 3:7–9	Matt. 3:7–10
Temptation of Jesus	Luke 4:1–13	Matt. 4:1–11
Beatitudes	Luke 6:20–23	Matt. 5:3–12
Love for enemies	Luke 6:27–36	Matt. 5:39–48; 7:12
On judging others	Luke 6:37–42	Matt. 7:1–5; 10:24; 15:14
On bearing fruit	Luke 6:43–45	Matt. 7:15–20
Parable of two builders	Luke 6:47–49	Matt. 7:24–27
Healing of a centurion's servant	Luke 7:1–10	Matt. 8:5–10, 13
John the Baptist questions Jesus	Luke 7:18–35	Matt. 11:2–19
The would-be disciples	Luke 9:57–60	Matt. 8:19–22
Jesus's missionary discourse	Luke 10:2–16	Matt. 9:37–38; 10:9–15; 11:21–23
Thanksgiving to the Father	Luke 10:21–24	Matt. 11:25–27; 13:16–17
The Lord's Prayer	Luke 11:2–4	Matt. 6:9–13
Asking and receiving	Luke 11:9–13	Matt. 7:7–11
Jesus identified with Beelzebul	Luke 11:14–23	Matt. 12:22–30
Return of an evil spirit	Luke 11:24–26	Matt. 12:43–45
The sign of Jonah	Luke 11:29–32	Matt. 12:38–42
On light	Luke 11:33–36	Matt. 5:15; 6:22–23
Woe to the Pharisees	Luke 11:37–52	Matt. 23:4–7, 13–36
Fear of humans and God	Luke 12:2–12	Matt. 10:19, 26–33; 12:32
Do not worry about life	Luke 12:22–34	Matt. 6:19–21, 25–33
Be ready for the master's return	Luke 12:39–46	Matt. 24:43–51
Divisions in the family	Luke 12:51–53	Matt. 10:34–36
Signs of the times	Luke 12:54–56	Matt. 16:2–3
Settle out of court	Luke 12:57–59	Matt. 5:25–26
Parable of leaven	Luke 13:20–21	Matt. 13:33
The narrow door	Luke 13:23–30	Matt. 7:13–14, 22–23; 8:11–12
Lament over Jerusalem	Luke 13:34–35	Matt. 23:37–39
Parable of the banquet	Luke 14:15–24	Matt. 22:1–14
Carrying the cross	Luke 14:26–27	Matt. 10:37–38
Parable of the lost sheep	Luke 15:1–7	Matt. 18:12–14
On serving two masters	Luke 16:13	Matt. 6:24
Role of the law and prophets	Luke 16:16–17	Matt. 5:18; 11:13
Rebuking and forgiving sin	Luke 17:1–6	Matt. 18:6–7, 15, 20–22
The day of the Son of Man	Luke 17:23–27, 33–37	Matt. 24:17–18, 26–28, 37–41
Parable of the talents	Luke 19:11–27	Matt. 25:14–30

how it got its name. Our best guess is that "Q" could be an abbreviation for *Quelle*, the German word for "source." In any case, scholars who follow this theory believe that the contents of Q can basically be identified with material that Matthew and Luke have in common but that is not found in the Gospel of Mark. A list of this material is provided in box 5.11. It is evident from this list that Q was essentially a collection of sayings, as there are only two brief stories about Jesus (temptation in the wilderness, healing of centurion's servant), while everything else recounts his teaching: parables, aphorisms, beatitudes, all sorts of pronouncements, and examples of every type of saying associated with Jesus. Think of it this way: if Q had been published in a "red letter" edition (a Bible that prints the words of Jesus in red ink), almost all the text would be in red.

We can only speculate as to the exact nature or origins of such a document. It seems likely that one of Jesus's disciples—possibly, but not necessarily, one of the Twelve—would have written down some favorite sayings of the Lord and that early Christians would have made copies of this "book of sayings" to pass around. Indeed, Papias, a second-century church leader, writes that Matthew the tax collector "collected the sayings in the Hebrew [or Aramaic] language and each one interpreted [or translated] them as he was able" (Eusebius, *Ecclesiastical History* 3.39). Papias apparently was talking about the book that we call the Gospel of Matthew, and in recent years his comments have been dismissed because (1) the Gospel of Matthew is not a collection of sayings; (2) it was not written in Hebrew or Aramaic; and (3) it almost certainly was not written or compiled by Matthew the tax collector. Recent scholars have wondered, however, whether Papias might have been confusing our "first gospel" with what we now call the Q source. Perhaps Matthew the tax collector was responsible for compiling the collection of sayings that we call "Q" and others (i.e., the authors of two of our Gospels) translated or interpreted these sayings by putting them into their Gospels.

But this is all speculation; there is much that we simply cannot know. Indeed, a few scholars think that Q might not have been a written source at all. Perhaps it was simply a memorized collection of sayings—a summary of the teaching of Jesus that Christians (or Christian leaders) learned by heart. That would explain why we no longer have any copies of it: physical copies never existed. But, again, this is speculation.

And, finally, we must emphasize that a number of scholars reject the Two-Source Hypothesis altogether in favor of a different solution to the Synoptic Puzzle. The primary competitor is probably a solution called the "Farrer Theory," according to which Mark's Gospel came first, Matthew modified Mark, and Luke drew on both Mark and Matthew. Another alternative is the "Two-Gospel Hypothesis" (sometimes called the "Griesbach Hypothesis"),

⊙ **EXPLORE 5.33**
Expanding Mark: How Matthew and Luke Arranged Their Gospels

⊙ **EXPLORE 5.28**
The Q Source in Contemporary Scholarship

⊙ **EXPLORE 5.27**
Evidence to Support the Two-Source Hypothesis

⊙ **EXPLORE 5.34**
Evidence to Support the Farrer Theory

⊙ **EXPLORE 5.35**
Evidence to Support the Two-Gospel Hypothesis

according to which Matthew wrote his Gospel first, then Luke drew on Matthew in creating his own compatible but distinctive work, and finally Mark had copies of both Matthew and Luke and produced a short, condensed Gospel using material from both of them. Both of these minority proposals attempt to account for the parallels and differences between the three Gospels without having to posit the existence of a hypothetical, now lost source. The key difference between the two is the order in which the three Gospels were written. The Farrer Theory maintains "Markan priority" and so has much in common with the Two-Source Hypothesis, rejecting only the existence of Q. The Two-Gospel Hypothesis rejects both Markan priority and the existence of Q and thus represents a more radical departure from the dominant paradigm.

Conclusion

In the second century, Tatian, a prominent Christian, decided that the church did not really need four Gospels; it was confusing to have four separate accounts of the life of Jesus, especially when they often reported the same events. Tatian set out to fix this by producing a synthesis of the four Gospels that combined their accounts into one extended narrative of Jesus's life. He called his work the *Diatessaron* (Greek, "through four"). It became very popular, especially in the Eastern Orthodox church, and for more than two hundred years it replaced the four Gospels in Syriac Bibles and lectionaries.

Eventually, Christian churches rejected the *Diatessaron*. Today, most churches teach that God wanted four people to write four different Gospels and that accepting the Bible as God's word means understanding and appreciating the distinctive stories that each Gospel tells. Still, the *Diatessaron* approach has continued to be employed in unofficial ways. For example, most motion pictures about the life of Jesus present a composite story based on pieces from all the Gospels, which is to say that the story of Jesus they tell is not one that is actually related by any individual biblical author.

At a popular level, most Christians today have some knowledge of "the story of Jesus," but what they know is usually a composite, *Diatessaron*-like story. Very few Christians are actually able to identify "the story of Jesus that Matthew wanted to tell," or "the story of Jesus that Mark wanted to tell," or that of Luke or John. Academic study of the New Testament works at remedying this in a manner that corresponds with the official interests of Christianity, even if those interests are not always evident in popular or practical expressions of the faith. As we turn now to look at each of the Gospels, we will seek to discern the portrait of Jesus that each evangelist offers. The goal is to appreciate the image of Jesus that each book offers and to understand the distinctive message that each author wanted to convey.

FOR FURTHER READING: **The Gospels**

Carroll, John T. *Jesus and the Gospels: An Introduction*. Louisville: Westminster John Knox, 2016.

Carter, Warren. *Telling Tales about Jesus: An Introduction to the New Testament Gospels*. Minneapolis: Fortress, 2016.

Cartlidge, David R., and David L. Dungan. *Documents and Images for the Study of the Gospels*. 3rd ed. Minneapolis: Fortress, 2015.

Powell, Mark Allan. *Fortress Introduction to the Gospels*. 2nd ed. Minneapolis: Fortress, 2018.

Puskas, Charles B., and David Crump. *An Introduction to the Gospels and Acts*. Grand Rapids: Eerdmans, 2008.

Senior, Donald, et al. *Invitation to the Gospels*. Mahwah, NJ: Paulist Press, 2002.

Strauss, Mark L. *Four Portraits, One Jesus: An Introduction to Jesus and the Gospels*. Grand Rapids: Zondervan, 2007.

Wenham, David, and Steve Walton. *Exploring the New Testament: A Guide to the Gospels & Acts*. 2nd ed. Downers Grove, IL: InterVarsity, 2011.

⊙ Go to www .IntroducingNT.com for summaries, videos, and other study tools.

6

Matthew

Here is a fun piece of Bible trivia: In Psalm 46 in the King James Version of the Bible the forty-sixth word from the beginning (not counting the psalm's superscription) is "shakes," and the forty-sixth word from the ending (not counting the "Selah") is "spear." The King James Bible was completed in 1610, the year that William Shakespeare celebrated his forty-sixth birthday. Many literature scholars think that the translators of this Bible, who were big fans of the Bard's work, snuck a birthday tribute to Shakespeare into the Word of God itself.

One does not have to read very far in the Gospel of Matthew to see that the author of our first Gospel likewise can play number games. When he relates the genealogy of Jesus, he arranges the names so that they fall into three sets of fourteen generations: there were fourteen generations from Abraham to David, fourteen from David to the exile, and fourteen from the exile to Jesus. Three fourteens! Many modern readers might respond, "So what?" But Matthew thinks that Jesus is the Messiah, and the Messiah is the son of David, and the name "David" can be written with Hebrew letters (*dwd*) that also served as numerals, and those numerals are 4, 6, 4, and $4 + 6 + 4 = 14$!

Matthew's Gospel is often called "the teacher's Gospel" because it focuses so heavily on the teaching ministry of Jesus and emphasizes so strongly the need for Christian leaders to understand the word (13:23) and to teach it to others (5:19; 28:19–20). But Matthew might just as easily be called "the accountant's Gospel," for its author is very interested in keeping track of things. People familiar with the Myers-Briggs Type Indicator would identify Matthew as a "high J"—that is, as a person who craves order and structure. Matthew loves triads, presenting examples or points in groups of three (e.g., three acts of piety in 6:1–18). He also likes doublets and dualism: two masters (6:24–25), two ways (7:13–14), two builders (7:24–27).

triad: a set of three.

doublet: in literature, a pair or duplication of references.

dualism: the tendency to separate phenomena into sharply opposed categories, with little room for anything in between.

119

There are things that we just don't get. Sometimes Matthew includes what appears to be the same material twice at different points in his Gospel: Jesus's words on divorce are included twice (5:31–32; 19:9), as are stories of the religious leaders seeking a sign from him (12:38–42; 16:1–4) or accusing him of operating with the power of Beelzebul (9:32–34; 12:22–24). Why would Matthew do that? Even more puzzling, characters sometimes get doubled: Mark's Gospel reports that Jesus healed a blind man at Jericho (10:46–52) and cast a legion of unclean spirits out of another man and into a herd of pigs (5:1–14)—a tale that biblical comedians like to call "the story of deviled ham"—but when Matthew tells those same stories, Jesus heals two blind men (20:29–34) and casts the legion of demons out of two men (8:28–33). And in Matthew's version of the Palm Sunday story, Jesus sits on two animals as he rides into the city (21:6–7). Is this some overly literal fulfillment of prophecy (21:5; cf. Zech. 9:9)? Did Matthew know something that Mark didn't? Or is there something special about the number "two"?

One thing is certain: Matthew is not a sloppy writer. He has a clear plan for his Gospel, and he is attentive to details. We just don't always know how far to press that. Jesus tells seven parables about the kingdom of heaven; is that because "seven" is a sacred number, or did that just happen to be the number of kingdom parables that Matthew knew? Matthew tells us twelve times that prophecy has been fulfilled; is that because "twelve" is a number for Israel, or is it just a coincidence? Matthew presents eight beatitudes in two groups of four, each group containing exactly thirty-six words in Greek and—well, actually, that one probably is just a coincidence, but with Matthew, one never knows for sure!

Overview

Matthew's Gospel opens with a genealogy that traces Jesus's descent from Abraham (1:1–17), followed by an account of Jesus's virgin birth and related events such as the visit of the magi (1:18–2:23). Then the narrative shifts to recount the beginning of Jesus's ministry as an adult: he is baptized by John (3:1–17) and tempted by Satan in the wilderness (4:1–11); then he begins to call disciples and go throughout Galilee preaching, teaching, and healing (4:12–25). He preaches the Sermon on the Mount (5:1–7:28), which focuses primarily on discipleship (i.e., the life expected of those who are faithful to God).

Matthew continues the story of Jesus's ministry by relating a series of healing stories (a leper, a centurion's servant, Peter's mother-in-law, two demoniacs, a paralytic). These are interspersed with anecdotes in which Jesus responds to questions that clarify or challenge the nature of his ministry (8:1–9:38). Jesus then appoints twelve of his followers to be apostles and sends them out on a

⊙ **EXPLORE 6.0**
Matthew: Outline of Contents

⊙ **EXPLORE 6.1**
Content Summary: Expanded Overview of the Gospel of Matthew

mission similar to his, instructing them with regard to persecution and the need for radical faithfulness (10:1–11:1). Opposition to Jesus begins to mount as he encounters doubt, apathy, and outright hostility from diverse parties: John the Baptist, the crowds, the Pharisees, and even his own family (11:2–12:50). He tells seven parables about the kingdom of heaven (13:1–53), and then he meets rejection in his own hometown (13:54–58). His ministry also attracts the attention of Herod, who has had John the Baptist put to death (14:1–12).

The story continues with an accent on miraculous deeds (multiplication of food, walking on water, exorcism of a demon from a Canaanite's daughter). These are interspersed with accounts that reveal the Pharisees to be blind guides who stand under God's judgment, and with accounts that show Jesus's own disciples to be people of little faith (14:13–16:12). But then Peter receives Jesus's blessing when he confesses Jesus to be the Messiah and Son of God

Fig. 6.1. The three magi. Only Matthew's Gospel tells the story of magi who come from the East to worship Jesus when he is born (2:1–12). (Bridgeman Images)

(16:13–20). After that the narrative shifts into a long section that emphasizes Jesus's instruction of his disciples (16:21–20:34): he repeatedly tells them he is going to suffer and die, a revelation that they find distressing; he teaches them about humility and self-denial; he allows three disciples a glimpse of his divine glory when he is transfigured before them on a mountain; and he instructs them on community life and other matters pertinent for those being prepared to live in the kingdom of heaven.

Jesus enters Jerusalem and challenges the religious leaders there (21:1–23:39): he overturns tables in the temple, questions the leaders' authority, tells parables against them, responds to a series of tests that they put before him,

Fig. 6.2. Exodus in reverse. In Matthew's Gospel righteous Israelites must flee into Egypt to escape a baby-killing monarch (2:13–15). This is the reverse of the traditional story in which Moses had to lead the Israelites out of Egypt to escape a baby-killing pharaoh (Exod. 1:15–22; 3:1–10). (Nalini Jayasuriya)

and lambastes them as fools and hypocrites destined for hell. Then Jesus retires to the Mount of Olives with his disciples and offers them private teaching regarding the last days, including information about his own return and a series of parables regarding the final judgment (24:1–25:46).

Matthew's Gospel concludes with an account of Jesus's passion and resurrection (26:1–28:20): he is anointed by an unnamed woman and shares a last meal with his disciples, who will betray, deny, and desert him; he is arrested, tried before Jewish and gentile leaders, crucified, and laid in a tomb; on the third day he rises from the dead, appears to a group of women, and then commissions his disciples to baptize and teach people from all nations.

Historical Background

Although it comes first in our New Testament, the Gospel of Matthew is not usually thought to have been the first Gospel written. Most scholars think that it was written after the Gospel of Mark. Since about 90 percent of the material in Mark's Gospel is also found in Matthew, it is possible to view Matthew as an expanded, second edition of Mark. But Matthew's book would not ultimately replace Mark's Gospel the way that a second edition of a work usually replaces earlier versions. Rather, Christians would read Matthew alongside Mark, excusing the redundancy and appreciating both books as offering compatible accounts of Jesus.

The book is anonymous, and its attribution to Matthew may owe in part to a mistaken or misunderstood comment from an early Christian leader. Around the middle of the second century the church leader Papias said that Matthew the tax collector, one of Jesus's twelve disciples, "collected the sayings in the Hebrew [or Aramaic] language and each one interpreted [or translated] them as he was able" (Eusebius, *Ecclesiastical History* 3.39). Subsequent church leaders took this comment as an indication that Matthew the tax collector wrote the book that now bears his name; indeed, this probably is what Papias meant. But the book that we know as the Gospel of Matthew is more than a collection of sayings. Furthermore, it is written in Greek, not Hebrew or Aramaic, and most scholars do not think that any of the other Gospel authors had copies of it to interpret or translate. Accordingly, many scholars simply dismiss the comment by Papias out of hand, claiming that he clearly did not know what he was talking about. It is possible, however, that Matthew the tax collector did have something to do with this Gospel. Perhaps he was the person responsible for compiling the now lost collection of sayings that scholars refer to as the Q source (see "Composition of the Gospels: The Synoptic Puzzle" in chap. 5), and maybe that is what confused Papias. But this remains speculative. Perhaps Matthew collected some of the sayings that ended up in Q, or maybe he collected some completely different sayings. Many scenarios are possible, and we simply cannot know for sure what Matthew the tax collector's ultimate contribution to this Gospel might have been. Very few scholars, at any rate, think that he was the author of the entire book in the form we now have. Nevertheless, scholars refer to the unknown author of

Fig. 6.3. Peter given keys. Matthew's Gospel grants a prominent role to the disciple Peter. In Matthew 16:19 Jesus tells Peter, "I will give you the keys to the kingdom of heaven, and whatever you bind on earth will be bound in heaven, and whatever you loose on earth will be loosed in heaven." (The Bridgeman Art Library International)

Box 6.1

Material Unique to Matthew's Gospel

This corresponds to what scholars sometimes refer to as the "M" material (see box 5.10).

Genealogy of Jesus (from Abraham)	1:2–17	Recovering the sinful member	18:15–20
Birth of Jesus (with focus on Joseph)	1:18–25	Peter asks about forgiveness	18:21–22
Visit of the magi	2:1–12	Parable of unforgiving servant	18:23–35
Flight to Egypt	2:13–21	Parable of laborers in vineyard	20:1–16
On fulfilling the law	5:17–20	Parable of two sons	21:28–32
The antitheses	5:21–24, 27–28, 33–38, 43	Prohibition of titles	23:7–12
On practicing piety	6:1–15, 16–18	Denunciations of Pharisees	23:15–22
Pearls before swine	7:6	Parable of bridesmaids	25:1–13
Mission limited to Israel	10:5–6	Description of last judgment	25:31–46
Invitation to rest	11:28–30	Death of Judas	27:3–10
Parables: weeds, treasure, pearl, net	13:24–30, 36–52	Pilate washes his hands	27:24–25
Peter tries to walk on water	14:28–31	Resuscitation of saints	27:52–53
Blessing of Peter	16:17–19	Guard at the tomb	27:62–66; 28:11–15
Peter pays the temple tax	17:24–27	The Great Commission	28:16–20

this book as "Matthew" anyway; it is traditional and convenient to do so, and no one knows what else to call him.

What we can know about this author must be surmised from the work itself. He obviously is a devout and educated Christian. He knows the Jewish Scriptures well and uses them in ways that might suggest some scribal training. Thus he is almost certainly a Jewish Christian, and perhaps he is a converted rabbi or synagogue leader. Among all of our Gospel authors, Matthew alone is adamant about reporting that the original ministry of Jesus was directed solely to Israel (10:5–6; 15:24; cf. 28:18–20).

As for date, his use of the phrase "to this day" (27:8; 28:15) implies that he is writing a generation or more after the time of Jesus (cf. Gen. 26:33; 2 Sam. 6:8), and his use of the Gospel of Mark indicates that he is writing after the publication and distribution of that book (usually thought to have been written around 65–73). A number of matters in Matthew's Gospel reflect the sort of concerns that Jewish people were dealing with in the decades after the destruction of the Jerusalem temple in 70 CE (cf. 24:1–2): How is God present with us? What is the continuing value of the Torah? How and when will God's promises to Israel be fulfilled?

The author of Matthew also seems to favor material that would appeal to people who lived in a more urban and prosperous setting than that of Jesus

▷ EXPLORE 6.39
Authorship of Matthew's Gospel

▷ EXPLORE 6.40
The Community of Matthew: Clues from the Gospel Itself

and his original disciples. It is often suggested that this Gospel might have been written in the city of Antioch, an important site in early Christianity (see Acts 11:25–26). Numerous details regarding the interpretation of this Gospel can be elucidated by the hypothesis that the book was written for believers in that setting, but it is not a sure thing, as other cities similar to Antioch could fit the bill as well.

Our best guess, then, is as follows: the book that we know as the Gospel of Matthew was written by an unknown Jewish Christian in Antioch or some similar Roman city some time after the destruction of the Jerusalem temple, most likely in the mid-80s.

What Is Distinctive about the Gospel of Matthew?

Perhaps the first step in understanding the Gospel of Matthew consists of recognizing how it is different from the other three Gospels. To get a good start on this, we should familiarize ourselves with what is unique to this Gospel. Box 6.1 lists stories and passages from Matthew that are not found anywhere else in the New Testament.

A review of this material provides a quick and easy guide to some things that are distinctive about Matthew. For example, the only two instances in the New Testament where Jesus talks about "the church" occur in passages on this list (16:17–19; 18:15–20): Jesus says that he intends to build a church, and he offers advice for how that church should make decisions and regulate its membership. Likewise, we may note that a number of stories on the "only in Matthew" list are ones in which Peter figures prominently (14:28–31; 16:17–19; 17:24–27; 18:21–22). That is interesting because if in fact Matthew's Gospel was written in Antioch, then it was produced in a community where Peter had actually lived (see Gal. 2:11–14).

There is another way to determine what is distinctive about Matthew: by setting the Gospels of Matthew and Mark side by side and noting differences that occur over and over again in the material that they have in common. If we follow the dominant source theories, we will have to conclude that Matthew did not just copy material from Mark word for word; rather, he made changes in what Mark had written, and these changes reveal what is distinctive about Matthew's version of the Gospel story. Box 6.2 provides a summary of changes often noted by "redaction critics," scholars committed to studying Matthew's editorial tendencies in order to discern his distinctive perspective. We should note, furthermore, that although the material is presented here as formulated by scholars who believe that Matthew had a copy of Mark's Gospel and used it as a source for his own work, the distinctive tendencies of Matthew would be noteworthy even if that were not the case. If, for example, Matthew was the

> EXPLORE 6.9
Distinctive Characteristics of Matthew's Gospel

> EXPLORE 6.20
The "Church" in Matthew

> EXPLORE 6.3
Passages from Mark Omitted by Matthew

> EXPLORE 6.44
Expanding Mark: How Matthew and Luke Arranged Their Gospels

Box 6.2

Matthew's Use of Mark

According to the dominant source theories, Matthew preserves about 90 percent of the stories and passages found in Mark's Gospel, but he edits this material in accord with certain principles. Studying these editorial changes is the work of redaction critics (see "Redaction Criticism" in chap. 3).

Organization

Some Markan material is moved about.
    Examples:
- Five miracle stories are moved to Matthew 8–9, where other miracle stories occur.
- The mission charge to the disciples is related immediately after they are selected (Matt. 10:1–42; cf. Mark 3:14–19; 6:7–13).

Abbreviation

Details or characters that are not immediately relevant are pruned away.
    Examples:
- the demoniac's chains and behavior (Matt. 8:28; cf. Mark 5:2–5)
- unroofing the tiles for the paralytic (Matt. 9:2; cf. Mark 2:2–5)
- the crowd and the disciples in the story of a woman's healing (Matt. 9:20–22; cf. Mark 5:24b–34)

Sophistication

Casual or colloquial expressions are rewritten in the more polished Greek of the educated class.
    Examples:
- Many instances of the "historical present" tense are changed (130 out of 151).
- Mark's repetitious use of words such as "and" and "immediately" is reduced.
- Clear antecedents are provided to pronouns that lack them.

Accuracy

Instances of questionable accuracy are corrected.

Examples:
- "King Herod" (Mark 6:14) becomes "Herod the tetrarch" (Matt. 14:1).
- Reference to Abiathar as high priest in Mark 2:26 is omitted (Matt. 12:4; cf. 1 Sam. 21:1–6).

Contextual Relevance

Some changes make things more relevant to Matthew's community.
    Examples:
- Matthew omits Mark's explanation of Jewish customs (Matt. 15:1–2; cf. Mark 7:3–4) because he is writing for Christians who are either ethnically Jewish or well acquainted with matters of Jewish tradition.
- Matthew often replaces the phrase "kingdom of God" with "kingdom of heaven" (e.g., Matt. 4:17; cf. Mark 1:15) because some Jews tried to avoid saying "God" out of respect for the sanctity of God's name.
- Where Mark uses "village" (*kōmē*), Matthew frequently uses "city" (*polis*) because he is writing for an urban community removed from rural settings.
- Matthew adds "silver" and "gold" to Jesus's injunction for the disciples to take no "copper" with them on their travels (Matt. 10:9; cf. Mark 6:8) because he is writing for a more prosperous community for which renunciation of "copper" might seem insignificant.

Character Portrayal

Matthew changes the way major characters are portrayed in the Gospel story, including Jesus, his disciples, and the religious leaders of Israel.

Jesus
- Questions that might imply a lack of knowledge on Jesus's part are omitted

(Mark 5:9, 30; 6:38; 8:23; 9:12, 16, 21, 33; 10:3; 14:14).

- Statements that might imply a lack of ability or authority on Jesus's part are modified (cf. Matt. 13:58 with Mark 6:5).
- References to Jesus exhibiting human emotions are dropped: pity (Mark 1:41), anger (Mark 3:5), sadness (Mark 3:5), wonder (Mark 6:6), indignation (Mark 10:14), love (Mark 10:21).
- Stories that might seem to portray Jesus as a magician are omitted (Mark 7:31–37; 8:22–26).

The Disciples of Jesus

- "No faith" is changed to "little faith" (cf. Matt. 8:26 with Mark 4:40).
- The theme of not understanding Jesus is adjusted so that the disciples are merely slow to understand (cf. Matt

16:12 with Mark 8:21; Matt 17:9–13 with Mark 9:9–13).

- Unseemly ambition is ascribed to the mother of James and John rather than to the disciples themselves (cf. Matt. 20:20 with Mark 10:35).
- References to the disciples "worshiping" Jesus and calling him "Lord" or "Son of God" are added to stories taken from Mark (cf. Matt. 14:32–33 with Mark 6:51–52).

The Religious Leaders of Israel

- A scribe whom Jesus praises in Mark (12:28–34) is depicted in Matthew as an opponent who puts Jesus to the test (22:34–40).
- Friendly religious leaders such as Jairus and Joseph of Arimathea are no longer identified as religious leaders in Matthew (cf. Matt. 9:18 with Mark 5:22; Matt. 27:57 with Mark 15:43).

first Gospel written, as some scholars hold, we would need to revise box 6.2 to present "Mark's Use of Matthew" rather than "Matthew's Use of Mark." That could be done—and the significant differences between the two Gospels would still be notable.

Many of these differences are simply stylistic, but they still serve to point out Matthew's priorities and approach to storytelling. For example, it is often said that Matthew takes more of a "just the facts" approach to narrative than Mark does; he is less concerned with telling stories in a lively or colorful manner than he is in simplifying material and organizing its presentation in a way that will establish certain key points. Other differences may reflect the audience that Matthew envisions for his Gospel: word choices in this Gospel seem intended to make the book more appealing to Jewish (or Jewish Christian) readers or more meaningful to readers who live in a fairly prosperous urban environment.

In any case, the most interesting differences that can be detected in Matthew-Mark parallel material are those that affect the way main characters in the story are presented. Jesus exhibits less human frailty in Matthew's Gospel than he does in Mark's. For example, statements that might imply a lack of knowledge or ability on his part are missing (cf. Mark 6:5 with Matt. 13:58). Likewise, the disciples of Jesus exhibit more potential for growth and leadership in Matthew's version of the story than they do in Mark's. Matthew's portrayal of the religious leaders of Israel, however, exhibits the opposite tendency: inevitably they come off worse in Matthew than they do in Mark.

Thus our recognition of what is distinctive about Matthew can be helped by taking note of what is found only in his Gospel and also by noticing how Matthew has apparently altered material taken from Mark. In addition, scholars often note that the very structure of Matthew's Gospel is distinctive. Matthew displays a penchant for stereotypical formulas and organizational patterns. Throughout his Gospel he makes use of a "fulfillment citation" to indicate that something in the story of Jesus "happened to fulfill what was written in the prophets" (see 1:22–23; 2:15, 17–18, 23; 4:14–16; 8:17; 12:17–21; 13:35; 21:4–5; 27:9–10; if 2:5–6 and 13:14–15 are added to this list, the fulfillment citation may be said to occur twelve times). Jesus also gives five great speeches in Matthew, each of which is followed by a formulaic transitional phrase (7:28; 11:1; 13:53; 19:1; 26:1); some scholars have thought that Matthew does this because Jews customarily thought of Torah as "the five books of Moses" and he wanted to provide a Christian parallel by offering five books (speeches) of Jesus. Matthew has a predilection for triads, organizing material into sets of threes. For example, the miracle stories in chapters 8–9 fall into three sets of three miracles, each followed by teaching on discipleship (8:1–17; 8:23–9:7; 9:18–24). Indeed, the basic outline for the entire Gospel story seems to be divided into three main parts, with the second and third parts introduced by another formulaic phrase, "From that time on, Jesus began . . ." (4:17; 16:21). The first part (1:1–4:16) serves as an introduction, presenting stories that help to identify who Jesus is; the second part (4:17–16:20) tells the story of Jesus's

The Presence of God in the Gospel of Matthew

God Is Present in Jesus

- when Jesus is born: "Emmanuel" = "God is with us" (1:23)
- Jesus is worshiped (2:11; 9:18; 14:33; 15:25; 20:20; 28:9, 17)

Jesus Is Present in the Church

- with little children, who are the greatest in the kingdom (18:5)
- with people who gather in his name to pray (18:20)
- with needy members of his spiritual family (25:37–40)
- with those who receive bread and wine in his name (26:26–28)
- with people who baptize, teach, and make disciples (28:19–20)

The Church Is Present in the World

- salt of the earth and light of the world (5:13–14)
- sheep in the midst of wolves (10:16)
- the gates of Hades will not stand (16:18)
- make disciples of all nations (28:19)

Jesus says to his followers, "Whoever welcomes you welcomes me, and whoever welcomes me welcomes the one who sent me" (Matt. 10:40).

ministry to Israel; the third part (16:21–28:20) deals with his journey to Jerusalem and subsequent passion and resurrection.

passion: in Christian theology, a term for the suffering and death of Jesus Christ.

Major Themes in the Gospel of Matthew

The Abiding Presence of God

Matthew's Gospel emphasizes that God has come to dwell with God's people and that mere human beings can now experience the transforming reality of God's presence in their lives. There is, of course, some sense in which God is not present on earth but rather is in heaven. Matthew has not abandoned that traditional affirmation (6:9; 23:22), but this Gospel is most interested in exploring the ways that God is present on earth. It answers the question "Where is God?" with a series of three propositions (see box 6.3). First, according to Matthew's Gospel, *God is present in Jesus*. This might not seem like a radical claim, since Jewish people would have recognized that God had been present in lots of good people throughout history: Moses, David, a host of prophets, and even certain gentiles such as Cyrus of Persia. But Matthew does not simply mean that Jesus was an agent of God or that God worked through him; rather, Matthew thinks that when Jesus was born, God entered the world as never before: God was now "with us" (with Israel or, perhaps, with humanity) in some unprecedented sense (1:23). In fact, Matthew thinks that it is appropriate for people to worship Jesus. As an adult, Jesus affirms the traditional teaching that one should not worship (*proskynein*) any entity other than the Lord God (4:10; cf. Deut. 6:13), but eight times in this Gospel people worship Jesus and are not rebuked for it (2:11; 8:2; 9:18; 14:33; 15:25; 20:20; 28:9; 28:17; see also 21:15–16). The point seems to be that God is present in Jesus in such a way that worshiping Jesus counts as worshiping God.

This affirmation of God's presence in Jesus might have settled the question "Where is God?" for people who lived while Jesus was still on earth, but for those who lived after Easter the question would be simply transformed: If God is present in Jesus, then where is Jesus? Matthew's answer is that, second, *Jesus is present in the church*. Jesus says in this Gospel that he will be in the midst of his followers when they come together in his name to pray (18:20) and that he will be with them as they go out into the world to make disciples of others (28:20; cf. 10:40). Indeed, the world will be judged according to how it treats members of his family, for what is done to them is done to him (25:40; cf. 10:41–42; 18:5).

Matthew's answer to someone seeking the presence of God might be, "Go to the church, and there you will find the God who is present in Jesus" (see 10:40). But Matthew does not really expect seekers to do this. Thus a third

⊙ **EXPLORE 6.11**
Jesus in the Gospel of Matthew

⊙ **EXPLORE 6.12**
The Disciples of Jesus in the Gospel of Matthew

⊙ **EXPLORE 6.24**
The Religious Leaders of Israel in Matthew's Narrative

⊙ **EXPLORE 6.41**
The Structure of Matthew's Gospel: Two Views

⊙ **EXPLORE 6.6**
Worship in the Gospel of Matthew

proposition: *the church is present in the world*. For Matthew, the church is not a static institution but rather a dynamic movement, an assembly of missionaries who go out into the world as sheep in the midst of wolves (10:16) in order to bring good news, healing, and life (10:7–8). Followers of Jesus will be the light of the world and the salt of the earth (5:13–14). The world may not appreciate them, but it will be a better place because of them. Indeed, the

Fig. 6.4. The Sermon on the Mount. This Italian fresco from the fifteenth century portrays Jesus teaching his disciples on a mountaintop.

church that Jesus will build will overcome the gates of Hades (16:18), moving triumphantly against the forces of death and evil.

Jesus as the Son of God

Matthew's Gospel places special emphasis on the identity of Jesus as the Son of God. As in Mark, in Matthew God speaks twice from heaven (at Jesus's baptism and at his transfiguration), and both times God calls Jesus "my son" (3:17; 17:5; cf. 2:15). But Matthew has expanded on this theme by adding a story of virgin birth that presents Jesus as God's Son in an almost literal sense (1:18) and by including accounts of the disciples confessing Jesus to be the Son of God (cf. Matt. 14:32–33 with Mark 6:51–52; Matt. 16:16 with Mark 8:29). Ultimately, Jesus's identity as God's Son in Matthew is closely linked to the story of his crucifixion: In one of his parables Jesus hints that the reason his enemies want to kill him is that he is the Son of God (21:33–46), and sure enough, later he is sentenced to death for claiming to be God's Son (26:63–66). On the cross he is mocked by opponents who claim that such a fate proves that he is not the Son of God (27:40, 43), but ironically the manner of his death leads others to confess that he is indeed the Son of God (27:54).

The Teaching of Jesus

The role of Jesus as a Jewish teacher or rabbi is more prominent in the Gospel of Matthew than in any other New Testament book. For the most part, this teaching of Jesus is presented in five large blocks of material, which constitute five speeches of Jesus. Scholars refer to these speeches by distinctive names:

- the Sermon on the Mount (chaps. 5–7)—on discipleship, trust in God, moral behavior
- the Missionary Discourse (chap. 10)—on mission, persecution, radical faithfulness
- the Parables Discourse (chap. 13)—on mysteries of the kingdom of heaven
- the Community Discourse (chap. 18)—on life in the church, forgiveness, and discipline
- the Eschatological Discourse (chaps. 24–25)—on the end times, the second coming, and the final judgment

All five speeches of Jesus are important, but the Sermon on the Mount receives the most attention because it offers a compendium of Jesus's teaching that has been extremely influential. It is here that one finds the Beatitudes (5:3–12), the Golden Rule (7:12), and the Lord's Prayer (6:9–13). Jesus urges

Hades: the underworld, or place where the dead dwell; in the New Testament, it sometimes appears to be synonymous with hell.

transfiguration: an event narrated in the Synoptic Gospels in which the physical appearance of Jesus is momentarily altered to allow his disciples a glimpse of his heavenly glory (Matt. 17:1–8; Mark 9:2–8; Luke 9:28–36).

⊘ **EXPLORE 6.16**
The Presence of God in the Gospel of Matthew

⊘ **EXPLORE 6.17**
Jesus as the Son of God in Matthew's Gospel

⊘ **EXPLORE 6.46**
Matthew's Beatitudes: A New Interpretation

⊘ **EXPLORE 6.47**
The Lord's Prayer

⊘ **EXPLORE 6.4**
Parallels between the Sermon on the Mount and the New Testament Epistles

people to "turn the other cheek" and to "go the second mile" (5:39, 41). He refers to "wolves in sheep's clothing" (7:15), to "serving two masters" (6:24), to storing up "treasure in heaven" (6:20), and to "casting pearls before swine" (7:6). These and other expressions from the Sermon on the Mount find common usage even among people who have little or no connection with Christianity.

Discipleship

Most of the teaching of Jesus in Matthew's Gospel consists of instructions for how God wants people to live. According to Matthew, a person becomes a disciple of Jesus in the post-Easter world by being taught to obey what Jesus commanded (28:19–20). The Sermon on the Mount, in particular, provides a summary of these commandments of Jesus that disciples are to be taught. Jesus wants his followers to be perfect (5:48), and such perfection is achieved by keeping even the most minute of God's commandments (5:18–19) in ways that stem from sincere motives (6:2–6, 16–18) and that reflect inner purity, not just external compliance (5:21–22, 27–28). Much of the discussion of this sermon in theological circles is focused on the question of whether it is realistic: Can any human being actually live this way? But the author of Matthew's Gospel would not have been troubled by such a question. The point for him is simply that Jesus has described the ethic of God's kingdom and that those who are seeking God's kingdom ought to do all they can to live in this manner (6:33). To the extent that the kingdom has drawn near (4:17), they will find some success—sufficient to be salt for the earth and light for the world (5:13–16). Their failures, however, may serve as reminders that the kingdom is not yet fully present; they need to pray for it to come so that God's rule over their own lives can be complete (6:7, 10). Thus the Sermon on the Mount presents an ethic that Christians are to live into, striving to live in the present as they are destined to live for eternity (6:33).

Interpretation of Scripture

According to Matthew, it is possible to know the Scriptures in a superficial sense without truly understanding them. Even Satan is able to quote Scripture, albeit with perverse intent (4:6). The religious leaders of Israel likewise possess an academic understanding of Scripture (2:3–6; 17:10; 19:7; 21:41–42), but Jesus repeatedly upbraids them for not knowing Scripture in some deeper sense (9:13; 12:3, 5, 7; 19:4; 21:16, 42; 22:29, 31, 43; 26:54). What is important is that people know the proper way to interpret Scripture. Matthew's attention to this matter is interesting to biblical scholars because Matthew himself does not always interpret Scripture in ways that would pass muster among exegetical

⊙ EXPLORE 6.45
Theological Interpretation of the Sermon on the Mount

⊙ EXPLORE 6.23
How to Interpret the Scriptures according to Matthew

Fig. 6.5. St. Matthew. The author of Matthew's Gospel is traditionally regarded as a scholar of Scripture. (The Bridgeman Art Library International)

experts today. He quotes verses with little concern for their original contexts, and sometimes he adds or changes words to bring out what he thinks is the intended meaning (see, e.g., 2:6, stitched together from Mic. 5:2 and 2 Sam. 5:2, with the words "by no means" added by Matthew to what the Old Testament texts actually say). For Matthew, the key to interpreting Scripture lies in the recognition that it is fulfilled in the life and teachings of Jesus (5:17). The revelation of God in Christ sheds light on the Scriptures and reveals their true meaning and intent.

Binding and Loosing

The Gospel of Matthew displays special concern for helping followers of Jesus to address questions of moral behavior. From other sources, we know that many matters of controversy arose within the early church. In particular, as more and more gentiles embraced the faith, many Christians came to view Jewish laws as archaic or irrelevant. In Matthew's Gospel, however, Jesus declares that all the commandments of the Jewish Torah (even the minor ones) will remain in full force "until heaven and earth pass away" (5:18). That seems clear enough, but then, elsewhere in Matthew, Jesus sets aside certain regulations and claims that those who insist on their validity are condemning the guiltless (9:10–17; 12:1–7; 15:1–11). In a set of verses referred to by scholars as "the antitheses," he repeatedly states his own understanding of God's will over against what people have heard in Jewish tradition (5:21–48). So, what's up? Is he contradicting his own principle?

Most likely Matthew is presenting the moral teaching of Jesus as consistent with the Jewish practice of "binding and loosing the law." Rabbis bound the law when they determined that a commandment was applicable to a particular situation, and they loosed the law when they determined that a word of Scripture, though eternally valid, was not applicable under certain circumstances. Thus Matthew's Gospel displays Jesus as making authoritative pronouncements

antitheses: six statements of Jesus in Matthew 5:21–48 in which he states his own view over and against that which people "have heard said."

Community Rules

Compare these guidelines from the Gospel of Matthew and from the *Community Rule* for the Qumran community (one of the Dead Sea Scrolls):

- "If another member of the church sins against you, go and point out the fault when the two of you are alone. If the member listens to you, you have regained that one. But if you are not listened to, take one or two others along with you, so that every word may be confirmed by the evidence of two or three witnesses. If the member refuses to listen to them, tell it to the church; and if the offender refuses to listen even to the church, let such a one be to you as a Gentile and a tax collector" (Matt. 18:15–17).
- "[You shall not] address [your] companion with anger, or ill-temper, or obduracy, or with envy prompted by the spirit of wickedness. [You shall] not hate him because of his uncircumcised heart, but [you shall] rebuke him on the very same day lest [you] incur guilt because of him. And, furthermore, let no [one] accuse his companion before the Congregation without having first admonished him in the presence of witnesses" (*Community Rule* 5:25–6:1).*

*The Complete Dead Sea Scrolls in English, 7th ed., trans. Geza Vermes (New York: Penguin, 2012).

regarding the applicability of biblical commandments. He binds the law prohibiting murder as applicable to anger and insults (5:21–23), and he binds the law prohibiting adultery as applicable to lust (5:27–28). Elsewhere, however, he looses certain Sabbath restrictions, indicating that they do not apply when they pose an unreasonable burden (12:5–8) or prevent one from doing good (12:11–12). The commandments themselves remain valid, but in certain circumstances they do not apply.

More to the point, Matthew presents Jesus as passing the authority to make such judgments on to his followers: whatever the church binds on earth will be bound in heaven, and whatever it looses on earth will be loosed in heaven (18:18). His expectation is that the church will exercise this authority with attention to the principles that Jesus articulates in this Gospel:

- allegiance to fulfilling Scripture, not abolishing it (5:17–19)
- commitment to doing to others as "you would have them do to you" (7:12)
- recognition of the divine preference for mercy over sacrifice (9:13; 12:7)
- refusal to make void God's word for sake of human tradition (15:6)
- prioritization of love for God and neighbor (22:34–40)
- attention to the "weightier matters of the law": justice, mercy, faith (23:23)

Such principles may allow for some discrepancy of interpretation, but Jesus indicates that God will hold believers accountable for living in accord with the judgments reached by their authorized leaders (16:19) or by the community as a whole (18:17–18).

Worship and Doubt, Faith and Understanding

Matthew portrays the disciples of Jesus as fallible followers who, in spite of their failings, are destined to become apostles of the church; indeed, they will sit on thrones judging the tribes of Israel (19:28). Jesus's pet name for his disciples in this Gospel is *oligopistoi*, "people of little faith" (6:30; 8:26; 14:31; 16:8; 17:20; used elsewhere only in Luke 12:28). They are filled with doubt (14:31; 28:17) and fear (8:24–26; 14:30; 17:6), and they often fail to meet Jesus's high expectations of them (e.g., 16:21–23; 17:14–17; 19:13–15). Still, Jesus indicates that a "little faith" is all that is required for people to accomplish what God expects of them (17:20). Furthermore, the disciples' doubts and fears are accompanied by worship; indeed, those seemingly incongruous phenomena are intertwined in this Gospel such that worship, doubt, and fear occur together (14:30–33). Even at the end of the story witnesses to the resurrection respond with a mixture of both fear and worship (28:8–9), and the community that receives the Great Commission is marked by both worship and doubt (28:17).

⊙ EXPLORE 6.22
Binding and Loosing in the Gospel of Matthew

⊙ EXPLORE 6.18
Disciples of Jesus as People of Little Faith in the Gospel of Matthew

⊙ EXPLORE 6.19
Fear, Joy, Worship, and Doubt in the Gospel of Matthew

⊙ EXPLORE 6.21
The Theme of Understanding in the Gospel of Matthew

Transcending all of these phenomena, however, is a special emphasis on understanding. In this Gospel the seed that falls on good soil in Jesus's parable of the sower is identified as "the one who hears the word and understands it" (13:23; cf. Mark 4:20; Luke 8:15). The disciples of Jesus, in spite of their doubt and little faith, are portrayed as growing in understanding as the narrative progresses (see 13:11–15, 51; 16:12; 17:13). Matthew's Gospel maintains that understanding is something that must be given by God (11:25; 13:11; 16:17), and often the disciples are portrayed as not understanding Jesus until he explains what they need to know. The exact purpose of this emphasis in Matthew is unclear, but he may be highlighting the significance of what we now call "Christian education": the great apostles of the church were ordinary people who, when taught by Jesus, received the understanding that would enable them to bear fruit (13:23; cf. 13:19). Indeed, they were able to go out into the world and teach others (28:19–20).

Hostility toward Jewish Leaders

Matthew's Gospel exhibits a pronounced hostility toward the religious leaders of Israel. These individuals are presented as opponents of Jesus in all four Gospels, but the level of antipathy is extraordinary in Matthew. For one thing, Matthew's Gospel does not seem to allow for exceptions. The other Gospels contain positive examples of Jewish leaders who are not opposed to Jesus (e.g., Mark 5:22; 12:28–34; 15:43; Luke 13:31; John 3:1–2), but in Matthew the Pharisees, Sadducees, scribes, priests, and elders seem to form a united front against Jesus, and everything that they do, say, think, or believe is wrong.

Matthew frequently uses the term "evil" to describe these religious leaders: they are evil people who are incapable of speaking or thinking anything good (12:34; cf. 9:4; 12:39, 45; 16:4; 22:18). This quality identifies them closely with Satan, the evil one (13:19, 38–39). Throughout Matthew's Gospel they are identified by epithets such as "brood of vipers" (3:7; 12:34; 23:33) and "child of hell" (23:15), which characterize them as offspring of the devil rather than as children of God. The meaning of such an identification becomes clear in a parable that Jesus tells: the world is like a field in which God has placed potentially good people and in which the devil has placed evil people (13:24–30, 36–43). Jesus explicitly identifies the Pharisees as being among these plants "that my heavenly Father has not planted"; they are not God's people, and they will be uprooted in time (15:13). Thus in Matthew's Gospel (unlike the others) Jesus never summons the religious leaders to repentance; he no more attempts to minister to them than he would to the demons that he exorcises. Rather, he counsels his disciples to "let them alone" (15:14). They provide

⊙ EXPLORE 6.24
The Religious Leaders of Israel in Matthew's Narrative

⊙ EXPLORE 6.26
Jewish Responsibility for the Death of Jesus in the Gospel of Matthew

Fig. 6.6. All nations. Matthew's Gospel concludes with a charge to make disciples "of all nations" (28:18–20). This charge, traditionally called the "Great Commission," would become the key biblical text for Christian evangelism, an aspect of the new religion that would distinguish it from Judaism, which tended to identify God's "chosen people" with one particular nation. (Bridgeman Images)

a paradigmatic example of people who will never enter the kingdom of heaven (5:20), and Jesus promises that they will not escape being sentenced to hell (23:33).

Scholars wonder why Matthew treats these religious leaders so harshly. It is often proposed that he is portraying them in the worst possible light because he is angry at contemporary Jews for refusing to believe in Jesus and for acting abusively toward Christians. Thus the polemic is informed not only by historical tensions between Jesus and Jewish leaders (ca. 30) but also by current tensions between Matthew's church and "the synagogue down the street" (ca. 85). This is certainly possible, but other scholars think that Matthew is more concerned with scoring a theological point through the literary rhetoric of his story. Matthew portrays the religious leaders of Israel as a personification of all that is opposed to God so that he can present the victory of Christ as a conquest of evil. The main point of the story is not that Jesus bested the Pharisees in various ideological contests; the more significant point is that God, through Jesus, overcame the ultimate powers of evil, even when they succeeded at doing their worst. Before leaving this point, we should note that Matthew's Gospel often has been accused of fostering anti-Semitism. Jesus tells the Jewish leaders that "the kingdom of God will be taken away from you" (21:43), and he tells a gentile centurion that "the heirs of the kingdom [the Jews?] will be thrown into outer darkness" (8:12). Finally, he portrays the people of Israel as a whole as taking responsibility for the murder of Christ, calling out, "His blood be on us and on our children!" (27:25). It is likely that Matthew meant this last verse to be read ironically: the blood of Christ brings forgiveness of sins (26:28), so the Jewish people are not evoking a curse upon themselves but instead are unwittingly praying for salvation (probably with words taken from the Christian liturgy). Nevertheless, the verse has not usually been read this way, and anti-Semitic people throughout history have used it and other texts from Matthew's Gospel to justify hatred and abuse of Jews, characterizing them as "Christ-killers" and as people accursed by God.

centurion: a Roman army officer, typically in charge of one hundred soldiers.

Conclusion

We have focused on what is distinctive about Matthew, but we should not lose track of the common tradition that this Gospel proclaims. If Matthew is understood to have taken material from Mark and other sources, then perhaps we should also note passages in which he did *not* make any serious alterations. And any list of "major themes" in Matthew could also include matters that are found in most or all of the Gospels: Jesus preached about the kingdom of God; he taught in parables; he welcomed sinners and outcasts; he worked miracles; he gave his life to save people from sin; he was raised from the dead; he predicted that he will return.

Scholars often have tried to characterize the Gospel of Matthew in terms of its most noticeable features. It has been called "a Christian Pentateuch," "a catechism," "an ecclesiastical handbook," and "a manual of discipline." It may have served its first readers in all those ways, but at a basic level Matthew is "a Gospel," an ancient biography that tells the story of Jesus, proclaiming his life and teaching as good news. It is a book of invitation, summoning the reader to seek God's kingdom and righteousness (6:33), to come to Jesus and experience rest (11:28), to hear his words and act on them (7:24), to understand the word and bear fruit (13:23), and to live a life of good works that bring glory to the Father in heaven (5:16).

Pentateuch: the first five books of the Bible: Genesis, Exodus, Leviticus, Numbers, Deuteronomy.

Boxall, Ian. *Discovering Matthew: Content, Interpretation, Reception.* Grand Rapids: Eerdmans, 2015.

Carter, Warren. *Matthew: Storyteller, Interpreter, Evangelist.* 2nd ed. Peabody, MA: Hendrickson, 2004.

Case-Winters, Anna. *Matthew: A Theological Commentary.* Belief Series. Louisville: Westminster John Knox, 2015.

Evans, Craig. *Matthew.* New Cambridge Bible Commentary. Cambridge: Cambridge University Press, 2012.

Harrington, Wilfrid J. *Reading Matthew for the First Time.* Mahwah, NJ: Paulist Press, 2014.

Luz, Ulrich. *The Theology of the Gospel of Matthew.* New Testament Theology. Cambridge: Cambridge University Press, 1995.

Senior, Donald. *What Are They Saying about Matthew?* Rev. ed. Mahwah, NJ: Paulist Press, 1995.

Talbert, Charles H. *Matthew.* Paideia. Grand Rapids: Baker Academic, 2010.

Wright, N. T. *Matthew for Everyone.* 2 vols. 2nd ed. Louisville: Westminster John Knox, 2004.

⊙ Go to www
.IntroducingNT.com
for summaries,
videos, and other
study tools.

7

Mark

What if people were asked to put together a compendium of "Jesus's Greatest Hits"? The lists would vary, of course, but many Christians would want to include the story of Jesus's birth (Luke 2:1–20), the parable of the good Samaritan (Luke 10:30–37), the parable of the prodigal son (Luke 15:11–32), the Lord's Prayer (Matt. 6:9–13), the Beatitudes (Matt. 5:3–10), the Golden Rule (Matt. 7:12), and maybe a few accounts of Jesus's encounters with memorable characters such as Zacchaeus (Luke 19:1–10), Mary and Martha (Luke 10:38–42), Thomas (John 20:19–29), and the Samaritan woman at the well (John 4:5–30). In terms of miracle stories, it would be hard to beat the raising of Lazarus (John 11:1–44) or the changing of water into wine (John 2:1–11). And we could not possibly leave out Jesus's teaching on "love for enemies" (Matt. 5:43–48) or "God so loved the world . . ." (John 3:16).

All these passages have one thing in common: they are not found in Mark's Gospel. The Gospel of Mark is the briefest of the four Gospels, and much of the material about Jesus that has been best-known and best-loved in Christian tradition is missing. There are a few gems here—the parable of the sower (4:1–9), the feeding of the five thousand (6:30–44), and the encounter with the rich young ruler (10:17–22)—but, for those familiar with the other Gospels, Mark may seem sparse, particularly with regard to its presentation of Jesus's teachings.

Furthermore, as we will see, Mark tells his stories of Jesus in ways that emphasize frailty, suffering, failure, and ambiguity; this has not endeared his Gospel to readers enamored of power, glory, success, or certainty.

Nevertheless, critics who study the Bible as literature often select Mark as the masterpiece among the four Gospels. His book is less complex than Matthew's and Luke's, and it is less "talky" (or philosophical) than John's. It works as a story told from beginning to end, the sort of story that one might have heard read aloud in a single sitting. Mark tells the story in an especially lively and colorful manner, offering us a fairly tightly constructed plot in which characters interact in sometimes surprising ways. All of this is to say that Mark's Gospel is less a compilation of miscellaneous hits than it is a single opus, a tale filled with mystery, conflict, irony, and pathos.

Overview

John the Baptist is preparing the way for the Lord (1:1–8). When Jesus is baptized by John, a voice from heaven calls him God's "beloved Son" (1:9–11). After being tempted by Satan, Jesus begins preaching the gospel of the kingdom of God (1:12–15) and calling disciples (1:16–20). Mark describes a day in his ministry: Jesus teaches with authority, exorcises an unclean spirit, heals many people, and gets up early the next morning to pray and continue this work (1:21–40). He becomes involved in a series of controversies over matters such as the authority to forgive sins, eating with tax collectors, fasting, and Sabbath laws (2:1–3:6).

Continuing his ministry, Jesus appoints twelve of his followers to be apostles (3:7–19). Tensions mount as his own family tries to restrain him and the Pharisees accuse him of using the power of Beelzebul (3:20–35). Jesus tells a series of parables, including the well-known parable of the sower (4:1–34). Then he works four miracles: he stills a storm at sea, casts a legion of unclean spirits out of a man and into a herd of pigs, heals a woman who has been hemorrhaging, and raises Jairus's daughter from the dead (4:34–5:43).

Jesus teaches in his hometown and in the surrounding villages (6:1–6). Then Jesus sends his disciples out on a mission, and while they are gone, Mark provides a retrospective report of how Herod killed John the Baptist (6:7–33). Jesus miraculously feeds five thousand people and walks on water (6:34–52). Then, after a controversy with the Pharisees over ritual purity (7:1–23), he is accosted by a Syrophoenician woman whose surprising faith obtains healing for her child (7:24–30). Jesus expands his ministry into gentile territory, going throughout the Decapolis, where he heals a deaf man (7:31–37) and feeds four thousand people (8:1–9). A tense discussion with his disciples reflects on the significance of the two feedings (8:10–21).

Jesus heals a blind man at Bethsaida (8:22–26), and Peter confesses that Jesus is the Messiah at Caesarea Philippi (8:27–30). This introduces a new phase of the narrative, in which Jesus instructs his disciples about his upcoming passion and its meaning for their vocation as his disciples (8:27–10:52). Three times he predicts his passion, and each time his disciples demonstrate some failure that prompts him to offer further instruction (8:27–9:1; 9:30–37; 10:32–45).

⊙ EXPLORE 7.0
Mark: Outline of
Contents

⊙ EXPLORE 7.1
Content Summary:
Expanded Overview
of the Gospel of Mark

Fig. 7.1. Jesus heals a paralytic. This sixth-century mosaic illustrates the story told in Mark 2:1–12. (Bridgeman Images)

Interspersed with this material are accounts of Jesus's transfiguration (9:2–13), the healing of a boy possessed by a malevolent spirit (9:14–29), and anecdotes that provide teaching on matters such as tolerance, radical faithfulness, divorce, and material possessions (9:38–10:31). The section concludes with Jesus healing another blind man (10:46–52).

Jesus enters Jerusalem on a donkey (11:1–11), curses a fig tree, and expels merchants from the temple (11:12–25). His authority is challenged in a series of encounters with religious leaders (11:27–12:37), against whom he tells the parable of wicked tenants (12:1–12). He castigates the scribes but praises a widow who gives all she has to the temple (12:38–44). Then he gives a long discourse on the end times and his second coming (13:1–37).

Mark concludes his Gospel with an account of Jesus's passion and resurrection. Jesus is anointed by an unnamed woman (14:1–11), and he shares a last supper with his disciples (14:17–25). Then he is betrayed, denied, and deserted by those disciples, as he is arrested and put on trial, first before the Sanhedrin and then before Pilate (14:26–15:20). When he is crucified, he speaks only once

Papias on the Gospel of Mark

Papias, a second-century Christian, reports the tradition that he heard regarding the Gospel of Mark:

> The elder also used to say: "Mark, who had been Peter's interpreter, wrote down carefully, but not in order, all that he remembered of the Lord's sayings and doings. For he had not heard the Lord or been one of his followers, but later, as I said, one of Peter's. Peter used to adapt his teaching to the occasion, without making a systematic arrangement of the Lord's sayings, so that Mark was quite justified in writing down some things just as he remembered them. For he had one purpose only—to leave out nothing that he had heard, and to make no misstatement about it."

Eusebius, *History of the Church*, trans. G. A. Williamson (London: Penguin, 1965), §3.39.15.

from the cross: "My God, my God, why have you forsaken me?" (15:34). On Easter morning some women come to the tomb in which his body was placed, and they are told that he has been raised from the dead (16:1–8).

Historical Background

Most scholars think that the Gospel of Mark was the first Gospel written and that it probably was produced sometime between 65 and 73, around the time of the Jewish war with Rome, and just after the Roman persecutions that took the lives of Peter, Paul, and many other Christians. Perhaps the deaths of those believers prompted the author to put into writing what had formerly been the subject of Christian preaching. Indeed, many readers notice that the basic outline of Mark's Gospel resembles brief accounts of Jesus's ministry offered by preachers such as Peter and Paul in the book of Acts (see Acts 10:36–41; 13:24–31).

The book is anonymous, and we can only guess at the identity of its author. By the beginning of the second century, however, Christians were writing "according to Mark" on manuscripts of the book. That offers us a pretty good clue to the author's identity, but "Mark" was a very common name (according to some, the single most common male name in the Roman Empire at the time). Nevertheless, around the middle of the second century, a Christian leader called Papias further identified the "Mark" who wrote this Gospel as "Peter's interpreter," indicating that he based his narrative on Peter's own remembrances (see box 7.1). The strong implication of Papias's remarks is that the author should be identified with the "Mark" who is mentioned in 1 Peter 5:13 as having been with the apostle Peter in Rome. Scholars don't quite know what to make of this tradition: it could be accurate, but the Gospel of Mark actually offers a less flattering portrait of Peter than does any other Gospel, and it also contains fewer stories about Peter or about matters that Peter would have witnessed than do any of the other Gospels.

In any case, church tradition has also identified the author of this Gospel with a person mentioned in the book of Acts and in some of Paul's letters, a man who is sometimes called "John Mark" and who is said to have been part of the early Christian community in Jerusalem (see box 7.2). This tradition fares better among modern scholars, since John Mark was at times a companion of Paul and the ideology of this Gospel reflects numerous Pauline themes and priorities (e.g., centrality of the cross, election of the undeserving, evangelization of gentiles). Indeed, Paul's influence can be seen in this Gospel much more clearly than in the Gospel of Luke, whose author is also frequently identified as one of Paul's companions.

Church tradition does exhibit a tendency to simplify matters, and so it is not surprising to find that the author of this Gospel is often identified as someone who fits all the possibilities above. Thus the John Mark we read about in Acts and in Paul's letters is declared to be the same Mark mentioned as being with Peter in Rome. According to tradition, this is the person identified by Papias as the author of the Gospel. He had been part of the earliest Christian church; he had traveled briefly with Paul; he had served as Peter's interpreter while the latter was in prison. What better person to write a Gospel?

Scholars do not discount the stated tradition completely, but they often prefer to stick to what can be known about the author from Mark's Gospel itself. The author is obviously a devout Christian who believes in Jesus as the Messiah and Son of God (1:1), and he appears to be writing for people who already know the basic Christian message and are favorably disposed to it. The book does not have a defensive tone, nor is there any element of suspense regarding how

---

Box 7.2

John Mark in the Early Church

The author of the Gospel of Mark has been identified popularly and traditionally with a Christian known as John Mark, who is mentioned in the book of Acts (12:12, 25; 13:5, 13; 15:37–39). What do we know about this person?

- John Mark was a young Christian who lived in Jerusalem, where his mother hosted meetings of the early church. He would have had opportunity as a child to meet Peter and all the rest of Jesus's disciples, in addition to Jesus's mother and brothers.
- John Mark was a relative of Barnabas, and he accompanied Paul and Barnabas on their first missionary journey. The rigors of the trip, however, proved to be too much for him, and he returned home. Paul refused to let Mark go on the next trip, but Barnabas took him on a separate missionary venture.
- Mark, the cousin of Barnabas, is later mentioned as being with Paul when the latter was in prison (Col. 4:10; cf. Philem. 24; 2 Tim. 4:11). This suggests that John Mark and Paul had reconciled.
- It is not clear whether John Mark is the same "Mark" mentioned as being with Peter in Rome in 1 Peter 5:13.

things are going to turn out. Mark seems to be recounting stories that people have heard before and will want to hear again.

It is interesting to note what needs to be explained and what Mark simply assumes his readers will know or believe. He assumes, on the one hand, that his readers regard the Scriptures of Israel as the word of God (see 7:8) and will understand what it means to say that Jesus is the Messiah (8:29), and that Jesus gives his life as a ransom (10:45). On the other hand, he does not assume that they have much knowledge of Jewish matters intrinsic to Palestine: he realizes that they may need some words of explanation concerning what Sadducees believe (12:18) or regarding what Pharisees mean by "eating with defiled hands" (7:2–5). Mark assumes that his readers do know the meaning of Latin words and concepts drawn from the Roman world ("legion" [5:9, 15]; "denarius" [12:15]; "praetorium" [15:16]; "centurion" [15:39]), but he regularly defines Aramaic words used by Jews in Palestine ("Boanerges" [3:17]; "talitha cum" [5:41]; "corban" [7:11]; "ephphatha" [7:34]; "Bartimaeus" [10:46]; "Abba" [14:36]; "Golgotha" [15:22]; "Eloi, Eloi, lema sabachthani" [15:34]).

From all of this we may surmise that Mark is probably writing for an audience of Roman Christians for whom the story of Jesus and his disciples is sacred history—sacred insofar as it is foundational for their religious faith, but history in that it happened some time ago among people who were quite different from them.

As noted above, most scholars think that the Gospel of Mark was written around the year 70, a few years before or after the temple in Jerusalem was destroyed by the Romans during the Jewish war with Rome. One reason for this is that in Mark 13:2 Jesus predicts the destruction of the temple, and many scholars think that Mark would be more likely to have included such a prediction in his Gospel if it had actually come to pass or at least seemed likely to come to pass. Another reason for supposing a date in the 65–73 range is that much of Mark's Gospel is concerned with offering comfort, courage, and counsel to Christians suffering violent persecution (e.g., 13:9–13), and the worst of the early persecutions came under the emperor Nero in the mid-60s. For this same reason, many scholars think that Mark's Gospel might have been written in Rome, addressed to believers reeling from the terrors unleashed on

---

legion: a unit of three thousand to six thousand soldiers in the Roman army.

denarius: a silver Roman coin equal to the typical wage for a day's labor.

praetorium: a Roman governor's or general's headquarters.

centurion: a Roman army officer, typically in charge of one hundred soldiers.

Box 7.3

Possible Sources for Mark's Gospel

- a collection of controversy stories, including those found now in 2:1–3:6
- a collection, or possibly two collections, of miracle stories, including many of those now found in chapters 4–8
- an apocalyptic tract containing much of what is now in chapter 13
- an early version of the passion narrative (the story of Jesus's death and resurrection)

them there (though, of course, those events would have traumatized believers elsewhere as well).

We cannot be certain exactly when or where Mark's Gospel was written. A few scholars do argue for an earlier date (before 60), and this is not impossible. In general, though, this Gospel appears to have been produced at a transition point between first-generation Christianity (the apostolic age) and second-generation Christianity (the postapostolic age). Its author had not known Jesus personally, but he was not far removed from those who had. He may have known people, such as Peter or Paul, who had been a part of the Christian movement from its earliest days. He also seems to have had access to some early source material, though the nature and extent of such materials are always difficult to determine (see box 7.3). In any case, Mark must have sensed a need to provide the church with a written account of the faith to which the passing generation of eyewitnesses and apostles had testified.

apostolic age: the time period between the crucifixion of Jesus and the deaths of his first followers.

postapostolic age: the time period related to the first or second generation after the deaths of Jesus's first followers.

What Is Distinctive about the Gospel of Mark?

Most of the content of Mark's Gospel is also found in either Matthew or Luke (or, in many cases, both Matthew and Luke). A small amount of material is found only in Mark (see box 7.4), but for the most part what is distinctive about this Gospel is its perspective and style.

Mark tells his story of Jesus with an urgency that surpasses what is found in the other Gospels. Everything seems to happen very quickly: the Greek word for "immediately" (*euthys*) is used forty-two times in this Gospel, eleven times in the first chapter alone. And the breathless anticipation with which Mark writes has theological implications. The first words of Jesus in this Gospel are "The time is fulfilled!" (1:15), and the story that follows is told in a manner to confirm that claim: the world is rapidly changing and will never be the same again. The events that have unfolded are of cosmic, ultimate significance, and the events that are about to unfold will be more momentous still (see 9:1; 13:28–30).

Mark's Gospel usually is said to be written in a style of Greek that is colloquial and unrefined, which is to say that he is not always attentive to matters that strict grammarians consider important (e.g., providing his pronouns with clear antecedents). One feature of his style that has attracted considerable attention is his abundant use of the "historical present": he begins a narrative in the past tense ("The Pharisees came up to Jesus . . .") and then continues it in the present tense ("and they

⊙ EXPLORE 7.7
Distinctive Characteristics of Mark's Gospel

Box 7.4

Material Unique to Mark's Gospel

- parable of seed growing secretly (4:26–29)
- healing of man who is deaf and mute (7:31–37)
- healing of blind man of Bethsaida (8:22–26)
- sayings on salt (9:49, 50b)
- flight of young man in the garden (14:51–52)

say to him . . ."). Mark does this 151 times, enough to drive a grammar teacher mad. Still, as many scholars note, the effect of writing this way is to "make the past come alive." Mark draws his readers into the action, reporting history as though it were occurring now rather than then.

Mark exhibits a special knack for storytelling in other respects as well. He makes notable use of a rhetorical technique known as "intercalation," wrapping one story around another to make what some pundits call a "literary sandwich." Four examples of this technique are presented in box 7.5. The rhetorical effect seems to be to invite the reader to look more closely at the two stories, to compare and contrast them. Thus the story of Jesus cursing the fig tree helps to interpret the account of his purging of the temple: like the fig tree, the temple no longer bears fruit (i.e., it does not produce what God intended it to produce), and so, like the fig tree, it is doomed.

The ending of Mark's Gospel is also distinctive—indeed, quite striking. It is Easter morning, and a group of women have come to the tomb to anoint the body of Jesus. A young man (probably an angel) tells the women that Jesus is risen and that they are to convey this message to his disciples. Then Mark's Gospel comes to a close with this sentence at 16:8:

> They went out and fled from the tomb, for terror and amazement had seized them; and they said nothing to anyone, for they were afraid.

⊘ EXPLORE 7.8
Three Prominent Rhetorical Devices in Mark's Gospel

This seems like an odd way to end a Gospel. One might well ask this: If the women really "said nothing to anyone," how did the disciples find out about the resurrection? And did anyone ever actually see the risen Jesus?

Box 7.5

Intercalation in the Gospel of Mark

Jesus's family sets out to seize him (3:21).
Religious leaders accuse Jesus of using the power of Beelzebul (3:22–30).
Jesus's family arrives and is rebuffed by him (3:31–35).

Jesus goes to heal the daughter of Jairus, a synagogue ruler (5:22–24).
A woman with hemorrhages is healed by touching Jesus's garment (5:25–34).
Jesus raises the daughter of Jairus from the dead (5:35–43).

Jesus sends his disciples out on a mission (6:7–13).
Mark gives an account of how Herod killed John the Baptist (6:14–29).
The disciples return with a report of their mission (6:30).

Jesus curses a fig tree for not bearing fruit (11:12–14).
Jesus attacks the temple, calling it a "den of robbers" (11:15–19).
The fig tree that Jesus cursed has withered and died (11:20–21).

This abrupt ending is so odd that some Christians sought to compose more suitable endings for the book, stitching together accounts of what happened next, based on material found elsewhere in the New Testament. The best known of these make-shift endings still appears as Mark 16:9–20 in English Bibles (usually enclosed in brackets or printed in italics at the bottom of the page). All of our oldest Greek manuscripts of Mark's Gospel, however, conclude with 16:8, which leaves us with two possibilities: (1) the ending of Mark got lost sometime before any of our oldest manuscripts were produced (in which case there is no way to know how this Gospel actually concluded); or (2) Mark deliberately ended his Gospel in this fashion to achieve some sort of rhetorical effect. Both theories have their advocates, but a majority of scholars favor the latter solution, which

Fig. 7.2. Jesus enters Jerusalem. After completing his ministry in Galilee, Jesus travels to Jerusalem and enters the city in a way that draws both criticism and acclaim. The story from Mark 11:1–10 is illustrated in this Russian icon from the seventeenth century. (The Bridgeman Art Library International)

then leaves us with more questions: What was the rhetorical effect that he had in mind? Why end the story with fear and silence?

This touches on another distinctive aspect of Mark's Gospel: it is imbued with a sense of mystery and ambiguity, and the story is told with a profound appreciation for letting things go unsaid (cf. 1:43–44; 5:43; 7:36; 8:26, 30; 9:9). Jesus doesn't mind leaving people in the dark (see 4:10–12), nor does Mark feel any compulsion to sort things out for the reader. We will note one example among dozens that could be cited. In Mark 8:14–21 Jesus tells his disciples, "Beware of the yeast of the Pharisees and the yeast of Herod." They don't understand what this means, and he becomes upset with them. What he does not do, however, is explain what he meant, and many readers might be left feeling as unenlightened as his disciples. We get that we are *supposed* to understand the metaphor of yeast, but *do* we understand it? It is interesting that both Matthew

Mark 16:8 (Abrupt
Ending of Mark)—
Did Jesus's Disciples
Ever Learn of the
Resurrection?

What Is Distinctive about the Gospel of Mark?   149

Fig. 7.3. The Last Supper. In Mark 12:17–31 Jesus shares a final Passover meal with his disciples the night before he is crucified. (© RMN-Grand Palais / Art Resource, NY)

and Luke amended Mark's story to let the reader know what Jesus meant; even more interesting, they interpreted the saying differently. Matthew tells us that Jesus was referring to the "teaching" of these religious leaders (Matt. 16:12); Luke says that he was referring to their "hypocrisy" (Luke 12:1). Mark was content to leave it unexplained; he does not mind leaving his readers to ask, "So what does it mean?" Or, sometimes, "What happened next?" Or, more important, "What now?"

Major Themes in the Gospel of Mark

A Very Human Portrait of Jesus

Mark's Gospel usually is said to offer the most human portrait of Jesus in our New Testament. Such a judgment is necessarily relative and is derived only by way of comparison with the other Gospels. If one were simply to read Mark without reference to any other book, Jesus would appear to be an extraordinary and, indeed, divine being. He often knows the future (e.g., 10:32–34; 13:2; 14:18–20, 27–30) or the inner thoughts of other people (e.g., 2:8; 12:15), and he is in direct and constant communication with God, who is pleased to call him "Son" (1:11; 9:7). He seems to make no mistakes and commit no sins, and he exhibits power over disease, nature, and unclean spirits. But he is also careful to distinguish himself from God (10:18), and he is depicted as a man subject to human weakness and frailty: he gets hungry (11:12), he does not know everything (13:32), and he is unable to work miracles for those who have no faith (6:5; cf. Matt. 13:58). He exhibits a full range of human emotions, including pity (1:41), anger (3:5), sadness (3:5), wonder (6:6), compassion (6:34), indignation (10:14), love (10:21), and anguish (14:34). He sometimes must struggle to know the will of God (14:36), and at one point in the story he even seems to change his mind, coming to a deeper understanding of God's plan in light of a woman's clever remark (7:24–30). Of course, some of these elements are present in the other Gospels also, and Mark certainly is not unique in portraying Jesus as a human being. All four Gospels attribute both human and divine attributes to Jesus, but most readers find the humanity of Jesus to be displayed with particular clarity in Mark's narrative.

The Centrality of the Cross

In the nineteenth century the scholar Martin Kähler described Mark's Gospel as "a passion narrative with an extended introduction" (on passion narratives, see "Passion and Resurrection Narratives" in chap. 5). The point of such a remark may be that although the Gospel of Mark is only half as long as either Matthew or Luke, the passion narrative in Mark is about the same length as it is in the other Gospels. Thus a greater percentage of Mark's total narrative is taken up with his account of Jesus's rejection, suffering, and death. But that's not all. In Mark's Gospel, the plot to kill Jesus is introduced early (3:6); in Matthew, it is introduced considerably later (12:14), and in Luke, later still (19:47). Thus most of Mark's story may be read as a prelude to what happens at the end, when Jesus dies on the cross. One long section of the story (8:22–10:52) seems to be organized around Jesus's predictions of his passion (8:31; 9:31; 10:33–34) and the disciples' inability to grasp the significance of the cross for human salvation and for their own discipleship (see box 7.6).

Since Mark's Gospel usually is regarded as the first of the four to be written, it is viewed as something of a transition between two major types of material in the New Testament: Paul's letters on the one hand, and the later Synoptic

passion: in Christian theology, a term for the suffering and death of Jesus Christ.

⊳ EXPLORE 7.11
The Passion of Jesus in the Gospel of Mark

Box 7.6

The Way of the Cross

Jesus heals blindness (Mark 8:22–26).			
Jesus predicts his passion.	8:31	9:30–31	10:32–34
The disciples misunderstand.	8:32–33	9:32–34	10:35–40
Jesus teaches the way of the cross.	8:34–38	9:35–37	10:41–45
Jesus heals blindness (Mark 10:46–52).			

Gospels (Matthew and Luke) on the other. In Paul's letters the focus on Jesus Christ is almost exclusively on the crucified and risen Lord. Nowhere in his letters does Paul mention that Jesus taught in parables, or that he worked miracles, or that he dined with outcasts, or that he argued with Pharisees over Sabbath laws; rather, Paul wants to pass on what he considers to be "of first importance": "that Christ died for our sins in accordance with the scriptures, and that he was buried, and that he was raised on the third day" (1 Cor. 15:3–4). The Gospels of Matthew and Luke differ radically from Paul in that most of their content is taken up with reporting things about Jesus that Paul does not include on his list of what is most important: they offer lengthy expositions of the teaching of Jesus and biographical accounts of his life and ministry prior to the passion. Mark is somewhere in between: he wants to report some aspects of Jesus's life (the things that Paul does not mention), but he wants to keep the focus from beginning to end on the story of Jesus's death on a cross.

Thematically, the crucifixion of Jesus is clearly what matters most to Mark. Ultimately, Jesus has not come to heal the sick or to argue with Pharisees; he has come to give his life (10:45). It is God's will that he do this (14:36); indeed, it appears to be God's will that he die on the cross as one who has been betrayed (14:44–45), deserted (14:50), denied (14:66–72), and forsaken (15:33–34). This is his destiny—what God wants to happen and what Satan wants to prevent (8:31–33). Mark does not spell out exactly why Jesus must do this or how his death serves God's purposes. In place of elaborate explanations we get two figurative images: ransom and covenant. The language of "ransom" (10:45) implies that his death somehow purchases human freedom, and the language of "covenant" (14:24) implies that it seals or establishes a relationship between humanity and God. How or why it does these things Mark does not say, but the cross of Christ is also very important to him for another reason: it serves as the primary symbol for the life of self-denial, service, and sacrifice that Jesus's followers are called to embrace (8:34).

ransom: the redemption of a prisoner or slave for a price; or, in Judaism, the offering of a substitute sacrifice.

covenant: an agreement or pact between God and human beings that establishes the terms of their ongoing relationship.

Secrecy

In Mark's Gospel Jesus speaks about "the secret [or mystery] of the kingdom of God," and his parables seem to function as a sort of code language that allows him to talk about God's kingdom in terms that only insiders will comprehend (4:10–12). That strikes many readers as odd, but the kingdom is not the only secret in this book. Jesus repeatedly tells people not to make known the miracles or healings that he performs (1:43–44; 5:43; 7:36; 8:26); sometimes they disobey him and tell people anyway (1:45; 7:36). He also instructs his disciples not to tell people that he is the Messiah (8:30), and he silences unclean spirits who would otherwise announce that he is the Son of God (1:23–25, 34;

⊙ EXPLORE 7.15
The Crucifixion of Jesus in the Gospel of Mark

Fig. 7.4. *Judas' Kiss.* This painting by Hungarian artist Tamas Galambos captures one of the most memorable moments in all literature: Judas betrays Jesus with a kiss (see Mark 14:43–46). In Mark's Gospel, Judas may be the worst of the lot, but all twelve of Jesus's disciples prove unfaithful (14:26–30, 50, 66–72). (The Bridgeman Art Library International)

3:11–12; cf. 5:7). Of course, God speaks twice from heaven, affirming Jesus's divine sonship, but the first time that this happens, only Jesus seems to hear the voice (1:11), and the second time, Jesus instructs those who witness the event not to tell anyone about it until after his resurrection (9:9). Thus it is no surprise that his identity remains a mystery to almost everyone throughout the story (see 1:27; 2:7; 4:41; 6:2–3, 14–16; 8:27–28). Only Peter confesses him to be the Messiah (8:29), and it is not at all clear that Peter understands what sort of messiah Jesus will be (cf. 8:31–33).

Scholars refer to this theme as the "messianic secret." At one point some scholars speculated that Mark might be using secrecy as a cover for reporting things about Jesus that had not occurred in history. He could fabricate stories about Jesus, attributing miracles and messianic claims to him, and assert that the reason that no one had known these things before was that he was only now revealing matters that had been kept a secret. This thesis has not fared well. For one thing, Mark's Gospel does not really seem like a blatantly dishonest work; for another, Mark seems more interested in making theological claims

messianic secret: in biblical studies, a term employed to describe the motif in Mark's Gospel according to which Jesus's identity appears to be intentionally shrouded in mystery.

Fig. 7.5. Stars will fall. When the long-awaited kingdom of God finally arrives, Jesus says, the heavens themselves will be shaken: "the sun will be darkened, and the moon will not give its light, and the stars will be falling from heaven" (Mark 13:24–25). (Bridgeman Images)

than historical ones. A modified version of the theory holds that Mark was using the secrecy motif as a way to explain why Jesus was not recognized as the Messiah (by the general public) during his lifetime: he intentionally kept his identity a secret. This explanation continues to have its advocates, but again, most modern interpreters do not think that Mark was primarily interested in historical questions.

Today most scholars understand the secrecy theme as a literary device that provides a theological interpretation of the story. In a nutshell, Mark does not think that any aspect of the Jesus story can be understood apart from the cross. Jesus tells people not to talk about his miracles or his glorious transfiguration because those elements of his biography must be understood in context, and the proper context for interpreting them does not come until the end of the story, when Jesus dies on the cross. Until then people may be impressed by his authoritative teaching (6:2–3; cf. 1:27) and awed by his miracles (4:41), but in this story no one is able to grasp what it means for Jesus to be the Messiah or Son of God before he is crucified. When Peter calls Jesus "messiah," he is ordered not to share this identification with anyone (8:29–30) because he is not thinking in terms of a messiah who will suffer and die (see 8:29–33), and until he is able to think in those terms, Jesus does not want him testifying. Mark seems to be convinced (as Paul was) that the cross is the starting point

⊙ EXPLORE 7.28
The "Messianic Secret" in Mark's Gospel

for understanding Jesus; the so-called secrecy theme serves to mute any proclamation or identification of Jesus that does not take the cross into account.

Proclamation of the Kingdom

Mark's story of Jesus is ultimately centered on the events of his death and resurrection, but prior to those climactic occurrences Jesus is presented as a preacher of the gospel. The content of his preaching, furthermore, can be summarized in a sentence: "The kingdom of God has come near" (1:14–15). The Greek word translated "has come near" (*ēngiken*) in this proclamation can mean either "has arrived" or "is soon to arrive," and most scholars believe that the ambiguity is intentional. In one sense, the power and presence of God's rule have already arrived in the person and ministry of Jesus, but in another sense, that rule will arrive soon when it is established through the cataclysmic, world-transforming events that Jesus says are about to occur.

There are both present and future aspects to God's kingdom. Let's consider the present aspect first. Jesus is claiming that God is ready and willing to rule people's lives, and he maintains that this is "good news"; people who realize this will respond with repentance and faith (1:15). The announcement has practical implications. First, the inbreaking of God's rule has brought an "invasion of purity" that challenges Israel's traditional view (as expressed through purity codes) that what is unclean must be kept separate from what is holy. Very soon after announcing the advent of God's kingdom, Jesus touches a leper; in this act Jesus does not become unclean, but rather the leper is cleansed (1:40–42). Similarly, he associates with sinners without worrying that they will contaminate him (2:15–17). One thing that Jesus means in proclaiming God's rule as a present reality is that "holiness" is now contagious in a way that "uncleanness" was before: what is holy now has the power to transform what is unclean.

A second implication of Jesus's proclamation of the kingdom in Mark is that the reality of God's rule creates possibilities for new obedience. People need not settle for what is merely acceptable. Moses recognized a need for divorce due to the hardness of people's hearts, and he set up procedures for such divorces to be obtained properly. But divorce was not part of God's original plan for humanity, and the nearness of God's kingdom renders it unnecessary for those whose lives are ruled by God (10:2–9). The same thinking undergirds other radical ideals of Jesus: those who trust in God to rule their lives should have no trouble divesting themselves of material possessions (10:21), or living as though they were slaves of others (10:43–44), or giving up their lives for the sake of Jesus and the gospel (8:35).

But there is also a future aspect to God's rule that has not yet been made manifest. The kingdom will not fully arrive until Jesus returns. His second coming will bring judgment on the wicked and on those who have been lax,

gospel: literally, "good news" (*euangelion*); the word was first used to describe the essential content of Christian proclamation and, later, was applied to books that present semibiographical accounts of Jesus ("the Gospels").

kingdom of God: a phrase typically used to describe the phenomenon of God ruling, wherever and whenever that might be.

but it will also bring deliverance and redemption for those who have trusted in God's rule (13:25–36). "You will be hated by all because of my name," Jesus says, "but the one who endures to the end will be saved" (13:13). As for when this final culmination of God's reign will occur, Mark sends mixed signals. In general, Mark wants to encourage readers always to live on the edge, expecting the end to come very soon (13:28–30; cf. 9:1) but realizing that it might not come as speedily as they hope (13:5–8, 21–22) and that, in any case, it cannot be predicted with certainty (13:32–33).

The Failures of the Disciples

⊙ EXPLORE 7.12
When Will Jesus
Return?

Another prominent theme in Mark's Gospel concerns his relentlessly negative portrayal of Jesus's disciples. It is often said that in Mark's version of the

Fig. 7.6. Jesus dies forsaken. Norwegian artist Edvard Munch indicates how Jesus was forsaken in his hour of death by showing people turning their backs on the cross in his painting of the crucifixion. Mark's Gospel makes a similar point in its narrative of those events: All of Jesus's disciples forsake him and run away (14:50). Judas betrays him (14:44–45), and Peter denies him (14:66–72). Friends and family who in other Gospels are said to be "near the cross of Jesus" are described in Mark as looking on "from a distance" (cf. Mark 15:40 with John 19:25). Finally, darkness covers the land, and Jesus cries out, "My God, my God, why have you forsaken me?" (15:33–34). (© 2017 Artists Rights Society (ARS), New York / Bridgeman Images)

Gospel story, the only thing the disciples of Jesus ever do right is leave their nets to follow him in the first place (see 1:16–20). After that they disappoint him at every turn. In the first half of the Gospel the disciples are remarkably obtuse, failing to grasp who Jesus is (4:35–41) or what he wants of them (8:14–21). Finally, about halfway through the Gospel, Peter does recognize that Jesus is the Messiah (8:29), but he seems to draw the wrong conclusions from this.

In the next section of the Gospel Jesus predicts his passion three times, and each time the disciples do something that indicates their failure to grasp the significance of a suffering messiah (see box 7.6):

- The first time, Peter rebukes Jesus outright, prompting Jesus to say, "Get behind me, Satan!" (8:31–33).
- The second time, the disciples remain oblivious to what Jesus has said, discussing among themselves which of them is the greatest (9:30–35).
- The third time, two of Jesus's disciples jockey for position, asking if they can be guaranteed seats at his right and left in glory (10:32–44).

This entire section of Mark, furthermore, is bracketed by stories of Jesus healing blind men (8:22–26; 10:46–52), an inclusio that highlights the disciples' need for spiritual enlightenment. With this background, what happens in the passion narrative is no surprise: Judas betrays Jesus (14:10–11, 44–45), Peter denies him (14:66–72), and the others all run away and desert him (14:50).

Why would Mark tell the story this way? A number of theories have been proposed, but the dominant thesis is that he wants to offer a narrative portrayal of Paul's theology of election and justification (cf. Rom. 3:22–24; 5:6–8; 2 Cor. 12:9). The disciples of Jesus, known to Mark's audience as heroes of the church, had nothing to commend themselves other than the fact that they had been chosen by Jesus. It is Jesus who calls them (1:16–20; 2:13–14; 3:13) and gathers them into his family (3:34–35). He offers them the secret of the kingdom (4:11) and sometimes provides them with private explanations of his teaching (4:10–20, 33–34; 7:17–23). He empowers them for mission (3:14–15; 6:7–13). He does all this even though they seem obtuse and self-obsessed and show few (if any) signs of improvement. In fact, he predicts that they will betray, deny, and forsake him, adding only that he will want them to rejoin him after his resurrection. And, sure enough, the word that goes out from the empty tomb is a word of invitation for the faithless disciples to come back and continue as before (16:7). Despite their failings, Jesus keeps them as his disciples. The point, for Mark, seems to be that discipleship is a relationship established by the call of Christ and defined by his own faithfulness, not by any merit that can be attributed to the disciples themselves.

inclusio: a literary device in which parallel expressions are used at the beginning and the ending of a literary unit.

election: in theology, the notion or doctrine that people may be chosen by God for salvation or some predetermined destiny.

justification: the act of being put into a right relationship with God.

⊙ EXPLORE 7.14
The Disciples of Jesus
in the Gospel of Mark

Fig. 7.7. *Women Arriving at the Tomb.* (He Qi / www.heqigallery.com)

Conclusion

Mark's Gospel is usually thought to have been written in a setting where the church had experienced violent persecution. At the very least, his readers probably were aware of what had happened in Rome under the emperor Nero: Christians had been tortured and crucified, fed to lions, and set on fire to serve as torches at night. Accordingly, many scholars believe that the community for which this Gospel was written consisted of those believers who were left—that is, the ones who had survived the persecution. The boldest and the bravest were gone. Those who remained included many people who had broken under pressure: some of them had denied Christ in order to be spared; some may have even betrayed other members of the church (cf. 13:12); many, perhaps most, may simply have become very quiet and hoped that no one would find any reason to connect them with this faith that brought such suffering and hardship. If this is the case, then Mark might be writing his Gospel to provide both comfort and challenge to these failures, cowards, and traitors. His treatment of many themes becomes meaningful in this light: the cross must be central to any true understanding of who Jesus is, and the failures of Jesus's original disciples may be recalled as a source of empathetic hope.

It is possible that some such impulse also provides the motivation for Mark leaving his Gospel story unfinished (unless, of course, he did finish it and the ending has simply been lost). Many scholars think that Mark ends his Gospel as he does because the readers themselves need to decide what happens next—for them. They know, of course, what happened to the original disciples of Jesus, that they met with Jesus after Easter and, despite their cowardice and denials, became witnesses for Christ throughout the world. But in telling their story, Mark chooses to end the tale at what, for his readers, is the critical juncture: he ends with an altar call, so to speak, for the readers need to decide whether they want to continue the story. When they weigh their own faithlessness to Jesus against his faithfulness to them, will they respond as the disciples did? According to this theory, the story ends in fear and silence because Mark wants his readers to realize the story is not over—it can't be over, yet. The readers need to ask, "So, what does it mean? What happens next? What now?"

FOR FURTHER READING: Mark

Beavis, Mary Ann. *Mark*. Paideia. Grand Rapids: Baker Academic, 2011.

Black, C. Clifton. *Mark*. Abingdon New Testament Commentaries. Nashville: Abingdon, 2011.

Bock, Darrell. *Mark*. New Cambridge Bible Commentary. Cambridge: Cambridge University Press, 2015.

Broadhead, Edwin K. *Mark*. Readings: A New Biblical Commentary. Sheffield: Sheffield Academic Press, 2001.

Harrington, Daniel J. *What Are They Saying about Mark?* Mahwah, NJ: Paulist Press, 2005.

Harrington, Wilfrid J. *Reading Mark for the First Time*. Mahwah, NJ: Paulist Press, 2013.

Moloney, Francis J. *Mark: Storyteller, Interpreter, Evangelist*. Peabody, MA: Hendrickson, 2004.

Placher, William C. *Mark: A Theological Commentary*. Belief Series. Louisville: Westminster John Knox, 2010.

Telford, W. R. *The Theology of the Gospel of Mark*. New Testament Theology. Cambridge: Cambridge University Press, 1999.

Wright, N. T. *Mark for Everyone*. 2nd ed. Louisville: Westminster John Knox, 2004.

⊙ Go to www
.IntroducingNT.com
for summaries,
videos, and other
study tools.

8

Luke

Let's start with some traditions concerning the author of our third Gospel. The most pervasive tradition is that the man who wrote this book (and the book of Acts) was a physician, a medical doctor. But he is also widely regarded as a historian—someone to be included among the ranks of Josephus, Herodotus, and other reporters of ancient history. And another long-standing tradition holds that the author of these two books was an artist—specifically, a painter who produced numerous portraits of the Virgin Mary that are treasured as sacred relics in churches scattered throughout Europe and the East. We may be forgiven for wondering if one person could be all of these things, but it is apparent from the work itself that he was a highly educated individual who appreciated both historical context and artistic elegance.

The French rationalist Ernest Renan called the Gospel of Luke "the most beautiful book in the world." One way to appreciate the impact that this book has had on religion and culture is to try to envision what Christianity would be like without it. Can we imagine Christmas without shepherds or a baby in a manger? Liturgy without the Magnificat? How many favorite Bible stories would we lose? Zacchaeus, Mary and Martha, the good Samaritan, the prodigal son—all would be gone forever.

Magnificat: a hymn in Luke 1:46–55, expressing the words of Mary on hearing that she would give birth to Jesus.

But, of course, we *do* have Luke's Gospel. It is the longest book in the New Testament and, from an aesthetic standpoint, probably the most beautiful. Certainly it has been the traditional favorite with artists over the years, and with historians. As for physicians, who knows?

Overview

After a brief dedication to Theophilus (1:1–4), Luke presents a long account of events related to the birth and childhood of Jesus, interspersed with hymns and parallel accounts of events related to the birth of John the Baptist (1:5–2:52). Then he reports Jesus's baptism by John (3:1–22), provides a genealogy for Jesus (3:23–38), and recounts Jesus's temptation by Satan (4:1–13). Jesus begins his ministry with an inaugural sermon at Nazareth (4:14–30). Luke then reports a number of miracle stories interspersed with accounts of Jesus calling disciples and engaging religious leaders in various controversies (4:31–6:16). He preaches the Sermon on the Plain (6:17–49), heals a centurion's servant (7:1–10), raises a widow's son from the dead (7:11–17), engages a question from John the Baptist (7:18–35), and responds positively to the devotion of a sinful woman who weeps at his feet in a Pharisee's house (7:36–50).

Luke notes that Jesus had a number of women followers (8:1–3), and then he relates a few parables by Jesus (8:4–18) and some words about his family (8:19–21). The account of Jesus's ministry continues with four miracle stories: calming a storm at sea, healing the Gerasene demoniac, healing a woman who has been hemorrhaging, and raising Jairus's daughter from the dead (8:22–56). Jesus then sends the twelve apostles out on a mission (9:1–9) and miraculously feeds five thousand people (9:10–17). After Peter confesses Jesus to be "the Messiah of God" (9:18–20), Jesus tells the disciples about his passion and instructs them regarding self-denial and service (9:21–50); at the same time, he reveals his glory through the transfiguration (9:28–36) and the healing of a boy possessed by an unclean spirit (9:37–43).

Next, Luke devotes a long section of his Gospel to the journey of Jesus and his disciples to Jerusalem (9:51–19:27). Along the way, Jesus is rejected by a Samaritan village (9:51–56), sends seventy followers out on a mission (10:1–20), and visits the homes of Mary and Martha (10:38–42) and Zacchaeus (19:1–10). He performs numerous healings (a crippled woman, a man with dropsy, ten lepers, a blind man). But mostly, Luke concentrates on reporting the teaching that Jesus offers his disciples along the way—including the Lord's Prayer (11:1–4), instruction on proper behavior at banquets (14:7–14), and many of Jesus's best-known parables (the good Samaritan, the friend at midnight, the rich fool, the great banquet, the lost sheep, the lost coin, the prodigal son, the shrewd manager, the rich man and Lazarus, the widow and judge, the Pharisee and tax collector, and the pounds).

Jesus enters Jerusalem (19:28–38) and weeps as he predicts its destruction (19:39–44). He challenges the religious leaders by cleansing the temple and telling the parable of the wicked tenants (19:45–20:19); then he responds to a series of challenges that they put to him, castigates their scribes, and praises a

⊙ **EXPLORE 8.0**
Luke: Outline of Contents

⊙ **EXPLORE 8.1**
Content Summary: Expanded Overview of the Gospel of Luke

Fig. 8.1. Blessed among women. Elizabeth greets Mary—both women are pregnant, and the baby in Elizabeth's womb (future John the Baptist) acknowledges the baby in Mary's womb (future Jesus). Elizabeth exclaims, "Blessed are you among women, and blessed is the fruit of your womb" (Luke 1:39–45). (Bridgeman Images)

widow for her offering (20:20–21:4). He predicts the destruction of the temple and offers a discourse on the end times (21:5–38).

Luke concludes his narrative with an account of Jesus's passion and resurrection (22:1–24:49). Jesus shares a last supper with his followers, prays in the garden, is arrested, and is crucified after being examined by both Jewish and Roman authorities. After his burial, he is raised from the dead and appears to women at the empty tomb, to two men on the road to Emmaus, and to his assembled disciples in Jerusalem. Finally, he blesses his disciples and ascends into heaven (24:50–53).

Historical Background

The Gospel of Luke is anonymous, as are all four of the New Testament Gospels, but in this case we have a powerful clue as to who its author might be. The person who wrote this Gospel also wrote the book of Acts (cf. Acts 1:1), and in that book he sometimes refers to himself in the first person as one of the apostle Paul's traveling companions (scholars refer to these texts as the "We

Passages": Acts 16:10–17; 20:5–15; 21:1–18; 27:1–28:16). By process of elimination, we may arrive at a fairly short list of Paul's known companions who are not mentioned by name elsewhere in Acts. Hypothetically, this would allow the author to be Epaphroditus or Titus or some other friend of Paul, possibly even someone whose name is never mentioned in the New Testament, but the early and unanimous tradition of the Christian church was that these books were written by Luke, who is referred to as "the beloved physician" in Colossians 4:14 (see also 2 Tim. 4:11; Philem. 24). Some scholars have suggested that the link with Paul might be a literary fiction in Acts, but the majority opinion is that there is no strong reason to challenge this tradition (provided one does not assume that Luke was actually a disciple or a close follower of Paul; see "Historical Background" in chap. 10).

Still, such attributions are far from certain, and so the key question for scholars is this: What can we surmise about the author of this book from the work itself? He is a well-educated writer who exhibits the richest vocabulary of any author in the Bible. Indeed, Luke-Acts utilizes some eight hundred words not found anywhere else in the New Testament (a feature that makes these two books somewhat infamous to beginning Greek students). He also seems to possess a better knowledge of both classical literature and the Hebrew Scriptures than do any of the other Gospel authors. With regard to the former, some scholars think that they can detect familiarity with the works of Homer and Virgil (and the poet Aratus, quoted in Acts 17:28), as well as with the writings of various philosophical schools (Cynicism, Epicureanism, Stoicism). With regard to the Scriptures, Luke integrates Old Testament concepts and patterns into his work, often using allusions and imagery that go beyond simple citation of individual verses. Scholars have debated whether he is a Hellenistic Jew who received a classical education or a gentile whose embrace of the Christian faith led to intense biblical study; the evidence can be read either way, although for what it's worth, "Luke the beloved physician" apparently was a gentile (Col. 4:14; cf. 4:11).

In any event, the author of Luke's Gospel tells us that he has done some research concerning the life and ministry of Jesus and that he is drawing on the previous work of those who were "eyewitnesses and servants of the word" (1:2). Many scholars think that he had a copy of the Gospel of Mark in addition to a copy of the Q source (an early collection of Jesus's sayings; see "Composition of the Gospels: The Synoptic Puzzle" in chap. 5) But his claim that many people have undertaken to write accounts of these events suggests that he probably had other written sources as well.

The book is addressed to someone named "Theophilus" (1:3; cf. Acts 1:1) in order to confirm the truth of matters in which he has already been instructed. We should not imagine, however, that this entire Gospel was written for the

Hellenistic: affected by Hellenism—that is, the influence of Greek and Roman culture, customs, philosophy, and modes of thought.

gentile: a person who is not Jewish.

⊙ EXPLORE 8.33
Authorship of Luke's Gospel

Fig. 8.2. Christ in the stable. Luke tells the well-known story of the birth of Jesus, celebrated by Christians on Christmas Eve, here depicted in a painting by Hungarian artist Pal Molnar. (The Bridgeman Art Library International)

benefit of one person. Most likely, Theophilus was the person responsible for commissioning the project, a wealthy patron who has put up the money to cover the considerable cost that the production and distribution of a work such as this would entail.

Scholars have no idea where this Gospel was written, but that matters little, since it appears to have been intended for widespread publication. As for when it was written, the book appears to come from a generation after that of Jesus's first disciples, since its author admits that he is reporting matters that were "handed on" by others (1:2–3). A few passages perhaps are intended to address questions or concerns raised by the destruction of Jerusalem in 70 CE (11:49–51; 13:34–35; 19:41–44; 21:20–24; 23:28–31), suggesting that it was written later than that; this would accord with Luke having a copy of Mark's Gospel, which was probably written sometime around 65–73. A handful of scholars do try to

⊙ EXPLORE 8.34
The Community of Luke: Clues from the Gospel and Acts

⊙ EXPLORE 8.8
Distinctive Characteristics of Luke's Gospel

Box 8.1

Material Unique to Luke's Gospel

This corresponds to what scholars sometimes refer to as the "L" material (see box 5.10).

Dedication to Theophilus	1:1–4
Promised birth of John	1:5–25
Announcement of Jesus's birth to Mary	1:26–38
Mary's visit to Elizabeth	1:39–56
Birth of John the Baptist	1:57–80
Birth of Jesus (with shepherds, manger)	2:1–20
Presentation of infant Jesus in temple	2:21–38
Childhood visit to Jerusalem	2:41–52
John's reply to questions	3:10–14
Genealogy of Jesus (to Adam)	3:23–38
Good news to the poor	4:14–23, 25–30
Miraculous catch of fish	5:1–11
Raising of widow's son at Nain	7:11–17
Encounter with homeless woman	7:36–50
Parable of two debtors	7:40–43
Ministering women	8:1–3
Rejection by Samaritan village	9:51–56
Return of the seventy missionaries	10:17–20
Parable of good Samaritan	10:29–37
Mary and Martha	10:38–42
Parable of friend at midnight	11:5–8
Parable of rich fool	12:13–21

Parable of severe and light beatings	12:47–48
Parable of barren tree	13:1–9
Healing of crippled woman	13:10–17
Healing of man with dropsy	14:1–6
Two parables for guests and hosts	14:7–14
Counting the cost (two parables)	14:28–33
Parable of lost coin	15:8–10
Parable of prodigal son	15:11–32
Parable of shrewd manager	16:1–12
Parable of rich man and Lazarus	16:19–31
Cleansing of ten lepers	17:11–19
Parable of widow and judge	18:1–8
Parable of Pharisee and tax collector	18:9–14
Story of Zacchaeus	19:1–10
Jesus weeps over Jerusalem	19:41–44
Reason for Peter's denial	22:31–32
Two swords	22:35–38
Jesus before Herod	23:6–12
Pilate declares Jesus innocent	23:13–16
Sayings associated with Jesus's death	23:28–31, 34, 43, 46
Jesus appears on road to Emmaus	24:13–35
Jesus appears to disciples	24:36–49
Jesus's ascension	24:50–53

date Luke's Gospel earlier than this (in the 60s), but the majority places it in the decade of the 80s, around the same time as the Gospel of Matthew.

What Is Distinctive about the Gospel of Luke?

As with Matthew, we might begin our investigation of what is distinctive about Luke's Gospel by first noting what is unique to this book and then proceeding to consider how Luke may have edited the material that he is thought to have taken from Mark. Then we will want to consider Luke's Gospel as a whole and note what is distinctive about its overall structure and arrangement.

infancy narrative:
the first two chapters of either Matthew or Luke that relate events associated with the birth and upbringing of Jesus.

A list of unique material in Luke's Gospel appears in box 8.1. The first thing we should note about this list is its length: about one-half of Luke's Gospel is composed of material that is found nowhere else. The book opens with a unique infancy narrative (chaps. 1–2), and Jesus commences his ministry with an inaugural sermon not recorded elsewhere (4:14–30). Luke also reports five miracle stories and a whopping seventeen parables not recounted anywhere else. Jesus's words from the cross are completely unique in this Gospel (see box 5.8). And Luke provides us with our only account of Jesus's ascension (or our only two accounts, since the story is repeated later in Acts 1:6–11). If we were to study just the material on this list, we would note several recurring topics or motifs: women are prominent (1:26–56; 2:36–38; 7:11–17, 36–50; 8:1–3; 10:38–42; 13:10–17; 18:1–8); Samaritans are mentioned repeatedly (9:51–56; 10:29–37; 17:11–19); Jerusalem is a frequent setting or focus (1:5–23; 2:21–38, 41–52; 9:51–56; 19:41–44; 24:13–53); and considerable attention is given to riches and poverty (1:52–53; 3:10–14; 4:14–30; 12:13–21; 14:12–14; 16:1–12, 19–31; 19:1–10).

Fig. 8.3. The return of the prodigal son. The seventeenth-century Dutch painter Rembrandt based one of his most famous paintings on a scene from this parable of Jesus recorded in Luke 15:11–32.

Another way to determine what is distinctive about Luke is to notice the editorial changes that he is thought to have made in material that he took from Mark's Gospel. According to the dominant source theories, Luke had a copy of the Gospel of Mark among his sources (cf. Luke 1:1), but he did not simply copy this material into his Gospel word for word. Rather, he made many of the same kinds of changes that Matthew is thought to have made, smoothing out unsophisticated language and deleting parochial references (e.g., Aramaic expressions). Luke does not change "kingdom of God" to "kingdom of heaven," as Matthew does, but (unlike Matthew) he does sometimes add notes to stories that provide historical or chronological information (3:1–2; 4:23; cf. 2:1–2). Thus, according to the dominant theories, Matthew wanted to alter Mark to appeal

Box 8.2

Luke's Use of Mark

According to the dominant source theories, Luke preserves only a little more than half of the Gospel of Mark, and he edits what he does preserve in accord with certain principles. Studying these editorial changes is the work of redaction critics (see "Redaction Criticism" in chap. 3).

Organization

Some Markan material is moved about.
Examples:

- The story of Jesus preaching in Nazareth is moved forward to provide the occasion for his inaugural sermon (Luke 4:16–30; cf. Mark 6:1–6).
- The disciples' dispute over who is the greatest is moved to take place at the final supper (Luke 22:24–27; cf. Mark 10:41–45).

Abbreviation

Luke omits from Mark's stories what he considers to be insignificant or inappropriate.
Examples:

- a comment on the incompetence of physicians (Luke 8:42–48; cf. Mark 5:26)
- conversation between Jesus and the father of a demoniac child (Luke 9:37–43; cf. Mark 9:21–24)
- the naked young man in the garden (Luke 22:47–53; cf. Mark 14:43–52)
- Note: Matthew's Gospel also omits this Markan material (Matt. 9:20–22; 17:14–18; 26:47–56).

Sophistication

Casual or colloquial expressions are rewritten in the more polished Greek of the educated class.
Examples:

- Instances of the "historical present" tense are changed (150 out of 151; he missed Mark 5:35 at Luke 8:49).
- Mark's repetitious use of words such as "and" and "immediately" is reduced.

- Clear antecedents are provided to pronouns that lack them.
- Use of syntactical constructions such as genitive absolutes and articular infinitives is increased (these portend a "higher class" of Greek).

Accuracy

Instances of questionable accuracy are corrected.
Examples:

- "King Herod" (Mark 6:14) becomes "Herod the tetrarch" (Luke 9:7).
- The reference to Abiathar as high priest in Mark 2:26 is omitted (Luke 6:4; cf. 1 Sam 21:1–6).

Contextual Relevance

Some changes make things more relevant to Luke's intended audience.
Examples:

- Probably because he is writing for a culturally diverse audience throughout the Roman Empire, Luke eliminates all eight of the Aramaic expressions found in Mark: "Boanerges" (3:17); "talitha cum" (5:41); "corban" (7:11); "ephphatha" (7:34); "Bartimaeus" (10:46); "Abba" (14:36); "Golgotha" (15:22); "Eloi, Eloi, lema sabachthani" (15:34).
- Notations providing broad historical/cultural context are introduced (cf. Luke 3:1–3 with Mark 1:4) because Luke wants the story he tells to be received as a work of "world history" with implications for all humanity.
- The word for "village" (kōmē) is often changed to that for "city" (polis) in order to give the story a more urban feel that transcends its setting in rural Palestine.
- The monetary value of coins is increased in order to keep the story relevant for those who live more prosperously than did Jesus and his original followers (cf. Luke 9:3, where the Greek

word *argyrion* means "silver," with Mark 6:8, where the Greek *chalkos* means "copper").

Character Portrayal

Luke changes the way major characters are portrayed in the Gospel story, including Jesus, his disciples, and his family.

Jesus

- Statements that imply a lack of ability or authority on Jesus's part are omitted (comment in Mark 6:5 does not appear in Luke 4:16–30).
- References to Jesus exhibiting human emotions are dropped: pity (Mark 1:41), anger (Mark 3:5), sadness (Mark 3:5), wonder (Mark 6:6), compassion (Mark 6:34), indignation (Mark 10:14), and love (Mark 10:21).
- Some stories in which Jesus acts in a somewhat violent way are omitted (cursing of the fig tree [Mark 11:12–14, 20–25; but cf. Luke 16:6–9]; overturning tables in the temple [Mark 11:15–17; cf. Luke 19:45–46]).

- Stories that might seem to portray Jesus as a magician are dropped (Mark 7:31–37; 8:22–26).

Disciples

- Stories of Jesus rebuking Peter (Mark 8:33), of James and John's presumptuous request (Mark 10:35–40), and of the disciples' flight at Jesus's arrest are eliminated.
- Peter's denial (Luke 22:31–34; Mark 14:29–31) and the disciples' sleep in Gethsemane (Luke 22:45–46; Mark 14:37–41) are muted and explained.
- Lack of understanding is attributed not to the disciples' unperceptive nature but instead to divine concealment (cf. Luke 9:45 with Mark 9:32; see Luke 18:34).

Jesus's family

- Reference to Jesus's family "coming to seize him" is dropped (Mark 3:21).
- Story of Jesus designating his "true family" is reworded to lessen the contrast with his earthly family (cf. Luke 8:19–21 with Mark 3:31–35).

to an ethnically Jewish readership, while Luke apparently wanted to appeal to a broader, more culturally diverse audience, one that would be likely to interpret the story of Jesus against the background of Roman history (see 2:1–2).

In chapter 6 we observed that when Mark and Matthew are set side by side, we can see differences in the way that major characters are presented (see box 6.2). A similar phenomenon can be detected with regard to Mark and Luke. This time there is no increased disparagement of Israel's religious leaders (as there was in Matthew), but Luke's material provides an even more positive portrayal of Jesus's disciples than does the Gospel of Matthew. Luke either eliminates or explains away a good number of passages in Mark that present the disciples as failures (e.g., Mark 8:33; 10:35–40). If Matthew edited Mark's material to tone down the negative portrayal of the disciples, Luke edited that material even more drastically to present the disciples in an overwhelmingly positive light. In the same vein, Luke also gives more positive attention to the earthly family of Jesus and softens negative comments that Mark's Gospel had made concerning them (cf. Luke 8:19–21 with Mark 3:31–35).

One more curiosity arises. If we follow the basic premise that Luke used Mark's Gospel as a source, we might well wonder at the amount of material Luke did not choose to retain. Whereas Matthew appears to incorporate about 500 of Mark's 649 verses into his Gospel, Luke retains only about 350 verses of Markan material. More to the point, Luke's Gospel contains none of the material in Mark 6:45–8:20 (sometimes called the "Great Omission") or in Mark 9:41–10:12 (sometimes called the "Little Omission"). Scholars are at a loss to explain this; it has even been suggested that Luke might have had a defective or incomplete copy of Mark's Gospel, but that is only speculation.

We may also discern what is distinctive about Luke's Gospel by examining the overall structure and arrangement of his Gospel. The first thing that we notice in this regard is that the entire first two chapters of Luke are composed of unique material that functions as something of a prologue or overture to the work. Indeed, they are written in a literary style different from that of the rest of this Gospel. The Greek is closer to the style of the Septuagint (the Greek translation of the Old Testament) and/or to the style of Greek that was used in synagogues. It seems that Luke wanted to begin his Gospel by writing in a lofty manner that would evoke religious or biblical associations. One does not need to know Greek, however, to recognize something else that is distinctive about these first two chapters of Luke: the narrative is repeatedly interrupted by poetry and hymns. A modern reader might think that Luke's Gospel was a musical: every time something important happens in the prologue, a character seems to burst spontaneously into song. Christian tradition has assigned Latin names to these hymns, which are widely used in the liturgies of many churches to this day:

Luke 1:42–45	the Ave Maria
Luke 1:46–55	the Magnificat
Luke 1:67–79	the Benedictus
Luke 2:14	the Gloria in Excelsis
Luke 2:29–32	the Nunc Dimittis

Why would Luke do this? Again, he seems determined to introduce this story in as masterful and impressive a manner as possible. Furthermore, many scholars believe the most important themes of Luke's Gospel are introduced in these first two chapters (and, indeed, in the hymns). Thus the analogy of an overture is appropriate: the reader hears snippets of everything that is to come, presented in an especially engaging and artistic fashion; then, as the story unfolds, these themes are reintroduced and developed more fully.

When we look at the rest of Luke's Gospel (chaps. 3–24), it becomes apparent that the story follows the same basic outline as the Gospel of Mark. Those

⊙ EXPLORE 8.3
Passages from Mark
Omitted by Luke

who accept the Two-Source Hypothesis think that Luke has adopted the basic narrative structure of Mark's Gospel and inserted other material (i.e., from the Q source and from the miscellaneous other sources that we call "L") into that framework at two key junctures:

Luke 3:1–6:19   draws primarily from Mark
Luke 6:20–8:3   draws primarily from Q
Luke 8:4–9:50   draws primarily from Mark
Luke 9:51–18:14 draws primarily from Q and L (interwoven)
Luke 18:15–24:7 draws primarily from Mark

Thus the Markan story of Jesus is "interrupted" by two relatively long sections largely devoted to the teaching of Jesus. The first of these (Luke 6:20–8:3) includes what is known as the "Sermon on the Plain" (Luke 6:20–49), teaching material from Q that corresponds closely to what is found in Matthew's much longer Sermon on the Mount (Matt. 5–7).

But most of the material that Luke has added to Mark is presented as part of a very long section of Luke's Gospel commonly referred to as the "Journey to Jerusalem" (9:51–19:40). This section of the book frequently receives special attention in the study of Luke. The journey functions as a literary device, such that much of the teaching of Jesus and many of Luke's unique stories concerning him are presented within the context of traveling, and specifically, traveling to Jerusalem (with some anticipation of all that will happen there: crucifixion, resurrection, ascension, outpouring of the Spirit). Some scholars have detected parallels between the wandering journey of Jesus and disciples in Luke and the wandering of the Israelites reported in Exodus, Numbers, and Deuteronomy. Others focus on journey motifs in classical literature (especially *The Odyssey*).

In any case, it is often said that the motif adds subtle nuances to the presentation of Jesus's teaching in Luke's Gospel. By comparison, we may recall that Matthew incorporated the non-Markan material into his Gospel by having Jesus deliver five long speeches or sermons (chaps. 5–7; 10; 13; 18; 24–25). Interpreters say that this gives Matthew's Gospel the atmosphere of a classroom: Jesus is a rabbi, instructing his disciples in thematic lessons. In Luke, however, discipleship seems more like an immersion experience of learning on the job: Jesus takes his disciples with him on a trip, and they learn from what he says and does along the way.

Finally, we should note that the Gospel of Luke is the only one of the four Gospels that has a sequel. Luke also wrote the book of Acts, and most scholars believe that he intended the two works to be read together. Some of the

Q source: according to the Two-Source Hypothesis, a now lost collection of Jesus's sayings that was used as a source for the Gospels of Matthew and Luke.

L material: material found only in Luke's Gospel, meaning that Luke did not derive it from Mark's Gospel or from the Q source, but rather from a variety of other, unknown sources.

> EXPLORE 8.10
Two Christmas Stories: Similarities and Differences

> EXPLORE 8.23
The Journey Motif in Luke

Excerpt from a Christmas Eve Sermon by Martin Luther

The inn was full. No one would release a room to this pregnant woman. She had to go to a cow stall and there bring forth the Maker of all creatures because nobody would give way.

Shame on you, wretched Bethlehem! The inn ought to have been burned with brimstone, for even though Mary had been a beggar maid or unwed, anybody at such a time would have been glad to give her a hand.

There are many of you in this congregation who think to yourselves: "If only I had been there! How quick I would have been to help the baby! I would have washed his linen! How happy I would have been to go with the shepherds to see the Lord lying in the manger!"

Yes you would! You say that because you know how great Christ is, but if you had been there at that time you would have done no better than the people of Bethlehem. Childish and silly thoughts are these!

Why don't you do it now? You have Christ in your neighbor. You ought to serve Him, for what you do to your neighbor in need you do to the Lord Christ Himself.

Quoted in Roland H. Bainton, *Here I Stand: A Life of Martin Luther* (1950; repr., Peabody, MA: Hendrickson, 2009), 365.

material in Luke's Gospel might be intended to prepare the readers for what is to come in the second volume.

Major Themes in the Gospel of Luke

Worship and Prayer

Luke's Gospel opens (1:8) and closes (24:53) with scenes of people worshiping God in the temple at Jerusalem, and, as we have noted, this Gospel also includes several liturgical hymns (1:46–55, 67–79; 2:14, 29–32). All told, there are twenty references in Luke to people worshiping or giving thanks to God (1:46, 64; 2:13, 20, 28, 37; 4:15; 5:25, 26; 7:16; 13:13; 17:15, 16; 18:11; 18:43 [twice]; 19:37; 23:47; 24:52, 53). This is far more than in any of the other Gospels. Furthermore, only Luke contains a story scolding people for failing to give thanks (17:11–19), and only Luke presents the death of Jesus on the cross as an occasion for people to glorify God (23:47; cf. John 12:28).

Likewise, Jesus prays far more often in this Gospel than in any of the others. He often withdraws to do this alone (4:42; 5:16; 6:12). Prayer is mentioned in association with Jesus's baptism (3:21) and transfiguration (9:28), and Jesus's relationship with his disciples is governed by prayer: he prays before he chooses them (6:12), before he questions them about his identity (9:18), and before he predicts Peter's denial (22:32). And it is only in this Gospel that Jesus's disciples ask him to teach them to pray (11:1). He does so not only by teaching them the Lord's Prayer (11:2–4)—found also in Matthew 6:9–13—but also through frequent encouragements to pray (18:1; 21:36; 22:40) and through parables about prayer not found anywhere else (11:5–8; 18:1–8, 9–14).

⊙ **EXPLORE 8.36**
Expanding Mark: How Matthew and Luke Arranged Their Gospels

⊙ **EXPLORE 8.5**
Worship in the Gospel of Luke

Fig. 8.4. The solitude of Christ. Luke depicts Jesus as frequently withdrawing to "deserted places" in order to spend time alone in prayer (4:42; 5:16), as depicted here in a painting by French artist Maurice Denis. On one occasion, Jesus spends the entire night in prayer to God (6:12). (Bridgeman Images)

Food

Many readers have noted a prominent "food motif" in the Gospel of Luke (and in the book of Acts as well). Luke mentions nineteen meals, thirteen of which are peculiar to his Gospel. Jesus frequently is portrayed as being present at meals (e.g., 5:29; 7:36; 14:1; 22:14; 24:30), and he gets criticized for eating too much ("a glutton and a drunkard" [7:34; cf. 5:33]) and for eating with the wrong people (tax collectors and sinners [5:30; 15:1–2]). Banquets figure prominently in his parables and teaching also, as he offers what on the surface appears to be instructions in social etiquette (7:44–46; 12:35–37; 14:7–24; 22:26–27).

What might be the purpose of such a theme? In a general sense, meals often symbolize nourishment and celebration, and in Luke's Gospel meals are depicted as occasions for healing (9:11–17), hospitality (10:5–7), fellowship (13:29), forgiveness (7:36–50), prophetic teaching (11:37–54), and reconciliation (15:23; 24:30–35). We also know that Christians in the early church met regularly for meals (Acts 2:42, 46), and thus many scholars think that Luke's use of food imagery might be meant to establish connections between his Gospel stories and Christian gatherings in his own day: what happens at meals in this Gospel corresponds to what can or should happen "at church."

Male-Female Parallels in the Gospel of Luke

Male		Female	
1:5–25	annunciation to Zechariah	1:26–38	annunciation to Mary
1:67–79	song of Zechariah	1:46–56	song of Mary
2:25–35	prophecy of Simeon	2:36–38	prophecy of Anna
4:27	man from Syria	4:25–26	woman from Sidon
4:31–37	demon in man rebuked	4:38	fever in woman rebuked
5:19–26	desperate man forgiven	7:35–50	desperate woman forgiven
6:12–16	list of male followers	8:1–3	list of female followers
7:1–10	man's servant saved from death	7:11–17	widow's son saved from death
11:32	men of Nineveh	11:31	queen of the South
13:18–19	man with a mustard seed	13:20–21	woman with yeast
14:1–4	man healed on Sabbath	13:10–17	woman healed on Sabbath
15:4–7	man loses a sheep	15:8–10	woman loses a coin
17:34	two men asleep	17:35	two women at mill

Ministry to the Excluded or Disadvantaged

Luke's Gospel shows special concern for outcasts, for victims of oppression, and for others who appear to be at a disadvantage in society. Its genealogy traces Jesus's lineage back to Adam in order to emphasize his connection with all humanity (3:23–38). Jesus challenges parochial attitudes that would limit God's care or blessings to any particular group or nation (4:24–27; cf. 2:32; 3:6, 8), and he insists that the gospel proclaimed in his name be a message of hope for all people (24:47; cf. 2:32). Within this inclusive paradigm, those who might be despised or simply overlooked receive special attention. Thus we find an abundance of unique material in Luke that challenges prejudicial attitudes toward Samaritans (9:51–56; 10:29–37; 17:11–19) and tax collectors (15:1–2; 18:9–14; 19:1–10; see also 5:27–32; 7:34).

This concern for the excluded may also explain the prominence of women in Luke's Gospel. There are numerous stories involving female characters (1:26–66; 2:36–38; 7:11–17, 36–50; 8:1–3, 42–48; 10:38–42; 11:27–28; 21:1–4; 23:27–31; 23:55–24:11), and Luke seems to go out of his way to include parallel references that demonstrate how Jesus's words and deeds apply to men and women alike (see box 8.4). A close connection is further established between "women and the word" in this Gospel: Mary the mother of Jesus is lauded three times on account of her faithfulness to the word (1:45; 8:21; 11:27–28; cf. 1:38); likewise, Mary the sister of Martha is defended and praised by Jesus for her decision to listen to his word (10:39, 42).

Luke's prevailing concern, however, is for "the poor," a category of people that seems to refer primarily to those who are economically deprived (though

▶ EXPLORE 8.39
Luke 22:14–34—The Last Supper and Other Suppers in the Gospel of Luke

people might be regarded as poor in other ways as well—e.g., lacking honor or prestige or power). Jesus says in his inaugural sermon that the purpose of his ministry is "to bring good news to the poor" and "to let the oppressed go free" (4:18; cf. 7:22). The poor and the oppressed are one and the same, for in this Gospel poverty is viewed as a consequence of injustice: the poor have too little because others have too much. Thus Luke's concern for the poor is accompanied by hostility toward the rich: God will provide the hungry with good things but will send the rich away empty (1:53); the poor are blessed (6:20–21) but the rich are doomed (6:24–25). In his parables Jesus depicts the rich as fools who think

Fig. 8.5. Women in the Gospel of Luke. Luke reports that many women followed Jesus, including Mary Magdalene, Joanna (the wife of Herod's steward Chuza), and Susanna (8:1–3). (The Bridgeman Art Library International)

that the essence of life is to be found in material possessions (12:16–21) or, worse, as persons destined to suffer eternal agony while the poor receive their comfort (16:19–31). God's kingdom brings a reversal of values and calls for a reversal of commitments (16:13–15). In this life, those who are faithful to God will divest themselves of material possessions (12:33; 14:33; 18:22) and will be generous in helping the poor (3:11; 14:13; 18:22; 19:8); in the life to come, the poor are the ones who will be supremely blessed (6:20; 14:21; 16:22).

Diverse Images for Jesus

Scholars have long noted that Luke's Gospel employs many different titles for Jesus and uses images for understanding Jesus drawn from both the Jewish and the Greco-Roman worlds. Luke is not the only New Testament author to do this, but his diversity of models is impressive and intriguing. First, he wants to

⊙ EXPLORE 8.4
Women in the Gospel of Luke

identify Jesus as the one who fulfills the expectations of Jewish religion based on many different passages in the Hebrew Scriptures (Luke 24:27; cf. 24:44): he is the Messiah (Luke 9:20), the Son of Man (22:69; cf. Acts 7:56), the prophet like Moses (Acts 3:22; 7:37), the servant of the Lord (22:37; cf. Acts 8:30–35), and (probably) the returned Elijah (cf. 7:11–17 with 1 Kings 17:17–24, and 24:50–51 with 2 Kings 2:9–10; see Mal. 4:5).

Fig. 8.6. Lazarus and the rich man. In Luke 16:19–31 Jesus tells a parable about a rich man who dines sumptuously every day while Lazarus, a poor beggar, lies outside his gate, where dogs lick his sores, here depicted in a fifteenth-century German painting. Upon death, Lazarus is carried to heaven to be united with Abraham, while the rich man is sent to the torments of hell. (The Barnes Foundation, Philadelphia, Pennsylvania, USA / Bridgeman Images)

⊙ EXPLORE 8.19
Jesus as Messiah, Lord, and Savior

Beyond this, Luke also seems to draw on a number of pagan images from the Greco-Roman world. His portrayal of Jesus has much in common with Hellenistic portrayals of philosophers, public benefactors, and figures known to Roman readers from Greek mythology. Of course, Luke believes that Jesus is more than just a philosopher or benefactor, and he clearly indicates that Jesus is a historical person, not a mythological one. Still, people familiar with the Hellenistic literature of the Greco-Roman world probably would have recognized some contact points that would enable them to connect Luke's story of Jesus with certain things that they already knew: they might recognize that Luke's Jesus is something like a philosopher or a benefactor, or one of the immortals from their myths (e.g., Hercules or Prometheus). Thus Luke seems inclined to provide his readers with a variety of entry points for obtaining a partial (if ultimately inadequate) understanding of who Jesus is.

Present Availability of Salvation

Luke emphasizes salvation as a reality to be experienced here and now. We may see this in, for instance, his repeated use of the word "today" (see box 8.5). Of course, salvation has a future aspect to it: when Jesus speaks to a man who is about to die, he uses "today" language to promise him life after death ("Today, you will be with me in Paradise" [23:43]). But in other cases, salvation has to do with life *before* death. For instance, when Jesus tells Zacchaeus that salvation has come to his house (19:9), his main point is probably not that Zacchaeus will go to heaven when he dies but rather that Zacchaeus has been set free from slavery to mammon and is going to discover what life is supposed to be.

Many scholars have said that Luke envisions salvation as primarily liberation (4:18). People need to be set free from certain things in order to experience life as God intends. Some people are ill and need to be healed; others are possessed by unclean spirits and need to be exorcized. Luke's Gospel uses the Greek word for "salvation" in describing what Jesus does for these people (e.g., 6:9; 8:36, 48, 50; 17:19; 18:42).

This emphasis on the present aspect of salvation may explain what would otherwise be peculiarities of Luke's Gospel. First, this Gospel seems to display a recognition that the parousia (second coming) of Jesus may not be imminent (12:38, 45; 19:11; 21:24); the book of Acts is evidence for this because, as the scholar Ernst Käsemann observed, "You do not write the history of the church if you are expecting the end of the world to come any day" (*Essays on*

mammon: money and things that money can buy.

⊙ EXPLORE 8.20
Jesus as the Promised One

⊙ EXPLORE 8.21
Jesus as Son and Servant in Luke

⊙ EXPLORE 8.22
Pagan Images for Jesus in the Gospel of Luke

Box 8.5

Luke's Use of "Today"

- "Today . . . a Savior is born" (2:11)
- "Today . . . this scripture is fulfilled" (4:21)
- "Today . . . we have seen strange things" (5:26)
- "Today . . . I must stay at your house" (19:5)
- "Today . . . salvation has come to this house" (19:9)
- "Today . . . you will be with me in Paradise" (23:43)

Box 8.6

Salvation in the Gospel of Luke

This chart lists the passages in Luke's Gospel in which the words *sōtēr* ("savior"), *sōtēria* ("salvation"), *sōtērion* ("salvation"), or *sōzein* ("to save") are used.

Text	Who Is to Be Saved?	Of What Does Salvation Consist?	Who or What Brings Salvation?	How Is Salvation Received?
1:47	Mary	blessedness (1:42, 48)	God	faith (1:45)
1:69, 71	Israel	rescue from enemies	God	———
1:77	the Lord's people	forgiveness	John (1:76)	———
2:11	shepherds	peace (2:24)	Christ	———
2:30	all people	revelation, glory	Jesus (1:27)	———
3:6	all flesh	forgiveness (3:3)	John	baptism
6:9	man with infirmity	healing	word of Jesus	———
7:50	sinner (7:37)	forgiveness	word of Jesus	faith
8:12	ones along the path	———	word of God	faith
8:36	demoniac	exorcism	word of Jesus	———
8:48	woman with infirmity	healing	power of Jesus	faith
8:50	Jairus's daughter	resuscitation	word of Jesus	faith
9:24	whoever	———	———	self-denial
13:23	a few	feasting in God's reign	———	effort
17:19	leper	being made clean	Jesus	faith
18:26	who?	entering God's reign	God	———
18:42	blind man	reception of sight	word of Jesus	faith
19:9, 10	Zacchaeus	being a child of Abraham	Jesus	renunciation

New Testament Themes [Philadelphia: Fortress, 1982], 28). Thus the eschatological urgency that characterizes Mark's Gospel (see "What Is Distinctive about the Gospel of Mark?" in chap. 7) is muted here: Jesus is indeed coming back, but maybe (probably?) not for a long time. This is also a shift away from the apostle Paul's perspective (Rom. 16:20; 1 Cor. 7:29; Phil. 4:5) and that of other New Testament writers (Heb. 10:37; James 5:8; Rev. 22:7, 12, 20) who seem to have assumed or at least hoped that Jesus would return within their own lifetimes. Luke has not abandoned that hope entirely, but, realistically, he seems to think that his readers are better served by "digging in for the long haul" and doing what they can to further God's work here on earth (24:47). This reckoning with what some theologians call "the delay of the parousia" is compatible with Luke's emphasis on present aspects of salvation: Christians should experience the consequences and manifestations of God's saving power here and now rather than simply waiting for Christ to rescue them from an imperfect world or longing for bliss in a life to come.

Another idiosyncrasy of Luke's Gospel is that it never directly connects salvation to the death of Jesus on the cross. In this Gospel, Jesus does not refer to

delay of the parousia: in theological studies, a term used for the problem faced by second-generation Christians who had to grapple with the fact that Jesus had not returned to his (original) followers as expected.

⊙ EXPLORE 8.14
The Passion of Jesus in the Gospel of Luke

his death as "a ransom" (cf. Mark 10:45) or talk about his blood being shed for the forgiveness of sins (cf. Matt. 26:28). No one ever calls Jesus "the Lamb of God," likening his death to an atoning sacrifice (cf. John 1:29, 35). Indeed, many scholars have observed that Jesus's death is presented almost as a martyrdom in Luke's Gospel, a noble but unfortunate occurrence that God quickly corrects through the resurrection. It is not quite that, for Luke does make clear that Jesus's death is necessary (9:22, 44; 18:31; 24:7), that it accords with the will of God (22:42), and that it is somehow connected with the initiation of a new covenant (22:20). Still, he does not indicate why it is necessary, or how it accomplishes God's will, or in what way it initiates a new covenant (or what that means).

Fig. 8.7. Pathos. Luke tells the story of Jesus's death with heart-rending emotion. His story of the passion presents Jesus as a heroic martyr and conveys a sort of "beautiful sadness" that arouses pity and promotes both repentance and praise (23:47–48). In *The Entombment*, an early twentieth-century rendering by French artist Charles Filiger, a disciple (Mary Magdalene?) stands by the dead body of Jesus, whose halo is decorated with pretty embroidery. Even in death (or especially in death?), Jesus inspires devotion. (The Bridgeman Art Library International)

Scholars often assume that Luke is simply not interested in "doing theology" in this regard. But again, this aspect of Luke's Gospel is compatible with his emphasis on present-day salvation: although Luke says almost nothing about how Jesus's death provides salvation (in the sense of life after death), he does say a great deal about how Jesus's life provides salvation (in the sense of deliverance from current distress). In this Gospel, Jesus is *born* a savior (2:11; cf. Matt. 1:21), and he saves people throughout his life on earth. Jesus even says that the reason he has come is to seek out people needing salvation and to save them (19:10)—that is, to set them free from whatever is preventing them from experiencing life as God intends. Furthermore, he continues to do this throughout the book of Acts, where his name becomes a vehicle for bringing saving power to those in need (2:21; 3:6, 16; 4:12; 10:43; 22:16).

Other Themes—Developed Further in Acts

We may note briefly here three other themes in Luke's Gospel that will be discussed further when we consider the book of Acts:

1. The *city of Jerusalem* receives considerable attention: Luke's Gospel begins and ends there (1:5–8; 24:52–53); Luke records childhood visits by Jesus to Jerusalem (2:22–52), devotes ten chapters to Jesus's journey to Jerusalem (9:51–19:40), recounts Jesus weeping over the city (19:41–44), relates stories of resurrection appearances in and around Jerusalem (24:1–43), and concludes with instructions for the disciples to stay in the city after Jesus leaves (24:44–49). See box 10.5.

2. Luke's Gospel emphasizes *the work of the Holy Spirit* more prominently than do the other Synoptic Gospels: people are filled with the Holy Spirit (1:15, 41, 67) and inspired by the Spirit (2:25–27); Jesus is conceived by the Spirit (1:35) and anointed with the Spirit (3:22; 4:1, 14, 18); Jesus says that God gives the Spirit to all who ask (11:13; cf. Matt. 7:11) and promises that his disciples will be clothed with the power of the Spirit (24:49).

3. Luke's Gospel *portrays the disciples of Jesus as role models* for leaders in the church. We have already noted that Luke plays down the negative attributes of the disciples evident in Mark and, to a lesser degree, in Matthew. But he actually goes even further, presenting the disciples as people who stand by Jesus in his trials (22:28–30) and who exhibit potential to become his loyal representatives (6:40). They do have some problems, but in this Gospel those problems are more of what would be associated with powerful or successful people than of the foibles of persons struggling with doubt or little faith (9:49–57; 22:14–27).

Conclusion

⊙ EXPLORE 10.10
Salvation in the Book of Acts

⊙ EXPLORE 10.18
The Name of Jesus in the Book of Acts

We noted at the start that Luke's Gospel has been a traditional favorite among both artists and historians. But what do theologians make of it? Many, quite frankly, are a little baffled by Luke's lack of a discernible, systematic approach to theology. Luke has been called "muddle-headed" by some frustrated scholars who think that he is more interested in recounting appealing stories or offering a panoply of memorable images than he is in outlining exactly what we are supposed to believe about a number of important subjects.

But Luke has his many fans. Christians who are enamored of liturgy are drawn to this Gospel. Evangelists love its tales of individuals who make life-changing decisions in response to the transforming power of the gospel. Social activists prize its devotion to justice and its clear call to work on behalf of oppressed and marginalized people. Pietists value its focus on spirituality and attention to personal prayer. In the modern church, however, people sometimes evince only one or two of those passions—pietists are not always enamored of liturgy, and evangelists are not always devoted to social action. What is perhaps most remarkable about Luke's Gospel is that all of these different concerns are held together in a way that seems completely natural. And this in a narrative that often is emotionally inspiring and aesthetically beautiful.

FOR FURTHER READING: Luke

Borgman, Paul. *The Way according to Luke: Hearing the Whole Story of Luke-Acts*. Grand Rapids: Eerdmans, 2006.

González, Justo L. *Luke: A Theological Commentary*. Belief Series. Louisville: Westminster John Knox, 2010.

Green, Joel B. *The Theology of the Gospel of Luke*. New Testament Theology. Cambridge: Cambridge University Press, 1995.

Harrington, Wilfrid J. *Reading Luke for the First Time*. Mahwah, NJ: Paulist Press, 2015.

Parsons, Mikeal C. *Luke*. Paideia. Grand Rapids: Baker Academic, 2015.

Powell, Mark Allan. *What Are They Saying about Luke?* Mahwah, NJ: Paulist Press, 1989.

Shillington, V. George. *An Introduction to the Study of Luke-Acts*. Harrisburg, PA: Trinity Press International, 2007.

Talbert, Charles H. *Reading Luke: A Literary and Theological Commentary on the Third Gospel*. Rev. ed. Reading the New Testament. Macon, GA: Smyth & Helwys, 2002.

Wright, N. T. *Luke for Everyone*. 2nd ed. Louisville: Westminster John Knox, 2004.

⊙ Go to www .IntroducingNT.com for summaries, videos, and other study tools.

9

John

The Gospel of John seems to invite comparisons with the other Gospels and, indeed, to draw comparisons that elevate it as superior to the other Gospels. Look at what some people have said about John's Gospel over the centuries:

- Clement of Alexandria (second century) said that while the other Gospels set forth "physical things," John wrote a "spiritual Gospel."
- Origen (early third century) called the Gospels "the firstfruits of all scripture" and John "the firstfruits of the Gospels."
- Augustine (fourth century) said that the Synoptic Gospels were Gospels "of the flesh," but John was "the Gospel of the Spirit."
- John Calvin (sixteenth century) said that while the Synoptic Gospels reveal the body of Jesus, the Gospel of John reveals the soul of Jesus.
- And Martin Luther (sixteenth century) wrote that John's Gospel is "far to be preferred over the other three because it will show you Christ and teach you everything you need to know."

Modern scholars object to some of this labeling because all four Gospels are concerned with spiritual things, and John's Gospel is no less concerned than the others with earthly matters (see 1:14). Still, the quotations just cited come from some pretty smart people—there must be something extraordinary about this Gospel to inspire such impressions.

Much of it is content; some is simply style. John's Gospel is a magisterial work of art, by any account one of the masterpieces of ancient literature. And as specifically religious literature, it has managed to transcend categories. The traditional favorite of both mystics and philosophers, John's Gospel has obvious appeal to both heart and mind. Scholars maintain that the meaning of this Gospel is so deep, and at times so elusive, that one can study the book for decades and still discover levels of thinking not noticed before. And yet John is traditionally the first book of the Bible placed in the hands of converts or inquirers; there is enough here that is simple and straightforward, and the numerous stories of persons engaging Jesus and sometimes (though not always) coming to faith in him provide an array of sufficiently diverse characters for readers at various stages of spiritual growth to find someone with whom they can identify.

In the early church, symbolic figures were chosen for each of the four Gospels: a man for Matthew, a lion for Mark, an ox for Luke, and for John an eagle. Whatever reasons determined the first three choices, no one has ever had to wonder about the symbol for John—this is a Gospel that soars!

Overview

The Gospel of John opens with a poetic prologue describing Jesus as the Word (Logos) of God made flesh (1:1–18). It continues with several stories that present different people engaging the question of who Jesus is and what that means. First, there is an account of how John the Baptist testified to Jesus as "the Lamb of God" (1:19–34); then we read a report of how Jesus's first disciples proclaimed him to be the Messiah, Son of God, and King of Israel (1:35–51). Jesus changes water into wine at a wedding in Cana (2:1–12) and expels merchants from the temple in Jerusalem (2:13–25). He speaks with a Pharisee, Nicodemus, about the need to be "born anew" (or "from above"), about God's love for the world, and about his own unique role as the Son of God (3:1–21). John the Baptist offers further testimony to Jesus as the Messiah, bridegroom, and Son of God (3:22–36). Then Jesus speaks with a Samaritan woman at a well, disclosing details of her private life and speaking of "living water" and true worship; many Samaritans come to believe that he is "the Savior of the world" (4:1–42). A royal official asks Jesus to come to Capernaum to heal his son, but Jesus performs the healing from a distance simply by speaking the word (4:43–54).

The next major section of this Gospel seems to be organized around Jewish festivals. On a Sabbath day Jesus heals a lame man by the pool of Bethzatha, which leads to a hostile confrontation with Jews (5:1–47). At Passover time Jesus feeds five thousand people, walks on water, and delivers a long discourse on the "bread of life" (6:1–71). When the Festival of Booths draws near, he goes to Jerusalem and engages in an extended disputation with Jews concerning his claims and origin: he says that he brings the truth that sets people free, but they want to kill him because they are children of the devil (7:1–52; 8:12–59). He halts the stoning of an adulterous woman (8:1–11), heals a man born blind

⊙ EXPLORE 9.0
John: Outline of Contents

⊙ EXPLORE 9.1
Content Summary: Expanded Overview of the Gospel of John

Fig. 9.1. Miracle at Cana. The first miracle that Jesus performs in John's Gospel occurs at a wedding party. The festivities were about to be spoiled when the hosts ran out of wine, but after his mother calls his attention to the problem, Jesus transforms six jugs full of water into jugs filled with wine. (Bridgeman Images)

(9:1–41), and delivers a discourse on his role as the good shepherd who brings abundant life (10:1–18). Finally, at the Festival of Dedication, Jesus continues to argue with the Jews, who are divided in their opinions about his identity and authority (10:19–42).

Jesus visits the home of Mary and Martha and raises their brother, Lazarus, from the dead; the miracle attracts so much attention that priests decide that both Jesus and Lazarus must die (11:1–57; 12:9–10). Mary is criticized by Judas for anointing Jesus with costly perfume (12:1–8). Jesus rides into Jerusalem on a donkey and speaks at length about his mission and impending death, prompting an audible response from God in heaven (12:12–50).

Jesus and his disciples gather for a final supper together, and he washes their feet (13:1–17) and predicts his betrayal (13:18–30). Then he delivers a long "farewell discourse" (13:31–16:33): among other things, he speaks of his death as glorification; gives his followers a new commandment to "love one another"; says that he goes to prepare dwelling places for them; claims that he and the Father are one and that no one comes to the Father except by him; promises that the Holy Spirit will come as an advocate and teacher; speaks of his disciples continuing to abide in him as branches on a vine; and describes

Box 9.1

Two Books in One

John's Gospel divides neatly into two parts:

- The Book of Signs (1:19–12:50)
- The Book of Glory (13:1–20:31)

The first part is called the "Book of Signs" because it relates stories of remarkable things Jesus did, which are repeatedly called "signs." The word "sign" (sēmeion) is used sixteen times in this part of John's Gospel, and then it is not used again until the end (20:30) in a passage that scholars think might have originally come at the end of chapter 12, as a conclusion to John's Book of Signs.

The second part of John's Gospel is called the "Book of Glory" because it deals with the last week of Jesus's life, when, in the words of this Gospel, the time for Jesus to be "glorified" had come (17:1; cf. 13:1; see also 7:39; 12:16, 23–24).

John's Gospel also opens with a prologue (1:1–18) and closes with an epilogue (21:1–25).

his death as a return to the Father, who sent him into this world. Then Jesus offers an extended prayer to the Father for his followers, pleading that they might be one, just as he and the Father are one (17:1–26).

John's Gospel next recounts Jesus's passion and resurrection (18:1–20:29): he is betrayed by Judas, denied by Peter, and interrogated by both Annas and Pilate; he is crucified and placed in a tomb; he rises from the dead and appears to Mary Magdalene and the other disciples, including Thomas, who has refused to believe without seeing him. The book appears to close (20:30–31), but an epilogue relates another incident in which, following a miraculous catch of fish, Jesus has private words for Peter and for the disciple whom he loves (21:1–25).

Historical Background

Historical circumstances attending the composition of John's Gospel are more complicated than those related to the other Gospels, as most scholars think that the book that we possess is a second, third, fourth, or fifth edition of a work that went through stages of development. The ancient tradition of the church (dating from the late second century) is that the Gospel of John was produced by one of Jesus's twelve disciples (the one named "John"), but those who accept this tradition usually think that the attribution applies only to the first edition of this Gospel. There is much discussion concerning which parts of the version currently in use might actually have been written by this disciple, and there is much debate over how heavily his work was edited by later contributors.

beloved disciple: an unnamed follower of Jesus whose written testimony is said to be incorporated into the Gospel of John (21:20, 24).

The first question is whether John had anything to do with this Gospel at all. The book itself is anonymous, but its final verses note that someone known as the "beloved disciple" (or the "disciple whom Jesus loved") offered testimony to "these things" and wrote them down (21:24; cf. 21:20). Church tradition has tended to associate this "beloved disciple" with John, in part because John is not otherwise mentioned in the book (except by way of one reference to "the sons of Zebedee" in the epilogue [21:2]), and it seems odd that so prominent a follower of Jesus would be left out of the story.

But is John the "beloved disciple"? In the Gospel of John the beloved disciple is not mentioned until 13:23, at the meal that Jesus shares with his disciples the night before he is crucified. After that he is mentioned several times, often in contexts where his role is compared to that of Peter (see box 9.3). If this beloved disciple is someone who was with Jesus throughout his public ministry, why doesn't the narrative mention him earlier (e.g., in stories set in Galilee, where John the son of Zebedee lived)? More to the point, why doesn't this Gospel describe events at which the disciple John would have been present (according to the other Gospels)? Accordingly, many scholars question whether the "beloved disciple" needs to be equated with John or, indeed, with any of the twelve disciples. Perhaps he was someone who lived near Jerusalem who joined

Box 9.2

The Apostle John in the New Testament

Christian tradition identifies the "beloved disciple," whose testimony is incorporated into the fourth New Testament Gospel, as John the son of Zebedee, one of Jesus's original twelve disciples. What do we know about this person from other New Testament writings?

- John and his brother James were among the first disciples called by Jesus. They were fishermen who left their nets and their father, Zebedee, when Jesus called them to follow him (Mark 1:19–20).
- Along with his brother James and the disciple Peter, John seems to have belonged to an inner circle among Jesus's followers. The trio of Peter, James, and John are invited to accompany Jesus when he raises Jairus's daughter from the dead (Mark 5:37), when he is transfigured on a mountaintop (Mark 9:2), and when he prays in Gethsemane (Mark 14:33). There is also an episode in which the three of them are said to question Jesus privately (Mark 13:3).
- James and John bore the nickname "Boanerges," meaning "sons of thunder" (Mark 3:17), and their headstrong ways sometimes got them in trouble with Jesus or the other disciples. In one instance they ask Jesus to guarantee them the two best seats in glory (Mark 10:35–41), and in another they offer to call down fire from heaven to destroy a Samaritan village that has refused hospitality to Jesus (Luke 9:51–55).
- John's brother (James) was the first of the twelve apostles to die as a martyr (Acts 12:2), and John went on to become a prominent missionary in the early church. He is specifically mentioned as testifying boldly before Jewish leaders in Jerusalem (see Acts 3:1–11; 4:1, 13, 19–20) and as a key missionary worker among the Samaritans (Acts 8:14–25). He became known as "a pillar of the church," one of three people whom the apostle Paul regarded as the key leaders of the Christian movement (Gal. 2:9).

Box 9.3

The Beloved Disciple in John's Gospel

- leans on Jesus's chest at the Last Supper (13:23)
- intermediary between Peter and Jesus (13:24–25)
- gains admittance for Peter to Pilate's court (18:15–16)
- entrusted with care of Jesus's mother (19:26–27)
- witness to blood and water flowing from Jesus's side (19:34–35)
- outruns Peter to the tomb on Easter morning (20:4)
- first to believe in the resurrection (20:8)
- identifies the risen Jesus for Peter (21:7)
- his fate should not be a matter of concern for Peter (21:21–23)
- wrote down these things; his testimony is true (21:24; cf. 19:35)

the group of Jesus's followers when Jesus came there to spend his last few days. Martin Luther actually proposed that the beloved disciple might be Lazarus, who is said to be with the group about a week before Jesus's crucifixion (12:1–2) and who is twice described as someone whom Jesus loved (11:5, 36). Other theories abound, and the identity of this beloved disciple has become one of the great unsolved mysteries of New Testament studies. Still, the traditional and most popular view, despite its difficulties, is that this person probably is to be identified as the disciple John, the fisherman who left his nets to follow Jesus (Mark 1:19–20) and who later became a pillar of the church (Gal. 2:9).

Most scholars, then, recognize that one of Jesus's disciples (possibly John) wrote a testimony to Jesus that is contained in this Gospel. But what, exactly, did he write? A few interpreters think that he wrote the book almost as we have it, though someone else appears to have brushed it up later and added some minor updates, including the epilogue (chap. 21), which assures readers that the beloved disciple's death should not be cause for concern (21:23). At the opposite end of the spectrum, some interpreters think that the original disciple (John or whoever) did little more than get the ball rolling. He probably was an uneducated man (cf. Acts 4:13), and although he might have written down a few things about Jesus, the Gospel of John that we now possess has been so thoroughly reworked that it is no longer possible to discern which nuggets of material stem from his original eyewitness testimony (the only exception being an explicit comment in 19:34–35 regarding a particular detail of Jesus's death). Most scholars, however, adopt a mediating position between these two extremes: they assume that the beloved disciple made a significant contribution to this Gospel, but they also recognize that what he wrote has been edited rather extensively. As evidence of such editing, scholars often note places where the "seams" still show:

- In chapter 8 Jesus is supposedly talking to "the Jews who had believed in him" (8:31), but then he suddenly begins addressing them as people who are seeking to kill him (8:37).

- In 11:2 the narrative reminds us that Mary was the person who anointed Jesus, but the story of Mary doing this is not told until later (12:1–8).
- In 14:31 Jesus brings his Farewell Discourse to a close, saying, "Rise, let us be on our way," but the discourse then continues unabated for two more chapters.

Farewell Discourse: in the Gospel of John, a final speech given by Jesus on the night of his arrest (chaps. 13–16).

These anomalies (and others) are taken as evidence that material in the otherwise carefully constructed work has been shifted about, with new material having been inserted at various points.

One popular theory suggests that the main editor responsible for this book was a person known as "John the Elder," who may have written the letters found toward the end of our New Testament (1 John, 2 John, 3 John). The fourth-century church historian Eusebius identifies John the Elder as a different person from John the apostle; the two were easily confused because they

⊙ EXPLORE 9.16
Three Persons Named John?

had the same name and were members of the same community. Actually, Eusebius says that John the Elder was a student or disciple of John the apostle (who had been a disciple of Jesus). Thus, according to one theory, the Fourth Gospel may actually be the product of two persons named "John": John the apostle (= the beloved disciple) wrote the "first draft," and his student John the Elder later produced an expanded, revised edition. But none of this is certain; indeed, some scholars think that Eusebius was mistaken in taking the apostle and the elder to be two different people.

This brings us to the question of sources—another matter on which

Fig. 9.2. Jesus and the Samaritan woman. Although Jews did not usually have any dealings with Samaritans, John's Gospel reports that Jesus had a memorable encounter with a Samaritan woman at a well (4:1–42). He demonstrated that he had prophetic knowledge of her private life and promised that he could give her "living water" so that she would never thirst again. (He Qi / www.heqigallery.com)

lack of certainty can be frustrating. There is, first, a basic disagreement among scholars as to whether the person with primary or final responsibility for producing this Gospel had copies of the other Gospels. If he did, that might explain why he doesn't bother to tell many of the stories found in those books (he wanted his Gospel to supplement theirs), but then we are left to wonder why he sometimes does tell overlapping stories (e.g., feeding five thousand, walking on water, anointing at Bethany). The issue is unresolved.

Another popular theory suggests that someone responsible for producing this Gospel had a copy of a now lost book that scholars call the "Signs Gospel." This book (if it existed) may have contained several miracle stories presented as numbered "signs" that Jesus performed (cf. 2:11; 4:54), and it would have concluded with the words now found in 20:30–31, indicating that Jesus also did many other signs that are not recorded in the book.

In sum, while many questions remain, most scholars affirm that the Gospel of John was produced in a community founded by one of Jesus's earliest followers, and that it was written, preserved, and edited by leaders who had close ties with the apostolic tradition. Wherever the community may have been located (tradition suggests Ephesus), clues within this Gospel indicate that the congregation was engaged in the task of defining themselves with regard to other Christians, the Jews, and the world at large. There are signals that the church has felt forced into adopting a defensive and competitive posture. Still, they are committed to being a community of love in an environment where they feel hated and persecuted by others (15:18–25; 16:33; 17:14).

Due to the complexity of its composition, this Gospel is difficult to date. It retains elements of very early eyewitness tradition not recorded elsewhere (e.g., the name of Malchus in 18:10), but it also evinces a developed understanding of faith that suggests a lengthy process of reflection. In shorthand fashion, the Gospel of John is usually said to have been produced in the 90s, since that is when the final redaction is likely to have taken place, but the scholars who say this generally recognize that much of the material in John comes from an earlier time.

As for the purpose of John's Gospel, scholars have proposed any number of aims that we might place on a list of multiple objectives: to defend the faith intellectually against criticisms brought by Jews; to convert Jews and/or Samaritans; to catechize new converts; to establish Jesus's superiority over other religious leaders (such as Moses and John the Baptist); to promote the credentials of the community's founder; to bring the community more in line with other Christian groups; to serve the liturgical needs of those who worship Jesus as the Son of God; to argue for particular doctrinal points; to sustain a counterculture fostered in opposition to the corrupt and unjust Roman world. The book's author(s) no doubt would have been happy to discover that the work had any or all of these effects, but certain passages in the text itself point to a more general and transcendent purpose:

- "I say these things so that you may be saved" (5:34).
- "You will know the truth, and the truth will make you free" (8:32).
- "I have said these things to you to keep you from stumbling" (16:1).

And the book concludes with an explicit indication of purpose:

- "These [things] are written so that you may come to believe [or, continue to believe] that Jesus is the Messiah, the Son of God, and that through believing you may have life in his name" (20:31).

We might say that the purpose of this Gospel is to do what it says Jesus came to do. Jesus came that people might be saved, set free, and kept from stumbling, and this Gospel seeks to inspire and sustain faith to those same ends. Jesus came so that people might have life (10:10), and this Gospel has been written so that people might have life in his name.

What Is Distinctive about the Gospel of John?

When asked to consider what is distinctive about John's Gospel, we might be tempted to answer, "Everything!" This is only a slight exaggeration, since more than 90 percent of the material in this book is without parallel in any of the other three Gospels. Still, it is the same basic story that is being told, and the testimony of John's Gospel is congruent with that of the Synoptic Gospels on all essential points: Jesus is the Messiah and Son of God; his life and teachings reveal God's character and will for humanity; his death and resurrection bring forgiveness of sins; salvation is found through faith in him; and a godly life is obtained through obedience to his commandments.

> ⊘ EXPLORE 9.4
> Distinctive Character-
> istics of John's Gospel

> ⊘ EXPLORE 9.7
> Comparison of John
> and the Synoptic
> Gospels

Possible Sources for John's Gospel

- a "Signs Gospel" that recorded seven or eight miracle stories (2:1–12; 4:46–54; 5:1–9; 6:1–13; 9:1–7; 11:1–44; 21:1–6; maybe 6:15–25) and may have included an account of the passion and resurrection
- a collection of remembrances of one called the "beloved disciple," dealing mostly with the last week of Jesus's life
- a body of material underlying the great discourses of Jesus, possibly sermons by the beloved disciple or another prominent member of the community

Nevertheless, to become aware of what is distinctive about this Gospel, students should first familiarize themselves with the data contained in boxes 9.5 and 9.6:

words from the cross: seven sayings of Jesus spoken during his crucifixion; see Mark 15:34 (Matt. 27:46); Luke 23:34, 43, 46; John 19:26–27, 28, 30.

- John's Gospel contains many stories not told elsewhere in the New Testament, and some of these stories are exceptionally long ones. We should also note that stories in John that are found in the other Gospels are sometimes told quite differently by John. John's account of the crucifixion includes three "words from the cross" not reported anywhere else and, conversely, includes no "words from the cross" that are reported in the other Gospels (see box 5.8).

- John's Gospel is also striking for what it does not include. Readers familiar with the story of Jesus from the other Gospels may find it hard to imagine a Jesus who never tells parables, casts out demons, or eats with outcasts, much less a Jesus who has almost nothing to say about the end times, the kingdom of God, or the call for God's people to deny themselves, love their neighbors, renounce their possessions, or help the poor. Some of this can be overstated: although the word "repentance" is never used, Jesus does tell a woman, "Do not sin again" (8:11); though Jesus does not tell actual parables, he does use figurative speech that is "parable-like" (4:35–37; 8:35; 10:1–5; 12:24; 16:21; cf. 10:6; 16:25). Still, an initial awareness of what is not found in John may alert us to how different this Gospel is and also may serve as a springboard for coming to a positive recognition of what John does have to offer.

John's Gospel is unique in other ways as well. It presents Jesus's ministry as extending over a three-year period and concentrates on happenings in and around Jerusalem; the other Gospels suggest a more compact time period and have a much heavier focus on events in Galilee. Whereas Jesus is noted for

---

Box 9.5

Some Stories about Jesus Unique to John's Gospel

- calling of Andrew, Philip, and Nathanael (1:35–51)
- changing of water into wine at Cana (2:1–12)
- conversation with Nicodemus (3:1–21)
- encounter with a Samaritan woman at a well (4:1–42)
- healing of a crippled man at Pool of Bethzatha (5:1–18)
- rescue of an adulterous woman from stoning (7:53–8:11)
- healing of a man born blind (9:1–41)
- raising of Lazarus (11:1–44)
- washing of disciples' feet (13:1–20)
- prayer for believers to be united (17:1–26)
- resurrection appearance to Thomas (20:24–29)

Material Not Found in John's Gospel

John's Gospel is notable for its lack of material that is very familiar in the other Gospels:

- no stories of Jesus's birth
- no mention of Jesus's baptism
- nothing about Jesus being tempted or tested by Satan
- no mention of Jesus eating with tax collectors and sinners
- no transfiguration of Jesus
- no parables
- no exorcisms
- no condemnations of the rich or words about helping the poor
- nothing about loving one's neighbor (or one's enemy)
- no call for people to repent (from either John the Baptist or Jesus)
- no call for disciples to deny themselves or renounce their possessions
- no predictions of Jerusalem's downfall (but cf. 2:19–22)
- no mention of Jesus instituting the Lord's Supper (but cf. 6:53–56)
- almost no mention of the kingdom of God (only in 3:3–5; but cf. 18:36)
- almost no references to a second coming (just once: 21:22–23; usually, 14:3, 18, 28 are read as Jesus coming for individuals at the hour of their death)

short, pithy sayings in the other Gospels, the Johannine Jesus delivers long, philosophical discourses (5:19–47; 6:25–70; 7:14–52; 8:12–59; 10:1–18, 22–39; 12:23–46; 14:1–16:33). Furthermore, where the Synoptic Gospels summarize the content of Jesus's proclamation as "the good news of the kingdom of God" (e.g., Matt. 4:23; Mark 1:14–15), in John, Jesus talks mostly about himself: he talks about his identity as the one who comes to reveal the Father and about what it means for people to believe in him, love him, obey him, and abide in him.

Finally, John is notable for its abundant use of symbolism. For example, in seven passages famously called the "'I am' Sayings," Jesus describes himself with metaphors:

"I am the bread of life" (6:35, 51)

"I am the light of the world" (8:12; 9:5)

"I am the door" (10:7, 9)

"I am the good shepherd" (10:11, 14)

"I am the resurrection and the life" (11:25)

"I am the way, the truth, and the life" (14:6)

"I am the true vine" (15:1, 5)

⊙ EXPLORE 9.10
Symbolism in the
Gospel of John

In such passages, the words "I am" themselves may be symbolic, recalling God's self-designation in Exodus 3:14; Deuteronomy 32:39; Isaiah 48:12.

The symbolism of John's Gospel is accompanied by an intriguing literary motif: misunderstanding. Characters in the story frequently misunderstand things Jesus says, such that the narrator or Jesus himself needs to clarify the matter (unless the correct meaning is assumed to be obvious). People think that Jesus is talking about the temple in Jerusalem when in fact he is speaking of his body as a temple (2:19–22). Jesus says that his friend Lazarus has "fallen asleep" (i.e., died), and Jesus's disciples think that Lazarus is getting some healthy rest (11:12). This device infuses the narrative with a dramatic irony that is alternately humorous and hopeful, peculiar and purposeful. At another level, the device serves to train readers to look more closely, to be aware that there may be deeper or multiple levels of meaning elsewhere as well.

Fig. 9.3. Foot-washing. John's Gospel reports that Mary of Bethany (sister of Martha and Lazarus) anointed Jesus's feet with perfume and wiped them with her hair (12:1–3). Perhaps this is what inspired Jesus a few days later to wash the feet of his disciples and to tell them to continue practicing this ritual as an illustration of the unselfish love that is to mark his followers (13:3–17). (J. Kirk Richards)

Thus readers are encouraged to look for symbolism even where it is not explicit, and much Johannine interpretation has been devoted to determining what is or is not symbolic and how that which is symbolic is to be understood. Why do the disciples catch 153 fish (21:11)? Does that number mean something? What do the "water and blood" that come from Jesus's side (19:35) stand for? Is it baptism and Eucharist (a popular Roman Catholic interpretation), or is it the gift of the Spirit and forgiveness of sins (a popular Baptist interpretation), or is it simply a gruesome detail having no symbolic meaning at all?

Major Themes in the Gospel of John

Jesus the True Revelation of God

In the Gospel of John, Jesus is the one who makes God known. He reveals God to humankind so that people might know God and be liberated and

Eucharist: from a Greek word meaning "thanksgiving"; the Christian rite or sacrament also known as the "Lord's Supper" or "Holy Communion."

▶ EXPLORE 9.11
Misunderstanding in the Gospel of John

transformed by that revelation. The prologue to John's Gospel introduces us to Jesus as the Son who makes the Father known (1:18) and as the Logos or Word of God made flesh (1:14). He has been with God from the beginning (1:1). John wants us to believe that the Word of God through which the heavens and the earth were created has now taken on human form and come to live for a time on earth. This ultimate expression of "who God is and what God says" reveals much more than prophets or Scripture or any other medium of revelation could ever convey. Theologians refer to this doctrine of God becoming human as the "incarnation"; it implies a notion of preexistence—that is, an understanding that the one who became known as Jesus Christ existed (as God) prior to the earthly life and ministry of Jesus. John's Gospel is the primary biblical text for the doctrines of incarnation and preexistence; those ideas are not found in Matthew, Mark, or Luke, though they may be evident in a few passages elsewhere in the New Testament (Phil. 2:5–8; Col. 1:15–20; Heb. 1:1–4; 2:9).

John's Gospel often speaks of God sending Jesus into the world, employing the same language that would have been used to describe an official or ruler sending an emissary (e.g., 3:16, 34; 7:28–29; in all, Jesus refers to God twenty-three times as "the one who sent me"). Thus Jesus is a messenger, but as the Word of God made flesh, he is also the message. He comes to reveal God, but he does this primarily through self-disclosure, by revealing himself (see 1:18).

We might summarize Jesus's role this way:

- Jesus *tells* people what God is like. He says that God loves the world (3:16), that God is true (3:33), that God is spirit (4:24), that God is active (5:17), that God gives the Holy Spirit (4:16), that God answers prayer (16:23), and much more.
- Jesus *shows* people what God is like. He does this through his deeds and mighty works. This may be one reason why his miracles are called "signs" (2:11; 4:54; 6:2, 14; 12:18). In some sense, the miracles are simply signs of legitimation, proving that Jesus has divine power and authority (see 3:2; 7:31; 9:16). Their effectiveness in this regard, however, is mixed: some people believe because of the signs (2:11, 23; 4:53–54; cf. 20:30–31); others do not (11:47; 12:37; cf. 4:48). In a deeper sense, the miracles are signs because, like the metaphors used by Jesus, they indicate something symbolic about who God is and what God does: God transforms the ordinary into the extraordinary (2:1–11) and offers people health (4:46–54), sustenance (6:2–14), and life (11:38–44; 12:17–18).
- Jesus *is* what God is like. Jesus reveals God through his very being. He not only discloses the truth but also *is* the truth (14:6). He can say, "Whoever has seen me has seen the Father" (14:9; cf. 12:45). According to John's Gospel, Jesus is the way, the truth, and the life (14:6); through him people

Logos: in Greek philosophy, a word referring to ultimate truth or reason; in John's Gospel, the term is used for the eternal divine entity that takes on flesh to become the human being Jesus Christ.

gain access to God, recognize God's authentic nature and intentions, and experience life as God intends.

Jesus as God

John's Gospel is the only one of the four to identify Jesus as God (but see box 4.5). Jesus not only was *with* God in the beginning but he also *was* God (1:1). After he rises from the dead, even his most stubborn disciple calls him "My Lord and my God!" (20:28). John's Gospel is nevertheless adamant in its insistence that Jesus is completely human: he feels grief (11:33–35), fatigue (4:6), and anguish (12:27; 13:21); he gets suspicious (2:24–25) and irritable (2:4; 6:26; 7:6–8; 8:25); he experiences thirst (19:28) and, most important, death (19:30, 33). Jesus also claims to be subordinate to the Father and completely dependent on God for everything (5:19, 30). Nevertheless, Jesus is God, for John's Gospel is able to speak of God in a twofold sense: there is God the Father, but there is also "God the Son" (1:18). Such language may have been disturbing to Jews (and Christians?) committed to monotheism, but John avoids compromising that principle by insisting on an essential unity of Father and Son. Jesus says, "I am in the Father and the Father is in me" (14:10–11) and "The Father and I are one" (10:30).

monotheism: the belief that there is only one God.

Scholars usually see John's Gospel as representing a transitional point between two ideological developments:

- Before John's Gospel, certain Jewish writings personified Wisdom as a divine mediator of God's person and intent (see Prov. 8:27, 29–30, 35–36; Wis. 7:25–26; 9:10).
- After John's Gospel, Christian theologians developed a doctrine of the Trinity, according to which God could be understood as three in one: Father, Son, and Holy Spirit (three persons, but only one God).

John's Gospel emerges from the milieu of Jewish Christianity and provides a link between these Jewish and Christian concepts. John's presentation of Jesus as "God the Son" may be inspired by the Jewish wisdom tradition, but it also points forward to the trinitarian view that would be articulated by later Christian theologians.

Jesus's Death Is His Glorification

John's Gospel refers to Jesus's death as the hour in which he is glorified (see 17:1; cf. 13:1; see also 7:39; 12:16, 23–24). In part, this may be because it is a prelude to his resurrection and his return to the Father, who sent him. But there is more: three times in this Gospel Jesus refers to his crucifixion as the occasion when he will be "lifted up" from the earth (3:14; 8:28; 12:32–34). Scholars cannot help but notice a parallel here to the three times in each of the other Gospels in which Jesus predicts his crucifixion (e.g., Mark 8:31–32; 9:31; 10:33–34), albeit without using the language of "lifted up." That language appears to employ a pun: the Greek word in question (*hypsoun*) can mean "lifted" (as when the soldiers took the cross on which Jesus was hung and raised it up from the ground) or "exalted" (in the sense of someone being praised or glorified). In John, the crucifixion itself becomes an act of glorification because it reveals the depth of God's love for humanity (3:14–17) and the depth of Jesus's love for his followers (10:11, 15; 13:1; 15:13). This concept of the crucifixion also affects the way that John tells the story. For one thing, Jesus remains in complete control of everything: no one takes his life from him; rather, he lays it down of his own accord (10:17–18). Further, when Jesus dies, he does not scream in pain (see Mark 15:37) or cry out "My God, my God, why have you forsaken me?" (see Matt. 27:46; Mark 15:34) but instead calmly declares, "It is finished" (19:30), which means, "What I came to do has been accomplished."

Fig. 9.4. Lifted up from the earth. In John's Gospel, Jesus speaks of his crucifixion as exaltation, through which he will be glorified, and by which he becomes the ultimate demonstration of God's gracious love for humanity (see 3:14; 8:28; 12:32–34). This perspective appears to have inspired Salvador Dali's famous painting *Christ of St. John of the Cross.* (© Glasgow City Council (Museums) / The Bridgeman Art Library International)

Salvation as Abundant Life

John's Gospel employs a rich and varied vocabulary for the phenomenon of salvation. Because of Jesus, people can become children of God (1:12), be saved (3:17; 5:34; 10:9; 12:47), enter God's kingdom (3:3–5), be born again (3:3), come to the Father (14:6), and be set free (8:32). In a basic sense, as noted above, Jesus has come that people might have life (10:10; cf. 3:14–17, 36; 5:39–40; 20:31; cf. 1 John 5:12). But what does all of this mean? We should note, first, that John

> ⊙ **EXPLORE 9.12**
> The Passion of Jesus
> in the Gospel of John

salvation: an act of God through which human beings are delivered from the power and consequences of sin.

eternal life: in biblical terms, life that is endless both qualitatively and quantitatively.

affirms the traditional concepts of salvation found almost everywhere in the New Testament. Jesus deals with the problem of sin by sacrificially laying down his life for others (10:11, 15, 17–18; 15:13) and taking away the sins of the world (1:29); he will likewise deal with the problem of death by raising people up on the last day (6:39–40, 54) so that they might live forever (11:25–26) in one of the many rooms of the Father's house (14:2–3). The main focus of John's Gospel, however, is on the way that Jesus affects quality of life in the here and now. In John's Gospel eternal life is more than just "life after death"; it is not only life that is endless in length but also life that is endless in value and meaning. The experience of eternal life is a present reality (3:36; 5:24). People can have this life, and have it abundantly, if they know the truth about God revealed in Jesus. What is this truth? Above all, Jesus reveals that God loves the world and desires to bless and to save rather than to punish or condemn (3:16–17). The very coming of Jesus is a demonstration of this love (3:16; cf. 1 John 4:9), and through his death on the cross Jesus reveals divine love at an unprecedented and unimaginable level: "Greater love has no one than this," he says (15:13; cf. 13:1). People who come to know this truth are set free (8:32); people who believe what Jesus reveals about the love of God have life that does not perish, life that is abundant and eternal.

Loving Jesus and Abiding in Christ

The beloved disciple and those who preserved his tradition believed that they were in a living relationship with Jesus Christ. The language that John's Gospel uses to describe the Christian life is intensely relational (1:11–12): being a Christian means not only believing in Jesus as one who is risen from the dead (see 20:24–29) but also loving him (8:42; 14:15, 21, 23; 16:27; 21:15–17) and abiding in him (6:56; 15:4–10). Believers are united to Jesus Christ in a spiritual relationship of love that sustains and empowers them (see 1:12). People are brought into this relationship by Jesus and at his initiative (15:3, 16), and they retain the connection by allowing his word to abide in them (15:7; cf. 5:38) and by keeping his commandments (15:10), especially the commandment to love one another (15:12, 17; cf. 13:34–35). As always in the Bible, love is not primarily an emotion but an action, exemplified here by Jesus's own humble acts of service on behalf of others (13:3–15; 15:13). Those who experience and exhibit this sort of love may remain in an abiding relationship with Jesus Christ and experience his joy (15:11; 17:13). Whatever they ask is granted (15:7; cf. 14:13–14; 15:16; 16:23–24). They are able to do the works that Jesus did (and even greater works) because Jesus is actually doing these things through them (14:12–13; cf. 15:5). They become one with him and with God and with one another (17:20–23).

The Paraclete

The Gospel of John also emphasizes the role of the Holy Spirit, who is referred to distinctively as the *paraklētos*, the "Paraclete" (14:16, 26; 15:26; 16:7; English Bibles variously translate this as "Comforter," "Counselor," "Advocate," or "Helper"). Jesus promises that the Spirit will come to his followers (7:37–39; 14:16–17; cf. 1:33), and after Easter he gives the Spirit to them (20:22). In John's Gospel, the primary role ascribed to the Spirit is that of revealing truth and teaching disciples what they need to know (14:25–26; 16:13); this is accomplished both by reminding believers of the truth revealed by Jesus (14:26) and by leading those believers into new revelation that they were not able to bear while Jesus

Fig. 9.5. The raising of Lazarus. The story in John's Gospel of Jesus raising his friend Lazarus from the dead (11:1–44) inspired this serigraph by Japanese artist Sadao Watanabe. (Photo © Boltin Picture Library / The Bridgeman Art Library International)

was with them (16:12–15). The Spirit testifies on Jesus's behalf (15:26) and counters the world's understanding of such things as sin and righteousness and judgment (16:8–11). Jesus tells his followers that it is actually to their advantage that he goes away because only then will he be able to send the Paraclete to them (16:7).

The World and the Jews

John's Gospel portrays the world as a hostile environment that hates Jesus and his followers (7:7; 15:18–19; 16:20; 17:14). The world is not intrinsically evil, for it came into being through God and, indeed, through the Word that became flesh in Jesus Christ (1:3, 14). God loves the world (3:16) and sent Jesus

Fig. 9.6. *Noli Me Tangere*. The Latin phrase that is the title of this Coptic icon derives from John 20:17, where the risen Jesus tells Mary Magdalene, "Do not touch me" (or, perhaps, "Do not hold me" or "Do not hold me back"). The reason for the prohibition was that he "had not yet ascended to the Father." Curiously, the phrase (which was well-known due to Roman Catholic liturgy) also became a motto of the American Revolution, where it was translated, not quite correctly, as "Don't tread on me" and employed with a very different meaning. (Bridgeman Images)

to be its savior (3:16–17; 4:42; cf. 1:29), but the world neither knew nor accepted him (1:10). The world is in fact ruled by the devil (12:31; 14:30; 16:11) and is unable to receive the Spirit of truth (14:17). Thus the community that produced this Gospel has little regard for the world, except as a mission field. Jesus sends his followers into the world (17:18; 20:21), but he makes clear that they do not belong to the world (17:14); they are to be in the world but not of it (17:15–16). Indeed, this Gospel does not seem to be greatly concerned with the beneficial or transforming effect that believers might have on the world (cf. Matt. 5:13–16; Acts 17:6); rather, the prevailing concern is for believers to be protected from the world's dangers and sanctified against its corruption (17:11–12, 17–19). Scholars have tended to interpret this aspect of John's Gospel as expressive of an early Christian community struggling to define itself in the milieu of the Roman Empire: conflicting claims regarding the authority and kingship of Jesus vis-à-vis that of Caesar created tensions between members of John's church and supporters of Roman imperialism.

John's Gospel also portrays the Jews as implacable opponents of Jesus and his followers. Of course, Jesus and his disciples were themselves Jews, and John's Gospel acknowledges this (4:9). Still, most of the time this Gospel uses the phrase "the Jews" to refer to a group of people that does not include Jesus or anyone associated with him. In the world of John's Gospel people must choose whether they are going to be disciples of Jesus or Moses (9:28), and confessing faith in Jesus is grounds for expulsion from the synagogue (9:22; 12:42; 16:2). Against this background, we cannot fail to notice that the portrayal of Jews in this Gospel seems harsh and polemical: the Jews are people who do not believe their own Scriptures (5:39–47) and whose basic allegiance to God has been sorely compromised (19:15). Compared to the world at large, the Jews are perhaps no worse than pagan people, but they are also no better. They have lost their status as the people of God (8:39, 42, 47), and so whatever can be said of "the world" in general can also be said of "the Jews" in particular. The devil is the ruler of the world (12:31; 14:30), and the devil is the father of the Jews (8:44). Scholars are quick to point out that the antipathy John's Gospel shows toward "the Jews" was never intended to convey a generic condemnation of an entire race or nation (all Jewish people everywhere); rather, what John's Gospel offers is a more specific attack on a particular expression of a rival religious movement (first-century Jewish synagogue religion). Nevertheless, polemical passages in John's Gospel often have been used to support anti-Semitism. Some Bible translators now render the word *Ioudaioi* in John's Gospel by some term other than "Jews" (e.g., "Judeans") in order to indicate that it refers to a specific group of people who lived at a particular place and time.

synagogue: a congregation of Jews who gather for worship, prayer, and Bible study, or the place where they gather for these purposes.

pagans: nonconverted gentiles, often associated by Jews and Christians with idolatry, polytheism, erratic religious beliefs, and an immoral lifestyle.

Loving One Another

John's Gospel has more to say about love than the other three Gospels combined. The word "love" occurs well over fifty times in this book, and yet there is no mention of loving one's neighbor (cf. Mark 12:31) or one's enemies (cf. Matt. 5:44; Luke 6:27). The focus, rather, is on loving one another—that is, on the love that believers have for one another (13:34–35; 15:12, 17). Jesus tells his followers that this is a "new commandment" (13:34; cf. 1 John 2:7–8) and that everyone will know who his followers are by the love they have for one another (13:35). How a Gospel with such a strong focus on love can also exhibit such hostility toward Jews and outsiders is a frequent subject for reflection. Still, Christians throughout the centuries have prized John's Gospel for its poetic and persuasive presentation of this simple ethic: "Love one another as I have loved you." The first of the Johannine Letters continues and expands on this theme (1 John 3:11–18; 4:7–21; see also 2 John 5–6).

Conclusion

The question is sometimes raised as to whether the community behind John's Gospel should be labeled a "sect." Was this Gospel written and preserved by Christians who were a community unto themselves, isolated if not alienated from other Christian groups? Parallels are drawn to the Jewish monastic community at Qumran, where the Dead Sea Scrolls were found: the group that lived there apparently regarded themselves as the only true believers in a world populated by pagans, apostates, and heretics. Like the Gospel of John, the Dead Sea Scrolls present community members as children of the light who belong to the truth, while castigating others (including other Jews) as children of darkness and falsehood.

John's Gospel does exhibit some marks of sectarian literature, such as a pronounced use of dualistic language, a tendency to differentiate between "us and them" (believers and unbelievers), and a strong emphasis on establishing and maintaining internal cohesion. Furthermore, John's Gospel is sufficiently distinctive to mark it as the product of a Christian group that had limited contact with other Christians. However, John's Gospel also insists that believers remain engaged with the world to which Christ has sent them (17:15–18), and it presents a grand vision of all believers being one in Christ (17:20–23).

Some scholars have suggested that John presents Peter and the beloved disciple as the representatives of two major strands of Christianity, thus acknowledging that his strand (the beloved disciple's community) is distinct from the norm (Petrine Christianity). But even if that were the case, there would be no reason to suspect hostility between these diverse expressions of the faith. In this Gospel the competition between Peter and the beloved disciple is a decidedly friendly one: the two leaders obviously respect each other and seek to outdo each other only in devotion and faithfulness to Christ (13:24–25; 18:15–16; 20:4; 21:7, 21–23).

⊙ EXPLORE 9.19
Competition among
the Pillars?

Furthermore, John's Gospel also exhibits a strong (if paradoxical) tendency to push outward, testing if not obliterating boundaries: the salvation that comes from the Jews (4:22) is also for Samaritans (4:39–42), Greeks (12:20–26), and "other sheep" (10:16)—the ambiguity of this last reference seems to invite application to anyone, anywhere. And whose sin does Jesus take away? Not just that of John's church members, or even of Christians in general. Jesus is the Lamb of God, who takes away the sin of the whole world (1:29). Could there be a more ecumenical (i.e., less sectarian) statement of Christian faith than that? In any case, the early church did not regard John's Gospel as a sectarian work. There never seems to have been any question that John's testimony to Christ, while distinctive, was wholly compatible with that offered by the Synoptic Gospels and other writings of the New Testament. John's understanding of the incarnation and divinity of Jesus became standard Christian doctrine; John's interest in freedom, truth, and glory became a mainstay of Christian theology; and John's tantalizing promises of receiving God's love and experiencing abundant life would appeal to a wide variety of new readers in every generation.

FOR FURTHER READING: John

Brant, Jo-Ann. *John*. Paideia. Grand Rapids: Baker Academic, 2011.

Edwards, Ruth B. *Discovering John: Content, Interpretation, Reception*. Grand Rapids: Eerdmans, 2015.

Harrington, Wilfrid J. *Reading John for the First Time*. Mahwah, NJ: Paulist Press, 2016.

Koester, Craig R. *The Word of Life: A Theology of John's Gospel*. Grand Rapids: Eerdmans, 2008.

Köstenberger, Andreas J. *Encountering John: The Gospel in Historical, Literary, and Theological Perspective*. 2nd ed. Encountering Biblical Studies. Grand Rapids: Baker Academic, 2013.

Neyrey, Jerome H. *The Gospel of John*. New Cambridge Bible Commentary. Cambridge: Cambridge University Press, 2006.

O'Day, Gail R., and Susan E. Hylen. *John*. Westminster Bible Companion. Louisville: Westminster John Knox, 2006.

Porter, Stanley E. *John, His Gospel, and His Jesus: In Pursuit of the Johannine Voice*. Grand Rapids: Eerdmans, 2015.

Sloyan, Gerard S. *What Are They Saying about John?* Rev. ed. Mahwah, NJ: Paulist Press, 2006.

Smith, D. Moody, Jr. *The Theology of the Gospel of John*. New Testament Theology. Cambridge: Cambridge University Press, 1995.

Wright, N. T. *John for Everyone*. 2 vols. 2nd ed. Louisville: Westminster John Knox, 2004.

⊚ Go to www
.IntroducingNT.com
for summaries,
videos, and other
study tools.

Peter Davidson

10

Acts

The book of Acts has everything but dinosaurs. It's got earthquakes (16:26), shipwrecks (27:41–44), avenging angels (12:23), harrowing escapes (9:23–25; 21:30–36), riots (19:23–41), murder plots (9:23; 23:12–15; 25:1–3), political intrigue (16:35–39; 22:24–29; 24:26–27), courtroom drama (23:1–10), and so much more. The book of Acts tells the story of the early Christian church with all the flair of an exciting adventure novel. Things start out rather calm—constant prayer (1:14) and some business to attend to (1:15–26)—then the Holy Spirit comes roaring into the room, igniting the pious with tongues of fire and causing them to behave in ways that lead onlookers to think they're drunk (2:1–13). From that point on, we know we are in for a bumpy ride.

The book of Acts has something else that is not all that common in the New Testament: humor. A maid is so overjoyed when Peter escapes from prison that she runs to tell everyone, leaving him on the doorstep, a wanted man, banging on the door to get in (12:13–16). Paul speaks to a group late into the night, going on so long that a young man falls asleep and tumbles out an upstairs window; he is allowed to go home, but the others are brought back upstairs—Paul isn't done yet (20:7–12). Some non-Christian exorcists decide that if the "name of Jesus" works for Paul, maybe it will work for them as well; however, the evil spirit that they try it on has other ideas, and—well, Ephesus would not soon forget the sight of a high priest's sons (seven of them) running naked from that house (19:13–17). These stories all have the quality of "Did you hear the one about . . . ?" They are not especially replete with theological meaning, but they do recall memorable moments in the early years of Christian development. They are examples of what early Christians would have regarded as "good stories," and of all the writers in the Bible, Luke seems most committed to the principle that good stories are worth telling.

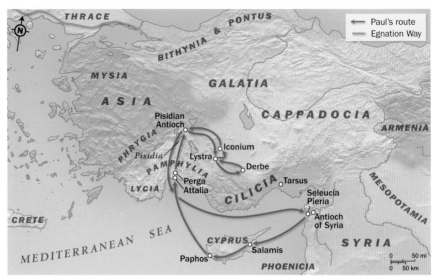

Map 10.1. Paul's first missionary journey.

apostle: "one who is sent" (*apostolos*); used for certain leaders among the earliest followers of Jesus, especially the twelve disciples and Paul.

The book of Acts may read like an adventure novel, but actually it is a history book. And Luke's ultimate interests are theological, or at least spiritual and pastoral. The book is sometimes called "Acts of the Apostles," but that name can be misleading. Luke does recount stories of the apostles (and other prominent church leaders), but he is most interested in recounting the acts of God. The book could almost be called "Acts of the Holy Spirit" or "Acts of the Risen Lord Jesus Christ."

Overview

The book of Acts opens with a preface to Theophilus (1:1–5), an account of Jesus's ascension (1:6–11), and a brief narrative of how Matthias was chosen to replace Judas Iscariot as the twelfth apostle (1:12–26). Then, on the day of Pentecost, the Holy Spirit fills 120 believers, who speak in tongues (2:1–13), and Peter preaches to the crowd, gaining many new converts (2:37–41). The marks of the early church are described (2:42–47). The healing of a lame man (3:1–10) leads to another sermon by Peter (3:11–26) and to the arrest of Peter and John by Jewish authorities (4:1–31). The Jerusalem church practices communal sharing of possessions, and two believers, Ananias and Sapphira, are struck dead by God for trying to take advantage of this arrangement (4:32–5:11). Luke then relates another arrest of the apostles and records that they were spared further suffering due to both miraculous intervention and the advice of a tolerant rabbi, Gamaliel (5:12–42). A dispute between Hellenists and Hebrews in the church leads to the appointment of seven men to exercise leadership in the community (6:1–7); one of them, Stephen, is stoned to death by hostile Jews after preaching a sermon accusing them of unfaithfulness (6:8–8:1).

⊙ EXPLORE 10.0
Acts: Outline of Contents

⊙ EXPLORE 10.1
Content Summary: Expanded Overview of the Book of Acts

Luke relates how the church expanded geographically and grew in ethnic diversity. Philip, one of the seven, brings the gospel to Samaria (where Peter has a confrontation with Simon Magus), and he also leads an Ethiopian eunuch to be baptized into the faith (8:2–40). A persecutor of the church, Saul (also known as Paul), has a vision of Jesus that transforms him into a passionate missionary for the faith (9:1–31). Peter heals Aeneas in Lydda (9:32–35), raises Dorcas (Tabitha) from the dead (9:36–43), and baptizes a gentile centurion, Cornelius, after receiving a vision about what is clean and unclean (10:1–11:18). Barnabas and Saul become leaders of a gentile mission at Antioch and take responsibility for a collection on behalf of Jerusalem famine victims (11:19–30; 12:24–25). Meanwhile, Herod kills James the disciple of Jesus and imprisons Peter (12:1–5), but an angel releases Peter (12:6–19). Herod later incurs God's wrath and dies a gruesome death (12:20–23).

Luke next reports the first missionary journey of Paul and Barnabas (13:1–14:28): they go to Cyprus and southeastern Asia Minor, preaching in synagogues but enjoying even greater success among gentiles. Paul strikes Elymas the magician blind, refuses worship when identified as a god, and is stoned and left for dead. The increasing number of gentile converts leads to a conference

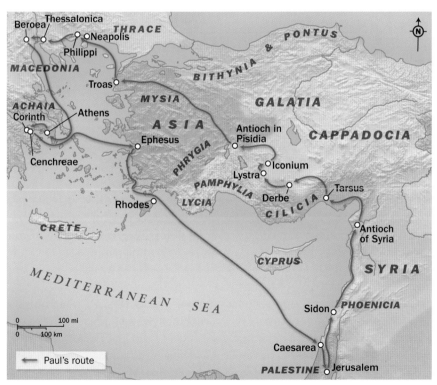

Map 10.2. Paul's second missionary journey.

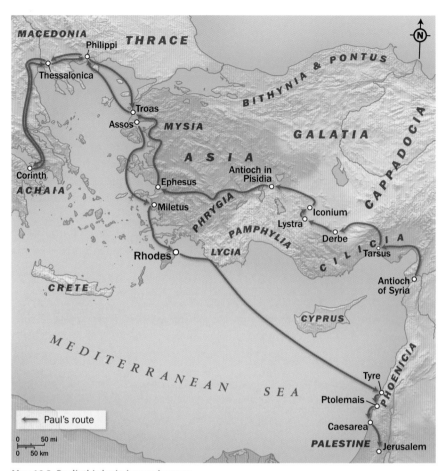

Map 10.3. Paul's third missionary journey.

in Jerusalem at which James the brother of Jesus proposes terms for the inclusion of gentiles in the church (15:1–35).

Luke reports a second missionary journey of Paul and Silas (15:36–18:22). Here they travel through Asia Minor and what is now Greece (Macedonia and Achaia); they meet a number of significant people (Timothy, Lydia, Aquila, Priscilla); found churches in Philippi, Thessalonica, Beroea, and Corinth; and encounter much hostility, including an imprisonment interrupted by an earthquake at Philippi. This section of the book also includes an account of Paul preaching on the Areopagus to philosophers in Athens (17:16–34).

Luke then reports a third missionary journey of Paul (18:23–21:14): he travels through Asia Minor and Greece, visiting many places where he has been before, but Luke focuses his account on events in Ephesus. There, a powerful preacher, Apollos, is instructed by Priscilla and Aquila; Paul brings the gift of the Spirit to former disciples of John the Baptist; seven sons of the priest Sceva are mauled by an evil spirit; and Paul survives a riot after Demetrius the silversmith convinces people that the city's economy and honor are threatened by the Christian affront to the Temple of Artemis. On the journey home, Paul preaches a fateful sermon in Troas (during which Eutychus falls out a window and must be miraculously revived), and he offers a farewell homily to the Ephesian elders in Miletus.

Luke devotes the last part of Acts to reporting on Paul's life as a prisoner (21:15–28:31). Paul is arrested in Jerusalem (21:17–36) and subsequently moved, first to Caesarea and then to Rome. He gives his testimony repeatedly, before the Jewish populace (22:1–22), before the council (23:1–10), before the governor Felix (24:1–27), before a later governor Festus (25:1–12), and finally before Festus's guests Agrippa and Bernice (25:13–26:32). The adventurous voyage to Rome involves a shipwreck on the island of Malta (27:1–28:10), but eventually Paul is brought to Rome, where he is placed under house arrest but allowed to preach freely for two years (28:11–31).

Historical Background

The book of Acts apparently was written by the same person who authored the Gospel of Luke (see Acts 1:1), the person whom the church has traditionally identified as Luke, a physician who is mentioned as being present with Paul in Colossians 4:14; Philemon 24; 2 Timothy 4:11. Is this tradition correct? The book itself is anonymous, but the author of Acts does seem to indicate that he personally accompanied Paul on some of his travels: in some portions of Acts (called the "We Passages"), he employs the pronoun "we" as though he himself is among Paul's company on those occasions (see 16:10–17; 20:5–15; 21:1–8; 27:1–28:16).

Still, the tradition of Acts being authored by one of Paul's companions has been challenged by scholars who think that the book is inaccurate in what it reports about Paul or who think that it misrepresents Paul theologically. Most scholars, however, do not think that the suggested anomalies pose a substantial challenge to the tradition that this book was written by someone who was only an occasional companion of Paul. We don't know much about Luke the physician, but there is no reason to think that he was a disciple of Paul, someone who knew everything about Paul, or someone whose theological commitments mirrored those of Paul in every respect. He may have been a Christian leader in his own right whose connections with Paul were limited to a few trips that they had taken together (and, possibly, one or two visits with the apostle while he was in prison).

Of course, most scholars will grant that this book (and Luke's Gospel) could have been written by some other occasional companion of Paul, perhaps someone whose name we wouldn't even recognize. Even so, "Luke" seems like a

⊙ EXPLORE 10.5
The "We Passages" in the Book of Acts

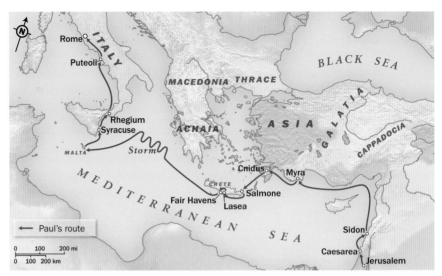

Map 10.4. Paul's journey to Rome.

persecution: a program or campaign to exterminate, drive away, or subjugate people based on their membership in a religious, ethnic, or social group.

good guess for which of Paul's many companions the author might have been, and, in any case, this is the name that everyone has decided to use.

Most scholars think that the book of Acts was written shortly after the Gospel of Luke and that it can be dated along with that Gospel to the mid-80s. One problem with such a dating is that Acts ends its account of church history in the early 60s: it does not tell us about the persecutions that came under Nero; it does not even mention the martyrdoms of its principal characters (James the brother of Jesus, Peter, Paul); and it does not say anything about the destruction of Jerusalem or describe what happened to the community of Christians there. Thus some scholars have thought that the book must have been written in the early 60s, before these things occurred. But then Luke's Gospel might have to be dated earlier than most people think, and if Luke used the Gospel of Mark as a source for his Gospel, then that book would have to be dated earlier still. None of this is impossible, and a few scholars do subscribe to a system of "early dating" that places the whole Mark-Luke-Acts complex within the lifetime of Paul (i.e., before 62–67, depending on which date for Paul's death one adopts). A majority of scholars, however, think that the perspective of these books fits better with the next generation of Christianity and that Luke is writing

Box 10.1

Possible Sources for the Book of Acts

- an Aramaic document describing the life of the early church in Jerusalem, used for chapters 1–12
- a collection of traditions from the church at Antioch, used for stories concerning Stephen and Barnabas (6:1–8:4; 11:19–30; 12:25–25:35)
- a travel diary, used for portions of the book recounting the journeys of Paul

Fig. 10.1. Pentecost. Acts 2:1–4 relates how the Holy Spirit descended on 120 believers, among them Jesus's disciples, "together with certain women, including Mary the mother of Jesus, as well as his brothers" (see 1:13–15). Divided tongues, as of fire, rested on each of them, and they began to speak in other languages through the power of the Spirit. (Bridgeman Images)

Acts some twenty years later than the events with which his book concludes; he ends the book where he does because he has fulfilled his goal of tracing the progress of the gospel from Jerusalem to Rome (see 1:8).

We must also note that a significant minority of scholars dates the book of Acts decades later than has been typical, perhaps around 120–30, or even as late as 150. These scholars think that they can detect dependence on writings by the Roman historian Josephus; they sometimes also argue that Acts is a response to second-century developments in Christian history, such as the challenges posed by a leader named "Marcion" (see "Development of the Canon" in chap. 3). This view has gained a hearing among scholars but has not carried the day; most still think that Acts must have been written before 90 because the author betrays no knowledge of Paul's letters (indeed, he never even says that Paul wrote letters). But, of course, that point has also been disputed: late-daters claim that Luke knew all of Paul's letters and specifically wrote Acts to provide a background that would temper some of Paul's more radical ideas and provide an orthodox context within which his letters could be interpreted.

We may also ask what Luke's purpose was in writing this book. A number of suggestions have been offered: (1) he wanted to offer an irenic portrayal of

Christian origins that would help to unify a church that was becoming increasingly diverse; (2) he wanted to demonstrate the political innocence of Christians in a way that would forestall further persecution from the Roman government (see 18:13–15; 23:29; 25:8, 18–19, 25; 26:31–32; cf. Luke 23:4, 14–15, 20, 22); (3) he wanted to convince pagans to adopt the new faith and/or challenge them to adopt the values and commitment to justice that this faith promoted; (4) he wanted to explain how Christianity had become a largely gentile religion in a way that would allow Christians to be viewed as the legitimate heirs of God's promises to Israel; and (5) he wanted to present a long-term theology of mission for a church that had come to recognize that the second coming of Christ might lie in the distant future. All of these points may be subsumed under a basic and obvious goal: Luke wrote the book of Acts because he wanted to tell the story of the church's early years in a way that would both inspire and challenge his readers.

What Sort of Book Is This?

The book of Acts is unique in the New Testament, but usually it is regarded as an example of "general history" (or "historiography"), a type of literature common in the Greco-Roman world. Many such histories were written to record the origins and progress of particular ethnic or national groups.

Books of this genre were not expected to be unbiased; in fact, such books openly celebrated the accomplishments of the subject group and promoted its ideals. A modern analogy might be drawn to a history of a particular institution or organization composed by that entity's public relations department: basic honesty is called for—the author is not supposed to invent things that have no basis in fact—but no one would fault such an author for glossing over potentially embarrassing incidents, dwelling on successes and victories, and putting the best possible construction on matters that might otherwise be construed as defeats or downfalls. Likewise, the story of the church in Acts is one of success, victory, growth, and triumph. We hear next to nothing about missions that fail, people who aren't healed, or prayers that aren't answered. Controversies are quickly resolved, and everything always seems to work out for the best. Luke is able to see a positive side to just about anything: the persecution that drives Christians out of their homeland spreads the gospel to new lands (8:1–4); the Jews' rejection of Jesus as the Messiah provides incentive for evangelizing gentiles (13:44–49).

All of this is to say that Luke is regarded as a competent historian when evaluated by the standards of his day. Still, modern scholars have to decide whether his book passes muster as a work of history when judged by our standards: Can modern historians view Acts as a reliable and accurate guide

Box 10.2

Potential Discrepancies between the Book of Acts and Paul's Letters

Many scholars claim that Luke's portrayal of Paul's life and theology does not agree with what Paul says in his letters. The following points are frequently raised:

- Paul says that he did not go to Jerusalem to consult with the apostles after his encounter with Christ (Gal. 1:15–18); Acts says that he did (Acts 9:10–30).
- Paul says that church leaders in Jerusalem endorsed his law-free mission to the gentiles and "added nothing" to it (Gal. 2:6–10); Acts says that they assigned Paul the task of promulgating a list of legal requirements for gentiles to keep (Acts 15:22–29).
- Paul claims that he lives like a gentile in order to win gentiles (1 Cor. 9:21); Acts presents Paul as utterly loyal to the law, never acting contrary to it (Acts 25:8; 28:17).
- Paul denounces reliance on Greek wisdom (1 Cor. 1:18–31); Acts presents him as friendly to philosophers and as drawing on Greek wisdom traditions to make common ground with them (Acts 17:22–31).
- Paul says that idol-worshipers are without excuse because knowledge of God has always been evident (Rom. 1:18–23); Acts presents Paul as saying that God has overlooked the worship of idols as a consequence of ignorance (Acts 17:29–30).

Of course, the significance of all of these points is disputed, and some scholars offer explanations for the apparent discrepancies.

---

to understanding the early years of Christianity? In a positive vein, modern historians do note numerous matters pertaining to geography, politics, and law on which Acts accurately reports what can be confirmed by other sources. The major point of contention, somewhat ironically, is raised by Christian theologians who maintain that Luke's portrayal of Paul's life and theology does not accord with what we ascertain regarding this pivotal figure from his own letters. For example, Paul's account of his various meetings with other apostles is hard to reconcile with what is reported in Acts (cf. Gal. 1:15–2:10 with Acts 9:10–30; 15:1–35). Also, comments that Paul makes about philosophers and idolaters in his letters reflect a somewhat different attitude than is exhibited in the comments that he makes in Acts (cf. 1 Cor. 1:18–31; Rom. 1:18–23 with Acts 17:22–31). Furthermore, scholars notice what Acts leaves out: Luke mentions or records numerous sermons and speeches of Paul in the book of Acts, but in all of those addresses Paul never once mentions justification by grace through faith, or the righteousness of God, or the redemptive value of suffering, or the union of believers in Christ, or any number of other matters that often dominate his letters. Indeed, the Paul of Acts never mentions the cross, nor does he ever indicate that Jesus's death has anything to do with salvation—a curious lapse in a book that focuses on the missionary work of a man who claims in one of his letters to have preached nothing but "Christ crucified" to that particular congregation (see 1 Cor. 1:22–24; 2:1–2).

Christ crucified: the main focus of Paul's preaching according to 1 Corinthians 1:22–24; 2:1–2; the phrase seems to be shorthand for what theologians call a "theology of the cross" (*theologia crucis*).

Of course, all of these matters might be explained one way or another. For one thing, Acts presents a "third-party perspective" on Paul, which we would expect to differ from Paul's own self-presentation. For another, most of the speeches in Acts are directed to non-Christians, whereas Paul's letters are written to believers—Paul might be expected to say things differently to one audience than to another. Still, scholars generally hold that the differences between the "Paul of Acts" and the "Paul of the Letters" reflect Luke's particular interests and agenda. Luke presents the Paul whom he wants us to know, highlighting those aspects of Paul that he most appreciates and leaving out matters that are not primary concerns for him. Thus Paul and other characters in Acts inevitably become spokespersons for Luke's own theological agenda: if honest in his depiction of what Paul and others said, he certainly is selective. Like any other ancient historian, Luke relates what he thinks is worthy of recollection, and, in Paul's case, his choices may differ from what Paul himself would have considered to be the highlights of his life and teaching.

The book of Acts does differ from ancient histories in one respect: it is a sequel or second volume to another work, the Gospel of Luke. When viewed as one work, Luke-Acts resembles certain Hellenistic biographies more closely than it does the works of "general history" with which Acts alone is usually compared. Diogenes Laertius (third century) wrote a number of biographies of eminent philosophers that report, first, on the life and teaching of the teacher (compare Luke's Gospel, with its account of Jesus) and, second, on the continuing mission and influence of that teacher's followers (compare Acts, with its account of the church).

> EXPLORE 10.8
Speeches in the Book of Acts

How to Write Speeches

In the book of Acts, Luke presents speeches by prominent church leaders. How did he know what the people said? About five hundred years before Luke wrote Acts, the Greek historian Thucydides wrote *History of the Peloponnesian War*. In the preface to that work he describes how he handled the difficult matter of reporting speeches:

> With reference to the speeches in this history, some were delivered before the war began, others while it was going on; some I heard myself, others I got from various quarters; it was in all cases difficult to carry them word for word in one's memory, so my habit has been to make the speakers say what was in my opinion demanded of them by the various occasions, of course adhering as closely as possible to the general sense of what they really said. (1.22.1)*

Many scholars believe that Luke followed a similar convention in reporting speeches in Acts. This would explain why there are no significant differences in vocabulary and style of the various speakers (or between the vocabulary and style of the speeches and the rest of Acts): Luke has relayed in his own words the "general sense" of what the speakers said.

*Thucydides, *The Peloponnesian War*, trans. Richard Crawley (London, J. M. Dent; New York, Dutton, 1910).

Box 10.4

Parallels between Luke's Gospel and the Book of Acts

Luke's Gospel	Acts
Preface to Theophilus (1:1–4)	Preface to Theophilus (1:1–5)
Spirit descends on Jesus as he prays (3:21–22)	Spirit comes to apostles as they pray (2:1–13)
Sermon declares prophecy fulfilled (4:16–27)	Sermon declares prophecy fulfilled (2:14–40)
Jesus heals a lame man (5:17–26)	Peter heals a lame man (3:1–10)
Religious leaders attack Jesus (5:29–6:11)	Religious leaders attack apostles (4:1–8:3)
Centurion invites Jesus to his house (7:1–10)	Centurion invites Peter to his house (10:1–23)
Jesus raises widow's son from death (7:11–17)	Peter raises widow from death (9:36–43)
Missionary journey to gentiles (10:1–12)	Missionary journeys to gentiles (13:1–19:20)
Jesus travels to Jerusalem (9:51–19:28)	Paul travels to Jerusalem (19:21–21:17)
Jesus is received favorably (19:37)	Paul is received favorably (21:17–20)
Jesus is devoted to the temple (19:45–48)	Paul is devoted to the temple (21:26)
Sadducees oppose Jesus, but scribes support him (20:27–39)	Sadducees oppose Paul, but Pharisees support him (23:6–9)
Jesus breaks bread and gives thanks (22:19)	Paul breaks bread and gives thanks (27:35)
Jesus is seized by an angry mob (22:54)	Paul is seized by an angry mob (21:30)
Jesus is slapped by high priest's aides (22:63–64)	Paul is slapped at high priest's command (23:2)
Jesus is tried four times and declared innocent three times (22:66–23:13)	Paul is tried four times and declared innocent three times (23:1–26:32)
Jesus is rejected by the Jews (23:18)	Paul is rejected by the Jews (21:36)
Jesus is regarded favorably by a centurion (23:47)	Paul is regarded favorably by a centurion (27:43)
Final confirmation that Scriptures have been fulfilled (24:45–47)	Final confirmation that Scriptures have been fulfilled (28:23–28)

The relationship between Luke and Acts is especially close. Many scholars have noted that Luke appears to have outlined the two narratives in ways that are remarkably similar. In the Gospel, the ministry of Jesus begins when the Holy Spirit comes upon him; then Jesus preaches a sermon claiming that a text from Isaiah explains why this has happened. In Acts, the mission of the church begins when the Holy Spirit descends upon the believers at Pentecost; then Peter preaches a sermon claiming that a text from Joel explains why this has happened. For a list of these and other parallels between the two books, see box 10.4. What do these parallels mean, and why would Luke arrange the two books this way? Perhaps it was simply an artistic way of telling the stories. Possibly he hoped that the similarities would serve a mnemonic function, helping people to remember key moments in the histories of Jesus and the church. Theologically, he may have wanted to present the church's life and mission as a reduplication of the life and work of Jesus. At the very least, scholars agree, Luke wanted the two books to be read together.

Pentecost: a Jewish harvest festival at which, according to Acts 2, the Holy Spirit came upon 120 early followers of Jesus, empowering them for mission and causing them to speak in tongues.

Major Themes in Acts

God Is in Control of History

The book of Acts emphasizes that God is sovereign over history: God determines what will happen, as well as when, where, and how it will happen. In both the Gospel of Luke and the book of Acts, God brings to pass events predicted in Scripture (Luke 1:20; 4:21; 21:24; 22:16; 24:44; Acts 1:16; 3:18; 13:27; 14:26). Times and seasons are set by God (Acts 1:7; 17:26), and God determines the fate, purpose, or destiny of people's lives (Acts 2:23; 10:42; 13:47–48; 17:31; 22:10). One of Luke's favorite words is the simple Greek term *dei*, which means "it is necessary"; he uses this word repeatedly to indicate that things must happen because God has willed them to happen. It was necessary for Jesus to die and rise from the dead (Acts 17:3; cf. Luke 9:22; 13:33; 17:25; 24:7, 26); it was also necessary for Judas to be replaced (1:22), for Paul to visit Rome (19:21; 23:11; 25:10; 27:24), for the gospel to be proclaimed to Jews first (13:46), and for Christians to experience tribulations (14:22) and to suffer for Christ's name (9:16). Curiously, Luke does not explain why such things are necessary, beyond the simple affirmation that they have been foretold in Scripture and are in accord with the will of God. Nevertheless, Luke apparently expects his readers to be comforted by the assurance that God is in charge and that everything is going according to plan.

Divine Guidance

Luke maintains that the God who is in charge of history offers divine guidance to those willing to submit to the predetermined plan. In the book of Acts, God directs people through the Holy Spirit (8:29, 39; 10:19; 11:12; 13:2–4; 16:6–7; 19:21; 20:22–23, 28), through prophets (11:28; 21:11), through angels (5:19; 8:26; 10:3, 7, 22; 11:13; 12:7–10, 23; 27:23–24), and through visions (10:3, 11–19; 11:5–10; 16:9–10). Such guidance is evidence that the God who predestined what has happened up to now (2:23; 4:28) is still in control and sometimes will reveal to people what must happen next.

predestination: the concept or doctrine that some or all events are predetermined by God, or that the destinies of individuals and nations may likewise be predetermined.

God Makes Promises and Keeps Them

As we have noted, Luke emphasizes that many of the events that he reports constitute the fulfillment of predictions and promises that God made in the Scriptures. The suffering of the Messiah (a difficult concept for Jews to grasp) should not have been unexpected, since it was foretold in Scripture (4:11, 24–28; 8:32–35; 13:27, 29; 17:3, 11). In addition, Luke finds scriptural promises for the resurrection of Jesus (2:25–28, 34–36; 3:18; cf. Luke 18:31–33; 20:17; 22:37, 69; 24:25, 27, 44), the outpouring of the Holy Spirit (2:16–21), and the ministry to gentiles (13:47;

⊙ EXPLORE 10.4
Distinctive Characteristics of the Book of Acts

15:15–17; 28:25–28; cf. Luke 24:45–47). The prior prediction of such events certainly proves that the occurrences were part of God's plan, but Luke may also have a broader purpose in mind: by demonstrating that God has been faithful to prior promises, he shows that God can be trusted to keep the promises that have not yet been fulfilled. The fact that Jesus had not returned as soon as many had expected may have prompted Luke to emphasize this theme: God has kept promises in the past and can be counted on to keep promises in the future.

God's Faithfulness to Israel

One specific issue that Luke wants to address in Acts is the question of

Fig. 10.2. A heavenly revelation. The book of Acts tells of Peter experiencing a vision from heaven while he was praying and fell into a trance (10:9–16). (Photo © The Fine Art Society, London, UK / Bridgeman Images)

whether God has been faithful to the covenant people of Israel. The destruction of the temple in Jerusalem and the blunt fact that most Jews did not believe in Jesus as the Messiah must have raised questions in this regard: Has God abandoned the "chosen people"? Luke suggests the opposite: God has fulfilled all of the divine promises to Israel, but many individual Jews abandoned God and opted out of the benefits that the fulfillment of those promises would bring. In his Gospel, Luke maintains that God visited the people of Israel with salvation and peace (1:68, 77–79), but tragically the people did not recognize the time of their visitation or the things that make for peace (19:41–44). Thus, according to Luke's Gospel, many of God's chosen people "rejected God's purpose for themselves" (7:30).

So too in Acts, Peter insists on two things: (1) God has been faithful in sending Jesus first to Israel (3:22, 26), and (2) those who do not listen to the one whom God has sent "will be utterly rooted out of the people" (3:23). The Paul of Acts also echoes these two points: the word of God is spoken first to the Jews, but

Fig. 10.3. The call of Paul. Luke tells the dramatic story of Paul's experience on the road to Damascus three times in the book of Acts (9:1–19; 22:3–16; 26:9–18). This painting by modern Chinese artist He Qi portrays what happened in a manner reminiscent of the call Moses received when he encountered a burning bush (Exod. 3:1–6). (He Qi / www.heqigallery.com)

sometimes they reject it and prove themselves "to be unworthy of eternal life" (13:46; cf. 18:6). Such language has a polemical edge to it, but Luke's main point seems to be that God cannot be blamed for the disasters that befall Israel (including the physical disaster of the destruction of Jerusalem and what Luke considers to be the spiritual disaster of Jews missing out on the salvation brought by the Messiah). Such catastrophes are not due to any lack of divine fealty or initiative but rather are simply a consequence of the same rebelliousness that Moses and the prophets decried throughout the history of Israel (3:22–23; 7:48–53; 28:25–28).

By the same token, however, the book of Acts insists that God's faithfulness has indeed been effective for a core group within Israel, since large groups of Jews do accept the gospel: three thousand in 2:41, five thousand in 4:4, and a great many more (including a "great many of the priests") in 6:7. Eventually, Acts reports that there are "myriads" of zealous believers among the Jews (21:20). For Luke, these Jewish Christians represent the "true remnant of Israel," and he regards them as sufficient in number to constitute the covenant people of God for whom the ancient promises are faithfully fulfilled.

Mission to Gentiles

While insisting that God has been faithful to Israel, the book of Acts clearly is interested also in celebrating and promoting the movement of Christianity into the gentile world. The author wants to make clear that this is no aberration: the salvation of the gentiles was prophesied in Scripture (2:17; 3:25; 13:47; 15:17; cf. Luke 2:32; 3:6), and the apostolic mission to the gentiles was authorized by Jesus (1:8; 9:15; 22:21; 26:17; cf. Luke 24:47); further, it has been conducted in accord with the prompting and guidance of the Holy Spirit (10:44; 11:12, 15; 15:8).

Theologically, Luke thinks that the gentile mission finds justification in the principle that God is not partisan (14:15–17; 17:22–31). If that is true, then we might think that it would have been a good idea regardless of whether Israel accepted the Christian gospel. Certain texts in Acts, however, seem to suggest that the gentile mission was a consequence of Israel's unfaithfulness: the Jews heard the gospel first, but because they did not listen, the gentiles were offered salvation instead (13:46; 18:6; 28:25–28). Theologians call this idea "supersessionism," and it has come to be viewed as a key element in anti-Semitism. Throughout the ages, people who hold to this view have often cited the passages in Acts that seem to support it.

Modern scholars frequently indicate that supporters of supersessionism tend to overlook one significant point: in the book of Acts, all the missionaries who bring the word of salvation to the gentiles—Peter, Stephen, Philip, James, Barnabas, Paul, Silas, Priscilla, Aquila, and the rest—are Jewish believers. Thus in some sense the successful mission to the gentiles in Acts is portrayed not as a replacement of mission to Israel but rather as a continuation of that mission. Those Jews whom Luke regards as most faithful to the messianic covenant (i.e., those who believe in Jesus) are fulfilling their role of being a blessing to the nations (Gen. 22:18) and a light to the gentiles (Isa. 49:6). In an ironic sense, the gentiles are offered salvation not because God's plan for Israel failed but rather because it succeeded: the restoration of Israel is accomplished through the repentance of a faithful remnant, allowing the next phase of God's plan to take effect.

Fig. 10.4. Ephesus. This reconstruction shows the great theater at Ephesus where a riot is said to have broken out as a result of Paul's success at converting gentiles to faith in Christ (Acts 19:23–41). See also fig. 17.2. (Balage Balogh / www.archaeologyillustrated.com)

Naturally, dialogue between Jews and Christians may still have to address the fact that Luke thinks that only Jews who believe in Jesus are part of the restored Israel (some people would call *that* view "supersessionist"). But Luke does not present the gentile mission as some "Plan B" that God adopts after getting angry and writing the Jews off. Rather, Luke presents the gentile mission as an outgrowth of Israel's faithfulness and obedience to God: a righteous remnant of the Jewish people accept their Messiah and act in accord with what he wanted them to do next, bringing salvation to all. Luke is careful to note that the church began as a completely Jewish, messianic movement within Israel and that "Christians" came along only later (11:26). He thinks that this is worth remembering.

Centrality of Jerusalem

The Jewish matrix for Christianity is preserved in Acts by a strong emphasis on the central role of Jerusalem. Luke established the importance of Jerusalem in his Gospel by presenting both Jesus and his disciples as devoted to the city and its temple (2:49; 13:33–35; 19:41–44; 24:52–53) and by structuring his Gospel so that much of the book is oriented toward Jerusalem as Jesus and his followers journey to that city. Now, in Acts, the reverse is true: the book is organized in such a way that everything proceeds out from Jerusalem. Jesus explicitly orders his disciples not to leave the city until they receive "the promise of the Father" (i.e., the Holy Spirit) (1:4), and after that happens, the mission of the church proceeds as he directed (1:8): first in Jerusalem, then in the broader area of Judea, then in Samaria, and finally to the rest of the world. Significantly,

The Centrality of Jerusalem in Luke-Acts

Gospel of Luke

- The story opens in Jerusalem (in the temple) (1:5–8).
- Jesus is brought to Jerusalem as a baby (2:22–38).
- Jesus is in Jerusalem at the age of twelve (2:41–50).
- There is a ten-chapter journey to Jerusalem (9:51–19:40; see especially 9:51, 53; 13:22; 17:11; 18:31; 19:11, 28).
- Jesus weeps over Jerusalem (19:41–44; also 13:33–35).
- Resurrection appearances occur in and around Jerusalem (24:13, 18, 33, 41–43).
- The mission to all nations begins with Jerusalem (24:47).
- Jesus tells disciples to stay in Jerusalem (24:49).
- The story closes in Jerusalem (in the temple) (24:52–53).

See also 5:17; 6:17; 9:31; 10:30; 13:4; 21:20, 24; 23:28.

Book of Acts

- Jesus orders his disciples not to leave Jerusalem (1:4).
- The mission to the ends of the earth begins in Jerusalem (1:8).
- Believers gather for prayer and planning in Jerusalem (1:12–26).
- The Holy Spirit comes to 120 believers in Jerusalem (2:1–4).

- Peter preaches to residents of Jerusalem, and three thousand are saved (2:5–41).
- The Jerusalem church is an ideal community (2:42–47; also 4:32–37).
- There are five chapters on the church in Jerusalem (3:1–8:1; see especially 4:5, 16; 5:16, 28; 6:7).
- The Samaritan mission receives the endorsement of the Jerusalem church (8:14–25).
- Paul's newfound devotion to Christ is recognized by the Jerusalem church (9:27–30).
- Peter reports to Jerusalem concerning the baptism of gentiles (11:1–18).
- The Jerusalem church sends Barnabas to check on the gentile mission in Antioch (11:19–26).
- Antioch Christians fund relief ministry for Jerusalem (11:27–30; also 12:25).
- The council in Jerusalem decides on the controversy over gentile conversions (15:1–29).
- Paul promulgates the decision of the Jerusalem council (16:4).
- Paul reports back to Jerusalem after the second missionary journey (18:22).
- Paul reports back to Jerusalem after the third missionary journey (21:17).
- Paul is arrested and put on trial in Jerusalem (21:27–23:11).

See also 8:27; 9:2, 13, 21; 10:39; 13:13, 27, 31; 19:21; 20:16, 22; 21:4–13; 25:1, 3, 7, 9, 15, 20, 24; 26:4, 10, 20; 28:17.

however, all missionaries—including Philip, Peter, and Paul—report back to Jerusalem, which seems to be "home base" in some spiritual sense even after its geographical importance has dwindled.

Lukan Generosity

The book of Acts continues the theme that we noted in Luke's Gospel of emphasizing God's acceptance of the poor, the marginalized, and any who might be considered outcasts. The early church is marked by a commitment to eliminating poverty (4:34) and by an inclusive vision that seeks to incorporate people from all nations, including such traditional enemies as Samaritans (8:4–25). In a broader sense, Luke is unusually generous in his portrayals of non-Christians; he seems intent on presenting almost all people, not just pitiable social outcasts but also potentially hostile unbelievers, in the best possible light. This applies most noticeably to Roman officials who, even when they are not Christians themselves, often are presented as just and sympathetic in their dealings with the Christian missionaries (18:12–16; 19:35–41; 23:10–35). Similarly, idolaters in Athens are depicted as "extremely religious" people who possess a sincere desire for truth (17:22–23, 32). Even the natives on the island of Malta are portrayed as kind and generous pagans who come to the aid of castaways (28:2, 10). Nonbelieving Jews are treated somewhat more harshly in Acts, but certain Jews who don't accept the Christian message are nevertheless presented as wise and responsible people (e.g., Gamaliel and those who heed his counsel [5:34–39]). In addition, the Jews and their leaders are to be excused for killing Jesus, since they acted in ignorance (3:17; cf. Luke 23:34).

Jesus Absent and Present

The book of Acts begins with an account of the ascension of Jesus, emphasizing his physical absence from the earth. Although he sometimes appears to people on earth in visions (9:3–5), he is now located in heaven, at the right hand of God (3:20–21; 7:55–56). Thus, in some sense, the book of Acts is devoted to describing the circumstances and conditions of living for Christ during the time of his absence (cf. Luke 5:35)—that is, the interim between his ascension and his parousia. The significance of this absence, however, is diminished by the fact that Jesus remains present in certain respects:

- *Through the Holy Spirit.* In former times the Holy Spirit inspired Scripture to be written, predicting numerous events to which Luke makes reference in Acts (1:16; 4:25; 7:51–52; 28:25–26). Now the Holy Spirit empowers people to be witnesses for Jesus in word and deed (1:8; 4:8, 31; 7:55), and the Holy Spirit directs the life and mission of the church (8:29; 10:19; 11:28; 13:2;

ascension: the event in which Jesus Christ left the physical earth and went up into heaven, as reported in Luke 24:50–51 and Acts 1:9.

parousia: the second coming of Christ.

15:28; 16:6; 20:23; 21:4, 11). The Spirit is described in very personal terms in Acts: people can lie to, test, or oppose the Spirit (5:3, 9; 7:51). But the Spirit is also closely connected to Jesus, such that what the Holy Spirit does on earth is to be regarded as the continuing activity of Jesus. In one place the book of Acts actually refers to the Holy Spirit as "the Spirit of Jesus" (16:7).

- *Through the word.* The "word of God" is personified in Acts as an active and powerful force, and readers are expected to regard what the word of God accomplishes on earth as another expression of the continuing activity of Jesus: the word grows, spreads, and increases (6:7; 12:24; 13:49; 19:20); it is sent to people for their salvation (13:26). In Acts, accepting or receiving the word of God is essentially the same thing as accepting Jesus or becoming a Christian (see 8:14; 11:1; cf. Luke 8:11).

- *Through the lives of his followers.* Jesus identifies his continuing presence on earth with the activity of those who believe in him: when the apostles or other followers of Jesus teach, preach, and heal people, the reader is expected to realize that it is Jesus teaching, preaching, and healing people through them (see, e.g., 9:34). Likewise, those who persecute the followers of Jesus are actually persecuting Jesus himself (9:5), for what is done to his followers is done to him.

- *Through the use of his name.* In Acts, people receive salvation (4:12), forgiveness of sins (10:43), and other divine benefits by calling on the name of Jesus (22:16; cf. 2:21) and having faith in the name of Jesus (3:16). The name stands for the person: to praise the name of Jesus is to praise Jesus (19:17); to oppose the name is to oppose Jesus (26:9); to suffer for the name is to suffer for Jesus (5:41; 9:16). The one essential difference is that the name remains present and accessible in a way that the literal person does not.

Luke begins the book of Acts by noting that in his first book (the Gospel of Luke) he wrote about what Jesus said and did "until the day when he was taken up to heaven" (1:2). Thus his second book continues that account by relating what Jesus has said and done since the day he was taken up: it relates what Jesus continues to say and do through the Holy Spirit, through the word of God, through the lives of his followers, and through the appropriate use of his name.

Salvation

As in the Gospel of Luke, the book of Acts emphasizes Jesus's identity as Savior (Acts 5:31; 13:23; cf. Luke 2:11). Salvation is bestowed by Jesus (2:33–40; 5:31; 13:23–39; 15:1–11; 16:30–31) and received through his name (2:21; 3:16; 4:12). In Acts, as in his Gospel, Luke does not seem interested in exploring how

⊙ EXPLORE 10.18
The Name of Jesus in the Book of Acts

Salvation in the Book of Acts

This chart lists the passages in the book of Acts in which the words *sōtēr* ("savior"), *sōtēria* ("salvation"), *sōtērion* ("salvation"), or *sōzein* ("to save") are used.

Text	Who Is to Be Saved?	Of What Does Salvation Consist?	Who or What Brings Salvation?	How Is Salvation Received?
2:21	everyone	escape from apocalypse	the Lord's name	calling
2:40	Jews (2:36)	forgiveness, Holy Spirit	exalted Jesus (2:33)	repentance, baptism (2:38)
2:47	additional numbers of believers	———	the Lord	
4:9	lame man (3:2)	being enabled to walk	name of Jesus (3:16)	faith (3:16)
4:12	people	———	name of Jesus	———
5:31	Israel	repentance, forgiveness	exalted Jesus	———
7:25	Israel	rescue from enemies	Moses	———
11:14	gentiles	Holy Spirit (11:15), repentance (11:18)	God (11:17)	faith (11:17)
13:23, 26	Israel, God-fearers (13:17, 26)	forgiveness, freedom (13:38–39)	risen Jesus (13:32–39)	faith (13:39)
13:47	gentiles	eternal life	———	
14:9	lame man	being enabled to walk	word of Paul	faith
15:1, 11	Jews, gentiles	———	the Lord Jesus	grace
16:30–31	jailer, family	———	the Lord Jesus	faith
27:20, 31	sailors, Paul	survival (27:23, 34, 44)	God (27:23)	obedience
28:28	gentiles	(spiritual) healing	God	listening

Jesus's death atoned for sins; instead, he simply affirms that God has made Jesus to be Lord and Christ (2:36) and authorized him to grant salvation to any whom he chooses to save. The content of this salvation is twofold. Eventually it will consist of "times of refreshing" (3:20) and "eternal life" (13:46) when Jesus returns to restore (3:19–21) and judge (17:30–31) all humanity (10:42). Right now, however, being saved might mean receiving forgiveness of sins (2:38; 5:31; 13:38–39), or the gift of the Holy Spirit (2:38; 11:15), or healing (4:9; 14:9–10), or simply being rescued from some sort of temporal distress (7:25; 27:22–24, 34, 44)—this is not always clear in English Bibles, where the Greek words for "saved" or "salvation" are sometimes translated as other expressions (e.g., 4:9, where *sesōtai*, "has been saved," is translated as "has been healed" in the NRSV). As in his Gospel, Luke's focus in Acts tends to be on accessing the saving power of God in this present world so that people might be liberated from whatever prevents them from experiencing life as God intends. This accent on present aspects of salvation may be influenced by a recognition that Jesus's parousia (second coming) could still be a long way off. The question then becomes, "How do we experience God's salvation and accomplish God's work in the meantime?

Charismatic Manifestations of the Spirit

The book of Acts speaks more about the Holy Spirit than does any other book of the Bible, making more than seventy references to the Spirit. It is somewhat surprising, therefore, that so little attention is paid to the quiet influence of the Spirit on people's lives. We hear almost nothing about the Spirit's role

Fig. 10.5. Paul, Silas, and Timothy. (© Look and Learn / Bridgeman Images)

Box 10.7

Church of Joy

In Acts, Luke emphasizes joy as a primary characteristic of the early church's life and mission:

- Disciples rejoice that they are considered worthy to suffer for Jesus's name (5:41).
- There is "great joy in that city" when the gospel comes to Samaria (8:8).
- The Ethiopian eunuch goes "on his way rejoicing" after being baptized (8:39).
- Barnabas rejoices when he witnesses God's grace in Antioch (11:23).
- The disciples are "filled with joy and with the Holy Spirit" (13:52).
- God blesses even pagan idol-worshipers by filling their hearts with joy (14:15–17).
- The conversion of gentiles brings "great joy to all the believers" (15:3).
- The gentiles rejoice when they hear the decision of the Jerusalem council (15:31).
- A jailer and his family rejoice after they are baptized (16:33–34).

This is a prominent theme in the Gospel of Luke as well (see 1:14, 44, 47, 58; 2:10; 6:23; 10:17, 20, 21; 13:17; 15:3–10, 32; 24:41, 52).

fruit of the Spirit: nine moral characteristics that Paul lists in Galatians 5:22–23: love, joy, peace, patience, kindness, generosity, faithfulness, gentleness, and self-control.

speaking in tongues (glossolalia): the phenomenon by which the Spirit enables a person to speak in known languages that the speaker has never learned (e.g., Acts 2:4–8) or in ecstatic languages unintelligible to any who do not possess the gift of interpretation (e.g., 1 Cor. 14:26–28).

in generating faith or in effecting an inner purification of believers: no one is "washed in the Spirit" (1 Cor. 6:11) or "sealed with the Spirit" (Eph. 4:30), nor is any reference made to the fruit of the Spirit that affects the moral character of individuals (Gal. 5:22–23) or to the unifying effect of the Spirit that binds all believers together into one body (1 Cor. 6:17; 12:13; Eph. 4:4; Phil. 1:27; 1 Pet. 3:8). The emphasis, rather, is on power and on external manifestations.

In Acts, people sometimes are said to be "filled with the Holy Spirit," and this typically occurs in a dramatic fashion that transforms their status with God and/or imbues them with power to become witnesses for Jesus (2:4; 4:31; 8:14–17; 10:44–48; 19:1–7; cf. 1:8; Luke 24:49). No exact pattern or set of qualifications for receiving the Spirit can be discerned: the gift of the Spirit is variously linked to prayer (4:31; 8:15; cf. Luke 11:13), the laying on of hands (8:17–18; 19:6), preaching (10:44), and baptism (2:38; 19:2–6; but see 8:15–16; 10:47). Sometimes those who are filled with the Spirit respond by speaking in tongues (unlearned languages) and prophesying (2:4–11; 10:45–46; 19:6). These phenomena are also mentioned as gifts of the Spirit in Paul's first letter to the Corinthians (see 1 Cor. 12; 14), though it is not clear that what is found there is identical to what we hear about in Acts (see "Spiritual Gifts" in chap. 14). The book of Acts also emphasizes the performance of "signs and wonders," spectacular miracles wrought by those who receive the Spirit's power (2:43; 4:30; 5:12; 6:8; 14:3; 15:12). Such actions place the apostles and other followers of Jesus in line with heroes of God such as Moses (7:36) and Jesus himself (2:22); they serve to authenticate the word of the gospel, proving that their bold proclamation is endorsed by spiritual powers not subject to human limitation—powers that usually are benevolent but that are not to be offended (5:1–11; 13:9–12).

Growth, Triumph, and Victorious Living

The book of Acts records the advance and progress of the church's mission, with emphasis on its successful expansion and on its transforming effect on society. Luke repeatedly stresses that the church is increasing numerically (1:15; 2:41; 4:4; 5:14; 6:7; 9:31; 11:21, 24; 12:24; 14:1; 16:5; 19:20; 28:30–31), as well as expanding geographically (1:8) and growing in terms of ethnic diversity (8:4–25; 10:44–48; 11:19–21). Christians become known in the empire as people who are "turning the world upside down" (17:6).

This motif of victorious transformation is also evident in the way that Acts depicts the lives of those who follow Jesus. In the Gospel of Luke, the apostles argued with one another over rank (9:46; 22:24); now in Acts, fellowship, good-will, and mutual dependence on God seem to be the rule (2:44–45; 4:32–35). Previously, Peter was a coward who denied that he even knew Jesus (Luke 22:54–62); now he boldly witnesses to Jesus in the face of persecution and death (Acts 4:8–12, 19–20; 5:29–32).

What has happened? In Luke's Gospel, Jesus indicated that when the disciples were "fully qualified," they would be like him, their teacher (6:40). In Acts, this appears to have been fulfilled: they are now like Jesus in word and deed. When disciples of Jesus speak in the book of Acts (but not in the Gospel of Luke, or in any other Gospel), the reader is almost always expected to regard what they say as wise, godly, and true. Likewise, the disciples and other church leaders in the book of Acts regularly do the kinds of extraordinary things associated with Jesus in the Gospel: they cast out demons (8:7; 16:18; 19:12), heal the sick (3:6–7; 5:16; 8:7; 9:34; 14:8–10; 19:12; 28:8–9), raise the dead (9:40), know the secret thoughts of others (5:3), predict the future (20:29–30), discern the hidden but true meaning of Scripture (1:15–22; 2:16–22, 25–32; 4:11, 24–26; 8:32–35; 13:32–37), interact freely with angels (5:19–20; 8:26; 12:7–10; 27:23–24), and even pass authoritative judgment on the wicked (5:1–10; 8:20–23; 13:9–11).

Just as people in Luke's Gospel could be healed by merely touching the hem of Jesus's garment (8:43–48), now in the book of Acts people can be healed by handkerchiefs or aprons that have touched Paul's skin (19:12). Peter becomes so renowned for his healing powers that people bring the sick out to the street on cots, hoping that just his shadow may fall on them and make them well (5:15–16). Even the persecution of believers becomes an occasion for victory: when disciples are savagely beaten, they rejoice that they have been counted worthy of suffering for Jesus (5:41); when they are imprisoned, they sing hymns (16:25). Nothing, it seems, can dampen their spirits or deter their confidence. And Luke shows again and again that this confidence is well placed, as God sends angels (5:19; 12:7), earthquakes (16:26), or whatever else is necessary to rescue them and allow the mission to go forward.

⊙ EXPLORE 10.23
Speaking in Tongues
in Acts and
1 Corinthians

⊙ EXPLORE 10.9
Miracles in Acts

⊙ EXPLORE 10.19
The Ministry of Peter
in the Book of Acts

Of course, there are also martyrs (7:54–8:1; 12:2), but their noble deaths do not impede the church's overall progress and mission. Indeed, when Stephen (the first martyr) dies, he does so in a way that clearly echoes the passion of Jesus himself:

Jesus: "Father, forgive them; for they do not know what they are doing" (Luke 23:34).
Stephen: "Lord, do not hold this sin against them" (Acts 7:60).
Jesus: "Father, into your hands I commend my spirit" (Luke 23:46).
Stephen: "Lord Jesus, receive my spirit" (Acts 7:59).

Thus, in death—as in life—the followers of Jesus in the book of Acts demonstrate that they have become like their master.

Conclusion

Is it realistic? That is the question that many people ask when they finish reading the book of Acts, and it is the question that many theologians and scholars have put to the book as well. Is the life of faith really like this? Most people do not experience miracles quite as spectacularly or as regularly as do the believers in this book. Most Christians do not experience the Spirit's power with the same intensity or receive the Spirit's guidance with the same clarity as is depicted here (e.g., divinely revealed street addresses [9:11; 10:5–6]). Some Christian readers find the comparison between Acts and our modern world to be depressing: Why can't the church be like this today? Where did we go wrong? But Luke would not want his book to depress anyone; the story is meant to be inspiring. He wants us to believe that the possibility of God's will being done is greater than we might imagine.

Luke is not telling the whole story. He says nothing, for instance, about the schisms in the church of Corinth or the false teachers in Galatia—problems that we know about from Paul's letters. If indeed Luke is writing in the mid-80s, he knows that the church has seen all sorts of scandals and schisms and that it has endured some very hard times. Not all the martyrs died as Stephen did; some went out screaming in agony, perhaps hurling curses at their enemies or directing unanswered prayers to God for deliverance. Others never got that far because they took a disgraceful but seemingly easier way out: denying the faith and/or betraying others. Luke knows all of this, of course, and he assumes that his readers know these things too. But such is not a part of the story that he wants to tell.

Instead he tells us something else. Sometimes miracles do happen. Sometimes prayers are answered, heroes are rescued, pagans are kind, martyrs die bravely, and people of faith turn the world upside down. Remember those times. Indeed, the basic message of Acts may be just that: Remember! Sometimes, God's will *is* done!

FOR FURTHER READING: **Acts**

Borgman, Paul. *The Way according to Luke: Hearing the Whole Story of Luke-Acts*. Grand Rapids: Eerdmans, 2006.

Gaventa, Beverly Roberts. *The Acts of the Apostles*. Abingdon New Testament Commentaries. Nashville: Abingdon, 2003.

González, Justo. *The Story Luke Tells: Luke's Unique Witness to the Gospel*. Grand Rapids: Eerdmans, 2015.

Jervell, Jacob. *The Theology of the Acts of the Apostles*. New Testament Theology. Cambridge: Cambridge University Press, 1996.

Kwon, Yon Gyong, ed. *A Commentary on Acts*. International Study Guides. Minneapolis: Fortress, 2015.

Parsons, Mikeal C. *Acts*. Paideia. Grand Rapids: Baker Academic, 2008.

Powell, Mark Allan. *What Are They Saying about Acts?* Mahwah, NJ: Paulist Press, 1991.

Shillington, V. George. *An Introduction to the Study of Luke-Acts*. Harrisburg, PA: Trinity Press International, 2007.

Talbert, Charles H. *Reading Acts: A Literary and Theological Commentary*. Rev. ed. Reading the New Testament. Macon, GA: Smyth & Helwys, 2005.

Wright, N. T. *Acts for Everyone*. 2 vols. 2nd ed. Louisville: Westminster John Knox, 2008.

⊙ Go to www .IntroducingNT.com for summaries, videos, and other study tools.

11

New Testament Letters

Sending a letter has become a remarkably simple process. Many people today send and receive numerous email messages every day, plus there are text messages that they transmit through their cell phones or other portable electronic wonders. It takes special time and attention to correspond the old-fashioned way, typing or writing a letter by hand, placing it in an envelope, addressing it, affixing postage, and then waiting several days for it to reach its destination.

Imagine what life was like in the Roman world. Not only were there no computers or internet but there also weren't any typewriters, or ballpoint pens, or paper, or mailboxes. It was a much more cumbersome process to produce a letter and see that it reached its intended recipients. Nevertheless, twenty-one of the twenty-seven books that make up our New Testament appear to be letters (in one sense or another), and we find at least nine other letters embedded in two of the other books (see Acts 15:23–29; 23:26–30; Rev. 2–3).

Arrangement of the Letters in the New Testament

The twenty-one letters are organized as follows: (1) letters by Paul to churches; (2) letters by Paul to individuals; (3) the anonymous letter to the Hebrews; (4) letters by James, Peter, John, and Jude. The letters in each of the first two categories (from Paul) are presented in order of length (longest to shortest), which may strike modern readers as somewhat arbitrary. Scholars would prefer to study these letters in chronological order (first to last), but since the letters are not dated, their chronological order is difficult to determine (see box 12.5). Some scholars (who might have too much time on their hands) have determined that the Greek text of Ephesians is actually a few words longer than the Greek text of Galatians, such that the order of those two letters should properly be reversed (as it is in at least one ancient list of New Testament writings that we possess).

The letters in the final category are arranged in the order that the authors' names are listed in Galatians 2:9 (James, Peter, John), with the short letter from Jude (who is not mentioned in Gal. 2:9) bringing up the rear. Curiously, most ancient Greek manuscripts of the New Testament present the letters of James, Peter, John, and Jude immediately after the book of Acts and before the letters of Paul. The order of the letters in our current Bibles follows that of later Latin manuscripts, though no one knows exactly when the change was made, or why.

Churches sometimes employ other labels to refer to particular groups of writings:

- The *Pastoral Letters* or *Pastoral Epistles* are the three letters addressed to colleagues of Paul entrusted with pastoral leadership of churches: 1 Timothy, 2 Timothy, Titus.
- The *Prison Letters (Epistles)* or *Captivity Letters (Epistles)* are the five letters that indicate they were written by Paul from prison: Ephesians, Philippians, Colossians, 2 Timothy, and Philemon.
- The *General Letters (Epistles)* or *Catholic Letters (Epistles)* are seven writings thought to be addressed to the church at large: James, 1 Peter, 2 Peter, 1 John, 2 John, 3 John, Jude.

The accuracy of these designations is questioned, but the labels are traditional and continue to be used.

How Letters Were Written

People would write on almost anything. We have found copies of letters written on clay tablets and on shards of pottery (called "ostraca") and on pieces of wood or animal skin. The most common writing material, however, was papyrus, a reedy plant that grew abundantly in the delta of the Nile. The core or pith of this plant can be cut into very thin strips; a writing surface was made by laying a horizontal row of strips on top of a vertical row and pressing the two layers together to form a sheet that was laid in the sun to dry. A typical sheet of papyrus measured about 9 ½ by 11 ½ inches (close to the dimensions of a modern sheet of letter-size paper) and could hold approximately two hundred words.

Pens for writing typically were made from sharpened reeds or sticks (pens from feather quills appear to have come along later). Ink was made from a combination of chimney soot and tree gum. It was kept in a dried cake but would liquefy slightly when touched with the moistened tip of the reed pen. Erasure was difficult—the ink had to be washed away—and so mistakes usually were blotched out in a rather unattractive manner. If the document was an important one, a mistake meant starting over.

⊙ EXPLORE 11.3
What's the Difference between a "Letter" and an "Epistle"?

Fig. 11.1. Papyrus. The writing material called "papyrus" was made from the fiber of these plants. (Todd Bolen / BiblePlaces.com)

Many people in the Roman Empire were illiterate. Those who could read probably could also write, but the task of composing a letter was sufficiently cumbersome that it was often delegated to persons trained in the craft—a secretary or scribe known as an "amanuensis." Thus Paul's letter to the Romans identifies Tertius as the one who is actually putting the words on paper (Rom. 16:22). At other places, Paul specifies that he is writing the concluding words in his own hand (1 Cor. 16:21; Gal. 6:11; Col. 4:18; 2 Thess. 3:17; cf. Philem. 19). This suggests that the rest of the letter has been written down by someone else.

What exactly did an amanuensis do? Sometimes the amanuensis took dictation, recording what the sender wanted to say by writing the words quickly with a stylus on a wax tablet (a form of shorthand was even in use for this purpose) and later copying the words more painstakingly in ink on papyrus. At other times, however, the amanuensis may have been given more freedom with regard to composition: the author of the letter explained in broad terms what was to be conveyed and allowed the amanuensis to devise the actual wording. Indeed, a skilled amanuensis would be trained in rhetoric, and the author of a letter might expect such a person to say "what I want to say better than I could ever say it myself." We have no way of knowing how much latitude the New Testament authors granted to the persons responsible for putting their words (or thoughts) into writing. Scholars note discernible stylistic differences in letters for which Paul is the designated author, but they also note that Paul sometimes chose words very carefully. The general assumption is that he would not have signed his name to anything that did not accurately express what he wanted to say.

Many of Paul's letters also list coauthors (or cosenders). For example, 1 Corinthians is from Paul and Sosthenes (1 Cor. 1:1), and 2 Corinthians is from Paul and Timothy (2 Cor. 1:1). We don't know what these people contributed to the actual content of the letters. Scholars usually assume that Paul bore the dominant responsibility, especially since he frequently claims that what he writes carries the weight of apostolic authority. A few scholars, however, have suggested that certain letters may come from "a Pauline school" that allowed coauthors to play a prominent role in crafting the letters. After all, Paul does trust other people to represent him in person when he sends them as his emissaries to deal with problems in various churches (see, e.g., 1 Cor. 4:17). Is it possible that he allowed them some leeway in shaping the content of his letters as well?

In any case, once a letter was written it had to be conveyed to the appropriate destination, and the Roman Empire had no postal service for individual citizens. Delivery of the letter was entrusted to someone who took responsibility not only for transporting it but also for seeing that it was read as intended (e.g., aloud to the entire congregation, as directed in 1 Thess. 5:27). In addition, the bearer of the letter may have been expected to explain various points in the letter that were unclear, respond to objections raised, and return to the sender with a report of how the letter was received. Paul seems to have entrusted Phoebe (a deacon in the church at Corinth) with the important job of delivering his letter to the Romans (Rom. 16:1–2). Titus (2 Cor. 8:16–18), Tychicus (Eph. 6:21; Col. 4:7–8), and Epaphroditus (Phil. 2:25–28) are similarly identified as bearers of other letters.

Typical Structure or Format for a Letter

In our modern world, both personal and professional letters follow typical patterns. It is common to open a letter with "Dear" followed by the name of the recipient, and to close a letter with "Sincerely" followed by the signature of the sender. Of course, there are variations in these patterns, some of which might reveal something about the character of the letter or the personality of the author. We would make inferences regarding the person who never used "Sincerely" but instead signed letters with "Yours in Christ" or "Keep on truckin'." The ancient world likewise had stereotypical patterns for letters. Archaeologists have unearthed thousands of letters from the New Testament period, and these can be examined to determine in what ways the New Testament letters are unique and in what ways they are typical.

---

apostolic authority: in Paul's letters, the claim that the author has the power and responsibility to instruct, exhort, and discipline persons who were brought to faith through his ministry.

deacon: a type of leader in the early church, the exact duties of which are unclear; the word means "one who serves" (*diakonos*).

Salutation

A letter typically opened with a salutation identifying the author and the recipient, followed by "greetings" (cf. Acts 15:23; James 1:1). The New Testament letters exhibit a strong tendency to substitute "grace" for "greetings." This may have been a bit of a pun, since the words look and sound similar in Greek ("greetings," *chaire*; "grace," *charis*). In any case, this use of "grace" instead of "greetings" seems to have been a peculiarity of Christian writing, and it may have served as an indicator to those in the know that what followed was written by a Christian. It is often thought that Paul originated the practice, since his letters are the earliest ones that we have exhibiting this feature. In a sense, the Christians were copying Jews in developing a distinctive salutation, for most Jewish letters from this period substitute "peace" (Hebrew, *shalom*, or the Greek equivalent, *eirēnē*) for "greetings." Indeed, the most common pattern for Christian writers seems to have been to use both "grace" and "peace," combining the traditional Jewish greeting with a transformed version of the Roman greeting. All the New Testament letters attributed to Paul open with some form of this "grace and peace" greeting, as do 1 Peter, 2 Peter, and 2 John.

> **grace:** the free and unmerited favor of God, as manifested in the salvation of sinners and the bestowal of undeserved blessings.

The New Testament letters also display a tendency for authors to expand the salutation with phrases that describe the sender and/or recipient in particular ways. Paul does not usually identify himself simply as "Paul" (1 Thess. 1:1); more often he is "Paul, an apostle of Christ Jesus by the will of God" (2 Cor. 1:1) or something even more elaborate than that (see Gal. 1:1). Likewise, he writes not just to "the church of God in Corinth" but also, more precisely, to "those who are sanctified in Christ Jesus, called to be saints" (1 Cor. 1:2). Paul and other writers in the New Testament seem so eager to preach the gospel that they jump the gate and work their preaching and theology into the very salutation of the letter itself.

> **saints:** people who are holy; some New Testament writers use the word as a virtual synonym for "Christians."

Hebrews and 1 John do not have opening salutations, which suggests to some that they are more like sermons or homilies than actual letters.

Thanksgiving

Letters in the Greco-Roman world often included a brief word of thanksgiving to the gods for good health, deliverance from calamity, or some other beneficence. Paul retains this feature in his letters, though it undergoes considerable development. The thanksgiving is offered to God in specifically Christian terms (e.g., "through Jesus Christ" [Rom. 1:8]), and the reason for the thanksgiving is also distinctive: Paul typically gives thanks for the faithfulness of the congregation to which he is writing and for the things God has done, is doing, and will continue to do for that congregation. There are instances in which some of the matters mentioned in the thanksgiving hint at topics that will be

Box 11.1

Types of Letters and Their Different Functions

Handbooks from the Greco-Roman world include instructions for writing different types of letters to accomplish different goals.

- *friendship*—shares memories and provides news between friends who are separated
- *prayer*—expresses the content of prayers said on the recipient's behalf
- *congratulations*—applauds the recipient for some accomplishment or honor
- *consolation*—expresses sympathy for those who have experienced suffering or loss
- *recommendation*—testifies to someone's abilities and/or character
- *inquiry*—requests information from the recipient
- *response*—responds to a letter of inquiry by supplying requested information
- *report*—informs the recipient of news that the sender deems relevant
- *supplication*—asks the recipient for some sort of favor
- *thanks*—expresses gratitude for a favor that has been promised or performed
- *excuse*—explains why the sender will not be able to do something that the recipient requested
- *didactic*—teaches the recipient about some topic
- *advice*—recommends one course of action over another
- *encouragement*—urges the recipient to be bold in pursuing some course of action
- *exhortation*—urges the recipient to avoid immorality and exhibit virtuous behavior
- *accusation*—claims that the recipient has an improper attitude or behavior
- *threat*—informs the recipient of consequences for behavior (especially if it continues)
- *defense*—seeks to defuse charges made against the sender by recipient or someone else
- *praise*—commends the recipient for exemplary behavior

The New Testament letters are longer than the letters that exemplify one or another of these types (but see Acts 15:23–29; 23:26–30). They usually are thought to represent "mixed types" for which there was no specific category in the handbooks. Still, all the New Testament letters incorporate aspects of these various letter types into their contents as they seek to accomplish the various functions that those types were intended to serve.

Indebted to David deSilva, *An Introduction to the New Testament* (Downers Grove, IL: InterVarsity, 2004), 533–34.

taken up in more detail later (e.g., 1 Cor. 1:4–7 is expanded on in 12:1–30). Thus, as with the salutations, Paul's prayers of thanksgiving tend to segue into preaching, and it is not always easy to tell when Paul is addressing God or the congregation on God's behalf. Some scholars think that the "thanksgiving" portion of 1 Thessalonians extends all the way to 3:13, taking up more than half the letter. Paul's letter to the Galatians, however, contains no thanksgiving, most likely because he was angry and disappointed with that church (nothing to be thankful about!—or so he felt at the moment).

Main Body

The main body of a letter had few fixed features, its structure being determined by what was appropriate for the particular content. Letters served a variety of purposes in the ancient world, and considerable variety is evident among letters in the New Testament as well. Galatians is a defensive letter written to rebuke its recipients, whereas Philippians is a letter of friendship written to thank a community for its faithfulness and support.

The New Testament letters also employ a variety of rhetorical styles, and many of them incorporate various subgenres of literature into their contents:

- hymns (Phil. 2:6–11; Col. 1:15–20)
- liturgical formulas (1 Cor. 6:11; Gal. 3:28; 4:6; Eph. 5:14)
- church traditions (1 Cor. 11:23–25; 15:1–7)
- creeds (1 Tim. 3:16; 2 Tim. 2:11–13)
- virtue/vice lists (Gal. 5:19–23; Eph. 4:31–32; Titus 1:7–10)
- household codes (Eph. 5:21–6:9; Col. 3:18–4:1; 1 Pet. 3:1–7)
- autobiography (Gal. 1:10–2:21; 1 Thess. 2:1–3:13)
- travelogues (Rom. 15:14–33)
- topical discussions (Rom. 13:1–7; 1 Cor. 7:1–40)
- chiasms (Rom. 5:12–21; Gal. 5:13–6:2)
- prayers (Phil. 1:9–11; 1 Thess. 3:11–13)

creeds: confessional statements summarizing key articles of faith.

chiasm: an organizing device for speaking or writing that arranges items in an "a, b, b, a" pattern—for example, "light and darkness, darkness and light."

Closing

The two most common conventions in the closing of Greco-Roman letters were a wish for good health (cf. 3 John 2) and an expression of "farewell" (cf. Acts 15:29). Curiously, the New Testament letters do not adhere to these conventions with any sort of regularity. Paul's letters tend to close somewhat haphazardly with mention of travel plans (e.g., 1 Cor. 16:5–9), greetings to specific individuals (e.g., Rom. 16:3–16), miscellaneous exhortations (1 Thess. 5:12–28), a recap of some significant point (e.g., Rom. 16:17–20; Gal. 6:15–16), a personal signature (e.g., Gal. 6:11), and finally a doxology (Rom. 16:25–27), benediction (Philem. 25), or closing prayer (2 Cor. 13:13). The non-Pauline letters tend to close more quickly, sometimes with brief greetings (Heb. 13:24; 1 Pet. 5:14; 2 John 13; 3 John 13) and a benediction or doxology (Heb. 13:20–21, 25; 1 Pet. 5:14; 2 Pet. 3:18; Jude 24–25).

doxology: a hymn or group of words that expresses praise to God.

benediction: a blessing, often offered at the conclusion of a document or worship service.

Finally, we may note one overall feature that is quite distinctive about the New Testament letters: their length. The typical length of personal letters from this period is around 90 words, but the shortest of the New Testament letters, 2 John and 3 John, contain 245 words and 219 words, respectively. The letters attributed to Paul average about 1,300 words in length, an incredible figure given that the learned letters of the Roman orator Cicero average no more than 295 words. Paul's letter to the Romans is 7,101 words long, quite a production given the time and trouble involved in producing such written correspondence in the ancient world.

Pseudepigraphy and the Question of Authorship

Few issues are more difficult for the beginning New Testament student (or even for the seasoned scholar) than that of pseudepigraphy, which involves the question of whether the New Testament letters were actually written by the people whose names they bear. The word *pseudepigraphy* literally means "false ascription" (not, as is often thought, "false writings"). Most scholars who use the term do not mean to imply that the works that they call "pseudepigraphic" are illegitimate or invalid. According to the dominant theory, the authors for some of these letters attributed their writings to famous church leaders who had not actually written them, but they did this in ways that were never intended to be misleading or dishonest. Still, not everyone is convinced that this theory holds up (at least not in every instance that it is applied), and some Christians remain opposed to allegations of pseudepigraphy in principle. The issue is complicated by confessional concerns and by different notions of what it means to view these writings as Scripture.

confessional concerns: matters of faith pertinent to particular religious groups or denominations.

Which Books?

Let's identify exactly which writings we are talking about. Of the twenty-one letters in the New Testament, four are anonymous and may be set aside for discussion elsewhere: Hebrews, 1 John, 2 John, and 3 John. There are church traditions about the authorship of these writings, which we will explore in the appropriate chapters of this book, but the letters themselves do not name their authors.

That leaves us with seventeen letters, and—good news!—seven of these are almost universally regarded as authentic letters of Paul: Romans, 1 Corinthians, 2 Corinthians, Galatians, Philippians, 1 Thessalonians, and Philemon. Together, these seven form a group typically referred to as the "undisputed letters of Paul." They receive special attention in New Testament scholarship and are often used together as the definitive resources for understanding Pauline theology.

deutero-Pauline letters: letters ascribed to Paul that are believed to have been written after Paul's death by persons who felt qualified to address the church in Paul's name.

But there are ten more letters in the New Testament, and these are the ones that are sometimes thought to be pseudepigraphic by some interpreters. Six of these letters state they are written by Paul, but that assertion is questioned: Ephesians, Colossians, 2 Thessalonians, 1 Timothy, 2 Timothy, and Titus. These six letters are best referred to as the "disputed letters of Paul." In the history of scholarship, however, they have often been called the "deutero-Pauline letters," meaning "secondary letters of Paul." That label has come to be regarded as unfair by some and as confusing by many. It may be unfair because it assumes that the letters are pseudepigraphic when, in fact, that is disputable. It can be confusing because people use the term with different meanings. Many interpreters who regard the six letters as pseudepigraphic call them "deutero-Pauline" because they are regarded as "secondary" in a chronological sense: they were written later than the undisputed letters of Paul. For other interpreters, however, the label "deutero-Pauline" seems to imply a value judgment: the "secondary letters" are less important or authoritative than Paul's "undisputed letters." Still others adopt a mediating position: the deutero-Pauline letters are less important for the specific task of "understanding how Paul thought," but they are not less important in any other sense (e.g., for receiving God's word of Scripture to the church).

Fig. 11.2. Reading a letter. This Roman fresco from the first century CE shows a young woman reading a letter that probably looks a lot like one of the letters now contained in our New Testament. (Bridgeman Images)

In any case, there are ten letters in the New Testament that are sometimes thought to be pseudepigraphic. The other four (in addition to the six disputed Pauline letters) are James (said to be written by James the brother of Jesus), 1 Peter and 2 Peter (said to be written by the apostle Peter, one of Jesus's twelve disciples), and Jude (said to be written by Jude the brother of James and thus also a brother of Jesus).

What Levels of Authenticity?

Now we should consider exactly what scholars mean when they say that one of these ten letters is either "authentic" or "pseudepigraphic." The chart provided in box 11.2 offers seven possible constructions, or levels, for how the names of prominent church leaders (Paul, James, Peter, or Jude) might become attached to such letters.

With regard to the ten suspect letters, scholars who argue for authenticity usually do not try to make a case for either literal authorship (level one) or dictation (level two). They usually grant that there are enough anomalies in these letters to rule out those possibilities. Rather, scholars who want to claim that one of these letters is authentic usually argue for some kind of "delegated authorship" (level three). For example, a scholar who claims that Ephesians or Colossians

⊙ EXPLORE 11.6
Pseudepigraphy as an Affront to Religious Faith

is an authentic letter of Paul might explain some of the apparent anomalies in those letters by saying that Paul granted disciples latitude in the crafting of the letters. Still, they would argue, Paul proposed the main thrust of the letters and approved their content, so it is fair to say that the letters were "authored" by Paul.

By the same token, scholars who argue that certain letters are pseudepigraphic usually do not jump all the way to level seven and claim that the letters are forgeries. More often they allege pseudepigraphy in terms of the in-between levels (four, five, six). For example, a few scholars have suggested that 2 Timothy might be an example of "posthumous authorship" (level four): the letter is pseudepigraphic only because Paul died before he could complete it, and one of his followers had to put into words what he had intended to say.

Many scholars who argue that letters in the New Testament are pseudepigraphic envision a scenario of "apprentice authorship" (level five), according to which disciples of a deceased church leader continue to write letters in his name to enable his tradition to continue after death. This appears to have been an established convention in some quarters of the ancient world. Disciples of the Greek philosopher Pythagoras continued to attribute all of their own writings to their master long after he was dead because they had learned so much from him that they thought he should receive credit for their insights. Thus many scholars think that some of the New Testament letters attributed to Paul were actually written by his (modest) disciples after his death. They weren't trying to fool anyone into thinking that a new letter from the deceased apostle had turned up; they were simply honoring their master by writing in his name so that his influence could continue to flourish.

Some scholars go a step further and attribute some of the New Testament letters to what might be termed "honorable pseudepigraphy" (level six). In such an instance, people who were not literally disciples of Paul—people who had never actually known him—might have considered themselves to be his spiritual disciples in an extended sense of the term, and so they may also have written letters in his name. Although such a practice may seem disingenuous to us, we know for certain that Christians did do this in the early church and that they did not see themselves as doing anything dishonest or disreputable. A bishop in the second century actually wrote a "Third Letter from Paul to the Corinthians," supplementing the teaching of 1 Corinthians and 2 Corinthians with what he was sure Paul would want to say about new crises that had arisen (e.g., gnosticism). Apparently he did not try to pass this work off as an authentic Pauline composition (the letter deals with matters of its current day, so who would have believed such a ruse?). Perhaps he was simply doing in the second century what Martin Luther King Jr. would do in the twentieth: the civil rights leader wrote a famous "Letter of St. Paul to the American Churches," expressing the apostle's views on racial prejudice and segregation. In any case,

Box 11.2

Authorship and Pseudepigraphy: Levels of Authenticity

1. *Literal authorship.* A church leader writes a letter in his own hand.

2. *Dictation.* A church leader dictates a letter almost word for word to an amanuensis.

3. *Delegated authorship.* A church leader describes the basic content of an intended letter to a disciple or to an amanuensis, who then writes the letter for the leader to approve and sign.

4. *Posthumous authorship.* A church leader dies, and his disciples finish a letter that he had intended to write, sending it posthumously in his name.

5. *Apprentice authorship.* A church leader dies, and disciples who had been authorized to speak for him while he was alive continue to do so by writing letters in his name years or decades after his death.

6. *Honorable pseudepigraphy.* A church leader dies, and admirers seek to honor him by writing letters in his name as a tribute to his influence and in a sincere belief that they are responsible bearers of his tradition.

7. *Forgery.* A church leader obtains sufficient prominence that, either before or after his death, people seek to exploit his legacy by forging letters in his name, presenting him as a supporter of their own ideas.

many scholars claim that it is not hard to imagine that, in the same vein, a well-meaning first-century admirer of Paul could have composed a second letter to the Thessalonians in Paul's name, or that other devout and sincere Christians could have composed letters in the names of Peter or James or Jude.

Nevertheless, we do know that outright forgeries sometimes were produced. People presented their own work under the name of a prominent church leader so that their ideas might obtain wider acceptance than they would have received otherwise. We see in 2 Thessalonians an explicit warning about forged letters that might be circulating under Paul's name (2 Thess. 2:2). The Muratorian Fragment, a document from the latter half of the second century, also refers to pseudepigraphic writings that are deemed illegitimate: "There is current also an epistle to the Laodiceans and another one to the Alexandrians, both forged in Paul's name to further the heresy of Marcion, and several others which cannot be received into the catholic church—for it is not fitting that gall be mixed with honey" (63–70).

Muratorian Fragment: a document from the latter half of the second century that lists which New Testament writings were considered to be Scripture at that time.

What Did the Early Church Think of Pseudepigraphy?

We noted that disciples of the Greek philosopher Pythagoras continued to publish works in his name long after he was dead. A later Greek writer, Porphyry, knew full well that this was the case but accepted those disciples' writings as genuine works of Pythagoras nonetheless. But did the Christian church have a similar attitude toward writings by Christians produced in the names of influential and prominent apostles? The bishop responsible for producing 3 Corinthians in the second century actually came under discipline when he confessed to being the author of that document. Whatever his intentions, the existence of the letter had confused people, and, as a result, the letter was condemned as spurious, and the bishop was required to resign in disgrace. This seems to indicate that the early church was not cavalier about such matters and evaluated pseudepigraphy differently than did the followers of Pythagoras. The church actually liked the content of 3 Corinthians and would have found it useful in combating gnosticism. The church rejected the letter for one reason only: it presented itself as a letter from Paul, though it was not a letter from Paul. Likewise, according to the late second-century theologian Tertullian, an Asian church elder who confessed to writing an apocryphal book called *Acts of Paul and Thecla* was deposed, even though he claimed to have done so out of great love for the apostle. The work itself remained popular in some circles for centuries (see fig. 12.1), but it was never recognized in any official sense as having the authority of Scripture. Thus many scholars maintain that no letter actually known to be pseudepigraphic would ever have been admitted to the New Testament canon.

Other scholars, however, suggest that the church developed its hard line against pseudepigraphy only because the practice was being abused. The problem of forgeries—documents promoting ideas that their putative authors would never have endorsed—led to a rejection of any sort of pseudepigraphy, including varieties that the church might previously have found acceptable. So some scholars maintain that the first-century church did not necessarily have a problem with people whose thought was in line with that of Paul writing works in Paul's name. This was an established convention in the world at the time, and books written in Paul's name under such conditions (especially ones written in the first two or three decades after his death) could have been viewed as part of the legitimate Pauline tradition and included as such in the New Testament canon. But this era of "acceptable pseudepigraphy" was fairly short and did not continue into the second century. This theory is attractive and seems reasonable to many scholars, but there is no certain evidence to support it: we have no record of anyone in the early church ever recognizing that a writing was pseudepigraphic (in any sense of the word) and still regarding it as authoritative.

How Are Decisions about Pseudepigraphy Made?

Discussion as to whether certain writings of the New Testament are pseudepigraphic or authentic tends to focus on six issues:

1. *Intrinsic probability.* Those who favor authenticity sometimes claim that letters encouraging ethical responsibility and moral virtue are not likely to have been produced by unscrupulous frauds. They insist that some of the New Testament letters thought to be pseudepigraphic cannot be explained as products of well-meaning Christians who did not think that they were doing anything dishonest. For example, the author of 2 Thessalonians goes

out of his way to ensure the readers that the letter actually is being written by Paul (3:17; cf. 2:2). If 2 Thessalonians is by Paul, fine; if not, if this letter is deemed to be pseudepigraphic, then it has to be viewed as a product of deliberate deceit. The question becomes, "Does it seem likely that the author of this letter would have been a person given to such tactics?"

2. *Reliability of church tradition.* Proponents of authenticity often argue that authorities in the early church are far more likely to have known the truth about these matters than we are today; we should not second-guess their decisions unless we have very good reasons for doing so. Hence the "conservative" position: tradition is innocent until proven guilty; the burden of proof is on those who want to establish pseudepigraphy. Many scholars, however, claim that church tradition is known to be in error about a great many matters (including authorship of the Gospels). Further, those who preserved these traditions often were uncritical, passing on what they wanted to believe was true without possessing the means or the inclination to evaluate the tradition scientifically. Hence the "liberal" position: tradition is suspect unless proven viable; the burden of proof is on those who want to claim authenticity.

3. *Language and style.* Scholars who suspect that a given letter is pseudepigraphic often indicate that it is written in a language and style the author would not have used. Do the letters ascribed to Peter really seem like the work of a Galilean fisherman? Or, with regard to the letters of Paul, literary analysts compare the language and style of possibly pseudepigraphic letters with the language and style of the undisputed letters (the ones we are sure that Paul wrote). The result? Some claim that the person who wrote Romans could not possibly have written Ephesians (or some of the other letters that bear Paul's name). Proponents of authenticity usually claim that linguistic and stylistic differences merely indicate that an author allowed an amanuensis or cowriter to take responsibility for some of the actual wording.

4. *Theological inconsistencies.* Some scholars claim that a letter must be pseudepigraphic if it conveys ideas with which the putative author would not have agreed. For example, Ephesians presents Paul as saying the Christian church is "built upon the foundation of the apostles" (Eph. 2:20), a point that some scholars think conflicts sharply with Paul's actual opinion that apostles are nothing special in the eyes of God (Gal. 2:6) and that Jesus Christ alone is the foundation for the church (1 Cor. 3:11). Proponents of authenticity typically minimize such discrepancies (e.g., they might claim that Eph. 2:20 does say that Jesus Christ is the "cornerstone," so the distinction is more one of imagery than substance). They also question the validity of assuming too much consistency for Paul, who admits that he was able to become "all things to all people" (1 Cor. 9:22) and so (on some matters) may have expressed his ideas in different ways to fit particular contexts.

⊙ EXPLORE 11.5
Pseudepigraphy and the Problem of Personal Reference

5. *Historical anachronism*. Some scholars argue that a letter must be pseudepigraphic if it reflects historical ideas or circumstances associated with a time later than the period when the putative author lived. For example, letters that reflect a fairly well-developed hierarchical form of church government are often said to reflect a period of the church a generation after the time of the first apostles. Proponents of authenticity tend to regard this as a circular argument: writings that depict a developed church structure are deemed pseudepigraphic because there is no evidence that such structure existed during the apostolic period; however, the claim that there is no early evidence for developed church structure is sustained by ascribing all writings that depict that type of structure to a later period.

6. *Biographical discrepancies*. Some scholars argue that certain letters ascribed to Paul might be pseudepigraphic because the presumed circumstances of their composition do not fit with what is known about Paul's biography from other letters or from the book of Acts. This comes up primarily in discussions of 1 Timothy and Titus, which presume missionary activity by Paul not reported elsewhere. Proponents of authenticity claim that there could be many gaps in our record of Paul's life; specifically, they sometimes claim that Paul may have had a "second career" as a missionary after the events reported in Acts (see "Final Years" in chap. 12).

second-career theory: in Pauline studies, the notion that the apostle was released from captivity in Rome and went on to do things not reported in the New Testament before being recaptured and executed later than has traditionally been thought.

Finally, we should note that proponents of authenticity often pursue a "divide and conquer" approach to defending letters against allegations of pseudepigraphy: they consider each potential problem one by one. By contrast, those who argue in favor of pseudepigraphy usually do so on the basis of cumulative evidence. They agree that explanations for individual considerations can be offered but maintain that pseudepigraphy provides one simple explanation for multiple anomalies that otherwise need to be accounted for in different and (they think) desperate ways.

Why Does This Matter?

The question of whether the New Testament letters were actually written by the persons whose names they bear becomes significant when we seek to define the historical contexts that the letters intended to address. The issue of authorship is inevitably linked to date of composition. If 1 Peter really was written by the apostle Peter, it may be addressing concerns in the Roman Empire around the time of Nero (just prior to Peter's martyrdom). If the letter is pseudepigraphic, it may be dealing with issues that arose decades later. Thus decisions about authorship and pseudepigraphy do end up affecting how particular passages in New Testament letters are interpreted. Such decisions become even more important for church historians and biblical theologians who want to read the New Testament letters as a chronological witness to developments in early Christianity. Pauline scholars, in particular, like to develop biographical accounts of Paul's life and thought, and such reconstructions depend on judgments regarding which letters were actually written by Paul and which might have been written by his followers or admirers after his death.

Conclusion

Letters were written for many purposes in the ancient world. One function, however, seems to have transcended all the rest: whatever else a letter did, it conveyed the personal presence of the one who sent it. Paul makes clear that his first choice was always to communicate with people in person (Rom. 1:9–15); letters were necessary because he could not always be where he wanted to be.

Letters were considered an effective substitute for the actual presence of the apostles or church leaders whose names they bore. A letter could convey the affection of Paul for his readers; it could also convey his authority over them, expressed sometimes in words of judgment or condemnation. Letters bridged the gap of physical space and brought the greetings, prayers, teaching, and benediction of prominent Christian leaders to those who hungered for the word of truth and hope of the gospel.

It is not so different for us, as readers of these letters today. The only essential difference is that the gap has grown larger: it is now temporal and cultural as well as spatial. Nevertheless, the New Testament letters can convey the power and the presence of ancient authors to modern readers. Those authors did not know about us. They never imagined that we would be reading their letters. Still, the letters themselves were designed to close gaps and make the authors present. And that still happens: when people read the New Testament today and hear Paul, James, Peter, or Jude speaking directly to them, the letters are working according to plan.

FOR FURTHER READING: **New Testament Letters**

Klauck, Hans-Josef. *Ancient Letters and the New Testament: A Guide to Context and Exegesis*. Waco: Baylor University Press, 2006.

Marshall, I. Howard, Stephen Travis, and Ian Paul. *Exploring the New Testament: A Guide to the Letters and Revelation*. Downers Grove, IL: InterVarsity, 2011.

Richards, E. Randolph. *Paul and First-Century Letter-Writing: Secretaries, Composition, and Collection*. Downers Grove, IL: InterVarsity, 2004.

Roetzel, Calvin J. *The Letters of Paul: Conversations in Context*. 6th ed. Louisville: Westminster John Knox, 2015.

Stirewalt, M. Luther, Jr. *Paul, the Letter Writer*. Grand Rapids: Eerdmans, 2003.

⊙ Go to www .IntroducingNT.com for summaries, videos, and other study tools.

ὍΑΓΙΟΣ ΠΑΥΛΟ**ϛ**

12

Paul

Religion professors sometimes like to stump their students with a trick question: Who was the founder of Christianity? The students, of course, say, "Jesus," and the professors respond, "No. It was Paul."

The point is that Jesus was a Jewish peasant who said and did some remarkable things in Galilee, but by the end of his career there was nothing on earth even remotely resembling a world religion. It was Paul who took the message of Jesus—and about Jesus—to the world. By the end of Paul's career the people who believed in Jesus were organized into churches, communities of faith that had confessions and liturgies and bishops and deacons. And these churches were scattered throughout the Roman Empire. Almost anywhere one went there were Christians—adherents of a new religion. "Paul did this," the religion professors will say. "Not Jesus."

This idea that Paul was the true founder of Christianity is an exaggeration. For one thing, it ignores the fact that there were many other apostles and missionaries involved in the spread of the Christian faith and the development of its various institutions. Beyond that, Paul clearly regarded himself as little more than an ambassador or emissary for Jesus, carrying out the directives of his Lord (cf. 2 Cor. 5:18–20). He makes no claim to be innovative in his doctrine or ideas; rather, he passes on what he has received (1 Cor. 15:3–9), and he considered his teaching to be consistent with what Jesus himself thought and did.

Still, Paul is a figure of monumental significance. Almost half the books of the New Testament are said to be written by him (thirteen out of twenty-seven), and more than half the book of Acts is devoted to recounting his exploits. He was largely (though not exclusively) responsible for expanding the Christian movement numerically and geographically and also for extending that movement along ethnic lines through the inclusion of gentiles.

doctrine: a belief or set of recognized beliefs held and taught by a church.

gentiles: people who are not Jewish.

A Remarkable Man

Whatever else we say about Paul, he does not appear to have been typical—he was not a "typical Jew" or a "typical Christian" or a "typical citizen of the Greco-Roman world." Paul was both controversial and persuasive. As is often noted, one reason Paul wrote so many letters is that people argued with him, and yet one reason we still have those letters is that his views usually prevailed.

He remains a towering figure of intellectual brilliance, regarded by secular and religious historians alike as one of the greatest moral teachers of history and as the most influential Christian theologian who has ever lived. Jonathan Edwards called Paul "the most fruitful and thrifty of the apostolic branches to shoot forth from the trunk of the risen Christ, so that the bigger part of the future tree came from this branch."

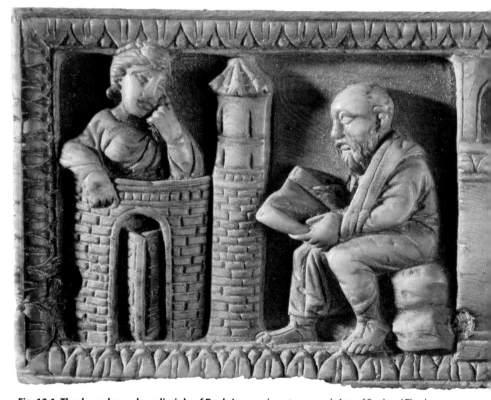

Fig. 12.1. Thecla—a legendary disciple of Paul. A second-century novel, *Acts of Paul and Thecla*, relates legendary tales of an otherwise unknown disciple of Paul who embraces his teaching on sexual abstinence and celibacy (cf. 1 Cor. 7:25–35). A woman named "Thecla" hears Paul's teaching and breaks her engagement to a wealthy man, who then seeks to have her executed. Thecla has many adventures that demonstrate how God protects those whom God favors, especially virgins. The picture above is of an eleventh-century ivory panel from a church in which the story of Thecla (listening attentively to Paul as he teaches) remained popular. (Erich Lessing / Art Resource, NY)

It is also worth noting that the letters of Paul usually are regarded as the only writings that we have from any Pharisee who belonged to what is called the Second Temple period of Judaism (515 BCE to 70 CE). True, the Roman historian Josephus claims that he was a Pharisee for a brief time (*Life* 2), but Paul was raised a Pharisee and continued to regard himself as a Pharisee throughout his entire life (Phil. 3:5). He remains an important figure for Jewish studies, though his ultimate identification with the Christian movement causes Jewish historians to question how truly representative a Pharisee he could have been (why didn't other Pharisees follow his lead or accept his arguments?).

In any case, there is more to Paul to consider. Although there is much in his letters that is difficult to understand (see 2 Pet. 3:16), there is also much that appeals to those who are not intellectuals or particularly interested in "theology" as such. There are passages of remarkable beauty—1 Corinthians 13 is on a par with Shakespeare—and there are sections so overtly inspiring that a million sermons could be offered to unfold their meaning for people in countless cultures and circumstances. There are also troubling texts in which Paul seems shortsighted or just plain mean: he condemns Jews (1 Thess. 2:14–16), accepts slavery (1 Cor. 7:21–22), and silences women (1 Cor. 14:34–35). Of course, various proposals have been offered to explain those texts, and we will note some of these in the chapters that follow.

In order to appreciate fully how remarkable this man Paul is, we should approach his writings in light of two sobering thoughts. First, we are reading the works of a martyr. Paul suffered gravely for proclaiming the gospel as he did and eventually died for his beliefs; he cared so deeply about what he had to say that he was willing to endure humiliation, tribulation, physical torment, and ultimately death in order to say it. Second, we are reading the works of a convert—in some sense of the term. As we will see, Paul did not abandon one religion (Judaism) to adopt another one (Christianity). But before he became a follower of Jesus, he actually tried to destroy the Christian church, employing violence against those who confessed the very faith for which he himself would later suffer violence. Something happened to transform him from an infamous enemy of that faith into its most prominent promoter and spokesperson. The biblical portrait is of a man willing to kill for his convictions transformed into a man willing to die for them.

The Life of Paul

Paul alludes to various aspects of his life in key portions of his undisputed letters: Philippians 3:4–6 (his upbringing); Galatians 1:13–17 (his calling); Galatians 1:18–2:14 (his trips to Jerusalem); 1 Thessalonians 2:1–12 (his ministry); 2 Corinthians 11:23–29 (his hardships). In addition, the book of Acts relates

Box 12.1

Sources for Studying Paul's Life and Thought

We have four sources for reconstructing Paul's life and thought:

- *seven undisputed letters*, acknowledged to have been written by Paul (Romans, 1 Corinthians, 2 Corinthians, Galatians, Philippians, 1 Thessalonians, Philemon)
- *six disputed letters*, believed by some but not by all to have been written by Paul (Ephesians, Colossians, 2 Thessalonians, 1 Timothy, 2 Timothy, Titus)
- *the book of Acts*, much of which was written about Paul a couple of decades after his death
- *traditions* from church history

The Primary Source

The undisputed letters are the most important of our sources, for in them we have what everyone agrees to be Paul's own statements about his life and thought. Still, since these letters are directed to specific occasions, we read only about topics that needed to be addressed. If the Corinthian church had not experienced problems with

regard to its celebration of the Lord's Supper (which Paul deals with in 1 Cor. 11), we would not know that Paul believed in that ritual or had any opinions about it one way or the other. Are we ignorant of other matters simply because no crises arose prompting Paul to comment on them?

Secondary Sources

The disputed letters can be an additional source for learning about Paul, but they are used sparingly in academic scholarship for the simple reason that whatever claims are made on the basis of what is said in these letters may not be accepted by those scholars who regard the works as pseudepigraphic. A similar caution holds for use of the book of Acts, since many scholars think that Luke's presentation of Paul in that book is colored by his own priorities and concerns. Church traditions regarding Paul are evaluated on an individual basis: some are taken seriously as preserving probable facts, while others are dismissed as conveying unverifiable legends.

numerous narratives of his life (7:58–8:3; 9:1–30; 11:25–30; 12:25–28:31) and presents speeches in which he offers brief summaries of his own biography (see especially 22:1–21; 26:2–23). The approach of academic scholarship is to look first at what Paul says in the letters and then at the material in Acts as a secondary and supplemental source (see box 12.1).

Early Years in Judaism

Whenever Paul reflects on his birth and upbringing, he emphasizes his Jewish identity (see Rom. 11:1; 2 Cor. 11:22; Gal. 1:13–14; Phil. 3:4–6). In his letters he does not tell us when or where he was born, but he does tell us that he was circumcised on the eighth day of his life, as was traditional among devout Jews. He was born and raised as "a member of the people of Israel," as "a descendant of Abraham," and more specifically as "a member of the tribe of Benjamin." He is proud to identify himself as "a Hebrew born of Hebrews" and, indeed, as a Pharisee. He maintains that he observed the Jewish law in

Fig. 12.2. Tarsus. The book of Acts reports that Paul was a native of Tarsus, a Roman city in the province of Cilicia (22:3). This picture shows the main street of that city, a road about twenty-three feet wide and paved with basalt; almost twenty-two hundred years old, the road is still in decent shape. Paul walked this road and conducted business in the shops that lined it on both sides. Growing up in the Hellenistic environment of Tarsus perhaps is what gave Paul the ability to communicate effectively with gentiles. (Todd Bolen / BiblePlaces.com)

a manner that was "blameless" and that he "advanced in Judaism" beyond many of his peers.

The book of Acts provides many more details about Paul's early life than what is related in the letters. First, Acts indicates that Paul's Jewish name was "Saul" (7:58–13:9; 22:7; 26:14). This was the name of Israel's first king, who had also belonged to the tribe of Benjamin and who was remembered as one of that tribe's more illustrious members. "Paul" was the apostle's Latin name. Saul did not come to be called "Paul" at the time of what has often been called his "conversion" or as a result of that event; rather, Saul/Paul seems to have had two names: his given Hebrew name (Saul) and a more Roman-sounding name (Paul) for use in the gentile world (similarly, his companion Silas was also called "Silvanus").

The book of Acts also tells us that Paul was brought up in Jerusalem, where he studied "at the feet of Gamaliel" (22:3), a famous rabbi of the era (see 5:34–39). Still, according to Acts, Paul was actually a native of Tarsus, the capital city of Cilicia (22:3; cf. 9:11; 21:39), and furthermore, he was a Roman citizen (16:37–38; 22:25–29). Some scholars suspect that this information from Acts is idealized, providing Paul with perfect pedigrees for both Jewish and Roman audiences. If he really did have such credentials (a student of Gamaliel, and a

Roman citizen), why doesn't he mention any of this in his letters, particularly in those instances where he lists things of which he could boast if he were so inclined (cf. 2 Cor. 11:16–12:13)? Still, there is nothing in Paul's letters that contradicts this information outright, and those letters do seem to be written by someone who is equally at home in Jewish and gentile environments (1 Cor. 9:19–23).

Persecutor of the Church

Paul tells us in his letters that he persecuted the early Christian church violently and tried to destroy it (1 Cor. 15:9; Gal. 1:13, 23; Phil. 3:6; cf. 1 Tim. 1:13; Acts 22:3–5, 19; 26:9–11). He never says exactly what it was about the new faith that provoked his ire, but he does say that he was driven by zeal for ancestral traditions, which apparently he believed were being challenged.

The book of Acts gives a specific example of Paul's persecution of the church: Paul (called "Saul") was present in Jerusalem for the murder of Stephen, often called "the first Christian martyr," tending to the coats of those who stoned him and approving of the deed (7:58; 8:1; 22:20). Acts further says that Paul ravaged the church, going from house to house and dragging men and women away to prison (8:3). Paul had believers bound and punished (tortured?) in order to force them to deny their faith, and when they would not do so, he voted to have them condemned to death (26:10–11; cf. 22:4, 19). Further, Acts tells us that Paul wanted to expand this persecution to other areas as well (9:1–2, 13–14, 21; 22:5). Again, these accounts in Acts merely amplify what Paul says in his letters; some scholars might consider the amplifications as narrative exaggerations, but there is nothing contradictory to Paul's self-testimony.

A Life-Changing Revelation

Paul says that he received a revelation from God that turned his life around (Gal. 1:15–16). What exactly happened? Paul says that the risen Jesus appeared to him in the same way that he had appeared to many of his followers in the days after his crucifixion (1 Cor. 15:3–8; cf. 9:1). He gives no details regarding what Jesus said or did, but as a result of the experience Paul's life was forever changed, and he would always regard the divine revelation that brought about this change as an act of unmerited grace that God had performed on his behalf (Rom. 1:5; 1 Cor. 15:10).

The book of Acts provides narrative descriptions of this pivotal event in Paul's life. It says that he was on his way to Damascus with warrants to arrest followers of Jesus when the dramatic event occurred. The story of that event is recounted three times in Acts with lively and colorful details not mentioned elsewhere (see 9:1–22; 22:6–21; 26:4–23).

Christians traditionally refer to this episode in Paul's life as his "conversion," but many scholars shy away from that term, since it implies quitting one religion to join another. From our perspective, it may seem like Paul became a Christian after Jesus appeared to him; we might at least say that he became a "Jewish Christian" or a "Christian Jew." But Paul himself does not use such language. He seems to have regarded what others have called his "conversion experience" as the reception of a prophetic call or simply as a moment of enlightenment: God corrected his misguided zeal (cf. Rom. 10:2) and gave him a new purpose in life. He went from being a Jew who did not know the truth about Jesus to being a Jew who did know the truth about Jesus, and he began proclaiming that truth in support of a faith he previously had tried to destroy.

Fig. 12.3. A life-changing revelation. Paul says in his letter to the Galatians that at a time when he was violently persecuting the church, God "was pleased to reveal his Son to me, so that I might proclaim him among the Gentiles" (1:15–16; cf. Acts 9:1–22). The event is commemorated here in a decoration by Fra Angelico in a fifteenth-century missal. (The Bridgeman Art Library International)

Interim Years

Paul indicates in his letters that the first few years following his encounter with Christ were spent in the region of Arabia and in the city of Damascus, in southern Syria (Gal. 1:15–24; cf. 2 Cor. 11:32–33). After three years he went to Jerusalem and stayed with Peter for fifteen days; he also met James the brother of Jesus at that time. Then he went into the regions of Syria and Cilicia and spent more than a decade there. Those years are often viewed as a time of formation for Paul, a period during which he honed his missionary skills and

Paul's "Conversion": A Change of Heart and Mind

Although Paul continued to regard himself as a loyal Jew and Pharisee after his encounter with the risen Christ, he does seem to have changed his thinking about some matters.

- *Jesus.* Paul had considered Jesus to be a false messiah; after his encounter he viewed Jesus as the true Messiah and, indeed, the Son of God (2 Cor. 1:19; Gal. 2:20).
- *The last days.* Paul had believed that God's Messiah would put an end to the old age of evil and initiate a new age of righteousness; after, he decided that this would occur in stages: the new age (ripe with possibility) had begun with the resurrection of Jesus, but the old age (with all its attendant problems) would continue until Jesus returned (Rom. 16:25; 1 Cor. 10:11; Gal. 1:4).
- *The cross.* Paul had considered death by crucifixion to be a shameful sign that one was cursed by God (Gal. 3:13); after, he understood the crucifixion of Jesus as a voluntary sacrifice that reconciled sinners with God (Rom. 5:6–10; Phil. 2:8).
- *The law.* Paul had believed that the law (Jewish Torah) kept people in a right standing with God (Gal. 2:16; 3:12); after, he decided that the law only reveals the extent of people's enslavement to the power of sin—a power that must be broken by Christ (Rom. 3:20b; 7:7–12).
- *Gentiles.* Paul had believed that gentiles were outside the covenant that God had made with Israel; after, he believed that gentiles and Jews were united as the people of God in Christ Jesus (Gal. 3:28).
- *Circumcision.* Paul had believed that circumcision was the rite through which people became part of Israel, an exclusive community of God's chosen people (Phil. 3:3–5); after, he believed that baptism was the rite through which people became part of the church, an inclusive community of Jews and gentiles put right with God through faith (Rom. 6:4).
- *Persecution.* Paul had considered his violent persecution of the church to be an indication of zeal for his religion (Phil. 3:6); after, he viewed Jewish hostility toward the church as sinful opposition that would incur God's wrath (1 Thess. 2:14–16).

developed his theological understanding of the gospel. For one thing, he became persuaded that uncircumcised gentiles could be put right with God through faith in Christ without first becoming Jews. It was this conviction that brought him back to Jerusalem after fourteen years to have "a private meeting" with leaders of the church. He shared the gospel that he was proclaiming among gentiles, and Peter, James, John, and others gave him their support. Sometime after this, however, a controversy erupted in Antioch, focused on whether gentile and Jewish believers could share table fellowship together (see box 16.5). Paul took one view, but Peter, Barnabas (Paul's coworker), and "people from James" took a different view.

The book of Acts also contains some information regarding these interim years of Paul's life: we read of his time in Damascus (9:19b–25), of a visit to Jerusalem (9:26–30), and of time spent in Tarsus and Antioch (9:30; 11:19–30). The information provided in these narratives goes beyond what Paul says in his letters, however, and sometimes seems to be in tension with Paul's own account. For example, in Acts, Paul seems to become well known among the believers in

What Did Paul Look Like?

Church tradition offers no descriptions of the physical appearance of Jesus, but one second-century work does provide a description of Paul (*Acts of Paul and Thecla* 3):

> Paul appeared to observers as "a man small of stature, with a bald head and crooked legs, in a good state of body, with eyebrows meeting and nose somewhat hooked."*

Is this accurate? The description is sufficiently early to be informed by actual memory and, furthermore, does not present a flattering portrait such as might suggest idealization. It also accords with passages from Paul's letters that suggest his outward appearance was unimpressive (2 Cor. 10:10; Gal. 4:13–15). Martin Luther voiced his own (uninformed) opinion on this subject: "I think that Paul was a pathetic, ugly, and scruffy little man—like Philipp." Luther apparently was referring to his friend Philipp Melanchthon.†

*W. Schneemelcher, *New Testament Apocrypha*, trans. R. McL. Wilson (Louisville: Westminster Press, 1964), 2:354.
†See Abraham Malherbe, "A Physical Description of Paul," in *Paul and the Popular Philosophers* (Minneapolis: Fortress, 1989), 165–70.

Jerusalem (9:26–29), which is not something we would have surmised from his letters (see Gal. 1:22). More to the point, Acts reports on an apostolic council in Jerusalem at which the question of gentile inclusion was discussed and a compromise decision reached: no circumcision required, but other restrictions would apply (15:1–35). If the meeting of this council is the same event as the "private meeting" that Paul says he had with church leaders in Galatians 2:1–10, then the two accounts of that meeting have to be regarded as widely diverse and probably irreconcilable. Some scholars think that the accounts refer to two completely different meetings: a private meeting between Paul and a few apostles in Galatians 2:1–10 and a churchwide apostolic council in Acts 15:1–35. If that is the case, we are left to wonder why Paul never mentions a council or a decision that Acts presents as foundational for his subsequent ministry.

However these matters are resolved, most scholars do not think that the account of the apostolic council reported in Acts 15 warrants much attention in a Pauline biography. Even those who defend the account as historically accurate will admit that, while Luke seems to have regarded what transpired there as extremely important, Paul does not appear to have taken it very seriously. There is no evidence in his letters that he ever favored or promulgated the decision that the book of Acts indicates was reached at that council.

Missionary Work in the Mediterranean World

We know from Paul's letters that eventually he left the areas of Syria and Cilicia, in which he had been at home for a considerable period of time, and ventured out into provinces of the Roman Empire north of the Mediterranean Sea. The bulk of this work appears to have occurred in four major areas: Galatia, Asia, Macedonia, and Achaia. As maps 10.1, 10.2, and 10.3 illustrate, these

circumcision: a surgical procedure that removes the foreskin of a penis; in the Jewish tradition, the rite is viewed as a sign of the covenant that God had made with Israel.

Map 12.1. Paul's world in his time.

areas correspond to modern-day Turkey and Greece. Paul also mentions that he proclaimed the gospel in Illyricum (Rom. 15:19), a region far to the north overlapping with what is now Albania, but nothing else is ever said about that particular evangelistic effort (either in Paul's letters or in the book of Acts).

Paul's letters provide a few clues as to how he went about his mission strategy. First, he appears to have targeted urban commercial centers as prime locations for founding churches that could help him take the gospel to the world. Four cities are mentioned repeatedly: Ephesus (in Asia), Philippi and Thessalonica (in Macedonia), and Corinth (in Achaia). All four cities were major cosmopolitan centers, situated on important trade routes around the Aegean Sea. Paul's emphasis on urban ministry affects his writing: scholars often note that whereas Jesus used agrarian images appropriate to rural life in Palestine (farming, fishing, shepherding), Paul uses images more appropriate to urban life: political identification (Phil. 3:20), commerce (Philem. 18), athletic competition (1 Cor. 9:24–27; Phil. 2:16), legal proceedings (Rom. 7:1; Gal. 3:15; 4:1–2), public festivities (1 Thess. 2:19), and even the slave trade (Rom. 7:14; 1 Cor. 7:22).

Second, Paul worked as the leader of a missionary team. Numerous assistants and emissaries are mentioned in his letters, though we are left to imagine what their job descriptions might have been. In some cases, trusted assistants such as Timothy (1 Cor. 4:17; 16:10; Phil. 2:19, 23; 1 Thess. 3:2, 6) and Titus (2 Cor. 7:6–8, 13–15) seem to function as his troubleshooters: he sends them

⊙ EXPLORE 12.0
Paul's Mission Sites

Map 12.2. Paul's world today.

to churches where there are problems, investing them with authority to act on his behalf in negotiating settlements.

Third, Paul indicates in his letters that he often supported himself financially by practicing a trade within the community (1 Cor. 9:14–15; 2 Cor. 11:9; 1 Thess. 2:9). In this way, he took care not to place any financial burden on the fledgling churches, and he avoided giving potential converts any reason to suspect that he was after their money (cf. 2 Cor. 2:17; Titus 1:11). Once a church was established, however, he drew on its resources to support his ministry in other locales (2 Cor. 11:8–9; Phil. 4:15–16).

Fourth, Paul insists that his missionary work is independent of any human (ecclesiastical) authority. He tries to be respectful of other church leaders (1 Cor. 3:4–6) and is even involved in taking up a collection for the church in Jerusalem (Rom. 15:25–26; 1 Cor. 16:1; 2 Cor. 8–9; Gal. 2:10), but he takes orders from no one but Jesus Christ (Gal. 1:1, 11–12). Perhaps for this reason, Paul indicates that his typical goal is to proclaim the gospel in new areas and to found churches in places where other missionaries have not worked—he does not want to "build on someone else's foundation" (Rom. 15:20; cf. 2 Cor. 10:13–16). He then assumes that he has a special relationship with his converts: they are his children in the faith (1 Cor. 4:15; Gal. 4:19), and he has apostolic authority over them (1 Cor. 5:3–5; 2 Cor. 10:8; 13:10). Accordingly, he strongly resents missionaries who, after he has moved on, come to churches that he established and undermine his authority while he is absent from the community (2 Cor. 11:4; Gal. 1:6–9).

apostolic authority: in Paul's letters, the claim that the author has the power and responsibility to instruct, exhort, and discipline persons who were brought to faith through his ministry.

Paul's letters reveal other scattered bits of information that might be useful in reconstructing a biography for this prominent period of his life. We learn, for instance, that he is currently not married and that he regards the single, celibate life as ideal for a Christian who is expecting Jesus to return soon (1 Cor. 7:7, 25–40; cf. 9:5). We also learn that he suffers from some sort of affliction that he calls his "thorn in the flesh" (2 Cor. 12:7–9), but despite many guesses, no one has ever been able to determine what this was (see box 15.3).

Paul's letters also contain several references to trials and tribulations that he endured while engaged in missionary work. He says that he was shamefully mistreated at Philippi (1 Thess. 2:2), that he fought with (metaphorical?) wild beasts in Ephesus (1 Cor. 15:32), and that he suffered such affliction in Asia as to despair of life itself (2 Cor. 1:8–9). And then, in one startling summary passage, he declares:

> Five times I have received from the Jews the forty lashes minus one. Three times I was beaten with rods. Once I received a stoning. Three times I was shipwrecked; for a night and a day I was adrift at sea; on frequent journeys, in danger from rivers, danger from bandits, danger from my own people, danger from Gentiles, danger in the city, danger in the wilderness, danger at sea, danger from false brothers and sisters; in toil and hardship, through many a sleepless night, hungry and thirsty, often without food, cold and naked. And, besides other things, I am under daily pressure because of my anxiety for all the churches. (2 Cor. 11:24–28)

The book of Acts fills out the picture of Paul's missionary work with colorful stories of the adventures that he and his colleagues had as they traveled about the Roman world. Most important to scholars, perhaps, Acts provides an itinerary for Paul's travels. It presents his work in such a way that he has been understood traditionally as embarking on three missionary journeys (see maps 10.1, 10.2, 10.3):

- *First Missionary Journey* (Acts 13:1–14:28)—to the island of Cyprus and to cities in southern Asia Minor, including Pisidian Antioch, Lystra, Derbe, and Iconium, for a total distance of about fourteen hundred miles
- *Second Missionary Journey* (Acts 15:36–18:32)—through Asia Minor to Macedonia (especially Philippi, Thessalonica, and Beroea), and then on to Achaia (especially Athens and Corinth), for a total distance of about twenty-eight hundred miles
- *Third Missionary Journey* (Acts 18:23–21:15)—through Galatia and Phrygia to Ephesus, then on to Macedonia and Achaia, for a total distance of about twenty-seven hundred miles

No such itinerary is discernible from Paul's letters, which make no reference to distinctive trips. Some scholars think that the scheme of three missionary

Fig. 12.4. Paul as martyr and letter writer. One of the most famous paintings of Paul is this one executed in 1612 by the Spanish artist El Greco. Paul is shown holding a sword as a symbol of his martyrdom and a letter inscribed in cursive Greek, "To Titus, ordained first bishop of the church of the Cretans."

journeys is a literary device created by Luke in order to organize the stories that he wanted to tell in Acts. More often, however, the itineraries are regarded as plausible and are employed as a general outline for making sense of this critical phase of Paul's life. In particular, Acts presents Paul as spending at least eighteen months in Corinth on his second journey (18:11; cf. 18:18) and as spending at least twenty-seven months in Ephesus on the third journey (19:8–10; cf. 20:31). These "long tenure" stays in key cities fit well with most reconstructions of Paul's life and ministry.

When it comes to mission strategy, the book of Acts also presents Paul as working a trade to support himself while seeking to evangelize certain communities. Acts tells us further that the particular trade that Paul practiced was some form of tent-making, a vocation that he shared with his friends and coworkers Priscilla and Aquila (18:3). This detail is generally accepted, with understanding that such an occupation would have placed Paul among the more fortunate members of the Roman Empire's impoverished population: he would have been poor, but he may have been a step above those who lived at a mere subsistence level.

More problematic is the claim in Acts that Paul typically went first to Jewish synagogues in each area where he worked and then turned to the gentiles only after the Jews had rejected his message (13:5–7, 13, 44–48; 14:1–7; 17:1–2, 10; 18:5–6; 19:8–9). We would never have gathered from Paul's letters that this was his approach; in the letters, Paul seems to indicate that God called him specifically to proclaim the gospel to gentiles and that this was one thing that set him apart from other missionaries (Rom. 11:13; Gal. 1:16; 2:7; but cf. 1 Cor. 9:20).

Another aspect of Paul's mission work that is especially striking in Acts is the prominence of the miracles that God works through him (on this, see "Growth, Triumph, and Victorious Living," in chap. 10). We do not hear about any of these specific miracles in Paul's letters: he never tells us that he cast spirits out of people (Acts 16:16–18) or that he healed the sick (Acts 14:8–10; 28:8), much less that his very handkerchiefs and aprons came to possess extraordinary divine power (Acts 19:12), or that he could punish opponents with curses that struck them blind (Acts 13:9–11). Paul does indicate in his letters that God worked "signs and wonders" through him, but he does so without getting any more specific about what those signs and wonders entailed (Rom. 15:19; 2 Cor. 12:12; cf. Acts 14:3; 15:12).

Many stories in Acts serve to illustrate the diverse trials and tribulations that Paul refers to in his letters. In Acts, Paul meets with opposition from local Jewish communities (13:45–50; 14:2, 4; 14:19; 17:5, 13; 18:12–13; cf. 1 Thess. 2:14–16), but he is also mocked by pagan philosophers (17:32) and attacked by merchants whose economic interests are threatened by the success of his ministry (16:16–24; 19:23–41). This seems dreadful enough, but when compared with what Paul says in 2 Corinthians 11:24–28 (quoted above), the record that Acts gives of Paul's trials actually seems a bit thin: there is a report in Acts of Paul receiving a stoning (14:19), but he is beaten with rods once (16:22–23) not thrice, and there is no account of him receiving the thirty-nine lashes (a dreadful punishment) that he says were meted out to him on five different occasions. Nor does Acts record any tales of Paul being repeatedly shipwrecked or frequently imprisoned (cf. 2 Cor. 11:23, 25); indeed, apart from one night

subsistence level: a standard of living that enables one to survive, albeit with no surplus and with little margin.

signs and wonders: spectacular acts (miracles) performed by people who access either divine or demonic supernatural power.

in jail at Philippi (16:23–26), the only references to imprisonment or shipwreck found in Acts come from a period of Paul's life after the time when 2 Corinthians would have been written. Scholars are left to conclude that either Luke was restrained in reporting on Paul's sufferings or that he simply did not know about many of these incidents.

Final Years

Paul's undisputed letters tell us nothing certain about what happened after the period of his missionary work in the areas surrounding the Aegean Sea. In one of his later letters he says that he wants to come to Rome and hints that he would like for the church there to assist him with a westward missionary journey all the way to Spain (Rom. 15:22–24). But did that happen?

The book of Acts reports that, after the period of Paul's great missionary work, he was arrested in Jerusalem, imprisoned for two years in Caesarea, and then, after a perilous sea voyage, was imprisoned for another two years in Rome (21:17–28:31). This information is generally accepted as a reliable postscript to what can be known about Paul's life from his letters. Some scholars believe

---

Box 12.4

Chronology of Paul's Life

A number of factors make exact dates difficult to determine. Here we look at the earliest and the latest dates that are typically suggested by Pauline scholars.

	Earliest Date	Latest Date
Call to be an apostle of Christ	32	36
Initial time in Arabia and Damascus	32–35	36–39
First visit to Jerusalem	35	39
Interim years in Cilicia and Syria	35–45	40–45
Private meeting with church leaders	45	46
First missionary journey	46–48	46–49
Apostolic council	48	49
Second missionary journey (includes one and a half years in Corinth)	49–51	50–52
Third missionary journey (includes two and a half years in Ephesus)	52–57	54–58
Arrested in Jerusalem	57	58
Prisoner in Caesarea	57–59	58–60
Voyage to Rome	59–60	60–61
Prisoner in Rome	60–62	61–63
"Second career" (not recognized by most scholars)	62–64	63–67
Death	62	67

that certain of Paul's letters perhaps were written while he was a prisoner in Rome, and if that is the case, those letters might be read as a witness to Paul's thoughts and priorities at this time. Even then, however, we would obtain few biographical details about his life situation.

We have to go outside the New Testament to find specific information concerning what happened to Paul after he was taken to Rome. Church tradition says that he was executed under the emperor Nero (Eusebius, *Ecclesiastical History* 2.22.3) and that he was killed in the same manner as was John the Baptist, by beheading (Tertullian, *Prescription against Heretics* 36). These traditions are generally accepted as reliable. Some church traditions, however, suggest that Paul was released for a time between his two-year imprisonment in Rome and his martyrdom under Nero, and that during that period his missionary work continued beyond what is reported in Acts. This idea first appears in the writings of Clement of Rome, about thirty years after Paul's death. Clement says that Paul "traveled to the extreme west" (*1 Clement* 5:7), which suggests to some that Paul actually did make it to Spain as he had intended (Rom. 15:23–24); a later witness, the Muratorian Fragment (ca. 180), explicitly mentions Spain rather than simply referring to "the extreme west." But this notion that Paul had a "second career" as a missionary between his imprisonment in Rome and his martyrdom has not found universal acceptance among scholars. Those who do accept the tradition think that positing a second career for Paul helps to account for anomalies in some of the Pauline letters that might otherwise cause those letters to be regarded as pseudepigraphic.

Chronology of Paul's Life and Letters

Neither Paul's letters nor the book of Acts provides dates that designate when the events to which they refer took place. Even the information that they do provide is sometimes ambiguous: When Paul says that he went to Jerusalem for a second time "after fourteen years" (Gal. 2:1), does he mean fourteen years after the first visit or fourteen years after his life-changing encounter with Christ? Yet certain points turn out to be surprisingly helpful. Acts 18:12 says that Paul was in Corinth (during his second missionary journey) when Gallio was the proconsul there. Roman records indicate that Gallio served as proconsul of Corinth from the summer of 51 to the summer of 52. Accordingly, most scholars working on a Pauline chronology situate Paul's eighteen-month stay in Corinth in the early 50s and then work forward and backward in an attempt to assign dates for other events in his life (see box 12.4).

The more pressing question for students of the New Testament may be, "When were the various letters written?" This question can be answered with

Muratorian Fragment: a document from the latter half of the second century that lists which New Testament writings were considered to be Scripture at that time.

> EXPLORE 12.8
Developing a Chronology for Paul

varying degrees of confidence for different letters (see box 12.5). Key issues (to be discussed in future chapters) include:

- Was Galatians written to southern Galatia or northern Galatia? This determines whether Galatians was one of Paul's earlier or later letters.
- Were the "prison letters" Philemon and Philippians written when Paul was in Caesarea or in Rome (the only two places of imprisonment mentioned in Acts), or were they perhaps written from somewhere like Ephesus, for which no imprisonment is mentioned in Acts?
- Are the six disputed letters to be regarded as authentic compositions produced during Paul's lifetime or as pseudepigraphic compositions produced after his death?

Box 12.5

Chronology of Paul's Letters

Earliest Suggested Date		Latest Suggested Date
46–48	**First Missionary Journey**	46–49
	Galatians—if addressed to "South Galatia"	
49–51	**Second Missionary Journey**	50–52
	1 Thessalonians	
	2 Thessalonians—if authentic	
52–57	**Third Missionary Journey**	54–58
	Galatians—if addressed to "North Galatia"	
	Philemon—if from Ephesus	
	and Colossians and/or Ephesians—if authentic	
	Philippians—if from Ephesus	
	1 Corinthians	
	2 Corinthians	
	Romans	
57–59	**Prisoner in Caesarea**	58–60
	Philemon—if from Caesarea	
	and Colossians and/or Ephesians—if authentic	
	Philippians—if from Caesarea	
59–60	**Prisoner in Rome**	61–63
	Philemon—if from Rome	
	and Colossians and/or Ephesians—if authentic	
	Philippians—if from Rome	
62–64	**"Second Career"**	63–67
	1 Timothy, 2 Timothy, and/or Titus—if authentic	
62	**Death of Paul**	67
62+	**The Post-Pauline Era**	67+
	2 Thessalonians—if pseudepigraphic	
	Colossians and/or Ephesians—if pseudepigraphic	
	1 Timothy, 2 Timothy, and/or Titus—if pseudepigraphic	

Paul's Theology

The following is a short summary of Paul's key theological ideas, as revealed in his seven undisputed letters.

Paul speaks often of the "gospel" (*euangelion*; literally, "good news") that has been revealed to him by God. In some sense this gospel is a message that can be conveyed through proclamation (Rom. 10:14–17), but it is also more than that. It is a dynamic force that Paul identifies as the "power of God for salvation to everyone who believes" (Rom. 1:16; cf. 1 Cor. 1:18). We will learn more about this gospel as we examine Paul's letters one by one, but we can note here that it is very much a gospel of Jesus Christ (Rom. 1:3–4).

Fig. 12.5. Paul the theologian. By all accounts, Paul was a brilliant thinker and an articulate interpreter of Scripture. No other individual has had a greater influence on Christian thought. (Bridgeman Images)

Paul believes that Jesus Christ has died for our sins (Rom. 4:25; 5:6–8; 1 Cor. 15:3; Gal. 1:4; 1 Thess. 5:10). Moreover, God raised Jesus from the dead (Rom. 4:24–25; 1 Cor. 15:4; Gal. 1:1; 1 Thess. 4:14). Jesus is now at the right hand of God in heaven, where he intercedes for believers (Rom. 8:34), and he will come again (1 Thess. 4:13–18). Those who confess that Jesus is Lord and place their trust in him will be saved (Rom. 10:9). After death they will live forever in a glorious realm that renders the troubles of this present life insignificant by comparison (Rom. 8:18). Furthermore, Paul believes that, in some sense, this wonderful new age of God has already begun. Through Jesus Christ, believers are reconciled with God (Rom. 5:8–11;

Box 12.6

Effects of the Christ Event

One Pauline scholar sees Paul using ten different images for describing what God accomplished in Jesus Christ:

- *Justification*. People stand before God acquitted and righteous (Rom. 3:21–26)
- *Salvation*. People are rescued from evil and wrath (Rom. 5:9; Phil. 3:20)
- *Reconciliation*. People are placed in a right relationship with God and one another (Rom. 5:10–11; 2 Cor. 5:18–19)
- *Expiation*. People have their sins blotted out or wiped away (Rom. 3:25)
- *Redemption*. People are bought out of slavery to sin and death (Rom. 8:18–23; 1 Cor. 7:23)
- *Freedom*. People are set free from sin, law, and self to live as God intended (Rom. 8:2; Gal. 5:1)
- *Sanctification*. People are made holy (1 Cor. 1:2, 30; 6:11)
- *Transformation*. People are being changed into the image of God (Rom. 12:2; 2 Cor. 3:18)
- *New creation*. People are given a new life in a new age (2 Cor. 5:17; Gal. 2:20; 6:15)
- *Glorification*. People share in the glory of God (Rom. 8:18, 21, 30; 1 Thess. 2:12)

See Joseph Fitzmyer, *Paul and His Theology*, 2nd ed. (Englewood Cliffs, NJ: Prentice Hall, 1989), 59–71.

cf. 2 Cor. 5:18–21). They are justified (made right with God) by faith (Rom. 3:24–26; Gal. 2:16). They become children of God (Rom. 8:14–17; Gal. 4:4–7) and receive the Holy Spirit (Rom. 5:5; 8:9; 1 Cor. 3:16; 2 Cor. 1:21–22; 5:5; Gal. 3:2–5; 4:6). Their lives are transformed in a way that can only be described as "a new creation" (2 Cor. 5:17).

Paul's interest in Jesus seems to have focused especially on the last week of his life—his institution of the Lord's Supper (1 Cor. 11:23–26) and especially his death, burial, and resurrection (1 Cor. 15:3–7). Since Paul knew disciples of Jesus, as well as James the brother of Jesus, he must have known some of the stories about Jesus that we find in our Gospels and probably other stories as well. He does cite words or instructions of Jesus in a few places (1 Cor. 7:10–11; 9:14; 11:23–25; 2 Cor. 12:9; cf. Acts 20:35), but for the most part he displays little interest in the details of Jesus's earthly life and ministry. He never mentions, for instance, that Jesus told parables or that he worked miracles or that he had numerous arguments with the Pharisees over various matters of the law (a striking omission, since Paul himself is a Pharisee). Paul's focus, rather, is on "Christ crucified" (1 Cor. 1:23) and on the risen Christ, who is Lord of all (Phil. 2:9–11). This, in fact, is what some scholars have in mind when they dub Paul "the real founder of Christianity." They claim that Paul transformed the gospel from the message *of* Jesus (i.e., the message about the reign of God that Jesus preached; see Mark 1:14–15) to a message *about* Jesus. But Paul himself probably would have regarded his emphasis on the latter part of Jesus's career as focusing on the events that brought to a climax everything that Jesus had sought to say and do in the years prior to those events.

new creation: an understanding of God's saving activity according to which, through Christ, people are given a new life in a new age that has already begun.

Lord's Supper: the ritual meal observed by Christians in a manner that commemorates Jesus's last supper with his disciples.

Box 12.7

The New Perspective on Paul

Toward the end of the twentieth century a revolution in Pauline studies brought to the fore an understanding of Paul's theology called the "new perspective." Basically, this view maintains that when Paul talks about justification "by faith apart from works prescribed by the law" (Rom. 3:28), his main point is not that people are put right with God through faith rather than through their own effort or obedience; his main point is that people can be put right with God without abiding by the legal codes that marked Israel as God's chosen people. Thus he is not so much contending against "works righteousness" as he is rejecting "ethnic privilege."

monotheism: the belief that there is only one God.

Theologically, Paul understands Jesus Christ to be the image of God (2 Cor. 4:4; Phil. 2:6; Col. 1:15; cf. 1 Cor. 15:49), the one who makes God visible and accessible to human beings. Jesus is the Son of God (Rom. 1:3–4; 8:3) and thus remains in some sense subordinate to God and distinct from God (1 Cor. 15:27–28). Thus Paul wants to respect Jewish monotheism: he does not mean to make Jesus into a second God, though at times he perhaps seems close to doing so (1 Cor. 8:6). He often quotes Scripture passages in which the word "Lord" originally referred to the God of Israel and interprets them in such a way that "Lord" now refers to Jesus Christ (see, e.g., the treatment of Joel 2:32 in Rom. 10:13; cf. Rom. 10:9). He also speaks of Christ as having been "in the form of God" and as having chosen not to regard "equality with God as something to be exploited" (Phil. 2:6; for discussion of how this passage is interpreted, see "Incarnation" in chap. 18). Paul clearly has an exalted view of Christ as one who is more than just a prophet, or even a messiah, or any other human servant of God.

We should also note the depth of Paul's religious feeling for Christ and the manner in which he speaks of Christ in relational terms. He is consumed with Jesus Christ and the gospel; he doesn't want to think or talk or write about anything else (see 1 Cor. 2:2; 2 Cor. 10:3–5; Phil. 3:7–8). He feels compelled to proclaim the gospel (1 Cor. 9:16), and he accepts his call to do so as a great honor: the gospel is a prized treasure with which he has been entrusted (Gal. 2:7; 1 Thess. 2:4). When he shares the gospel with others, he is fulfilling the purpose for which he was born (Rom. 1:1; Gal. 1:15). And Paul is committed not simply to a cause or an ideology but rather to a person: he *knows* Jesus Christ (Phil. 3:7–10) and can say, "It is no longer I who live, but it is Christ who lives in me" (Gal. 2:20). He is not claiming to be exceptional in this regard; rather, union with Christ is a reality to be experienced by all believers (Rom. 6:5; 8:10; 1 Cor. 6:17; 2 Cor. 13:5; cf. Col. 3:3). Paul speaks of Christians as "those who are *in* Christ Jesus" (Rom. 8:1; 16:7; 2 Cor. 5:17) and describes the church as "the body of Christ" (Rom. 12:4–5; 1 Cor. 12:27). Accordingly, Paul's gospel is very much a message for a community; it is good news for the church, the new people of God formed in Christ and empowered by the Holy Spirit.

⊙ EXPLORE 12.12
The New Perspective
on Paul: A Brief Essay

Paul's theology is eminently practical in that everything he believes about God and Christ has direct implications for how people live in the present world. Simply put, those who experience God's salvation through Christ are to live not for themselves but rather for Christ, who died and was raised for them (2 Cor. 5:14–15), and "the only thing that counts is faith working through love" (Gal. 5:6). Paul devotes generous portions of his letters to instruction on moral and behavioral matters. He addresses controversial issues (e.g., Rom. 14:5–6; 1 Cor. 8:1–13; 12:1–14:40) and lists both virtues to be pursued and vices to be avoided (Rom. 1:29–31; 13:13; 1 Cor. 5:10–11; 6:9–10; 2 Cor. 6:6–7; Gal. 5:19–23).

How does Paul determine what sort of behavior is appropriate for those who are now in Christ? There is no question that his ethical positions are informed by the Hebrew Scriptures—the moral commandments of Torah—but Paul also claims that Christians are no longer "under the law" (Rom. 6:14–15; 1 Cor. 9:20; Gal. 3:23–25), and interpreters struggle to determine exactly what he means by that (see "Obedience of Faith" in chap. 13, and "Christ and the Law: The Real Issue" in chap. 16). In a few instances, Paul makes reference to a human "conscience" that may serve as a moral guide (Rom. 2:15; 2 Cor. 1:12; 4:2), but this cannot be absolute, since conscience can be weak and is easily defiled (1 Cor. 8:7–12; 10:25–29).

Ultimately, Paul's ethics are shaped by the expectation that believers will imitate Christ with regard to sacrificial humility: they will seek the good of others rather than what is pleasing or beneficial to themselves (Rom. 15:1–3; Phil. 2:4–8). Thus for Paul the cross becomes the emblem not only of Christian salvation but also of Christian conduct. Furthermore, for Paul all ethics are community ethics, for the individual believer is united spiritually with others in such a way that all individual actions have consequences for others (1 Cor. 12:11–26). Paul's ethics are also shaped by an expectation that Christ is coming soon and that the time remaining to do what must be accomplished in this world is short (Rom. 13:11–14; 1 Cor. 7:29–31; 1 Thess. 4:13–5:11). And, finally, Paul is certain that believers have divine assistance in living as God would have them live; they are transformed from within, by a renewing of their minds (Rom. 12:1), and they are imbued with the Holy Spirit, who produces in them the fruit that is pleasing to God (Gal. 5:22–23).

the law: "the law of Moses" or any regulations that the Jewish people understood as delineating faithfulness to God in terms of the covenant that God made with Israel.

humility: the quality of consciously seeking what is best for others rather than what is best for oneself.

Conclusion

Perhaps the best word to describe Paul is *multifaceted*. There appear to have been many sides to this man, and those who think that they have him figured out may be surprised to discover there is more to Paul than they have taken into account.

Paul spoke in tongues (1 Cor. 14:18). He experienced celestial visions in which he was transported to the heavenly realm (2 Cor. 12:1–7). He received revelations from the Lord (Gal. 2:2) and sometimes expected people to regard his rulings on certain matters as bearing the mark of divine authority (1 Cor. 14:37–38; cf. 7:12, 39–40). He was a man who prayed much (Rom. 1:9–10; 1 Thess. 1:2–3; 3:10), sometimes with troubled longing (Rom. 8:26) but often with joyful praise (Phil. 1:3–4). He was also a man given to unabashed emotion and sentiment: he recounts without embarrassment the times that he has been moved to tears (2 Cor. 2:4; Phil. 3:18), and he speaks openly of his affection for those who are dear to him (2 Cor. 7:2–4; Gal. 4:19–20; Phil. 4:1; 1 Thess. 2:17–20; Philem. 4–7). Of course, he can also be roused to anger, and he is not shy about expressing that emotion (1 Cor. 4:19–21; 2 Cor. 11:12–15; Gal. 1:9; 3:1; 5:12).

Paul often seems to embody a confident faith that many would regard as idealistic: he has learned to be content in any and all circumstances, and he knows that he can do all things through Christ, who strengthens him (Phil. 4:11–13). In other ways, however, he seems remarkably down-to-earth. In his letters he deals with the most mundane matters in ways that are realistic and evocative of common sense. Note, for instance, his counsel to spouses not to deprive one another of conjugal rights but rather to grant access to each other's bodies for fulfillment, as needed, of sexual desires (1 Cor. 7:3–5). Such advice may seem a bit crass to some, but the point remains: he is able to recognize the need for dealing with practical concerns in a realistic manner.

At other times, Paul can seem to be a morass of contradictions. He can appear to be a champion of women's rights in one instance (Rom. 16:1–2; Gal. 3:28) and a proponent of patriarchal chauvinism in another (1 Cor. 11:1–16). At one point he seems to question the validity of all human authority figures (Gal. 2:6), but elsewhere he urges his readers to show respect for those who are over them in the Lord (1 Thess. 5:12–13) and even to be subject to pagan political rulers because all authorities have been instituted by God (Rom. 13:1–7). He is adamant that the gospel that he proclaims was revealed to him directly by Jesus Christ without further consultation with anyone (Gal. 1:11–12), but he also describes the essentials of that gospel as a tradition handed on to him by others (1 Cor. 15:3). He can adopt a tolerant "agree to disagree" attitude on some controversial issues (Rom. 14:5), but he seeks to lay down the law in an absolute sense on other matters (1 Cor. 7:17; 11:16; 14:33–36). He is capable both of commending gentleness (Gal. 5:23; 6:1; Phil. 4:5) and of threatening people with harsh discipline (1 Cor. 4:21; 5:1–5; 2 Cor. 13:2). He emphasizes grace and forgiveness, but he insists that people reap what they sow (Gal. 6:6–10) and says that wrongdoers will not inherit the kingdom of God (1 Cor. 6:9).

The point is not that such tendencies cannot be reconciled but rather that, unless they are recognized, our understanding of Paul may be one-sided or incomplete. There is more to Paul than meets the eye. The depth and complexity of his life and thought are what make him one of the most fascinating figures in human history and, after Jesus himself, the most important figure in the history of Christianity.

FOR FURTHER READING: Paul

Bird, Michael F. *Paul: An Anomalous Jew*. Grand Rapids: Eerdmans, 2016.

Capes, David B., Rodney Reeves, and E. Randolph Richards. *Rediscovering Paul: An Introduction to His World, Letters, and Theology*. Downers Grove, IL: IVP Academic, 2007.

Longenecker, Bruce, and Todd D. Still. *Thinking through Paul: A Survey of His Life, Letters, and Theology*. Grand Rapids: Zondervan, 2014.

McRay, John. *Paul: His Life and Teaching*. Grand Rapids: Baker Academic, 2003.

Porter, Stanley E. *The Apostle Paul: His Life, Thought, and Letters*. Grand Rapids: Eerdmans, 2016.

Sanders, E. P. *Paul: The Apostle's Life, Letters, and Thought*. Minneapolis: Fortress, 2015.

Schreiner, Thomas R. *Paul, Apostle of God's Glory in Christ: A Pauline Theology*. Downers Grove, IL: InterVarsity, 2001.

Sumney, Jerry L. *Paul: Apostle and Fellow Traveler*. Louisville: Abingdon, 2014.

Taylor, Walter F., Jr. *Paul: Apostle to the Nations*. Minneapolis: Fortress, 2012.

Witherup, Ronald D. *Responses to 101 Questions on Paul*. Mahwah, NJ: Paulist Press, 2003.

Wright, N. T. *Paul and His Recent Interpreters*. Minneapolis: Fortress, 2015.

⊙ Go to www
.IntroducingNT.com
for summaries,
videos, and other
study tools.

Romans

In the year 386 a young pagan named "Augustine" was converted to Christianity by reading two verses from Paul's letter to the Romans (13:13–14). He says, "I had no wish to read further; there was no need to. For it was as though my heart was filled with a light of confidence and all the shadows of my doubt were swept away."

Over eleven centuries later, in 1515, the Protestant Reformation began with the meditations of an Augustinian monk, Martin Luther, on another text from that same letter (Rom. 1:17). Luther later called the letter "a gate of heaven" and testified that through reading it he had felt himself "to be reborn and to have gone through open doors into paradise."

A couple centuries after that, in 1738, a young Anglican, John Wesley, heard a church leader read aloud from a commentary on Romans that Luther had written. It was the turning point of his life. "I felt my heart was strangely warmed," he later wrote of the experience. "I felt that I did trust in Christ, Christ alone for my salvation."

Your experience with Romans may be different, but no one can doubt the enormous impact that this book has had in the history of Christianity. It certainly has been one of the most influential books of the Bible for the development of Christian doctrine and theology. This is not to say that it has been the most popular. Romans has a reputation for being Paul's most difficult letter; it captures the apostle at his most brilliant, engaged in some heavy-duty thinking.

Romans may be the only letter of Paul written to people he doesn't know (but cf. Col. 2:1). Usually he writes to churches that he started, addressing his own converts. This time, he writes to introduce himself to a church that he has never visited. Although it comes first among Paul's letters in our New Testament, it was written later than most of the letters that follow it. Nevertheless, it can

Protestant Reformation: the religious movement of the sixteenth century that sought to reform the Roman Catholic Church and that led to the establishment of the Protestant churches.

Box 13.1

The Conversion of Augustine

From a hidden depth a profound self-examination had dredged up a heap of all my misery. . . . I threw myself down under a certain fig-tree and let my tears flow freely. . . . Suddenly I heard a voice from the nearby house chanting as if it might be a boy or a girl (I do not know which), saying and repeating over and over again "Pick up and read, pick up and read." At once my countenance changed, and I began to think intently whether there might be some sort of children's game in which such a chant is used. But I could not remember having heard of one. I checked the flood of tears and stood up. . . . I hurried back to the place where . . . I had put down the book of the apostle when I got up. I seized it, opened it, and in silence read the first passage on which my eyes lit: "Not in riots and drunken parties, not in eroticism and indecencies, not in strife and rivalry, but put on the Lord Jesus Christ and make no provision for the flesh in its lusts" [Rom. 13:13–14]. I neither wished nor needed to read further. At once, with the last words of this sentence, it was as if a light of relief from all anxiety flooded into my heart. All the shadows of doubt were dispelled.

Augustine, *Confessions*, 8.12.28–30, trans. Henry Chadwick (Oxford: Oxford University Press, 1991), 153.

offer a good starting point for understanding Paul precisely because it offers a mature and articulate presentation of some of his key ideas. John Calvin said that when Christians come to understand this letter, they have a passageway opened for them to understand the whole of Scripture.

Overview

The letter begins with Paul greeting the Romans (1:1–7), giving thanks for their renowned faith (1:8–10), and stating his intention to visit them soon (1:11–15). Then, in 1:16–17, he offers what many regard as a sort of "thesis statement" for the letter: the gospel that he preaches conveys the power of God for salvation to everyone who has faith, to Jews first but also to gentiles. This gospel reveals "the righteousness of God . . . through faith for faith." This thesis is then developed in two stages.

First, Paul claims that both gentiles and Jews are under the wrath of God (1:18–3:20). The gentiles may not have had Scripture (the law) to guide them in doing God's will, but this does not excuse their behavior, for by worshiping idols and engaging in homosexual acts they have failed to live according to what should be obvious from nature. They violate human conscience, ignoring the "law written on their hearts" (2:15). The Jews, meanwhile, have had Scripture to guide them, but they have not obeyed it.

Next, Paul claims that both gentiles and Jews are the beneficiaries of God's grace (3:21–5:21). The Old Testament patriarch Abraham becomes an example of how people may be reckoned as righteous because of their faith. Likewise, God's action in Jesus Christ has restored human beings to a right relationship

⊙ EXPLORE 13.0
Romans: Outline of
Contents

with God, such that they are "justified by faith" (5:1). Through Jesus Christ both Jews and gentiles may enjoy peace with God and live in confident hope of eternal life.

Having summarized the gospel that he preaches in this way, Paul takes up several potential questions (or objections). If salvation comes by grace, why shouldn't people just "continue in sin in order that grace may abound" (6:1–7:6)? What now is the role of the law? Does it still have a place in the lives of Christians (7:7–8:39)? And what about God's covenant promises to the Jews? Are those nullified by a gospel that places Jews and gentiles on even terms (chaps. 9–11)? In answering these questions, Paul develops a number of themes: he maintains that the righteousness of God works an inner transformation in believers such that, through baptism, they die to sin and come alive to Christ (6:11). The law serves to show people their sin, but true obedience to God's will comes with a life that is lived "according to the spirit" rather than "according to the flesh"; the Spirit of God makes possible what mere human effort cannot achieve (8:3–4). And as for the promises to Israel, Paul remains confident that "all Israel will be saved" (11:26) while also maintaining that "not all Israelites truly belong to Israel" (9:6).

Finally, Paul addresses the Roman Christians with a number of exhortations regarding the Christian life, a life marked by inner transformation that yields conformity to the will of God (12:1–2). They are to live in harmony with one another, recognizing the different gifts that various members exercise within the community (12:3–13). They are also to live peacefully with society (12:14–13:10), respecting the authority of the secular government (13:1–7). And with regard to various matters of controversy, particularly those that arise from the clash of Jewish and gentile traditions, they are to respect divergent opinions (14:5) and avoid passing judgment on one another (14:10). Paul counsels those who accept the full implications of the gospel that he preaches (he calls them "the strong in faith") to be patient with those who continue to follow various rules and restrictions that he considers unnecessary (14:1–15:13).

The letter concludes with a description of Paul's travel plans (15:14–32), a list of greetings to various individuals (16:1–24), and a final doxology (16:25–27).

Historical Background

We do not know when Christianity came to Rome or who was responsible for the first missionary work there. Perhaps churches were established gradually as Christians moved from other places to the capital city of the empire. In any case, there appear to have been a surprising number of believers in Rome by the year 49. In that year, the emperor Claudius expelled a segment of the Jewish population due to what the historian Suetonius calls "a disturbance over Chrestus" (*Life of*

Claudius 25). It is widely believed that by "Chrestus" Suetonius means *Christos* (Greek for "Christ") and that the Jews expelled included ones who believed in Jesus (see Acts 18:2). Thus within twenty years of the crucifixion of Jesus, there appear to have been enough Christians in Rome to create a disturbance worthy of the emperor's attention. In any case, Claudius died in 54, and after his death the Jews whom he had expelled (including Jewish Christians) began to trickle back.

Paul writes to the Christians in Rome a few years later, probably around 57 or 58. He appears to be in Corinth and is near the end of what would be his third missionary journey (see Acts 18:23–21:15, especially 20:2–3). He tells the church in Rome of his plans to make a trip to Jerusalem to deliver an offering that has been collected for "the poor among the saints" (15:25–26). After that, he hopes to visit the Roman Christians before he embarks on another ambitious missionary venture, westward to Spain (15:23–24, 28). The hopeful and joyful manner in which he announces these plans (15:29, 32) has a tragic ring for those who know the rest of the story: according to the book of Acts, Paul's trip to Jerusalem ended with his arrest (21:17–33), and when he did arrive in Rome, it was as a prisoner under guard (28:16).

Against this background of events, scholars are able to discern a number of specific reasons why Paul might have written this letter: he wants to introduce himself to the Roman Christians in preparation for his visit; he wants to garner support for his eventual work in Spain; he wants to solicit their prayers regarding his upcoming trip to Jerusalem; and he wants to offer pastoral counsel concerning problems that have arisen or might arise within the congregation.

Still, Paul could have accomplished such purposes with a much shorter and less complicated letter. The real question concerns why he would write this letter—his magnum opus, so to speak—to this particular group of people. A few scholars have said that he didn't write it for them, or at least not just for them; rather, he intended to produce a generic summary of his views that could be copied and distributed to lots of churches. Most scholars, however, prefer

collection for Jerusalem: a fundraising effort conducted by the apostle Paul among gentile believers on behalf of Jewish believers in Jerusalem.

Christianity Comes to Rome

We don't know when or how the Christian faith took root in the city of Rome, though for many centuries that city would serve as a focal point and virtual headquarters for the Christian religion. Two of our earliest references to Christianity in Rome offer different views on the phenomenon:

"Your faith is proclaimed throughout the world"; "you yourselves are full of goodness, filled with all knowledge, and able to instruct one another."—Paul (Rom. 1:8; 15:14)

"A most mischievous superstition . . . broke out . . . in Rome, where all things hideous and shameful from every part of the world find their centre and become popular."—Tacitus (*Annals* 15.44)*

*Complete Works of Tacitus, trans. Alfred John Church, William Jackson Brodribb (New York: Modern Library, 1942).

Fig. 13.1. Ancient Rome. This artist's reproduction of the Roman Forum displays the might of a city that ruled the world. (Balage Balogh / www.archaeologyillustrated.com)

to look for reasons why the contents of this letter would be pertinent to the particular situation of the Romans.

Much of the letter is devoted to discussing implications of Paul's claim that the gospel puts Jews and gentiles on the same footing, with regard to both their need for salvation and God's provision of that salvation through Christ. How would that message fit with Paul's particular agenda for the Roman Christians? At least three answers can be given, and they are not mutually exclusive. Paul may have written this letter the way he did for any or all of these reasons:

1. Since Paul is personally unknown to most of these Christians but wants them to sponsor his mission trip to Spain, he needs to explain key tenets of the ministry that he hopes they will agree to support. He says that he wants to be "sent on" by the Roman Christians (15:24), implying that he has hopes for their financial support for his work in the west. But Paul also seems to think that the Roman Christians might be suspicious of him. He needs to clear up points on which he has been misrepresented (3:8) and to anticipate objections that might arise (3:1, 3, 5, 8; 6:1, 15; 7:7, 13; 11:1, 11). Basically, he writes to set the record straight concerning his famous "law-free gospel" and to answer the questions that always come up (Did God renege on promises to Israel? Does "law-free" mean "anything goes"?).

⊙ EXPLORE 13.9
Recycling Romans?

Condemnation of Homosexual Acts

In Romans 1:26–27 Paul refers to women and men who engage in what he regards as shameless sex acts with same-sex partners. He says these acts are "unnatural" and a consummation of "degrading passions." These verses offer what is usually regarded as the most clear "generic condemnation" of homosexual activity in the Bible. Their relevance for ethical teaching on homosexual relations in our modern world has been a subject of much debate.

In Roman cities homosexuality was closely associated with promiscuous and exploitative activity, including prostitution, orgies, and sex with minors. Little was known of what is now called "sexual orientation," and people were not generally classed as having a basic "heterosexual" or "homosexual" identity. Thus some scholars suggest that the best analogy for the behavior condemned by Paul might be "homosexual acts engaged in by heterosexual people." Paul's words, they say, would not necessarily apply to responsible partnerships between persons who are homosexual in terms of a basic (possibly genetic) orientation.

While support for this view seems to be increasing, many biblical scholars have not been convinced. They would say that Paul denounces the behavior not because it is promiscuous or exploitative but rather because it is "unnatural." The point for Paul seems to be that such actions violate God's original design for humanity. These scholars say that if Paul knew everything we know about sexual orientation, he would no doubt regard a "homosexual orientation" (even if genetically determined) as an unfortunate predisposition toward sin, as an inclination of the flesh that needs to be resisted or overcome by those who "walk not according to the flesh but according to the Spirit" (8:4).

Other biblical texts in which homosexual acts are mentioned include Genesis 19:1–9; Leviticus 18:22; 20:13; Judges 19:22–25; 1 Corinthians 6:9; 1 Timothy 1:10.

2. Paul's mind is on the upcoming trip to Jerusalem, and he is rehearsing the summary and defense of his gospel that he may need to offer there. He asks the Roman Christians to pray not only that he will be kept safe "from the unbelievers" as he travels to Jerusalem but also that the offering that he is bringing will be acceptable to the Jerusalem saints (15:30–31). That last part seems odd. Why wouldn't the offering be acceptable? Do churches usually turn away money? We know, however, that Paul previously quarreled with representatives of the Jerusalem church (Gal. 2:12–13) and that his ministry among the gentiles has been a source of contention in those quarters (Gal. 2:4; Acts 15:1–5). Paul hopes that the gift that he is bringing will symbolize the mutual interdependence of gentile and Jewish Christians (Rom. 15:27). Acceptance of the gift would imply that the Jewish Christians in Jerusalem recognize the legitimacy of the gentile churches that Paul founded in Macedonia and Achaia. People in the Jerusalem church who are opposed to Paul and to his ministry may see this as an opportunity to make a statement: "Let's tell Paul and his gentile Christians that we don't want their help." Thus, according to this theory, Paul writes to the Romans what he plans to say (if necessary) to the Christians in Jerusalem. He is, at least, rehearsing his defense. Beyond

that, he may also hope that some influential persons in the Roman church will serve as intermediaries with their counterparts in Jerusalem, paving the way for him to be received favorably there.

3. Paul wants to effect reconciliation among Jews and gentiles in the Roman church itself. If indeed the Jewish Christians had been expelled for a time but are now making their way back, there could have been a power shift in the interim: the gentiles are now in charge. Any number of issues discussed in the letter could be informed by Paul's sensitivity to such dynamics (see, e.g., the tensions between the "strong" and the "weak" in Rom. 14). Much of the letter seems to be addressed to gentile believers (1:13; 11:13), and since Paul thinks that he has been called by God to be the "apostle to the Gentiles" (1:5; 11:13; cf. Gal. 2:7–8), he may consider it his charge to speak pastorally to gentile believers whether they know him personally or not (15:15–16).

Major Themes in Romans

The letter is long and complex. Here we note some of its key themes.

Righteousness of God

Paul claims that the gospel he preaches (and summarizes in this letter) reveals "the righteousness of God" (1:17; cf. 3:21–22). This is a rich concept, for Paul is able to speak of righteousness as something that God displays (3:25), reckons (4:3, 6), and imparts (10:3). We will explore a bit more about the latter two concepts below, under the heading "Obedience of Faith." For now, let us focus on the first: righteousness is something that God *displays*. Paul wants to

---

Box 13.4

Phoebe, Prisca, Junia

The number and prominence of the women mentioned in Romans 16 is striking: ten are mentioned in verses 1, 3, 6, 7, 12, 13, 15. Three of these are especially noteworthy:

- *Phoebe*. Paul sends the letter with her and commends her to the congregation. He identifies her as a deacon in her home church and a benefactor of many (16:1–2).
- *Prisca*. She is singled out as one who, along with her husband, risked her life for Paul and earned the thanks of all churches of the gentiles (16:3). We hear of her elsewhere (Acts 18:2, 18, 26; 1 Cor. 16:19; 2 Tim. 4:19).
- *Junia*. She is said to be "prominent among the apostles" (16:7). Nineteenth-century scholars, perhaps unable to believe that Paul could have called a woman an apostle, treated the accusative *Iounian* in the Greek text as a form not of the female name "Junia" but of a male name "Junias"—a name for which there is no ancient evidence.

Box 13.5

Some Key Verses in Romans

These passages underscore some of the key points Paul makes in his letter to the Romans.

- "I am not ashamed of the gospel; it is the power of God for salvation to everyone who has faith" (1:16).
- "All have sinned and fall short of the glory of God" (3:23).
- "The wages of sin is death, but the free gift of God is eternal life in Christ Jesus our Lord" (6:23).
- "There is therefore now no condemnation for those who are in Christ Jesus" (8:1).
- "We know that all things work together for good for those who love God, who are called according to his purpose" (8:28).
- "I am convinced that neither death, nor life, nor angels, nor rulers, nor things present, nor things to come, nor powers, nor height, nor depth, nor anything else in all creation, will be able to separate us from the love of God in Christ Jesus our Lord" (8:38–39).
- "Do not be conformed to this world, but be transformed by the renewing of your minds" (12:2).
- "Do not be overcome by evil, but overcome evil with good" (12:21).

righteousness of God: in Paul's writings, the essential quality of God comprising justice, faithfulness, love, and generosity, which God graciously imparts to others through faith.

justification by grace: the idea or doctrine that God has acted graciously through Jesus Christ in a manner that allows people to be put right with God through faith.

emphasize that what God does through Jesus Christ demonstrates that God is righteous. In showing grace to all humanity, God displays the righteous qualities of faithfulness and generosity: God is faithful to the covenant made with Israel because God gives Jews a means of salvation through faith in their Messiah (3:3–4). And God is generous beyond all measure in offering this same means of salvation to gentiles. Paul says that such faithfulness and generosity prove God's love (5:8), and the greatness of that love is seen in the means through which God's gracious salvation of the undeserving is accomplished: Christ died for the ungodly (5:6), giving his very life to reconcile with God those who at the time were God's enemies (5:10).

Justification by Grace

Paul declares in Romans that people are justified by faith (3:28; 5:1), a point that also figures heavily in his letter to the Galatians (see Gal. 2:16; 3:24). The term *justification* derives from the covenant language of Israel: to be justified means to be in a right relationship with God. Justification is closely related to forgiveness (cf. Rom. 3:26 with 4:6–8), but it is more than mere acquittal; it implies and effects the restoration of a relationship. It is, in that sense, more closely linked to reconciliation (Rom. 5:8–11; cf. 2 Cor. 5:18–21). Paul says that people are justified or put in a right relationship with God by faith. The Christian doctrine of "justification by grace" or "justification by faith" derives from this teaching of Paul, usually assuming that "faith" implies trust in God's gracious, unmerited favor. Some interpreters, however, have noted that the Greek word translated as "faith" (*pistis*) in English Bibles can also mean "faithfulness."

Furthermore, the biblical texts do not specify whose faith or faithfulness puts people right with God. The question thus arises as to whether what justifies people is their own faith in God, or God's faithfulness to the divine promises, or indeed Christ's faithful obedience to God's will. Paul himself does not seem bothered by this ambiguity. Throughout Romans he presents justification as a consequence of divine faithfulness (4:25; 5:18) but seems always to assume that those who are justified trust God's promises, believe the gospel, and strive to be faithful in their response to what God has done (5:1–2; 10:10). This topic will come up again in Paul's letter to the Galatians (see chap. 16, "Christ and the Law: The Real Issue").

Obedience of Faith

In the prescript of this letter Paul says that as an apostle he has been sent by God to bring about "the obedience of faith" (1:5). As the letter progresses, we get a better idea what he means by this. Paul wants all people—Jews and gentiles—to live in a way that is pleasing to God, but he thinks that the Jews failed to do this, and he believes that the gentiles will do no better if they are simply shown the Scriptures and told to live according to God's law. True obedience to the will of God comes through faith, as a result of being reconciled

---

Box 13.6

Models for Understanding Justification

In Romans and in his other letters Paul seems to draw on different images to explain how the death and resurrection of Jesus Christ can justify people, or make them right with God (Rom. 3:24–26, 30; 4:24–5:1; 5:9, 16–21; cf. 1 Cor. 6:11; Gal. 2:21; 3:11–14).

- *Substitution.* All people are guilty of not living as God requires, and the penalty is (eternal) death; Jesus is completely innocent but dies on the cross to take the penalty for everyone else (see Rom. 3:23–24; 5:6–8; 6:23).
- *Redemption.* People are like slaves, owned by some hostile power (sin, death, the devil); the purchase price for freedom is the blood of Christ, and God pays this so that people can now belong to God (see Rom. 3:24; 8:23; 1 Cor. 1:30; 6:20; 7:23).
- *Reconciliation.* People have been unfaithful to God in ways that have severely damaged the divine-human relationship; Jesus comes as the mediator and offers his own life to restore the broken relationship (see Rom. 5:10; 2 Cor. 5:18–20).
- *Atonement.* People have sinned against God, who demands sacrifices of blood to nullify the consequences of sin; Jesus dies on a cross to offer one supreme sacrifice for the sins of all (see Rom. 3:25).
- *Participation.* People live under the power of sin and death, and the only way out is to die and rise to new life. Through baptism, people are united with Christ, participating in his death and (ultimately) in his resurrection (see Rom. 6:1–11; Gal. 2:19–20).

See also Bart D. Ehrman, *The New Testament: A Historical Introduction to the Early Christian Writings*, 6th ed. (Oxford: Oxford University Press, 2016), 406–10.

sanctification: the
act or process of
being made holy or
sinless.

with God (5:10) and receiving the gift of God's Spirit (8:4). For Paul, one consequence of being justified by faith (5:1) is "sanctification" (6:22), being made holy or righteous by God. When Paul says that Christ makes people righteous (5:18–19; cf. 2 Cor. 5:21), he means this in a double sense: (1) people can now be counted as righteous even though they continue to struggle and fail to live as God wishes (theologians call this "imputed righteousness"); and (2) people can now be transformed so that they actually are able to please God in ways that would not be possible otherwise (theologians call this "effective righteousness"). Both seem to be a part of what Paul means by "sanctification" and "obedience of faith": by trusting in what God has done through Jesus Christ, people are reconciled with God and set on a path to godly living.

Universal Availability of Salvation

Paul proclaims a gospel that promises "salvation to everyone who has faith, to the Jew first and also to the Greek" (1:16). The idea that divine blessings once available only to Israel are now offered through Christ to all people runs like a thread through this letter (1:5, 17; 3:21–23, 29–30; 4:16; 5:18; 10:4, 12; 11:32). Indeed, some scholars think that this might be Paul's main point, and they claim that the significance of the matter has often been missed. Since the Protestant Reformation, the central theme of Paul's letter to the Romans has often been identified as exposition of the idea that people are justified (or made righteous) before God by faith rather than by performing good works. In recent years, however, a number of scholars have said that this is, at best, only a subsidiary point. Paul's main point is that because people are justified by faith rather than through obedience to the covenant law of Israel, salvation

---

Box 13.7

The End of the Law

In Romans, Paul says that Christ is "the end of the law" (10:4). What does he mean?

Perhaps he means that Christ is the goal or fulfillment of the law, the one to whom the law was pointing all along and the one who accomplishes the purposes of God that the law was intended to produce. Or he might mean that the coming of Christ marks a termination of the law in God's plan. But if that is the case, then in what sense has Christ put an end to the law? Has the law been terminated simply as a means to being made right with God, or has it also been done away with as an adequate expression of God's will?

And what law or laws are we talking about? Is the Mosaic law as a whole to be disregarded by Christians, since God's will can now be discerned through a transformed and renewed mind (12:2)? Or are Christians released only from keeping certain laws, ones that are pertinent to Jewish identity (such as dietary and Sabbath regulations)? Are some laws generic and timeless (13:9), and if so, how do we know which ones these are?

For a survey of how these and other questions have been answered, see Veronica Koperski, *What Are They Saying about Paul and the Law?* (Mahwah, NJ: Paulist Press, 2001).

Fig. 13.2. The second Adam. In Romans, Paul presents Jesus as a second Adam who reverses the effects of original sin for humanity. The first Adam responded to temptation (symbolized here by Eve with her apple) with disobedience; the second Adam responds with obedience: "Just as one man's trespass led to condemnation for all, so one man's act of righteousness leads to justification and life for all" (Rom. 5:18). (The Bridgeman Art Library International)

is now equally available to all. This position is a part of what is called "the new perspective on Paul" (see box 13.8). According to this view, Paul expounds the doctrine of justification by grace as a means to an end; what interests him most is the universal scope of the gospel and the implications of such universal inclusion for Christian faith and practice.

Death and Resurrection

Paul closely connects justification and salvation with the death and resurrection of Christ, and he does so in a way that brings out present and future dimensions of Christian experience. He interprets Christian baptism as a participation in the death and resurrection of Christ (6:3–4). Through Christ's death, believers have been put right with God, justified by faith so that they enjoy peace with God in their lives here and now (5:1, 6–9). Because of Christ's resurrection, believers experience the newness of a life free from bondage to sin (6:4–11), and ultimately they will be saved from a life that is marked by suffering for a life of glory marked by the fulfillment of hope (5:2–5; 8:18–25). Paul uses a variety of verb tenses when speaking about these matters. In the English Bible (NRSV), we read that "we *were* reconciled" (5:10), "we *are* justified" (5:1), and "we *will be* saved" (5:9, 10; 10:9, 13; but cf. 8:24). What God has done in the past affects both our current life and our future status. This is Paul's way of expressing the "already / not yet" dynamic of Christian experience that is also evident in Jesus's teaching about the kingdom of God (see box 4.2, and "Proclamation of the Kingdom" in chap. 7).

God and Israel

Paul devotes three chapters of this letter to discussing questions raised by the stark fact that most Jewish people did not accept the gospel of Christ. How could such a development fit into God's plan, and what would ultimately become of God's chosen people, Israel? In thinking about these matters, Paul maintains that Scripture does allow for this seeming anomaly: he cites precedents and prophecies to assure his readers that Israel's rejection of Christ and possible loss of salvation does not mean that the word of God has failed (9:6). He also maintains that election is God's business: God can choose to accept or reject whomever God wishes (9:18), and people have no right to question God's decisions (9:20). Nevertheless, God's faithfulness is evident in the remnant of Jews who have accepted the gospel, a remnant of which Paul himself is a part (11:1–6).

⊙ EXPLORE 12.12
The New Perspective
on Paul: A Brief Essay

Box 13.8

The New Perspective on Paul: An Example

What does this verse mean?

> For we hold that a person is justified by faith, apart from works prescribed by the law. (Rom. 3:28)

Traditional Interpretation

People are put right with God by trusting in what God has graciously done through Jesus Christ rather than by doing things that would earn God's favor. In this view, "works prescribed by the law" = meritorious acts of human achievement (keeping commandments, performing good works, etc.).

New Perspective

People are put right with God by trusting in what God has graciously done through Jesus Christ rather than by being faithful to the covenant that God made with Israel. In this view, "works prescribed by the law" = covenant markers that identify Jews as belonging to God's chosen nation (circumcision, Sabbath observance, dietary restrictions, etc.).

Fig. 13.3. The whole creation. In Romans 8, Paul maintains that all creation is in bondage to decay and yearns for the freedom and glory of God's salvation (8:19–22). In these few verses he offers a broad vision of redemption (8:23) that encompasses more than individual lives or even humanity as a whole; "the glory to be revealed" (8:18) will involve a restoration of the earth itself.

Beyond these initial observations, Paul claims that Israel's rejection of Christ has served a good purpose, facilitating the spread of the gospel to the rest of the world (11:11–24). He holds out hope that many Jews will recover from what will turn out to have been a temporary misstep and will come to faith in Christ after all. Indeed, he yearns for this with such passion that he would give up his own salvation in order to make it happen (9:3). Finally, Paul declares confidently that "all Israel will be saved" (11:26), but it is not clear what he means by this. Some interpreters think that Paul is speaking prophetically of a literal conversion of Jews to come about in the end times. Others think that he is entertaining the notion that God's mercy will extend to the Jews whether they accept Christ or not, since "the gifts and calling of God are irrevocable" (11:29). Still others question whether Paul is using the term "Israel" to refer to an ethnic group (see 9:6; cf. 2:29); the point could be that God's covenant promises will be fulfilled for those who accept Israel's Messiah (be they Jews or gentiles), and in that sense "all Israel" will be saved.

Obedience to the Government

Paul's words regarding obedience to the governing authorities in Romans 13:1–7 are often cited in discussions of church-state relations. He says that Christians should not resist political rulers, for these have been put in place by God. This advice invites comparison with what is said elsewhere in the Bible. In the Gospel of Luke, the devil claims to be responsible for installing rulers over

Box 13.9

The Rhetoric of Romans

Paul's letter to the Romans often is examined with an interest in how the apostle chooses to make his points.

- He uses testimony lists of biblical citations, in which a string of verses are quoted in rapid succession (e.g., 3:10–18 quotes Ps. 14:1–3; Ps. 53:1–2; Ps. 5:9; Ps. 140:3; Ps. 10:7; Isa. 59:7–8; Ps. 36:1).
- He employs creative techniques of biblical interpretation (e.g., arguing in 4:9–12 that, since Abraham had not been circumcised when he first trusted in God, we must conclude that uncircumcised gentiles may be put right with God through faith).
- He draws on key concepts from Stoic philosophy, including his appeal to conscience (2:15) and to "natural law" (1:26).
- He employs a rhetorical style of argument known as "diatribe," responding to questions posed by an imaginary dialogue partner (e.g., 3:1; 6:1).
- He offers analogies from daily life to explain theological points (e.g., grafting a branch from a wild olive tree onto the root of a cultivated tree = incorporating gentiles into the people of God rooted in the history of Israel).

the kingdoms of the earth (Luke 4:4–5), and in the book of Acts, Christians declare, "We must obey God rather than any human authority" (Acts 5:29). The presupposition of Paul's counsel seems to be that the authorities to be respected are carrying out their divine mandate to administer justice, punishing wrongdoers and supporting those who do right (Rom. 13:3–4). Scholars often suggest that Paul wrote these words during the first half of the reign of the emperor Nero, when the Roman government was exercising relatively good behavior. Within a few years, that emperor would turn out to be a tyrant responsible for monstrous injustice, much of which was directed specifically against Christians. In fact, Paul himself would die as a martyr in the waves of persecution that this particular governing authority instituted.

Accommodation for the Weak

Paul's discussion of "the weak" and "the strong" in chapter 14 of Romans has become a touchstone for Christian ethics. Paul taught that the Jewish dietary laws were no longer relevant for those who were justified by faith; throughout his ministry he was adamant that such restrictions not be imposed upon gentiles (see Gal. 2:14). But now he deals with a complicating factor: if a person believes (erroneously) that eating certain foods is sinful, then it actually is sinful for that particular person to consume those foods (14:23). The strong in faith know that "nothing is unclean in itself" (14:14), but the weak in faith do not know this, and they should not be tempted or encouraged to do what they themselves believe is wrong. Those who are strong must not do anything that will prove to be a hindrance to those who are weak, even if this means giving up food that it would be appropriate for them to eat otherwise.

> EXPLORE 13.18
Romans 13:1–7—
Church and State:
The Ethic of
Subordination

Thus Paul counsels the Roman Christians to evaluate their behavior in broader terms than "what is acceptable or allowed." They must consider the effects that their actions have on others and strive to avoid doing anything that might be perceived as evil (14:16) or that might cause another to stumble (14:21). This matter also comes up in 1 Corinthians 8–10.

Why Not Sin?

In Romans, Paul addresses issues of sin and grace. If God forgives sin, someone might ask, why would anyone want to stop sinning? If there is no limit to God's grace, why not just "sin all the more, that grace may abound" (see 6:1)?

Paul thinks that these are questions that only an unconverted person would ask. Those who have actually received God's grace and been put right with God through faith know better. The will to sin has been broken: they have died to sin (6:2) and been freed from its hold over them (6:6–7).

Paul claims that his gospel actually provides a better motivation for obedience than the law ever did: inner renewal (12:2) rather than fear of condemnation (8:1). Those who have been reconciled with God through the death of Jesus are no longer God's enemies (5:10), and they may now be expected to offer themselves in obedience to God out of spiritual worship (12:1).

Even so, Paul reminds his readers that "no condemnation" (8:1) does not mean "no accountability" (14:12). We will still stand before the judgment seat of God (14:10).

Fig. 13.4. Olive tree. Paul says that gentile Christians have been joined to God's people Israel in the same way that branches from a wild olive tree can be grafted on to the trunk of a cultivated olive tree (Rom. 11:17–24). (Todd Bolen / BiblePlaces.com)

Box 13.11

Romans 8 in Classic Literature

Two verses from Paul's letter to the Romans:

- "We know that the whole creation has been groaning in labor pains until now" (8:22).
- "All things work together for good for those who love God, who are called according to his purpose" (8:28).

From *The Return of the Native* by Thomas Harvey (1878):

- Clym bemoans the travails of life: "I get up every morning and see the whole creation groaning and travailing in pain, as St. Paul says."

From *Wuthering Heights* by Emily Brontë (1847):

- Joseph the servant exclaims, "Thank Hivin for all! All warks togither for gooid tuh them as is chozzen, and piked aht forr' th' rubbidge! Yah knaw what t' Scripture ses."

Conclusion

A prominent Roman Catholic scholar once said that it would be only "a slight exaggeration to say that Western Christianity is divided into Catholic and Protestant churches today because of Paul's letter to the Romans and disputes over how it is to be interpreted" (Raymond E. Brown, *An Introduction to the New Testament* [New York: Doubleday, 1997], 559). In fact, the first Protestant textbook on Christian doctrine ever written organized its topics according to an outline of Romans (Philipp Melanchthon, *Loci communes*, published in 1521). In the twentieth century, the theological giant Karl Barth began his program of neoorthodoxy with a commentary on Romans (1933). And in the present day, Paul's letter to the Romans is usually regarded as "home base" for Lutheran theologians, though it is vigorously studied by Christians of all persuasions. The most widely used and highly respected critical commentaries on the letter include volumes by a Roman Catholic (Joseph Fitzmyer), two Methodists (James Dunn, Robert Jewett), and two Baptists (Douglas Moo, Thomas Schreiner). Clearly the letter has been a theological sounding board for Christians of all persuasions.

In addition to the themes touched on in this chapter, Paul's letter to "God's beloved in Rome" (1:7) gets consulted for theological questions regarding baptism (6:3–4), original sin (5:12–21), predestination (8:29–30; 9:11–12; 11:25–26), and numerous other subjects. Despite the heady character of this letter, however, faith was not just an intellectual exercise for Paul. He expects those who believe the gospel that he presents here to be "transformed by the renewing of [their] minds" (12:2). They will think differently about themselves (12:3), other believers (12:16), total strangers (12:13), and their enemies (12:19–21).

Paul certainly did not want his message to be a source of division: his plea (12:16) and prayer (15:5) is for his readers to "live in harmony with one another." There are some matters on which Christians can simply agree to disagree: "Let all be fully convinced in their own minds" (14:5). In any case, they should not pass judgment on one another (14:10–13) but rather must make every effort to live peaceably with all (12:18) so that all believers may "with one voice glorify the God and Father of our Lord Jesus Christ" (15:6).

FOR FURTHER READING: **Romans**

Cobb, John B., Jr., and David J. Lull. *Romans*. Chalice Commentaries for Today. St. Louis: Chalice, 2005.

Haacker, Klaus. *The Theology of Paul's Letter to the Romans*. New Testament Theology. Cambridge: Cambridge University Press, 2003.

Keck, Leander. *Romans*. Abingdon New Testament Commentaries. Nashville: Abingdon, 2005.

Lancaster, Sarah Heaner. *Romans: A Theological Commentary*. Belief Series. Louisville: Westminster John Knox, 2015.

Matera, Frank J. *Romans*. Paideia. Grand Rapids: Baker Academic, 2010.

Moo, Douglas J. *Encountering the Book of Romans: A Theological Survey*. 2nd ed. Encountering Biblical Studies. Grand Rapids: Baker Academic, 2014.

Talbert, Charles H. *Romans*. Smith & Helwys Bible Commentary. Macon, GA: Smyth & Helwys, 2002.

Thistleton, Anthony C. *Discovering Romans: Content, Interpretation, Reception*. Grand Rapids: Eerdmans, 2016.

Wright, N. T. *Paul for Everyone: Romans*. 2 vols. 2nd ed. Louisville: Westminster John Knox, 2005.

⊙ Go to www .IntroducingNT.com for summaries, videos, and other study tools.

14

1 Corinthians

Denominational politics, doctrinal disputes, liturgical preferences—why can't Christians just learn to get along? It is an old question, as old as Christianity itself. The letter in our New Testament called "1 Corinthians" reveals that church conflict is nothing new.

Paul's first letter to the Corinthians is perhaps best known for some of its individual passages. Many know it as "the book that gets read at weddings" (see 1 Cor. 13). Some think of it as "the book with all that stuff about speaking in tongues" (see 1 Cor. 12; 14). But taken as a whole, the letter may be popularly regarded as Paul's epistle to "that church with problems." All churches have problems, of course, but 1 Corinthians seems to deal with nothing but problems, one right after another. Some of those problems sound just like ones encountered in congregations today; others are linked to cultural situations that may seem foreign to modern readers.

It is a letter explicitly addressed to spiritual babies—Paul can give them only milk, since they are not ready for solid food (3:1–2). Students may think that this promises an easy read, but things are not that simple. For one thing, these are babies who are "sanctified in Christ Jesus, called to be saints" (1:2), which means that Paul has high expectations of them. He wants to offer them spiritual wisdom that surpasses anything discernible through mere human wisdom (2:13–14). They have tremendous potential: they have the "mind of Christ" (2:16; cf. Phil. 2:5).

A couple of other matters complicate our study of this letter. First, Paul apparently wrote several letters to this fractious church, some of which have been lost to us. The letter that we know as 1 Corinthians actually appears to be his second letter to the church—yes, that's confusing, but at least 1 Corinthians was written prior to the letter that we know as 2 Corinthians (so it is the first

saints: people who are holy; some New Testament writers use the word as a virtual synonym for "Christians."

of the letters that we still have). Our 2 Corinthians usually is identified as Paul's fourth letter to the church, at least in part, but let's leave that aside until our next chapter (if you can't wait, see the summary in box 15.1).

The Corinthians also wrote to Paul, but we do not have copies of what they sent him. Sometimes he seems to cite things that they said (6:12, 13; 7:1; 8:1, 4, 8; 9:4; 10:23; 14:22; possibly 14:34–35) and then responds by correcting or condemning their position (see box 14.1). Thus some verses in this letter express views that Paul wants his readers to reject rather than adopt. By paying attention to context, interpreters usually can tell which passages these are, but disagreements do occur, and such disagreements can lead to (you guessed it) church conflict.

Overview

After the customary opening (1:1–3) and thanksgiving (1:4–9), Paul takes up a few matters that have been brought to his attention by some members of the church whom he refers to as "Chloe's people" (1:11). The first of these is that there are factions in the church, with different members claiming to follow various human leaders (1:10–4:21). After dealing with this problem at length, Paul touches briefly on three other matters that Chloe's people probably reported to him: a man is living in a sexual relationship with his stepmother (5:1–13); members of the church are suing one another in secular courts (6:1–8); and some members evince an "anything goes" philosophy that justifies visiting prostitutes and other immoral behavior (6:9–20).

Paul turns next to questions that the Corinthians have asked him in a letter (7:1). First, he considers the question of whether sexual abstinence might not always be the best policy (even for married people), and he offers some extended teaching on marriage, divorce, and celibacy (7:1–40). Then he takes up the question of whether it is appropriate for Christians to eat food that was dedicated to idols, and this leads into a general discussion of Christian freedom and responsibility (8:1–11:1). Interposed into this latter discussion is an excursus in which Paul discusses his own rights as an apostle (9:1–14) and his decision to waive those rights (9:15–27). Finally, he turns his attention to several issues that have arisen with regard to Christian worship: the importance of head coverings for women (11:2–16), proper conduct at the Lord's Supper (11:17–34), and the role of spiritual gifts such as prophecy and speaking in tongues (12:1–14:40). Embedded in the discussion of spiritual gifts is a poetic ode to love (13:1–13).

Having addressed the questions presented to him, Paul continues to instruct the Corinthians regarding what he considers to be matters "of first importance" (15:3): the death, burial, and resurrection of Christ (15:1–58). Then he offers

⊘ EXPLORE 14.0
1 Corinthians: Outline of Contents

a few words regarding the collection that he is taking for Jerusalem (16:1–4) and concludes the letter with comments on travel plans (16:5–12) and some final exhortations and greetings (16:13–24).

Historical Background

In New Testament times, much of modern-day Greece was divided into two Roman provinces, Macedonia and Achaia (see map 14.1). The capital of Macedonia was Thessalonica, and the capital of Achaia was Corinth, one of the largest and most prosperous cities of the ancient world. Corinth, about fifty miles from Athens, often was viewed as a crass antithesis to that intellectual center. The city, after all, had been settled by freed slaves as recently as 44 BCE. A poet of the day summed up what may have been a popular sentiment: "What inhabitants, O luckless city, have you received? . . . Alas for the great calamity to Greece! . . . Such a crowd of scoundrelly slaves!" (Crinagoras, *Greek Anthology* 9.284).

Still, Corinth had what seemed to be an ideal location. The city was situated on a narrow strip of land: the Adriatic Sea lay to the west and the Aegean Sea to the east. Several Roman emperors proposed cutting a canal across the isthmus to allow ships to pass back and forth from Italy to Asia. The Corinthians

---

Box 14.1

Point/Counterpoint in 1 Corinthians

Paul is engaged in dialogue with the Corinthians, sometimes quoting things that they have said to him and then responding to them. His response qualifies or rejects the Corinthian viewpoint that he has just described. Here are a few examples:

	The Corinthians Say	Paul Responds
6:12	"All things are lawful."	"Not all things are beneficial."
6:13	"Food is meant for the stomach, and the stomach for food" (i.e., it is only natural to satisfy one's appetites).	"God will destroy both" (i.e., God will judge people who satisfy sinful appetites).
7:1–5	"It is well for a man not to touch a woman" (i.e., even married persons should practice celibacy).	Husbands and wives should grant each other "conjugal rights," lest there be temptation to sexual immorality.
8:1	"All of us possess knowledge."	"Knowledge puffs up, but love builds up."

For other examples, see 8:4, 8; 9:4; 10:23. Some scholars also think that the words about women keeping silent in church in 14:34–35 describe the Corinthians' own view rather than that of Paul (whose responses would then come in 14:36); otherwise, those comments seem to be in tension with 1 Corinthians 11:5, Paul's attitude in Galatians 3:28, and reports in Acts 2:17–18; 21:9.

Fig. 14.1. The city of Corinth. (Balage Balogh / www.archaeologyillustrated.com)

would have loved that, but in the meantime they did the next best thing. They established ports on either side of their little strip of land with a very nice road (called the "Diolkos") between them. A ship could unload at either port and have its cargo and crew transferred by land to another ship just nine miles away. In fact, smaller ships were sometimes hoisted out of the water and pulled along the road on rollers to be deposited back into the ocean on the other side. Although this was labor intensive, many trading companies considered the Corinthian option preferable to sending their ships all the way around Achaia by way of the Mediterranean Sea.

Corinth was famous for a number of other things. The city produced a metal compound called "Corinthian bronze" that was highly valued. It hosted an annual competition, the Isthmian games, which was second only to the Olympian games in popularity. Corinth also prided itself on being a haven for the newly rich, offering enterprising men and women their best shot at upward social mobility. Further, Corinth was proud of its reputation as a city that was open to new ideas and tolerant of diversity. By New Testament times, the city of Corinth had come to be associated with lavish lifestyles and conspicuous consumption. It was also famous for its amusements: theaters, temples, casinos, and brothels. Throughout the empire, the expression "to act like a Corinthian" came to be Roman slang for engaging in sexual promiscuity (Crinagoras, *Greek Anthology* 9.284).

⊙ EXPLORE 14.10
Corinthian Bronze

Map 14.1. Achaia.

According to the book of Acts, Paul stayed in Corinth for at least eighteen months on his second missionary journey, when Gallio was the proconsul there (18:1–17). This places his sojourn in the city somewhere between 50 and 53. He lived with Aquila and Priscilla, a married couple with whom he apparently had a lot in common: they were Jewish Christians, and, like Paul, they made their living as tentmakers or leatherworkers (Acts 18:2–3; cf. 1 Cor. 16:19). Paul evangelized the city with his companions Silas (sometimes called "Silvanus") and Timothy (Acts 18:5; 2 Cor. 1:19). The congregation that emerged was diverse ethnically and socially. Most of Paul's converts were gentiles (1 Cor. 12:2), but not all. Crispus (1 Cor. 1:14; cf. Acts 18:8) and Sosthenes (1 Cor. 1:1; cf. Acts 18:17) had been leaders of Jewish synagogues. Most of the Corinthian Christians also appear to have come from the lower classes (1 Cor. 1:26), but not all. Gaius (1 Cor. 1:14) had a house big enough to host gatherings of the entire church (Rom. 16:23), and Erastus was the city treasurer (Rom. 16:23; 2 Tim. 4:20). As we will see, the social integration of persons from different ethnic groups and economic classes may have been one significant cause of conflict in the church.

Sometime after founding the church, Paul wrote the Corinthians a letter to which he makes brief reference in 1 Corinthians 5:9 (see box 15.1). We know almost nothing about this "lost letter," except that one thing Paul told the Corinthians in the letter was to avoid association with sexually immoral people (by which he meant immoral Christians). In any case, Paul heard back from them

Fig. 14.2. The Corinthian canal—then and now. Corinth is situated on a narrow strip of land separating the Aegean Sea from the Adriatic Sea. In Paul's day, boats sometimes were put on rollers and hauled across the land for nine miles. Many centuries later (in 1893), a canal was finally dug, fulfilling a plan that had been proposed but never carried out by numerous Roman emperors. (*top*, Craig Koester; *bottom*, Todd Bolen / BiblePlaces.com)

Box 14.2

Say What? Some Puzzles in 1 Corinthians

Some matters discussed in 1 Corinthians are baffling to scholars and casual Bible readers alike.

- Paul says that women should wear head coverings in church as "a symbol of authority . . . because of the angels" (11:10). What do the angels have to do with it? Is Paul afraid that the angels might lust after the earth women (cf. Gen. 6:4)? Are these good angels or bad angels (demons)? Or are human messengers being referred to as angels? Many theories have been advanced, but no one knows for sure what this means.
- Paul refers to people "who receive baptism on behalf of the dead" (15:29). What was this ritual, and what was it meant to accomplish? Was it a vicarious baptism for people who had already died? Was Paul for it or against it? A "baptism for the dead" is practiced today among Mormons but not by any other group that views 1 Corinthians as Scripture. One reason: no one knows for sure what Paul is talking about.

in two ways. First, he received a visit from some folks he refers to as "Chloe's people" (1:11)—possibly servants or family members of a woman who was a member of the church. Second, he received a letter from the church asking him questions about a number of matters (see 7:1, 25; 8:1, 4; 12:1; 16:1, 12). This letter appears to have been hand-delivered by three church members—Stephanas, Fortunatus, and Achaicus (16:15–18)—who no doubt supplied some information orally as well. In response to these reports, Paul wrote the letter that we know as 1 Corinthians (though it was actually his second letter to the church). He was in Ephesus at the time (16:8), and our best guess places the year of composition somewhere between 53 and 57. The letter is cowritten with Sosthenes (1:1), who, according to the book of Acts, had been beaten publicly by an angry mob when the proconsul Gallio had refused to rule against Paul on his initial visit to the city (Acts 18:12–17).

Major Themes in 1 Corinthians

Church Unity

Paul is concerned that there are divisions in the church (1:10–11; 11:18–19). Members identify themselves in terms of allegiance to one or another prominent leader. Some identify themselves as disciples of Paul, though he has not authorized them to do so (1:12; 3:4); others follow Apollos (1:12; 3:4–6, 22; 4:6; 16:12; cf. Acts 18:24–19:1; Titus 3:13) or Peter, here called "Cephas" (1:12; 3:22; 9:5; 15:5; cf. Gal. 2:7–9, 11–14). Paul does not side with "the Paul party" but rather condemns all factions for placing too much attention on mere human beings (3:5–7, 21–23), which inevitably leads to "jealousy and quarreling" (3:3). In contrast to this image of a divided church, Paul offers two images of his

Cephas: an Aramaic word meaning "Rock," the Greek form of which is "Peter"; a nickname given by Jesus to Simon, one of his disciples.

own. First, the congregation should know that it is "God's temple" (3:16–17); God's Holy Spirit dwells in the community as a whole. There is only one Spirit, given to all, and whatever one individual or faction does to destroy the unity of the congregation is an assault on God's holy dwelling place. Second, Paul says that the church is "the body of Christ" and the individual members are like various body parts: hands, feet, ears, eyes (12:12–27; cf. Rom. 12:4–5; Eph. 4:14–16). The parts are quite different from one another, but all are needed and important. Thus Paul presents the unity of the church not as an ideal or goal to be realized but rather as an accomplished reality that needs to be recognized (12:27): all individuals (and various factions) are connected to one another whether they know it or not (and whether they like it or not). When any one part of the body suffers, the whole body is affected. The church must learn to act as the unified entity that it actually is.

Wisdom and Power

Paul is troubled that the Corinthians are enamored of worldly wisdom and power. In fact, this may be a root cause for the divisions in the church: the Corinthians seek to identify with the human leaders whom they regard as the most wise and powerful. This matter will come up again in 2 Corinthians, where Paul takes on a group of interlopers who made a big splash in this congregation apparently by flaunting their wisdom and power as signs of divine blessing and authority (2 Cor. 10–12). The bottom line, Paul insists in 1 Corinthians, is that what God considers wise and strong does not accord with the world's judgments on such matters (1:19–20). Exhibit A is "Christ crucified" (1:23–24): God's greatest act of wisdom and power was accomplished by what appears to the world to be an exhibition of weakness and folly (1:18; cf. 2 Cor. 13:4). The cross of Christ alone should be enough to get the Corinthians to rethink their value system, but Paul suggests that they also take a good look at themselves: they are not the wisest or most powerful people around, yet God chose them (1:26–27). Finally, he offers himself as an example: he is not ashamed to admit that he is a fool (4:9–10; cf. 2 Cor. 11:16–17) and a weakling (2:3; 4:9–10; cf. 2 Cor. 10:10; 11:30; 12:5, 9–10; 13:4, 9) by worldly standards. All of these considerations reveal a God who prizes what the world rejects, who works through what the world regards as weak and foolish (1:18–29; 2:14; 3:18–20; cf. 2 Cor. 12:9–10; 13:4). The Corinthians' high evaluation of wisdom and power represents a fundamental misunderstanding of the gospel.

Christ crucified: the main focus of Paul's preaching according to 1 Corinthians 1:22–24; 2:1–2; the phrase seems to be shorthand for what theologians call a "theology of the cross" (*theologia crucis*).

Christ Crucified

⊙ EXPLORE 14.18
1 Corinthians 3:16; 6:19–20—Temple of God Imagery

Paul says that when he was with the Corinthians, he decided to know nothing among them "except Jesus Christ, and him crucified" (2:2; cf. 1:23; 11:26).

Many interpreters have noted that if this really was the case, his congregation didn't seem to get the message. They at least failed to realize what the message of the cross means for their daily lives. As people who experienced miracles (12:10, 28; cf. 2 Cor. 12:12) and received all sorts of exciting spiritual gifts (1:7; 2:12; 12:4–10), the Corinthians seemed to think that they were already enjoying the full benefits of salvation, living a glorious life that could be characterized by freedom from want or trouble. Paul mocks such attitudes, addressing those whom he knows to be spiritual infants (3:1) with sarcasm: "Already you have all you want! Already you have become rich!" (4:8). Look at yourselves, he tells them. You live like kings because of Christ! Not like us poor apostles, who have to suffer hardship for the sake of the gospel. Not you! We are treated like garbage in this world, but you are like kings (4:8–13)! In reality, Paul thinks that Christians live in a world where the forces of evil remain powerful (5:5; 7:5; 8:5; 10:20–21; cf. 2 Cor. 2:11; 4:4; 11:14–15; 12:7), the experience of God's presence is limited (7:7; 8:2; 13:9, 12; 15:50, 53; cf. 2 Cor. 5:6), temptations to sin are rampant (7:28; 10:12; cf. 2 Cor. 11:3; 12:21), and hardship and suffering are to be expected (15:30–32; cf. 2 Cor. 1:8–9; 4:7–12; 6:4–5; 7:5; 8:2; 11:23–29; 12:7, 10). The problem, Paul says, is that the Corinthians are intent on identifying only with the risen Christ, not with the crucified Christ. Paul makes clear elsewhere that life in the present world is marked by a participation in the death of Jesus (Rom. 6:3–5; Gal. 2:19–20; Phil. 3:10; cf. 1 Cor. 11:26; 15:31; 2 Cor. 1:5–6; 4:8–12). That is why he decided to know nothing among them but "Christ crucified": the message of the cross was what they needed to hear.

Resurrection of the Body

Chapter 15 of 1 Corinthians is often regarded as a theological high point of the New Testament. Paul waxes eloquent about the resurrection of Christ, providing a list of historical witnesses to that event (15:5–8) and claiming that if Christ had not been raised, then preaching would be vain, faith would be futile, people would still be in their sins (15:14–17), and Christians would be the most pitiable people on earth (15:19). The point that Paul really wants to make, however, is not simply that Christ rose from the dead but that he did so as the "firstfruits" of a resurrection that eventually will include all who belong to him (15:23). One major concern for Paul is to show that those who have died in Christ have not perished (15:18). Death has lost its sting (15:54–57) because, as the final and ultimate enemy of God, death will be destroyed in the victorious reign of Christ (15:24–26). But Paul also insists that this will be a resurrection of the body, not just the soul or spirit. The actual bodies of believers will be raised and transformed from something perishable to something imperishable (15:35–54).

firstfruits: an agricultural term for crops collected at the beginning of the harvest season; Jesus is called the "firstfruits of the resurrection" because his resurrection is thought to precede and anticipate the general resurrection of all.

⊙ EXPLORE 14.14
A Practical Question about Resurrection

Fig. 14.3. One body in Christ. Paul tells the Corinthians that they are interconnected in Christ (1 Cor. 12:1–27). (The Bridgeman Art Library International)

This is a very important point for Paul, and we might wonder why it demands so much attention. It is possible that some of the Corinthians interpreted resurrection as a spiritual experience in which people could participate here and now—an exaltation to a higher plane of spiritual living that they believed had become a reality (4:8–13; 15:12, 19). Paul will return to this theme in 2 Corinthians, where he says that Christians are like fragile jars of clay that contain a precious treasure (2 Cor. 4:7). The outer shell—the human body—is frail, subject to decay, temptation, sickness, and pain. How can anyone living in such a body claim to have already attained some heavenly plane of existence? Rather, believers currently live under a burden, longing to be clothed with heavenly glorified bodies (2 Cor. 5:1–10). In 1 Corinthians, Paul says that Christ's resurrection grants assurance that they will be so clothed; just as Christ was raised with a new, transformed body, so all who belong to him will be raised with new bodies that are glorious, powerful, spiritual, and immortal (15:43–44, 53–54). But this will happen at Christ's second coming, not before (15:23, 51–52). By failing to understand that resurrection is future (15:20–34) and corporeal (15:35–50), the Corinthians have exaggerated the benefits of their current situation and failed to grasp the significance of what God ultimately has in store for them. The doctrine also has practical consequences: those who do not believe in a resurrection of the body are likely to lapse into moral indifference, but those who do believe in such a resurrection will persevere and remain faithful, even when experiencing trials (15:32).

Christian Freedom

Paul addresses what he considers to be an egregious misunderstanding of Christian freedom, which some Corinthians have interpreted as license to do as they please. Some of them apparently go to prostitutes (6:16–18), and one member of the church is living in an incestuous relationship with his stepmother (5:1). The latter incident actually seems to have become an occasion for boasting (5:2, 6). Why would the congregation be proud of a church member openly doing what most people in the world would have regarded as immoral? The likely answer is that some of the Corinthians construe such permissiveness as a radical enactment of the gospel. "All things are lawful for me!" they say (6:12; cf. 10:23). Where would they have gotten such a notion? It is possible that they got it from Paul himself. In some of his other letters Paul does talk about Christians being free from the law (Rom. 4:15; 6:14; 7:4, 6; 10:4; Gal. 3:24; 5:18). In those passages, however, his point is that Christian behavior is not to be equated with simply obeying rules: Christians live by the Spirit in a new covenant of grace, and they do what is right because it is right, not just because it is required. The Corinthians, it seems, heard only half of what Paul said and missed the point. In any case, he now clarifies his position: the question a Christian should ask is not "Am I allowed to do this?" but rather "Is this a good thing to do?" Even if all things are lawful (allowed), the Christian wants to do only those things that are beneficial (6:12), that build up the community (10:23), and that bring glory to God (6:20). Paul also notes, with some irony, that the Corinthian concept of freedom leads to what is actually bondage: those who adopt a "do as you please" attitude toward life end up becoming slaves to their own passions, dominated by compulsive desires that are neither fulfilling nor healthy (6:12).

the law: "the law of Moses" or any regulations that the Jewish people understood as delineating faithfulness to God in terms of the covenant that God made with Israel.

Some Practical Matters

The Lord's Supper

The community gathers regularly for a common meal or "love feast" (cf. Jude 12) at which the Lord's Supper is observed (11:17–34). This is a full meal—sort of like a potluck dinner with the Lord's Supper at the end. The food, however, is not getting distributed equitably (11:21). Why not? There could be many reasons, but since Paul says that they should "wait for one another" (11:33), many interpreters think that the problem arose from people arriving at different times and eating in shifts. The wealthier members of the church came early and shared with one another whatever they had brought. Members of the lower classes, who labored until dark, came later, bringing whatever meager contributions they could afford. They arrived to find that the elite had already enjoyed a nice banquet and were sated with expensive food and sometimes drunk on fine spirits (11:21). There might be some leftovers, but the second-shift meal for latecomers (probably the great majority of the congregation) was a decidedly lower-class affair. This may have seemed appropriate to those familiar with Greco-Roman banquets, at which servants always ate separately and considered it a privilege to receive scraps from the feast as a supplement to what they would have had otherwise. Paul, however, thinks that replicating such inequities at this meal shows "contempt for the church of God" (11:22). He is appalled that a meal meant to be eaten in remembrance of Jesus (11:24) has become an occasion for humiliating the poor (11:22). The meal is intended to mark the institution of a new covenant (11:25), and the sharing (Greek, *koinōnia*) of the bread and wine is to be done in a way that conveys unity, not division (10:16–17).

Excommunication

In 1 Corinthians 5 Paul instructs the church regarding one of their members, a man who is living in a sinful relationship: "Drive out the wicked person from among you!" (5:13). They should not associate with him anymore; they should not even eat with him (5:11). Paul indicates that excluding this man from Christian fellowship will be tantamount to handing him over to Satan "for the destruction of the flesh" (5:5), by which he may mean that the person will no longer be under God's protection, and so his flesh will be more susceptible to the ravages of disease and death (cf. 11:30). Paul hopes that this drastic action will bring about the

---

Box 14.3

Better to Marry Than to Burn

In 1 Corinthians 7:9 Paul counsels young people to marry if they are not able to practice self-control. It is "better to marry than to burn" (KJV; or, in the NRSV translation, "to be aflame with passion").

Chaucer uses the line to somewhat humorous effect in his famous *Canterbury Tales* (3.49–52). The sassy and oft-widowed Wife of Bath justifies her need for a sixth marriage:

> ". . . th' apostle seith that I am free
> To wedde, a Goddes half, where it liketh me.
> He seith that to be wedded is no synne;
> Bet is to be wedded than to brynne."

repentance necessary for the man to be saved (5:5), but his broader concern is to preserve the purity of the community as a whole (5:6–7). If these words seem harsh, they may be only a sample of the sorts of punishment that Paul threatens to mete out when he visits the congregation (4:18–21; cf. 2 Cor. 12:20–13:4).

Within Christianity, the practice of expelling unrepentant persons from the church (and sometimes ostracizing them socially) is called "excommunication" because the excluded persons are no longer allowed to commune or partake of the Lord's Supper. Christian churches typically cite 1 Corinthians 5 as theological justification for the practice and refer to Matthew 18:15–17 as outlining a procedure by which the disciplinary removal is to be carried out (see also 2 Cor. 2:6–11; Gal. 6:1).

Sexual Morality

Paul considers numerous matters related to sexual conduct in 1 Corinthians (especially in chaps. 5–7, but also 10:8). Talk about a divisive issue! There are people in this church who see nothing wrong with having sex with prostitutes (6:15–18), and there are people who think that having sex is always wrong, even for married couples (7:1). What these extremists have in common is a commitment to being spiritual. Some of the Corinthians apparently think that Christians can do as they please with their bodies, since the spirit is all that matters; others claim that Christians should try to avoid anything that involves the flesh, since only spiritual activities bring glory to God. One group seems to regard fleshly bodies as irrelevant, while the other seems to regard them as inherently dirty or bad. Paul rejects both positions: bodies do matter (6:13, 15, 19), and they are not intrinsically bad—they can be used for God's glory (6:20). Ultimately, Paul thinks that the Corinthians' misplaced values regarding sexual matters stem from a misguided understanding of spirituality, one that could be corrected if they understood his teaching on resurrection of the body (see "Resurrection of the Body" above). In the middle of his discussion of sexual matters he suddenly declares, "God raised the Lord and will also raise us" (6:14). His point is that the risen Christ is the firstfruits of a resurrection that will involve transformed bodies, not just liberated souls. This indicates that "the Lord is for the body" (contra those who think that the body is bad) and "the body is for the Lord" (contra those who think that the body is irrelevant) (6:13).

Paul's basic stance is that sexual relations are acceptable only within marriage (7:2) but that within marriage sexual relations are not to be denied (7:3–4). He also takes the following positions:

⊙ EXPLORE 14.7
Divorce in 1 Corinthians and in the Bible

- *Celibacy* is preferable to marriage (7:6–8, 25–28, 32–34, 37–38, 39–40), but it requires the gift of being able to maintain sexual abstinence (7:7, 9, 36).

- *Divorce* is to be avoided if at all possible (7:10–13, 16), and when it does occur, the divorced persons should remain unmarried unless they reconcile (7:11).
- *Marriage* should be between believers ("in the Lord" [7:39]), but if one ends up married to an unbeliever, that union should stand unless the unbeliever ends it (7:12–16).

In discussing these matters, Paul keeps in mind biblical commandments (7:19) and draws on sayings of Jesus (7:10). He also offers what are simply his own opinions (7:12, 25), albeit the opinions of one who claims to have the Spirit of God (7:25, 40). He appears to be operating with at least three guiding principles: (1) the personal conduct of individual Christians affects the community as a whole; (2) Christians are to live as persons who assume that the

Fig. 14.4. Marketplace at Corinth. In Paul's day the streets of Corinth were lined with small shops like this one. It is likely that Paul used such a shop for his tent-making and leather-working business. In addition, it was in shops like these that controversial "idol meat" was sold. Jews and Christians knew that animals often were butchered in sacrificial rites at local temples, and buyers could not know for certain that meat sold in the marketplace had not come from such a sacrifice. (Craig Koester)

Lord is coming soon (7:29–31); and (3) Christians ought to make decisions in light of what will enable them to be of greatest service to the Lord (7:32–35).

Food Sacrificed to Idols

Paul devotes considerable attention to the question of whether Christians should eat food sacrificed to idols (chaps. 8–10). There may be a couple of different issues involved here. In Roman society the gods were blessed and propitiated at virtually all public events, including birthdays, weddings, banquets, business parties, and other affairs that Christians who had any dealings with non-Christians might be invited to attend. Paul does not think that Christians should remain aloof from people outside the church (5:10) or adopt judgmental attitudes toward them (5:12). Still, he sounds a word of caution with regard to participation in pagan social activities. He believes that offering sacrifices to pagan gods is like sacrificing to demons and doing so has a powerful and negative effect on the person involved (8:4–5; 10:20). Just as Christians share in the body and blood of Christ when they consume bread and wine at the Lord's Supper, so they may become partners with demons if they eat and drink food at a meal that involves the worship of idols (10:14–22).

A related matter concerns the consumption of food bought in the general marketplace. Almost all the meat sold in the Roman markets came from animals slaughtered in homage to some god. This made sense: if an animal was going to be killed anyway, why not butcher it as a sacrifice to an idol and score a few points with the deity for which that idol stood? Many Jews refused to purchase or consume such food, instead obtaining their meat from "kosher shops." The question for the Corinthian Christians was, "Should we be as scrupulous as Jews on this matter?" Paul thinks that food is basically just food, and Christians who do not acknowledge the pagan idols or gods should be able to eat meat from the general market with a clear conscience (10:25–27). Still, he qualifies this advice with a special concern: those whose faith is strong enough to eat the "idol food" without acknowledging the idols must be sensitive to believers whose faith is not so strong (8:7, 9). Those who know that there is nothing intrinsically wrong with eating "idol meat" should nevertheless give up their right to eat such food if doing so would compromise their witness to unbelievers, scandalize other Christians, or tempt less mature converts to become involved in what, for them, actually would be pagan worship (8:10–13; 10:27–28, 32–33).

This willingness to give up one's rights for the sake of others may be Paul's dominant concern with regard to this whole "food sacrificed to idols" controversy. He begins his discussion of the topic by insisting that love must trump knowledge as a guide to Christian behavior (8:1–3), and he ends it with an exhortation for those with superior knowledge to seek what is advantageous to others, not themselves (12:24, 31). In the middle he embarks on a long excursus

idol food: food available for consumption that had been used in a sacrifice to a pagan god or idol.

pagan: Greco-Roman religion and culture as viewed from the perspective of Jews and Christians, who tended to associate what was "pagan" with erratic religious beliefs and an immoral lifestyle.

Box 14.4

1 Corinthians 13—King James Version

[1]Though I speak with the tongues of men and of angels, and have not charity, I am become as sounding brass, or a tinkling cymbal.

[2]And though I have *the gift of* prophecy, and understand all mysteries, and all knowledge; and though I have all faith, so that I could remove mountains, and have not charity, I am nothing.

[3]And though I bestow all my goods to feed *the poor*, and though I give my body to be burned, and have not charity, it profiteth me nothing.

[4]Charity suffereth long, *and* is kind; charity envieth not; charity vaunteth not itself, is not puffed up,

[5]Doth not behave itself unseemly, seeketh not her own, is not easily provoked, thinketh no evil; [6]Rejoiceth not in iniquity, but rejoiceth in the truth;

[7]Beareth all things, believeth all things, hopeth all things, endureth all things.

[8]Charity never faileth: but whether *there be* prophecies, they shall fail; whether *there be* tongues, they shall cease; whether *there be* knowledge, it shall vanish away.

[9]For we know in part, and we prophesy in part.

[10]But when that which is perfect is come, then that which is in part shall be done away.

[11]When I was a child, I spake as a child, I understood as a child, I thought as a child: but when I became a man, I put away childish things.

[12]For now we see through a glass, darkly; but then face to face: now I know in part; but then shall I know even as also I am known.

[13]And now abideth faith, hope, charity, these three; but the greatest of these *is* charity.

regarding his own rights as an apostle. He has the right to be married (like Peter and the other apostles), but he surrenders this for the sake of his mission (9:5). He has the right to be paid a salary by the Corinthians, but he has foregone that as well (9:6–14). The Corinthians who don't think they should have to give up good market food just because others are unperceptive might want to think twice before telling *him*, "We have a right to our food and drink" (9:4). His life bears witness to the deeper recognition that being a Christian is not a matter of insisting on one's rights (9:12, 15, 18); rather, it is a matter of doing whatever is necessary "for the sake of the gospel" (9:23) and of doing everything "for the glory of God" (10:31).

Love

One of the best-known and most beloved passages in all of scripture is 1 Corinthians 13, a poetic tribute to love. The Greek word for "love" used here is *agapē*. It refers to love that is not necessarily dependent on the loveliness of its object and that in fact confers goodness on that object: the beloved becomes lovely by virtue of being loved.

Paul defines this love in terms of unselfish behavior. One shows *agapē* love by treating other people in ways that put their interests ahead of one's own (13:4–7).

Without such love nothing else matters, for all human achievements and knowledge are only transitory (13:1–3, 8–12). Only three things unite humans with God throughout eternity: faith, hope, and love—and the greatest of these is love (13:13).

Like Psalm 23, this chapter of Paul's letter to the Corinthians is treasured for its literary and artistic beauty. As such, it often is cited in the traditional language of the King James Version, which translates *agapē* as "charity" rather than "love" (see box 14.4).

Spiritual Gifts

Paul devotes three chapters of this letter to a discussion of "spiritual gifts," by which he seems to mean manifestations of the Holy Spirit (12:7) activated by God (12:6) in the lives of individual church members (12:11) for the common good (12:7). Paul can speak of "gifts" (Greek, *charismata*) in a broader sense to encompass many things: it is a gift when God enables one to practice sexual abstinence (7:7) or endows people with attributes that qualify them to be

Fig. 14.5. Singing in the Spirit. This depiction of Pentecostal worship displays a scene that is lively yet orderly. So Paul's words in 1 Corinthians encourage singing praises with both mind and spirit (14:15) and envision a liturgy in which hymns and Scripture lessons are interspersed with messages from people who speak in tongues and/or deliver prophetic revelations (14:26–33). (Bridgeman Images)

leaders in the church (12:28; cf. Rom. 12:6–8). The focus of 1 Corinthians 12–14, however, seems to be on something more specific: the gifts he is talking about here are typically exercised when the church comes together (14:26) and God speaks or acts in remarkable ways through various individuals for the edification of the community (7:7; 14:12, 26–27, 29–30). Paul lists nine of these gifts: the utterance of wisdom, the utterance of knowledge, faith, healing, the working of miracles, prophecy, the discernment of spirits, various kinds of tongues, and

⊘ EXPLORE 14.8
Spiritual Gifts in 1 Corinthians and the New Testament

speaking in
tongues (glos-
solalia): the phe-
nomenon by which
the Spirit enables a
person to speak in
known languages
that the speaker has
never learned (e.g.,
Acts 2:4–8) or in
ecstatic languages
unintelligible to any
who do not possess
the gift of interpre-
tation (e.g., 1 Cor.
14:26–28).

the interpretation of tongues (12:8–10). Of these, the gift of tongues receives the most attention because it is the one that has been a source of controversy within the church.

The topic of speaking in tongues (glossolalia) also comes up in the book of Acts (2:4; 10:46; 19:6), though the phenomenon described there may be somewhat different from what is mentioned in 1 Corinthians. In Acts believers are miraculously inspired to speak in languages that they have never learned but that are understandable to hearers who know these languages (2:6–7), whereas in 1 Corinthians there is no indication that the "tongues" are potentially recognizable languages (14:2, 9, 23)—the ecstatic speech may in fact be regarded as the language of angels (13:1), unintelligible to any human being. Further, the incidents of speaking in tongues in Acts appear to have been single occurrences; there is no indication in Acts that those who spoke in tongues on any one occasion ever did so again. In 1 Corinthians, however, those who possess this gift seem to be able to speak in tongues any time they choose (14:15, 18, 27).

We are not sure why the gift of tongues has become problematic in Corinth. Possibly it is being exercised in ways that are disruptive to worship, or perhaps those who are exercising the gift are trying to show off how spiritual they are. It seems also that some people in the community are overreacting to these problems by trying to prohibit speaking in tongues altogether (14:39). In any case, it is no accident that Paul interrupts his discussion of spiritual gifts twice, once to present his stirring analogy of the church as the diverse but unified body of Christ (12:22–27), and a second time to extol love as the "more excellent way" (12:31) without which nothing else matters (13:1–13).

As for more specific counsel on the spiritual gifts, Paul says that the public exercise of such gifts should edify the whole community (12:7; 14:12, 26). This basically excludes tongues, since unintelligible messages are intrinsically unedifying (14:2, 4, 6–11, 16–19, 23). There is also some concern about how ecstatic speech will be perceived by unbelievers (14:23; cf. Acts 2:13). Paul does, however, allow the public use of tongues when someone is present who possesses the gift of being able to interpret the divine language (14:5, 13, 26–27). And he not only allows but also encourages speaking in tongues in private for the purpose of self-edification (14:4–5). He himself speaks in tongues, more than any of them (14:18), and his wish is for them all to do so as well (14:5). Still, those who have been showing off their spiritual prowess by delivering ecstatic but unintelligible messages to the community would do well to seek "the greater gifts" (12:31)—those that better serve the community. Prophecy (speaking God's word in normal, understandable words) may be less exotic, but it is generally more helpful (14:1–5, 22–25, 29). And, as a bottom line, Paul simply insists that everything be done "decently and in order" (14:40) because "God is not a God of disorder but of peace" (14:33).

⊙ EXPLORE 14.9
Speaking in Tongues
in 1 Corinthians and
Acts

Conclusion

Paul's first letter to the Corinthians is almost as long as his letter to the Romans and, along with that letter, is regarded as one of his major works. To some extent, Romans is more theoretical, presenting key theological ideas in a fairly systematic way; 1 Corinthians is more practical, focused on specific issues that have arisen in a particular context. Taken together, the letters offer us a portrait of Paul as theologian and pastor, and what stands out is how interconnected those roles are for him: Romans reveals him to be pastoral in addressing theological issues, and 1 Corinthians reveals him to be theological in dealing with pastoral concerns.

But Paul's adventures with the Corinthians have only just begun! After writing 1 Corinthians he would visit the church again, write them at least two more letters, and continue to grapple with their problems (which, unfortunately, did not subside but actually grew worse). Eventually he would spend a considerable amount of time in the city, for it was from Corinth that he would write his letter to the Romans. If problems still existed in the church at that point, he does not mention them to the Roman Christians; he does, however, warn the church in Rome to "keep an eye on those who cause dissensions and offenses" (Rom. 16:17). Apparently he has seen enough conflict in Corinth to last him a lifetime. Nip that stuff in the bud, he tells the Romans. Otherwise, it could be Corinth all over again.

pastoral concern: concern for the physical, emotional, and spiritual well-being of persons for whom one feels responsible.

FOR FURTHER READING: 1 Corinthians

Crocker, Cornelia Cyss. *Reading 1 Corinthians in the Twenty-First Century*. New York: T&T Clark International, 2004.

Furnish, Victor Paul. *The Theology of the First Letter to the Corinthians*. New Testament Theology. Cambridge: Cambridge University Press, 1999.

Keener, Craig S. *1–2 Corinthians*. New Cambridge Bible Commentary. New York: Cambridge University Press, 2005.

Lull, David. *1 Corinthians*. Chalice Commentaries for Today. St. Louis: Chalice, 2007.

Perkins, Pheme. *First Corinthians*. Paideia. Grand Rapids: Baker Academic, 2012.

Proctor, John. *First and Second Corinthians*. Westminster Bible Companion. Louisville: Westminster John Knox, 2015.

Talbert, Charles H. *Reading Corinthians: A Literary and Theological Commentary*. Rev. ed. Reading the New Testament. Macon, GA: Smyth & Helwys, 2002.

Wright, N. T. *Paul for Everyone: 1 Corinthians*. 2nd ed. Louisville: Westminster John Knox, 2004.

⊙ Go to www .IntroducingNT.com for summaries, videos, and other study tools.

15

2 Corinthians

Sequels can be disappointing. There is a blockbuster Hollywood movie, and next summer we get a lackluster follow-up. There is a breakthrough rock album, and a year later the band delivers its "sophomore slump."

About a year after writing 1 Corinthians, another letter emerged from the pen of the apostle Paul, a letter that we know as 2 Corinthians. It has all the marks of a typical sequel: hasty production and sloppy composition. A book review editor for the *Corinthian Post* may have thought that the apostle had lost his touch. The former letter (1 Corinthians) was organized topically, whereas this one seems to wander all over the place: Paul jumps around in his thinking, goes off on tangents, and then returns to finish a point that we had almost forgotten about. The letter is also marked by abrupt changes in tone: Paul is hurt (2:1–4), happy (7:13–16), hopeful (1:7, 10), and horrified (11:13–21). Why can't he just pick a mood and stick with it?

Some people think that 2 Corinthians was written on the move, that Paul dictated it over a period of days or weeks, responding as the occasion suited him. Others think that 2 Corinthians is not a letter at all but rather a compilation of bits and pieces from various letters that Paul wrote at different times, in which case (to use our Hollywood sequel analogy) there may have been many deleted scenes that ended up on the cutting-room floor.

The bottom line, however, is that 2 Corinthians has not been a disappointment to scholars, ministers, or everyday Christians. It has become one of Paul's most read and studied works. There are passages of incredible beauty, such as the opening prayer in 1:3–7 and the testimony to Christian hope in 4:16–5:5. And there are rich theological passages, including some of the Bible's earliest references to the preexistence (8:9) and divinity of Christ (4:4) and to the work

preexistence: the Christian doctrine that the person now known as Jesus Christ existed (as the Son of God) before he became the man Jesus who lived and died on earth.

of God that is accomplished through him (5:17–19). It's enough to make us wish we had sequels to all of Paul's letters.

Overview

The letter begins with a typical opening (1:1–2) and prayer (1:3–7), to which Paul appends a brief report on how God delivered him and his companions from a terrible ordeal that they faced in the Roman province of Asia (1:8–11). After this he offers a somewhat defensive explanation for his recent dealings with the church, including his rationale for canceling a promised visit and for writing them an unusually harsh letter instead (1:12–2:13). This leads to an extended commentary on what Paul considers to be the meaning and value of his ministry among the Corinthians (2:14–6:13). Paul discusses both the character and the content of that ministry, emphasizing what God has accomplished through him and his associates. Then he exhorts the Corinthians to avoid partnerships with unbelievers (6:14–7:1), insists that he has always had their best interests at heart (7:2–4), and returns at last to the subject of his recent relations with the community (7:5–16, picking up from 2:13): he rejoices that the difficult letter that he sent them did bring them to repentance, and he affirms his newfound confidence in them. On a new note, Paul takes up the subject of the collection that he is taking for Jerusalem, and he offers a number of incentives for his readers to contribute generously to this cause (8:1–9:15). Then the tone of the letter changes abruptly as he returns to a lengthy defense of his ministry, employing bitter sarcasm as he compares himself to a group of "super-apostles" (11:5; 12:11) who have maligned him in the Corinthian church (10:1–13:10). The letter ends with a few quick exhortations (13:11–12) and a final benediction (13:13).

super-apostles: opponents of Paul in Corinth, discussed in 2 Corinthians; they apparently were rhetorically gifted and claimed that their abilities and successes marked them as more commendable leaders than Paul.

Historical Background

Let's pick up Paul's adventures with Corinth where we left off in the last chapter. Paul founded the church in Corinth and, after leaving, wrote a now lost letter to the congregation (mentioned in 1 Cor. 5:9). Then, while he was in Ephesus, he received two different reports of various problems in the church and wrote the letter that we know as 1 Corinthians in an attempt to adjudicate those matters.

After that things really got messy. Paul had said that he was going to take a trip to Macedonia and then visit the Corinthian church on his way back to Ephesus (1 Cor. 16:5–7). He changed his mind and decided to visit Corinth on his way to Macedonia as well (2 Cor. 1:15–16). Perhaps he caught them unawares; in any event, the visit did not go well. He had some kind of confrontation with people who he believed were sinning (2 Cor. 13:2), and someone in the church

⊘ **EXPLORE 15.0** 2 Corinthians: Outline of Contents

Correspondence with the Corinthians

Paul made at least two visits to the church at Corinth and wrote at least four letters to the Corinthians.

- First visit: Paul founds the church (Acts 18:1–18; 2 Cor. 1:19)

Letter 1 (referred to in 1 Cor. 5:9)

– Could it be found in 2 Corinthians 6:14–7:1 (see box 15.2)?

- Paul receives distressing reports of problems in Corinth:
  - an oral report from Chloe's people (1 Cor. 1:11)
  - a written letter from the church (1 Cor. 7:1)

Letter 2 (1 Corinthians)

- Second visit: a painful confrontation (2 Cor. 2:5; 7:12; 13:2)

Letter 3 (referred to in 2 Cor. 2:3–4; 7:12)

– Could it be found in 2 Corinthians 10–13 (see box 15.2)?

- Paul receives Titus's report of goodwill in Corinth (2 Cor. 7:6–7).

Letter 4 (2 Corinthians, or at least 2 Cor. 1:1–6:13; 7:2–16)

- Was there a Letter 5 (on super-apostles)?
  - Could it be found in 2 Corinthians 10–13?
- Was there a Letter 6 (on fundraising)?
  - Could it be found in 2 Corinthians 8–9 (or just 2 Cor. 8)?
- Was there a Letter 7 (also on fundraising)?
  - Could it be found in 2 Corinthians 9 (separate from 2 Cor. 8)?

did something intended to hurt or humiliate him, something that later he would claim actually hurt the entire congregation (2 Cor. 2:5). Paul left in a huff and canceled his plans to visit them on the return trip (1 Cor. 16:6–7). This exacerbated tensions and led to accusations that he was unreliable (2 Cor. 1:15–23). His explanation for the change of plans is telling: he says that he canceled the trip to avoid "another painful visit" (2 Cor. 2:1); he simply could not bear suffering more hurt from those who should make him rejoice. He also wanted to spare the Corinthians the pain that he knew he would inflict on them if he came to them at this particular time (2 Cor. 1:23; 2:1–3). Without knowing all the details, we can tell that Paul's relationship with the church had deteriorated.

We get a hint in the last few chapters of 2 Corinthians as to what part of the problem might have been. At some point, a group of people whom Paul sarcastically refers to as the "super-apostles" (11:5; 12:11) arrived in Corinth; whether they were already there at the time of his unannounced painful visit to the church, we cannot say. We know nothing about these super-apostles except what can be gathered from Paul's comments: they were of Jewish ancestry (11:22), and they presented themselves as ministers of Christ (11:23). Paul, however, regarded them as ministers of Satan in disguise (11:13–15): they presented the Corinthians with a different Jesus, preached a different gospel, and imparted a different spirit (11:4).

The conflict between Paul and the super-apostles appears to have been more a contest of authority than a disagreement over particular doctrines or practices. Indeed, a major issue seems to have been the question of what constitutes a basis for authority within the church. Paul claimed that the super-apostles employed worldly standards for excellence in order to establish themselves and promote their authority. They in turn maligned Paul as appearing bold in his letters but not in person (10:1). They said, "His bodily presence is weak, and his speech contemptible" (10:10), a remark that has given rise to much speculation. To what were they referring when they criticized his "bodily presence"? Was Paul of short stature or of slight build? Did he have some kind of physical disability (cf. 12:7–9)? And what was wrong with his speech? Did he stutter or have a speech impediment? Was he a lousy preacher? We cannot know, but what seems obvious is that the super-apostles claimed that he lacked charisma. Compared to what the Greco-Roman world had to offer in the way of skilled orators and public presenters, Paul was unimpressive. Paul, of course, said as much about himself (1 Cor. 2:1–5; 2 Cor. 11:6), but he did not draw the same conclusions from his lack of showmanship that the super-apostles wanted the Corinthians to draw (2 Cor. 11:5; 12:11).

After Paul decided to forgo "another painful visit" to Corinth, he attempted to resolve problems in the church by writing them a desperate and difficult letter. This was actually his third composition to the church, and, like the first letter (referred to in 1 Cor. 5:9), it has been lost (but see box 15.2). Paul refers to the letter a few times in the letter that we know as 2 Corinthians (see 2:3–4, 9; 7:12), and Bible readers sometimes simply assume that he is referring in those passages to the letter that we know as 1 Corinthians. This is an understandable misconception; however, a closer look reveals that Paul is referring to a different letter, one that he wrote after 1 Corinthians and after his subsequent painful visit to the church. In this difficult letter ("Letter 3" in box 15.1) he apparently gave the church an ultimatum, challenging them to prove their obedience to him by disciplining the individual who had wronged him (2 Cor. 2:9; 7:12). Paul says that he wrote this letter "out of much distress and anguish of heart and with many tears" (2 Cor. 2:4), and he indicates that, after sending it by way of Titus, he regretted having done so (2 Cor. 7:8).

From 2 Corinthians we learn that around this time Paul also experienced a terrible trial in Asia (probably in the city of Ephesus). The opposition to his ministry brought on some sort of "deadly peril" that led Paul and his associates

Box 15.2

The Lost Letters: Have They Been Found?

Paul wrote at least four letters to the Corinthians, but we have only two in our Bibles. Many Christians have longed to discover copies of the missing letters, the ones identified as Letter 1 and Letter 3 in box 15.1.

Today, many scholars believe that those letters have been found and that they were right under our noses all along. A prominent theory holds that the letter known as 2 Corinthians is actually a patchwork epistle containing not only the work identified as Letter 4 in box 15.1 but also other letters:

- Second Corinthians 6:14–7:1 may be an excerpt from Letter 1. In its present context, this passage forms an odd interruption in Paul's train of thought; it also deals with the general topic that Paul says he addressed in his first letter to the Corinthians (1 Cor. 5:9).
- Second Corinthians 10–13 may be from Letter 3. These four chapters are laced with harsh rebukes and bitter sarcasm that seem out of place in what is otherwise a letter of reconciliation and renewed confidence; they are more characteristic of what we would expect to find in the difficult letter that Paul says he was sorry he had to write (2 Cor. 7:8).

There is no solid evidence to support these proposals; they just make sense to some people who think that 2 Corinthians reads more consistently and smoothly when these sections are taken out and read as separate compositions.

There have been variations and expansions on these proposals: some suggest that 2 Corinthians 6:14–7:1 is part of a totally different letter that wasn't even written by Paul; some think that 2 Corinthians 10–13 is from a fifth letter that Paul wrote to the Corinthians after things turned bad again.

The "patchwork epistle" theory has also been employed with regard to 2 Corinthians 8–9, which deals with the collection that Paul is taking for Jerusalem. These often are regarded as a separate fundraising letter that Paul may have written to the church on that subject, or even as two letters on the subject (chap. 8 addressed to Corinth, and chap. 9 presenting a similar appeal to the province of Achaia).

---

to believe that they were going to die (1:8–9). Most scholars think that they were imprisoned for their faith, and some think that Paul may have written his letter to the Philippians or some of the other "prison letters" at this time. In any case, the experience provided Paul with some perspective on ministry that is evident in his subsequent communications with the Corinthians. After the ordeal had passed, he left Ephesus for missionary work in Troas and then moved on to Macedonia, still anxious to hear from the Corinthians (2:12–13).

At last Titus (who had carried Paul's challenging [but now lost] letter to the Corinthians) arrived with incredibly good news: the Corinthians had repented of all the ways in which they had grieved Paul (7:9–11), and they had disciplined the guilty party who had treated him so badly (2:6–7). Paul was overjoyed (7:4), and his confidence in the church was restored (7:16). In response, he wrote to the church a fourth time, expressing his relief and joy at their favorable response and encouraging them to forgive and console the one who had been

Prison or Captivity Letters (Epistles): five letters attributed to Paul that are said to have been written from prison: Ephesians, Philippians, Colossians, 2 Timothy, and Philemon.

disciplined (2:6–10). This fourth letter was sent from Macedonia (2:13; 7:5) sometime between 55 and 58. We call it "2 Corinthians."

Such, in broad outline, is the history of Paul's dealings with Corinth up to the time that he wrote 2 Corinthians. There is, however, one potentially complicating factor. As we noted, some scholars believe that the letter that we currently know as 2 Corinthians is actually a composite containing various letters and notes that Paul sent to the Corinthians at different times. By this reckoning, only the first seven chapters represent Paul's fourth letter to the church (or perhaps just 1:1–6:13; 7:2–16); chapters 8 and 9 might be additional letters that he sent regarding the collection for Jerusalem; and the last four chapters (10–13) perhaps represent still another letter dealing with the problem of the super-apostles. These theories become very complicated, with numerous variations (see boxes 15.1 and 15.2).

Major Themes in 2 Corinthians

Paul's Ministry

Paul devotes the bulk of this letter to discussing the character and content of his ministry. He emphasizes, first of all, the integrity with which his ministry is always carried out (7:2). He and his associates are not "peddlers of God's word" (2:17) or self-promoters (4:5) who falsify God's word (4:2) to their own advantage. They operate with sincerity (1:12; 2:17) and with complete openness (4:2), enduring hardships (6:4–5) and exhibiting virtues (6:6–7) that reveal them to be true servants of God (6:4) and ambassadors for Christ (5:20). Second, Paul stresses that he has developed a close personal relationship with the Corinthians. He seems to be as committed to them emotionally as he is professionally, speaking openly of his affection for them (2:4; 6:12; 11:11) and of the personal pain that he experiences when they are in conflict (2:1–4). Indeed, he remains solicitous of them, styling their relationship as one of not-quite-requited love (6:11–13; 7:2; cf. 12:15).

More important, Paul stresses that his ministry is of God: he has been sent by God to do God's work, and God is working through him to accomplish it (2:14, 17; 3:4–6; 4:1, 7; 5:2, 18, 20). That work itself is glorious; it is a spiritual ministry that brings a new covenant (3:6) and more: a new creation (5:17). Indeed, what God is doing through Paul reveals a glory that surpasses anything previously envisioned (3:7–18). And yet this is a ministry carried out by mere humans, by mortal beings who suffer trials and tribulations (4:16; 5:2–4; 6:4–10; see also 11:21–33). Just as precious treasure might be contained in nondescript jars of clay, so too the glorious gospel of God is advanced by frail and fragile agents whose lives exhibit the paradoxes that such a gospel entails (4:7–12).

Fundraising

Paul devotes two chapters of this letter to the collection that he is taking up for Jerusalem, making 2 Corinthians 8–9 the most extensive discussion of fundraising in the New Testament. Paul had agreed with leaders among the Jewish Christians in Jerusalem that he would collect an offering from the gentile churches that he founded for "the poor" in Jerusalem (Gal. 2:10; cf. Acts 11:29–30; 24:17). This was not simply an act of charity but also an opportunity to demonstrate the unity of gentile and Jewish believers. Paul mentions the collection elsewhere (Rom. 15:25–27; 1 Cor. 16:1–4), and, we might assume, he often solicited donations with words similar to what we find here. Indeed, since chapter 9 seems to introduce the subject as though it were a new topic, some scholars think that we are in possession of two letters that Paul wrote concerning this offering (2 Cor. 8 to the city of Corinth and 2 Cor. 9 to the whole province of Achaia). Be that as it may, these two

Fig. 15.1. Jars of clay. Earthen jugs were common in Paul's world. Paul likens human beings to clay jars in which someone has placed a priceless treasure: the spirit is precious, but the flesh is weak; life is eternal, but in this present world we are frail beings subject to the powers of death and decay. (Jim Yancey)

chapters are often used by Christian churches to teach financial stewardship and encourage generous giving.

Paul presents the opportunity to give as a privilege—a favor from God (8:1–2)—and he promotes a principle of sharing resources so that there might be neither excess nor want among God's people (8:13–15). Since "God loves a cheerful giver" (9:7), participation in the offering is to be voluntary (9:5), and contributions are to be offered according to individual means (8:3, 11–13). Still, in order to motivate the Corinthians to give generously (8:7) Paul points to the liberality of their neighbors the Macedonians (8:1–5). They don't want to be outdone by the Macedonians, do they? Then he goes on to say that he has actually bragged to the Macedonians about them, and he hopes that they won't embarrass him by failing to come up with what he expects (8:24; 9:2–4). On a deeper level, however, Paul hopes that their generosity will be inspired by the sacrifice of Christ (8:9). Further, the ultimate rationale for such giving lies in his belief that people are stewards or caretakers of all that they have received from God (see 1 Cor. 4:1–2). If the Corinthians realize how abundantly they have been blessed with God's gifts (9:8; cf. 1 Cor. 4:7), they will want to use what they have received to help others and to bring glory to God, who has been so generous to them (9:12–14).

Apostolic Authority

Throughout 2 Corinthians Paul emphasizes and defends his authority as an apostle. To appreciate this fully, we need to go back to his earlier correspondence with the church and notice the authoritative manner in which he speaks in 1 Corinthians. In that letter he claims to have the authority to excommunicate members of the church from afar (5:3–5). He issues rulings on matters for which there is no clear "word of the Lord" (7:12, 25, 40; cf. 7:10), and he insists that only those who accept what he has to say in his letters are to be recognized as prophets in the church (14:37–38). He offers himself to the church as an ideal role model, blatantly calling on the Corinthians, "Be imitators of me, as I am of Christ" (11:1; cf. 4:16). It is not difficult to imagine that such statements appeared heavy-handed to some in the church or that they might

Box 15.3

Paul in Christian Legends

Throughout the centuries, many speculative legends about Paul have been inspired by comments that he makes in 2 Corinthians.

- *Short of stature.* Second Corinthians 10:10 says that Paul had a weak bodily presence. A common tradition took this to mean that he was unusually short. Paul's very name comes from a Latin word (*paulus*) meaning "small," and this may have helped to feed traditions about his height. In any case, John Chrysostom (fourth century) called Paul "the man of three cubits," identifying him as only four feet six inches tall. Medieval artwork typically portrays Paul as the shortest man in a painting or scene.
- *Thorn in the flesh.* Second Corinthians 12:7–10 refers to an unidentified affliction from which Paul suffered as his "thorn in the flesh." What was this problem? One second-century writing says that Paul was congenitally bowlegged. Tertullian (second–third centuries) says that Paul had chronic headaches. Clement of Alexandria (second–third centuries) suggests that Paul may have had a difficult wife (although 1 Cor. 7:7 indicates that he was unmarried). John Chrysostom (fourth century) thought that the thorn was Alexander the coppersmith (see 2 Tim. 4:14) or one of Paul's other opponents. Martin Luther and John Calvin thought that Paul might be referring metaphorically to sexual temptations that he experienced as a result of his commitment to celibacy. Others have suggested a guilty conscience over persecuting the church (see 1 Cor. 15:9) or anguish over Jewish rejection of the gospel (see Rom. 9:1–3). Still others have suggested a speech impediment (to explain 2 Cor. 10:10) or poor eyesight (to explain Gal. 4:15; 6:11) or epilepsy (to explain Acts 9:3–4). A few have even proposed that Paul was possessed by a demon (taking the words "messenger of Satan" in 2 Cor. 12:7 literally).
- *Spirit journeys.* Second Corinthians 12:2–4 relates a visionary experience in which Paul (describing himself in the third person) was transported to heavenly realms. Many apocryphal tales report additional "spirit journeys" undertaken by Paul. A Greek writing from the third century tells of how he visited hell and brokered a deal for all torments to be suspended for one day each week (on Sundays); thus even the damned have Paul to thank for getting them a day off.

have provided Paul's opponents with grist for painting him as an egotistical self-promoter. And if Paul can claim that kind of authority, what is to prevent others from claiming it as well?

In 2 Corinthians we see that this potential for a power struggle has come to fruition. There are now people in the Corinthian church who, Paul says, are "disguising themselves as apostles of Christ" (11:13). This raises the question, "How does one know a true apostle from a false one?" Paul says in 1 Corinthians that apostles must be appointed in the church by God (12:28); one cannot simply choose to be an apostle. Taking the two letters together, we find that Paul mentions four qualifications for apostleship:

1. He refers to "the signs of a true apostle," reminding the Corinthians of signs and wonders and mighty works (miracles?) that he did in their midst (2 Cor. 12:12).

2. He identifies true apostles as people who have "seen the Lord"—that is, who were witnesses to the risen Jesus (1 Cor. 9:1). This may explain why Paul included himself on the short list of persons to whom the risen Jesus appeared in his discussion of Christ's resurrection in 1 Corinthians 15:3–8; it may also explain why he says "*last* of all . . . he appeared to me" (1 Cor. 15:8). The appearances are over and done; Paul doesn't want there to be any volunteer apostles (like these folks in Corinth?) suddenly claiming that Jesus appeared to them too.

3. He describes the role of an apostle as founding churches. He is an apostle to the Corinthians because they are his converts (his "work in the Lord") and, accordingly, the seal of his apostleship (1 Cor. 9:1–2). He is their father in the faith (1 Cor. 4:14–15) and has earned the right to address (and discipline) them as his children (1 Cor. 4:14; 2 Cor. 6:13; 12:14). Thus in 2 Corinthians he mocks would-be apostles who try to establish their authority with letters of recommendation (2 Cor. 3:1). The Corinthian believers themselves are Paul's letter of recommendation, written on human hearts by Christ, using the Spirit of God as ink (2 Cor. 3:2–3). For this reason, Paul is particularly perturbed that the super-apostles (who in fact are not apostles) have overstepped their bounds by coming into his "sphere of action" and trying to establish themselves by building on what he has done (2 Cor. 10:13–16). Hypothetically, if these people want commendation from the Lord (2 Cor. 10:18), they should set out for lands where the gospel has not yet been proclaimed (2 Cor. 10:16), make new converts for the faith, and exercise authority over churches that they themselves founded.

4. He thinks of apostles as persons who serve as spokespersons for an authoritative tradition. In 1 Corinthians Paul said that he "handed on" to

⊙ EXPLORE 15.3
Collection for Jerusalem

⊙ EXPLORE 15.9
Generous Giving: Stewardship Principles from 2 Corinthians

the Corinthians what he "in turn had received" (1 Cor. 15:3; cf. 11:2, 23). Now in 2 Corinthians he suggests that the "false apostles" (2 Cor. 11:13) are proclaiming "a different gospel" (2 Cor. 11:4; cf. Gal. 1:6–8)—that is, a gospel different from the one that has been handed on. Paul admits that he might be untrained in speech, but he claims that he is not deficient "in knowledge" (2 Cor. 11:6). Knowledge of what? Most likely he means that he is a reliable apostle because, unlike these interlopers, he has legitimate knowledge of what God has done in Jesus Christ.

Such general ideas of what it means to be an apostle may not have been absolute for Paul. In Romans 16:7 he refers to Andronicus and Junia as "prominent among the apostles," though there is no indication that either of them worked miracles, saw the risen Jesus, or founded a church. The context in Corinth clearly is one of conflict, which may have colored Paul's remarks.

In any event, in 2 Corinthians Paul yields none of his apostolic authority to his rivals, nor does he ease up on any of his grandiose claims. He has been given divine power to punish the disobedient (10:2–6), and he lets the Corinthians know that they will experience the full weight of this punitive authority if they don't live right (13:1–2). This grieves him, because ultimately the authority that the Lord has given to him is for building up, not tearing down (10:8; 12:19; 13:10; cf. Jer. 1:10). If he seems harsh with the Corinthians, he says, it is only

Fig. 15.2. The Erastus Inscription. This pavement stone in Corinth still bears the name of Erastus, the city treasurer mentioned in the New Testament as belonging to the Corinthian church (Rom. 16:23; 2 Tim. 4:20). (Todd Bolen / BiblePlaces.com)

Plutarch on Self-Commendation

But those who are forced to speak in their own praise are made more endurable by another proce-dure as well: not to lay claim to everything, but to unburden themselves, as it were, of honor, letting part of it rest with chance and part with God.

Plutarch, *Moralia*, vol. 7, trans. Philip H. De Lacy and Benedict Einarson, Loeb Classical Library (Cambridge, MA: Harvard University Press, 1959), §542E (On Praising Oneself Inoffensively 11).

because they are so obstinate (12:20–21) and so easily fooled by those who take advantage of them (11:19–20).

Boasting

Paul is generally opposed to self-commendation and boasting; it is unseemly (Rom. 1:30; 1 Cor. 13:4) and credits mere human beings with what should be attributed to God (Rom. 3:27; 11:18; 1 Cor. 1:29; 3:21–23; 4:7; 9:16). His usual slogan is "Let the one who boasts, boast in the Lord" (1 Cor. 1:31; 2 Cor. 10:17; cf. Jer. 9:24; see also Gal. 6:14). In 2 Corinthians, however, Paul brags quite a bit about himself and his credentials: he has authority over the Corinthians (10:8); he comes from good Israelite stock (11:22); he is an exceptional minister of Christ (11:23); he has made sacrifices and endured hardships for the sake of the gospel (11:23–29); he has received visions and revelations from the Lord (12:1–7); and he has worked signs and wonders (12:12).

Why is Paul so given to praising himself? He says that he has been forced into it because the super-apostles have offered unfounded claims to superiority (10:10; 11:5–6; 12:11). He has been forced into it also because the Corinthians, who should be commending him, have not done so (12:11; cf. 5:12). He often brags about them (1:14; 7:4, 14; 8:7; 9:2–3), but they don't return the favor. He is forced to commend himself because no one else will do so. This may seem a bit silly, and apparently that's the whole point! Paul admits that he is a fool to talk this way (11:1, 16–19, 21, 23; 12:11). An obvious implication of such an admission is that the super-apostles are fools when they talk this way too. Apparently the super-apostles were big on commendation (3:1; 10:18; 11:13), comparing themselves to others to see who measured up (10:12; 11:12). They liked to call attention to their abilities and achievements in ways that Paul thought evaluated them "according to human standards" (11:18). By admitting to his own foolishness, Paul exposes theirs. With biting irony, he says (in effect), "I am nothing, but that doesn't make me inferior to them" (see 12:11). The difference is that Paul is well aware that he is nothing (cf. 1 Cor. 3:7), whereas the super-apostles do not seem to have grasped the reality of their nothingness.

Finally, Paul turns the table on his opponents by suggesting a different contest: Instead of comparing strengths, why not compare weaknesses? After all, he rea-sons, our inadequacies are what ultimately prove that it is God who is responsible

Fig. 15.3. Paul being lowered in a basket. This colorful incident from Paul's biography is mentioned in Acts 9:23–25 and 2 Corinthians 11:32–33. Most people would not brag about having fled or hidden from their enemies, but Paul employs this as an example of how God uses those who are weak in this world. (The Bridgeman Art Library International)

for our accomplishments. If we really want to establish which of us is being used by God, we should check to see which of us is the most inadequate. Paul, of course, assumes that the super-apostles will not join him in this venture; human failings and weaknesses are things that they try to deny or cover up. So Paul goes it alone: he talks about a humiliating incident when he had to be smuggled out of a city in a basket (11:32–33); he reminds the Corinthians of an affliction that he has to put up with (12:7); and he admits to times when God has rejected his prayer requests (12:8–9). He boasts gladly of things that expose his weakness, things that prove he is nothing, because these are what should grant the Corinthians absolute assurance that it is God who is responsible for all that comes of his ministry (12:9–10).

Conclusion

In theological circles, the super-apostles with whom Paul contends in 2 Corinthians would come to be viewed as the primary paragons of what is called *theologia gloriae*, a "theology of glory." Simply stated, this refers to a way of understanding the gospel that views faith in Christ as a means to self-betterment, success, and the attainment of power. Martin Luther was especially adamant about condemning such theological constructions, contending that the apostle Paul proclaimed *theologia crucis*, a "theology of the cross." According to the latter understanding, faith in Christ implies an immersion into a life of service and sacrifice, a life marked by vulnerability and recognition of one's failings.

But what happened next? Did Paul win his battle with the super-apostles? Did the Corinthian church finally get its act together in a way befitting his "full confidence" in them (7:16)? We have two reasons to believe that matters were resolved to Paul's satisfaction. First, his letters to the Corinthians (at least two of them) were copied and preserved—somebody in the church had high regard for Paul's words. Second, Paul wrote his letter to the Romans from Corinth within a year of writing 2 Corinthians to Corinth. In Romans he indicates that the funds for Jerusalem have been successfully collected (Rom. 15:25–26), and he passes on greetings from prominent Corinthian Christians with whom he seems to be on good terms (Rom. 16:1, 23). All of this hints at a happy ending.

Prepare for the sequel. About forty years later—three decades after Paul's death—another letter to Corinth appeared, this one ascribed to Clement, who is said to be a bishop of Rome. He complains that the Corinthian congregation is divided into factions. He also says, "It is a shameful report, beloved, extremely shameful and unworthy of your training in Christ, that on account of one or two persons the steadfast and ancient church of the Corinthians is being disloyal to the elders!" (*1 Clement* 47:6).

Factions in the church? Troublemakers undermining the authority of established leaders? Where have we heard that before?

FOR FURTHER READING: **2 Corinthians**

Collins, Raymond F. *Second Corinthians*. Paideia. Grand Rapids: Baker Academic, 2013.

Keener, Craig S. *1–2 Corinthians*. New Cambridge Bible Commentary. New York: Cambridge University Press, 2005.

Murphy-O'Connor, Jerome. *The Theology of the Second Letter to the Corinthians*. New Testament Theology. Cambridge: Cambridge University Press, 1991.

Proctor, John. *First and Second Corinthians*. Westminster Bible Companion. Louisville: Westminster John Knox, 2015.

Roetzel, Calvin J. *2 Corinthians*. Abingdon New Testament Commentaries. Nashville: Abingdon, 2007.

Talbert, Charles H. *Reading Corinthians: A Literary and Theological Commentary*. Rev. ed. Reading the New Testament. Macon, GA: Smyth & Helwys, 2003.

Wan, Sze-Kar. *Power in Weakness: The Second Letter of Paul to the Corinthians*. The New Testament in Context. Harrisburg, PA: Trinity Press International, 2000.

Wright, N. T. *Paul for Everyone: 2 Corinthians*. 2nd ed. Louisville: Westminster John Knox, 2004.

⊙ Go to www .IntroducingNT.com for summaries, videos, and other study tools.

16

Galatians

"You foolish Galatians!" Paul rails against the recipients of his most intense and combative letter (3:1). And that's how the poor Galatians have been remembered ever since. They are the buffoons of the Bible, or at least of the New Testament. They probably said and did many things that were not foolish (4:12–15), but Christians know them best for this, their walk-on role as targets of a blistering rebuke from an apostle dumbfounded by their folly.

Some of Paul's other letters also address situations in which individuals or entire congregations have disappointed him, but the Letter to the Galatians stands out from the pack. These people have aroused his ire in a manner that surpasses anything we find elsewhere. Why? What could be worse than, say, the Corinthians getting drunk at the Lord's Supper (1 Cor. 11:20–21)?

The Galatians want to be circumcised! That seems to be the crux of this crisis (5:2–3). And why is that such a big deal? Paul himself says, "Neither circumcision nor uncircumcision counts for anything" (5:6; also 6:15). We might think, then, that Paul would regard circumcision as merely superfluous, a ritual that is meaningless but basically harmless (provided the knife doesn't slip!; see 5:12). But, no, it's a much bigger deal than that. Paul maintains that the Galatians are deserting God and perverting the gospel of Christ (1:6–7).

circumcision: a surgical procedure that removes the foreskin of a penis; in the Jewish tradition, the rite is viewed as a sign of the covenant that God had made with Israel.

The Letter to the Galatians is known as Paul's "angry letter." He is not interested in engaging his opponents in a polite debate over the issue of circumcision. It is too late for that—things have already become personal. His opponents have attacked his credibility and impugned his integrity. Paul is angry with these opponents, and he is angry with the Galatians for listening to them.

This is Paul's only letter that does not open with words of thanksgiving for the recipients (cf., e.g., Rom. 1:8–10; 1 Cor. 1:4–9; 2 Cor. 1:3–11; Phil. 1:3–11;

1 Thess. 1:2–5; Philem. 4–7). Is this because he can find nothing to be thankful for? Or is he just too worked up to realize that he has left out what normal decorum would commend?

Overview

After a customary salutation (1:1–4), Paul immediately declares his astonishment that the Galatians are deserting God and embracing a false message that perverts the gospel of Christ (1:6–9). He then turns defensive, responding to charges that he is a people-pleaser (1:10). He recounts segments of his autobiography to counter allegations that he picked up the gospel message secondhand, or that he does not proclaim the gospel in a manner approved by other apostles (1:11–2:10). Continuing in the autobiographical mode, he relates an incident at Antioch that set him at odds with Peter (called "Cephas," his Aramaic name) and other respected church leaders (2:11–14). Reporting that incident serves as a segue to a discussion of matters at hand, for it brings into sharp focus a question that the Galatians themselves need to consider: whether one is made right with God by doing works of the law or by trusting in Jesus Christ (2:15–21).

Cephas: an Aramaic word meaning "Rock," the Greek form of which is "Peter"; a nickname given by Jesus to Simon, one of his disciples.

Box 16.1

Circumcision

Circumcision is a surgical procedure that removes the foreskin of a penis. It has been and still is practiced by many cultures for a variety of reasons: it is sometimes cosmetic or linked to health concerns, but in many traditions the rite has taken on symbolic meaning connected with puberty, fertility, or spiritual devotion.

In ancient Israel male children typically were circumcised on the eighth day of their life (Gen. 17:12; Lev. 12:3). Both Jesus (Luke 1:59; 2:21) and Paul (Phil. 3:5) are said to have been circumcised in keeping with this sacred tradition, which still is practiced by Jewish people today.

In Israelite and Jewish religion circumcision was regarded as "the sign of the covenant": males were circumcised to indicate that they belonged to the chosen people of God, that they were heirs of the promises to Abraham, and that they intended to keep the Torah, given by God to Moses. Prophets sometimes spoke of circumcision in symbolic terms, accusing those who were stubborn or unreceptive of having an uncircumcised ear (Jer. 6:10) or an uncircumcised heart (Lev. 26:41).

The apostle Paul favors the symbolic meaning of circumcision (Rom. 2:29) but regards the physical act as irrelevant, since all people are now made right with God through Christ (1 Cor. 7:19; Gal. 5:6; 6:15). Paul's strong opposition to circumcision voiced in certain passages (e.g., Gal. 5:2) has nothing to do with the value of the act itself: he is not opposed to Jews (or gentiles) observing religious traditions that they find meaningful, but he is incensed by the notion that any such tradition is necessary to affect one's status with God, which, for Paul, is maintained solely by grace through faith.

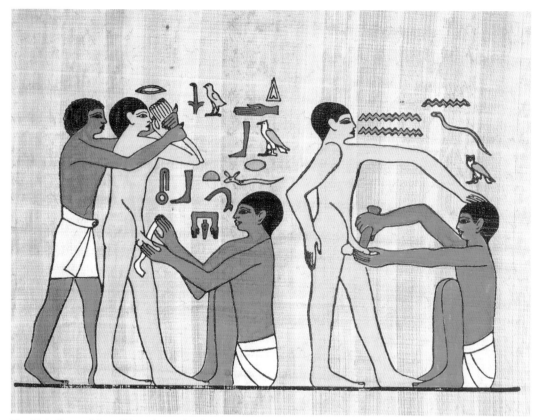

Fig. 16.1. Circumcision. Although it is often known as a practice associated with Judaism, this reconstructed relief from an Egyptian tomb (third millennium BCE) shows that circumcision was a ritual practiced among other peoples as well. (Bridgeman Images)

Seizing the offensive, Paul tells the Galatians that they are fools for allowing anyone to convince them that the crucified Christ is insufficient for them. With a number of arguments, many of them drawn from Scripture, he reiterates his point that trusting in Christ is incompatible with relying on works of the law as a means to receiving God's Spirit or being declared righteous by God (3:1–18). He considers the true purpose of the law (3:19–4:11) and then turns conciliatory, appealing to the Galatians as his children in the faith and calling them to turn back from a course that will lead them into bondage (4:12–5:1). He warns them against accepting circumcision as a qualification for belonging to God and vents his anger against those who urge them to do so (5:2–12).

Finally, Paul launches into a soaring treatise on the meaning of freedom, emphasizing its paradoxical fulfillment in loving service rather than in self-indulgence. He identifies the outcome and evidence of true freedom with the fruit that the Holy Spirit bears in people whose lives have been transformed by God's grace (5:13–25). He then concludes the letter with a quick series of

⊙ EXPLORE 16.0
Galatians: Outline of Contents

⊙ EXPLORE 16.8
Circumcision in the Biblical Period

exhortations (5:26–6:10) and a summary paragraph written in his own hand, exalting the cross of Jesus (6:11–18).

Historical Background

The Letter to the Galatians is written by Paul to a number of congregations in a Roman province located in modern-day Turkey (1:2). Although the Romans called the entire province "Galatia," the only people in the area who called themselves "Galatians" were descendants of Celtic tribes that had settled in the northern part of the province. According to the book of Acts, Paul visited some cities in the southern part of Galatia on his first missionary journey (see Acts 13:14–15; 14:1; all the cities mentioned are in the south). He does not appear to have ventured north to where the people known as the "Galatians" lived. He might have done this, however, on his second journey a few years later (see Acts 16:6; 18:23; the northern part of the province could be included here, though it is not specifically mentioned).

According to the book of Acts, an important council was held in Jerusalem in between Paul's first two missionary journeys to deal with some of the same issues that are addressed in the Letter to the Galatians (see Acts 15). Biblical scholars want to know whether Paul wrote the letter before or after that council. Since he addresses the people to whom he is writing as "Galatians" (3:1), not just "residents of Galatia," it is often thought that the letter is addressed to

---

Box 16.2

Northern and Southern Galatian Theories

"Northern Galatian Theory"—Sequence of Events

- Paul evangelizes cities in southern Galatia (Acts 13:14–15; 14:1).
- Conference takes place in Jerusalem (Acts 15; Gal. 2:1–10).
- Paul evangelizes Galatian tribes in northern Galatia (Acts 16:6; 18:5).
- Paul writes the Letter to the Galatians to churches in northern Galatia.

The Northern Galatian Theory recognizes that the people usually known as the "Galatians" lived in the northern part of the province visited by Paul after the Jerusalem conference.

"Southern Galatian Theory"—Sequence of Events

- Paul evangelizes cities in southern Galatia (Acts 13:14–15; 14:1).
- Paul meets with church leaders in Jerusalem (Gal. 2:1–10).
- Paul writes the Letter to the Galatians to churches in southern Galatia.
- Conference takes place in Jerusalem (Acts 15).

The Southern Galatian Theory resolves what would be inconsistencies between Galatians 2:1–10 and Acts 15 that would arise if these passages were viewed as describing the same event.

people in the northern part of the province. In that case, it would have to have been composed after the council (since Paul had not visited the northern part of the province on his first trip to the area). Initially this does seem to make sense because in Galatians 2:1–10 Paul talks about a meeting that he had with apostles in Jerusalem, which often is understood to be his own account of that famous council. The problem, however, is that Paul's description of this meeting differs in key respects from the description of the Jerusalem council in Acts 15. For this reason, some scholars think that the meeting Paul describes in Galatians 2:1–10 is not the Jerusalem council but rather an earlier, different event. The assumption, then, is that Paul probably wrote Galatians before the Jerusalem council occurred (since, on this reckoning, he does not mention that council). The problem with this suggestion is that if Paul wrote the letter that early, it would have to have been addressed to the southern Galatian cities that he visited on his first journey. It then seems odd that he would address his recipients as "Galatians" (3:1), a term more appropriate for the people in the north (see box 16.2).

The Northern Galatian Theory is preferred by most scholars who do not feel constrained to defend the accuracy of what Luke reports in Acts or to reconcile Paul's account of the Jerusalem meeting with what is presented there. Then the letter is assumed to have been written in the mid-50s, possibly from Ephesus. That would mean it was written around the same time as Romans, a work with which it has much in common thematically and theologically. But those who think that Paul is writing to people in southern Galatia hold that the letter was probably written around 48, possibly from Antioch in Syria, to which Paul returned at the conclusion of his first journey. Then it could be the earliest of all the letters we possess; indeed, it could be the oldest surviving Christian document of any kind.

All we know for certain is that the people to whom this letter was written were gentiles who had been introduced to Christianity by Paul but who had since become attracted to ideas that Paul rejected. Paul notes

Map 16.1. Northern and southern Galatia.

Did Paul Have Bad Eyesight?

- He says that he suffered from a "physical infirmity" (Gal. 4:13) and from a "thorn" in the flesh (2 Cor. 12:7).
- He says that the Galatians would have given him their own eyes to help him had it been possible (Gal. 4:15).
- His handwriting is recognizable because of the exceptionally large letters that he makes (Gal. 6:11).
- He is said to have been temporarily blinded (Acts 9:8), and when his sight is restored, "something like scales" fall from his eyes (Acts 9:18).
- He fails to recognize the high priest when appearing before the Jewish council in Jerusalem (Acts 23:4–5).

Such considerations have led to speculation: Did he have cataracts or some other eye problem? Was he partially blind?

that it was because of a physical infirmity that he first proclaimed the gospel to them (4:13). Apparently he had intended to go elsewhere, but some problem (possibly with his eyes; see 4:15) caused him to be laid up for a while. Making the best of things, he turned his evangelistic efforts toward those who inhabited the area where he was recuperating. They received him with goodwill and accepted the gospel. After he moved on, however, some other teachers came to the area, proclaiming a rival version of the faith. These interlopers undermined Paul's understanding of the gospel and turned some of the Galatians against Paul himself.

What was this "rival version" of the Christian faith? In the early years of Christianity, there appear to have been some Jews who believed in Jesus but who thought that salvation in Christ was for Jewish people only. They believed that gentiles who wanted to become Christians first needed to become Jews. Gentiles attracted to Christianity should be circumcised and commit themselves to living in accord with the Torah (Jewish law). Then as converted, law-observant Jews they could receive the salvation that Jesus the Jewish Messiah had accomplished for Israel. Advocates of such an understanding of Christianity have traditionally been called "Judaizers."

We don't know how widespread this vision of a law-observant Jewish Christianity was in the first century, since there are only scattered and sometimes obscure references to it in the New Testament (Acts 15:1–2, 5; Gal. 2:4, 11–14; Phil. 3:2). It is also possible that those who called for gentiles to accept circumcision and keep the Jewish law did so with varying degrees of intensity. There is no indication that Paul's opponents in Galatia made salvation dependent on circumcision or acceptance of the law. Perhaps they simply told the Galatian Christians that being circumcised and following the law was a commendable "next step" to take, the way to a deeper and fuller realization of their faith.

Torah: the law of Moses, as contained in the Pentateuch.

Judaizer: a term sometimes used by scholars to describe Christians who insisted that gentile Christians be circumcised and observe other practices that had traditionally identified Jews as the covenant people of God.

Box 16.4

The Polemic of Galatians

More than any other letter, Galatians shows Paul on the attack. As one who apparently has been maligned by his opponents, he shows that he can give as good as he gets. Here are some of the charges that he makes against his opponents:

- They upset and confuse the Galatians (1:7; 5:10).
- They pervert the gospel of Christ (1:7).
- They have bewitched the Galatians (3:1).
- They are manipulative, trying to secure the Galatians' loyalty by first courting them and then making them feel excluded (4:17).
- They prevent the Galatians from obeying the truth (5:7).
- Their real motivation is to avoid persecution from Jews (6:12).
- They are hypocrites who don't obey the law themselves (6:13).
- They want to boast of their success at getting the Galatians circumcised (6:13).

Twice in this letter Paul levels a curse against his opponents (1:8–9), and once he says that he wishes they would castrate themselves (5:12).

Such details would have mattered little to Paul. He maintains that any reliance on the law as a means to obtaining a right (or better) relationship with God is incompatible with the gospel of grace and faith in Christ.

Major Themes in Galatians

Paul's Claim to Authority

Before Paul explains why the proponents of circumcision are misguided, he has to deal with another matter. His opponents have muddied the waters by attacking him personally. Thus he needs to reestablish his credentials as one whose words carry authority. The basic allegation seems to be that Paul misunderstood or at least misrepresented the gospel message that he received from the apostles and other leaders of the church. His opponents probably remind people that he came in late, as one who had never known the earthly Jesus. Dependent on others, he possessed only a derivative authority and should be listened to only when his ideas matched those of people who really knew what they were talking about—people such as Peter and John, who had been among Jesus's original disciples, or Jesus's brother James, who now led the church in Jerusalem.

Paul has a twofold response to this charge: (1) he did not derive his understanding of the gospel from the other apostles; and (2) his understanding of the gospel does not differ substantially from theirs.

Let's take the second point first. Paul states for the record that he has shared his understanding of the gospel with James, Peter, and John and that they have given it their endorsement (2:6). He says that he met with these church leaders in

Fig. 16.2. Paul and Peter embrace. Paul and Peter appear to have had a somewhat feisty relationship. They respected each other, but they did not always agree or get along (Gal. 2:11–14), and sometimes they were viewed as competitors (1 Cor. 1:12; 3:21–23). Thus the image of Paul and Peter embracing each other became a motif in certain periods of Christian art—a symbol of reconciliation or especially of ecumenical unity. This example comes from a twelfth-century mosaic in Sicily. (The Bridgeman Art Library International)

Jerusalem and specifically discussed the question of circumcision with them. He even brought Titus, an uncircumcised gentile Christian, to the meeting with him, and all of these church leaders agreed with Paul: neither Titus nor (by implication) any other gentile should be compelled to be circumcised (2:3).

This, we might think, would be all that Paul needed to say. Indeed, we might assume that he would call on people such as Peter and James to back him up. Perhaps he could get them to send reference letters to the Galatians on his behalf, letting them know that, contrary to what they have been told, Paul's gospel does indeed meet with their approval (cf. 2 Cor. 3:1). But this is not at all the route that he wants to take.

Rather, Paul's main point in responding to the charge against him is the first one listed above. In effect, he claims that it doesn't matter whether his gospel has the support of prominent church leaders, because the message that he proclaims is one that he received directly from Jesus himself, by way of divine revelation (1:11–12; cf. 1:1). Paul seems to be saying, "My opponents are dead wrong when they say that the gospel I preach contradicts that of the apostles, but even if they were right, it wouldn't matter. The gospel that I preach does not need their endorsement—it comes from God."

To drive this point home, Paul voluntarily shares a story that his opponents would likely have used against him (or perhaps he offers his version of an

Box 16.5

The Incident at Antioch

The crisis at Antioch, reported by Paul in Galatians 2, was sparked by the issue of table fellowship: representatives of James (brother of Jesus and leader of the Jerusalem church) encouraged the Jewish Christians in that community to observe Jewish dietary laws, even though this required them to separate themselves from the gentile Christians when the community shared meals together, including, we might assume, celebrations of the Lord's Supper.

Such a policy probably was presented as a mediating "separate but equal" position: let the gentiles who become Christians live as gentiles, and the Jews who become Christians live as Jews. Paul would have none of it, rejecting both parts of that proposal as hypocrisy (Gal. 2:13).

Let the gentiles who become Christians live as gentiles. Paul thinks that it is hypocritical to claim that the policy of separate tables allows gentiles to live as gentiles, because the actual effect is to "compel the Gentiles to live like Jews" (Gal. 2:14). He does not explain exactly why that is the case, but the point may be that the policy marginalizes gentiles within the community and puts social pressure on them to become law observant like the respected church leaders who eat at the Jewish Christian table.

Let the Jews who become Christians live as Jews. Paul claims that Jews who become Christians actually live as gentiles in the only sense that matters: they live as people who have been justified by faith in Jesus Christ, just as the gentiles are (2:15–16). It is hypocritical for Jews to live as gentiles in this sense (trusting in Christ for justification) and still claim to be living as Jews just because they keep dietary laws.

❚ ❚ ❚

The book of *Jubilees*, written around the time of Jesus (give or take fifty years), offers this advice to Jews:

- Separate yourselves from the gentiles, and do not eat with them.
- Do not perform deeds like theirs, and do not become associates of theirs, because their deeds are defiled, and all of their ways are contaminated, and despicable, and abominable. (*Jubilees* 22:16)

Compared to that standard, Paul's opponents probably thought that they were being generous in sharing a meal with gentiles, albeit at separate tables. But Paul thought that "the truth of the gospel" demanded that Jews and gentiles eat together without any distinction (Gal. 2:11–14; see also 3:28).

incident that they actually were using against him). There was one time when he found himself publicly at odds with Peter and, by implication, with James, on whose counsel Peter appears to have been operating. It happened at Antioch, Paul's home base of operations, and though it is not clear that Paul won the argument in that setting, he recounts the event with absolute confidence that he was right and the early church's most highly respected leaders were wrong (2:11–14). Paul's mandate for authority then comes from the truth of the gospel itself and requires no endorsement from particular church officials (see box 16.5).

Christ and the Law: The Real Issue

Having defended his own credibility and asserted his authority as one commissioned by God to speak on these matters, Paul takes up the issue at hand. He maintains that the Galatians will be deserting God and "turning to a different gospel" (1:6) if they accept circumcision and commit to keeping the Jewish law. His arguments in support of this position are sometimes difficult to follow, drawing heavily on interpretations of Scripture that may not be immediately obvious to modern readers. By way of summary, however, we may say that he wants to make four critical points, probably being offered in response to things that his opponents have said.

Point One: Justification Is by Faith, Not Works

justification: the act of being put into a right relationship with God.

Paul insists people are justified or made right with God through faith in Jesus Christ or through the faith(fulness) of Jesus Christ (the Greek phrase that Paul uses can be translated either way) and not by doing works of the law (2:16–17). His opponents may have been telling the Galatians that living in accord with the Jewish law would put them in a right relationship with God, or at least that it would keep them in a right relationship with God or in some way improve their status with God by bringing them to a higher plane. Paul claims that such a teaching nullifies "the grace of God" and, to be blunt, means that "Christ died for nothing" (2:21). Why? It makes justification depend on what human beings do rather than on what God has done through the cross, which is all-sufficient for making people as right with God as they ever can be or need to be. Accordingly, gentiles who think that their status with God can be improved by getting circumcised and keeping the Jewish law are not just fooling themselves; they also are, ironically, jeopardizing the very status with God that they hoped to improve. They have "fallen away from grace" (5:4). A right relationship with God depends not on doing works of the law but rather on trusting in the absolute sufficiency of God's grace.

works of the law: (1) meritorious acts of human achievement (keeping commandments, performing good works, etc.); or (2) covenant markers that identify Jews as belonging to God's chosen nation (circumcision, Sabbath observance, dietary restrictions, etc.).

grace: the free and unmerited favor of God, as manifested in the salvation of sinners and the bestowal of undeserved blessings.

Throughout history this point would receive more attention in theological studies than any of Paul's other arguments. It would become the basis for what is variously called the doctrine of "justification by grace" or "justification by faith" (with occasional argument as to which label is the more appropriate). Protestant theologians in particular would sometimes identify that doctrine (perhaps hyperbolically) as the heart of Pauline theology or even as the heart of Christian theology. On justification by grace/faith, see also "Justification by Grace" in chapter 13, on Romans.

What to Do with Gentiles?

Widespread conversion of gentiles forced the early Christian church to face several important questions. Robert Gundry lists these:

- Should gentile Christians be required to submit to circumcision and practice the Jewish way of life, as gentile proselytes to Judaism were required to do?
- To those gentile Christians unwilling to become wholly Jewish, should the church grant a second-class citizenship, as for gentile "God-fearers" in Judaism?
- What makes a person Christian: faith in Christ solely, or faith in Christ plus adherence to the principles and practices of Judaism?

See Robert H. Gundry, *A Survey of the New Testament*, 5th ed. (Grand Rapids: Zondervan, 2012), 388.

Point Two: God's Favor Is Universal in Scope

Paul believes that God's action in Jesus Christ has effectively removed distinctions between Jews and gentiles, since all are now children of God through faith (3:26). His opponents probably argued that Christianity is grounded in the Jewish tradition, which includes the practice of circumcision and fidelity to Torah. Those who expect to receive the benefits of a Jewish Messiah ought to become part of the Jewish community. But Paul says no to such thinking; the message of the gospel is that such distinctions have been removed for all who are in Christ (3:28). Paul's opponents' claim that the good news is that gentiles can become part of the favored group, whereas Paul claims that the good news is that there is no favored group. A primary function of Torah had always been to mark Jews off as a separate and special people, so if gentile Christians were to become circumcised and begin keeping the Jewish law, they would be perpetuating this notion of exclusion, failing to recognize the universal scope of God's favor that brought the gospel to them in the first place.

Point Three: The Fullness of Time Has Come

Paul believes that a radical shift in history has coincided with the coming of Christ, such that a new phase in the great plan of God is now in effect. His opponents no doubt made much of the fact that God gave circumcision as a "sign of the covenant" to Abraham (Gen. 17:11) and later articulated terms of that covenant in the law given to Moses (Deut. 5:1–21). Therefore, if gentiles want to be people of the covenant (as Jews are), they should accept the sign of that covenant and commit themselves to its terms. But Paul argues that a new era has dawned, making that covenant obsolete. He tells the Galatians that God sent Christ "when the fullness of time had come . . . in order to redeem those who were under the law" (4:4–5). He speaks of the bygone era as a time "before faith came." Back then, people were both guarded and imprisoned by the law (3:23), but things are different "now that faith has come" (3:25). Thus accepting circumcision and living in accord with the law are not only passé but also grossly inappropriate for anyone in the current phase of God's plan. Paul uses the analogy of a child who is an heir to a fabulous estate. While a minor, the child must live under the authority of the servant appointed as tutor or guardian, but when the fullness of time comes (so to speak), the child will no longer be under that authority. Paul is suggesting that for the Galatians to receive circumcision and begin living under the law would be like a full-grown heir submitting to the will of the servant who had been given temporary authority over the heir during childhood (4:1–7).

Some Complicated Arguments

Some of the arguments that Paul uses in Galatians are difficult to follow. Perhaps these simplified reconstructions will help.

Christ Became a Curse (3:10–14)

The Bible teaches that anyone who does not keep all things written in the law is under a curse (see Deut. 27:26). So, Paul reasons, everyone is under this curse. But Scripture also says that anyone who "hangs on a tree" is cursed (see Deut. 21:23). This means that when Jesus was crucified (hung on a tree) he became a curse, and when he died the curse died with him. In this way, Christ redeemed those who were under the curse of the law.

Christ Is the Sole Beneficiary (3:15–18, 27–29)

The Bible says that God made covenant promises to Abraham and his offspring (Gen. 12:7; 22:17–18). The word "covenant" can also refer to a person's "last will and testament," and the collective noun "offspring" (referring to all descendants of Abraham) can also be read as a singular noun referring to one particular individual. So, with a bit of wordplay Paul proposes that God's covenant with Abraham is like a person's will and that the beneficiary of that will is only one person, Jesus Christ. The law of Moses was given long after Abraham and does not annul Christ's inheritance as the sole beneficiary of the promise to Abraham. Furthermore, although Christ is the sole heir to the promise, people who trust in Christ can be clothed with Christ through baptism (Gal. 3:27) and become one in Christ (3:28). By virtue of being "in Christ" they too become Abraham's singular offspring and heirs of the promise (3:29).

Two Mothers Stand for Two Covenants (4:21–31)

The Bible reports that Abraham had children by two women: his son Isaac was born to his wife, Sarah, and was his heir; another son, Ishmael, was born to the slave woman Hagar and so was not his heir (see Gen. 16:15; 21:2, 9–10). These women, Paul suggests in Galatians, provide an allegory for understanding two covenants. People who trust in the covenant of the law (given by Moses on Sinai) are like the child of Hagar: they are physically descended from Abraham but are not heirs to the promise; indeed, they are enslaved to the law (Gal. 4:25; cf. 2:4; 5:1). But those who trust in Christ are children of a new covenant, and they are like Isaac, true heirs for whom God's promise to Abraham is being fulfilled.

Point Four: The Spirit Produces What the Law Cannot Effect

Paul believes that God has given the Holy Spirit to people (3:2) so that Christ may be formed in them (4:19), and the benefits of receiving the Spirit exceed anything that could be accomplished by being circumcised and keeping the Jewish law. His opponents may have presented "keeping Torah" as a path to holiness and virtue: the Galatians should be circumcised and live in accord with the Jewish law because that law expresses how God wants people to live. But Paul's position is that the law is impotent: it describes holiness but cannot effect holiness. He reminds the Galatians that God gave them the Spirit when they first believed the gospel (3:2), and he assures them that God continues to supply them with the Spirit and to work miracles among them, not because they do works of the law but rather because they place their trust in what they heard from the first: the gospel of Christ crucified (3:1–5; cf. 1 Cor. 1:23; 2:2). Paul says that the whole law may be summarized in the command "You shall love your neighbor as yourself" (5:14; cf. Lev. 19:18), and in order to fulfill this, he encourages the Galatians to "live by the Spirit" (5:16). Sinful behavior results from human desires and passions (called "the desires of the flesh" in 5:16–17). These are bent on selfish indulgence rather than on serving others, and they inevitably lead to all sorts of vices and unholy activities. The law tells people that these things are wrong but offers nothing in the way of controlling the flesh or extinguishing its desires. When a person belongs to Christ Jesus, however, the desires and passions of the flesh are "crucified" (5:24), and Christ now lives in and through that person (2:20). The Spirit takes over and produces a rich harvest of virtuous fruit (5:22–23; see fig. 16.3). The result is nothing short of "a new creation" (6:15; cf. 2 Cor. 5:17).

Christ crucified: the main focus of Paul's preaching according to 1 Corinthians 1:22–24; 2:1–2; the phrase seems to be shorthand for what theologians call a "theology of the cross" (*theologia crucis*).

new creation: an understanding of God's saving activity according to which, through Christ, people are given a new life in a new age that has already begun.

Conclusion

Students might be excused for wondering whether Paul's letter to the Galatians has enduring significance for Christian churches. In our day, few people who believe in Jesus are Jewish, and the proposal that Christians should keep Jewish laws may seem odd. The idea that people have to convert to Judaism before they can

---

Box 16.8

Distinctions Cancelled

Diogenes Laertius says that Socrates, the wisest of the wise, is reported to have said there were three blessings for which he was grateful to Fortune: "First, that I was born a human being and not one of the brutes; next, that I was born a man and not a woman; third, a Greek and not a barbarian."*

Paul writes, "There is no longer Jew or Greek, there is no longer slave or free, there is no longer male and female; for all of you are one in Christ Jesus" (Gal. 3:28).

*Diogenes Laertius, *Lives of Eminent Philosophers*, trans. R. D. Hicks (Cambridge, MA: Harvard University Press, 1925), §1.33.

Fig. 16.3. Fruit of the Spirit. In Galatians 5:22–23 Paul lists nine things that he claims are produced within believers by the Spirit of God: love, joy, peace, patience, kindness, generosity, faithfulness, gentleness, and self-control. His point seems to be that people cannot learn how to evince these virtues simply by trying harder or by following rules, but when people are transformed by the Spirit of God, they become people for whom such virtues are authentic expressions of their new identity. (Bridgeman Images)

become Christians seems especially odd. And yet, Paul's letter to the Galatians has continued to be one of the most read and discussed books of the New Testament.

Along with Romans, this letter became central to the doctrinal controversies that characterized the Protestant Reformation. Martin Luther, John Calvin, and other Reformers understood what Paul says about "works of the law" as implying an impotence of human merit to overcome the effects of original sin or attain salvation. They argued that although "good works" may be the expected fruit of the Holy Spirit evident in a Christian life, such works cannot establish, maintain, or improve one's standing with God, which is dependent solely on the grace of God in Jesus Christ. Some modern scholars question whether this was Paul's main point, but few would argue that Paul would disagree with such an application of his position, and the teaching that people are saved (justified) by trusting in God's grace rather than by performing meritorious good works has become standard within most Christian circles today.

⊙ **EXPLORE 16.12**
Galatians 3:28 in Roman and Jewish Perspective

The letter's declaration of God's universal favor has also sparked continuing discussion, as it is generally thought that Paul opens a topic on which much more could be said. In Galatians 3:28 Paul declares, "There is no longer Jew or Greek, there is no longer slave or free, there is no longer male and female; for all of you are one in Christ Jesus." He cites three types of distinctions that should no longer be made, but his letter addresses only one of these in depth: the distinction between Jews and gentiles. Christians throughout history have sought to apply what Paul says about Jews and gentiles to the other distinctions as well. What do his bold words about God's universal favor have to say about distinctions made on the basis of social class or gender? And do they have implications for other sorts of distinctions?

Finally, Galatians has often been called the "Christian Magna Carta" because of its strong affirmation of Christian freedom. In Galatians 5:1 Paul declares, "For freedom, Christ has set us free. Stand firm, therefore, and do not submit again to a yoke of slavery." And, then, just a few verses later, in 5:13, he says, "You were called to freedom, brothers and sisters; only do not use your freedom as an opportunity for self-indulgence, but through love become slaves to one another." This portrait of liberty has been one of the most celebrated aspects of Paul's letter to the Galatians. The paradoxical notion that one is really free only when one is "free to serve" has struck a chord throughout the ages with Christians of many stripes, including preachers, poets, politicians, and philosophers.

FOR FURTHER READING: **Galatians**

Bedford, Nancy. *Galatians: A Theological Commentary.* Belief Series. Louisville: Westminster John Knox, 2016.

Cousar, Charles B. *Reading Galatians, Philippians, and 1 Thessalonians: A Literary and Theological Commentary.* Reading the New Testament. Macon, GA: Smyth & Helwys, 2001.

Dunn, James D. G. *The Theology of Paul's Letter to the Galatians.* New Testament Theology. Cambridge: Cambridge University Press, 1993.

Oakes, Peter. *Galatians.* Paideia. Grand Rapids: Baker Academic, 2015.

Weidman, Frederick W. *Galatians.* Westminster Bible Companion. Louisville: Westminster John Knox, 2012.

Wright, N. T. *Paul for Everyone: Galatians and Thessalonians.* 2nd ed. Louisville: Westminster John Knox, 2004.

⊘ Go to www
.IntroducingNT.com
for summaries,
videos, and other
study tools.

17

Ephesians

Good times! Paul's letter to the Ephesians portrays the present as a time of blessing (1:3), when believers feel like they are already in heaven (2:6). Everything is going as planned (1:9–10; 3:8–10), and it can get only better from here (2:7). Most of all, this is a time of peace: the walls that divide people have come down, and hostility has given way to reconciliation (2:14–17). There is a profound sense of "oneness" (4:4–6).

Of course, this is the church that we're talking about, not the world at large. Still, the idyllic picture of Christian community may seem at odds with what we observe in other letters of Paul: factionalism (1 Cor. 1:11–12); arguments (Rom. 14:1–6); heresy (Gal. 1:6–7); scandalous behavior (1 Cor. 5:1); painful confrontations (Gal. 2:11); persecution (1 Thess. 2:14; 3:4); and a generous amount of gossip, backbiting, and instances of people meddling in one another's affairs (2 Cor. 12:20; 1 Thess. 4:11). So when did things get so peaceful?

At first glance, Ephesians appears to be addressed to a church in which there is no conflict. But wait—there is indeed conflict. In fact, there is a war going on, but it is not a war with enemies made of flesh and blood. The battle now is against "spiritual forces of evil in the heavenly places" (6:12), against the devil (6:11) and his minions, the principalities and powers that exercise their influence in a dimension not perceptible to human senses (2:2; 3:10). The saints of God are children of light, bringing what is good and right and true into a realm that must otherwise be described as "this present darkness" (5:8–9; 6:12).

In Ephesians the focus has shifted from the mundane to the ethereal. The instances of friction and harassment that have troubled the church before may

saints: people who are holy; some New Testament writers use the word as a virtual synonym for "Christians."

or may not have died down, but they pale in significance when one looks at the big picture. The emphasis of this letter is on the universal significance of what God has done in Jesus Christ, and "universal" is meant here in a literal sense: the focus is on what Christ means not simply for Christians or even for all humanity but rather for everything in heaven and on earth (1:9–10, 20–23).

We call this writing "the letter of Paul to the Ephesians," although, as we will see, many interpreters do not think that Paul wrote it, some do not think that it was written to the Ephesians, and quite a few do not even think that it is a letter.

Overview

After a fairly typical salutation (1:1–2), the author (who identifies himself as "Paul, an apostle of Christ Jesus") presents an elegant blessing of God that serves as a liturgical overture to the letter (1:3–14). He declares that God is bringing to fulfillment a plan to gather all things in Christ: those who were destined to be God's blameless children have been forgiven their trespasses as a result of the redemption that comes through Christ's blood, and they have been sealed with the Holy Spirit as a pledge of further redemption still to come. The blessing segues into a thanksgiving as the writer acknowledges his recipients' faith and love (1:15–17). He prays that they might be fully enlightened with regard to what God has in store for them and with regard to what the power of the risen and exalted Christ will accomplish in and through the church, which is his body (1:18–23). Once dead in trespasses, they have been saved by grace and exalted with Christ to fulfill their destiny as people created for a life of good works (2:1–10). By reconciling all people to God through the cross, Christ has created a new humanity, marked by peace rather than hostility; this is manifest in the church, where Jews and gentiles alike have access to God and, indeed, compose what is now God's spiritual dwelling place (2:11–22). This new unity of humanity is "the mystery of Christ," revealed to Paul when he was commissioned by God; now the church's role in the divine drama is to make the mystery known, not only to the world of unbelievers but also to spiritual powers in heavenly places (3:1–13). The author prays again that his readers might comprehend the immeasurable love of Christ manifested in all of this (3:14–19), and he offers a brief doxology to conclude the first part of the letter (3:20–21).

The second half of the letter explicates practical implications of what was proclaimed in the first part: the readers are urged to live a life worthy of their calling (4:1), which means life with others in a community that functions as a single entity (4:2–16). The specifics of such a life are spelled out with reference to a number of behaviors that will set those in the church apart from others,

⊙ EXPLORE 17.0
Ephesians: Outline of Contents

as imitators of God and children of light (4:17–5:20). A series of household instructions indicates how they are to conduct themselves in family and social relationships (5:21–6:9), and an appeal to guard against the wiles of the devil encourages the readers to be dressed in spiritual armor provided by God (6:10–17). The letter concludes with exhortations to prayer (6:18–19), a commendation of Tychicus, the letter carrier (6:20–21), and a double benediction (6:23–24).

Historical Background

The city of Ephesus is located in what is now western Turkey, across the Aegean Sea from Athens (see map 17.1). In New Testament times it was both the capital city and the leading commercial center in the Roman province of Asia (not to be confused with the continent of Asia today). Even today visitors thrill to see the ruins of an amphitheater that seated perhaps as many as twenty-five thousand people (possibly referred to in Acts 19:29–30); Ephesus was also home to the magnificent Temple of Artemis (referred to in Acts

Fig. 17.1. Ephesus gate. The ruins of ancient Ephesus provide some indication of the grandeur that the city must have had in the days of Paul. This magnificent gateway was built about the same time that Jesus was born (4–2 BCE). An inscription on the gate dedicates the structure to Caesar Augustus, who is identified as "Son of God." Paul passed through this gate (and beneath that inscription) whenever he entered the city. (Todd Bolen / BiblePlaces.com)

Map 17.1. Pauline cities around the Aegean Sea.

19:27), one of the fabled seven wonders of the world (see fig. 17.2). It was a thoroughly Roman city that had often earned the title of *neōkoros* for the region, meaning that it served as the official headquarters for the imperial cult, in charge of festivities and rituals honoring and worshiping the emperor. A brief letter to the church in Ephesus is found in Revelation 2:1–7, which portrays the Christian community there as orthodox and faithful but lacking in the love and works that it had exhibited "at first."

The book of Acts says that Paul paid a brief visit to Ephesus on his second missionary journey (18:19–21) and returned on his third journey (19:1–41; cf. 20:17–38) to spend between two and three years there (19:10; 20:31). All Asia heard the word of the Lord (19:10), but the introduction of Christianity to this pagan setting caused "no little disturbance" among those whose livelihood depended on practices Christians denounced as demonic or idolatrous (19:23–41). Paul's time in Ephesus usually is dated in the early to mid-50s, and he is believed to have written 1 Corinthians from there (possibly other letters as well). He refers to times of trouble in the city (1 Cor. 15:32; 2 Cor. 1:8), and it is often thought that he was imprisoned there for a time. He says that he had many adversaries in Ephesus but that there was also "a wide door for effective work" that justified a considerable expense of time in this location (1 Cor. 16:8–9).

Given Paul's close association with the church in Ephesus and his relatively long tenure in the city, it is not surprising that we find a letter from Paul to "the saints who are in Ephesus" (1:1) in our New Testament. What is surprising, however, is that the contents of that letter betray no hint of that well-established relationship. There are no references to the specific circumstances of that community or to Paul's previous ministry among them. Typically, Paul likes to reminisce about such things (e.g., 1 Cor. 2:1; Gal. 4:12–15; 1 Thess. 2:1–12). In Ephesians there are no personal greetings to individual members of the church; by contrast, when Paul wrote to the Romans, he greeted twenty-six individuals by name (Rom. 16:3–15), and that was in a letter to a church that he had never visited. The Letter to the Ephesians has an impersonal tone: Paul says, "I have heard of your faith in the Lord Jesus" (1:15; cf. 4:21) and indicates that,

⊙ EXPLORE 17.7
Artemis of the Ephesians

Fig. 17.2. The Temple of Artemis. *Above*, a reconstruction of the famed Temple of Artemis in Ephesus, listed by Plutarch as one of the seven wonders of the ancient world. According to Acts, the mere suggestion that Paul's preaching might detract from the temple's glory caused an anti-Christian riot (see Acts 19:23–41). *Below*, all that remains of the temple today. See also figs. 1.5, 10.4. (Balage Balogh / www.archaeologyillustrated.com; Todd Bolen / BiblePlaces.com)

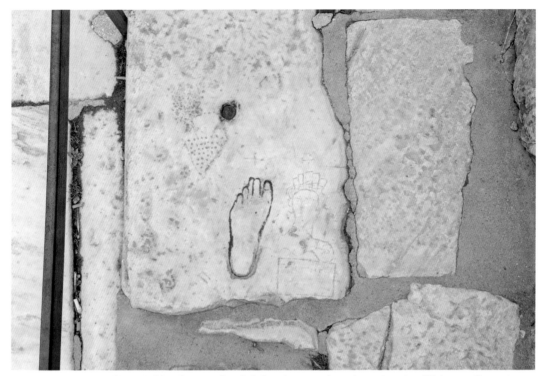

Fig. 17.3. Directions to a brothel. A paving stone from the ancient city of Ephesus still reveals a prominent advertisement for one of the city's brothels: the images of a foot ("walk this direction"), a woman, and a bill of sale (or price list) are still visible on the two-thousand-year-old sign. It was in this secular environment that the Christian community tried to advance the ethic of marriage spelled out in Ephesians 5:21–33. (Todd Bolen / BiblePlaces.com)

surely, they have also heard about him and his commission from God (3:2). Such comments suggest that the author and recipients know one another by reputation only, but in fact Paul had spent from two to three years in Ephesus as a very visible leader of that church (Acts 20:31).

We may need to look beyond the text of English Bibles to find an explanation for this curious state of affairs. The words "in Ephesus" that are found in Ephesians 1:1 in almost all English translations of the Bible actually do not appear in the oldest and most consistently reliable Greek manuscripts. If those ancient manuscripts are correct, then the letter that we call "Ephesians" may not have presented Paul's words to the church in Ephesus as such but rather to "the saints who are faithful in Christ Jesus" (wherever they might be).

Many scholars think that this letter was written probably as a general address intended for widespread distribution. They sometimes question whether it should properly be called a "letter" at all, since it is more like a homily or theological tract to which an epistolary opening and closing have been attached. It could have been a circular pamphlet sent to many churches, and the copy

⊙ EXPLORE 10.27
Acts 19:23–41—
Temple of Artemis

⊙ EXPLORE 19.21
The Letter from
Laodicea

sent to Ephesus simply happens to be one that survived. One second-century commentator, Marcion, actually refers to what we know as "the Letter to the Ephesians" as "the Letter to the Laodiceans," indicating his belief that it had been addressed to the church in Laodicea (for an indication that some

Parallels between Ephesians and Colossians

Similar topics are treated, often in the same order and sometimes with identical wording.

Topic	Ephesians	Colossians
Redemption and forgiveness	1:7	1:14–20
All things in heaven and earth are in Christ	1:10	1:20
I have heard of your faith	1:15	1:4
I thank God always for you	1:16	1:3
Pray that God will give you wisdom	1:17	1:9
Riches of a glorious inheritance/mystery	1:18	1:27
God made you alive	2:5	2:13
Aliens reconciled through Christ's death	2:12–13	1:21–22
Christ has abolished the law	2:15	2:14
Paul is suffering for their sake	3:1	1:24
Divine commission given to Paul	3:2	1:25
Divine mystery made known to Paul	3:3	1:26
Paul a servant of the gospel	3:7	1:23, 25
Lead a worthy life	4:1	1:10
Humility, meekness, patience	4:2	3:12
Bear with one another	4:2	3:13
Christ is head of the body	4:15–16	2:19
Put off old nature, put on new nature	4:22–32	3:5–10, 12
Let there be no immorality among you	5:3–6	3:5–9
Walk wisely and make the most of your time	5:15	4:5
Sing psalms, hymns, and spiritual songs	5:19	3:16
Give thanks to God	5:20	3:17
Tables of household duties	5:21–6:9	3:18–4:1
for wives	5:22–24	3:18
for husbands	5:25–33	3:19
for children	6:1–3	3:20
for fathers	6:4	3:21
for slaves	6:5–8	3:22–25
for masters	6:9	4:1
Paul the prisoner exhorts persistence in prayer	6:18–20	4:2–3
Tychicus will inform church about Paul	6:21	4:7
Tychicus sent to encourage their hearts	6:22	4:8

Indebted to Charles B. Puskas Jr., *The Letters of Paul: An Introduction* (Collegeville, MN: Liturgical Press, 1993), 130–31.

Box 17.2

Distinctive Aspects of Ephesians

Ephesians is different in certain ways from what are called Paul's "undisputed letters."

Distinctive Wording

- It contains extremely long sentences (in Greek, 1:3–14 is one sentence, as are 1:15–23; 3:1–7).
- It makes repetitive use of adjectives and synonyms (1:19 uses four words for "power").
- It makes abundant use of the word "all" (about fifty times).
- It uses "devil" (4:27; 6:11) instead of "Satan" (Rom. 16:20; 1 Cor. 5:5; 7:5; 2 Cor. 2:11; 11:14; 12:7; 1 Thess. 2:18).
- It refers to Paul as "least of all the saints" (3:8) rather than as "least of the apostles" (1 Cor. 15:9).
- Christ (4:11) rather than God (1 Cor. 12:28) is the one who appoints apostles, prophets, and others in the church.
- The church is the body with Christ as head (1:22–23; cf. Col. 1:18) rather than being the whole body of Christ with the head as one of its members (1 Cor. 12:20–21, 27).
- Readers are told to imitate God (5:1) rather than Paul (1 Cor. 4:6; 11:1; Phil. 3:17; but cf. 1 Thess. 1:6).
- It uses "kingdom of Christ and of God" (5:5; cf. Col. 1:13) rather than "kingdom of God" (Rom. 14:17; 1 Cor. 4:20; 6:9, 10; 15:50; Gal. 5:21; 1 Thess. 2:12).
- People are "saved" by faith (2:5, 8) rather than "justified" by faith (Rom. 3:28; 5:1; Gal. 2:16; 3:24).
- It speaks of works as "good works" (2:9–10) rather than as "works of the law" (Gal. 2:16; 3:2, 5, 10, 12).
- It uses "church" for the universal church (1:22; 3:10, 21; 5:23, 24, 25, 27, 29, 32) rather than for a local congregation (e.g., Rom. 16:23; 1 Cor. 4:17; 14:23; but cf. 1 Cor. 10:32; 15:9).

- It refers to Christ as "the Beloved" (1:6), an expression not used for Christ in Paul's undisputed letters (but cf. Col. 1:13).
- It speaks of "the heavenly places" (1:3, 20; 2:6; 3:10; 6:12) rather than simply "heaven" (1 Cor. 8:5; 2 Cor. 12:2; Phil. 3:20) or "the heavens" (2 Cor. 5:1).
- The church is built on the foundation of the apostles and prophets, with Christ as cornerstone (2:19–20), rather than on the foundation of Christ alone (1 Cor. 3:10–11).

Distinctive Concepts

- The second coming of Christ has faded in significance, since the power and glory of heaven are experienced now (1:3; 2:4–7; cf. Rom. 8:18–25; 2 Cor. 4:7–18).
- Jews and gentiles are merged equally into a new humanity (2:14–16) as opposed to gentiles being provisionally grafted into the tree of Israel (Rom. 11:13–21).
- Marriage is highly esteemed (5:21–23) rather than being merely allowed for the sake of controlling lust (1 Cor. 7:8–9).
- The law is said to have been abolished by Christ (2:15) rather than being described as something that the coming of faith has not overthrown (Rom. 3:31).
- The reconciliation of Jews and gentiles is depicted as an accomplished reality (2:11–18) rather than as a future hope (Rom. 11:25–32).
- Salvation is a present reality (2:7–10) rather than a future hope (Rom. 5:9–10; 10:9, 13; 1 Cor. 3:15; 5:5; but cf. Rom. 8:24; 1 Cor. 1:18; 15:2; 2 Cor. 2:15).
- Exaltation of believers to heaven is a present reality (2:6) rather than a future hope (1 Cor. 15:23; 1 Thess. 4:16–17).

letter from Paul had been sent there, see Col. 4:16). Nevertheless, although we have manuscripts that do not mention any specific church in the address, all manuscripts that do specify a church mention Ephesus. The letter (if we may call it that) came to be closely associated with the Ephesian church at a very early time, suggesting perhaps that this was the location in which it was most prominently read and valued.

In any case, the work that we now know as "the Letter to the Ephesians" indicates that Paul is writing from prison (3:1; 4:1; 6:20). There is quite a bit of discussion as to which imprisonment is meant, since Paul apparently was locked up several times (2 Cor. 6:5; 11:23). There is also considerable doubt among scholars as to whether this book actually was written by Paul; the prison identification is sometimes taken as a bit of romantic fiction—the sort of device that a pseudonymous author might use so that readers would receive the book as the testimony of someone who suffered for the faith.

pseudonymous author: an author who uses a pseudonym (fictitious name); the author of a pseudepigraphic writing.

This question of Pauline authenticity is determinative for understanding the historical origins of the letter, but we must first note two other matters.

1. Ephesians is remarkably similar to the letter of Paul to the Colossians (see box 17.1); in fact, the two writings have been called "literary siblings." Somewhere between one-half and one-third of the 155 verses in Ephesians have close parallels to the material found in Colossians, often to the point of occurring in the same order of presentation. A few passages are repeated almost word for word (cf. Eph. 1:4 with Col. 1:22; Eph. 1:15 with Col. 1:4; Eph. 6:21–22 with Col. 4:7–8). Most scholars believe that Colossians was written first and that whoever wrote Ephesians was familiar with the contents of Colossians. One possibility is that Paul wrote both letters: first, he wrote Colossians to a specific congregation, and then he produced Ephesians as a more general letter dealing with the same subject matter. Another possibility, however, is that someone had a copy of Colossians (which, as we will see in chap. 19, may or may not have been written by Paul) and used it as a template to create Ephesians—a letter that sounds like one that Paul would have written but with more general application.

2. Ephesians is remarkably dissimilar to what are called the "undisputed letters of Paul" (i.e., the seven letters that all scholars agree are written by him). Box 17.2 lists some of the distinctive anomalies that characterize this letter. A number of these matters might be regarded as minor stylistic quirks, but others seem to convey differences that could be theologically significant. Scholars differ in their assessment of whether such features present Ephesians as actually inconsistent with Paul's undisputed letters or as simply different from them. They also differ in their understanding of whether such features can be adequately explained (e.g., by claiming

⊙ **EXPLORE 17.13**
Literary Siblings: Relationship of Ephesians to Colossians

amanuensis: a secretary or trained scribe who writes letters for other people.

that Paul allowed an amanuensis considerable freedom in crafting the letter, or that the Ephesian context required different language and imagery, or that Paul's ideas had developed over time).

Given the two matters just described (similarity with Colossians, dissimilarity with the seven undisputed letters), many different scenarios have been proposed regarding the authorship or origin of the book we know as Paul's letter to the Ephesians. These proposals fall into three basic categories:

1. Some scholars think that Paul did write Ephesians. If so, he produced it probably around the same time as Colossians and Philemon, sending all three compositions to the province of Asia by way of Tychicus (Eph. 6:21; Col. 4:7). He may have written these letters during his Roman imprisonment in the early 60s or possibly during an earlier imprisonment (e.g., in Caesarea or even in Ephesus itself).

2. Some scholars think that one of Paul's disciples or companions wrote Ephesians in the years after Paul's death, perhaps to provide the church with a generic statement of what the apostle would have wanted to write to them had he lived. In this case, the letter might be dated to the decade of the 70s or maybe even to the 80s.

3. Some scholars think that a later admirer of Paul (albeit someone who had not actually known him) wrote Ephesians in Paul's name in order to continue the apostle's legacy and to gain an audience for work that might not have drawn as much attention otherwise. Scholars who hold to this view often date the letter to the early 90s.

There are possible variations on these views. If Paul wrote Colossians but not Ephesians then, as indicated above, the person responsible for Ephesians may have used Colossians as a template. Or if Paul wrote neither of the letters then both Ephesians and Colossians perhaps were produced by the same devoted disciple or later admirer of Paul. Or the letters could have been produced by two completely different pseudonymous writers, with one using the work of the other.

One point on which most scholars agree is that Ephesians appears to be addressed to a mainly gentile readership (2:11–12; 3:1). The overall purpose of the letter is to offer encouragement to these believers by articulating God's plan for them and exhorting them to fulfill the role that they have been chosen to play in that plan. The focus is on the identity of believers in Christ and in the church and in the world: the author wants his readers to realize who they are and to pursue the values and lifestyle appropriate to that identity (2:10).

⊙ EXPLORE 17.12
Authorship of
Ephesians

Major Themes in Ephesians

The Mysterious Plan of God

The Greek word *mystērion* ("mystery") is used six times in Ephesians (1:9; 3:3, 4, 9; 5:32; 6:19), always with reference to something divine. We perhaps think of a mystery as something puzzling that needs to be figured out, but the Greek term has a different connotation: it refers to something hidden that cannot possibly be figured out, but can be known only if revealed by someone possessing inside information. A *divine* mystery can be revealed only by God (3:5), though in this case God has commissioned Paul and other "holy apostles and prophets" to disclose the mystery to the church (3:1–5, 8–9; 6:19). God also has chosen the church to reveal the mystery to the world and, indeed, to the cosmic powers of the universe (3:9–11).

The mystery concerns God's plan to unite all things in Christ (1:9–10). In particular, God plans to unite all *people* in Christ, including those who traditionally have been identified as "Jews" or "gentiles" (3:5–6) but who may

cosmic powers: spiritual beings, perhaps associated with stars and other heavenly bodies (see Eph. 6:12).

Powerful Spiritual Beings

The cosmic dimension of Christ's victory over powerful spiritual beings is emphasized in Ephesians (see 1:20–21; 3:10) and also in Colossians (see 1:13; 2:10, 15). We read about:

- rulers (Eph. 1:21; 2:2; 3:10; 6:12; Col. 1:16; 2:10, 15; cf. Rom. 8:38; 1 Cor. 15:24)
- authorities (Eph. 1:21; 3:10; 6:12; Col. 1:13, 16; 2:10, 15; cf. 1 Cor. 15:24)
- powers (Eph. 1:21; cf. Rom. 8:38; 1 Cor. 15:24)
- cosmic powers (Eph. 6:12)
- dominions (Eph. 1:21; Col. 1:16)
- thrones (Col. 1:16)

Six different designations are used in Greek, though English Bibles do not translate the words consistently; the phrase "elemental spirits of the universe" (Col. 2:8, 20) seems generic.

Who or what are these spiritual beings? The author and original readers of Ephesians would have believed that they were living creatures, not biological entities "of blood and flesh" (Eph. 6:12), but just as real as humans or animals. Angels and demons may be the best-known examples of such beings, along with the devil, who is called "the ruler of the power of the air" (2:2) and elsewhere in the New Testament is referred to as "the god of this world" (2 Cor. 4:4). Jews and Christians often identified the gods of other religions as powerful spiritual beings as well, not denying their existence but rather identifying them as inferior rivals to the one true God.

In Ephesians these powerful spiritual beings are presented as evil forces intent on dominating people's lives and influencing world affairs. They are the true enemies of believers (6:12). Ephesians says that Christ has been elevated to a position of dominance over them (1:20–21), that the church shares in this exaltation (1:22–23; 2:6; 3:10), and that God equips believers for the ongoing struggle against such spiritual forces of evil in "this present darkness" (6:12).

now be identified as a "new humanity" (2:15). This has been God's intention all along, "hidden for ages" (3:9; cf. 3:5) but coming to fruition now in "the fullness of time" (1:10).

The plan seems to be accomplished in (at least) two stages: crucifixion and exaltation. First, the death of Jesus on the cross has effected a forgiveness of trespasses so that all people are now on equal footing before God (1:7; 2:4, 13, 16–18). There is no longer any divine preference for Israel, for Christ has broken down the dividing wall that separated Jews from gentiles and has abolished the law that set Jews apart (2:14–15). This reference to a "dividing wall" invokes the image of an actual wall in the Jerusalem temple that literally separated the "Court of the Gentiles" from the inner sanctuaries to which only Jews could be admitted; the Jewish law that Christ has abolished served as a metaphorical dividing wall because it defined the terms of a covenant that applied to Israel only. The cross of Christ creates a new way to be human, a way that does not privilege one national or ethnic group above another.

Fig. 17.4. The dividing wall. This picture shows a contemporary view of the wall around the old city of Jerusalem. In Paul's day a similar wall surrounded the temple court, into which only Jews were admitted. An inscription on that wall read, "No man of another nation is to enter within the fence and enclosure round the temple, and whoever is caught will have himself to blame that his death ensues." Ephesians 2:14 uses this "dividing wall" as a metaphor for things that separate humans. Christ creates "one new humanity" in which all people are reconciled and hostility gives way to peace (Eph. 2:15–16). (Todd Bolen / BiblePlaces.com)

The second stage of God's plan to unify all reality in Christ came with the exaltation of Christ, with his resurrection and subsequent installment in heaven as God's supreme agent, with authority over all other powers and principalities (1:19–22). Jesus Christ now possesses immeasurable power to eradicate the oppressive influence of all spiritual forces that have held people captive (1:21–22; 2:1–2; 4:8; 6:12).

According to Ephesians, there are two signs that this plan of God is being realized. The first sign is the Holy Spirit (1:13). Without going into detail, the author of this letter assumes that his readers will know that they have been marked with the seal of the Spirit (1:13–14; 4:30) and will agree that this is a reliable sign that God's plan is working out. But then there is a second, ultimate sign that God's plan is unfolding: the unity of the church (4:4–6, 11–16), especially the unity of Jews and gentiles in the church (2:11–21). The peace (2:14–15; 4:3) and lack of hostility (2:14) that the church exhibits serve as a revelation even to the cosmic powers of the universe that God's mysterious plan has taken effect (3:10–11).

Elevation of the Church

Attention is often paid to the ecclesiology of Ephesians, for there is considerable focus on the nature and function of the church. We may note, first, that in this letter the word "church" (Greek, *ekklēsia*) is never used to refer to a local congregation but is used only with reference to "the universal church" (1:22; 3:10, 21; 5:23, 24, 25, 27, 29, 32). The "church" in Ephesians is synonymous with "all people who have been reconciled with God through Jesus Christ."

The devotion of Christ to the church is emphasized; indeed, the sexual intimacy of a husband and wife may be construed as a living metaphor for the loving union of Christ and the church (5:31–32). Elsewhere Paul says that Christ died for sinners (Rom. 5:6, 8) or even for all (2 Cor. 5:14–15); in Ephesians Christ died for the church (5:25). Christ has also sanctified the church (through cleansing by the washing of water with the word—a baptismal image) in order to present the church to himself in splendor without spot or blemish (5:25–26). Thus the unity and the holiness of the church appear to have been the goal of Christ's suffering and death, and he continues to nourish and cherish the church toward these outcomes (5:29). As indicated above, the church has a central place in God's plan for the unity of all creation. That plan was executed for the church (1:22) and is now being carried out through the church (3:10).

The church in Ephesians is both a spiritual and an earthly institution. Spiritually, the church is the body of Christ (1:22–23; 4:12; cf. Rom. 12:4–8; 1 Cor. 12:12–27) or the body of which Christ is the head (5:23; cf. Col. 1:18). This image implies interdependence between Christ and the church: the body would,

ecclesiology: beliefs and ideas about the nature and function of the church, or of the Christian community in general.

Box 17.4

A Life Worthy of the Calling

Ephesians 4:1–6:18 offers these "dos and don'ts" with regard to Christian behavior.

Do

- be humble and gentle (4:2)
- be patient, bearing with one another in love (4:2)
- make every effort to maintain unity and peace (4:3)
- speak the truth in love to others in the body (4:15)
- speak truth, not falsehood, to neighbors (4:25)
- work honestly at manual labor (4:28)
- be sufficiently productive to share with the needy (4:28)
- speak only words that impart grace and edify others (4:29)
- be kind to one another (4:32)
- be tenderhearted, forgiving one another (4:32)
- be imitators of God (5:1)
- live in love, as Christ loved us (5:2)
- offer thanksgiving (5:4)
- try to find out what is pleasing to the Lord (5:10)
- expose the secret and shameful works of darkness (5:11–12)
- be careful to live wisely (5:15)
- make the most of the time (5:16)
- understand what the will of the Lord is (5:17)
- be filled with the Spirit (5:18)
- sing psalms and hymns and spiritual songs (5:19)
- give thanks to God at all times and for everything (5:20)
- be subject to one another in reverence for Christ (5:21)
- be strong in the Lord and stand firm (6:10, 14)
- pray at all times (6:18)

Don't

- be tossed about by every wind of doctrine (4:14)
- fall prey to people's trickery, craftiness, or deceitful scheming (4:14)
- pursue licentiousness or impure practices (4:19–20)
- yield to lust (4:22)
- let the sun go down on your anger (4:26)
- make room for the devil (4:27)
- steal (4:28)
- let evil talk come out of your mouth (4:29)
- grieve the Holy Spirit of God (4:30)
- hold on to bitterness, wrath, anger, wrangling, slander, or malice (4:31)
- even mention fornication, impurity of any kind, or greed (5:3)
- make any allowance for obscene, silly, or vulgar talk (5:4)
- let anyone deceive you with empty words (5:6)
- associate with deceivers or the disobedient (5:7)
- take part in the unfruitful works of darkness (5:11)
- be foolish (5:17)
- get drunk with wine (5:18)

of course, be dead without its head, but the head also needs its body in order to function. In another somewhat strange or mixed metaphor, the church is described as a living building, one that grows into a holy temple that serves as the dwelling place of God (2:19–22). But the church is also an earthly institution, with a fairly well-defined polity and governance. There are apostles and prophets (2:20; 3:5; 4:11), in addition to evangelists, pastors, and teachers (4:11) who apparently serve particular functions in accord with their gifts. The actual work of ministry, however, is not carried out by these officers or leaders but rather is entrusted to "the saints"—that is, to the laity who compose the rank-and-file membership of various congregations. The task of church leaders is to "equip the saints for the work of ministry" so that all may come to experience God's plan for unity in its fullness (4:12–13).

The oneness of the church also seems to provide the touchstone for moral conduct in Ephesians: all thirty-six ethical imperatives provided in 4:1–6:20 seem related to the affirmation that "we are members of one another" (4:25) (see box 17.4). Accordingly, believers should treat one another as extensions of themselves (see 5:28–30). This might be regarded as a metaphysical actualization of the Golden Rule: the point is not simply that one should "do to others as you would have them do to you" (Matt. 7:12); the point now is that what you do to others you actually do to yourself. This is never truer than with regard to members of one's own household (see box 17.5). Indeed, Ephesians seems to regard the Christian household as a miniature version of the church (which may be called the "household of God"; see 2:19; cf. 1 Tim. 3:15).

Idealized Status of Believers

Ephesians describes the present status of Christians in terms of an idealistic spiritual reality, giving expression to a view that theologians call "realized eschatology." It was God's plan before the foundation of the world for people to be "holy and blameless before him in love" (1:4), and those who make up the church are destined to be "without blemish" (5:27). Such an ideal has not been fully realized, but according to Ephesians there is some sense in which perfection has been obtained. Since the church is the body of Christ, when God raised Christ from the dead and seated him in heaven, the church was exalted with him (1:20); already now, those who believe in Christ have been raised up and are seated with him in the heavenly places (2:6; cf. 1:3). They are empowered, furthermore, to actualize the implications of this spiritual exaltation in their daily lives on earth. The same power that raised Jesus from the dead and exalted him is available for those who believe (1:19–20) and is able to accomplish far more than they could ever imagine (3:20); they need only come to know the immeasurable greatness of this power (1:17–19). When they do, they will live in unity and holiness, manifesting their true spiritual identity in their current lives; for believers, to live in this way is simply a matter of being who they are, of becoming the people they have always been destined to be (2:10).

Some interpreters think that this motif is at odds with the teaching of Paul found elsewhere. In other letters Paul mocks those who believe that they have been elevated to some ideal status in this life (1 Cor. 4:8–13), and he emphasizes identification with the crucified Christ rather than with the risen Lord (Rom.

realized eschatology: the belief that blessings and benefits typically associated with the end times can be experienced as a present reality.

⊘ EXPLORE 17.9
Ephesians 6:1–4—
Parenting Advice
from Paul and Ben
Sira

⊘ EXPLORE 17.6
Ephesians 5:21–6:9
and Other House-
hold Tables in the
New Testament

Box 17.5

The Christian Household

Ephesians 5:21–6:9 presents a modified *Haustafel*, or table of household duties, appropriate for Christians, who also belong to the household of God (2:19). Such tables were common in Greco-Roman writings, but this one is distinctive in that it includes directives to the more powerful members of the household: the instructions are for not just wives but also husbands, not just children but also fathers, not just slaves but also masters.

These directives seem antiquated and oppressive to many modern readers, who believe that wives are to be equal partners in a marriage, not subjects of the husband's domain; children should be taught respect rather than blind obedience; slaves should be emancipated, not intimidated into obedience.

The early Christians were not so radical as to deny the basic ranking of responsibilities that society assigned to such relationships (but see Gal. 3:28). Nevertheless, the traditional *Haustafel* is set here within a context of *mutual* submission (Eph. 5:21), and the overall focus is shifted toward responsibilities of the more powerful party—this in keeping with the servant ethic encouraged by Jesus in the Gospels (Mark 10:41–45; John 13:1–7). Most notable, perhaps, is the notion that husbands are to love their wives in the same way that Christ loved the church: they are to put their wives' wants and needs ahead of their own, giving of themselves in selfless service. This call to husbands probably is based on a social distinction rather than on gender characteristics: the main point is that the impact of Christ's universal call to self-denial is proportionately related to status and power (cf. Mark 8:34).

Other examples of *Haustafeln* are found in Colossians 3:18–4:1; 1 Timothy 2:8–15; 5:1–2; 6:1–2; Titus 2:1–10; 1 Peter 2:13–3:7 (see also two letters by other early church leaders: *1 Clement* 1:3; 21:6–9; Polycarp, *To the Philippians* 4:1–6:2).

theology of glory: a way of understanding the gospel that views faith in Christ as a means to self-betterment, success, and attainment of power.

theology of the cross: a way of understanding the gospel that views faith in Christ as an immersion into a life of service and sacrifice.

⊙ **EXPLORE 19.15** "Realized Eschatology": What Would Paul Think?

6:3–5; 1 Cor. 2:2; 15:31; Gal. 2:19–20; Phil. 3:10); the triumphalist understanding advanced in Ephesians is said to have more in common with the ideas of the "super-apostles" confronted by Paul in Corinth (2 Cor. 11:5; 12:11) than with anything that Paul himself would have promulgated. Indeed, some have identified Ephesians (and sometimes Colossians) as works that promote a "theology of glory" rather than the "theology of the cross" that Paul preferred.

Those who place Ephesians within the Pauline corpus, however, think that the apparent discrepancy can be explained in terms of context. In 2 Corinthians Paul was resisting the notion that life in Christ meant a reprieve from service or suffering. In Ephesians the point is that those who are in Christ are no longer subject to the control of spiritual enemies; they need not fear magical incantations or curses that may be invoked on them by their non-Christian neighbors, nor do they need to worry about incurring the wrath of Roman deities whose favors they no longer curry. Christ has exalted them spiritually above such powers. The idealism, furthermore, is balanced by an awareness that human action is still required: believers must clothe themselves with the new self that God provides (4:24); they must "take up" the armor of God (6:13); they must exert effort at maintaining the unity of the Spirit in the bond of peace (4:3);

they must be faithful in prayer (6:18); and they must be deliberate about leading a life worthy of that to which they have been called (4:1).

Conclusion

Other distinctive themes in Ephesians include an emphasis on growth in knowledge (1:17–18; 3:5, 18; 4:17–24; 5:10, 17) and on speaking the truth (4:15, 21, 25; 5:9, 11–14; 6:14). Ephesians also has a more liturgical feel than any letters except Hebrews and 1 Peter; it strikes many as being saturated with the language and practice of prayer (1:13–14, 16–19; 3:13–21; 5:19–20; 6:18–20). The word *agapē* ("love") is used more often here than in any letter except 1 Corinthians and 1 John (see 1:4, 15; 2:4; 3:17, 19; 4:2, 15, 16; 5:2; 6:23; also the verb "to love" in 5:25, 28, 33; 6:24).

Some have noted a penchant in Ephesians for describing the Christian position with reference to body posture. With regard to the heavenly kingdom, believers are seated (2:6; cf. 1:20), fully at rest because they are saved by grace and their position in paradise is assured. With regard to this world, believers are exhorted to walk, actively moving toward the goal of holiness that is their destiny (the Greek verb for "walk" [*peripatein*] is translated as "live" in the NRSV and other English Bibles in 4:1, 17; 5:2, 8, 15; cf. 2:2, 10). And finally, with regard to the devil, believers are called to stand (6:11, 14), holding firm against the opposition, clothed in God's armor and shielded by faith (6:10–17).

FOR FURTHER READING: **Ephesians**

Lincoln, Andrew, and A. J. M. Wedderburn. *The Theology of the Later Pauline Letters.* New Testament Theology. Cambridge: Cambridge University Press, 1993.

Perkins, Pheme. *Ephesians.* Abingdon New Testament Commentaries. Nashville: Abingdon, 1997.

Talbert, Charles H. *Ephesians and Colossians.* Paideia. Grand Rapids: Baker Academic, 2007.

Verhey, Allen, and Joseph S. Harvard. *Ephesians: A Theological Commentary.* Belief Series. Louisville: Westminster John Knox, 2011.

Wright, N. T. *Paul for Everyone: The Prison Letters; Ephesians, Philippians, Colossians, and Philemon.* 2nd ed. Louisville: Westminster John Knox, 2004.

⊙ Go to www
.IntroducingNT.com
for summaries,
videos, and other
study tools.

18

Philippians

"Rejoice in the Lord always," Paul exclaims in what is probably his most upbeat letter, "again, I will say, Rejoice" (Phil. 4:4). This brief letter to the Philippians not only contains a magnificent example of what may have been an early Christian hymn (2:6–11) but also is laced with happy and confident passages just begging to be turned into gospel choruses for rousing revival meetings or amusing ditties for kids at summer camp. There is, of course, much more to the letter. "Beware of the dogs . . . who mutilate the flesh" (3:2). No one ever turns *that* into a camp song. But on the whole, Philippians is a positive and upbeat letter. Prominent topics include friendship (1:3, 7–8; 4:1, 15), contentment (4:11–12), thanksgiving (1:3; 4:6), peace (4:7, 9), joy (1:4, 18; 2:2, 17–18, 28, 29; 3:1; 4:1, 4, 10), unity (1:27; 2:2, 14; 4:2), spiritual growth (1:6, 9–11, 25; 2:12–13; 3:12–15), perseverance (1:27; 2:16; 3:16; 4:1), and the certainty of answered prayer (1:3–6, 19; 4:6, 19).

The tone of this letter is all the more remarkable when we consider that it was written from prison. Paul is under arrest (1:7, 13–14, 17), and he realizes that this time he might not get off with a beating (cf. 2 Cor. 6:4–5; 11:23–24). The end of his life could be near (1:20), but that prospect does not extinguish his enthusiasm. He has given up everything for Christ, and he regards as mere rubbish things that many people would value (3:7–8). He has long since learned to be content in any and every circumstance (4:11–12), including, apparently, prison. What is death to a person whose goal (3:12) is to know the power of Christ's resurrection and to attain resurrection from the dead (3:10–11)? For such a person, living can only mean continuing to serve and love Christ, and dying can only bring gain (1:21).

Fig. 18.1. Philippi. (Balage Balogh / www.archaeologyillustrated.com)

Overview

The letter opens with a customary but brief salutation (1:1–2) and a report of Paul's prayers of thanksgiving for the church (1:3–11). Paul then fills the Philippians in on the circumstances regarding his current imprisonment: it has served to advance the gospel (1:12–18), but he looks forward to being set free in response to their prayers (1:19–26). After these preliminaries he offers an extended appeal for humility and unity in the church (1:27–2:18): they are to live in a manner worthy of the gospel, even though this means suffering (1:27–30), and they are to follow the example of Christ Jesus in setting aside personal interests for the sake of others (2:1–18). Embedded in this appeal is a poetic account of how Christ "emptied himself" for the sake of humanity and was subsequently exalted by God to become Lord of all (2:6–11). Paul then discusses his hopes for future visits to the church and provides an update on the status of one of their members, Epaphroditus, who became ill while visiting Paul (2:19–30). At this point the letter seems to be winding down (3:1), but instead of concluding, Paul launches into another major appeal, warning the Philippians against false teachers and calling on them to imitate him as one who suffers for Christ in hope of the resurrection (3:1–4:1). Embedded in this appeal is a brief autobiographical section in which Paul lists personal attributes and achievements that might be considered badges of honor in the Jewish world, but that he denounces as "rubbish" for the sake of knowing Christ and

⊙ EXPLORE 18.0
Philippians: Outline
of Contents

obtaining the righteousness of God that comes through faith (3:4–11). Then he offers a series of pastoral exhortations (4:2–9), expresses his thanks to the church for the concern and support that they have offered him (4:10–20), and concludes with final greetings (4:21–23).

Historical Background

Paul's letter to the Philippians is addressed to Christians in the Roman colony of Philippi, a medium-sized farming community whose unpretentious appearance was no measure of its ultimate significance in world history. Philippi is located in what is now northern Greece, about one hundred miles east of Thessalonica. In Paul's day both cities belonged to the Roman province of Macedonia. Thessalonica was the capital (see map 17.1), but Philippi was also an important site because, like Thessalonica, it was a stop along the Via Egnatia, a Roman road that stretched from the Bosporus Strait across modern-day Bulgaria, Greece, and Albania to the Adriatic Sea (see fig. 20.1). Philippi was just ten miles inland from Neapolis, the eastern port through which people (and goods) from Asia came into Macedonia when arriving by sea. Thus the town of Philippi, though surrounded by farmlands, was located at the junction where the route inland from the sea connected with the major thoroughfare of the Via Egnatia.

Via Egnatia: a road constructed by the Romans in the second century BCE; it crossed the Roman provinces of Illyricum, Macedonia, and Thrace.

Some four hundred years before Paul, Philip II (the father of Alexander the Great) had conquered this area, and in naming Philippi after himself he must have had a sense of the city's potential importance. The Romans took over two centuries later, and then in 42 BCE Philippi earned renown as the site where Marc Antony and Octavian (later to become Caesar Augustus) defeated Brutus and Cassius, the assassins of Julius Caesar. Veterans of the victorious armies were settled here, and Philippi became something of a retirement community for military personnel, a pleasant haven where former soldiers could enjoy a decent standard of living augmented by conferral of Roman citizenship and consequent exemption from all taxes. Of course, not all the population would have been so blessed, but the value that came to be placed on Roman

---

Box 18.1

Bishops and Deacons

Paul mentions "bishops and deacons" in his opening salutation to the Philippians (1:1). Much more is said elsewhere in the New Testament about the qualifications and responsibilities of persons holding such church offices (1 Tim. 3:1–13; Titus 1:7–9). We do not know, however, whether the terms meant the same thing in every locale. The word "bishop" (in Greek, *episkopos*) means "overseer," and the word "deacon" (in Greek, *diakonos*) means "one who serves." At the time Paul wrote to the Philippians, these words may have been fairly generic designations for church leaders rather than technical terms for particular orders of clergy.

citizenship in this locale (see Acts 16:37–38) adds poignancy to Paul's comment in Philippians that Christians enjoy a far greater citizenship "in heaven" (3:20; cf. 2 Cor. 5:1–2).

Then around 50–51 CE something happened that no one had seen coming but that determined what would become the city's greatest claim to fame. The apostle Paul arrived and founded a very small church. Why is that so important? It was the first church on European soil (cf. 4:15). As a result, to this day Philippi is known less for being the site of a famous battle than for being "the birthplace of Western Christianity." According to the book of Acts, Paul and his companions first brought the gospel to Europe in response to a vision that Paul had of a Macedonian man pleading for help (Acts 16:6–10). They landed at the port of Neapolis, traveled up to Philippi, and remained there for "some days" (Acts 16:11–12). Paul's own letters reveal that he would remember those days as a time of suffering, when he and his coworkers were "shamefully mistreated" (1 Thess. 2:2; cf. Acts 16:16–40). Nevertheless, his converts in the city proved exceptionally loyal, supporting him financially as he ministered elsewhere (Phil. 4:10, 16; 2 Cor. 11:8–9) and contributing to his collection for Jerusalem in ways that exceeded all expectations (2 Cor. 8:1–4; 9:1–5). His letter to them is written to acknowledge receipt of yet another gift, for now they are supporting him in his time of imprisonment (Phil. 4:10, 18).

Fig. 18.2. Paul and Lydia. According to the book of Acts, Paul's first convert in the city of Philippi was a woman named "Lydia," whom he met at a prayer meeting by a river (16:11–15). A dealer in textiles ("purple goods"), Lydia apparently was a wealthy woman, and she hosted Paul and his missionary team while they worked in the city. These stained-glass windows of Paul and Lydia appear in a modern church in Philippi; the two are remembered as cofounders of the congregation. (Todd Bolen / BiblePlaces.com)

Box 18.2

Hymns in New Testament Letters

The New Testament often mentions Christians singing hymns and spiritual songs (Acts 16:25; 1 Cor. 14:15, 26; Col. 3:16; Eph. 5:19; Heb. 2:12; James 5:13). Still, it does not contain a song-book or hymnal comparable to the book of Psalms in the Old Testament. Instead we find liturgical materials woven into other books. Notable examples are found in the Gospel of Luke (1:46–55, 67–79; 2:14, 29–32) and the book of Revelation (1:5–6; 4:8, 11; 5:9–14; 7:10–12, 15–17; 11:15–18; 12:10–12; 15:3–4; 16:5–7; 19:1–8; 22:13). Some of the letters attributed to Paul also appear to draw on hymns from the early church. Here are some often-cited examples:

- Rom. 11:33–36: a doxology on the inscrutability of God
- 1 Cor. 13: an exposition on the superiority of love
- Eph. 1:3–14: a doxology on the redemptive work of God in Christ
- Eph. 5:14: a verse promising the life and light of Christ to believers
- Phil. 2:6–11: a doxology on the self-abasement and the ensuing exaltation of Christ
- Col. 1:15–20: an exposition on the person of Christ and God's work through him
- 1 Tim. 3:16: a short litany on the coming of Christ to earth and his return to heaven
- 2 Tim. 2:11–13: a promise that suffering for Christ leads to glory

We would love to know more about the particular circumstances under which Paul wrote Philippians, but details escape us. All that we know for certain is that he is in prison (1:7, 13–14, 17). When might this have been, and where? Paul appears to have experienced some such captivity in Ephesus (1 Cor. 15:32; 2 Cor. 1:8–9), in Caesarea (Acts 23:23–26:30), and in Rome (Acts 28:16–31). Since in Philippians he mentions the "imperial guard" (1:13) and the "emperor's household" (4:22), many readers think that he is writing to the Philippians from Rome, but such terms could be used to refer to authorities in other cities as well. Since he indicates that there is a good deal of back-and-forth travel between Philippi and his current location (2:19–28), many think that he is in Ephesus (about a one-week journey from Philippi), but longer trips between Philippi and either Rome or Caesarea are also feasible. To complicate matters further, it seems likely that Paul was in prison in other locations and at other times as well (see 2 Cor. 11:23, which mentions multiple imprisonments in a letter written before Paul was jailed in Caesarea or Rome). Scholarship remains divided on the question of where (and when) Paul wrote this letter. The lack of resolution is frustrating to those who want to place Paul's letters in chronological order and trace the development of themes from one letter to the next. It is, however, a matter of little concern for understanding his letter to the Philippians in its own right. If Philippians was written from Ephesus, it is one of Paul's earlier letters (ca. 54–56); if from Rome, it is one of his last (ca. 61–63; a letter from Caesarea would be dated ca. 58–60). We wish that we knew which was the case, but either way, the messages that Paul wants to convey in the letter are fairly clear.

> EXPLORE 18.5
> Paul in Prison

Trouble in Philippi

Paul's letter to the Philippians is not particularly polemical, but references to opponents or enemies do appear here and there.

Text	Comment	Possible Reference
1:15–18	Some proclaim Christ out of false motives: envy, rivalry, and selfish ambition.	Christian missionaries who compete with Paul and create factions in the church (cf. 1 Cor. 1:11–13)
1:28–30	Opponents cause the Philippians to suffer the same struggles that Paul experienced as a missionary in the city.	Nonbelievers who persecute Christians (cf. Acts 16:19–39; 2 Cor. 1:8–9; 6:4–5; 11:23–26)
3:2	Evil workers (whom Paul calls "dogs") insist on "mutilating the flesh."	Jewish Christians who say that all Christians must be circumcised (cf. Gal. 5:2–12)
3:18–19	Many live as "enemies of the cross," having their belly as their god, glorying in their shame, and setting their minds on earthly things.	Christians who seek power and glory apart from suffering and service (cf. 1 Cor. 1:18–2:5; 2 Cor. 10–12)

Note that only the second reference (1:28–30) is to troublemakers who are definitely in Philippi. The first reference (1:15–18) is to people in the area where Paul is in prison. The last two references could be to troublemakers who are in Philippi, but it is possible that Paul is simply warning the Philippians about the kinds of people who have caused trouble elsewhere: the Judaizers in Galatia (see "Historical Background" in chap. 16) and the "super-apostles" in Corinth (see "Historical Background" in chap. 15).

We may note in passing a couple of oddities about the letter. One section (3:1b–4:3) has a markedly different tone than the rest (warnings against enemies in a letter that is otherwise happy and upbeat). And one passage seems to indicate that Epaphroditus has just arrived (4:18), whereas another implies that he has been with Paul for a considerable period of time (2:25–30). For these and other reasons, some scholars wonder if the letter in our possession might be a composite of two or three letters that Paul wrote to the Philippians.

Nevertheless, the letter as we have it fits the general form for what is called a "friendship letter." Paul's main purpose in writing may be simply to update his friends and ministry partners on his personal situation (1:12–26), to ease their minds with regard to the health of Epaphroditus (2:25–30), and to thank them for the gift that Epaphroditus delivered (4:10–20). He offers words of consolation as an antidote for any discouragement that they might be feeling over his imprisonment or their own suffering. Intertwined with such concerns is some teaching on matters relevant to the church's situation, so that they will not be intimidated by their enemies (1:28), led astray by false teachers (3:2), or hindered by internal dissension (4:2–3). It is possible that the emphasis on joy has been prompted by such concerns: Paul stresses positive responses to the gospel not because he happens to be feeling particularly happy or confident at this point in time but because this church is in danger of allowing anxiety to

⊙ EXPLORE 18.9
How Many Letters to Philippi?

get the better of them. The matters provoking such anxiety are not trivial, and Paul is willing to deal with them. Still, most scholars think that the primary focus of the letter is not on addressing problems but rather on cementing and celebrating the relationship that Paul enjoys with the Philippians in Christ.

Major Themes in Philippians

Incarnation

In Christian theology the term *incarnation* refers to the doctrine that Jesus was God come to earth as a human being. The key biblical passages for this doctrine are John 1:1–18 and Philippians 2:6–11. The passage in Philippians is particularly interesting because it is so early, indicating that Christians had some notion of incarnation before any of the Gospels were written. Indeed, if Paul is quoting from liturgical materials already in existence by this time, then the idea is even earlier. The passage describes the career of Christ Jesus in three stages:

Fig. 18.3. Philippian jail. Paul's letter to the Philippians is written from prison (in Ephesus or Colossae or Rome), but Paul also spent a night in jail while he was in Philippi (see Acts 16:12–40). This picture shows a cell in the ancient city similar to the one in which Paul would have been kept. Most jails at the time were dark chambers in which prisoners were held until their trial. Prisoners often were kept in chains for additional security. (Craig Koester)

- first, he was in "the form of God" (2:6);
- second, he was born in human likeness, and he lived and died as a human being (2:7–8);
- third, he was exalted by God to be Lord of all (2:9–11).

Theologians discuss and debate many details of what Paul intends to say in this passage, but most recognize that the text contains one of the earliest references in Christian literature to the concept of preexistence—that is, the idea that Christ existed (in the form of God) before he became the man Jesus who lived and died on earth.

In Christian theology, the concept of incarnation would raise questions about the nature of Christ and of God: How can there be only one God if Jesus has "the form of God" and "equality with God" (2:6)? Why do Christians worship Jesus and say that he is their Lord (2:10–11; cf. Rom. 14:11)? In terms of official doctrine, Christians would not sort these things out for hundreds of years, finally reaching tentative agreements at the councils of Nicaea in 325 and Chalcedon in 451. At those meetings, churches endorsed views that are now called the doctrine of "the Trinity" and the doctrine of "the two natures of Christ." But Paul's letter to the Philippians reveals that the sentiments that were later worked out intellectually were being expressed in Christian devotion and worship from a very early time.

Box 18.4

The Christ Hymn

The most celebrated passage in Paul's letter to the Philippians is 2:6–11, often called the "Christ Hymn." Its poetic quality marks it as material that probably was used in early Christian worship as a creed or responsive reading or, indeed, as an actual hymn that was put to music and sung or chanted. Paul might have composed the piece himself, or he might be quoting material familiar to the Philippians from their liturgy.

Here is one of several ways in which the text might be arranged in verses that resemble a modern hymn:

Though he was in the form of God
He did not regard equality with God
As something to be exploited
But emptied himself
Taking the form of a slave
Being born in human likeness
And being found in human form
He humbled himself
And became obedient unto death—
    even death on a cross!
Therefore God also highly exalted him
And gave him the name
That is above every name
So that at the name of Jesus

Every knee should bend
In heaven and on earth and under the
    earth
And every tongue should confess
That Jesus Christ is Lord
To the glory of God the Father.

The focus of the hymn is on Christ Jesus (2:6), but it celebrates his career with allusions to the Old Testament. The voluntary humiliation of Christ in the first part draws on Isaiah 52:13–53:12, and the universal submission to him at the end quotes from Isaiah 45:23 (cf. Rom. 14:11). Also, Christ's willingness to give up his "equality with God" may be seen as a contrast to Adam's desire to attain equality with God in Genesis 3:1–7 (cf. Rom. 5:12–19).

Around 110, Pliny the Younger, a Roman governor, wrote a letter to the emperor Trajan to inform him of Christians. He said that when Christians gather at their meetings, they "chant verses alternately amongst themselves in honor of Christ as if to a God" (Epistulae 10.96). The "Christ Hymn" of Philippians 2:6–11 seems like a perfect example of the sort of liturgical material that this Roman governor heard the Christians using.

Humility

Paul urges the Philippians to do nothing from selfish ambition but rather to place the interests of others ahead of their own (2:3–4). He calls this self-effacing attitude "humility" (2:3), which is not to be equated with low self-esteem (thinking ill of oneself). Humility refers to putting others first and consciously seeking what is best for others rather than what is best for oneself. This is closely connected to what Paul means by "love" (Rom. 12:10; 14:15; 1 Cor. 13:4–7; Gal. 5:13; cf. Phil. 1:9, 16; 2:1–2), and it is also closely connected to what he means by people having "the mind of Christ" (1 Cor. 2:16; cf. Rom. 12:2; Phil. 2:5). The promotion of humility as a defining mark of Christian character runs through all of Paul's letters, but it seems to receive special attention in Philippians. Indeed, most of the letter can be read in light of this theme.

The reason Paul quotes from the "Christ Hymn" (2:6–11) in this letter is to remind the Philippians of the all-time best example for humility: Christ Jesus did not exploit his prerogatives as one who was equal with God, but rather "emptied himself" and "humbled himself" by becoming human. And he didn't just become human: he became obedient unto death. And he didn't just become obedient unto death: he became obedient unto death on a cross (2:6–8). "Let the same mind be in you," Paul tells the Philippians (2:5). Christ Jesus is the ultimate paradigm for one who puts the interests of others first, and his followers are to emulate him in this regard (cf. Mark 8:34; 10:43–45).

To show that it can be done, Paul cites other examples: Timothy shows a genuine and unselfish interest in the Philippians' welfare (2:19–24), and their own Epaphroditus risked everything for the sake of others (2:25–30). And Paul himself can be their role model (3:17; 4:9): he rejoices when his rivals succeed, as long as Christ is preached (1:17–18); when he considers matters of life and death, it is with regard to what will prove most fruitful for others (1:22–25); he rejoices that the Philippians have sent him a gift, not because he needs the money but rather because they will profit from having shown such kindness (4:14, 17, 19). Just as Christ Jesus emptied himself for the sake of humankind, Paul is willing to be poured out as a sacrifice for the Philippians (2:17). He gives up his legitimate reasons for claiming earthly honor in a way that echoes Christ's decision not to exploit a much greater divine honor (3:4–8). Paul feels that he can invite the Philippians to imitate him in this regard because he knows that he is imitating Christ (3:17; cf. 1 Cor. 11:1).

Paul accompanies his plea for humility with a promise of ultimate exaltation. God exalted Christ Jesus (2:9–11), and Paul's hope likewise is in the power of Christ's resurrection (3:10–11). His call to put others ahead of self cuts against the grain of conventional wisdom but is grounded in a sublime paradox recognized in many strands of early Christian tradition: those who humble themselves will be exalted (Matt. 23:11–12; Luke 14:11; 18:14; James 4:10; 1 Pet. 5:6).

Rubbish and Christ

In Philippians 3 Paul warns the believers against people who insist that circumcision is necessary to belong to God (3:2). This is an issue that he dealt with at length elsewhere (see Gal. 5:2–12). Now he insists, ironically, that it is those who trust in Christ who have become "the circumcision"—that is, the true people of God (Phil. 3:3). To drive the point home, Paul turns to autobiography, contrasting his identification with God as an exemplary (blameless!) Jew and the identification with God that he now enjoys through knowing Christ Jesus as his Lord (3:4–7). He does not mean to disparage the former, but he does allow that, as wonderful as his Jewish legacy might be, it is mere rubbish (literally, "dung") compared to what is available through Christ (3:8). In a few verses, Paul sketches what has been called the essence of his theology: through faith in Jesus Christ, one may be justified (3:9), sanctified (3:10), and glorified (3:11). His words in these verses ring with the dialectic of what is "already" and what is "not yet"—a hallmark of his theological position. His advice to the Philippians emerges from that dialectic: "hold fast to what we have attained" (3:16) and "press on toward the goal" that lies ahead (3:14).

Suffering

Philippians offers some reflection on the inevitability and potential value of human suffering. The main point is simply that although Christians suffer on account of their faith, ultimately they will be united with Christ in a world beyond death (1:21, 23, 28; 3:10–11, 14, 20–21; cf. Rom. 8:18). Paul knows that the Philippians are experiencing opposition to their faith (1:27–29). He reminds them that he suffered the same when he first came to them (1:30) and, of course, that he is suffering still as a prisoner for Christ (1:17). Paul does not try to answer the question of why such bad things happen to good people; he simply recognizes that they do, and he encourages hope in the promise of ultimate vindication (3:14, 20–21; 4:19). Beyond this, however, he does indicate that suffering can have positive effects (cf. Rom. 8:28). His imprisonment has actually served to advance the gospel by emboldening others and providing even his captors with an inspiring and powerful testimony to Christ (1:12–14). And there is more. In some undefined way, Paul thinks

Fig. 18.4. Running for the prize. Track and field events were especially popular in the Greco-Roman world. In Philippians, Paul uses the analogy of a footrace to speak of the perseverance that attends the Christian life (2:16; 3:14). A runner must move forward with single-minded focus on the prize; in the same manner, the believer is drawn toward God in Christ, forgetting what lies behind and pressing on toward the heavenly goal. (The Bridgeman Art Library International)

that Christians who suffer for their faith are actually sharing in the sufferings of Christ (3:10). The experience bonds them to Christ in a way that makes them "like him in his death," which in turn enables them to know the power of his resurrection (3:10–11). For this reason, Paul tells the Philippians that they may view their suffering for Christ as a favor from God: it is a privilege that God has granted them (1:29; cf. Acts 5:41).

Fellowship

Paul stresses Christian "fellowship" (Greek, *koinōnia*; used in 1:5; 2:1; 3:10) in this letter, first with regard to the fellowship that he shares with the Philippians, and second with regard to the fellowship that he wants them to have with one another. Scholars have often noted that this letter exhibits a strong penchant for Greek words that begin with the prefix *syn-* (meaning "together" or "with," similar to the English prefix *co-*). Paul attaches this prefix to all sorts of words throughout the letter, to verbs such as "struggle" (1:27; 4:3) and "rejoice" (2:17, 18), and to nouns such as "sharer" (1:7), "soul" (2:2), "soldier" (2:25), and "imitator" (3:17). In 4:3 four different words bear the *syn-* prefix, such that the verse might be translated, "I urge you, my *co*-companion, to *co*-assist these women, for they have *co*-struggled with me in the gospel, together with Clement and the rest of my *co*-workers." Clearly Paul wants to emphasize for the Philippians that "we are all in this together." No other church has shared with him in "the matter of giving and receiving" as this one has done (4:15); they are his partners in the gospel (1:5) who share in God's grace with him (1:7).

In other letters, Paul often describes his relationship with the recipients as that of a father addressing his children (1 Cor. 4:14; 2 Cor. 6:13; 12:14; Gal. 4:19; 1 Thess. 2:11; cf. Philem. 10); in this letter, Paul

---

Box 18.6

Friendship and Sharing

"The proverb says, 'the possessions of friends are shared'—and it says this correctly, for friendship consists in sharing, and siblings and comrades hold all things in common" (Aristotle, *Nicomachean Ethics* 8.9.1–2).*

"All who believed were together and had all things in common" (Acts 2:44).

*Quoted in Robert H. Gundry, *A Survey of the New Testament*, 5th ed. (Grand Rapids: Zondervan, 2012), 341.

Euodia and Syntyche

Near the close of his letter to the Philippians, Paul urges two women, Euodia and Syntyche, to "be of the same mind in the Lord," and he appeals to someone else in the church (his "loyal companion") to help them (4:2–3). The women are coworkers of Paul, and apparently they have had a falling out. This could be a personal matter—a spat that requires an impartial mediator to help facilitate conflict resolution. Or, since the women appear to be prominent in the church (4:3), they could be leaders of major factions with different ideas on congregational policies and programs. Their inability to see eye to eye could pose a threat to the unity of the church as a whole. Some interpreters think that the rift between Euodia and Syntyche might be a primary reason for Paul's attention to the themes of unity and humility throughout the letter. Although he does not address the two women by name until the end, other verses perhaps are quietly addressed to them and to their followers as well (see 1:27; 2:1–5, 14–15; 3:15–16).

Christology: a branch of theology that focuses on the person and work of Jesus Christ, understood as an eternal divine figure.

repeatedly refers to the Philippians as his siblings (1:12, 14; 2:25; 3:1, 13, 17; 4:1, 8, 21), and he speaks of their relationship as a partnership (1:5). He emphasizes that as faithful followers of Christ, they have had common experiences (1:29–30), and as fellow citizens of heaven, they share a common hope and destiny (3:20). Indeed, he seems to feel that they are "with him" in his imprisonment (1:7), sharing now in his distress (4:14) as they have shared (and continue to share) in his joy. They are one another's cause for joy (2:17–18; 4:1). Still, Paul says that his joy will be complete only when they come to experience the same level of accord with one another that they have experienced up to now with him (2:2).

Conclusion

Philippians is studied by scholars as a theological resource that deals with complex topics such as incarnational Christology and the meaning of suffering, and it is expounded by preachers as a motivational tract that encourages humility and harmony. Still, it is perhaps valued most highly at a popular level as an inspirational example of Christian optimism. Many individual verses stand out as favorites in the canons of Christian piety.

- Early in this letter, Paul promises the Philippians, "The one who began a good work among you will bring it to completion by the day of Jesus Christ" (1:6).
- Then at the close he asserts, "My God will fully satisfy every need of yours according to his riches in glory in Christ Jesus" (4:19).
- Along the way he confesses his own confidence: "I can do all things through him who strengthens me" (4:13).
- And he assures the Philippians, "The peace of God, which surpasses all understanding, will keep your hearts and minds in Christ Jesus" (4:7).

We know from other letters that Paul was not always this cheerful or congenial (see 2 Cor. 2:4; Gal. 3:1–3), but Philippians stands as a testimony to his transcendent confidence and hope. The affirmative, perhaps idealistic, outlook of Paul's letter to the Philippians is summarized in one verse, where he urges his readers to focus on positive aspects of life and faith:

> Whatever is true, whatever is honorable,
> whatever is just, whatever is pure,
> whatever is pleasing, whatever is commendable,
> if there is any excellence
> and if there is anything worthy of praise,
> think about these things. (4:8)

FOR FURTHER READING: Philippians

Cousar, Charles B. *Reading Galatians, Philippians, and 1 Thessalonians: A Literary and Theological Commentary*. Reading the New Testament. Macon, GA: Smyth & Helwys, 2001.

Donfried, Karl P., and I. Howard Marshall. *The Theology of the Shorter Pauline Letters*. New Testament Theology. Cambridge: Cambridge University Press, 1993.

Fowl, Stephen E. *Philippians*. Two Horizons Commentary. Grand Rapids: Eerdmans, 2005.

Migliore, Daniel L. *Philippians & Philemon: A Theological Commentary*. Belief Series. Louisville: Westminster John Knox, 2014.

Osiek, Carolyn. *Philippians, Philemon*. Abingdon New Testament Commentaries. Nashville: Abingdon, 2000.

Tamez, Elsa, et al. *Philippians, Colossians, Philemon*. Wisdom Commentary. Collegeville, MN: Liturgical Press, 2016.

Thompson, James W., and Bruce W. Longenecker. *Philippians and Philemon*. Paideia. Grand Rapids: Baker Academic, 2016.

Weidman, Frederick W. *Philippians, First and Second Thessalonians, and Philemon*. Westminster Bible Companion. Louisville: Westminster John Knox, 2013.

Wright, N. T. *Paul for Everyone: The Prison Letters; Ephesians, Philippians, Colossians, and Philemon*. 2nd ed. Louisville: Westminster John Knox, 2004.

⊙ Go to www
.IntroducingNT.com
for summaries,
videos, and other
study tools.

19

Colossians

"Think globally, act locally." That could be the motto of the Letter to the Colossians. This letter adopts a cosmic perspective that views human existence from the vantage point of one who knows the secrets of the universe. It sweeps across time, taking us from the start of creation (1:15–17) to the end of the age (3:4), stopping along the way to reveal the meaning of life (1:27; 3:4), the source of all wisdom and knowledge (2:2–3), the reason for order in the universe (1:17), and humanity's only hope for peace (1:20; 3:15). It encourages us to lift our sights from earth to heaven, to "set your minds on things that are above" (3:2), and to view life from the perspective of eternity. Still, this letter is exceptionally well grounded in the affairs of daily living. Its universal perspective on power, wisdom, and faith has specific implications for how the members of one local community ought to conduct themselves (3:5–4:6)—how they should act toward one another (3:13), toward family members (3:18–4:1), and toward "outsiders" (4:5–6).

This letter is attributed to the apostle Paul (1:1, 23) and appears to close with his personal mark of authentication (4:18; cf. 1 Cor. 16:21; Gal. 6:11; 2 Thess. 3:17). Nevertheless, its authorship is a matter of dispute among scholars, in part because its cosmic perspective transcends the usual contours of what Paul provides in letters that are more confidently attributed to him.

Overview

Colossians begins with a typical salutation and greeting (1:1–2). A prayer of thanksgiving for the readers' faith and love emphasizes that the gospel they heard from Paul's fellow servant Epaphras has been growing in them and bearing fruit (1:3–8). The authors (identified as Paul and Timothy) continue to pray that the

⊙ EXPLORE 19.0
Colossians: Outline
of Contents

Colossians might be filled with knowledge of God's will, grow in knowledge of God, and be strengthened by God, who is responsible for their current position and status (1:9–14). This opening prayer segues into a liturgical meditation on the magnificence of Christ as the "firstborn of all creation" and the "firstborn from the dead." Christ is "the image of the invisible God" and the one in whom "the fullness of God was pleased to dwell"; all things were created in him and through him and for him, and in him all things hold together (1:15–20).

The letter goes on to present theological implications of the foregoing exposition of who Christ is and what he has done (1:21–2:23). The Colossians are assured of their perfection before God, provided they continue in the faith, and it is to this end that Paul has been willing to suffer and toil on their behalf, in accord with his commission from God to make known the mystery of "Christ in you, the hope of glory" (1:21–2:7). The Colossians are then warned about being deceived by empty philosophy that suggests that their baptism into Christ has been inadequate to secure their position with God, or that religious observances or experiences will enable them to grow into the fullness that is found in Christ alone (2:8–23). Such philosophy is denounced as representing mere human tradition (2:8, 22) and as being in accord with spiritual powers that Christ has vanquished (2:8, 15, 20).

The letter continues by turning to ethical implications of the recipients' status in Christ (3:1–4:6). The Colossians should focus completely on the heavenly kingdom to which they now belong, reject practices that marked their lives before Christ, and pursue conduct that befits God's chosen ones (3:1–17). A specific table of household duties spells out responsibilities of wives, husbands, children, fathers, slaves, and masters (3:18–4:1). They should devote themselves to prayer and exercise wisdom in their relations with outsiders (4:2–6). The letter concludes with instructions and greetings (4:7–17) and with a final greeting from Paul in his own hand (4:18).

Historical Background

In New Testament times the city of Colossae was a relatively small town in western Asia Minor (modern-day Turkey). It had close connections with two

---

Box 19.1

Nailed to the Cross

Colossians 2:14 uses a memorable image for how God forgave human trespasses (2:13) through Christ's death. When a person was crucified, the Roman executioners attached to the cross a list of the condemned person's crimes. Colossians says that the record of human failings—the list of all accusations that could be brought against human beings—was "nailed to the cross" of Christ. This is a colorful way of saying "Jesus died for our sins." See also Colossians 1:14, 20, 22.

other cities, Laodicea (10 miles to the west) and Hierapolis (16 miles northwest), both of which are mentioned in this letter (2:1; 4:13, 15–16). All three cities were situated in the valley of the Lycus River, about 110 miles east of Ephesus (see map 17.1). They were part of the Roman province of Asia and were commercial centers for textile industries. Colossae, in particular, was known for its production of scarlet-dyed wool.

Fig. 19.1. Tree of knowledge. According to Genesis 2:17, the tree that bore the forbidden fruit in the garden of Eden was "the tree of knowledge of good and evil." The Letter to the Colossians is written to believers who are tempted to supplement the fruit that the gospel is bearing with wisdom and knowledge that they think will bring them to another level of spiritual maturity (1:6; 2:8). (Suad Al-Attar)

mystery religions: popular religious cults that flourished during the Hellenistic era and tended to keep their doctrines and practices secret from outsiders.

elemental spirits of the universe: a generic term for powerful spiritual beings (Col. 2:8, 20).

The area was renowned as a haven for exotic spiritual pursuits. Numerous pagan cults and "mystery religions" were popular here, including those that involved devotion to the mother goddess Cybele (whose cult was centered in Hierapolis) or the worship of various astral deities (sun, moon, and stars). The latter, in particular, may have been what gave rise to this letter's references to "the elemental spirits of the universe" (2:8, 20). Colossae also had a sizable Jewish population, though reports indicate that the Jewish settlers were thoroughly Hellenized (i.e., integrated into the Greco-Roman culture).

At one time Colossae had been the largest of the three cities in the Lycus Valley, but by the time of Paul, Colossae was in decline, having lost out to the much more prosperous Laodicea. The worst, however, was yet to come: around 61 CE an earthquake devastated the region. Laodicea appears to have had the money to rebuild, but the situation may have been worse for the smaller communities. We have no sure data as to what happened to the town of Colossae or to the Christian community there.

The only reference to Colossae in the New Testament is found in the opening line of this letter (1:2). The book of Acts indicates that Paul passed through the region of Phrygia (i.e., Asia) on both his second (16:6) and third (18:23; cf. 19:1) missionary journeys, but it makes no mention of Colossae, Hierapolis, or Laodicea, and it says nothing about Paul's winning converts or founding

---

Box 19.2

What Was the "Colossian Heresy"?

More than forty proposals have been offered regarding the nature of the philosophy that the Letter to the Colossians seeks to oppose. Here are some sample suggestions:

- a Jewish Christian movement that insisted that gentile Christians must be circumcised and keep the law of Moses, similar to the "Judaizers" opposed by Paul in Galatians (cf. Gal. 3:19; 4:3–9)
- an esoteric and rigorous form of Judaism, comparable to that practiced by the Essenes at Qumran
- a mystical form of Judaism, like the Merkabah tradition, so named because asceticism and strict adherence to the law allowed devotees to travel in the spirit to the heavenly throne room in a celestial chariot called a *merkabah*
- a syncretistic religious amalgam of beliefs, combining elements from Jewish tradition with elements of astral religion
- some variety of a Greco-Roman "mystery religion," which emphasized the hidden nature of spiritual truth revealed only to the spiritually elite
- incipient gnosticism, a precursor of what would develop into prominent antimaterialist religious systems in the second century CE
- Pythagorean philosophy, based on the teaching of Pythagoras (sixth century BCE), who thought that the sun, moon, and stars were spirits that control human destiny and that the human soul must be purified through ascetic practices

churches in the province. Likewise, the Letter to the Colossians indicates that the Christians in this area had not seen Paul "face to face" (2:1); they appear to have been taught the gospel by Epaphras (1:7–8), who "worked hard" in Colossae, Laodicea, and Hierapolis and who is now said to be with Paul (4:12–13).

The Letter to the Colossians presupposes a particular situation: the readers are in danger of being deceived by "plausible arguments" (2:4) and taken captive through "philosophy and empty deceit" (2:8). Scholars have devoted much attention to trying to spell out exactly what this seductive ideology may have been, but the letter provides only generalities. What is sometimes called the "Colossian heresy" seems to have had something to do with appeasing or revering the "elemental spirits of the universe" (2:8, 20), which might be equated with the "rulers and authorities" mentioned in 2:15 or even with the "angels" referred to in 2:18. The reference to "worship of angels" in the latter verse is intriguing. If spiritual powers were thought to control human destiny, the Colossian Christians might be tempted to believe that honoring them as minor deities could help to ensure positive outcomes in life. Or perhaps they were simply invoking the help and protection of angels in ways that the author of this letter considers inappropriate and polemically dismisses as "worship." It is also possible that the phrase "worship of angels" refers to worship offered *by* angels; in that case, the point could be that the Colossian Christians are being invited to participate in mystical rites that will transport them spiritually to a heavenly plane where they can worship God in the company of the hosts of heaven (cf. Ezek. 1:4–28; 1 Cor. 11:10; 2 Cor. 12:1–5; Heb. 12:22–23). Either way, this teaching also seems to have encouraged or required ascetic practices and ritual observances: dietary restrictions (2:16); festival and Sabbath observance

heresy: false teaching, or teaching that does not conform to the official standards of a religious community.

⊙ EXPLORE 19.12
Literary Siblings: Relationship of Ephesians to Colossians

Box 19.3

Colossians and Philemon

Similarities

- Both Colossians and Philemon are said to be written from prison (Col. 4:3, 18; cf. 1:24; Philem. 9, 10, 13).
- Both are said to be coauthored by Paul and Timothy (Col. 1:1; Philem. 1).
- Both letters mention many of the same individuals: Archippus (Col. 4:17; Philem. 2), Onesimus (Col. 4:9; Philem. 10), Epaphras (Col. 1:7; 4:12–13; Philem. 23), Mark (Col. 4:10; Philem. 24), Aristarchus (Col. 4:10; Philem. 24), Demas (Col. 4:14; Philem. 24), and Luke (Col. 4:14; Philem. 24).

Differences

- Philemon indicates that Epaphras is in prison with Paul, and Aristarchus is not (23–24); Colossians gives the impression that it is the other way around (4:10, 12).
- Colossians makes no mention of an impending visit from Paul, while Philemon indicates that Paul hopes to come to visit soon (22).

(2:16); self-abasement (2:18); taboos regarding what to handle, taste, or touch (2:21); and quite possibly circumcision (2:11). Paul, or whoever is responsible for this letter, deems all these things unnecessary for saints in Christ; such things are a mere shadow of the substance to be found in Christ (2:17).

The proponents of this philosophy may have been proselytizing the Colossian Christians from within the church as fellow believers or from outside the church as adherents to a rival religion. Or perhaps the letter is simply issuing a generic warning regarding ideas in the region to which Christians might be attracted. Either way, the basic claim of the "Colossian heresy" seems to have been that something more than faith in Christ was needed for people to survive (or at least to grow or mature) in a world ruled by powerful supernatural beings. The primary purpose of the letter is to caution readers against such a notion.

As for the specific circumstances of the letter's composition, most scholars believe that Colossians is either one of the last letters in the New Testament to have been written by Paul or one of the first of the pseudepigraphic letters to have been written in his name. Decisions about these circumstances are based on comparisons between Colossians and other letters.

First, Colossians bears many close parallels to Ephesians (see box 17.1). Indeed, most scholars think that Colossians was written first and then used as a template for Ephesians, which offers an expanded and more general version of content that is more context specific in Colossians.

Second, Colossians appears to be closely tied to Paul's brief letter to Philemon (see box 19.3). Two different explanations are offered for this: (1) Paul wrote Colossians around the same time that he wrote Philemon and under similar circumstances; or (2) someone else had a copy of Paul's letter to Philemon and borrowed the personal references to make a pseudepigraphic letter to the Colossians appear to be an authentic Pauline composition.

Third, Colossians may be compared with the "undisputed letters" of Paul—that is, letters that all scholars recognize as being written by the apostle (see

---

Box 19.4

Distinctive Aspects of Colossians

Distinctive Style

Compared to the undisputed letters, Colossians uses more long sentences (1:3–8 and 2:8–15 are each just one sentence in Greek), more redundant adjectives (e.g., "holy and blameless and irreproachable" [1:22]), far more participles and relative clauses, and far fewer conjunctions.

Distinctive Theology

Compared to the undisputed letters, Colossians is said to evince a higher Christology, a more developed ecclesiology, and a more "realized" view of eschatology (i.e., more emphasis on present benefits than future hope).

box 19.4). There are some stylistic differences, but these might be explained by Paul's use of an amanuensis or secretary. At a deeper level, the letter expresses some theological ideas that seem to be enhanced or developed beyond what Paul says elsewhere. The points seem to be on a trajectory with Pauline thought but taken a step further than in the undisputed letters (see box 19.5). Again, there could be two explanations for this state of affairs: (1) Paul has developed his ideas further than in some of his other letters, prompted perhaps by the necessity of responding to the philosophy that he wants to combat in Colossae; or (2) someone else is developing Paul's thoughts in ways that are intended to be faithful to his views and thus attributable to him.

Decisions regarding the historical origins of Colossians ultimately depend on the question of whether the letter was actually written by Paul or produced pseudepigraphically after his death.

- Some scholars think that Paul did write Colossians. If so, the usual view is that he wrote the letter late in his life (to account for the development of ideas) but that he also probably wrote it before 61, when the city of Colossae was destroyed by an earthquake. A popular suggestion is that Paul wrote Colossians and Philemon (and possibly Ephesians) early in his Roman imprisonment (ca. 60). A few scholars suggest composition during an earlier imprisonment (e.g., in Caesarea or in Ephesus).

- Some scholars think that a disciple (Timothy, the letter's coauthor?) might have written the letter for Paul shortly after his death, putting into words what Paul would have wanted to say. Then the letter might be dated to the late 60s, allowing time for some development of Pauline ideas on the part of one of his closest companions.

- Some scholars think that a devoted follower of Paul might have composed Colossians a couple of decades after his death, placing the letter in the 80s and allowing more time for development of ideas reflective of second-generation Christianity. One version of this theory suggests that the letter may have been produced by a school of Pauline disciples.

The decision about whether Paul wrote Colossians usually depends on the amount of latitude an interpreter is willing to grant Paul with regard to consistency of expression and development of thought. The question becomes "Is it possible (or likely) that the person responsible for the undisputed letters could also have thought this way and allowed his thoughts to be expressed in this manner?" Whichever proposal is adopted, the theological teaching of Colossians usually is viewed as offering a progression from what is found in other letters of Paul, but a progression that remains understandable within the Pauline tradition (see box 19.5). The question of who was responsible for this

⊙ EXPLORE 19.11
Authorship of Colossians

Development of Pauline Ideas in Colossians

The Letter to the Colossians seems to expand on many ideas found in other (undisputed) letters of Paul, taking the points a step further or to another level.

- Romans says that believers have died and been buried with Christ through baptism and will someday be united with him in resurrection (6:4–6); Colossians says that believers have already "been raised with Christ" through baptism (2:12; cf. 3:1; but see also Rom. 6:11).
- Romans says that believers have died to sin (6:2); Colossians says that they have "died to the elemental spirits of the universe" (2:20).
- Romans says that no spiritual being or power will "be able to separate us from the love of God in Christ" (8:39); Colossians says that Christ disarmed the spiritual rulers and authorities and "made a public example of them, triumphing over them" (2:15; cf. 1 Cor. 15:24).
- First Corinthians says that Jesus Christ is the one "through whom are all things and through whom we exist" (8:6); Colossians presents Christ as the one in whom "all things in heaven and on earth were created" (1:16) and in whom "all things hold together" (1:17).
- Second Corinthians says that Paul's sufferings manifest the death of Jesus in Paul's body (4:8–12); Colossians says that Paul's sufferings serve the vicarious function of "completing what is lacking in Christ's afflictions for the sake of his body, that is, the church" (1:24).
- Philippians refers to Christ as being "in the form of God" (2:6); Colossians refers to Christ as "the image of the invisible God" (1:15) and as the one in whom "the whole fullness of deity dwells bodily" (2:9).

Are these points on which Paul has further developed his own thinking? Or are they instances of a pseudonymous author building on Paul's ideas?

progression (Paul himself, one of his disciples, or later followers) is important to church historians and to biographers of Paul. We do not, however, need to answer this question with certainty to understand the basic message of the letter or the key points its author wanted to make.

Major Themes in Colossians

The Cosmic Christ

redemption: a theological term derived from commerce (where it means "purchase" or "buying back").

Colossians speaks of Jesus Christ in exalted terms: he is not only the Lord of the church but also the ruler of the universe (1:15–17); he is not just the Savior of humankind but also the one who reconciles all things in heaven and on earth (1:20). The person of Christ is described as one who is "the image of the invisible God" (1:15) in whom "all the fullness of God was pleased to dwell" (1:19; cf. 2:9). The work of Christ includes his traditional role as God's agent of redemption (1:14) but is expanded to include serving also as God's agent of creation: all things in heaven and on earth, visible and invisible, were created "through him and for him" (1:16).

Fig. 19.2. The cosmic Christ.

The key verses that present this high estimate of Christ are found in a passage that probably derives from an early Christian confession or hymn—material that has come to be known as the "Colossian Hymn" (1:15–20). Paul (or whoever the writer may be) feels no need to debate these points or to convince the readers that this is who Jesus Christ is. He simply quotes liturgical material well known to the readers as a way to introduce the points that he wants to make next. Thus we can be reasonably confident that this understanding of Christ as a divine figure with universal preeminence was widely accepted among Christians by the time this letter was written (cf. John 1:1–18; Heb. 1:1–4).

The main point in quoting this hymn is simply to remind the Colossians of their own confession that Christ has preeminence over all things (1:18). They need not worry about any of the spirits or powers that are said to dominate this earth, for it was Christ who created those powers (1:16), and it is Christ who rules them (2:10) and who has now disarmed them (2:15). Likewise, the Colossians need not be concerned about rules or practices that will make them more acceptable to God, for Christ has already reconciled them with God through the blood of his cross (1:20), and he will present them to God as "holy and blameless and irreproachable" through his death (1:22). Why would they need physical circumcision when Christ has already given them a spiritual circumcision, removing "the flesh" from their minds (2:11)? Why be concerned about vision journeys to worship angels (or to worship with angels) when Christ has already raised them up "to share in the inheritance of the saints in light" (1:12)? The status of Christ as the one through whom all things are created (1:15–16), sustained (1:17), and redeemed (1:18–20) rules out their need for anything else.

Colossian Hymn: the poetic passage in Colossians 1:15–20 that exalts Christ as the image of the invisible God, the ruler of the universe, and the one who reconciles all things in heaven and on earth.

⊘ EXPLORE 19.17 Divine Wisdom and the "Colossian Hymn"

Box 19.6

Worldwide Evangelism: Is Paul Exaggerating?

In the Gospel of Matthew, Jesus tells his disciples that the gospel "will be proclaimed throughout the world, as a testimony to all nations; and then the end will come" (24:14). The Letter to the Colossians seems to indicate that this mission has been fulfilled. The gospel "has been proclaimed to every creature under heaven" (1:23) and "is bearing fruit and growing in the whole world" (1:6).

There were people in the world at the time who had not heard of Jesus Christ, as well as entire nations (including ones known to Paul) to which no Christian missionary had traveled. So what do we make of this extraordinary claim?

Most scholars take the words as an example of hyperbole—that is, an obvious exaggeration used for rhetorical effect (e.g., when someone in our modern society says, "I've told you a million times . . ."). In 1 Thessalonians Paul likewise tells the readers that the news of their faith has become known not just in their own country, or in the neighboring province, but "in every place" (1:8).

Realized Eschatology

Colossians is one of a handful of New Testament documents to emphasize what theologians call "realized eschatology," the belief that blessings and benefits associated with the end times are available already in this present life. In this regard, the letter may be compared with the Gospel of John (see "Salvation as Abundant Life" in chap. 9) and especially with the Letter to the Ephesians (see "Idealized Status of Believers" in chap. 17).

Colossians presents what God has done as a completed action, with immediate consequences for those who believe in Christ. The emphasis is on what has already transpired rather than on what is still to come: believers have already been rescued from the power of darkness (1:13); they have already been transferred to the kingdom of God's beloved Son (1:13); they have already been raised with Christ (2:12; 3:1). The spiritual powers that might oppose them have already been disarmed, and Christ has already made a public display of his triumph over them (2:15). This last reference draws on the image of Roman conquerors parading their vanquished foes through the streets after winning a decisive victory. We might have guessed that a biblical author would use this image to describe something scheduled to occur on judgment day or in the interim following Christ's return (see 1 Cor. 15:23–26), but Colossians says that it has already occurred. When? Colossians is not primarily concerned with temporal chronology (cf. 1 Cor. 15:23–24; 2 Thess. 2:2–3); the point could be that this public triumph is something that has already occurred—in the future! Realized eschatology typically adopts an eternal perspective rather than a historical one, and from the perspective of eternity, what is still future to us may be regarded as accomplished. The point, at any rate, is to stress the absolute

Fig. 19.3. Realized eschatology. The Colossian Christians have been raised with Christ, and they share in the inheritance of the saints in the light (Col. 1:12; cf. Eph. 2:6). (The Bridgeman Art Library International)

certainty of God's accomplishment, an appreciation of which impacts life in the present.

The claim that the Colossians "have been raised with Christ" (2:12; 3:1) is likewise meant in a spiritual sense: believers still live on the earth and must be concerned about life and relationships within the structures that this world affords (3:18–4:1). Their status as people who have already been raised is something that is currently "hidden" (3:3) and that will be revealed only when Christ returns (3:4); it is experienced in the present "through faith" (2:12). The point seems to be that the Colossians should count their resurrection with Christ as an assured reality that defines their values and shapes their life decisions (3:1–3), even though it may appear to be still future from the pedantic perspective of human history.

The specific point of emphasizing realized eschatology in the Colossian context is to assure these readers that no power in the universe is able to affect believers who have put their trust in Christ. The elemental spirits may control destinies in this world (that point is not argued), but those who have been baptized into Christ have died and been raised to a new life in a kingdom that lies beyond those spirits' jurisdiction (1:13).

⊙ **EXPLORE 19.15** "Realized Eschatology": What Would Paul Think?

Fig. 19.4. Disrobing for baptism. (The Bridgeman Art Library International)

Knowledge and Maturity

There is a notable emphasis in Colossians on growth in knowledge and on developing spiritual maturity (1:9–10, 28; 2:2; 4:12). Does this emphasis imply that the Colossians are particularly ignorant or especially immature (cf. 1 Cor. 3:1–3)? To the contrary, the ironic point made throughout this letter is that the Colossian Christians have already learned everything they need to know (1:7; 2:6–7); the gospel itself is growing and bearing fruit in them (1:5–6), and if they just remain steadfast, Christ will present them to God as "holy and blameless and irreproachable" (1:22–23)—it would be hard to become more "mature" than that! They have come to fullness in Christ (2:10), in whom the fullness of God dwells (1:19; 2:9).

The issue, perhaps, is that proponents of the philosophy that the letter seeks to counter are advocating programs and practices that will enable these believers to reach a more advanced level in their spiritual development. But in Christ, the Colossians already have "all the treasures of wisdom and knowledge" (2:3).

Slaves and Masters

Colossians 3:18–4:1 presents a *Haustafel* (table of household responsibilities) similar to the one in Ephesians 5:21–6:9. This one emphasizes the duties of slaves, perhaps because of a recent issue in the congregation in which Onesimus, the slave of Philemon, had run away from his master, only to be sent back to him by Paul (Philem. 8–18; cf. Col. 4:9). As in Paul's approach to that situation, the attitude toward slavery here is ambiguous.

On the one hand, slaves are instructed to obey their masters in everything (3:22; on this, cf. Eph. 6:5; 1 Tim. 6:1–2; Titus 2:9–10; 1 Pet. 2:18–21). On the other hand, masters are instructed to treat their slaves justly and fairly and to do so in recognition of their equality before God (Col. 4:1). For those whom Christ has clothed with a new way of being human (3:10), the distinction between "slave and free" has become ultimately meaningless (3:11).

The new ideas have "only an appearance of wisdom" with no real value (2:23). Those who promote such things are "puffed up without cause by a human way of thinking" (2:18), and the failure of their program becomes clear when one looks at the results: it has led these supposedly advanced spiritual people to condemn (2:16) and disqualify (2:18) those whom God has redeemed (1:14) and reconciled (1:22).

Real growth comes from God (2:19; cf. 1:6; 3:10): the body grows, and one need only remain a part of that body to grow to full maturity. The body is the church, with Christ as its head (1:18, 22, 24; 2:17, 19; 3:15). Growth and maturity, according to Colossians, involve not the discovery of anything new but rather continuing in Christ and remaining steadfast with regard to what they have been taught (2:6–7). Such maturity becomes evident in the fruit that it bears: lives worthy of the Lord, marked by good works (1:10; cf. Eph. 4:1). Christian maturity leads not to judging others but rather to love and peace and thanksgiving (3:14–15; cf. 2:2).

The latter portion of Colossians explicates some specific consequences of growth in knowledge and maturity (3:1–4:1). The vices to be avoided (3:5, 8–9) are exemplary of an old way of being human that the Colossians are to "strip off," and the virtues to be exhibited (3:12–15) are exemplary of a new way of being human with which the Colossians are to clothe themselves (3:9–10). This metaphor of taking off and putting on clothing invokes the image of early Christian baptisms, in which the initiates shed their garments and then were clothed with a new white robe to symbolize their transformed identity in Christ. The new humanity granted in baptism affects relationships, for there is no longer to be any discrimination on the basis of origin or status (3:11). Thus Colossians concludes with what may be our earliest example of a Christian *Haustafel* ("household table"): the family and social relationships that mark the daily lives of believers are to be conducted under the lordship of Jesus Christ (for discussion of a similar *Haustafel*, see box 17.5).

⊙ EXPLORE 19.5
Colossians 3:18–4:1 and Other Household Tables in the New Testament

⊙ EXPLORE 19.8
Colossians 3:20–21 — Parenting Advice from Paul and Ben Sira

Archippus the Procrastinator?

It has become a bit of a puzzle and source for jokes in New Testament studies: What was Archippus's unfinished task?

Archippus appears to have been a family member of Philemon who lived in or near Colossae. Paul calls him a "fellow soldier" in his personal letter to Philemon (v. 2).

In Colossians, he is the only member of the community to be mentioned by name, and this is only because he is to receive a private message from Paul: "Say to Archippus, 'See that you complete the task you received in the Lord'" (4:17).

Is this simple encouragement or a discreet rebuke? Has Archippus been slow to fulfill some duty? This was, and remains, a private matter, but interpreters throughout the ages have taken the word to Archippus as a directive for all procrastinators.

Ecology

The Letter to the Colossians gives ample consideration to the place of human beings in the universe and to the relationship of people to their environment. Whatever the specific concerns of the original author might have been, modern interpreters have found the book to be a pivotal text for consideration of ecological issues. Theologians and scientists have found its "cosmic Christology" provocative for an era in which we know infinitely more about the vastness of space and time than anyone knew when this letter was composed. Ecological awareness, furthermore, is driven by the Colossian position that everything in heaven and on earth was created through Christ, in Christ, and for Christ (1:16). Although there is a directive here that believers are not to focus their minds on earthly concerns (3:2), there is also the remarkable affirmation that Christ is the one in whom all things in the universe (including the natural environment) "hold together" (1:17). The reasoning for many theologians, then, goes something like this: if Christ is responsible for keeping the environment sound (holding it together), and if the church is the body of which Christ is the head (1:18; 2:19), then the church must view the protection and preservation of the natural world as a primary calling. Believers are to "seek the things that are above, where Christ is" (3:1), but if it is Christ's agenda to maintain the coherence of all things created through him and for him, then caring for the earth becomes a heavenly concern.

Conclusion

The Letter to the Colossians has contributed significantly to the development of Christian doctrine, especially Christology. While Protestant Christianity has often looked on Romans and Galatians as the theological high points in the Pauline corpus, Roman Catholic and Eastern Orthodox traditions have tended

⊘ EXPLORE 19.22
Colossians and the
Nicene Creed

to bestow that honor on Colossians and Ephesians. The letter has also been a favorite among Christian "mystics" who appreciate the emphasis on mystery and spiritual knowledge (in Christian tradition, believers identified as "mystics" have typically been ones who seek union with God through prayer and contemplation in a manner that transcends intellectual explanation). And apart from any considerations of theology or doctrine, Colossians is often said to exhibit a liturgical, celebrative style of writing that contrasts notably with the often argumentative, didactic tone of many Pauline letters. For all of its emphasis on the high position that believers in Christ now hold, the letter encourages compassion rather than hostility toward those who are still estranged, as they once were, doing the evil deeds they once did (1:21). "Conduct yourselves wisely among outsiders," the author counsels. "Let your speech always be gracious, seasoned with salt" (4:5–6).

FOR FURTHER READING: Colossians

Barclay, John M. G. *Colossians and Philemon*. T&T Clark Study Guides. New York: T&T Clark International, 2004.

Hay, David M. *Colossians*. Abingdon New Testament Commentaries. Nashville: Abingdon, 2000.

Lincoln, Andrew, and A. J. Wedderburn. *The Theology of the Later Pauline Letters*. New Testament Theology. Cambridge: Cambridge University Press, 1993.

Talbert, Charles H. *Ephesians and Colossians*. Paideia. Grand Rapids: Baker Academic, 2007.

Tamez, Elsa, et al. *Philippians, Colossians, Philemon*. Wisdom Commentary. Collegeville, MN: Liturgical Press, 2016.

Thompson, Marianne Meye. *Colossians and Philemon*. Two Horizons Commentary. Grand Rapids: Eerdmans, 2005.

Wright, N. T. *Paul for Everyone: The Prison Letters; Ephesians, Philippians, Colossians, and Philemon*. 2nd ed. Louisville: Westminster John Knox, 2004.

⊘ Go to www .IntroducingNT.com for summaries, videos, and other study tools.

20

1 Thessalonians

This may be where it all began. Most New Testament scholars believe that Paul's first letter to the Thessalonians is the earliest of any of his letters that have been preserved for us. If they are right, then almost certainly it was written before any of the other books now found in our New Testament, which would make it the earliest surviving Christian writing of any kind. The letter ostensibly is sent from "Paul, Silvanus, and Timothy," but first-person singular references pop up often enough (2:18; 3:5; 5:27) to indicate that Paul is the primary author.

The man who wrote this letter, the apostle Paul, was an avid student of Scripture: the law of Moses, the psalms of David, the oracles of the prophets. It seems unlikely that he could have imagined that people would one day be reading this letter alongside those works, regarding his own words as Scripture. He certainly did not imagine that people would be doing that two thousand years later, for he did not think it likely that anyone would still be around two thousand years hence—or two hundred years, or even twenty years, for that matter. The man who wrote 1 Thessalonians expected Jesus Christ to return soon, and assumed that he would be alive to see it happen (4:17).

What was it like to be a Christian in those very early days? In this letter, Paul tells us. He even tells us how he practiced his ministry, how he went about the task of spreading what he calls "the gospel of God" (2:2). The focus, we will see, is not simply on the message he shared but also on the manner in which he shared it.

Overview

After a brief salutation (1:1), Paul and his companions give thanks to God for the Thessalonians' faithfulness (1:2–3). They recall the powerful spiritual

> ⊙ EXPLORE 20.0
> 1 Thessalonians: Out-
> line of Contents

387

transformation that occurred in the lives of the letters' recipients: the Thessalonians responded to the gospel by turning to God from idols and, despite persecution, became an inspiring example to believers everywhere (1:4–10). Paul reminds them of the purity and integrity with which he conducted his ministry among them (2:1–12), and also of the conviction with which they accepted the gospel as the very word of God (2:13). He tells them that the suffering that they have had to endure from gentiles is analogous to what Christian Jews have had to experience from Jews who reject Christ (2:14–16). Although he regrets not having been able to visit them, he has received word from Timothy of their continuing steadfastness (2:17–3:10). Paul concludes this "thanksgiving" portion of his letter with a threefold benediction (3:11–13). He then offers the Thessalonians advice on a few matters. He reminds them that they must be pure and holy with regard to sexuality (4:1–8). He says that they should live quiet, productive lives, marked by mutual love for other believers and commendable behavior toward outsiders (4:9–12). Paul then takes up a topic that apparently has been troubling the Thessalonians: the fate of those who have died. He assures them that the departed will not miss out on the resurrection, or even on the parousia (the second coming of Christ): when Christ returns, the dead in Christ will rise to meet him in the air, and then believers who are alive will be caught up in the air to join them (4:13–18). Exactly when and how this will occur cannot be known, but the assurance is that both those who live and those who die in Christ are destined for salvation (5:1–11). Having offered this

---

Box 20.1

Evangelical Reminders

One striking characteristic of 1 Thessalonians is the number of times that Paul reminds his readers of things that they already know.

- "You know what kind of persons we proved to be" (1:5).
- "You yourselves know . . . our coming to you was not in vain" (2:1).
- "As you know, we had courage in our God" (2:2).
- "As you know . . . we never came with words of flattery or with a pretext for greed" (2:5).
- "You remember our labor and toil" (2:9).
- "You are witnesses . . . how pure, upright, and blameless our conduct was" (2:10).
- "As you know, we dealt with each one of you like a father with his children" (2:11).
- "You yourselves know that this is what we are destined for" (3:3).
- "We told you beforehand that we were to suffer . . . so it turned out, as you know" (3:4).
- "You know what instructions we gave you" (4:2).
- "The Lord is an avenger . . . as we have already told you" (4:6).
- "Concerning love . . . you do not need to have anyone write to you" (4:9).
- "Work with your hands, as we directed you" (4:11).
- "Concerning the times and seasons . . . you do not need to have anything written to you" (5:1).
- "You yourselves know very well that the day of the Lord will come like a thief" (5:2).

encouragement, Paul concludes the letter with a number of final exhortations, blessings, and greetings (5:12–28).

Historical Background

In New Testament times, the region that is now known as Greece consisted of two provinces: Macedonia in the north and Achaia in the south. The cities of Thessalonica and Philippi were in Macedonia, and Athens and Corinth were in Achaia (see map 17.1). The apostle Paul spent quite a bit of time in Greece on what are traditionally called his second and third missionary journeys, and he wrote letters to three of the four cities just named. Thessalonica (modern-day Thessaloniki or Salonika) was the capital city of Macedonia, and it was in many respects the most important city of the region. It was located at the crossing of four major roads and also possessed one of the best natural harbors on the northern Aegean Sea. A bustling metropolis with a population that may have ranged as high as one hundred thousand, the city appears to have been home to a wide variety of religious groups: archaeology reveals multiple shrines and temples for deities such as Isis, Osiris, Serapis, and Cabirus.

Paul's second missionary journey brought him to Thessalonica around 48–51. According to the book of Acts, he crossed over to Europe from what is now western Turkey. He landed at Neapolis (see map 14.1) and went first to Philippi, where he managed to found the church to which he would later write his letter to the Philippians (Acts 16:11–40). Then he moved down the Via Egnatia about one hundred miles west to Thessalonica (Acts 17:1). He appears to have stayed in this city for several months, receiving financial assistance on at least two occasions from the new church in Philippi that he had just left behind (Phil. 4:16).

Via Egnatia: a road constructed by the Romans in the second century BCE; it crossed the Roman provinces of Illyricum, Macedonia, and Thrace.

The brief sketch of Paul's Thessalonian ministry in the book of Acts focuses on his preaching in the Jewish synagogue (17:2–4), but comments in his first letter to the Thessalonians indicate that his ministry in the city must have taken on a broader compass. Paul refers to the recipients of 1 Thessalonians as people who "turned to God from idols" (1:9). He also mentions that he and his companions "worked night and day" while proclaiming the gospel to the Thessalonians (2:9), which perhaps offers a literal description of how the evangelization of these gentile idol-worshipers took place. Many Roman cities, including Thessalonica, featured market buildings called *insulae* that contained shops on the ground floor and living quarters for the shopkeepers on the floors above (see fig. 20.2). The shops opened out onto the street and became principal sites for social interaction in addition to commerce. Many scholars think that Paul, Timothy, and Silas (= Silvanus) rented an *insula* shop in Thessalonica where they could practice their trade as leatherworkers or tent-makers (Acts 18:3). Paul may have preached in synagogues on Sabbath days,

Fig. 20.1. Via Egnatia. This is the actual road that Paul walked as he traveled from Philippi to Thessalonica. The Via Egnatia was a major land route across northern Greece and Asia Minor (modern-day Turkey). A tribute to Roman engineering, it also proved to be a great boon to Christian missionaries in spreading the gospel. (Craig Koester)

but on the other six days of the week Paul and his friends turned their leather shop into an arena for religious dialogue, offering their Christian testimony to clients, customers, colleagues, and curious passersby. They apparently did this with great success, for Paul's letter refers to the market encounters rather than to the synagogue engagements as the primary context out of which the church at Thessalonica was born.

We may wonder, of course, how Paul went about persuading gentiles to worship the Jewish God and to become followers of the Jewish Messiah. In this letter he makes frequent mention of matters that he addressed while among the Thessalonians, and some of the points seem similar to the teachings of philosophical schools that were popular in the Greco-Roman world. For example, Paul says that he directed the Thessalonians to aspire to live quietly, to mind their own affairs, and to work with their hands (4:11); this is advice that might just as well have been offered by the Epicureans. Thus Paul may have established some contact with these gentiles by presenting Christianity as a meaningful moral system that allows people to live with integrity and dignity. But, of course,

Epicureans: adherents of Epicureanism, a philosophical system that emphasized free will, questioned fate, and encouraged the attainment of true pleasure through avoidance of anxiety, concentration on the present, and enjoyment of all things in moderation.

Paul would want to say that the Christian faith is much more than just "good advice," and this letter makes clear that he also taught the Thessalonians about topics more specific to Christian doctrine—for example, that there is only one true and living God (1:9), and that Jesus is the Son of God (1:10), who died for them (4:10, 14), and whom God raised from the dead (1:10; 4:14). The point that comes up more than anything else, however, is the Christian declaration that Jesus is coming again to rescue people from God's wrath (1:10; 2:19; 3:13; 4:15–17; 5:2–5, 23). This appears to have been a matter of special interest to the Thessalonians—a dominant, driving concern of their faith. In any event, Paul appears to have brought the Thessalonians quite a ways in a short period of time. He was in the city less than a year, and yet by the time he left, there were leaders in the church who had responsibility for admonishing others in the Lord (5:12). It is somewhat amazing to realize that these trusted and respected church leaders apparently were persons who a few months earlier had never even heard of Jesus.

Fig. 20.2. A Roman *insula*. These remains of a Roman *insula* in the city of Ostia may look similar to the building in Thessalonica where Paul is likely to have worked while spreading the gospel. (Dennis Jarvis, CC BY-SA 2.0)

Box 20.2

The Jews and God's Wrath

In one section of 1 Thessalonians, Paul goes off on a brief tangent of condemnation against "the Jews" (2:14–16). He levels six charges: (1) they persecuted Christians in Judea; (2) they killed the Lord Jesus; (3) they killed the prophets; (4) they drove Paul and his companions out—probably a reference to forcing them to leave Macedonia (cf. Acts 17:5, 13–14); (5) they displease God; and (6) they "oppose everyone" by hindering the Christian evangelization of gentiles. Paul says that by doing such things, the Jews have been "filling up the measure of their sins" and that now God's wrath has overtaken them at last.

These verses have had a terrible influence in Christian history, inspiring anti-Semitism and lending support to centuries of mistreatment of Jewish people at the hands of gentiles versed in the Christian Scriptures.

Scholars note that the verses are not typical of Paul. Elsewhere Paul identifies *himself* as a persecutor of the church (Gal. 1:22–23; cf. Acts 7:58). Instead of blaming the Jews for killing Jesus, he attributes the death of Jesus to "the rulers of this age" (1 Cor. 2:8), by which he probably means evil spiritual powers (cf. Col. 2:15). And rather than speaking of anyone incurring God's wrath for killing Jesus, Paul normally speaks of Jesus giving his life voluntarily in order that people might be saved from God's wrath (Rom. 5:6–9).

Paul was often in conflict with his fellow Jews, and he claims to have suffered at their hands (2 Cor. 11:24). Still, the attitude expressed in 1 Thessalonians 2:14–16 seems markedly different from his statements about God's continued dealings with Israel elsewhere (Rom. 9:1–5; 10:1–4; 11:25–32). A few scholars wonder whether these verses (1 Thess. 2:14–16) might have been written by someone other than Paul and inserted into this letter at a later date, but there is no direct evidence in any of our manuscripts to support that supposition. More often, the verses are regarded as "polemical hyperbole"—an angry rant that exemplifies the rhetorical tactics of the day but surely does not represent Paul's full or reasoned view on the subject. It is possible that he understood such rhetoric as being in line with Israel's own Scriptures, which contain numerous passages that speak words of condemnation against God's chosen people (cf. Deut. 32; 2 Chron. 36:15–21; Amos 6:1–8).

Other New Testament examples of polemical rants against Jews are found in Matthew 23:13–39; John 8:39–47; Acts 7:51–53.

After Paul, Timothy, and Silas had spent a few months in this city, they were suddenly forced to leave. Separated from the Thessalonians, they were distraught and worried about what would become of the new believers in the midst of the persecution that they were experiencing (2:14; 3:3–4). The nature of that persecution is not described. It is not impossible that it involved physical violence, such as Paul later would indicate had befallen him throughout his ministry (cf. 2 Cor. 6:4–5; 11:23–25). But it is also possible that the tribulation took the form of social ostracism and public shaming. In any event, Paul knew that Satan, the tempter, was behind this distress, and he wondered whether the young Christians would be able to withstand the trial (3:5). He tried repeatedly to come to them, but Satan thwarted his plans (2:18). At last he managed to send Timothy to them (3:2–3), and Timothy returned with good news: the

Box 20.3

Faith, Love, and Hope

Paul mentions faith, love, and hope at the beginning and the end of 1 Thessalonians:

- "We always give thanks . . . constantly remembering . . . your work of faith and labor of love and steadfastness of hope in our Lord Jesus Christ" (1:2–3).
- "Put on the breastplate of faith and love, and for a helmet the hope of salvation" (5:8).

Paul talks about "faith, hope, and love" in 1 Corinthians 13:13, and he lists "love" last because, he says, it is the most important of the three. In 1 Thessalonians, however, he lists "hope" last because, for this church at this time, the message of hope seems to be what is most important. Paul says that Timothy has brought him a good report regarding the Thessalonians' "faith and love" (3:6), but he does not mention any good report about them excelling in hope. When he goes on to say that he wants to restore what is lacking in their faith (3:10), many interpreters assume that he is speaking of the missing element of hope. The Thessalonians are famous for their faith (1:8), and they abound in love (3:12; 4:9–10), but they need to be encouraged with a message of hope (4:13, 18).

Thessalonians were standing firm in the Lord (3:8), and they continued to think well of Paul and his companions (3:6).

It was in response to this news that Paul (with Silas and Timothy) wrote the letter that we know as 1 Thessalonians. The date for the letter's composition is somewhere between 49 and 52, if we assume that he is writing "a short time" after founding the church (see 2:17). By now he is probably in the city of Corinth, living with his friends and fellow tentmakers Aquila and Priscilla and spending days in the Corinthian marketplace attempting to replicate the evangelistic success that he had achieved in Philippi and Thessalonica (see Acts 18:1–4).

The primary purpose of Paul's first letter to the Thessalonians is to celebrate and cement the good relationship that he has with the believers in the community. The letter has a general tone of "reminding," alerting the Thessalonians to the continued relevance of what they have seen and heard and know to be true (see box 20.1). But Paul also wants to respond to one new matter that has come up, a question that has precipitated a faith crisis within the community. Not surprisingly, it is a question involving the Thessalonians' favorite subject: the second coming of Christ.

Major Themes in 1 Thessalonians

The Conduct of Paul's Ministry

Paul reminds the Thessalonians of the way he and his companions behaved (1:5; 2:1–12). They showed courage in the midst of opposition (2:2) and did not

Fig. 20.3. Marketplace evangelism. In many Latin American countries, villagers gather in the marketplace to share their ideas and philosophies while working with their hands. A similar scenario is described by Paul, who brought the gospel to the Thessalonians while working at his craft (tent-making) in the market. (© The Alfredo Ramos Martínez Research Project, reproduced by permission. Photo © Christie's Images / Bridgeman Images)

compromise God's message to earn approval from mere mortals (2:3–6). They cared so deeply for the Thessalonians that they worked overtime to earn their own keep and not be a burden on anyone (2:8–9). Their conduct was "pure, upright, and blameless" (2:10). They did not even make the sort of demands that might have been appropriate for them to make as apostles; they chose to forgo what would have been their due, for they preferred to regard the Thessalonians as family rather than as students or disciples.

Indeed, family imagery in this letter is both pervasive and diverse. First, Paul and his companions say that while they were with the Thessalonians they filled the role of parents; they were as tender and gentle as a nursing mother (2:7), and they offered each individual fatherly advice and encouragement (2:11). Then, when forcibly separated from the Thessalonians, they felt as though *they* were the children—the anguish made them feel like orphans (2:17). And now, writing the letter, they regard the Thessalonians as their "brothers and sisters": the sibling terminology is used a remarkable fifteen times in what is a fairly short letter (1:4; 2:1, 9, 14, 17; 3:2, 7; 4:1, 6, 9, 10, 13; 5:1, 12, 26).

Why does Paul spend so much time explicating the depth of his devotion for the Thessalonians and reminiscing about the nobility of his ministry and motives? Some scholars wonder whether he might be on the defensive. Perhaps he has opponents or detractors in the city who are deriding his ministry in ways that he wants to negate. It is also possible that some of the Thessalonians might blame him for the persecutions that they are suffering, persecutions that he himself has managed to avoid by leaving town; thus Paul goes out of his way to let them know that he has suffered for their sake (2:2), that he remains concerned for them (2:17–3:5), and that in some sense he continues to share in their distress (3:4, 7).

It is also possible, however, that Paul offers this recap of his ministry not for defensive reasons but rather as a model for the Thessalonian Christians to follow as they become imitators of him, sharing the word with others (1:6–8). Furthermore, Paul may want to remind the Thessalonians how well they were treated as a way of honoring them: they have suffered the shame of being reviled by their own compatriots (2:14), but they were (and still are) deemed worthy of exemplary devotion from three prominent church leaders. Whatever their fellow citizens might say about them, Paul, Timothy, and Silas say, "You are our glory and joy!" (2:20; cf. 3:8–9).

Honor and Shame

Several points in this letter may be read in light of a concern just mentioned: the Thessalonians have been shamed by their compatriots, and Paul wants to offer them a somewhat ironic restoration of honor. The reason for the shaming probably was that the new Christians repudiated much that was (literally) sacred to gentile society: they did not join in festivities associated with the city's temples and shrines; they did not honor the emperor with worshipful tributes or accolades; they did not participate in banquets and parties and other amusements. As a result, while the Jews of Thessalonica would have viewed the Thessalonian Christians as heretics, the gentile population probably styled them as irreligious, unpatriotic, and antisocial. Becoming a Christian in mid-first-century Thessalonica almost certainly meant a loss of esteem and social prestige.

Paul wants to tell the Thessalonian Christians that although they are not honored in the eyes of this world, they are honored in the eyes of God. He also goes out of his way to assure them that they are highly regarded among other believers: their story is told as an inspiring example of faith in churches throughout Macedonia and Achaia and, indeed, "in every place" (1:7–9). Further, he suggests that their unbelieving neighbors (the ones who shame them) are the ones behaving in a manner that is truly unworthy of honor: they mistreat others (2:2) and live as people who do not know God, controlled by lustful passions (4:5). All of this will be exposed when the day of God's wrath arrives: utter destruction will come upon those who blithely talk of "peace and security" (5:3–4).

Thus the Thessalonian Christians should not be concerned with what their doomed neighbors think, but Paul does offer two practical suggestions that might help their situation. First, the Thessalonian believers ought to build one another up, for this provides an affirmation of honor within the community that

honor: the positive status that one has in the eyes of those whom one considers to be significant.

shame: negative status, implying disgrace and unworthiness.

Fig. 20.4. The dead will rise. An Italian work from the fifteenth century illustrates Paul's assurances in 1 Thessalonians 4:13–18. (The Bridgeman Art Library International)

they no longer enjoy in society at large (4:18; 5:11, 14). Second, they should be careful about their behavior toward outsiders: if they refrain from meddling in the affairs of others and if they remain good, productive citizens (4:11–12), they may mute some of the criticisms leveled against them. So they must look beyond their current situation to their ultimate destiny (5:9; cf. 3:3), but in the meantime they are to abound in love and do good for one another (3:12) and to outsiders as well (5:15).

Sexual Morality

Paul offers the Thessalonians advice regarding how they are to live in order to please God (4:1; cf. 2:9). First, he emphasizes that they are to be holy and honorable in matters of sexual morality: they are to abstain from sexual relations outside of marriage and from anything that is exploitative or expressive of lustful passion (4:3–7). Had the Thessalonian believers been Jewish converts, they would have needed little instruction in this regard, but for gentiles who

Box 20.4

Good Grief

In 1 Thessalonians 4:13 Paul says that he does not want the believers to "grieve as others do who have no hope." A popular text for Christian funerals and memorial services, this passage typically is interpreted as encouraging a distinctive, Christian grief that is grounded in the promise of life after death. Paul does not say that the Thessalonians should not grieve for their lost loved ones—that would be unrealistic and unhealthy. Rather, he says that their grief should be different from the grief of people who have no hope of ever seeing their loved ones again. The Christian Thessalonians are not to be "uninformed about those who have died." They know that the dead in Christ will rise and that all who believe, living and dead, will be reunited to be with the Lord forever (4:16–18). Such knowledge does not cancel out the grief or sorrow of experiencing the loss of loved ones in this life, but Paul nevertheless urges the grief-stricken Thessalonians to "encourage one another with these words" (4:18).

until a short time ago did not know God (cf. 4:5), chastity and monogamy may have seemed like novel ideas. Paul has told them all of this before (4:2), but either because of something Timothy told him or simply because of his own intuition or knowledge of human nature, he figures that it is worth mentioning again. He also emphasizes that this teaching is not based on human authority but rather comes directly from God (4:8).

Working for a Living

Paul urges the Thessalonian believers to work with their hands and be dependent on no one (4:11–12). This charge seems to pick up on the example that he and his companions set by working night and day so as not to be burdens on anyone (2:9). There appear to have been idlers in the Thessalonian community who needed to be admonished to work for a living (5:14). Such a problem perhaps resulted simply from laziness, but many interpreters have wondered whether the idleness in the Thessalonian community was connected to the church's expectation of an imminent second coming. Perhaps some church members had quit their jobs in eager anticipation of the end times, and now Paul needs to tell them that loitering for Jesus is not an appropriate way to await his coming. This matter will come up again in another letter addressed to this community (2 Thess. 3:6–13; see box 21.3).

Death of Believers Prior to the Parousia

Near the end of 1 Thessalonians Paul takes up a question that seems to have been troubling the congregation. Some persons in the church have died, and the

Box 20.5

Tombstone Inscription

A legend on tombstones in the Roman Empire read:

Non Fui
Fui
Non Sum
Non Curo

Translation: I didn't exist / I did exist / I don't exist / I don't care.

Caught Up in the Clouds

In some circles, 1 Thessalonians is valued for providing the primary biblical reference (or "proof text") for what is called the "rapture":

> The Lord himself, with a cry of command, with the archangel's call and with the sound of God's trumpet, will descend from heaven, and the dead in Christ will rise first. Then we who are alive, who are left, will be caught up in the clouds together with them to meet the Lord in the air. (1 Thess. 4:16–17)

The Greek word translated as "caught up" (*harpazein*) in this passage is used elsewhere to describe people being snatched by God's Spirit (Acts 8:39) or transported into heaven (2 Cor. 12:2–4). Paul seems to be saying that all Christians (alive and dead) will be miraculously lifted up into heaven by God (see also 2 Cor. 12:2, 4; and cf. Matt. 24:40–41; Luke 17:34–35).

The Greek word translated as "meet" (*apantēsis*) in the phrase "meet the Lord" is often used with reference to a custom of the day. People expecting an important visitor often went out from house or city to intercept and escort the approaching traveler on the final leg of the journey (Matt. 25:6; Acts 28:15). Thus Paul might be saying that as Jesus returns, all Christians (living and dead) will rise into heaven to meet him halfway; they will then join him in a triumphant procession as he continues his descent to earth.

The term *rapture* (an English word formed from the Latin for "caught up") has come to be associated with one particular scenario of end-time events: the notion that faithful Christians will be taken up into heaven at some point before the return of Christ, while others are left behind to deal with a time of unprecedented tribulation. Christians who say that they "believe in the rapture" often mean that they accept this particular doctrine of a miraculous pretribulation deliverance of believers. Christians who say that they "don't believe in the rapture" may nevertheless expect to be caught up in the clouds to meet the Lord Jesus when he returns; they just don't accept the particular scenario for a pretribulation deliverance with which the term *rapture* has come to be associated.

grief-stricken Thessalonians wonder whether this means that their loved ones will miss out on what Paul has promised them. No, Paul says, when Christ returns, the dead in Christ will rise and then all believers, living and dead, will be caught up in the clouds to meet the Lord in the air (4:16–17). This all seems fairly clear; in fact, to many scholars it seems a bit too clear. In a letter that is largely devoted to reminding people of things that they already know, 1 Thessalonians 4:13–18 stands out as the one section of the letter in which Paul provides new information. But it seems like such a basic matter. Did the Thessalonians really not know that the dead would be raised to new life? Had Paul neglected to tell them that? And even if that were the case, couldn't Timothy have told them while he was visiting them? Why was this a matter that required a word from Paul himself?

Some scholars think that the presentation of this question indicates how primitive Paul's theology may have been at the outset of his ministry. He naively assumes that he will still be alive at the time Christ returns (note 4:17: "we who are alive"). Perhaps in those early years he was so eagerly awaiting the second coming that he hadn't even stopped to think about what would happen to people who died. He had never even talked about it with Timothy or Silas, but now that the Thessalonians broached the question, he had to think it through and come up with an answer: Of course! The dead will be raised, just as Jesus was.

That's one explanation. Another one, preferred by a number of scholars, suggests that the Thessalonians' question was not about the resurrection of the dead (a subject on which they surely would have received prior instruction) but instead about the chronology of events in the end times. The concern was not that their loved ones would miss the resurrection but rather that they would miss the parousia. The dearly departed had been waiting every day for Jesus to come, and now they had died. Of course, they would be raised to new life, but what a disappointment it would be for them if the resurrection came after

parousia: the second coming of Christ.

Box 20.7

Kissing Christians

Paul closes his letter to the Thessalonians with this exhortation: "Greet all the brothers and sisters [*adelphoi*] with a holy kiss" (5:26). He closes three of his later letters with the more generic exhortation, "Greet one another with a holy kiss" (Rom. 16:16; 1 Cor. 16:20; 2 Cor. 13:12).

In the early years of Christianity, followers of Jesus were noted for kissing one another (probably, though not necessarily, on the lips) and for making the exchange of such greetings a part of their public liturgy. Paul's emphasis that this greeting was to be a "*holy* kiss" (cf. 1 Pet. 5:14) makes clear that nothing erotic was implied. Still, the practice was a novel one.

In the biblical world, kissing appears to have been commonplace between family members (Gen. 27:26–27; Exod. 18:7) and friends (1 Sam. 20:41). Men kissed men (2 Sam. 20:9) and women kissed women (Ruth 1:9, 14) as expressions of welcome (Gen. 29:13; Exod. 4:27), favor (2 Sam. 15:5), blessing (Gen. 48:9–10; 2 Sam. 19:39), farewell (Gen. 31:28, 55; 1 Kings 19:20), grief (Gen. 50:1), and reconciliation (Gen. 33:4; 45:15). However, there does not appear to have been any precedent in Jewish or Greco-Roman society for kissing between men and women who were not either relatives (Gen. 29:11–12) or lovers (Song 1:2; 8:1).

The New Testament contains references to kisses similar to what is found elsewhere in the Bible (Mark 14:45; Luke 15:20; Acts 20:37), but it also introduces this new concept of a "holy kiss" that might be shared by believers regardless of gender, rank, or race. This practice probably can be traced to the teaching of Jesus that identified his followers as family members (Mark 3:35). Based on this idea, a greeting shared between literal brothers and sisters became a symbolic act expressing the spiritual relationship between those who were one family in Christ.

In the second century, the ritual exchange of a "kiss of peace" became a standard component of the Sunday morning liturgy (see Justin Martyr, *First Apology* 66).

For more on this subject, see Michael Philip Penn, *Kissing Christians: Ritual and Community in the Late Ancient Church* (Philadelphia: University of Pennsylvania Press, 2005).

the parousia and they missed the great event that they had longed to behold. Thus Paul assures the Thessalonians that the dead in Christ will rise *before* Jesus comes, and they will not miss a thing. According to this view, Paul may have given the Thessalonians general information about both the resurrection and the parousia previously, but he now needs to fill them in on some details (that perhaps Timothy had been unable to provide).

Conclusion

Much more could be said about Paul's first letter to the Thessalonians, short as it is. Theologians are interested in the correspondence not only for its contribution to eschatology (study of the end times) but also for what it has to offer regarding such themes as election (1:4), predestination (3:3; 5:9), sanctification (4:3; 5:23), the word of God (1:5, 6, 8; 2:13; 4:15, 18), and the gospel (1:5; 2:2, 4, 8, 9; 3:2). The letter refers to these subjects without offering much in the way of teaching on them—a point of frustration for theologians—but it is notable that what are often regarded as "advanced Christian teachings" are referenced so casually in what usually is taken to be the earliest surviving Christian document. The letter typically is dated somewhere between fifteen and twenty years after the crucifixion of Jesus. In that short span of time a movement that began with a small circle of Jewish peasants in rural Galilee became a somewhat organized religion with gentile adherents in major cities of the Roman Empire. The simple fact that there is a Christian church in Thessalonica is remarkable; that this church already evinces an awareness of many key issues that would be debated among intellectuals for the next two millennia is truly amazing.

Still, for Christians who are not professional theologians, Paul's first letter to the Thessalonians has probably been valued more for its contributions to spiritual life than to Christian doctrine. This letter is saturated with prayer, and it describes prayer as a continuous activity: Paul and his companions constantly remember the Thessalonians as they give thanks to God (1:2), they pray "night and day" that they might see them again (3:10), and they invite the Thessalonians to "pray without ceasing" (5:17). Further, the Thessalonians are urged to "rejoice always" (5:16) and to "give thanks in all circumstances" (5:18). Such references ("constantly," "night and day," "without ceasing," "always," "all circumstances") envision prayer as an attitude and a lifestyle, not simply a verbal activity. Finally, we should note that 1 Thessalonians appears in our Bibles as the first of two letters from Paul to this church. Scholars have mixed opinions about the nature of the relationship between the two letters (did Paul write them both?), but all agree that they are indeed related. Similar themes are addressed and similar points are made, but with intriguing twists.

FOR FURTHER READING: 1 Thessalonians

Cousar, Charles B. *Reading Galatians, Philippians, and 1 Thessalonians: A Literary and Theological Commentary*. Reading the New Testament. Macon, GA: Smyth & Helwys, 2001.

Donfried, Karl P., and I. Howard Marshall. *The Theology of the Shorter Pauline Letters*. New Testament Theology. Cambridge: Cambridge University Press, 1993.

Furnish, Victor Paul. *1 Thessalonians, 2 Thessalonians*. Abingdon New Testament Commentaries. Nashville: Abingdon, 2004.

Gillman, Florence M., Mary Ann Beavis, and HyeRan Kim-Cragg. *1–2 Thessalonians*. Wisdom Commentary. Collegeville, MN: Liturgical Press, 2016.

Johnson, Andy. *1 & 2 Thessalonians*. Two Horizons Commentary. Grand Rapids: Eerdmans, 2016.

Weidman, Frederick W. *Philippians, First and Second Thessalonians, and Philemon*. Westminster Bible Companion. Louisville: Westminster John Knox, 2013.

Wright, N. T. *Paul for Everyone: Galatians and Thessalonians*. 2nd ed. Louisville: Westminster John Knox, 2004.

⊙ Go to www
.IntroducingNT.com
for summaries,
videos, and other
study tools.

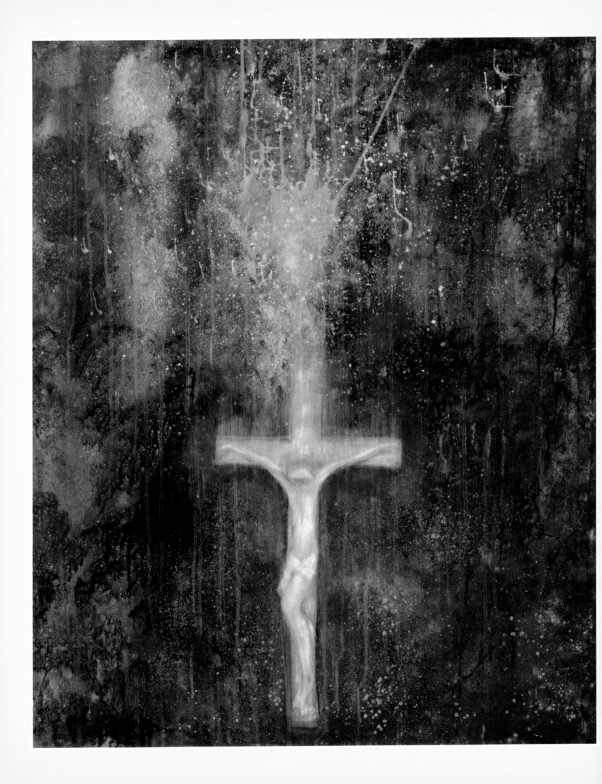

21

2 Thessalonians

Rock bands and other popular music artists often perform "cover versions" of songs with which their audience is already familiar. The trick is not to copy the song exactly but rather to reinvent it in creative and interesting ways without losing those features that made the piece appealing in the first place. Indeed, some artists have been known to do cover versions of their own songs, revising past hits sufficiently to gain them a new hearing for a new day.

The New Testament letter known as 2 Thessalonians might be thought of as "a cover version" of the letter known as 1 Thessalonians. The content and format are remarkably similar, but the tone has changed. The first letter mentioned destruction that will come upon unbelievers on the day of judgment (1 Thess. 5:3); the second seems to relish such condemnation (2 Thess. 1:6–9; 2:11–12). The first letter said that idlers should be admonished (1 Thess. 5:14; cf. 4:11); the second says that they should be denied food (2 Thess. 3:10). The first letter said that everyone in the community was to hear what the letter said (1 Thess. 5:27); the second says that they are to obey what it says or else be shunned by other church members (2 Thess. 3:14).

Much (but not all) of what is found in 2 Thessalonians comes across as a harsher version of what was said more gently in the letter that we examined in the preceding chapter. A key question becomes whether the author is Paul restating his own material in a more strident vein or is someone else reshaping one of the apostle's "greatest hits" (the letter known as 1 Thessalonians) in a more stern and forbidding style.

Overview

A brief salutation (1:1–2) identifies 2 Thessalonians as being from Paul, Silvanus, and Timothy, who testify to how the Thessalonians' mutual love and

Fig. 21.1. The day of the Lord. A rumor circulated among the Thessalonians that the "day of the Lord" had already come. The apostle Paul's teaching on the topic reveals his belief that it would be a day that no one could miss (see 1 Cor. 15:51–57; 1 Thess. 4:13–18). (The Bridgeman Art Library International)

faithfulness in persecution have inspired pride and thanksgiving among the churches of God (1:3–4). This is followed by a promise that God will wreak vengeance on those who afflict the Thessalonians, punishing them with eternal destruction on the day of judgment (1:5–12). The mention of that day leads to instruction on a significant issue: some people have been telling the Thessalonians that the "day of the Lord" has already arrived (2:1–2). The authors assure them that this is not the case and that, indeed, that day will not come until after the "lawless one" mounts a final and futile opposition to God (2:3–12). The authors are confident that the Thessalonians will not be among those deceived by this satanic foe, provided they hold fast to what Paul taught them (2:13–15). They offer the Thessalonians their blessing in this regard (2:16–17),

⊙ EXPLORE 21.0
2 Thessalonians: Out-
line of Contents

ask for their prayers in return (3:1–2), repeat the affirmation of confidence (3:3–4), and offer another blessing, similar to the first (3:5). Then the letter turns to another topic, addressing the problem of idleness: the Thessalonians ought to follow the example of productive labor that Paul set for them, and they should avoid association with believers who do not follow this example (3:6–15). The letter closes with two benedictions and some words in Paul's own handwriting by which the readers will be able to recognize the authenticity of this letter as coming from him rather than from someone using his name to mislead them (3:16–18).

Historical Background

Our knowledge regarding the historical background of this letter is uncertain. Let's start with a brief review of what we do know. Thessalonica was the capital city for the Roman province of Macedonia (located in what is now northern Greece). Paul founded a church composed mainly of gentiles in this city sometime around 48–51. He was forced to leave the city amid growing persecution, and he wrote the letter that we now know as 1 Thessalonians to the struggling church that he had left behind.

What happened next? One possible scenario is pretty straightforward. A few months after writing 1 Thessalonians, Paul received word back from the church that a new crisis had erupted: the Thessalonians were so eager and excited about the imminent return of Christ that some of them had bought in on a rumor that "the day of the Lord is already here" (2 Thess. 2:2). We

---

Box 21.1

What Was the Rumor?

The Thessalonians were shaken and alarmed by a rumor that "the day of the Lord is already here" (2 Thess. 2:2). What did they think had happened?

- Did they think that the persecutions that they were experiencing were the "birth pangs" indicating that the second coming was certain to occur within a matter of days (cf. 1 Thess. 5:3)?
- Did they think that Jesus had already come back and was putting together his kingdom somewhere on earth?
- Did they think that something like the "rapture" had occurred and that they had been left behind (cf. 1 Thess. 4:15–17)?
- Did they think that Christ had returned in some mystical sense, perhaps embodied in the spiritual unity of the community?
- Did they think that the "day of the Lord" was something that did not require a literal second coming but rather could be realized spiritually through a life of faith that overcomes all difficulties (cf. 1 Cor. 4:8)?

Fig. 21.2. Hell awaits. According to 2 Thessalonians 1:7–9, evildoers and the enemies of faithful Christians will suffer the vengeance of God. (The Bridgeman Art Library International)

are not certain exactly what they thought this meant (see box 21.1) or where they would have gotten this notion (an enthusiastic prophecy by one of their members, or a forged letter from someone claiming to be Paul, or a misinterpretation of the teaching in 1 Thessalonians?). In any case, Paul realized that it was time to write them another letter to sort things out. According to this scenario, the letter known as 2 Thessalonians was written from Corinth by Paul and his companions a few months after 1 Thessalonians, some time between 50 and 53. The main point of the letter comes in 2:1–12, where Paul teaches the Thessalonians about what must happen before the day of the Lord arrives.

For many students of the Bible, the scenario outlined above provides a reasonable historical context for understanding this letter. It certainly is the context within which the letter has been understood throughout most of church history. In modern times, however, an alternative scenario has been suggested and has garnered significant support. According to this view, the letter was not actually written by Paul, and it may not have been written to the Thessalonians.

⊙ EXPLORE 21.5
Authorship of
2 Thessalonians

It comes from a later time, years after Paul's death, when Christians regarded the apostle's writings as authoritative treatises, almost on a par with Scripture. By that time, as Christians had continued to think about the second coming of Christ, they had come up with ideas that never would have occurred to Paul, ideas developed in response to things that had happened in the Roman Empire. Some of these ideas are presented in the book of Revelation and in the Synoptic Gospels (Matt. 24:1–44; Mark 13:3–37; Luke 21:7–36), books that were written two to four decades after Paul wrote 1 Thessalonians. So, according to this suggestion, some Christian who is unknown to us wrote a new "letter from Paul" expressing these ideas about the second coming. The person who did this apparently had a copy of 1 Thessalonians and used it as a model for creating a composition that would read like something that Paul would have written. Although the letter is ostensibly addressed to "the church of the Thessalonians," it probably was intended for circulation among Christians throughout the Roman Empire. If this is the case, then we don't know who wrote the letter, or where, or when (though proponents of this view think that some date in the 80s seems likely). Still, the main point of the letter is once again assumed to be the teaching about the end times presented in 2:1–12.

In sum, questions regarding the best context for understanding 2 Thessalonians revolve around the issue of whether this is actually a letter from Paul. If 2 Thessalonians is by Paul, then it should be read as one of his earliest compositions—indeed, it is likely to be the second earliest Christian writing that we possess—and it may be read as a virtual postscript to 1 Thessalonians dealing with a particular crisis that arose in one early Christian congregation. If 2 Thessalonians is not by Paul, then it should be understood as presenting generic instruction on what had become a matter of interest decades later.

Major Themes in 2 Thessalonians

The Certainty of Judgment

The author of 2 Thessalonians assures the Christian believers that those who are persecuting them will have to answer to God for their misdeeds (1:6). When the Lord Jesus comes, accompanied by angels, he will bring "flaming fire" and will wreak a terrible vengeance on those who do not know God and on those who do not obey the gospel (1:7–8). Thus all opponents of Christianity—gentile and Jew alike—will "suffer the punishment of eternal destruction," separated from God's presence forever (1:9). A number of scholars have noted that Paul does write elsewhere about judgment and the wrath of God (Rom. 1:18; 2:5–8; 12:19; 1 Thess. 1:10; 2:16), but usually he does not relish the eventual suffering of his enemies as he is sometimes thought to do here. Nevertheless, the accent in

Fig. 21.3. The lawless one. In this fifteenth-century Italian fresco, the devil tells a prominent teacher what to say. (The Bridgeman Art Library International)

this section of the letter (1:5–12) perhaps is not on the negative aspects of judgment but rather is on the relief of the afflicted (1:6–7) and on the vindication of Jesus, whose name will be glorified at last (1:10, 12).

The Coming of the "Lawless One"

The most significant "new content" in 2 Thessalonians concerns the teaching that the day of the Lord (2:2)—the second coming of Jesus Christ (2:1)—will not occur until after "the rebellion comes" and "the lawless one is revealed" (2:3). This lawless one may already be present: the "mystery of lawlessness" concerning him is already at work (2:7). For the moment, however, he is being restrained by someone or something (2:6–7). After this restraint is removed, the lawless one will be revealed. He will take his seat in the temple of God and declare himself to be God (2:4). And then the Lord Jesus will blow him away—literally (2:8; cf. Isa. 11:4)!

We do not know for certain what this means. Scholars who think that Paul wrote 2 Thessalonians usually assume that he had filled the Thessalonians in on details that are unavailable to us (see 2:5–6). Interpreters often have assumed that some of the references in this section of the letter are to recent or current events in the Roman Empire, but there are many guesses as to which events those might be: various offenses to Christianity associated with Caligula (37–41), Nero (54–68), or Domitian (81–96) would qualify, especially if the letter is regarded as pseudepigraphic (and thus as difficult to date). In any case, if the imagery is based on the author's visions of the future, then identifications with figures from his own time might be beside the point: the text might be intended simply to offer Christians a somewhat hazy and ambiguous forecast of things to come, with confidence that those who love the truth (cf. 2:10) will be able to figure it out when it happens. It is possible (though by no means certain) that some of the imagery is symbolic: the "temple" could be a metaphor for God's presence or dwelling place (cf. 1 Cor. 3:16; 6:19). In any case, the main point of the passage seems to be to establish a chronology of events that disprove the notion that the day of the Lord is already here: the restraining agency has not

Box 21.2

Who (or What) Is the Restrainer?

Second Thessalonians 2:6–7 indicates that the "lawless one" is currently being restrained by someone or something that eventually will be removed. The Thessalonians knew who or what this restrainer was (2:5–6). Interpreters since then have had to guess:

- God or God's power
- the Holy Spirit
- Satan
- the angel Apollyon (Rev. 9:11)
- the archangel Michael (Jude 1:9; Rev. 12:7)
- the Christian church
- some prominent Christian leader (Paul himself or James of Jerusalem)
- the gentile mission, which had to be completed first (cf. Mark 13:10)
- the Roman Empire and/or the emperor (cf. Rom. 13:1–7)

Such ideas are sometimes combined: 2:6 seems to speak of a restraining force ("what is now restraining him"), while 2:7 seems to speak of a person ("the one who now restrains").

In the fifth century, Augustine's comment on 2:6–7 was, "I must admit that the meaning of this completely escapes me" (*The City of God* 20.19). Modern scholars have fared no better than Augustine in their analysis of this puzzle.

---

yet been removed; therefore, the lawless one has not been revealed; therefore, the day of the Lord has not arrived.

There are a few points of contact between what is presented here and in other New Testament writings. The "lawless one" described in this passage may be analogous to the antichrist referred to in the Johannine Letters (1 John 2:18; cf. 1 John 2:22; 4:3; 2 John 7) and to the beast mentioned in Revelation (Rev. 11:7; 13:1–18), though all these figures seem to be distinctive in some aspects. The idea that people in the last days will be deceived by satanic signs and wonders resonates with some ideas presented in the Synoptic Gospels (Matt. 24:24; Mark 13:22), as does the claim that the end-times scenario will involve a great act of apostasy in the temple (Matt. 24:15; Mark 13:14). The unique element in 2 Thessalonians is the reference to someone or something that restrains the lawless one until the appointed time (2:7–8)—a point that apparently is not made elsewhere.

signs and wonders: spectacular acts (miracles) performed by people who access either divine or demonic supernatural power.

The Problem of Idleness

The author of 2 Thessalonians addresses a problem of idleness that was mentioned in the first letter addressed to this church (2 Thess. 3:6–12; cf. 1 Thess. 4:11; 5:14). This time a command is given: "Anyone unwilling to work should not eat" (3:10). It was common in those days for Christians to share a common meal together (see Acts 2:42, 46; 1 Cor. 11:33; Gal. 2:12), and some lazy

⊙ EXPLORE 21.4
Antecedents for an Antichrist

Box 21.3

Christian Freeloaders

The generosity of early Christian communities was sometimes put to the test by persons who sought support beyond what was necessary or reasonable.

Some churches practiced a communal lifestyle: members pooled their money and possessions and lived out of a common purse (cf. Acts 2:44–45; 4:32–35). But the book of Acts also reveals that there were unscrupulous people who tried to take advantage of this arrangement (5:1–11).

Problems also arose with traveling missionaries. In keeping with the words of Jesus recorded in Matthew's Gospel, transient preachers were to receive support from the communities that they visited (10:7–15). But a Christian document from around 100 (*Didache* 11:3–6), just fifteen years after the Gospel of Matthew was written, suggests limits for such support:

> Act toward the apostles and prophets as the gospel decrees. Let every apostle who comes to you be welcomed as the Lord. But he should not remain more than a day. If he must, he may stay one more. But if he stays three days, he is a false prophet. When an apostle leaves, he should take nothing except bread, until he arrives at his night's lodging. If he asks for money, he is a false prophet.*

The situation addressed in 2 Thessalonians 3:6–13 may reflect similar tensions in the early church involving the appropriate role of charity. We know from Paul's letters that the Thessalonian Christians (and other believers in Macedonia) were particularly noted for their generosity; indeed, they were known for giving "beyond their means" and for being generous in ways that they could scarcely afford (2 Cor. 8:2–4). It is not hard to imagine that there were people willing to take advantage of the community's well-intentioned but naive altruism.

*Bart D. Ehrman, *The Apostolic Fathers*, 2 vols., Loeb Classical Library (Cambridge, MA: Harvard University Press, 2003), 1:435.

individuals may have viewed the provision of free food as a way to survive off the largesse of the community. It is also possible that some people tried to offer spiritual rationalizations for not being gainfully employed: they were devoting themselves to prayer or to "waiting on the Lord" (see box 21.3). Yet another possibility is that this rebuke of idleness is addressed to rich persons who had no need to work for a living and so spent their lives as "mere busybodies, not doing any work" (3:11). Whatever the situation, the point, obviously, is not that persons who are unable to work (or unable to find work) should be deprived of food; rather, those who are *unwilling* to work are to be excluded from the community meal. Paul, Timothy, and Silas (= Silvanus) set an example for all by holding down full-time jobs as manual laborers while evangelizing the city and founding the church (3:6–9).

Conclusion

Although 2 Thessalonians perhaps lacks the warmth and affection of the first letter addressed to the church at Thessalonica, it does convey a fundamentally positive message. The harsh tone must be understood against the backdrop of the letter's two most prominent concerns: virulent persecution of Christians on account of their faith and an alarming misinterpretation of doctrine that threatens to undermine that faith.

The letter tries to put a positive spin on the afflictions that the believers have had to endure: not only will the Thessalonian believers be vindicated by God's justice on the final day, but already, in the present, their suffering is having positive effects. Their endurance in these trials has made them steadfast, so that their faith is growing abundantly and their love for one another is increasing (1:3–4). The first letter written to the Thessalonians maintained that God's faithful people are destined to suffer (1 Thess. 3:3–4); now the second letter to them reveals why: persecutions and afflictions are intended to make believers "worthy of the kingdom of God" (2 Thess. 1:5). The eschatological teaching in 2 Thessalonians also conveys a fundamentally positive message: Christians are encouraged to view themselves as living in what might be regarded as an initial phase of the end times. The events of the last days seem to be under way (2:7), but they have only just begun. The coming of Christ is soon, but not immediate. The time that remains is not to be wasted on fanatical speculation or idle anticipation. The Thessalonians should look forward to their almost imminent deliverance, but they should view the waiting period as a time to be used productively for Christian growth and mission, as a time for "doing what is right" (3:13).

FOR FURTHER READING: 2 Thessalonians

Donfried, Karl P., and I. Howard Marshall. *The Theology of the Shorter Pauline Letters.* New Testament Theology. Cambridge: Cambridge University Press, 1993.

Furnish, Victor Paul. *1 Thessalonians, 2 Thessalonians.* Abingdon New Testament Commentaries. Nashville: Abingdon, 2004.

Gillman, Florence M., Mary Ann Beavis, and HyeRan Kim-Cragg. *1–2 Thessalonians.* Wisdom Commentary. Collegeville, MN: Liturgical Press, 2016.

Johnson, Andy. *1 & 2 Thessalonians.* Two Horizons Commentary. Grand Rapids: Eerdmans, 2016.

Menken, Maarten J. J. *2 Thessalonians.* New Testament Readings. London: Routledge, 1994.

Weidman, Frederick W. *Philippians, First and Second Thessalonians, and Philemon.* Westminster Bible Companion. Louisville: Westminster John Knox, 2013.

Wright, N. T. *Paul for Everyone: Galatians and Thessalonians.* 2nd ed. Louisville: Westminster John Knox, 2004.

⊙ Go to www .IntroducingNT.com for summaries, videos, and other study tools.

22

The Pastoral Letters:
1 Timothy, 2 Timothy, Titus

In our world today, most churches have pastors. They might be called "ministers" or "priests," and they might be addressed as "Reverend" or "Father" or "Brother" or "Sister," but whatever the nomenclature, such individuals are in charge of providing the congregation with pastoral ministry. We don't know exactly when or how these official leadership positions developed in the early Christian church, but three letters in the New Testament—1 Timothy, 2 Timothy, and Titus—are commonly called the "Pastoral Letters" because they are addressed to individuals charged with oversight of congregations. Two of these letters are specifically addressed to Timothy and one is addressed to Titus; all three indicate that they were written by Paul, though as we will see, many interpreters think that they are pseudepigraphic.

The Pastoral Letters differ from most other letters ascribed to Paul in that they are addressed to individuals; the only other letter from Paul to an individual is Philemon, a brief note that deals with a personal matter rather than with issues of pastoral leadership. The Pastoral Letters have other things in common as well, which is why they usually are treated together. There is benefit to considering each of these three letters individually, but at an introductory level, it can be helpful to learn what they have to offer as a group, as three letters that are similar to one another in both style and content.

Overview

1 Timothy

After an opening salutation and greeting (1:1–2), the author (identified as Paul) urges Timothy to curtail those who teach false doctrines and to

Fig. 22.1. Three generations. Timothy is the Bible's preeminent example of a Christian raised in the faith. The author of 2 Timothy says, "I am reminded of your sincere faith, a faith that lived first in your grandmother Lois and your mother Eunice and now, I am sure, lives in you" (1:5). (HIP / Art Resource, NY)

promote faithful instruction that recognizes the proper role of the law (1:3–11). Paul's own story as a former blasphemer saved by Christ Jesus is a testimony to the extent of divine mercy (1:12–17). Other persons who have suffered "shipwreck in the faith" exemplify the judgment that comes on those who reject conscience and continue to blaspheme (1:18–20). The letter encourages fervent prayer, especially for those in authority (2:1–4), and quotes a confession that describes Christ as "the mediator" whose herald and apostle Paul is (2:5–7). It offers gender-specific instructions regarding the roles of men and women, emphasizing that the latter should dress modestly and learn "in silence with full submission" (2:8–15). It then provides summary qualifications for church leaders (3:1–15), including bishops (3:1–7) and deacons (3:8–13).

After another quotation from a Christian confession or hymn (3:16), the letter issues further warnings about false teachers (4:1–5), along with positive exhortations regarding Timothy's own behavior and ministry (4:6–5:2). This leads to specific advice concerning widows (5:3–16), elders (5:17–20), and slaves (6:1–2), along with more personal exhortations to Timothy (5:21–25). The topic of false teaching is taken up again, with specific attention to the corrupting influence of money (6:3–10). The letter concludes with charges for Timothy to be faithful (6:11–16), some advice for the wealthy (6:17–19), and a final charge for Timothy to guard what has been entrusted him against what is "falsely called knowledge" (6:20–21).

2 Timothy

The letter opens with a salutation and greeting (1:1–2). The author (identified as Paul) gives thanks for the faith of Timothy (1:3–5) and offers words of encouragement for his continued zeal (1:6–7). Timothy is told not to be ashamed of Paul's gospel or of the suffering that it brings (1:8–14). Paul's status as a prisoner has caused many to turn away, but Timothy should follow the positive examples of Paul and a certain Onesiphorus (1:15–18). Indeed, Timothy is charged with seeing that Paul's teaching gets passed on (2:1–2). He is urged to faithfulness with analogies from daily life (a soldier, an athlete, a farmer) and with lines quoted from a Christian confession or hymn (2:3–13). Timothy is to avoid those things that have been the downfall of false teachers, and he is to strive for the qualities that will allow God to use him as a favored vessel (2:14–26). He is warned about distressing times to come and of false teachers who will take advantage of others during those times (3:1–9). As things go from bad to worse, he must remember Paul's own life and ministry and commit

---

Box 22.1

Timothy: A Biographical Sketch

Timothy, the son of a gentile man and a Jewish woman, lived in the town of Lystra in southeastern Asia Minor; his mother was a believer, but his father was not (Acts 16:1). Timothy embraced the Christian faith, and Paul recruited him as a companion for his second missionary journey, circumcising him so as not to offend the Jews (Acts 16:3). Toward the end of that journey, Paul sent him back to Macedonia to strengthen the Thessalonians (1 Thess. 3:2). Timothy then rejoined Paul in Corinth, bringing him good news about the Thessalonian church (Acts 18:5; 1 Thess. 3:6) and helping him to evangelize the Corinthians (2 Cor. 1:19). Later, he accompanied Paul on his third missionary journey and thus was with Paul during his lengthy stay in Ephesus (Acts 19). Paul sent him once again to Macedonia (Acts 19:22) and repeatedly to Corinth (1 Cor. 4:17; 16:10). Timothy later spent a winter with Paul in Corinth (from which Romans was written; see Rom. 16:21) and then went on to Troas, where Paul spent a week with him on his way to Jerusalem (Acts 20:4–5).

After this we lose track of Timothy. He may have continued ministering in Troas, where Paul's own work had been cut short due to crises in Corinth (2 Cor. 2:12–13). Later on he may have gone to Rome to be of service to Paul during his imprisonment there (see Phil. 1:1; Col. 1:1; 4:10; Philem. 1 [but were these letters written from Rome?]). He himself may have been imprisoned at some time (see Heb. 13:23), but we have no information as to when or where this would have been.

The two letters addressed to Timothy add only minor details to this portrait: his mother's name was Eunice, and his grandmother, also a believer, was named Lois (2 Tim. 1:5); he was young in comparison to Paul (1 Tim. 4:12; 5:1); he suffered from frequent illnesses (1 Tim. 5:23); and he had received a spiritual gift through prophecy and the laying on of hands (1 Tim. 4:14; 2 Tim. 1:6).

In artwork, Timothy is often depicted as holding a rod or bat because, according to one church tradition, he was beaten to death by opponents at the age of eighty.

Titus: A Biographical Sketch

Titus was a gentile Christian, possibly from Antioch, who was brought to Jerusalem by Paul and Barnabas as a sort of test case for the church in deciding whether gentile converts to Christianity needed to be circumcised (Gal. 2:1–3). The extent of his involvement with Paul's subsequent missionary work is unknown, but Paul did come to regard him as a "partner and co-worker" (2 Cor. 8:23), and he appears to have been with Paul during portions of what is called the third missionary journey. In the mid-50s Paul sent him from Ephesus to Corinth, carrying a painful letter that Paul had written to that church. He was successful in mediating a reconciliation between Paul and the congregation, and he brought Paul news of this in Macedonia (see 2 Cor. 2:4, 13; 7:6–8, 13–15). Later, Titus would return to the Corinthian church as one of the agents responsible for administering the offering Paul was collecting for Jerusalem (2 Cor. 8:6, 16–18, 23; 9:5; cf. 12:18). We know nothing else for certain, though there are references in the Pastoral Letters to Titus conducting ministry in Dalmatia (2 Tim. 4:10) and in Crete (Titus 1:5).

himself wholeheartedly to learning and teaching the Scriptures (3:10–17). The need for Timothy's diligence and persistence in such faithful ministry is made more urgent by the certainty of God's judgment (4:1–5) and by the fact that Paul's own days on earth are coming to an end (4:6–8). As the letter winds to a close, it offers some personal instructions and provides updated information regarding various individuals and circumstances (4:9–18). It concludes with greetings and a benediction (4:19–22).

Titus

The letter opens with an unusually expansive salutation, which identifies the writer as Paul (1:1–4). The author indicates that Titus is to appoint elders in the towns of Crete and lists qualifications for the office of bishop (1:5–9). These instructions segue into a description of the corrupt persons whom the bishops will need to refute (1:10–16), followed by specific advice regarding what Titus is to say to older men, older women, younger men, and slaves (2:1–10). The letter then provides a stirring summary of the gospel and its consequences for human behavior (2:11–14). Titus is exhorted to declare these things in a manner that is both authoritative and tactful (2:15–3:2). This leads to a second summary of the gospel message, one that provides personal testimony to the salvation that Paul and Titus share in Christ (3:3–7). Titus is to insist on this message and avoid "stupid controversies" and things that cause divisions (3:8–11). The letter concludes with some discussion of future plans, final greetings, and a benediction (3:12–15).

Historical Background

Timothy and Titus, to whom these letters are addressed, are known to us from other references in the New Testament. Both were among Paul's inner circle of assistants, persons he is known to have entrusted with significant roles in shaping and leading the early church.

Timothy is the better known of the two, and three things stand out with regard to what we learn of him elsewhere. First, Paul seems to have sent Timothy on frequent missions, including ones that involved dealing with difficult situations (1 Cor. 4:17; 16:10; Phil. 2:19, 23; 1 Thess. 3:2, 6). Second, Timothy is listed as the coauthor of many of Paul's letters: 2 Corinthians, Philippians, Colossians, 1 Thessalonians, 2 Thessalonians, and Philemon (see also Rom. 16:21). Third, Paul pays tribute to Timothy with words that identify him as a specially valued colleague (1 Cor. 16:10; Phil. 2:19–23; 1 Thess. 3:2): he says that Timothy is "like a son" to him (Phil. 2:22; cf. 1 Cor. 4:17) and insists, "I have no one like him" (Phil. 2:20; see box 22.1).

Titus is never mentioned in the book of Acts, but his name does come up in Paul's letter to the Galatians and his second letter to the Corinthians. Titus was one of the first gentiles to be attracted to the Christian faith, and he became one of Paul's principal examples for how a gentile could be put right with God through faith in Christ without first becoming Jewish (Gal. 2:1–3; cf. Rom. 3:28–29; Gal. 2:16; 3:11). Like Timothy (whose mother was Jewish), Titus became one of Paul's emissaries, visiting churches as his representative and serving as something of a troubleshooter in dealing with difficult situations (2 Cor. 7:6–8, 13–15; see box 22.2).

The letters addressed to these individuals presume particular situations in the life of Paul, but those situations do not quite fit with what we know of Paul's career from his other letters and from the book of Acts.

- The Letter to Titus presumes that Paul and Titus had been ministering together in Crete but that Paul has left, entrusting Titus to continue the work (1:5); Paul is now writing to Titus from some unspecified location (possibly Ephesus), and he plans to spend the winter in Nicopolis, where he hopes that Titus will be able to join him (3:12).
- The First Letter to Timothy presumes that Paul and Timothy had been ministering together in Ephesus but that Paul has now left there for Macedonia; he is writing back to Timothy, who is now in charge of the Ephesian church (1:3).
- The Second Letter to Timothy presumes that Paul is in prison in Rome (1:16–17; 2:9; 4:16), where he expects to be executed (4:6); he wants Timothy to come to him (4:9, 13).

Scholars working out a Pauline biography have long noted that these scenarios do not quite fit with their reconstructions of Paul's career. For example, there is no indication anywhere else in the New Testament that Paul sought to evangelize the island of Crete (cf. Titus 1:5) or that he left Timothy in charge of the church in Ephesus while engaged in a mission in Macedonia (cf. 1 Tim. 1:3). Likewise, some of the information on Paul's judicial hearing in Rome provided in 2 Timothy (4:16–17) is not attested elsewhere, and many scholars think that Timothy actually was with Paul in Rome from the start of his imprisonment there.

The matter gets very complicated, but scholars who think that Paul wrote the Pastoral Letters generally follow one of two proposals for dealing with the biographical anomalies. When these two proposals are added to a third suggestion, that the letters are pseudepigraphic, three scenarios for the historical situations behind these letters emerge.

Scenario One: "Gaps in the Record" Theory

According to this proposal, we are simply missing key information about Paul's life and ministry. Neither the outline of travels in the book of Acts nor the occasional references to trips and locations mentioned in Paul's letters allow us to develop a comprehensive account of his missionary work. Thus the presumed situations for the Pastoral Letters described above should be taken at face value, as evidence of otherwise undocumented moments in Paul's career. According to this theory, 1 Timothy and Titus can be dated to the mid-50s, when Paul spent time in the general area of the Aegean Sea, while 2 Timothy can be dated to the time of his imprisonment in Rome in the early 60s.

Scenario Two: "Second Career" Theory

According to this proposal, all three Pastoral Letters can be assigned to a period of Paul's life later than what is reported in the book of Acts or alluded to in any of his other letters. This theory depends on a hypothesis that Paul survived the imprisonment in Rome that we hear about in Acts. He was released from captivity and went on to have a second career as a missionary, going places and doing things that are not mentioned elsewhere in the New Testament. The primary support for this theory comes from a letter ostensibly sent by the Roman bishop Clement to the Corinthian church around the end of the first century. This letter indicates that Paul took the gospel to "the extreme west" (1 Clement 5:6–7). Clement apparently thought that Paul had gone to Spain, which he would have had to have done after his imprisonment in Rome (cf. Rom. 15:22–24). If Paul did survive the imprisonment to go to Spain, this theory holds, he also could have returned to Ephesus with Timothy and gone to Crete with Titus, writing back to his associates after leaving them in those locations. Then, after he was arrested again, he could have served a second imprisonment in Rome and written 2 Timothy before being executed. According to this theory, all three Pastoral Letters can be dated to the mid-60s—that is, to a time later than the traditional date for Paul's death.

Scenario Three: "Pseudepigraphic Composition" Theory

For a number of literary and theological reasons, many scholars believe that the three Pastoral Letters can be regarded as pseudepigraphic, and if so, then the "presumed situations" described above may be regarded as literary constructs. The letters actually were written by some unknown person (or persons) at a time when Paul, Timothy, and Titus were dead and gone, but not forgotten. The letters try to articulate what Paul would say to his famous colleagues if he (and they) were still around, grappling with issues that, in reality, had become matters of concern for Christians of a later time. Most interpreters who follow this view date the letters late in the first century (80–100) or possibly to some time in the first quarter of the second century (100–125).

There are other complicating factors. Some scholars think that the Pastoral Letters could be pseudepigraphic expansions on brief notes that Paul actually did write to Timothy and Titus; thus nuggets of material from authentic Pauline letters are contained within our current pseudepigraphic letters. And many scholars have suggested that only 1 Timothy and Titus are pseudepigraphic, while 2 Timothy may be an authentic Pauline letter that later was used as a template for producing the two pseudepigraphic works.

Whatever view is adopted concerning the historical situations for the Pastoral Letters, the overall purpose of the letters seems clear. The letters want to ensure that the Pauline tradition gets carried forward in the face of competing ideas: the preservation of that tradition is now being entrusted to emissaries and to faithful leaders they appoint. In addition, all three letters have a strong parenetic character: they are filled with exhortations to good behavior, for conduct appropriate within "the household of God" (1 Tim. 3:15; cf. Eph. 2:19).

authentic: in discussions of authorship, "not pseudepigraphic"—that is, written by the person to whom a work is ascribed.

parenetic: containing advice, counsel, or exhortations intended to motivate or persuade.

⊙ EXPLORE 22.13
Authorship of the Pastoral Letters.

Box 22.3

Did Paul Write the Pastoral Letters? Why Doubt It?

For these reasons, some scholars do not think that Paul wrote the Pastoral Letters:

- The language and style are not typical of Paul's letters.
- Certain theological ideas are different from what Paul expresses elsewhere.
- The description of church government seems too developed for Paul's lifetime.
- The teaching opposed in these letters is not something that Paul deals with elsewhere.
- The manner of dealing with false teaching is not characteristic of Paul.
- Historical circumstances presumed for the letters do not find support elsewhere.

All of these points, however, are disputed, and many scholars believe that Paul did write the Pastoral Letters.

Box 22.4

Proposed Historical Situations for the Pastoral Letters

	Titus	1 Timothy	2 Timothy
If there are gaps in our record of Paul's career	by Paul from Ephesus (?) to Titus in Crete, ca. 52–56	by Paul from Macedonia to Timothy in Ephesus, ca. 52–56	by Paul from prison in Rome to Timothy, ca. 60–64
If Paul had a "second career"	same as above but ca. 63–66	same as above but ca. 63–66	same as above but ca. 65–67
If all three letters are by the same pseudonymous author	by an unknown admirer of Paul from an unknown location to Christians in general, late first or early second century		
If the letters are expansions of Pauline notes	brief personal references in all three letters, same as first row above; bulk of all three letters, same as third row above		
If 2 Timothy was written first and by a different author	by admirer of Paul with a copy of 2 Timothy from an unknown location to Christians in general, late first or early second century		same as first row above, or, written by Pauline admirer shortly after his death

Major Themes in the Pastoral Letters

Church Government

The appointment of church officers and leaders is a primary concern in the Pastoral Letters, especially in 1 Timothy and Titus (see 1 Tim. 3:1–13; 5:3–22; 2 Tim. 2:2; Titus 1:5–7). Several offices are mentioned, but we don't know what their various functions were. Bible readers today should not assume that the designations for church officials used in these letters correspond to ecclesiastical roles that bear those same designations in the modern world. A person who was called a "bishop" in some parts of the early church might have had a role more similar to what we call a "deacon" or a "pastor" today—we simply do not know what these terms specified. In Titus *bishop* and *elder* appear to be interchangeable terms for the same leadership position, but in 1 Timothy *bishop*, *deacon*, and *widow* represent at least three different offices within the community, and *elder* might be a fourth role (or *elder* may be a generic term for leaders of all sorts). The exact responsibilities of these various leaders are not spelled out, but 1 Timothy describes the bishop's job as "[taking] care of God's church" in a manner analogous to managing a household (3:4–5; cf. 3:15), and Titus describes the bishop as "God's steward" (1:7), implying that bishops are appointed by God to attend to various matters on God's behalf. In terms of a bishop's duties, proclamation and teaching receive the most attention (1 Tim. 3:2; 5:17–18; Titus 1:9).

Both 1 Timothy and Titus focus on qualifications for these church offices (1 Tim. 3:1–13; Titus 1:5–9). The emphasis clearly is on character: all the officers are to be responsible and respectable persons whose lives may be described as "blameless" (Titus 1:6) and "above reproach" (1 Tim. 3:2), persons whose example will reflect favorably on the church in the public eye (1 Tim. 3:7). They must be thoroughly grounded in the faith (1 Tim. 3:6, 9–10; Titus 1:9) and capable of demonstrating self-restraint with regard to temper and passions (1 Tim. 3:2–3, 8, 11; Titus 1:7–8). In particular, their family life must be in order; parenting skills are a prime indicator of whether one has the competence for church leadership (1 Tim. 3:4–5, 12; Titus 1:6), since the church may be construed as "the household of God" (1 Tim. 3:15). And they must not be greedy or lovers of money (1 Tim. 3:3, 8; Titus 1:7), for "the love of money is a root of all kinds of evil" (1 Tim. 6:10). The general advice to Timothy with regard to church leaders is, "Do not ordain anyone hastily" (1 Tim. 5:22); a shortage of leadership in the church is preferable to appointment of leaders who may disgrace the community (cf. 1 Tim. 5:19–20).

False Teaching and Sound Doctrine

All three Pastoral Letters exhibit concern to correct false teaching in the church (1 Tim. 1:3–7; 4:1–3, 7; 6:3–5; 2 Tim. 2:14, 16–18, 25–26; 3:6–9; 4:3–4; Titus 1:9–16). All three also place an emphasis on sound doctrine (1 Tim. 1:10; 2 Tim. 4:3; Titus 1:9, 13; 2:1), on knowledge of the truth (1 Tim. 2:4; 4:3; 2 Tim. 2:25; 3:7; Titus 1:1; cf. 1 Tim. 3:15; 6:5; 2 Tim. 2:15, 18; 3:8; 4:4; Titus 1:14), and on persons accepting orthodox teaching (1 Tim. 1:10; 4:6; 6:3; 2 Tim. 1:13) so that they can be "sound in faith" (Titus 1:13; 2:2).

doctrine: a belief or set of recognized beliefs held and taught by a church.

The specific brand of false teaching opposed in these letters is difficult to determine; it appears to involve a mixture of ideas, some drawn from Jewish circles and others drawn from what later became known as gnosticism. The letters actually spend less time describing the teaching that is to be rejected than they do disparaging the teachers responsible for those ideas. The methods, morals, and motives of these teachers are put on display as examples of what Christians should avoid. The problem, however, is not just that such teachers exist but also that there are people in the church willing to listen to them. The folly of such teaching eventually becomes evident to all (2 Tim. 3:9; cf. 1 Tim. 5:24–25), but in the short term, plenty of people have "itching ears" and want "teachers to suit their own desires" (2 Tim. 4:3)—that is, teachers who will tell them what they want to hear. For example, some of the false teachers "make their way into households and captivate silly women" who, because they are "overwhelmed by sin and swayed by all kinds of desires," take these teachers seriously (2 Tim. 3:6). Apparently, the teachers enroll these naive women in programs that promise a gradual revelation of spiritual knowledge; the women may pay fees for help in attaining successive levels of so-called spiritual maturity, and so they end up "always being instructed" without ever actually arriving at "knowledge of the truth" (2 Tim. 3:7).

⊙ **EXPLORE 22.5**
Church Leaders in the New Testament

Fig. 22.2. *No Tengan Miedo*. This work was originally produced to celebrate a papal visit to Cuba in 1998, and its title (Spanish for "Do not be afraid") is taken from the pontiff's remarks on that occasion. The painting depicts church authorities as figures who promise protection and security in an otherwise fearsome world. Likewise, the Pastoral Letters indicate that bishops, deacons, and elders will make the church a bulwark of truth to protect believers from those who would lead them astray. (Bridgeman Images)

The response to this crisis of false teaching, then, must be twofold: first, the teachers themselves need to be silenced (Titus 1:11), and second, the Christian congregations need to be protected from the influences of such persons. Titus is to rebuke the troublemakers sharply (Titus 1:13); he is to declare what is right and to reprove "with all authority" those who do not accept it (Titus 2:15). He is not to be drawn into argument with people who cause divisions; rather, he

Box 22.5

Concern for Social Respectability in the Pastoral Letters

The Pastoral Letters exhibit special concern for the social respectability of Christians:

- A bishop is to be someone "well thought of by outsiders" (1 Tim. 3:7).
- Slaves are to accept their lot so that "the name of God and the teaching may not be blasphemed" (1 Tim. 6:1).
- Young women are to be submissive to their husbands "so that the word of God may not be discredited" (Titus 2:5).
- Young widows should remarry "so as to give the adversary no occasion to revile us" (1 Tim. 5:14; cf. Titus 2:8).

In general, Christians are to be productive and obedient, good citizens whose lives are free of anything offensive or scandalous (1 Tim. 2:1–3, 9–10; 3:2–13; 2 Tim. 2:22–25; Titus 1:5–8; 2:3–10; 3:1–2, 14). The virtue of "self-control" receives particular emphasis (2 Tim. 1:7; Titus 1:8; 2:5–6, 12). Thus these letters make clear that Christianity is not socially subversive and that the gospel has a certain "civilizing function": it trains those who would otherwise be "vicious brutes" (Titus 1:12; cf. 3:3) to live in ways that are "self-controlled, upright, and godly" (Titus 2:11–12).

should simply give them two warnings and, after that, be done with them (Titus 3:10–11). Likewise, Timothy is to "instruct people not to teach any different doctrine" than that which Paul imparted to him (1 Tim. 1:3). He is to be insistent (1 Tim. 4:11) and persistent (2 Tim. 4:2) in seeing that this tradition is maintained.

In terms of caring for the congregations, a primary strategy seems to be the appointment of prominent and exemplary leaders who will proclaim sound doctrine and teach the tradition inherited from Paul (see preceding section). Beyond this, Timothy is told to set an example for the believers through his own teaching and lifestyle (1 Tim. 4:12, 16). And, in addition to exhortation and teaching, he is to give attention to the public reading of Scripture (1 Tim. 4:13). He has relied on Scripture since childhood; now he is to rely on it in public ministry (2 Tim. 3:15–16).

The overall emphasis, then, is on teaching sound doctrine so that the church might be a bulwark of truth (1 Tim. 3:15) against the novel speculations of those who want to divide the church with "profane chatter" (2 Tim. 2:16–17) or "stupid controversies" (2 Tim. 2:23; Titus 3:9). Sound doctrine seems to take two forms: (1) brief and easily memorized creedal statements that summarize key ideas in the church's teaching about Christ (see 1 Tim. 2:5–6; 3:16; 2 Tim. 2:11–13; Titus 2:11–14); and (2) specific instructions about moral behavior (Titus 2:1–10; cf. 1 Tim. 3:14–15). The latter directions are important because these letters suggest that moral conduct is the proof of correct belief. The false teachers profess to know God, but they deny God by their actions (Titus 1:16). Sound doctrine, by contrast, leads to "love that comes from a pure heart, a good conscience, and sincere faith" (1 Tim. 1:5); it is "teaching that is in accordance with godliness" (1 Tim. 6:3). Orthodoxy ("right thinking")

⊙ **EXPLORE 22.18**
What Was the False Teaching Opposed by the Pastoral Letters?

leads to orthopraxis ("right behavior"). Thus the Pastoral Letters insist that those who have come to believe in God devote themselves to good works (Titus 3:8; cf. 1:16; 2:7; 3:14; also 1 Tim. 2:10; 5:10, 25; 6:18; 2 Tim. 2:21; 3:17). If Paul's colleagues show themselves to be models of good works and, in their teaching, display the integrity, gravity, and sound speech that their opponents' teaching lacks, the opponents "will be put to shame, having nothing evil to say" (Titus 2:7–8).

Women and Ministry

The Pastoral Letters evince attitudes toward women and the role of women in church and society that have been the focus of much discussion. In general, women are to concentrate on bearing children (1 Tim. 2:15; 5:14), managing their households (1 Tim. 5:14; Titus 2:5), and being submissive to their husbands (1 Tim. 2:11; Titus 2:5). In terms of ministry, there is an office in the church for aged widows (1 Tim. 5:9–10), and some women may also serve as deacons (1 Tim. 3:11), but women should not be permitted to teach or to have authority over men (1 Tim. 2:12). Not surprisingly, this theme has been considered problematic by many Christians: it seems sexist and unreasonable, and it is expressed in language that seems unduly harsh (e.g., 1 Tim. 5:6). Numerous proposals have attempted to deal with the matter. Some Christians regard what the Pastoral Letters say about women as indicative of divinely mandated gender roles; others interpret those comments as socially conditioned remarks for a particular venue rather than as timeless truth that applies in every setting.

Fig. 22.3. The reading of Scripture. A primary charge to Timothy and other pastoral leaders is to give attention to the public reading of Scripture (1 Tim. 4:13). These "sacred writings" are inspired by God and will be the pastor's most helpful tool for ministry, useful for teaching, reproof, correction, and training in righteousness (2 Tim. 3:15–16). (Bridgeman Images)

Suffering and Shame

⊙ EXPLORE 22.10
Women and Ministry
in the Pastoral Letters

In 2 Timothy Paul's final words from prison are presented in a way that calls for fortitude in the face of suffering and shame. For many people in

Box 22.6

The Office of Widows

The office of widows receives special attention in the First Letter to Timothy (5:3–16). The idea behind this vocation was that widows who had no family members to care for them could be supported financially by the church while devoting themselves to prayer and good works. But two problems seem to have arisen:

- Some church members were taking advantage of the program and abdicating their personal responsibility to care for family members (1 Tim. 5:4, 8).
- Some younger widows apparently were taken into the program and then they dropped out, deciding to remarry.

Thus Timothy is told to limit enrollment in the program to those who are "real widows"—that is, those who have been "left alone" with no one to care for them (1 Tim. 5:1, 3, 5, 16). He is also to limit enrollment to widows over sixty years of age and to women who have demonstrated a capacity for the life of prayer and good works that are expected of those in the program.

For more on this intriguing office, see Bonnie Bowman Thurston, *The Widows: A Women's Ministry in the Early Church* (Philadelphia: Fortress, 1989).

Roman society, the humiliation of "being chained like a criminal" (2:9) would be an almost unbearable disgrace, and 2 Timothy acknowledges that many of Paul's associates deserted him in the face of such hardship (4:10, 16). Readers familiar with the passion story of Jesus may recall how Jesus was deserted by his closest followers in his hour of trial (Mark 14:27, 50). Still, 2 Timothy makes clear that Paul is not ashamed of any humiliation that he has suffered (1:12; cf. 3:10–11), and the letter also names Onesiphorus as a positive example of one who was not ashamed of Paul's chains (1:16). Beyond this, 2 Timothy indicates that "all who want to live a godly life in Christ Jesus will be persecuted" (3:12). Timothy is invited to join Paul in "suffering for the gospel" (1:8).

Within this context of persecution, humiliation, and possible martyrdom, messages of good news are proclaimed. First, the word of God is not chained (2 Tim. 2:9); thus those who harm God's messengers will not thwart the purposes of God. Second, suffering for the sake of the gospel can serve God's purposes, helping to bring salvation to others (2 Tim. 2:10). Third, a glorious reward awaits those who suffer for Christ: those who endure hardship and humiliation now will reign with Christ in glory forever (2 Tim. 2:12; 4:18). Fourth, even those who fail to endure will be protected by Christ's inestimable mercy; outright apostasy may bring people into condemnation (2 Tim. 2:12; 4:14), but the weak and cowardly should know that the faithfulness of Christ to his followers is greater than their faithlessness to him (2 Tim. 2:13; cf. 4:16).

⊘ EXPLORE 22.11
Polemic against False Teachers in the Pastoral Letters

Fig. 22.4. Women in the church. This nineteenth-century German painting shows women fulfilling roles in the church that would be pleasing to the author of the Pastoral Letters: praying, listening, learning.

Box 22.7

Married Only Once?

The letter of 1 Timothy indicates that bishops (3:2) and deacons (3:12) are to be married only once (or, literally, to be "the husband of one wife"). What does this mean? Four suggestions:

- They are not to practice polygamy. This seems to be obvious, but perhaps it needed to be stated, given converts from many cultures.
- They are to practice fidelity, fulfilling the role of husband only for the woman to whom they are actually married. Again, this seems to be an obvious expectation, though no doubt an important one.
- They are not to remarry after being divorced. This seems consistent with Paul's teaching elsewhere (1 Cor. 7:10–11; cf. Mark 10:11–12).
- They are not to remarry after being widowed. This seems stricter than Paul's usual policy (Rom. 7:1–3; 1 Cor. 7:39). Still, Paul does say elsewhere that it is best not to remarry (1 Cor. 7:8, 32–35, 40), and the bishops and deacons may be expected to model ideal behavior beyond what would be requirements for all.

Most scholars assume that at least the first two ideas would be included in what is intended here; the third and/or fourth ideas might be intended as well.

Conclusion

The Pastoral Letters have fallen on hard times in the modern church and in modern society. At the very least, these letters might not sit well with people in a climate that tries to resist polemic and stereotyping. In 1 Timothy there is reference to superstitious legends as "old wives' tales" (4:7). The Letter to Titus indicates that Jews ("those of the circumcision") are especially given to being "rebellious people, idle talkers and deceivers" (1:10), and it agrees with a popular stereotype that natives of Crete are "always liars, vicious brutes, lazy gluttons" (1:12–13, citing a verse by Epimenides of Knossus from the sixth century BCE). Such language usually is considered rude and inappropriate in our modern culture. Likewise, the penchant in these letters for *ad hominem* attacks on ideological opponents (1 Tim. 4:1–2; 6:3–5; 2 Tim. 3:2–9; Titus 1:10–16; 3:10–11) may strike modern readers as petty or mean.

ad hominem: attacking an opponent's character rather than addressing his or her arguments.

Even the household directions in these letters base their instructions on specific (and not very complimentary) assumptions regarding age and gender (1 Tim. 2:8–15; 5:1–16; 6:1–2; Titus 2:2–10). They move away from the ideal of "mutual submission" found in other letters attributed to Paul (Eph. 5:21), instead giving advice that is one-sided: wives are to submit to their husbands (Titus 2:5; cf. 1 Tim. 2:11), but nothing is said about the husbands' responsibilities for their wives (cf. Eph. 5:25–33; Col. 3:19); slaves are to submit completely to their masters (1 Tim. 6:1–2; Titus 2:9–10), but nothing is said

⊙ **EXPLORE 22.20**
Household Tables in the Pastoral Letters and Elsewhere in the New Testament

about the masters' attitude or behavior toward their slaves (cf. Eph. 6:9; Col. 4:1).

At a deeper level, the Pastoral Letters as a whole (especially 1 Timothy and Titus) are often viewed as domesticating Paul in a way that takes the edge off radical, countercultural Christianity. They are said to advance "the institutional church," emphasizing ecclesiological order and structure; some Protestants have complained that they are a stark example of "early catholicism." Such assessments, of course, have not altered the universal affirmation of Christian communities that the Pastoral Letters are inspired and authoritative Scripture. Within churches of all denominations, preachers, teachers, and everyday believers continue to engage these letters as Scripture, including those passages that they find awkward or challenging.

The Pastoral Letters are probably best understood as compositions written under duress: they engage two severe threats to the evolving Christian religion. One of these threats, violent persecution, is simply embraced as an inevitable consequence of adopting a faith that is at odds with the ways of the world. The second threat, however, is more insidious because it comes from within: the threat of "heresy," representations of faith that claim to be authentic but, if accepted, would redefine the substance of what the developing religion claims to be true. One New Testament scholar suggests that the early Christian response to heresy involved the triad of "clergy, creeds, and canon," and he thinks that some rudimentary form of all three can be seen in the Pastoral Letters (see Bart Ehrman, *The New Testament: A Historical Introduction to the Early Christian Writings*, 6th ed. [New York: Oxford University Press, 2016], 454–56).

> **heresy:** false teaching, or teaching that does not conform to the official standards of a religious community.

- *Clergy*: the church developed a more controlled administrative structure, with recognized leaders who could determine and declare what sort of teaching was acceptable (cf. 1 Tim. 3:1–2; 5:17; 2 Tim. 2:2; Titus 1:9).
- *Creeds*: the church identified summary statements of accepted belief and doctrine (cf. 1 Tim. 2:5–6; 3:16; 2 Tim. 2:11–13; Titus 2:11–14).
- *Canon*: the church designated certain writings as authoritative and appealed to these as a hedge against ideas that could be declared "unscriptural" (cf. 1 Tim. 4:13; 2 Tim. 3:16).

Thus the Pastoral Letters often are regarded as coming from a difficult but necessary stage in the development of the Christian religion: the church is becoming more institutionalized and more authoritarian in an effort to forestall revision of the faith for which Paul was willing to suffer and die. Interestingly, the book of Revelation praises the church in Ephesus (to which 1 Timothy appears to be directed) for having rejected false teachers (Rev. 2:2); a second-century writing to that same church from Ignatius of Antioch (ca. 110) likewise affirms that the Ephesian Christians remained steadfast in faith, avoiding the attraction of unorthodox ideas (Ignatius, *To the Ephesians* 8:1).

FOR FURTHER READING: **The Pastoral Letters**

Harding, Mark. *What Are They Saying about the Pastoral Epistles?* Mahwah, NJ: Paulist Press, 2001.

Huizenga, Annette Bourland. *1–2 Timothy, Titus.* Wisdom Commentary. Collegeville, MN: Liturgical Press, 2016.

Krause, Deborah. *1 Timothy.* Readings: A New Biblical Commentary. London: T&T Clark, 2004.

Long, Thomas G. *1 & 2 Timothy and Titus: A Theological Commentary.* Belief Series. Louisville: Westminster John Knox, 2016.

Wall, Robert W., and Richard B. Steele. *1 and 2 Timothy and Titus.* Two Horizons Commentary. Grand Rapids: Eerdmans, 2016.

Wright, N. T. *Paul for Everyone: The Pastoral Letters; 1 Timothy, 2 Timothy, and Titus.* 2nd ed. Louisville: Westminster John Knox, 2004.

Young, Frances. *The Theology of the Pastoral Letters.* New Testament Theology. Cambridge: Cambridge University Press, 1994.

⊚ Go to www .IntroducingNT.com for summaries, videos, and other study tools.

23

Philemon

"You owe me one." "One hand washes the other." "I'll scratch your back if you scratch mine." Such quotations from modern life express a basic notion of reciprocity—the idea that people can (and probably should) do things for one another in ways that are mutually beneficial.

This idea was even more pronounced in the Roman world than it is in ours. In that society, friendship was defined more often with reference to an exchange of favors than with regard to compatible personality types. People could be close friends in what we might regard as a professional sense even if they had never met. Social relationships were construed in terms of patronage, and people were remarkably adept at keeping track of who owed favors to whom.

Paul's letter to Philemon is the shortest of all of his letters (335 words in Greek), and it is the only undisputed letter of Paul addressed primarily to an individual rather than to a congregation. It is a personal letter between friends, and yet it is written from a perspective that clearly understands friendship in terms of reciprocity. Philemon owes Paul a favor, and Paul writes to request a favor from him. But there is a twist: the favor that Paul seeks is not for himself; rather, it is for a slave, a person at the bottom of the social ladder who had no right to ask anyone for anything. Paul uses Philemon's obligation to him to make an appeal on behalf of someone to whom Philemon owes nothing—indeed, on behalf of someone who appears to have incurred Philemon's wrath.

Overview

After a brief salutation and blessing (vv. 1–3), Paul offers a prayer of thanksgiving for Philemon's faith and for how he has refreshed "the hearts of the saints" (vv. 4–7). Then he turns to the matter at hand: an appeal on behalf of Philemon's

⊙ EXPLORE 23.0
Philemon: Outline of Contents

slave Onesimus (vv. 8–21). Paul says that Onesimus has become like a son to him during his imprisonment (v. 10), but he is now sending Onesimus back (v. 12). He does so reluctantly and hints that Philemon might allow Onesimus to return to him (vv. 13–14). In any case, Paul wants Onesimus to receive a favorable reception, and he offers to repay any debt that Philemon has incurred because of him, though Philemon also owes a great debt to Paul—his "own self" (vv. 15–19). Paul expresses confidence in Philemon's obedience (v. 21) and asks him to have a guest room prepared for when he comes to visit (v. 22). He closes the letter with a series of greetings from his companions (vv. 23–24).

Historical Background

Paul is in prison (vv. 1, 9, 23), and several of his coworkers are with him (vv. 1, 23). He is writing to a friend named "Philemon." This letter does not say where Philemon lives, but since two members of his household (Archippus [v. 2] and Onesimus [vv. 10–16]) are also mentioned by Paul in Colossians 4:9, 17, we probably can conclude that he lives in or near Colossae. Philemon apparently is a wealthy and influential man, since he owns slaves (vv. 15–16) and is able to host gatherings of the church in his home (v. 2). Paul knows Philemon

---

Box 23.1

An All-Star Cast

The brief letter to Philemon features cameo appearances by some very big names. All the folks who send greetings in verses 23–24 are mentioned elsewhere in the New Testament.

- *Epaphras* (Col. 1:7; 4:12): the missionary who evangelized Colossae, Laodicea, and Hierapolis.
- *Mark* (Acts 12:12, 25; 15:37, 39; Col. 4:10; 2 Tim. 4:11; possibly 1 Pet. 5:13): also known as John Mark, a relative of Barnabas; Paul has troubles with him in Acts, but letters ascribed to Paul indicate that they are on good terms at a later point in his ministry; he is identified in church tradition as the author of the Gospel of Mark.
- *Aristarchus* (Acts 19:29; 20:4; 27:2; Col. 4:10): from Thessalonica, a long-time companion of Paul who was sometimes imprisoned with him.
- *Demas* (Col. 4:14; 2 Tim. 4:10): a sometime companion of Paul who, according to 2 Timothy, later deserted him.
- *Luke* (Col. 4:14; 2 Tim. 4:11; possibly all of the "We Passages" in Acts 16:10–17; 20:5–15; 21:1–18; 27:1–28:16): known as the "beloved physician," he is traditionally identified as the author of the Gospel of Luke and the book of Acts and as a companion of Paul on portions of his first and third missionary journeys and his voyage to Rome.
- And, of course, in verse 1, the letter's cowriter, *Timothy* (Acts 16:1, 3; 17:14–15; 18:5; 19:22; 20:4; Rom. 16:21; 1 Cor. 4:17; 16:10; 2 Cor. 1:1, 19; Phil. 1:1; 2:19; Col. 1:1; 1 Thess. 1:1; 3:2, 6; 2 Thess. 1:1; 1 Tim. 1:2, 18; 6:20; 2 Tim. 1:2).

Fig. 23.1 Paul in prison. The sword in Paul's cell is meant to symbolize his impending martyrdom.

well enough to call him a "dear friend and co-worker" (v. 1), but they are not exactly equals. The relationship is one of apostle to disciple: Paul apparently was responsible, directly or indirectly, for Philemon's coming to Christ, and for this reason Philemon owes Paul his very "self" (v. 19). Paul assumes that he has authority over Philemon in matters of faith and duty (v. 8).

Slavery in the Roman World

The institution of slavery was deeply ingrained in Roman society. Roman conquests often led to the enslavement of resident populations, and slave hunters captured victims in provinces not yet overtaken by Rome (cf. 1 Tim. 1:10; Rev. 18:13). Individuals could be sentenced to slavery as punishment for various offenses, and entire families were sold into slavery when someone defaulted on a debt. Since children born to slaves were automatically slaves themselves, the passage of generations guaranteed growth of a large slave population. By the time of Paul, between one-fourth and one-third of all people in the empire were slaves.

The life and condition of slaves seems to have varied enormously. Social decorum encouraged humane treatment, and the extreme abuse or killing of slaves was prohibited by law. Still, the welfare of slaves generally depended on the disposition of their masters. In some cases—notably, for slaves who worked in mines or rowed the oars of galley ships—the conditions of life were appalling. In other instances, however, slaves were given an education and provided with a lifestyle that they probably would not have been able to attain on their own. Indeed, many persons willingly sold themselves into slavery in exchange for being taught a trade or obtaining employment that would improve their lot in life.

Slavery was not always permanent. In some cases, slaves were paid a wage and allowed to purchase their freedom after a period of time; in other cases, slaves were automatically freed when they reached the age of thirty. Nevertheless, slaves had few legal rights. They could be beaten at the discretion of their master, they could not legally marry, and any children they produced were the property of their master (cf. Matt. 18:25, 34; 24:48–51; 25:30). They had virtually no autonomy—no ability to make decisions regarding their own lives or destinies—and in a world that valued honor above all else, they occupied the bottom tier of the social pyramid. A slave was a person with no honor—a person who literally lived in disgrace.

But now a problematic situation has arisen: one of Philemon's slaves, Onesimus, is with Paul, and Paul has come to value him personally and professionally. Paul says that Onesimus is like a son to him ("my own heart" he calls him [v. 12]) and affirms that Onesimus is useful to him and could continue to be of service to him, especially during his time of imprisonment (vv. 10–13). Onesimus is also a Christian, probably as a result of Paul's ministry (cf. v. 10 with 1 Cor. 4:14–15). Indeed, the language of Paul's letter suggests that Onesimus has only recently come to Christ: his status has changed from "useless" to "useful" (v. 11) and from being only a slave to being "a beloved brother" (v. 16). But there is a wrinkle in all of this: Philemon apparently believes that Onesimus has wronged him in some way, most likely in a way that caused him financial loss (v. 18).

Thus Paul writes to make an appeal on behalf of Onesimus (v. 9) and to urge Philemon to welcome his slave back in a manner befitting the gospel. He is to receive Onesimus as he would receive Paul himself (v. 17). Paul even offers to stand good for whatever debt Philemon has incurred on account of Onesimus, putting a guarantee to that effect in his own handwriting (v. 19). It is possible that Paul had the financial resources to do this (cf. Phil. 4:12), but he probably wants

⊙ EXPLORE 23.5
Paul in Prison

⊙ EXPLORE 23.6
Prison Conditions in the Roman World

Philemon to count the loss as a partial repayment of the inestimable debt that Philemon owes Paul for his salvation.

There has been much speculation with regard to the details of the Onesimus situation. Almost all scholars assume that Onesimus has run away from his master. Some think that he also robbed him (to finance the escape?) and that this is the financial loss to which Paul refers (v. 18). Or perhaps Onesimus mismanaged some business interest for Philemon in a manner that caused a loss, and that is what prompted him to run away. In either case, he could be in big trouble, for runaway slaves often were punished severely or even executed as an example to other slaves. Another possibility (since the text does not actually say that Onesimus ran away) is that Onesimus was simply out of town representing Phi-

io fiz iacob.   iofeph.   hymaclito

lef fiz iacob uendirette iofeph lur frere a tref paſſaul e il lamenetette en egypce.

Fig. 23.2. Joseph sold into slavery. The social institution of slavery is prevalent throughout the stretch of biblical history. The Old Testament records a story in which Joseph, patriarch of one of the twelve tribes of Israel, was sold into slavery by his brothers, the patriarchs of the other eleven tribes (Gen. 37:12–36). (Bridgeman Images)

lemon on some business matter and, because the deal went bad, was afraid to return home. Still, whether he fled or merely tarried, his time away from home has been noticed and can have only compounded the problem. Paul tries to put a positive spin on this part of the situation by pointing out that the time when Onesimus was absent from his master did eventuate in his conversion. In Paul's mind, there is sometimes a "reason" that things happen the way they do (v. 15), a hidden divine purpose that lies behind the mundane or apparently random events of this life (cf. Rom. 8:28).

Some information from the Roman world may help us to understand why Paul would write a letter such as this one. First, Roman law required that fugitive slaves be returned to their masters, so if Onesimus actually was "on the run" from Philemon, Paul would have been obligated by law to send him back. More to the point, however, Roman jurisprudence allowed a slave who was on the outs with his or her master to seek arbitration with a colleague or friend of that master; in such instances, the slave was not considered to be a fugitive and could be granted sanctuary under the mediator's care until the difficulty was resolved. Something of this nature seems to provide a reasonable context for understanding Paul's letter to Philemon: Onesimus has sought out his master's friend for assistance in resolving a dispute. He is willing to return home to Philemon, but he wants to do so with a letter from Paul encouraging his possibly angry master to be more favorably disposed toward him than he might have been otherwise.

Paul provides Onesimus with such a letter but seems to take things a step or two further. He asks Philemon for a favor: "Let me have this benefit from

Sanctuary for a Runaway Servant

A letter from Pliny the Younger, written in the late first century, offers an appeal to a certain Sabinianus on behalf of a runaway servant. It makes for an interesting comparison to Paul's letter to Philemon, written on behalf of Onesimus.

> To Sabinianus. Your freedman, whom you lately mentioned as having displeased you, has been with me; he threw himself at my feet and clung there with as much submission as he could have done at yours. He earnestly requested me with many tears, and even with the eloquence of silent sorrow, to intercede for him; in short, he convinced me by his whole behavior, that he sincerely repents of his fault. And I am persuaded he is thoroughly reformed, because he seems entirely sensible of his delinquency. I know you are angry with him, and I know too, it is not without reason; but clemency can never exert itself with more applause, than when [the cause for resentment is most just]. You once had an affection for this man, and, I hope, will have again: in the meanwhile, let me only prevail with you to pardon him. If he should incur your displeasure hereafter, you will have so much the stronger plea in excuse for your anger, as you show yourself more exorable to him now. Allow something to his youth, to his tears, and to your own natural mildness of temper: do not make him uneasy any longer, and I will add too, do not make yourself so; for a man of your benevolence of heart cannot be angry without feeling great uneasiness. I am afraid, were I to join my entreaties with his, I should seem rather to compel, than request you to forgive him. Yet I will not scruple to do it; and so much the more fully and freely as I have very sharply and severely reproved him, positively threatening never to interpose again in his behalf. But though it was proper to say this to him, in order to make him more fearful of offending, I do not say it to you. I may, perhaps, again have occasion to entreat you upon his account, and again obtain your forgiveness; supposing, I mean, his error should be such as may become me to intercede for, and you to pardon. Farewell.

Pliny (the Younger), *Letters*, 2 vols., trans. William Melmoth, revised by W. M. L. Hutchinson, Loeb Classical Library (London: Heinemann, 1915), 2:166–67.

Fig. 23.3. Men in chains. This Roman stela portrays men who became slaves because they were taken as prisoners in a war. But people could become slaves for many reasons, defaulting on debt being the most common one. Between one-fourth and one-third of the people in the Roman Empire were slaves. (© Ashmolean Museum, University of Oxford, UK / The Bridgeman Art Library International)

you in the Lord" (v. 20). What exactly does he want? The strong hint is that he would like for Philemon, as a voluntary good deed (v. 14), to send Onesimus back to Paul to be of service to him (v. 13). While in prison, Paul probably needed to rely on people on the outside to tend to his needs (bring him food, changes of clothing, etc.). Still, he seems to have had a number of persons with him who could do those things (v. 24), and he expects to be released soon (v. 22). Thus he must be thinking long term: Onesimus can join his team and aid him in his missionary work of spreading the gospel. It may be that Paul is also suggesting that Philemon grant Onesimus his freedom.

Paul is probably writing to Philemon from Ephesus around 54–55, or from Caesarea around 58–60, or from Rome around 60–61. Scholars debate which of these options is best, but none of them can be

Was Paul an Old Man?

In his letter to Philemon, Paul says that he writes to his friend as a *presbytēs*, an "old man" (v. 9). This statement is intriguing because it is the only reference in the New Testament to Paul's age. How old was he? What would qualify as an "old man" in those days?

Some scholars suggest that he is not necessarily referring to chronological age but rather to his status as a leader or "elder" in the church. But Paul never refers to himself as a church "elder" in any other instance, and writers who do refer to themselves that way use slightly different Greek words to do so (cf. 1 Pet. 5:1; 2 John 1; 3 John 1).

A few scholars have speculated that there might be an error in our manuscripts here. Paul did not write "elder" or "old man" but rather another word that looks very similar in Greek. They suggest that perhaps he referred to himself as a *presbeutēs* ("ambassador"; cf. *presbeuein* in 2 Cor. 5:20; Eph. 6:20), and a later copyist mistook that word for *presbytēs* ("old man" and "elder"). But this is simply a guess for which there is no actual evidence; we have no manuscripts in which the word *presbeutēs* ("ambassador") occurs here.

Paul Is Witty

Paul chooses his words carefully in his letter to Philemon, using language in ways that are provocative and witty.

- *Euphemism.* Paul refers to Onesimus's problematic absence from the household (due to flight or failure to return home on schedule) simply as a time when Onesimus and Philemon have been "separated" for a while (v. 15).
- *Paradoxical tact.* Paul says that he is not going to mention the debt that Philemon owes to him (v. 19), but of course, in stating that he is not going to mention it, he actually does mention it.
- *Pun.* Paul indicates that Onesimus was once "useless" but is now truly "useful" (v. 11); the word "useless" (*achrēstos*) sounds like a word that means "without Christ" (*achristos*); the word "useful" (*euchrēstos*) is a synonym for a word that serves as Onesimus's proper name (*onēsimos*).
- *Wordplay.* Paul refers to Onesimus as "my own heart" (v. 12) and then calls on Philemon to "refresh my heart" (v. 20), giving the latter reference a double meaning: refresh Onesimus (who is Paul's heart), and refresh Paul's heart by sending Onesimus back to him.

ruled out with certainty, and such precision is not needed to understand the letter's essential points and message.

Major Themes in Philemon

Powers of Persuasion

Paul employs a number of persuasive tactics in this brief letter to ensure that Philemon will comply. For one thing, he brackets his personal message for Philemon with salutations and greetings for the entire church, indicating that the letter is to be read to the community (vv. 2, 25). Thus there will be public knowledge of the request that Paul is making, and the whole congregation will know whether Philemon responds as Paul hopes. Then Paul plays on Philemon's reputation for generosity (vv. 4–7) and reminds Philemon that he is indebted to Paul for his very salvation (v. 19). He even plays the "sympathy card" by reminding Philemon three times that he is in prison (vv. 1, 9, 23) and by indicating that the favor he asks would be a nice thing to do for an "old man" (v. 9). In short, Paul manages in a few sentences to place Philemon in a position in which it would be rather awkward for him to deny this request of his "dear friend" (v. 1), especially one who is planning to come and visit him soon (v. 22). We don't know whether Paul resorted to what we might consider to be manipulative tactics because he suspected that Philemon needed this sort of pressure, or because the situation was particularly delicate, or simply because this was how requests were made in that culture.

Paul's Attitude toward Slavery

Paul's letter to Philemon affords scholars an opportunity to investigate further the attitude of Paul toward slavery. In Galatians 3:28 Paul says that "there is no longer slave or free . . . for all of you are one in Christ Jesus." But does this mean that Christians should reject the institution altogether, refuse to own slaves, and work for the emancipation of slaves? In 1 Corinthians 7:21–24 Paul seems to regard the status of slavery as simply irrelevant: since all are equal in the eyes of God, it doesn't matter what state one occupies in this life. A number of other letters present Paul as insisting that slaves be obedient and loyal to their masters (Eph. 6:5–8; Col. 3:22–25; 1 Tim. 6:1–2; Titus 2:9–10), but not all scholars believe that Paul authored those letters.

Against this background, there is debate about what Paul wants Philemon to do. Obviously he wants Philemon to be magnanimous in welcoming Onesimus back, despite any loss or injury that Philemon might have suffered (v. 17). But beyond that, what is the favor (v. 20) that Paul wants Philemon to do for him? Some scholars have thought that Paul wants Philemon to present Onesimus to Paul as a gift, so that Onesimus would now become Paul's slave and serve him in his imprisonment (v. 13). More often, however, the suggestion is that Paul wants Philemon to set Onesimus free so that he can return to Paul and serve willingly among Paul's company in a manner similar to Paul's other companions and disciples. Paul does not say this outright, but many interpreters think that this is what he means when he expresses confidence that Philemon will do "more than" what has been explicitly requested of him (v. 21). Further, Paul's insistence that Philemon now regard Onesimus as "a beloved brother . . . both in the flesh and in the Lord" (v. 16) implies that Philemon is to regard the slave as his equal.

In any case, many modern interpreters have expressed disappointment that Paul was not more forthright in denouncing the social institution of human slavery. Paul believed the distinction between Jew and gentile to be spiritually irrelevant (Gal. 3:28), and he acted on this belief by insisting on the abolition of practices that perpetrated such a distinction (Gal. 2:11–14). Why didn't he draw similar conclusions with regard to slavery? He might at least have forbidden Christians from participating in the institution. He might have told Philemon in unequivocal terms that it was wrong to keep a human being as a slave and that, to please Christ, he needed to set Onesimus free.

Rather than focus on what Paul does not do, many interpreters want to emphasize the positive steps against slavery that are offered in this letter. Paul insists that Philemon is not to regard Onesimus as mere property but rather is to "welcome him as you would welcome me" (v. 17). Thus it is often said that Paul lays the groundwork for the abolition of slavery or implies that such abolition would be a good thing. Nevertheless, many Bible-believing Christians

⊘ EXPLORE 23.10
Where Was Paul When He Wrote to Philemon?

⊘ EXPLORE 23.11
Paul's Persuasive Tactics in the Letter to Philemon

⊘ EXPLORE 23.7
New Testament References to Slaves and Slavery

An Excerpt from Uncle Tom's Cabin

In chapter 11 of *Uncle Tom's Cabin* (1852), by Harriet Beecher Stowe, a slave named George lets it be known that he is planning to escape. Mr. Wilson, a sympathetic white man, responds:

> Why, George, no—no—it won't do; this way of talking is wicked—unscriptural. George, you've got a hard master—in fact, he is—well he conducts himself reprehensibly—I can't pretend to defend him. But you know how the angel commanded Hagar to return to her mistress, and submit herself under her hand; and the apostle sent back Onesimus to his master.

The biblical references are to Genesis 16 and Paul's letter to Philemon. George replies:

> Don't quote Bible at me that way, Mr. Wilson . . . don't! for my wife is a Christian, and I mean to be, if ever I get to where I can; but to quote Bible to a fellow in my circumstances, is enough to make him give it up altogether. I appeal to God Almighty;—I'm willing to go with the case to Him, and ask Him if I do wrong to seek my freedom.

throughout history did end up condoning slavery as a viable social institution, with full confidence that the Bible did not prohibit the ownership of slaves. The Letter to Philemon often was studied and quoted in debates over slavery, and abolitionists always had to contend with the fact that in this letter Paul does return a slave to his master without prohibiting the continuance of slavery.

Most scholars today think that Paul did not approve of slavery and that his appeal to Philemon on behalf of Onesimus was merely couched in language appropriate for addressing a prominent and powerful individual with regard to a "touchy subject." Still, if Paul had been less subtle in stating his views on the matter, the history of Western Christianity (particularly in the United States) might have been very different.

Conclusion

Whatever limitations may have attended Paul's approach to slavery as a systemic social institution, he does go out of his way to assist one particular slave. He values Onesimus (vv. 11–12) and regards him as an equal (vv. 16–17). And his appeal on behalf of Onesimus is perhaps all the more poignant when we recall that he is making that appeal as a prisoner: it is because of Christ that Paul has lost his own freedom, and it is for Christ's sake that he now seeks the freedom of another. We cannot know for certain whether Philemon did as Paul requested, but, as many scholars have pointed out, it seems unlikely that any copies of this letter would have been preserved if it had not proven effective and been met with a favorable response.

A possible postscript to the story surfaces some fifty years later via the writings of the church leader Ignatius of Antioch. Ignatius reveals that the bishop of the church of Ephesus at that time (ca. 110) was a man named "Onesimus"

(Ignatius, *To the Ephesians* 1:3). Could this be the same person? Did Onesimus the one-time slave end up becoming bishop of one of the world's most prominent churches? If Onesimus was a teenager at the time of Paul, he could have been alive at the time when Ignatius wrote. As some scholars point out, the name Onesimus was frequently (though not always) a slave's name, and it would not be very likely for another slave named "Onesimus" to rise to such prominence in this same geographical region in so short a period of time. And it makes good sense to presume that the slave who became a bishop would be the one who came from the prominent household of Philemon and who had served as a trusted assistant to Paul the apostle, since both of those factors would help to explain his accession. Still, Ignatius tells us nothing of Bishop Onesimus's credentials, nor does he indicate that the Onesimus whom he knows is the one who knew Paul. The bottom line is that we cannot know whether this is the same Onesimus, and scholars usually do not take the potential connection very seriously. But what a great conclusion to the story it would make: Philemon's errant slave, now the bishop of Ephesus!

FOR FURTHER READING: Philemon

Barclay, John M. G. *Colossians and Philemon*. New Testament Guides. Sheffield: Sheffield Academic Press, 2001.

Donfried, Karl P., and I. Howard Marshall. *The Theology of the Shorter Pauline Letters*. New Testament Theology. Cambridge: Cambridge University Press, 1993.

Migliore, Daniel L. *Philippians & Philemon: A Theological Commentary*. Belief Series. Louisville: Westminster John Knox, 2014.

Osiek, Carolyn. *Philippians, Philemon*. Abingdon New Testament Commentaries. Nashville: Abingdon, 2000.

Tamez, Elsa, et al. *Philippians, Colossians, Philemon*. Wisdom Commentary. Collegeville, MN: Liturgical Press, 2016.

Thompson, James W., and Bruce W. Longenecker. *Philippians and Philemon*. Paideia. Grand Rapids: Baker Academic, 2016.

Thompson, Marianne Meye. *Colossians and Philemon*. Two Horizons Commentary. Grand Rapids: Eerdmans, 2005.

Weidman, Frederick W. *Philippians, First and Second Thessalonians, and Philemon*. Westminster Bible Companion. Louisville: Westminster John Knox, 2013.

Wright, N. T. *Paul for Everyone: The Prison Letters; Ephesians, Philippians, Colossians, and Philemon*. 2nd ed. Louisville: Westminster John Knox, 2004.

⊙ Go to www
.IntroducingNT.com
for summaries,
videos, and other
study tools.

Hebrews

Almost every year a motion picture is released that garners rave reviews from professional critics but still flops at the box office. Critical acclaim does not guarantee a popular reception.

Among New Testament writings, the Letter to the Hebrews may provide our best example of a critic's favorite. Scholars claim that Hebrews is written in more polished and eloquent Greek than any other book of the Bible. It presents a carefully constructed argument that employs Hellenistic rhetorical strategies in an impressive and effective manner. It also displays intriguing examples of Christian exegesis that demonstrate both apologetic and dogmatic approaches to the Old Testament Scriptures. Christian doctrine and theology owe much to this letter. It is invariably described as a masterpiece.

Still, Hebrews doesn't top many popularity lists for Christians who just want to do some inspirational Bible reading. The letter has an unfortunate reputation for being long and stodgy, intellectual and difficult to understand, or even—dare we say it?—boring. Some people will say that Hebrews, apart from a few passages (e.g., 4:12—a favorite of Bible readers who are fond of "memory verses"), doesn't really get good until the last three chapters. Then, at last, it becomes considerably more accessible, as well as inspirational, practical, and relevant.

One problem for contemporary readers may be that those first ten chapters deal with subjects that seem arcane to them: Jewish sacrifices, purification rituals, the priesthood. Indeed, a major focus is on an obscure biblical character, Melchizedek, who makes but a cameo appearance in Old Testament history (Gen. 14:18–20; Ps. 110:4). What does this have to do with us? It may help to know that the first readers of Hebrews probably asked that same question. Melchizedek was not a major figure to them either. And the sacrificial rituals that are the focus of this letter are not those of the Jerusalem temple but rather rites of an earlier wilderness tabernacle; they are rituals that had not been performed in Israel for over a millennium. In a certain sense, then, the contents of Hebrews were arcane from the start. Still, the critics were impressed, and over the years persistent Christians have found real substance in this letter: teaching that not only reveals who Christ is but also discloses who they are (and can be) in relation to him.

Overview

The letter (or sermon) opens with an eloquent prologue that presents God's Son as the definitive revelation of God (1:1–3). The author proposes that the Son is superior to angels (1:4–14) and then issues a plea for the readers not to drift away from the truth that they have received (2:1–4). Returning to the theme of the Son's superiority, the author explains that the temporary humiliation of Jesus was necessary for human salvation and led to his glorious exaltation (2:5–18). He argues that Jesus is also superior to Moses (3:1–6), which leads to a warning not to rebel and fail to enter into God's rest as did some of those who were delivered from Egypt under Moses (3:7–19). The readers should make every effort to enter God's Sabbath rest (4:1–11). This exhortation is punctuated by a reminder of the piercing power of God's word to reveal secret intentions of the heart (4:12–13).

The author then launches into a long exposition on the role of Jesus as high priest (4:14–10:39). First, the author shows that Jesus possesses two qualifications for being such a priest (4:14–5:10): he is able to sympathize with humans, and he has been appointed by God to be a priest after the order of Melchizedek. This gives way to another excursus: the author rebukes the readers for their spiritual immaturity, urges them to press on toward perfection, and expresses confidence that they will persevere (5:11–6:20).

Returning to the main theme, the author expounds on what is meant by identifying Jesus as a priest according to the order of Melchizedek (7:1–28). He then spells out the implications of what he has been saying: the earthly sanctuary where priests offer sacrifices is only a sketch or shadow of the heavenly one, and the old covenant has been made obsolete by the new and better covenant in Jesus (8:1–13). These points are elaborated through a treatise on the many ways in which the sacrifice of Christ is superior to the sacrifices of the Levitical priests (9:1–10:18).

⊙ EXPLORE 24.0
Hebrews: Outline of Contents

⊙ EXPLORE 24.13
Structure of Hebrews

The author concludes his theological homily on Christ's high priesthood by exhorting readers to respond appropriately (10:19–39). He then offers a roll call of biblical heroes whose lives have testified to faith as "the assurance of things hoped for" (11:1–40). They constitute a great "cloud of witnesses," to which Jesus may be added as the ultimate example of one who proved faithful in suffering and prepared the way for others to follow (12:1–3). The author urges readers to endure their trials and reflects briefly on the positive role that suffering can play when viewed as discipline from a loving God (12:4–11). These exhortations to faithfulness give way to a contrast between the covenants of Mount Sinai and Mount Zion: the readers are receiving a kingdom that cannot be shaken, but those who fail to obtain the grace of God offered through this new covenant will not escape God's judgment (12:12–29).

The letter begins to draw to a close with numerous admonitions (13:1–17): the readers ought to follow the example of former leaders; they need to avoid getting caught up in strange doctrines; they should be willing to suffer ostracism for their faith; they are to worship God with praise and good works; and they should submit to their current leaders. The book closes in the typical style of a letter, with prayer requests, benedictions, and personal greetings (13:18–25).

Historical Background

Although this book is traditionally called the "Letter to the Hebrews," it doesn't look very much like a letter, at least not until the very end. It closes like a letter, but it doesn't open like one. The author refers to his work as a "word of exhortation" (13:22), using exactly the same term employed in Acts 13:15 of a

---

Box 24.1

Why Don't the Quotations Match?

Astute Bible readers sometimes note that Old Testament passages quoted in the Letter to the Hebrews do not quite match what is actually said in the Old Testament itself. For example:

Psalm 8:5: "lower than God"
Hebrews 2:7: "lower than the angels"

The Letter to the Hebrews regularly quotes from the Septuagint, a Greek translation of the Old Testament. Almost all modern Bibles contain translations of the Old Testament done from the Hebrew, not from the Septuagint (so as not to produce a translation of a translation).

The Hebrew word in Psalm 8:5 is *elohim*, which usually means "God," though it might sometimes mean "angels." Almost all Bible translators have thought that the psalmist intended the word to mean "God," and almost all English Bibles translate Psalm 8:5 as "lower than God." The Septuagint, however, translates *elohim* with the Greek word for "angels" in this one verse, and the author of Hebrews relied on that somewhat idiosyncratic translation in making his point.

Something similar happens a number of other times in the letter. For example, in Psalm 40:6 we read "you have given me an open ear" in modern translations of the Old Testament, but Hebrews 10:5 follows a Septuagint reading in quoting the text as "a body you have prepared for me."

sermon. Perhaps that is what Hebrews is: a sermon, preached from afar and sent through the mail to those who needed to hear it. A few scholars have thought that chapters 1–12 make up the original sermon—an elegant treatise structured with alternating patterns of exposition and exhortation—and chapter 13 is a personal note affixed to this sermon when it was sent to the congregation for which it had been composed.

But who were those intended recipients? The letter (let's call it that) reveals a number of things about its readers:

- They are Christians (3:6; 4:14; 10:23).
- They are either Jewish Christians or at least Christians with a strong interest in sacrificial practices and other matters of Jewish faith.
- They heard the message of salvation from people who heard it from Jesus (2:3); thus they are second-generation Christians, but not third- or fourth-generation Christians.
- They have witnessed signs and wonders and various miracles and have received diverse gifts of the Holy Spirit (2:4).
- They are sufficiently educated and astute to understand arguments that employ both Hellenistic rhetoric and allusive reasoning based on the Jewish Scriptures.
- They have gone through a hard time that required them to endure abuse, persecution, and suffering (10:32–33).
- Some of them had property that was plundered (10:34), but thus far the abuse has not involved bloodshed (12:4).
- They have been exemplary in good works (6:10), such as showing compassion to those who suffer (10:34).
- They nevertheless have now become "dull in understanding" (5:11) and potentially "sluggish" (6:12; cf. 12:12).
- They seem to be in danger of apostasy, renouncing their faith or drifting away from the truth (2:1–3; 3:12–14; 4:1; 10:35–36); some are already neglecting to meet with the community (10:25).

apostasy: the abandonment or renunciation of one's religious faith.

Taking all of these points together, many scholars have surmised that the crisis this letter wants to address is a specific temptation for some Christians to embrace what the author regards as outmoded aspects of the Jewish religion or even a return to that religion in a way that compromises their Christian confession. Most scholars today think that Hebrews was written for a mixed audience of Jewish and gentile Christians, either in Jerusalem or (and this is the dominant theory) in Rome. The specific situation eludes us, but the author of Hebrews seems to view the Jewish religion (or aspects thereof) as

⊙ EXPLORE 24.14
The Audience for the Letter to the Hebrews

a primary competitor for the hearts, minds, and souls of the letter's intended audience. This could account for two motifs that are emphasized repeatedly: the superiority of Christ and the dire consequences of apostasy. Those two themes seem interwoven throughout the letter. Perhaps that is because the author feared that the readers might prove susceptible to one specific form of apostasy, adopting Judaism in a way that failed to reckon with or appreciate the unqualified supremacy of Christ.

The King James Version of the Bible titles this work "The Epistle of Paul the Apostle to the Hebrews," but the attribution to Paul was a guess, and probably not a very good one. The letter itself is anonymous, and its distinctive style and theology set it apart from Paul's writings. The Letter to the Hebrews actually had some trouble in gaining acceptance as part of the Christian canon because of its anonymity. It eventually came to be regarded as Scripture on the strength of intrinsic factors (sound theology, eloquent presentation), but the question "Who wrote the Letter to the Hebrews?" has continued to draw the interest of interpreters throughout the ages, like some great unsolved detective story. There are clues, but they are inconclusive. And there are suspects: the history of interpretation has provided a long list of impressive possible authors, including the famously eloquent Apollos (see Acts 18:24–25), the beloved physician and

canon: literally, "rule" or "standard"; used by religious groups to refer to an authoritative list of books that are officially accepted as Scripture.

Box 24.2

The Basics of Faith

Hebrews 6:1–2 lists six matters as "basic teaching" that mature Christians should have down pat. It is a little embarrassing that we lack clarity regarding things that are supposed to be so obvious that no instruction is necessary, but sometimes that is the case.

- *Repentance from dead works.* Believers should reject "dead works," but what are those? The reference may be to sinful behaviors that lead to death, or it could be to ritual practices of the Jewish religion that Christ has rendered obsolete. See also Hebrews 9:14.
- *Faith toward God.* Believers should trust radically in God and in God's promises (cf. Heb. 11:1–12:2).
- *Baptisms.* Why is this in the plural? Perhaps it refers to various purification rites practiced by Jews (cf. Heb. 9:10). Did the readers of this letter practice those rituals? Or did they have some variant understanding of Christian baptism as an action practiced more than once or for diverse functions (cf. 1 Cor. 15:29, a verse that also refers to some primitive baptismal practice about which we have no knowledge)?
- *Laying on of hands.* This refers to a rite through which human touch accompanies or imparts divine authorization or empowerment (cf. 2 Tim. 1:6), but it could be practiced for a variety of reasons: conveying the gift of the Holy Spirit to believers (Acts 8:17; 19:6); commissioning leaders (Acts 6:6; 1 Tim. 5:22); healing the sick (Acts 9:12; 28:8).
- *Resurrection of the dead.* All persons will be raised to new life when Christ returns.
- *Eternal judgment.* God will judge all people, granting them salvation or condemnation (cf. Heb. 9:27; 10:26–27; 13:4).

putative evangelist Luke (Col. 4:14), Paul's traveling companion Barnabas (Acts 13–14) or his tent-making colleague Priscilla (Acts 18:2–3), and the late-first-century bishop Clement of Rome. The case remains open, and most current scholars would agree with the verdict reached more than seventeen hundred years ago by Origen, a prominent teacher of the early church. After investigating the matter, he concluded, "Who wrote this epistle? Only God knows!" (reported in Eusebius, *Ecclesiastical History* 6.25.13).

We probably can assume, however, that the author of Hebrews was a person of prominence in the early church. He (assuming a male author, though that is not absolutely certain) knew people who had known Jesus (2:3) and was well educated with regard to both Greek rhetoric and the Jewish Scriptures. The author also knew the readers personally and assumed a mandate to speak to them authoritatively, even though he does not appear to have been the founder of their community. Indeed, the author was planning to visit the readers soon (13:19, 23), which may indicate that he exercised a supervisory role for the congregation beyond that of its local leaders (13:7, 17, 24).

Since the author and the readers apparently belong to a second generation of believers (2:3), and since they have been believers for a while (5:12; 10:32), the letter is usually thought to have been written at least as late as 50 (or, more often, as late as 60). It probably had to have been written before 90, since Clement of Rome knows it and cites it in a letter that was written probably around 96 (*1 Clement* 36:1–5; cf. Heb. 1:3–5, 7, 13). Efforts to determine a more precise date usually focus on the question of whether Hebrews was written before or after 70, when the temple in Jerusalem was destroyed. Since the letter never mentions the temple (using instead the ancient tabernacle for all of its sacrificial imagery), some scholars reason that the temple was no longer a viable institution, that it had been destroyed. But others maintain that if the temple had been destroyed, the author surely would have mentioned this to clinch his argument that the Jewish sacrificial system was now obsolete (8:13). Readers sometimes note that the letter refers to sacrifices in the present tense, as though they are still being offered (7:8; 8:3; 9:6–7, 9, 13; 13:11), but this is not as conclusive as it may at first seem, since the Greek language sometimes uses the present tense for describing historical acts. Both Josephus (*Jewish Antiquities* 4.102–50, 151–87) and Clement of Rome (*1 Clement* 41) talk about sacrifices in the present tense in writings produced after the temple destruction (and in any case, Hebrews is actually referring to sacrifices offered in the ancient tabernacle). Still, many scholars do find the reasoning of Hebrews 10:2 to be highly suggestive of a pre-70 date: the argument seems to turn on an insistence that the offering of sacrifices (identical or similar to those offered in the tabernacle) was still taking place at the time when this letter was being written.

⊙ **EXPLORE 24.11**
Hebrews in the Christian Canon

⊙ **EXPLORE 24.7**
Hebrews and Paul: Some Parallels

⊙ **EXPLORE 24.12**
Authorship of Hebrews

The bottom line is that we know less about the historical circumstances for this letter (if indeed it is a letter) than for almost any other New Testament book. It was written by an unknown, eloquent, and probably prominent Christian to a group of Jewish and/or gentile Christians in some city (unknown to us, but possibly Rome) between 50 and 90 (possibly, but not certainly, before 70). The purpose of the composition, however, is fairly clear: it proclaims the superiority of Christ as the divine Son of God, and the superiority of faith in Christ over all other confessions, especially Jewish religion. It does so, negatively, to forestall apostasy (i.e., to persuade Christians not to abandon their faith) and, positively, to encourage perseverance appropriate to receiving the favor and benefits of God bestowed on those who are faithful. Such perseverance is justified in light of what the earthly Son has done to bring believers into God's favor, and it is sustained through the intercessions that the exalted Son continues to offer on their behalf.

Major Themes in Hebrews

Christianity and Judaism

As Christianity developed, different conceptions emerged regarding how this new faith should be understood relative to its parent, Judaism. At one

---

Box 24.3

The First Christian Platonist?

In the fourth century BCE, the Greek philosopher Plato introduced a two-tiered scheme of reality that appears to have been influential for the author of Hebrews. Plato claimed that the world of "ideas" is the most real and true world and that the physical world in which we live contains only representations of those ideas that are in some sense less real and less true.

Jews who were attracted to this notion often translated it into a contrast between what was heavenly and what was earthly (though that is not exactly the same thing). The writings of Philo of Alexandria, produced around the same time as the Letter to the Hebrews, provide illustrations of Jewish Platonism. Philo read Genesis 1:26–27 as reporting the creation of the "idea" (or "ideal form") of humanity and Genesis 2:7 as reporting the creation of a material representation of this idea (a physical man formed from the dust of the earth).

Likewise, the author of Hebrews has sometimes been called "the first Christian Platonist." He argues that the Jewish tabernacle is only "a sketch and shadow" of a heavenly sanctuary in which Jesus exercises his office as high priest (8:5–6; cf. 9:23; 10:1). The earthly sanctuary made by human hands is only a material representation of the more real, heavenly sanctuary, which was not made by hands.

Obviously, a more true and more real salvation is to be obtained in the heavenly sanctuary than in the earthly one. Notably, Hebrews does not denigrate what is physical as evil or wrong: the contrast between earthly and heavenly is not between "bad" and "good" (as it would be in gnosticism); it is between "good" and "better."

extreme, some Christians appear to have insisted that Christianity was a subset of Judaism. One could not be a Christian without being a Jew. Gentiles who became Christians should get circumcised (become Jews) and observe all the traditional Jewish rituals and regulations. Paul likely was dealing with people who thought this way when he wrote his letter to the Galatians (see "Historical Background" in chap. 16). The opposite extreme, however, held that Judaism was a false religion. The Jewish God was evil and the Jewish Scriptures were to be rejected. This view was favored by the second-century Christian Marcion and was also prominent among gnostics (see "On the Horizon: Gnosticism" in chap. 1, and "Development of the Canon" in chap. 3). The Letter to the Hebrews steers a course between these approaches, stressing the continuity of Christianity with Judaism while also emphasizing the supremacy of Christianity over Judaism.

The continuity of Christian and Jewish religions is evident in that the God who has now spoken through the Son is the same God who spoke through the Jewish prophets (1:1–2). The Jewish Scriptures are quoted authoritatively throughout Hebrews as reliable expressions of God's will and plan (see, e.g., 1:5–12; 4:3, 7; 7:21; 8:8–12). Thus Hebrews affirms that Christians and Jews worship the same God and read the same Bible.

Hebrews also insists, however, that Christianity is superior to Judaism in two highly significant ways. First, Jesus Christ is superior to all other figures from Israel's illustrious history, including Moses (3:1–6), Joshua (4:1–11), Aaron (4:14–5:10), and Levi (7:1–22). He is more glorious than angels (1:4–11; 2:5–18), and he brings a revelation superior to that of prophets (1:1–3). Second, the salvation that Jesus brings is superior to that which Israel attained through the old covenant (8:1–13). He offers a superior sacrifice (10:1–18) in a superior tabernacle (9:1–28) and can be said to save people "completely" (7:25).

In making this case, the author of Hebrews draws on two traditions of thought. In terms informed by an almost rabbinic understanding of the Jewish Scriptures, he claims that Christ provides the fulfillment of the new covenant that historic Judaism has promised (8:7–13). In terms informed by Hellenistic Judaism or Greek philosophy, he claims that Christ offers the true, eternal salvation for which Judaism provides a lesser, earthly representation (8:5–6; 9:23; 10:1).

salvation: an act of God through which human beings are delivered from the power and consequences of sin.

covenant: an agreement or pact between God and human beings that establishes the terms of their ongoing relationship.

⊙ EXPLORE 24.15 Use of the Old Testament in Hebrews

Box 24.4

Something Better

A prominent theme in Hebrews is that in Jesus Christ, God has provided "something better" (11:40):

- better things (6:9)
- a better hope (7:19)
- a better covenant (7:22; 8:6)
- better promises (8:6)
- better sacrifices (9:23)
- better possessions (10:34)
- a better country (11:16)
- a better resurrection (11:35)
- a better word (12:24)

Christology

The Letter to the Hebrews says, "Jesus Christ is the same yesterday and today and forever" (13:8). This letter's portrait of who Jesus Christ is and its sketch of what Jesus Christ means for humanity are broad and nearly comprehensive: much of what is affirmed about Christ in other books of the New Testament is found here, but that information is supplemented by distinctive elements and particular nuances that have been influential on Christian theology.

Hebrews speaks of Christ's preexistence (1:2; 10:5), incarnation (2:14–18; 10:5–7), sacrificial death (1:3; 2:9; 7:27), resurrection (1:3), heavenly intercession (7:23–25; cf. 2:18; 8:1–2), and return for judgment (9:27–28; 10:25). The first two items on this list (preexistence and incarnation) express the idea that the person now known as Jesus Christ existed as a divine being (the Son of God) prior to becoming a human being (see also John 1:1–2, 14; Phil. 2:5–7). The fifth element on the list (heavenly intercession) refers to the notion that Jesus Christ is currently in heaven, where he prays for his followers in ways that support and sustain them on earth (see also Rom. 8:34; 1 John 2:1).

Fig. 24.1. Christ and the angels. Why does the Letter to the Hebrews emphasize that Jesus is to be exalted over angels (1:5–2:18)? At least three answers have been proposed:

- Some of the letter's intended recipients may have been tempted to worship angels (cf. Col. 2:18; Rev. 19:10; 22:9).
- Some of the recipients may have displayed a mistaken tendency to think of Jesus as an angel.
- Angels are identified in Hebrews as mediators of the covenant (2:2; cf. Gal. 3:19), and Jesus is said to bring a greater salvation through a new covenant (8:6–13).

(Manu Sassoonian / Art Resource, NY)

Hebrews testifies to what would become standard Christian dogma regarding "the two natures of Christ": Jesus Christ is to be confessed as both fully divine and fully human (see box 24.5). Jesus is actually equated with God in

⊘ EXPLORE 24.4
Images and Titles for
Jesus in Hebrews

Hebrews 1:8 (cf. John 20:28; Titus 2:13; see box 4.5), and he is said to represent the "exact imprint of God's very being" (1:3; cf. Col. 1:15; 2:9). He is presented as the agent through whom God created the worlds and sustains all things (cf. John 1:3; 1 Cor. 8:6; Col. 1:16–17). Some scholars have wondered whether this presentation of Christ might have been influenced by Jewish writings that personified Wisdom as the agent of God. The Wisdom of Solomon (a book belonging to the Apocrypha, or deuterocanonical writings; see "The Effects of Hellenism on the New Testament World" in chap. 2) says that Wisdom is "a reflection of eternal light, a spotless mirror of the working of God, and an image of God's goodness" (Wis. 7:25–26; cf. Heb. 1:3). Elsewhere, Wisdom is identified as an active agent in creation (Prov. 8:22–23; Wis. 7:22; 9:9) and in the ongoing preservation of the created realm (Wis. 7:27; 8:1). Thus Hebrews might be understood as applying to the Son what some Jewish writings were attributing to Wisdom.

But Hebrews also presents Jesus as fully and profoundly human—a person who, like other human beings (2:11, 17–18), had to be made perfect or complete through obedience to God (2:10; 5:8). Such obedience, furthermore, was something that he had to learn (5:8). The notion of Jesus needing to learn things (to grow in knowledge or wisdom) is rare in the Bible (cf. Luke 2:52), and the idea of Jesus needing to learn obedience (to grow in faithfulness to

---

Box 24.5

The Divine and Human Christ in Hebrews

The Divine Christ

- the one through whom worlds were created (1:2)
- the mirror image (reflection) of God's glory (1:3)
- the exact imprint of God's very being (1:3)
- the one who sustains all things (1:3)
- seated at the right hand of God in glory (1:3)
- superior to angels (1:4) and worshiped by them (1:6)
- without sin (4:15) and able to sanctify others (2:11)
- will return to save those who wait eagerly for him (9:28; 10:37)

The Human Christ

- a person of flesh and blood, like all children of God (2:14; cf. 2:11)
- became like us in every respect (2:17)
- was tested by what he suffered (2:18)
- is able to sympathize (or empathize) with our weaknesses (4:15)
- was tested (or tempted) in every respect as we are (4:15)
- offered prayers to God with loud cries and tears and reverent submission (5:7)
- learned obedience through suffering (5:8; cf. 2:10)
- an example of perseverance that others can follow (12:1–3)

God) is unique to Hebrews. The book makes clear that Jesus did not sin (4:15) but nevertheless alleges that a prolonged process of testing (4:15) and suffering (5:7–9) brought Jesus to progressive levels of faithfulness that marked growth in obedience and, eventually, perfection.

The humanity of Christ is theologically significant in this book because

- being human allows Christ to suffer and die and thus to offer an ultimate sacrifice for sin and destroy the power of death (2:14–15; 7:27);
- being human enables Christ to identify with human beings in every respect so that he is able to sympathize mercifully with the weak and wayward (2:17; 4:15; cf. 5:1–2); and
- being human allows Christ to become a credible example for others who suffer testing and must persevere as he did (12:1–3).

Jesus as High Priest

One of the most striking aspects of Hebrews is its prominent identification of Jesus as high priest (2:17; 3:1; 4:14; 5:5, 10; 6:20; 7:26; 8:1; 9:11; 10:21). At first,

---

Box 24.6

Perfection in Hebrews

The Letter to the Hebrews often speaks of perfection:

- We (the readers) are encouraged to "go on toward perfection" (6:1).
- The hope of being made perfect was not fulfilled for even the most faithful heroes of the Bible (11:40).
- Religious rules and rituals cannot make people perfect (7:11, 19; 9:9; 10:1).

What can we do?

- Jesus Christ is the "perfecter of our faith" (12:2).
- Christ himself was made perfect (2:10; 5:8–9; 7:28).
- Then, by a single offering (his death), Christ made perfect for all time those who are sanctified by him (10:14).
- The spirits of the righteous enrolled in heaven have now been made perfect by Christ (12:23), and we look forward to joining them (13:14).

The perfection envisioned here is not simply or primarily moral perfection; Jesus was without sin (4:15), but he still needed to be made perfect. Rather, the idea is completion—people becoming all that they are meant to be. The discipline of learning obedience through suffering contributes to a process of perfection here on earth (5:8–9; 12:11), but this is but a temporal realization of the complete and more glorious salvation that has been accomplished in the heavenly realm.

See David Peterson, *Hebrews and Perfection: An Examination of the Concept of Perfection in the "Epistle to the Hebrews"* (Cambridge: Cambridge University Press, 1982).

Fig. 24.2. Melchizedek. This depiction of Melchizedek, the priest who appears to Abraham (Gen. 14:18–20), is from the Verdun Altar in the Klosterneuburg Monastery in Austria, constructed in 1181. (Erich Lessing / Art Resource, NY)

such an identification may seem surprising because the historical Jesus certainly was not a priest and, indeed, seems to have been critical of temple practices and at odds with the Jerusalem priesthood (Mark 11:15–18). The author gets around this by an appeal to the obscure Old Testament figure of Melchizedek (Gen. 14:18–20; Ps. 110:4). In the Bible, Melchizedek is identified as a priest centuries before the hereditary order of the Levitical priesthood was established; thus, for the author of Hebrews, Jesus can be a nonhereditary priest "according to the order of Melchizedek" (5:6, 10; 6:20; 7:17; cf. Ps. 110:4). Since Melchizedek came first chronologically, he should be deemed greater than the later Levitical priests; furthermore, Abraham paid tithes to Melchizedek, which effectively means that all of Abraham's descendants (including Levi and all of the Levitical priests) paid homage to Melchizedek as well (7:9–10). The fact that neither the genealogy nor the death of Melchizedek is reported in the Bible indicates that the superior priesthood that he represents is an eternal one, having neither beginning nor end (7:3). What better candidate could there be for such a priesthood than the preexistent and ever-living Jesus?

The image of Jesus as a "priest" is almost absent elsewhere in the New Testament; the closest we get to such thinking is John 17:19, where Jesus sanctifies himself so that others might also be sanctified (see also John 10:36). The more common motif pictures Jesus not as a priest but rather as a sacrificial animal (John 1:29, 36; Rom. 3:25; 1 John 2:2). Curiously, Hebrews does not substitute one image for the other but instead doubles up on them, providing us with one of the most astonishing mixed metaphors of all time: Jesus is both the priest and the sacrifice; he offers his own sinless blood, which is obviously a much greater sacrifice than the blood of sheep or goats (9:12–14; 10:4–10; 13:12). He does so, furthermore, in the superior heavenly sanctuary rather than in an earthly tabernacle (8:1–2; 9:24). So we have a better priest offering a better sacrifice in a better sanctuary. The result is that the priestly ministry of Jesus offers a once-for-all purification from sin; it never needs to be repeated (9:25–26), and since the need for subsequent sacrifices has been eradicated, the entire sacrificial system is rendered obsolete. The ministry of Jesus as high priest continues, however, as he offers heavenly intercession for his followers, supporting them before God with prayer and supplication (7:25).

Fig. 24.3. Jesus the high priest. (© Radiant Light / Bridgeman Images)

Rest

The Letter to the Hebrews uses the concept of "divine rest" as an image for salvation (4:1–11). It speaks of the "rest" that God promised to Israel in the biblical stories of Moses and Joshua—the rest that Israel was to experience after the exodus and conquest of Canaan. Subsequent history has made clear that this rest was not received. Quoting Psalm 95:7–11, the author of Hebrews

Box 24.7

Two Favorite Terms in Hebrews

Eternal

- eternal salvation (5:9)
- eternal judgment (6:2)
- eternal redemption (9:12)
- eternal Spirit (9:14)
- eternal inheritance (9:15)
- eternal covenant (13:20)

Heavenly

- heavenly calling (3:1)
- heavenly gift (6:4)
- heavenly sanctuary (8:5)
- heavenly things (9:23)
- heavenly country (11:16)
- heavenly Jerusalem (12:22)

Fig. 24.4. the tabernacle. The tabernacle, a portable sanctuary, served as the primary place for worship and sacrifices during Israel's wilderness period (see Exod. 25–30; 35–40). According to the Letter to the Hebrews, the earthly tabernacle has a heavenly counterpart (8:2, 5; 9:23). (Becky Bardon / BiblePlaces.com)

says that the reason was that the Israelites did not listen to God's voice: they were unbelieving (3:12, 19), rebellious (3:16), disobedient (4:6, 11), and hard of heart (3:13, 15; 4:7). The importance of hearing God's voice today is exponentially greater because the rest that remains for God's people is not simply that of Canaan; it is the Sabbath rest of God (4:9–11; cf. Gen. 2:2).

Sabbath: a day of the week set aside for worship and for rest from normal endeavors.

Pilgrim People

The Letter to the Hebrews employs a pilgrimage motif to present Christians as people on a journey. One possible reason that the author uses the tabernacle rather than the temple for his descriptions of Israelite sacrifices is that it better serves this theme. The tabernacle (described in Exod. 25–27) was a portable worship space, a tent with curtains and screens hung over a wooden framework. The Israelites carried this with them, along with the ark of the covenant, which was placed behind a curtain to symbolize God's presence with the people (cf. Heb. 6:19; 9:3; 10:20), and an altar on which sacrifices could be offered (cf. Heb. 7:13; 9:4; 13:10). But, according to Hebrews, the journey of God's people to the promised land of Canaan was only a temporal and earthly representation of the greater spiritual journey of God's people toward an eternal city in a heavenly country (11:16). People who believe in Christ are on this ultimate journey, and the author of Hebrews offers a litany of examples for his readers to consider when troubles beset them and the notion of turning back crosses their minds:

- The first example, somewhat ironically, is their own history. They have endured hard struggles in previous times and proven that they are not people who shrink back and are lost; rather, they are people who persevere and are saved (10:32–39).
- The second example is the witness to faith provided by heroes of the Bible who have borne all manner of suffering and shame in mere anticipation of what is now at last becoming a reality (11:1–12:1).
- The third and greatest example is Jesus, for whom the joy of exaltation to God's presence proved sufficient for him to endure hostility without growing weary or losing heart (12:2–3). As one tested in every way as we are (4:15), Jesus established himself as a "pioneer" who can guide those on the journey that he has completed (2:10; 12:2).

Suffering and Shame

The Christian pilgrimage depicted in Hebrews is marked by a paradoxically positive evaluation of suffering and shame. Suffering may be a form of discipline (12:4–13). God may sometimes punish people through suffering, but God also teaches or trains people through suffering. The experience of trials may serve to strengthen commitment and to advance disciples who are following Jesus in a trek toward perfect obedience (2:10; 5:7–9; cf. Rom. 5:3–4; James 1:2–3; 1 Pet. 1:6–7; 4:12–16). Thus Hebrews can encourage its readers to consider any loss of status or social reputation that they have experienced because of their faith as an ironic badge of honor. Since God disciplines those whom God favors (12:5–6), such trials may be viewed as an indication of God's approval.

shame: negative status, implying disgrace and unworthiness.

honor: the positive status that one has in the eyes of those whom one considers to be significant.

Stern Warnings

The Letter to the Hebrews is also noted for the intensity of its warnings against apostasy, which seem to go beyond what is usually said in Scripture or confessed by the church. Three passages stand out:

- Hebrews 6:4–6 says that it is impossible for those who have been enlightened (come to faith in Christ) and then fallen away to be restored to repentance.
- Hebrews 10:26–31 makes clear that those who willfully persist in sin after receiving knowledge of the truth in Christ will discover that no sacrifice for those sins remains, and indeed they will suffer a worse punishment of hellfire than those who sinned without such knowledge.
- Hebrews 12:16–17 confirms the teaching that apostates cannot be restored to faith, offering an analogy to Esau, who repented of giving away his birthright and then sought to recover the blessing only to find that his repentance was rejected and his tears were shed in vain.

⊙ EXPLORE 24.17
Honor and Shame in Hebrews

The Christian church has struggled with these texts almost since the time they were written. Some scholars speculate that these texts might have arisen as a reflection on the tradition of an "unforgivable sin" referenced in the Synoptic stories of Jesus (Matt. 12:31–32; Luke 12:10). Still, the assertion that those who fall away from the faith cannot be forgiven or restored seems to conflict with biblical teaching elsewhere (Matt. 18:12–14, 15, 21–22; Luke 15; John 6:39–40; 10:27–29; Gal. 6:1; James 5:19–20; 1 Pet. 1:4–5; 2 Pet. 3:9; 1 John 2:1), as well as with the Gospel tradition that the apostles themselves had been apostates, recovered after deserting and denying Jesus (e.g., Mark 14:50, 66–72; 16:7; cf. Luke 22:31–34). It also runs counter to numerous doctrines held by various Christian churches and denominations (justification by grace, election, eternal security).

Many interpreters take these passages as instances of prophetic hyperbole, a rhetorical ploy according to which God's spokesperson insists that divine patience has come to an end even though, inevitably, God turns out to be more merciful than anyone had a right to expect (something like this also seems to inform Paul's seemingly absolute but inevitably revocable rejections of Israel in Acts 13:46–47; 18:6; 28:25–28). In any case, this much is clear: the readers of Hebrews are expected to recognize that "it is a fearful thing to fall into the hands of the living God" (10:31; cf. 12:29); they are to consider what Jesus Christ has done for them and ask, "How can we escape if we neglect so great a salvation?" (2:3).

Conclusion

We have noted a few problems that Christian readers have had with the Letter to the Hebrews over the years. The book was slow to be accepted into the canon, in part because it was anonymous. It has not always been appreciated at a popular level because of its intellectual cast and seemingly arcane subject matter. Its threats of condemnation regarding apostasy seem to go too far, denouncing the backslidden in a way that rules out any possibility of their recovery. To these, we might add a couple more modern concerns: first, a writing dedicated to establishing the superiority of Christianity over Judaism may not sit well with people in an era that emphasizes interreligious tolerance, cooperation, and dialogue; second, recent interpreters have detected some tension between the claim in Hebrews that God's new covenant through Christ has rendered the old covenant with Israel obsolete (8:13) and Paul's insistence that "the gifts and calling of God are irrevocable" (Rom. 11:29). The letter is sometimes thought to support supersessionism—the exaltation of Christians at the expense of Jews, whom God is thought to have rejected.

Still, we may focus on the positive contributions that Hebrews offers the Christian church and individual believers. Above all, its theology has helped

justification by grace: the idea or doctrine that God has acted graciously through Jesus Christ in a manner that allows people to be put right with God through faith.

election: in theology, the notion or doctrine that people may be chosen by God for salvation or some predetermined destiny.

eternal security: the idea or doctrine in some Christian traditions that those who find salvation through Jesus Christ can never lose that salvation.

to define orthodox positions on the identity of Christ and on the meaning of his death and exaltation. Beyond these doctrinal considerations, however, the book has retained a special appeal for Christians who think of themselves as pilgrims dedicated to following Jesus. For many, it becomes a guidebook for a trek that leads them "outside the camp" of social acceptance and respectability (13:13). Ostracized by relatives and neighbors, they find themselves in the midst of a new community composed of historical saints (12:1), incognito angels (13:2), and fellow outcasts (10:32–34). It is a trek marked by struggles and suffering (10:32), but one that is undertaken with joy (10:34; 12:2) and thanksgiving (12:28; 13:15). For those who are convinced that there is "no lasting city" on earth (13:14), no created thing that cannot and will not be shaken (12:26–28), Jesus remains the pioneer whose life, death, and exaltation open a pathway to eternity.

FOR FURTHER READING: Hebrews

Beavis, Mary Ann, and HyeRan Kim-Cragg. *Hebrews*. Wisdom Commentary. Collegeville, MN: Liturgical Press, 2016.

Donelson, Lewis R. *From Hebrews to Revelation: A Theological Introduction*. Louisville: Westminster John Knox, 2001.

Hagner, Donald A. *Encountering the Book of Hebrews*. Grand Rapids: Baker Academic, 2002.

Harrington, Daniel J. *What Are They Saying about the Letter to the Hebrews?* Mahwah, NJ: Paulist Press, 2005.

Isaacs, Marie E. *Reading Hebrews and James: A Literary and Theological Commentary*. Reading the New Testament. Macon, GA: Smyth & Helwys, 2002.

Jobes, Karen. *Letters to the Church: A Survey of Hebrews and the General Epistles*. Grand Rapids: Zondervan, 2011.

Lincoln, Andrew. *Hebrews: A Guide*. New York: T&T Clark, 2006.

Lindars, Barnabas. *The Theology of the Letter to the Hebrews*. New Testament Theology. Cambridge: Cambridge University Press, 1991.

Long, D. Stephen. *Hebrews: A Theological Commentary*. Belief Series. Louisville: Westminster John Knox, 2011.

Puskas, Charles B. *Hebrews, the General Letters, and Revelation: An Introduction*. Eugene, OR: Cascade, 2016.

Schenck, Kenneth. *Understanding the Book of Hebrews: The Story behind the Sermon*. Louisville: Westminster John Knox, 2003.

Thompson, James W. *Hebrews*. Paideia. Grand Rapids: Baker Academic, 2008.

Wright, N. T. *Hebrews for Everyone*. 2nd ed. Louisville: Westminster John Knox, 2004.

⊙ Go to www
.IntroducingNT.com
for summaries,
videos, and other
study tools.

25

James

In one of the most famous poems in American literature, "The Road Not Taken," Robert Frost writes of two roads that "diverged in a yellow wood" and reflects on how his choice of the one less traveled made "all the difference" for his subsequent life. This theme of divergent roads also figured in the teaching of Jesus, where the difference is amplified: the well-trodden path often leads to destruction, while the less popular road leads to life (Matt. 7:13–14). An early Christian writing, the *Didache* (ca. 100–120), seized on this theme as its controlling motif: there are two paths (one of life, one of death), and people must choose between them. No one can walk in two different directions at once; likewise, believers should not be "of two minds" with regard to which path they want to follow (*Didache* 2:4; 4:4).

The Letter of James is the biblical book most attentive to this theme: it presents Christianity as a way of life (not just a system of beliefs), and it warns Christians against the danger of being "double-minded" (1:8; 4:8), of trying to maintain simultaneous friendships with God and with the world (4:4). Though it is unmistakably Christian, the book has a very Jewish feel to it. Jesus is mentioned by name only twice (1:1; 2:1; cf. 5:7–8), and there are no references to the saving effects of his death and resurrection or to the gift and work of God's Holy Spirit. Instead, there are a lot of "dos and don'ts" (59 imperative verbs in just 108 verses). The book provides a guidebook for following the path to life (1:12) and avoiding the way that leads to death (5:19–20), and in so doing it offers something more: a fundamental consideration of the nature of faith (2:17–18, 26) and the character of true religion (1:27).

Overview

The letter opens with a salutation identifying it as correspondence from James to "the twelve tribes in the Dispersion" (1:1). It then offers some quick evangelical counsel or advice on different subjects: trials that test one's faith (1:2–4); divine guidance (1:5–8); the value of poverty and the ephemeral character of riches (1:9–11); resisting temptation (1:12–16); God's generosity (1:17–18); anger (1:19–21); acting on God's word (1:22–25); controlling one's tongue (1:26); and the marks of pure religion (1:27).

The letter then presents a series of short essays on various topics, some of which have already been mentioned. First, James discusses how attitudes and practices that show partiality to the rich violate the royal command, "You shall love your neighbor as yourself" (2:1–13). Next, he maintains that faith must be revealed or demonstrated in action, for "faith without works is dead" (2:14–26). He issues a warning to those who aspire to be teachers (3:1), which leads to a homily on the power of speech and the need for all people to control what they say (3:2–12). He then reflects on two types of wisdom—that which is of God and that which is of the world—and calls his readers to repent of being double-minded with regard to these incompatible philosophies (3:13–4:10).

⊙ EXPLORE 25.0
James: Outline of Contents

⊙ EXPLORE 25.13
Was James the Son of Joseph and Mary?

The letter concludes with another series of evangelical counsels on various topics: speaking evil against one's neighbor (4:11–12); the arrogance of human planning (4:13–16); sins of omission (4:17); condemnation of the wealthy

---

Box 25.1

James and Other Brothers of Jesus

The Synoptic Gospels report that Jesus had four brothers—James, Joses, Judas, and Simon—plus an unknown number of sisters whose names are also unknown (Mark 6:3). Since James is listed first, he is often thought to be the oldest of these brothers, although perhaps he is listed first simply because he was the one who became best known.

The Gospels indicate that the brothers of Jesus did not "believe in him" during the time of his ministry (John 7:5). At one point they attempt to seize him and take him home for a forced retirement from doing and saying things that are leading people to think he is "beside himself" (Mark 3:21, 31–35). The Gospel of John even presents Jesus on the cross choosing one of his disciples to care for his mother after his death, which seems like an affront to James and his other brothers (John 19:25–27).

After Easter, things changed. Paul mentions in 1 Corinthians that the risen Jesus appeared to James (1 Cor. 15:7). The book of Acts indicates that the brothers of Jesus (all of them?) were part of the early church in Jerusalem (Acts 1:14) and, apparently, were present for the great event on the day of Pentecost (Acts 2:1–4). A short while later, James appears to be the leader of the church in Jerusalem (Acts 12:17; 21:18). He presides over the apostolic council described in Acts 15 and offers a final authoritative ruling that he expects to be disseminated and accepted by Christians everywhere (Acts 15:19–29; 21:25).

James's importance as a leader in the church is also acknowledged by Paul in Galatians, albeit somewhat grudgingly (Gal. 1:19; 2:6, 9). Paul disagreed sharply with James's policies regarding the continued relevance of certain markers of Jewish identity within the Christian community (Gal. 2:11–14). Still, he devoted a considerable portion of his ministry to supervising a collection for Christians in Jerusalem, where James was the recognized leader (Rom. 15:25–29; 2 Cor. 8–9).

(5:1–6); patience and endurance (5:7–11); swearing oaths (5:12); prayer and healing (5:13–18); and restoration of backslidden sinners (5:19–20).

Historical Background

The first verse of this letter says that it is written by "James, a servant of God and of the Lord Jesus Christ," and directed to "the twelve tribes in the Dispersion." Accordingly, the letter is traditionally attributed to Jesus's brother James, who became the leader of the church in Jerusalem. This individual is known to us from the Gospel stories, the book of Acts, and occasional references in Paul's letters. He is sometimes called "James of Jerusalem" or "James the Just" (a nickname that was widely used for him in early Christianity, at least as early as the second century). The view that James wrote this letter and sent it to Christians who lived outside Palestine ("in the Dispersion") is still widely held by many Christians and scholars today, but it was questioned in the early church and has continued to be debated throughout history.

The letter may, in any case, be linked to three major strands or traditions that seem to have influenced its ideas and literary style.

The Jewish historian Josephus reports that James was murdered in 62 (see *Jewish Antiquities* 20.199–201). During an interim between on-site Roman rulers (when "Festus was dead and Albinus was still on the way"), the high priest Ananus II seized the opportunity to move against those whom he considered to be "lawbreakers." He convened the judges of the Sanhedrin and delivered James and certain others to be stoned. Josephus notes that "the inhabitants of the city who were considered to be the most fair-minded and who were strict in their observance of the law were offended at this." Furthermore, Josephus maintains that the action was judged to be illegal, and Ananus II subsequently was deposed by the new procurator on this account. A later Christian tradition, reported by Clement of Alexandria (third century), says that James was killed by being thrown off the pinnacle of the temple, but this account is generally regarded as legendary.

Other traditions about James emphasize his traditional Jewish piety and his devotion to the law. Eusebius (fourth century) reports that he received his nickname "the Just" because he lived as a Nazirite, an ascetic who was especially devoted to God. Another oft-repeated tradition (reported by Eusebius) holds that James spent so much time praying in the temple that his knees became as calloused as those of a camel.

The apocryphal *Gospel of Thomas* (first or second century) contains an overwhelmingly positive affirmation of James. In one curious passage, Jesus's disciples ask him who their leader will be after he departs; he answers, "You are to go to James the Just, for whose sake heaven and earth came into being" (*Gospel of Thomas* 12).

We have only a little information about the other brothers of Jesus. Paul refers to them as Christian missionaries, noting specifically that (unlike him) they were married and often accompanied by their wives (1 Cor. 9:5). Judas (= Jude) is the putative author of another New Testament letter.

Jerome on the Authorship of James

Jerome, the fourth-century scholar responsible for producing the Vulgate (a Latin translation of the Bible), indicates that the authorship of James was debated in his day, though he did not seem troubled by that fact:

> James, who is called the brother of the Lord . . . wrote a single epistle, which is reckoned among the seven Catholic Epistles and even this is claimed by some to have been published by some one else under his name, and gradually, as time went on, to have gained authority.

Jerome, *Lives of Illustrious Men 2*, in *Nicene and Post-Nicene Fathers*, Series 2, ed. Philip Schaff and Henry Wace (1890–1900; repr., Grand Rapids: Eerdmans, 1979), 3:361.

---

wisdom literature: biblical and other ancient materials that focus on common-sense observations about life; examples include the books of Proverbs, Job, and Ecclesiastes.

Apocrypha: books of the Old Testament whose status as Scripture is disputed by Protestant, Roman Catholic, and Eastern Orthodox Christians.

diatribe: a rhetorical device derived from Greek philosophy in which an author argues with an imaginary opponent by proposing objections and then responding to them.

First, the Letter of James has much in common with Jewish wisdom literature. Some examples of this literature are found in the Old Testament (Proverbs, Ecclesiastes, Job), and a strong overlap of themes can be found between James and these writings. Even closer analogies can be found between James and other examples of Jewish wisdom literature, such as the books of Sirach and Wisdom of Solomon, part of what Protestants term the "Apocrypha" and Roman Catholics call the "deuterocanonical writings" (see "The Effects of Hellenism on the New Testament World" in chap. 2). Like these wisdom writings, James appeals to what is usually called "common sense": he attempts to reason with his readers (2:14; 4:13; 5:1), and he uses secular examples and images drawn from the world at large (e.g., 3:3–4, 11). Thus James maintains that the behavior he advocates is not only what God demands but also the wisest course of action (3:13).

Second, the Letter of James shows many rhetorical and stylistic similarities to Greco-Roman literature, especially those philosophical writings that employ the literary technique called "diatribe." James engages his readers in direct conversation, addressing them as "you," with an occasional switch to "we" for the purpose of contrast (3:1) or to describe universal tendencies (3:3, 9). He makes ample use of rhetorical questions (2:14, 21; 3:13; 4:1–5) and, at times, appears to be dialoguing with an imaginary opponent, refuting claims that such a person might make (1:13; 2:18; 4:13)—a common feature of the diatribe style that was also adopted by Paul in some of his letters.

Third, the Letter of James draws more heavily than any other New Testament letter on sayings of Jesus. There are numerous passages in James that echo words attributed to Jesus in the Synoptic Gospels (particularly sayings contained in the Sermon on the Mount). Scholars who study these parallels generally conclude that James is not quoting directly from the Gospels (the wording is not that precise); rather, he appears to have independent knowledge of many things that Jesus said. It is interesting, however, that the letter never actually tells us that Jesus said these things; instead, the sayings are simply presented as James's own teaching rather than as "Jesus quotes." Why would this be? One possibility is that the author has so integrated the ideas of Jesus

⊘ EXPLORE 25.12
Authorship of James

⊘ EXPLORE 25.4
Parallels between James and Proverbs

into his teaching that he naturally draws on those ideas when offering advice without conscious awareness that he is doing so (cf. Paul's words in Rom. 12:14, which seem to reflect the teaching of Jesus in Matt. 5:44 without explicitly quoting Jesus).

To whom might this letter have been written? James is the first of seven writings in the New Testament that traditionally are called "The General Letters (Epistles)" or "The Catholic Letters (Epistles)" because it has been said that they were addressed to the whole church rather than to specific individuals or congregations (here the word *catholic* simply means "universal" or "general"). Indeed, after the first verse, the "letter" of James does not seem very much like a letter at all. It conveys no personal news and mentions no one by name; it makes no reference to specific situations, past or present;

Box 25.3

James and the Wisdom Tradition

The Letter of James exhibits these common features of wisdom literature.

James Tries to Reason with His Readers

- He uses expressions such as "Come now, you who say . . ." (4:13) and "Come now, you rich people . . ." (5:1).
- His letter is peppered with words such as "because" and "for," which introduce reasons for the points that he is making (1:3, 20, 23; 2:10–11, 13, 26; 3:1–2, 16; 4:14), and words such as "therefore" and "so," which introduce conclusions to be derived from what he has said (1:21; 2:17, 23; 4:12, 17; 5:7, 16).
- Sometimes James asks his readers to consider the benefit or profit of their actions: "What good is it?" (2:14); "What is the good of that?" (2:16; see also 1:16, 20, 26; 2:20, 26; 4:5).

James Uses Secular Images Drawn from the World at Large

- the billowing sea (1:6)
- the scorching sun (1:11)
- a reflection in a mirror (1:23–24)
- a bit in a horse's mouth (3:3)
- a ship's rudder (3:4)
- a forest fire (3:5)
- domestication of animals (3:7)
- a freshwater spring (3:11)
- a fig tree (3:12)
- a grapevine (3:12)
- salt water (3:12)
- a vanishing mist (4:14)
- the rainy seasons for crops (5:7)

In both of these ways, James presents his teaching as "common sense": he is advocating the wisest course of action, as should be obvious from logical reasoning and observation of nature.

there is no hint of the author's particular relationship with the readers or basis for addressing them. And then, when we get to the end, we find that there is not even a formal closing or signature (cf. the ending of 1 John). Accordingly, most interpreters regard James as a general treatise or series of short homilies rather than a letter in the traditional sense. This does not mean, however, that it was simply intended for "all people everywhere" (or even for all Christians everywhere). The author has a "target audience" in mind, and he indicates as much by addressing his work to "the twelve tribes in the Dispersion" (1:1). That designation can be interpreted in different ways (see box 25.4), but consideration of the letter's literary influences discussed above suggests an audience of Christian readers who are appreciative of both the Jewish wisdom traditions and Hellenistic rhetoric.

Beyond this, projections concerning the historical circumstances that gave rise to the letter depend on decisions regarding its author. If the letter is attributed to James of Jerusalem, then he probably sent it to Christians who had been scattered due to persecutions in the area (Acts 8:1; 11:19) or to congregations that had been established by missionaries sent out from Jerusalem. As for the date, such a letter could have been written almost anytime prior to 62, when James was killed, but a date in the mid-50s might make the most sense, given apparent connections to ideas expressed in some of Paul's letters that were written during that period. If the letter is not attributed to James of Jerusalem, the circumstances of its composition become impossible to determine. Scholars who regard the letter as pseudepigraphic usually assume that it was written

⊙ EXPLORE 25.3
Parallels between James and the Sermon on the Mount

Twelve Tribes in the Dispersion

The Letter of James is addressed to "the twelve tribes in the Dispersion." What does that mean? For Christians, these terms had both literal and metaphorical levels of meaning.

	Literal	Metaphorical
Twelve tribes	Jewish descendants of Abraham	Christians, who are the new Israel, under the twelve apostles
Dispersion	Jews who live outside Palestine	Christians who live on earth, apart from their home in heaven

Most scholars think that James uses these words in a way that combines the literal and metaphorical senses. The letter was written not for Jews (the "twelve tribes" in a literal sense) but rather for Christians (2:1). Still, it may have been written for Jewish Christians (i.e., Christians who belong to the literal twelve tribes), or at least for Christians who have a strong appreciation of their Jewish heritage. And as for the Dispersion, even if the letter can be read as speaking generically to Christians who live anywhere on earth (in a diaspora from heaven), its original application may have been for Christians who lived outside Palestine, where the Jesus movement had begun.

Fig. 25.1. The mirror analogy. This bas-relief panel from a second-century grave monument displays a woman fixing her hair with the aid of an ancient mirror (probably a sheet of polished bronze). James says that people who are "hearers of the word and not doers" are like those who look into a mirror and then forget what they were like (1:23–24). The point seems to be that a mirror reveals one's appearance while one is actually looking into it; likewise, James says, the Scripture speaks to some people only while they are actually reading (or hearing) it. Believers should not use the Bible in such a cavalier way but rather should allow its words to shape their lives and conduct at all times. (The Bridgeman Art Library International)

a few decades after James's death, possibly in the period of 80–100, but they admit that all of this is uncertain.

The purpose of the letter is to offer evangelical counsel and pastoral exhortation to believers who might be tempted to compromise their faith through devotion to the world.

pastoral exhortation: advice motivated by concern for the physical, emotional, and spiritual well-being of persons for whom one feels responsible.

Major Themes in James

Trials and Temptations

The Letter of James opens with a declaration that the readers should "consider it nothing but joy" when they face trials of any kind, since the testing

Propositions about God in the Letter of James

The Letter of James is primarily concerned with ethical teaching, but the principles that it espouses do assume a generic theological foundation. Thus the letter also offers several propositions about God's nature and character:

- God gives to all, "generously and ungrudgingly" (1:5).
- God has promised "a crown of life" to those who love God (1:12).
- God cannot be tempted by evil, and God tempts no one (1:13).
- God is "the Father of lights, with whom there is no variation or shadow" (1:17).
- God created us by "the word of truth" (1:18).
- God favors the poor (2:5).
- God is one (2:19).
- God is the "Lord and Father" and has made humans in the likeness of God (3:9).
- God answers the prayers of the righteous (4:2–3; 5:16–18).
- God yearns jealously for our spiritual devotion (4:5).
- God "opposes the proud, but gives grace to the humble" (4:6, 10).
- God draws near to those who draw near to God (4:8).
- God is both lawgiver and judge, able to save and destroy (4:12).
- God's will trumps all human plans (4:13–15).
- God hears the cries of the exploited and oppressed (5:4).
- God is compassionate and merciful to the patient (5:11).
- God heals the sick and forgives sins (5:15).

It is often noted that although all of these points are important for Christians, they are not specifically Christian declarations. These things would also be confessed by Jews (and, for that matter, by deists, Muslims, and adherents of other religions).

As for Jesus Christ, this letter tells us only that he is our "glorious Lord" (2:1; cf. 1:1) and that his coming (as judge) is near (5:7–9).

---

beatitude: any statement of divine blessing (though the term has come to be associated more specifically with the blessings offered by Jesus in Matt. 5:3–12 and Luke 6:20–23).

of their faith helps them to mature (1:2–4). A few verses later, the letter pronounces a beatitude on any who endure temptation, promising to them the "crown of life" (1:12). These thoughts are related: in the Greek text, the same word (*peirasmos*) is used for what the NRSV translates as "trials" in 1:2 and "temptation" in 1:12. Thus James promotes the common idea that the testing of faith is ultimately beneficial to believers, but he develops that concept as applying specifically to the sort of testing that comes from resisting temptation to sin. Most writings that deal with the testing of faith focus on external trials, such as the hardships of life and, especially, the persecutions that come as a result of faith (see Rom. 5:3–4; Heb. 12:3–12; 1 Pet. 1:6–7). James would grant the benefit of those things also—"trials of any kind" (1:2; cf. 5:10–11)—but he seems especially focused on the tests to faith that come from within.

James emphasizes that God is not the source of any temptation to sin (1:13; cf. Sir. 15:11–13). The culprit, rather, is "one's own desire" (1:14)—the human heart, which is enticed by pleasure (4:1–3) and selfish ambition (3:14, 16). Nevertheless, the person who is tempted to sin should view that temptation as a test: yielding to temptation gives birth to sin, which, when fully grown, gives birth to death (1:15). But those who submit to God (4:7) and purify their hearts (4:8) make the joyful discovery that the devil flees from those who resist him (4:7) and that God draws near to those who draw near to God (4:8). In this way, temptation to sin, though it does not come from God, may become a trial that, like other trials, helps believers toward their goal of being "mature and complete, lacking in nothing" (1:4).

Wisdom from Above

The wisdom tradition in Jewish literature is often contrasted with the prophetic tradition in that the former deals more with what can be known through reason and observation (what should be apparent to all), whereas the latter presents revealed truth ("Thus says the LORD . . ."). Such a distinction, however, is somewhat simplistic.

Fig. 25.2. Divine wisdom. Jesus is depicted here as "the embodiment of Divine Wisdom." The artist, Sophie Hacker, explains, "The face is geometrically proportionate (a 'divine circle'); the nose is seen as the root of wisdom and is elongated accordingly." (The Bridgeman Art Library International)

The Letter of James, which has much in common with the Jewish wisdom tradition, is specifically interested in "wisdom from above" (3:17)—that is, wisdom that must be given by God (1:5). Such wisdom often is compatible with what should be generally apparent (since God is the source of all truth), but it also transcends and even contradicts conventional ways of thinking, which are driven by envy and selfish ambition and should be dismissed as "earthly, unspiritual, devilish" (3:15).

The content of the wisdom from above is primarily ethical: how people ought to live in relation to God and to one another. Such wisdom favors humility (1:9; 4:10), meekness (1:21), mercy (2:13), gentleness (3:13), peace (3:18), and patience (5:7–8, 10) while decrying envy, selfish ambition, and boasting (3:14–16). It promotes endurance in trials (1:3–4; 5:11) and moral fortitude in the face of temptation (1:12–16). It involves controlling one's tongue (1:26; 3:5–10) and being quick to listen, slow to speak, and slow to anger (1:19), as opposed to cursing those made in God's likeness (3:9–10) and grumbling or speaking evil against one another (4:11; 5:9). God wants people to love their neighbors (2:8), to care for orphans and widows (1:27), to clothe the naked and feed the hungry (2:14–15), and to avoid both the lure of wealth (1:9–11) and the tendency to show favoritism to the wealthy (2:1–9). James summarizes the "wisdom from above" in one verse: it is "first pure, then peaceable, gentle, willing to yield, full of mercy and good fruits, without a trace of partiality or hypocrisy" (3:17).

Readers may note that there is nothing here exclusive to Christian teaching; many secular authorities would commend this behavior as well. But James maintains that such a lifestyle requires knowledge of God. For example, people who know that God is generous and just are able to live unselfishly in ways that promote cooperation and peace (3:13–18); people who lack this understanding inevitably buy into the world's system of competition, acquisitiveness, and lust, which ultimately leads to adultery, murder, and war (4:1–4). Thus the

Box 25.6

The Royal Command of Love

The Letter of James does not just contain teaching similar to the sayings of Jesus; it also adopts the hermeneutic of Jesus, maintaining that love is the key to fulfilling God's law and doing God's will.

Jesus said that love for God and love for neighbor are the greatest commandments, the ones on which "all the law and the prophets" depend (Matt. 22:36–40; cf. Mark 12:29–31; Luke 10:25–28). He summarized ethics with what has come to be known as the Golden Rule: "Do to others as you would have them do to you" (Matt. 7:12).

James likewise identifies "You shall love your neighbor as yourself" (Lev. 19:18) as "the royal law" (2:8), "the law of liberty" (1:25; 2:12), and "the perfect law" (1:25). Faced with the prospect of keeping the whole law, with all its various points, believers do well to concentrate on this commandment (2:8–10).

James further interprets this royal law in context. He appears to have examined the Old Testament section in which the command to love one's neighbor appears and incorporated more of what that part of the Bible says into his moral exhortations:

- Leviticus 19:12 forbids swearing false oaths (cf. James 5:12).
- Leviticus 19:13 forbids withholding wages from laborers (cf. James 5:4).
- Leviticus 19:15 forbids showing partiality to the rich (cf. James 2:1–12).
- Leviticus 19:16 forbids slander and evil talk (cf. James 4:11–12).
- Leviticus 19:17 commends reproof as a way to reconciliation (cf. James 5:20).
- Leviticus 19:18a discourages vengeance and grudge-holding (cf. James 5:9).
- Leviticus 19:18b says to love neighbor as self (cf. James 2:8).

See Luke Timothy Johnson, *Brother of Jesus, Friend of God: Studies in the Letter of James* (Grand Rapids: Eerdmans, 2004), 123–35.

wisdom from above is a philosophy based on friendship with God, and, conversely, friendship with the world is enmity with God (4:4). The real problem for believers is what James calls "double-mindedness" (1:8; 4:8; cf. Sir. 1:28): people try to retain friendship both with God and with the world, embracing the generosity of God while at the same time striving to fulfill self-interests. Such double-mindedness involves halfhearted commitment and compromise unbecoming of those who are truly wise and understanding (3:13).

Faith and Works

The most renowned section of the Letter of James is the one in which the author addresses anyone who might say, "I have faith but not works" (see 2:14). He responds by insisting that faith without works is dead (2:17, 26) and, indeed, by declaring that "a person is justified by works and not by faith alone" (2:24). This seems to be a direct contradiction to the teaching of Paul that "a person is justified by faith apart from works prescribed by the law" (Rom. 3:28; cf. Gal. 2:16). James even seizes on a key biblical passage that Paul employed to make his point and interprets it in a way that makes the opposite point. Paul says that Abraham was justified by faith and not by works because he "believed God, and it was reckoned to him as righteousness" (Rom. 4:3; Gal. 3:6; cf. Gen. 15:6). James points out that Abraham not only believed God but also acted on that belief by offering his son Isaac. Thus Abraham was justified not by faith alone but rather by faith "brought to completion by the works" (James 2:22; cf. 2:24).

Most theologians agree that there is no real argument here. Paul and James appear to be talking past each other, using words such as "justification," "works," and "faith" to mean different things. For instance, James wants to insist on the necessity of "good works" or acts of obedience to God; Paul is concerned with establishing the nonnecessity of "works prescribed by the law," by which many scholars think he means circumcision and other ritual requirements that grant Jews a privileged position. More to the point, James seems to think of faith as mere intellectual assent, the act of knowing or believing certain things to be true (see James 2:19). For Paul, faith is a radical orientation toward God that transforms one's entire being and produces a "new creation" (2 Cor. 5:17). The notion of faith that does not affect one's actions (or lifestyle) would be literally unthinkable for Paul; he would not dignify such a phenomenon by calling it "faith."

It is true that many interpreters throughout history (famously, Martin Luther) have thought that James and Paul disagreed with each other on this fundamental point. Today, it is generally recognized that many things in Paul's letters indicate that he would agree with the point that James is trying to make (though he might have worded it differently). Paul's concept of "faith working through love" (Gal. 5:6) is not much different from James's notion of faith "brought to completion" by works (James 2:22). Paul's insistence that faith without love is

Fig. 25.3. Resist the devil. James offers a simple prescription for facing trials and temptations: "Resist the devil and he will flee from you. Draw near to God, and he will draw near to you" (4:7–8). (Bridgeman Images)

nothing (1 Cor. 13:2) is not much different from James's claim that faith without works is dead (James 2:26). And Paul's assertion that "it is not the hearers of the law who are righteous in God's sight, but the doers of the law who will be justified" (Rom. 2:13) concurs well with James's call for believers to be "doers of the word, and not merely hearers" (James 1:22; cf. 1:23, 25; 4:11).

Given the foregoing comparison, James is now thought to be responding not to Paul but, more likely, to a misunderstanding of Paul. It could be that James himself has misunderstood Paul and is trying to counter what he thinks that Paul is teaching. Or, since he does not mention Paul by name, it could be that he is responding to others who are using Paul's ideas or slogans in ways that Paul himself would not have intended. Or he might be contending against an imaginary opponent, indicating what he would say to some hypothetical person who claimed to have saving faith without works (2:14) (compare Paul's hypothetical response to an outlandish position in Rom. 6:1–4).

In any case, James's words should be read on their own terms and not simply evaluated in terms of their compatibility with the words of Paul or other teachers. What James wants to promote is consistency of belief and action or, indeed, of speech (verbal confession) and conduct. Christians are to practice what they preach (cf. Matt. 23:2–3), and they need to think through the implications of their faith commitments for every aspect of their lives in this world. This would be a significant point even if James were simply focused on the relationship of individual faith to personal conduct. In truth, however, he seems to have moved already to another plane, to a consideration of what the faith of the entire community has to say about its social responsibilities in the world at large (cf. Matt. 5:13–14).

Rich and Poor

The Letter of James evinces the twin themes of "concern for the poor" and "hostility toward the rich." Indeed, these themes are emphasized more in James than in any other writings of the New Testament except for Luke and Acts, books written by someone who had a high opinion of the man James and of the church that he led in Jerusalem. Like those writings, the Letter of James denounces wealthy persons who attain or preserve their position at the expense of others. Rich landholders drag debtors into court and confiscate their property or force them into slavery (2:6). Rich employers exploit their laborers, defrauding them of wages by either not paying them at all or not paying them what is fair (5:4). These fools live in luxury and pleasure without taking into account the terrible judgment of God: no one wants to be the plumpest calf in the stall when the butcher arrives. So James calls out with ironic delight, "Come now, you rich people, weep and wail for the miseries that are coming to you. . . . You have fattened your hearts in a day of slaughter" (5:1, 5). In passages such as this, the Letter of James has less in common with the Jewish wisdom tradition than with prophetic writings of the Old Testament (cf. Isa. 3:11–15; 5:8–10; 9:18–10:4; Amos 2:6–7; 5:11–12; 6:4–6; 8:5–6; Mic. 2:1–5).

The treatment of this theme, however, goes beyond condemnation of easy targets (a corrupt and uncaring upper class that oppresses the poor without mercy). James also upbraids Christian congregations that show partiality or favoritism to wealthy persons (2:1–4). Some rich people, then, are religious individuals who participate in the Christian assemblies. In this regard, James has a few more things to say:

- Riches do not last, and the rich will not be rich forever (1:9–11; 4:13–14).
- Pure and undefiled religion involves caring for widows and orphans and keeping oneself unstained by the world (1:27).
- God has "chosen the poor in this world to be rich in faith and to be heirs of the kingdom" (2:5).

What, then, should rich Christians do? They should boast in "being brought low" (1:10)—that is, take pride in losing their status as "rich people" and in becoming people of humble means and lowly circumstances. Simply put, they should give

Fig. 25.4. Friend to the poor. This Byzantine mosaic from the twelfth century portrays Jesus healing the poor, the crippled, and the blind. In the Letter of James, helping the poor is a mark of "pure religion" (1:27–2:5). (The Bridgeman Art Library International)

away their money, use it to care for the needy and to serve God rather than spend it on fine clothing or gold rings (2:2) or hoard it for an uncertain future. They should also reevaluate their priorities so that their life plans are concerned not with how to make money but instead with how to fulfill the will of God (4:13–15).

James's attitude toward the rich is in keeping with the overall perspective of his letter. First, the rich believers may be understood as a prime example of those who are double-minded: they are trying to be a part of God's community, but they still cling to the value system of the world. Second, James's expectation of the rich is simply that they obey the royal commandment, "You shall love your neighbor as yourself," the law by which they will be judged (2:8, 12; cf. 1:25). What does this commandment mean for people who have more than they need, when others have less? For James, the answer is obvious.

Finally, let's return briefly to the thought that God "has chosen the poor in the world to be rich in faith and to be heirs of the kingdom" (2:5). James goes beyond calling the rich to repentance and divestment; he declares that God has a preference for the poor, both in this life and the next. This means, at least, that God takes the side of the poor because God is kind and helps those in need, and

Box 25.7

Rich and Poor in James

The Poor

- the lowly (1:9)
- orphans and widows (1:27)
- persons dressed in dirty clothes or naked (2:2, 15)
- those who lack daily food (2:15)
- day laborers defrauded of wages (5:4)
- dishonored by those who show partiality (2:3–4, 6, 9)
- will be raised up (1:9)
- focus of concern for pure and undefiled religion (1:27)
- bodily needs will be met by believers whose faith is not dead (2:14–17)
- chosen by God to be rich in faith (2:5)
- heirs of the kingdom promised to those who love God (2:5)
- cries have reached the ears of the Lord of hosts (5:4)

The Rich

- persons with gold rings and fine clothes (2:2)
- receive preferred treatment even in the church (2:3)

- live in luxury and pleasure (5:5)
- plan for a year how to do business and make money (4:13)
- oppress others and drag them into court (2:6)
- blaspheme the name of Christ (2:7)
- defraud workers of fair wages (5:4)
- condemn and murder the righteous, who do not resist (5:6)
- will disappear like a flower in the field (1:10)
- a mist that appears for a while and then vanishes (4:14)
- should boast in being brought low (1:10)
- should weep and wail for the miseries coming to them (5:1)
- riches will rot and clothes will be moth-eaten (5:2)
- gold and silver will rust and eat their flesh like fire (5:3)
- have fattened their hearts in a day of slaughter (5:5)

because God is just and defends those who are oppressed. Beyond this, it also seems to imply that the poor are intrinsically more godly, more likely to have a spirit that responds to God with the love and devotion that God both desires and rewards (4:5; cf. 1:12; 2:5). This could be because the poor are less likely to be "double-minded" (1:8; 4:8), stained by the world (1:27), or distracted by material concerns (4:2–4, 13–15). Or it may simply be that God gives the poor an added measure of faith, blessing them with a generous spiritual gift more precious than any worldly object of desire (cf. 1:17; 4:3).

Conclusion

Both the Letter of James and its titular author have had a tough time earning respect in Christian history. There has been little outright hostility; more often, they have faced the ignominy of "faint praise": the man James is an "acknowledged" pillar of the church, though that does not necessarily mean anything to God (so Paul,

Abraham Lincoln's Second Inaugural Address

President Abraham Lincoln alluded to James 1:27 in what could be his second-most-famous speech (after that little address at Gettysburg):

> With malice toward none, with charity for all, with firmness in the right as God gives us to see the right, let us strive on to finish the work we are in, to bind up the nation's wounds, to care for him who shall have borne the battle and for his widow and his orphan, to do all which may achieve and cherish a just and lasting peace among ourselves and with all nations.

He and the nation were specifically mindful of the widows and orphans of fallen Civil War soldiers.

The full verse in James reads, "Religion that is pure and undefiled before God, the Father, is this: to care for orphans and widows in their distress, and to keep oneself unstained by the world."

Social Gospel movement: a movement among American Protestant Christians claiming that the gospel of Jesus Christ necessitates work in the area of social reform, particularly with regard to living conditions among the urban working class.

liberation theology: a movement in Christian theology, developed mainly by twentieth-century Latin American Roman Catholics, that emphasizes liberation from oppression.

in Gal. 2:6, 9); his letter contains many good things, provided one is looking for "straw" rather than gold (so Martin Luther). How would James have responded to such assessments? Perhaps he would have considered it a joy to suffer affronts sure to produce endurance and train him in humility (1:2–4; 4:6; 5:11).

In any case, the Letter of James has come to the fore now and then in Christian history, being given pride of place in, for instance, the "Social Gospel" movement of the nineteenth and early twentieth centuries and among liberation theologians in the twentieth. It may be largely because of James that many theologians now speak not only of orthodoxy ("right thinking" or "correct doctrine") but also of orthopraxis ("right practice" or "correct behavior"), and specifically of the orthopraxis of the church as a whole in a way that transcends concerns for personal morality. It is also largely due to James that many theologians now speak of "God's preferential option for the poor" and discuss the accompanying motif of faith being expressed through social (and sometimes, political) action. The Letter of James has also been prized by various peace movements for its keen insight into the reasons for conflict, war, and strife (3:18–4:3).

The Letter of James has come increasingly to be regarded as a book of the church: it depicts the practical life of a community where people pray for one another and confess their sins to one another (5:16), and where people are committed to social ministry on behalf of those in distress (1:27). It is a community where the suffering and the cheerful gather for prayer and praise, a place where diseases are healed, sins are forgiven, and souls are saved from death (5:15, 20; cf. 1:21). The community is composed of people who love the Lord (1:12; 2:5) and who are committed to loving their neighbors (2:8). But they are also sinners (4:8; 5:16; cf. 1:21; 2:9–10; 3:9–10; 4:4, 17; 5:15, 19–20), people who struggle with temptation (1:12–16) and sometimes yield to partiality (2:1–4, 9), pride (3:14; 4:5–6, 13, 16), and worldly cravings (4:1–3). The whole tone of the letter, therefore, assumes readers who are open to correction, who have God's seed

(>) EXPLORE 25.11
An "Epistle of Straw":
What Martin Luther
Said about James

implanted in them (1:21) but who want to draw closer to God and experience spiritual growth and intimacy (4:5, 8). The letter is written for believers who truly do want to be friends with God (cf. 2:23) but need the sort of evangelical exhortation that the book provides if they are to avoid double-mindedness and overcome the temptation to be friends with the world (4:4, 8).

evangelical: pertaining to or in keeping with the Christian gospel and its teachings.

Finally, the lasting appeal of James may be attributed to its unflinching realism. While espousing the highest of ideals, the book manages to keep its feet on the ground: it urges believers to make every effort to "bridle their tongues" (1:26) while recognizing how terribly difficult this is to do (3:7–8). This is a winsome characteristic of wisdom literature, evident also in the *Didache* (mentioned at the start of this chapter). That book pulls out all the stops to implore Christians to follow the right path in every possible way, and then at one point it simply concludes, "If you can bear the entire yoke of the Lord, you will be perfect; but if you cannot, do as much as you can" (*Didache* 6:2). Likewise, James insists that temptation must be resisted, and he declares that sin leads to death (1:14–15), but he also acknowledges that "all of us make many mistakes" (3:2). So Christians will sin, and they need to confess their sins to one another (5:16) and let their leaders pray for them so that their sins may be forgiven (5:15). We all make many mistakes, but the path that leads to life is not traveled alone (cf. 5:19–20).

FOR FURTHER READING: James

Batten, Alicia J. *What Are They Saying about the Letter of James?* Mahwah, NJ: Paulist Press, 2009.

Chester, Andrew, and Ralph P. Martin. *The Theology of James, Peter, and Jude*. New Testament Theology. Cambridge: Cambridge University Press, 1994.

Donelson, Lewis R. *From Hebrews to Revelation: A Theological Introduction*. Louisville: Westminster John Knox, 2001.

Isaacs, Marie E. *Reading Hebrews and James: A Literary and Theological Commentary*. Reading the New Testament. Macon, GA: Smyth & Helwys, 2002.

Jobes, Karen. *Letters to the Church: A Survey of Hebrews and the General Epistles*. Grand Rapids: Zondervan, 2011.

Johnson, Luke Timothy. *Brother of Jesus, Friend of God: Studies in the Letter of James*. Grand Rapids: Eerdmans, 2004.

Painter, John, and David deSilva. *James and Jude*. Paideia. Grand Rapids: Baker Academic, 2012.

Puskas, Charles B. *Hebrews, the General Letters, and Revelation: An Introduction*. Eugene, OR: Cascade, 2016.

Wright, N. T. *The Early Christian Letters for Everyone: James, Peter, John, and Jude*. 2nd ed. Louisville: Westminster John Knox, 2004.

⊙ Go to www .IntroducingNT.com for summaries, videos, and other study tools.

PETRVS APOSTOLVS

26

1 Peter

The hope of heaven has been a staple in gospel music of all varieties. African American spirituals such as "Swing Low, Sweet Chariot" and "When the Saints Go Marchin' In" focus on the prospect of leaving this world behind for a better life beyond. One of the all-time classics of Southern gospel music is the song "This World Is Not My Home," written in 1946 by J. R. Baxter Jr. and recorded by the Stamps Quartet. In the early 1970s Larry Norman released what is sometimes regarded as the first Christian rock album, a record bearing the provocative title *Only Visiting This Planet*. Fifteen years later the somewhat more secular rock band U2 enjoyed an enormous hit with a gospel-like song called "I Still Haven't Found What I'm Looking For." Its composer, Bono, explained that it was based on his conviction as a Christian that the longings of the human soul can never be satisfied by the pleasures that this earthly world affords.

The common theme in all of these works is not simply that "heaven will be great" but also that Christians who have placed their hope in heaven can never truly be at home on earth. Historically, this perspective has been especially meaningful to Christians beset by troubles and hardships, particularly when those difficulties do not seem to be ameliorated by their faith and may even come as a result of that faith. The letter known as 1 Peter addresses this theme in words that have inspired millions of struggling believers throughout the ages.

Overview

The letter opens with a salutation that identifies the author as "Peter, an apostle of Jesus Christ," and designates the readers as "exiles of the Dispersion" who inhabit five regions of Asia Minor (1:1–2). It continues with an eloquent blessing

⊙ EXPLORE 26.0
1 Peter: Outline of Contents

of God that segues into a call for the readers to rejoice in the salvation that God is providing for them (1:3–9): they have received a new birth and await their glorious inheritance with hope, faith, and love that cannot be tarnished by suffering temporary trials. What prophets predicted is now a reality, announced through the gospel (1:10–12). Therefore, the readers should discipline themselves for lives appropriate to the gospel, lives marked by obedient holiness, reverent fear, mutual love, and continued spiritual growth rather than by the ignorant desires and futile ways of their former lives (1:13–2:3). Their identity as God's chosen people allows them now to be built into a living house for God to inhabit (2:4–10).

The author exhorts the readers as aliens and exiles to abstain from evil and to conduct themselves honorably (2:11–12). They are to honor the emperor, as instituted by God (2:13–17). Further instructions are provided for slaves (2:18–25), wives (3:1–6), and husbands (3:7). In general, they should conduct themselves in ways that do not invite opposition, and they should regard as a blessing any abuse that they suffer for doing good (3:8–17). In this way they follow the example of Christ, whose suffering secured salvation for the baptized and led to a vindication over all angels and spiritual powers (3:18–22). In keeping with this, their intention must be to live in a distinctive way, as stewards of God's grace and gifts, ready to give an account of themselves in the final judgment, which is near (4:1–11).

The next section of the letter seems to recapitulate previous exhortations regarding the proper response to suffering (4:12–19). The readers should not be surprised by the "fiery ordeal" that tests them; indeed, they should rejoice insofar as they share Christ's suffering and suffer in accordance with God's will. Then the author speaks "as an elder" to encourage church leaders to exercise their office responsibly and to urge others to submit to their leadership (5:1–5). He exhorts everyone to humility and steadfastness, and he assures his readers that even though their adversary the devil is on the prowl, God's deliverance is near (5:6–11). The letter closes with greetings and a benediction (5:12–14).

Historical Background

This letter presents itself as being written by the apostle Peter, one of Jesus's original twelve disciples, who now regards himself as an elder in the church (5:1). He is sending it from Rome (referred to as "Babylon" in 5:13; cf. Rev. 17:1, 5) to Christians in Asia Minor (1:1).

Cephas: an Aramaic word meaning "Rock," the Greek form of which is "Peter"; a nickname given by Jesus to Simon, one of his disciples.

Peter is probably the most celebrated of all Jesus's disciples. Often called "Simon" or "Simon Peter" (but referred to as "Cephas" by Paul), he is always listed first among the twelve (Matt. 10:2; Mark 3:16; Luke 6:14; Acts 1:13). He figures prominently in many Gospel stories (see, e.g., Matt. 14:22–33; Mark

Fig. 26.1. St. Peter. This mosaic of the apostle Peter pronouncing a blessing is found on the crypt of Peter (regarded as his tomb) in St. Peter's Basilica in Rome. (The Bridgeman Art Library International)

14:53–72). Peter is singled out as one who will have a distinctive role in the post-Easter church (Matt. 16:17–19; Luke 22:31–32), and various biblical traditions indicate that the risen Lord appeared privately to him (Luke 24:34; 1 Cor. 15:5; cf. John 21:15–19). Peter plays a leading role in the ministry of the early church described in the book of Acts (see Acts 1–5; 8:14–25; 9:32–11:18; 12:1–19), and he is also mentioned as a missionary and "pillar of the church" in Paul's letters (1 Cor. 9:5; Gal. 2:9). Fairly reliable church tradition indicates that Peter was martyred in Rome under the emperor Nero around 64–68. Not surprisingly, numerous pseudepigraphic works were produced in his name, including a *Gospel of Peter*, an *Acts of Peter*, and an *Apocalypse of Peter*, none of which appear to bear any connection to the actual apostle or to be expressive of his thoughts. Many scholars view the New Testament letter known as 2 Peter as a pseudepigraphic work as well.

authentic: in discussions of authorship, "not pseudepigraphic"—that is, written by the person to whom a work is ascribed.

The Letter of 1 Peter has a greater claim to authenticity. Scholars remain divided over the question of whether it is pseudepigraphic. Many scholars think that this letter might actually have been written by the apostle a few years before his martyrdom; others suspect that it may have come from a circle of Peter's followers who wanted to articulate his ideas with new relevance a decade or two after his death. In either case, the letter is regarded as expressive of a "Petrine perspective" associated with Rome in the last third of the first century.

Ironically, perhaps what is most noteworthy about this "Petrine perspective" is that it seems to lack anything overtly distinctive. The ideology of 1 Peter seems to be generically expressive of "mainstream Christianity," an integrated faith that provides a synthesis of numerous strands of tradition: some elements may derive from the Galilean ministry of Jesus, others from concerns of the Jerusalem church, still others from the theological witness of Paul. Interpreters

---

Martyrdom of Peter

Christian tradition holds that Peter was martyred in Rome under the emperor Nero, that he was put to death by crucifixion, and, specifically, that he was crucified upside down.

The Gospel of John records a prediction by Jesus concerning "the kind of death" by which Peter would glorify God: "When you grow old, you will stretch out your hands, and someone else will fasten a belt around you and take you where you do not wish to go" (21:18–19). The reference to outstretched hands seems like an allusion to crucifixion (though not, actually, to upside-down crucifixion).

Around the year 96, the bishop Clement writes from Rome, "Because of jealousy and envy the greatest and most upright pillars were persecuted, and they struggled in the contest even to death. . . . Peter bore up under hardships not just once or twice, but many times; and having thus borne his witness he went to the place of glory that he deserved" (1 Clement 5:2–4).* About one hundred years later, Tertullian states that Nero was the one responsible for the apostles' deaths (Antidote for the Scorpion's Sting 15). He refers to Rome as a fortunate church "where Peter endures a passion like his Lord's! where Paul wins his crown in a death like John's!" (Prescription against Heretics 36).† The reference to Peter having "a passion like his Lord's" probably refers, again, to crucifixion (Paul's death was like that of John the Baptist, because he was beheaded).

The idea that Peter was crucified upside down actually comes from the apocryphal Acts of Peter, a fanciful second-century work that usually is given little credibility by religious scholars. In this case, however, the work devotes several paragraphs to explaining why Peter was crucified in this manner: Peter himself requested it because it would convey an elaborate and esoteric symbolism likening his death to a birth process, with imagery supposedly recalling Adam. This all seems way too complicated and not at all persuasive—but that simply begs the question of what the author of this work hoped to gain by such far-fetched explanations. Many scholars surmise that the author never would have brought the matter up at all unless there was something that needed to be explained.

Elsewhere, the Roman historian Josephus does note that soldiers sometimes amused themselves by crucifying criminals in different positions as a means of furthering their humiliation. Thus it is possible that the Acts of Peter did not invent this detail about Peter's death but rather tried (somewhat desperately) to supply theological reasons for something that many Christians knew and found traumatic. Thus the upside-down crucifixion of Peter might be regarded as an actual historical event that went unmentioned in earlier sources whose authors hoped that the detail could be forgotten.

*Bart D. Ehrman, The Apostolic Fathers, vol.1, Loeb Classical Library (Cambridge, MA: Harvard University Press, 2003).
†Ante-Nicene Fathers, ed. A. Roberts and J. Donaldson, 10 vols., (1885–96; Repr., Grand Rapids, Eerdmans, 1986–89), 3:260.

have long noted that almost every verse of 1 Peter can be read as a parallel passage to some other New Testament writing (see box 26.2). The letter also seems to draw on numerous liturgical and catechetical materials; it is peppered with snatches of hymns or creeds (1:18–21; 2:21–25; 3:18–22), and it seems to employ homiletic or apologetic conventions that had achieved widespread use (e.g., the discussion in 2:4–10 uses many of the same Scripture texts that feature in Rom. 9:25–33; likewise, 5:5–9 offers a sequence of exhortations similar to James 4:6–10).

As an apostolic missive from Rome, 1 Peter is addressed specifically to "the exiles of the Dispersion in Pontus, Galatia, Cappadocia, Asia, and Bithynia." All of these regions are located in Asia Minor (what now is Turkey; see map 26.1), and they are probably listed in the order in which the letter was delivered to them (carried, apparently, by Silvanus; see 5:12). The Romans did not actually distinguish between "Pontus" and "Bithynia" (having established a single province that incorporated both areas), so the terminology used here perhaps reflects traditional territories rather than the official (imposed) political designations. In any case, 1 Peter appears to have been composed as a "circular letter" intended for multiple congregations (cf. Acts 15:23–29; Col. 4:16).

creeds: confessional statements summarizing key articles of faith.

Dispersion: typically, Jews (including Jewish Christians) living outside Palestine (synonymous with "Diaspora"), but 1 Peter seems to apply the term to gentiles.

⊙ EXPLORE 26.13
Authorship of 1 Peter

Map 26.1. Asia Minor: Provinces addressed in 1 Peter.

Box 26.2

Parallels between 1 Peter and Other New Testament Writings

1:1	Heb. 11:13; James 1:1	2:2–6	Eph. 2:18–22	3:1–6	1 Tim. 2:9–11
1:2	Heb. 12:24	2:5	Rom. 12:1	3:8–9	Rom. 12:16–17
1:3	Eph. 1:3	2:6–8	Rom. 9:32–33	3:9	Luke 6:28; Heb. 12:17
1:3–5	Titus 3:4–7	2:7	Matt. 21:42	3:14	Matt. 5:10
1:4	Matt. 6:20	2:9	Titus 2:14; Rev. 1:6; 5:10	3:18	Rom. 6:10; Eph. 2:18; Heb. 9:28
1:6–7	Rom. 5:3–5; James 1:2–3	2:10	Rom. 9:25		
1:10–12	Eph. 3:2–6	2:11	Heb. 11:13; James 4:1	3:22	Eph. 1:20–22; Col. 2:15
1:12	Matt. 13:17	2:12	Matt. 5:16	4:8	James 5:20
1:14	Rom. 12:2; Eph. 2:2–3	2:13–17	Rom. 13:1–7	4:10–11	Rom. 12:6–7
1:17	Luke 11:2	2:16	Gal. 5:13	4:13	Matt. 5:10
1:20	Eph. 1:4	2:19–20	Luke 6:32–33	4:14	Matt. 5:11; Heb. 13:13
1:22	Rom. 12:9–10	2:24	Rom. 6:2, 11; Heb. 10:10	5:2	Acts 20:28
1:23–2:2	James 1:10–11, 18–22	2:25	Heb. 13:20	5:4	Heb. 13:20
2:1	Eph. 4:25, 31; Titus 3:1; James 1:21	3:1	Eph. 5:22	5:5–9	James 4:6–10

What do we know of the areas to which 1 Peter was sent? Two of the regions are familiar to New Testament students: Galatia is an area to which Paul also wrote a well-known letter; Asia is the province in which Ephesus and Colossae were located. But we know almost nothing about the spread of Christianity into Pontus, Cappadocia, or Bithynia. Curiously, the book of Acts says that the Spirit of Jesus actually prohibited Paul and his company from taking the gospel to Bithynia (Acts 16:7). Still, one way or another the faith spread to these regions, and by the time 1 Peter was written there were churches that had become sufficiently well established to have elders who were paid salaries (see 1 Pet. 5:1–2).

The description of the recipients as "exiles of the Dispersion" is interesting because such language typically was used to describe Jews who lived outside Palestine (in the Diaspora; see "The Effects of Hellenism on the New Testament World" in chap. 2). The Letter of James uses a similar description to refer to Jewish Christians who live outside Palestine (James 1:1; see box 25.4). The recipients of 1 Peter, however, are almost certainly gentile Christians: there are frequent references to their pagan background (1:14, 18; 4:3–4) and a clear assertion that before their conversion they were not God's people (2:10). Interpreters conclude that the Jewish language of exile is being applied to these believers metaphorically (they are in a diaspora from their true home, the promised land of heaven). Other Jewish categories are also applied to them (2:9), and the letter sometimes uses "gentile" in a nonliteral sense to mean "pagan" or "unbeliever" (2:12; 4:3). The Christian readers of 1 Peter may be literal gentiles (in terms of ethnic identification), but apparently they no longer think of themselves as being gentiles; now they see themselves as part of Israel, God's chosen people.

⊙ EXPLORE 26.14
Resident Aliens: A Social Class?

Why would the apostle Peter (or others writing in his name) send a letter from Rome to the gentile believers in these provinces? The main purposes of the letter are clearly stated: to encourage the readers, to testify to them concerning what constitutes "the true grace of God," and to exhort them to stand fast in that grace (5:12). Thus the genre of this letter is often described as parenesis, a type of teaching that seeks to motivate an audience to live in accord with what they already know to be true. But we can go further. One of the more noticeable aspects of 1 Peter is the repeated reference to suffering (1:6, 11; 2:19–21, 23; 3:14, 17–18; 4:1, 13, 15–16, 19; 5:1, 9–10). This, no doubt, indicates why the readers need the motivation that this letter seeks to provide: they are undergoing hard times. Much attention has focused on this element of the letter's context. Scholars have attempted to link the composition of 1 Peter to some known crisis or wave of persecution that affected believers in Asia Minor around

Fig. 26.2. Shepherd of souls. A depiction of Christ from the catacombs in Sousse, Tunisia. In 1 Peter, Christ is presented as "the shepherd and guardian of your souls" (2:25). (Bridgeman Images)

the time this letter was written. In recent years, however, most scholars have become convinced that the variety of suffering being addressed in 1 Peter is social ostracism and general harassment rather than official or government-led persecution of the church. As far as we know, Christians in Asia Minor did not endure state-sponsored persecution until the second century. This letter, furthermore, never mentions persecution per se; rather, it speaks of suffering as a common experience that should be regarded as the expected lot of anyone who is a Christian (4:12), anywhere in the world (5:9).

With regard to date, on the one hand, if this letter actually was written by Peter, it was composed probably in the early to mid-60s, after Peter came to

Rome but before Nero began his violent attacks on believers (given the remarks about the emperor in 2:13–14). Or we might say that it was written after Paul wrote his letter to the Romans (since Paul does not include Peter among the persons whom he greets in the city, Peter probably was not in Rome at the time) but before Paul was brought to Rome under house arrest (since 1 Peter does not mention Paul or provide any update on his situation, Paul probably was not in the city at the time). On the other hand, if 1 Peter is pseudepigraphic, it could have been written almost anytime in the latter three decades of the first century, though a time before 89 may seem more likely (given the remarks in 2:13–14), since that is when Domitian began to vent his hostility toward Christians.

In either case, the letter addresses gentile Christians in Asia Minor who are suffering for their faith. It seeks to provide them with apostolic encouragement from a revered leader, the apostle Peter, who knows a thing or two about suffering (5:1) and who can testify to them about God's grace and exhort them, with integrity, to remain steadfast.

Major Themes in 1 Peter

Suffering Abuse for Christ

Numerous texts in 1 Peter refer to abuse that the readers are suffering. Most of the references seem to imply "verbal abuse": Christians are maligned as though they are evildoers (2:12; cf. 3:16) and reviled for bearing the name of Christ (4:14; cf. 4:16). In a culture that prioritized honor and shame as pivotal social values, such defamation would be experienced as more than mere annoyance: these Christians have experienced a loss of status and social reputation. In some instances, the abuse may also have turned physical, as in the case of

---

Box 26.3

Silvanus and Mark in 1 Peter

Two of Paul's colleagues appear to be associated with the writing of 1 Peter.

- *Silvanus.* The letter from Peter is to be delivered to churches by Silvanus (5:12). This probably is the same Silvanus (= Silas) who, according to the book of Acts, previously was entrusted with delivering a different circular letter following the apostolic council (see Acts 15:22–29). Elsewhere in the New Testament, Silvanus/Silas is closely linked with Paul (Acts 15:40; 17:14–15; 18:5; 2 Cor. 1:19) and is even listed as coauthor of two Pauline letters (1 Thess. 1:1; 2 Thess. 1:1).
- *Mark.* Peter sends greetings to the churches from Mark, who is identified as Peter's "son" (5:13). The latter ascription usually has been taken metaphorically, and this "Mark" traditionally has been identified with John Mark, whose mother knew Peter in Jerusalem (Acts 12:11–12). This Mark, a relative of Barnabas (Col. 4:10), had also been a colleague of Paul for a time, but Paul became dissatisfied with him and replaced him with none other than Silvanus/Silas (see Acts 12:25; 15:37, 39; cf. 2 Tim. 4:11; Philem. 24).

Christian slaves being beaten by their masters for doing what is right in God's eyes (2:19–20). Even apart from such violence, however, social shaming alone could qualify as a "fiery ordeal" (4:12).

The root cause of this abuse seems to be caught up with the letter's identification of its readers as "aliens and exiles" (2:11; cf. 1:1, 17). Their conversion to Christ has led them to cut off ties with former associations, and so they have come to be regarded as social misfits or deviants (4:3–4). They may have been viewed as impious for refusing to give the gods their due, as unpatriotic for neglecting to worship the emperor, and as antisocial for avoiding the various rites and festivities that constituted social life in a pagan world.

By way of advice, 1 Peter makes several points:

- Jesus predicted such suffering for his followers; the readers should neither be surprised by it nor think that they have done anything wrong to bring it upon themselves (4:12; 5:9).

Fig. 26.3. Christ's descent into hell. Two curious passages in 1 Peter speak of Christ preaching to "spirits in prison" and to "the dead" (3:19–20; 4:6). These references gave rise to a Christian tradition that Jesus descended into hell to rescue lost souls. This doctrine is sometimes called "the harrowing of hell." (The Bridgeman Art Library International)

- Such suffering may accord with God's will in that it is allowed by God (3:17), but it does not come from God; it is caused by unrighteous people and by the devil (5:8).
- God cares for those who suffer (5:7) and protects them (1:4–5).
- The time of suffering will be short (1:6; 5:10), for the end of all things is near (4:7; cf. 1:5).
- Those who have caused suffering will be defeated and punished (4:5, 17–18).
- Those who have endured unjust suffering will be blessed and rewarded (1:7, 11, 13; 2:19–20; 3:9, 14; 4:14; 5:4, 10).

Beyond these assurances, the letter encourages the readers to adopt a particular perspective toward their suffering.

First, they should know that trials can be a proving ground for faith, serving to refine it just as precious metals are purified in a hot fire (1:6–7; cf. 4:1). This image for the refinement of faith (or character) was common in Jewish wisdom literature (see Prov. 17:3; Wis. 3:4–6; Sir. 2:5).

Second, and at a deeper level, the readers are urged to understand what is happening to them as sharing in the suffering of Christ (4:13). Throughout the letter Jesus is consistently portrayed as one who suffers (1:11, 19; 2:22–24; 3:18; 4:1), and the Christian who suffers is said to follow in his footsteps (2:21; cf. 3:17–18). This idea is common in Christian writings (cf. Rom. 8:17; Phil. 3:10–11; 2 Tim. 2:11–12). A practical implication is that believers ought to suffer in the same manner that Christ did, thus not seeking retaliation against their foes (2:21–23; 3:9) and totally trusting in God (2:23; cf. 1:13, 21; 2:19).

Finally, 1 Peter also offers readers two practical suggestions that might help to make life more bearable for them:

1. The church should become an alternative community of support, a substitute family termed the "household of God" (4:17; cf. Eph. 2:19; 1 Tim. 3:15). The readers are urged to love and honor one another as a family of believers (2:17; cf. 1:22; 3:8) and to regard all other Christians in the world as their brothers and sisters (5:9).
2. The readers are to behave respectfully in ways that "give the lie" to the false accusations being made against them (2:15–16; cf. 1:15–16). They should be careful not to antagonize the opposition unnecessarily, but they should show by their deeds that their faith is genuine (2:12; 3:12) and be ready to give a defense of the gospel that sustains them when the occasion presents itself (3:15–16). They must show that they are different

wisdom literature: biblical and other ancient materials that focus on common-sense observations about life; examples include the books of Proverbs, Job, and Ecclesiastes.

⊘ EXPLORE 26.15
Honor and Shame in
1 Peter

Fig. 26.4. The sin of personal adornment. The author of 1 Peter warns believers against the sin of personal adornment: hairstyles, fashionable clothing, and jewelry are manifestations of vanity (3:3).

in a positive way, that they not only have given up those aspects of the pagan life that their neighbors still find appealing (4:3–4) but also have rid themselves of vices that are more universally regarded as undesirable (2:1; cf. 3:9). They should concentrate on conducting themselves honorably, so that those who malign them will see their honorable deeds and be put to shame (3:16) or possibly be converted (2:12).

In short, those who suffer abuse because they are Christians should not be intimidated by such harassment (3:14) or consider it a disgrace (4:16). Rather, they should cast their anxiety upon God (5:7), realize that the Spirit of God is with them (4:14), set their hope on what is coming (1:13), and discipline themselves for faithful living in what is currently a dangerous world (5:8).

Christians as the New Israel

In 1 Peter Christians are described with terminology and categories traditionally used for Israel. Gentiles who believe in Jesus are identified as "a chosen race, a royal priesthood, a holy nation, God's own people" (2:9). Christian believers also represent a new temple, a spiritual house for God composed of living stones (individual believers) where sacrifices acceptable to God are offered through Jesus Christ (2:5). The salvation of God promised by Israel's prophets is being received by people who love Jesus and who believe in him (1:8–10). In fact, the Jewish Scriptures were inspired by the Spirit of Christ and written for the benefit of those who believe the Christian gospel (1:11–12).

The author of 1 Peter does not spell out a clear rationale for why Christians are now to be regarded as the new Israel or chosen people of God. The thinking probably is that because Jesus is the Jewish Messiah, people who believe in him and follow him are brought into the special relationship that God has always had with the Jewish people (regardless of ethnic identification). The letter does not speak explicitly of a transfer of privileges (from Jews to Christians) but rather stresses the inclusion of Christians in the blessings of Israel. Many interpreters, however, have thought that such a transfer is implied, and 1 Peter is then read as a key text in support of supersessionism, the doctrine that Christians have replaced or superseded Jews as the chosen people of God.

supersessionism: the idea or teaching that Christians have replaced Jews as the chosen people of God.

Whether or not that is the case, we may at least affirm that the emphasis in 1 Peter is not on demotion of traditional Israel (the fate and destiny of Jews who do not accept Jesus is never mentioned) but instead on the accession of others: the grace (1:10, 13; 4:10; 5:10, 12) and the mercy (1:3; 2:10) of God have made salvation available to all through the death and resurrection of Jesus Christ (1:3, 11; 2:21–24; 3:18, 21). And 1 Peter also wants to emphasize that Christians have inherited the expectations and responsibilities of being God's people along with the privileges: like Israel of old, those who are brought to God through Christ (3:18) are to be holy, for God is holy (1:15–16; cf. Lev. 11:45).

Box 26.4

Images for the Church in 1 Peter

- *the Dispersion*—exiles on earth, separated from the true home in heaven (1:1, 17; 2:11)
- *the new Israel*—a chosen race and a holy nation (2:9; cf. Deut. 7:6; 10:15; Isa. 43:20); God's own people (2:9; cf. Exod. 19:5; Isa. 43:21)
- *a priesthood of all believers*—a holy priesthood (2:5); a royal priesthood (2:9; cf. Exod. 19:6)
- *a living temple*—a spiritual house made of living stones where spiritual sacrifices are offered (2:5; cf. 1 Cor. 3:16)
- *a flock of sheep*—tended by pastors (= shepherds) with Christ as chief shepherd (2:25; 5:3–4; cf. John 10:11; 21:15–19; Acts 20:28; Isa. 40:11; Ezek. 34:12)
- *a woman*—"your sister church in Babylon" (5:13), referring to an individual congregation as a woman (literally, "she who is in Babylon"; cf. 2 John 1)

Finally, we should note that Christians are portrayed not simply as the new Israel in 1 Peter but specifically as the "Dispersion" (1:1)—that is, as Israel-in-exile or as Israel-in-the-Diaspora. This metaphor of dispersion is appropriate because the readers' situation is one of both peril (1:6–7; 2:11–12, 15, 18–20; 3:13–4:6; 4:12–19; 5:8–9) and privilege (1:3–5, 9–12; 1:13–2:10). Christians may be God's elect—chosen, destined, and sanctified (1:2; cf. 2:9)—but they are also exiles (1:1; cf. 1:17; 2:11). At a practical level, the metaphor of dispersion works in two specific ways: (1) a primary danger that the readers face is assimilation to the surrounding culture (the temptation that confronted Israel in the Diaspora); and (2) the return from exile to the homeland (in this case, the Christian pilgrimage from earth to heaven) involves a journey of faith accompanied by many trials (as did that of Israel from Babylon to Palestine).

the elect: those chosen by God, predestined for salvation or some special purpose.

exiles: in Israelite history, the Jewish people who spent fifty years in Babylon after they were deported from their homeland in 587 BCE and before they (or their descendants) were allowed to return in 537 BCE.

Baptism and Spiritual Growth

In 1 Peter baptism is mentioned in connection with the appeal or pledge to God that believers offer and the salvation that they receive through the resurrection of Christ (3:21). Many interpreters have thought that much more of the letter can be related to the general theme of baptism or at least that its contents could be especially meaningful for the newly baptized. The author addresses his readers as persons who have begun a new life (1:3, 23) and acquired a new identity (1:21; 2:10, 25). They are urged to discipline themselves (1:13; 4:7; 5:8) for a way of life appropriate to that identity (1:15; 2:12). They are like newborn infants who have only tasted the Lord's goodness but who will "grow into salvation" if they continue to be nourished with pure spiritual milk (2:2–3; contrast this with 1 Cor. 3:2 and Heb. 5:12–13, where supposedly mature readers are rebuked for being such babies that they still need milk). The readers of 1 Peter are Christians in process, or "under construction," as the metaphor of being built into a not-yet-completed house implies (2:4–5). A key word for such people is "hope" (1:3, 13, 21; 3:15): the readers can look back on a futile and dubious past (1:18; 2:25; 4:3), and they can look forward to an absolutely certain future (1:4–5; 5:10), but the present is a time of "living hope" (1:3). They are already receiving the outcome of their faith (1:9), and this is only the beginning of what God has for them (1:13).

baptism: a religious rite involving symbolic washing with water; it sometimes signifies repentance, purification, or acceptance into the community of God's people.

Submission to Earthly Authorities

In 1 Peter 2:13–3:7 we find a fairly long *Haustafel* ("household table") that may be compared with similar ones elsewhere in the New Testament (Eph. 5:21–6:9; Col. 3:18–4:1; 1 Tim. 2:8–15; 5:1–2; 6:1–2; Titus 2:1–10; see box 17.5). What is particularly striking about this table is its emphasis on submission to non-Christian authorities: the Roman emperor, masters who are not believers,

⊙ EXPLORE 26.12
What John Calvin Said about Women as the "Weaker Sex"

Box 26.5

The Weaker Vessel: Women and Wives in 1 Peter

One passage in 1 Peter instructs men to show consideration to their wives, "paying honor to the woman as the weaker sex" (3:7). Such language may strike modern readers as quaint or ill-advised. Peter's intentions may be noble, but most women do not like being referred to as "the weaker sex." In the ancient world, of course, such inferiority could be, and often was, stated without controversy. Plato declares, "A woman is weaker than a man" (*Republic* 5.455D).*

The expression used in 3:7 literally means "the weaker vessel." The word "vessel" (*skeuos*) comes from pottery (cf. 2 Cor. 4:7; 1 Thess. 4:4). Peter's point seems to be that men and women are like clay jars that hold God's precious gift of life: both are fragile, but the female vessel tends to be even more frail. The only point of comparison seems to be physical strength, since the preceding verses (3:1–2) indicate that wives may be stronger than their husbands in other ways (e.g., spiritually or intellectually or morally). Of course, healthy women sometimes are physically stronger than less-healthy men, but the basic point seems to be that men should typically be courteous and considerate of women with regard to workload and other matters that could strain or damage the physical body.

In a broader sense, the reference may be applied to "social power." Within Roman society, men had certain rights and privileges that women did not. Peter may have been noting that men, who often are physically stronger than women, also possess more power in society. Given this situation (which he neither blesses nor critiques), he urges men to "show consideration" to women and to "honor" them as joint heirs of God's grace. In other words, men are to yield power to women, granting them an equality in Christ that is not recognized by society at large (cf. Gal. 3:28).

*Plato, *The Republic*, trans. Paul Shorey, Loeb Classical Library (Cambridge, MA: Harvard University Press, 1969).

husbands who do not respect their wives' commitment to the Christian faith. A great deal of attention is devoted to exhorting those who lack social power to accept the authority of those who have it (2:13, 18; 3:1); relatively little attention is paid to instructing the persons in authority to exercise their power responsibly (e.g., there are no directions for Christian masters regarding treatment of their slaves; cf. Eph. 6:9; Col. 4:1). This could be partly due to the actual composition of the Christian communities to which the letter is addressed (more slaves than masters, more wives than husbands). It also may be that subservient positions were the ones that the author regarded as most Christlike (2:21–24): slaves and wives get the most attention because they are the ones that all believers should emulate, humbling themselves in selfless service (3:8; 5:2, 6).

Many scholars, however, suggest another explanation for the unbalanced presentation: the author believes that Christians need to demonstrate that their faith is not a threat to the social order. The Christian religion had potential for being perceived as a radically subversive social movement. At the end of the first century, the Greek author Plutarch stated that "a married woman should worship and recognize the gods whom her husband holds dear, and these alone" (*Advice on Marriage* 19); Christian wives would be in defiance of

⊙ EXPLORE 26.5
1 Peter 3:1–7 and Other Household Tables in the New Testament

such conventional wisdom, as would Christian slaves with regard to the gods of their pagan masters. Thus 1 Peter urges believers to show the world that, although there are some matters on which Christians will not compromise, the religion does not as a general rule cause people to become insubordinate, rebellious, or insolent. The letter does not deal with the question of social transformation (creating a society that is more just) but simply offers counsel to believers in circumstances for which the hierarchical arrangement is a given. Nevertheless, many social critics have complained that the stance of 1 Peter encourages accommodation in a way that inevitably favors maintenance of the status quo. In Christian theology, the teaching of 1 Peter on this subject is usually considered alongside other biblical texts that offer alternative perspectives on political and hierarchical power (e.g., Mark 10:42–44; John 15:18–19; Acts 5:29; 1 John 2:15–17; Rev. 13; 17–18).

Conclusion

The letter known as 1 Peter offers us a striking portrayal of the final stage of faith development for one of the most fascinating religious figures in world history. By any account, the man Peter is an amazing figure—an uneducated Galilean fisherman who ended up being revered and honored by millions of people for over two thousand years. He is known to most as "Saint Peter." One of the world's largest and most magnificent churches is named after him (the Basilica of St. Peter in Vatican City, home parish to the pope). He has been memorialized in thousands of sculptures and paintings and stained-glass windows, and even at a crass popular level he is assigned a role in jokes and stories as the man who stands at the "pearly gates," determining who should be admitted to the kingdom of heaven. How did this happen? How did this simple fisherman become such an important person?

One of the more intriguing aspects of Peter's legacy is that even after he had come to be regarded as a hero and martyr, the church preserved traditions that cast him in a less than favorable light. In the Gospel stories, Peter often comes off as an impetuous and overly confident buffoon, as someone who repeatedly gets things wrong. He is the one who tried to walk on water but sank because of fear and doubt (Matt. 14:28–31). He is the one who earned Jesus's most stinging rebuke, "Get behind me, Satan!" (Mark 8:33). And, of course, he is the one who is remembered for denying three times that he even knew who Jesus was (Mark 14:66–72). The letter known as 1 Peter serves as almost irrefutable evidence that this story had a second act. Free of bluster, it offers exactly the sort of sober advice that Peter himself once needed to hear: following Jesus does not guarantee a trouble-free life, and it might even make things worse. Still, fear is not a helpful or necessary response. If Peter himself

⊘ EXPLORE 26.16
1 Peter 2:13–17—
Church and State:
The Ethic of
Subordination

⊘ EXPLORE 1.17
Pliny the Younger on
Persecution of
Christians

Box 26.6

Postscript to 1 Peter: Persecution in Bithynia-Pontus

What became of the Christians to whom 1 Peter was addressed? Around 112, Pliny the Younger, a Roman governor, wrote to the emperor Trajan concerning the status of Christianity in Bithynia-Pontus, two of the areas named in 1 Peter 1:1. Pliny's letter provides information about the churches addressed by 1 Peter a few decades later.

On the one hand, we learn that the church in this region has continued to grow and prosper. Pliny notes that "many persons of every age, every rank, and also of both sexes" were associated with the faith, and he complains that "the contagion of this superstition has spread not only to the cities but also to the villages and farms."

On the other hand, it is clear that the suffering of the believers has also increased, for now they are experiencing deliberate persecution at the instigation of the Roman state. Pliny reports:

> The method I have observed towards those who have been brought before me as Christians is this: I asked them whether they were Christians; if they admitted it . . . I ordered them to be at once punished: for I was persuaded, whatever the nature of their opinions might be, a contumacious and inflexible obstinacy certainly deserved correction. . . .
>
> An anonymous information was laid before me containing a charge against several persons, who upon examination denied they were Christians, or had ever been so. They repeated after me an invocation to the gods, and offered religious rites with wine and incense before your statue . . . and even reviled the name of Christ: whereas there is no forcing, it is said, those who are really Christians into any of these compliances: I thought it proper, therefore, to discharge them.
>
> Some among those who were accused . . . at first confessed themselves Christians, but immediately after denied it; the rest owned indeed that they had been of that number formerly, but had now . . . renounced that error. . . .
>
> After receiving this account, I judged it so much the more necessary to endeavor to extort the real truth, by putting two female slaves to the torture, who were said to officiate in their religious rites: but all I could discover was evidence of an absurd and extravagant superstition.

A. N. Sherwin-White, *The Letters of Pliny* (Oxford: Oxford University Press, 1966).

wrote this letter, then we may surmise that he had learned his lessons well; if the letter is pseudepigraphic, it nevertheless reflects the unanimous opinion of second-generation Christians that Peter's own journey of faith had taken him beyond doubt and denial. Either way, the letter presents Peter as someone who can be regarded as a faithful apostle and elder of the church (1:1; 5:1), having much to offer his younger siblings in the faith (cf. Luke 22:31–32).

FOR FURTHER READING: 1 Peter

Callan, Terrance D., and Duane F. Watson. *First and Second Peter*. Paideia. Grand Rapids: Baker Academic, 2012.

Chester, Andrew, and Ralph P. Martin. *The Theology of James, Peter, and Jude*. New Testament Theology. Cambridge: Cambridge University Press, 1994.

Donelson, Lewis R. *From Hebrews to Revelation: A Theological Introduction*. Louisville: Westminster John Knox, 2001.

González, Catherine Gunsalus. *1 & 2 Peter and Jude: A Theological Commentary*. Belief Series. Louisville: Westminster John Knox, 2014.

Green, Joel B. *1 Peter*. Two Horizons Commentary. Grand Rapids: Eerdmans, 2007.

Harner, Philip B. *What Are They Saying about the Catholic Epistles?* Mahwah, NJ: Paulist Press, 2004.

Jobes, Karen. *Letters to the Church: A Survey of Hebrews and the General Epistles*. Grand Rapids: Zondervan, 2011.

Puskas, Charles B. *Hebrews, the General Letters, and Revelation: An Introduction*. Eugene, OR: Cascade, 2016.

Wright, N. T. *The Early Christian Letters for Everyone: James, Peter, John, and Jude*. 2nd ed. Louisville: Westminster John Knox, 2004.

⊙ Go to www
.IntroducingNT.com
for summaries,
videos, and other
study tools.

27

2 Peter

Plagiarism is taken very seriously nowadays. Any student who copies large segments of someone else's work and presents it as his or her own is likely to suffer harsh penalties. In the ancient world, however, the standards were different. One of the most interesting aspects of the New Testament letter known as 2 Peter is that it borrows heavily from another New Testament letter, the one attributed to Jude, a brother of Jesus. By most estimates, about nineteen of Jude's twenty-five verses have been reworked to reappear somewhere in 2 Peter (see box 27.1). This was, of course, noticed in ancient times, although back then most authorities thought that Jude had borrowed from 2 Peter instead of the other way around. Either way, it doesn't appear to have bothered anyone. Imitation may truly have been regarded as the sincerest form of flattery.

Students who want to understand the New Testament writings in terms of their historical sequence might prefer to read the chapter on Jude prior to reading this one. It is not necessary to do this, however, for the original readers of 2 Peter probably would not have known the Letter of Jude or been aware that the author of the work that they were reading had borrowed so freely from an earlier composition.

Overview

The Letter of 2 Peter opens with a traditional salutation and blessing, identifying it as a message from the apostle "Simeon Peter" to all believers who share his faith (1:1–2). The author declares that God has provided believers with everything necessary for a godly life, and he exhorts them to capitalize on this in fruitful ways that will confirm their election (1:3–11). His own death is near, and he is writing to them so that, after he is gone, they will be able to recall those things that they know now to be true (1:12–15). He was a witness to the transfiguration of Jesus,

> ⊙ **EXPLORE 27.0**
> 2 Peter: Outline of
> Contents

497

Box 27.1

Parallels between Jude and 2 Peter

Jude		2 Peter	
v. 4	stole into the community	2:1	bring in opinions secretly
v. 4	long ago designated for condemnation	2:3	condemnation pronounced long ago
v. 4	pervert the grace of God	2:2	way of truth is maligned
v. 4	licentiousness	2:2	licentious ways
v. 4	deny our Master	2:1	even deny the Master
v. 6	angels kept in chains in deepest darkness for judgment	2:4	angels kept in chains in deepest darkness until judgment
v. 7	Sodom and Gomorrah serve as an example	2:6	Sodom and Gomorrah made an example
v. 7	unnatural lust	2:10	depraved lust
v. 8	defile the flesh, reject authority, and slander the glorious ones	2:10	indulge their flesh, despise authority, and slander the glorious ones
v. 9	archangel did not bring a condemnation of slander	2:11	angels do not bring a slanderous judgment
v. 10	slander what they do not understand	2:12	slander what they do not understand
v. 10	like irrational animals, live by instinct, and are destroyed	2:12	like irrational animals, creatures of instinct, will be destroyed
v. 11	"Woe to them!"	2:14	"Accursed children!"
v. 11	abandon themselves to Balaam's error	2:15	follow the way of Balaam
v. 11	error for the sake of gain	2:15	wages of doing wrong
v. 12	blemishes on your love-feasts	2:13	blemishes (at your feasts)
v. 12	feast with you without fear	2:13	revel while they feast with you
v. 12	waterless clouds	2:17	waterless springs
v. 12	clouds carried along by the winds	2:17	mists driven by a storm
v. 13	deepest darkness reserved for them	2:17	deepest darkness reserved for them
v. 16	bombastic, flatter people	2:18	bombastic, entice people
v. 17	remember predictions of apostles	3:2	remember commandments spoken through apostles
v. 18	in the last time, scoffers will come, indulging their own lusts	3:3	in the last days, scoffers will come, indulging their own lusts

which confirms the truth of Christ's power and coming, to which Spirit-inspired prophecies also attest (1:16–21). The author then announces that false teachers will arise in the church, marked by both "destructive opinions" and "licentious ways" (2:1–3a). He provides a brief history of God's judgment on the wicked to make clear that these false teachers will also be condemned (2:3b–10a). Then he launches a blistering attack on the teachers, describing them as greedy, immoral reprobates who promise freedom but deliver slavery (2:10b–22). The author says that he is writing to remind the readers to hold fast to the tradition delivered to them by prophets and apostles (3:1–2). Next, he turns his attention to the second coming of Jesus, dispelling arguments that scoffers use to reject its relevance (3:3–9) and exhorting the readers to live in anticipation of the fiery judgment and glorious salvation that it will bring (3:10–13). The letter concludes with a few final exhortations and a doxology to Jesus Christ (3:14–18).

Historical Background

The New Testament letter known as 2 Peter leaves no doubt that it is to be read as correspondence from the apostle Peter (see 1:1, 16–18), but a majority of New Testament scholars think that the book is pseudepigraphic, written quite some time after Peter's death. In fact, many scholars who are reluctant to grant that any other writing of the New Testament might be pseudepigraphic make an exception in the case of this one book.

There are at least three reasons for this. First, the arguments in favor of pseudepigraphy seem to be exceptionally strong (see box 27.2). Second, attribution of this letter to the apostle Peter does not have the support of church tradition (the letter is not even mentioned in writings of the Western church until the third century, and even then it is referred to as a "disputed writing"). Third, many Christians have less trouble accepting this letter as pseudepigraphic because of the type of work that it appears to be: most scholars think that this letter employs an ancient genre of literature called "testament."

What was a "testament"? Basically, a testament presented the final words of some heroic figure as a deathbed soliloquy that provided insight on matters of contemporary relevance. These books were always pseudepigraphic, and they were popular not because readers thought that someone had actually discovered a long-lost message from a figure of the past but because sometimes the works really did seem to capture the essence of what the heroic individual stood for and to express what he or she might have wanted to say to the current generation. We have copies of numerous testaments, including the *Testament of Moses*, the *Testament of Job*, the *Testaments of the Three Patriarchs* (Abraham, Isaac, Jacob), the *Testaments of the Twelve Patriarchs* (the twelve sons of Jacob), and many more. Such books were read widely by Jews in the Second Temple period and by both Jews and Christians in the first two centuries of the Christian era. Scholars have observed that 2 Peter contains the key elements of this genre of literature (see box 27.3).

The only problem with viewing 2 Peter in these terms is that testaments usually were not incorporated into the format of a letter. Still, the dominant view of New Testament scholarship is that 2 Peter was written as "a testament in letter form." Indeed, the combination of two genres (letter and testament) may be what got 2 Peter in trouble: because it looks like a letter rather than a testament, its pseudonymity seemed like a mark of forgery rather than a literary device. As a result, 2 Peter had a harder time gaining admittance to the canon than did books that were completely anonymous (Hebrews). It even met with

testament: here, a genre of literature that provides a fictitious but pious account of a famous person's dying words, presented in a manner pertinent to present circumstances.

Second Temple period: the era in Jewish history between the dedication of the second Jerusalem temple in 515 BCE and its destruction in 70 CE.

⊙ EXPLORE 27.8
Authorship of 2 Peter

Box 27.2

Did Peter Write 2 Peter?

Most scholars believe the letter called "2 Peter" was written pseudepigraphically some years after the death of the apostle Peter. Here are a few reasons why:

- It does not appear to be written by the same person who wrote 1 Peter.
- It exhibits a reliance on Jude, which they think was written after (or close to) the time of Peter's death.
- It is written from a strongly Hellenistic perspective inconsistent with what might be attributed to a person of Palestinian Jewish background.
- It regards the second coming of Christ as something that might not occur for thousands of years (3:8).
- It looks back on the time of the apostles as a sacred bygone era (3:2, 4).
- It refers to Paul's letters as a collection of writings that are being interpreted as Scripture (3:15–16).
- It seeks to address the concerns of Christians a generation or more after Peter's death.

These points are disputed by scholars who think that Peter did write the letter.

proleptically:
anachronistic but anticipatory; one speaks proleptically when one speaks in a manner that has little meaning for present circumstances but will become more relevant in another time and place.

more resistance than the similar Letter of Jude, which church leaders did not like nearly as much but which they had no reason to suspect was pseudepigraphic (see "Historical Background" in chap. 29).

A few scholars do think that 2 Peter can be regarded as a letter composed by the apostle Peter, written around 62–65, and sent by him from Rome to the same churches in Asia Minor to which he had written 1 Peter (see 1 Pet. 1:1; cf. 2 Pet. 3:1). The assumption for 2 Peter, then, is that Peter knew that his martyrdom was near (1:14) and wanted to summon his readers' loyalty to his legacy and to warn them proleptically about future heretical teachers who he knew would come to them (2:1). This scenario takes everything in the letter at face value, but among modern New Testament scholars this is very much a minority position.

More often, 2 Peter is regarded as the latest book in the New Testament. The author assumes that his readers know the letters of Paul as a group or collection of writings that are studied, interpreted, and misinterpreted *as Scripture* within the Christian church (3:15–16). Thus many scholars conclude that 2 Peter was written in the second century, possibly a full generation later than any other New Testament book. An intermediate view holds that the letter is pseudepigraphic but was written somewhat earlier, around 80–100. This allows for it to have been written by a disciple of Peter—that is, someone who actually had known the apostle and felt authorized to speak in his name.

A primary purpose of the letter is to warn readers about false teachers and to counter the effects of "destructive opinions" (2:1). A comparison of 2 Peter with Jude reveals that the people spreading dangerous ideas in both contexts appear to have several things in common:

EXPLORE 27.6
2 Peter in the Christian Canon

- They are members of the Christian community who have gone astray (2 Pet. 2:15, 21–22; Jude 12).
- They operate surreptitiously in a manner that shows no respect for authority structures (2 Pet. 2:1, 10; Jude 4, 8).
- They profit from what they are doing and so may be governed by a love for money (2 Pet. 2:3; Jude 11).
- They entice or flatter people, fooling them into thinking that they have their interests at heart (2 Pet. 2:14, 18; Jude 16).
- They exhibit a lifestyle marked by shocking moral laxity (2 Pet. 2:10, 13; Jude 8, 18).
- They lure people into licentiousness, which may very well involve sexual exploitation (2 Pet. 2:2, 10, 14, 18; Jude 7–8, 16).

The author of 2 Peter also adds a couple of new allegations regarding his opponents that go beyond what is said of the troublemakers encountered in Jude:

- They scoff at the promise of Christ's coming and seem to reject out of hand the notion that God will intervene in the world's affairs or bring judgment (3:3–9).
- They appear to rely on idiosyncratic interpretations of Scripture, twisting Old Testament prophecies and certain obscure passages in Paul's letters to garner support for their ideas (1:20–21; 3:16).

Although various suggestions have been made, scholars are unsure as to the historical identification of the teachers repudiated in this letter. What is clear is that 2 Peter addresses the problem of Christians living in a pluralistic society. The believers addressed in this letter are used to contending with the corruption of a world that is opposed to God (1:4; 2:20; cf. 2:8), but now the danger to their faith is coming from within the community itself. The dangerous

⊙ EXPLORE 27.11
Who Were the False
Teachers in 2 Peter?

Box 27.3

2 Peter as a Testament

The New Testament letter known as 2 Peter contains the four key elements of a Jewish testament:

- A heroic person offers a précis of his teaching or ideas (1:3–11).
- The hero announces that his death is near (1:14).
- The hero urges readers of the testament to remember his message after he is gone (1:12–13, 15).
- The hero predicts what will happen after his death, describing circumstances that have become reality for readers of the testament, and offers advice for how his ideas will apply in those circumstances (2:1–3; 3:1–4).

ideas that the false teachers present in an enticing way are a threat not only to "unsteady souls" and recent converts (2:14, 18) but also to the more mature believers who are stable and established in the faith (1:12; 3:17).

In sum, the letter known as 2 Peter appears to be a communication from some representative of orthodox Christianity written in Peter's name to urge believers to hold to traditional apostolic teaching, particularly with regard to eschatology and ethics (1:12, 15; 3:1–2). The author seeks to refute skepticism with regard to Christ's return and the concomitant judgment (1:16; 3:1–4, 9), and he encourages his readers to strive for the true godliness that is to be the mark of all true believers (1:3–18). In doing this, the letter explicitly claims that it is offering nothing new: the goal is simply to remind the readers of what they already know (1:12), lest they lose their stability (3:17).

Fig. 27.1. Peter old and wise. Once a feisty and impetuous fisherman, Peter came to be regarded as an elder statesman of Christianity. The letter known as 2 Peter presents his experienced counsel as the antithesis of troubling innovations. (The Bridgeman Art Library International)

Major Themes in 2 Peter

The Delay of the Parousia

When Jesus did not return as soon as expected, many Christians perhaps asked the question that 2 Peter attributes to scoffers: "Where is the promise of his coming?" (3:4). The letter's response is threefold: (1) the promise of Christ's return is not derived from speculative myths (1:16) but rather is grounded in the actual experiences of the apostles, of trustworthy people such as Peter, who saw Jesus transfigured before him in what was essentially a preview of the parousia (1:17–18); (2) fulfillment of the promise appears to be slow in coming only when viewed from a human point of view, but "with the Lord one day is like a thousand years" (3:8); and (3) the reason Jesus has not returned yet is that God is merciful and wants to give more people a chance to repent (3:9). This last point leads to the startling conclusion that humans can hasten the time:

the readers are to imagine that Christ wants to return but is reluctant to do so when this would bring condemnation to so many. If Christians are earnest in evangelism, and if more people are brought to the godliness that comes from knowing Christ (1:3), then, indeed, the parousia might come.

The Certainty of Judgment

Apparently, the false teachers reasoned that if Christ was not going to return (at least, not anytime soon), they need not fear divine judgment (3:3–4). To counter this, the author cites biblical precedents that show God does intervene violently in history (2:4–6). In fact, God destroyed the world once before, at the time of the flood (2:5; 3:5–6), and will do so again. This time, however, the end will come by fire (3:7, 10–12). This destructive judgment will be followed by a more positive re-creation of a new heaven and a new earth (3:13; cf. Rev. 21:1), for God not only punishes the unrighteous but also rescues the godly (2:9). Still, the emphatic point for this letter is that there will be accountability, and this means that the ungodly will be condemned (2:9–10; 3:7, 16), including the false teachers and their followers (2:1, 3, 12, 17).

Godliness

The assault on false teaching in 2 Peter is set within the framework of a call for Christians to grow in godliness—that is, to lead lives pleasing to God. The problem, according to this letter, is that the world is a dark place (1:19); it has been corrupted by lust (1:4) and is characterized by licentiousness and lawlessness (2:7–8). Still, it is possible to escape from this corruption (1:4) and lead a virtuous life (1:5–9). How? The letter claims that God's power provides everything needed for life and godliness and that this is accessed through knowledge of God (1:2–3). Thus 2 Peter posits a close connection between knowing and doing, between orthodoxy and orthopraxis, between theology (beliefs, doctrine, ideology) and ethics (behavior, conduct, practice).

The letter wants to stress both the prospect for growth and the danger of

---

Box 27.4

Barren Fig-Tree: Excerpt from a Sermon by John Bunyan

John Bunyan (author of *Pilgrim's Progress*) preached a sermon in 1673 on Luke 13:6–9, stressing the limits of God's forbearance—a prominent theme in 2 Peter.

> Barren Fig-tree, Dost thou hear?
> the Ax is laid to thy roots,
> the Lord Jesus prays God to spare thee;
> Hath he been digging about thee?
> Hath he been dunging of thee?
> O Barren Fig-tree, Now thou art come
>   to the point;
> if thou shalt now become good,
> if thou shalt after a gracious manner
>   suck in the Gospel-dung,
> and if thou shalt bring forth fruit unto
>   God . . . Well!
> But if not, the fire is the last.
> Fruit or the Fire!
> Fruit or the Fire, Barren Fig-tree!

Fig. 27.2. This time by fire. The eventual destruction of heaven and earth envisioned by 2 Peter seems to depict the consignment of present-day creation to the fires of hell (3:7, 10, 12). The Christian hope is for new heavens and a new earth, where righteousness is at home (3:13). (The Bridgeman Art Library International)

backsliding. On the one hand, those who move backward, who escape the world's defilements only to become overcome by them once again, are in a worse state than if they had never known the way of righteousness (2:20–21). On the other hand, those who move forward will become participants in the divine nature (1:4), which probably means that they will possess the immortality and moral perfection attributable to God (cf. 3:14). The point seems to be that Christians can have righteous lives already in this world full of corruption, and they can grow in the grace and knowledge of God while waiting for new heavens and a new earth, where "righteousness is at home" (3:13).

EXPLORE 27.5
Judgment Day in the Bible

EXPLORE 27.4
Godliness and Knowledge in 2 Peter

Conclusion

The letter of 2 Peter often is valued as a witness to the developing life of the Christian church as it moved into the postapostolic era. We see a church that is searching for some way to define what is acceptable and what is not. Scripture might provide the standard for making such determinations, but Scripture needs to be properly interpreted (1:20–21; 3:16). Likewise, apostolic tradition may provide some basis for defining what is orthodox (1:1; 3:2), but this assumes a clear understanding of what the apostles taught. Church history eventually would show that most Christian groups make a claim for their teachings being scriptural and apostolic (including groups with widely divergent views, and ones that are labeled "heretical"). Over time, most Christian sects devised strategies for evaluating the acceptability of ideas or behaviors: they developed hierarchies of leadership authorized to make such determinations, and they adopted creeds or confessional statements definitive of what was considered normative. In 2 Peter we get a snapshot of a church in which such measures have not been fully implemented. Thus the struggle against perceived heresy is not from the top down but rather from the bottom up: the author of 2 Peter does not try to silence the teachers by issuing official and authoritative declarations but, instead, makes his appeal to their audience. One thing that this snapshot reveals is that, at this point in church history, maintenance of orthodoxy was more a matter of persuasion than of pronouncement.

postapostolic age: the time period related to the first or second generation after the deaths of Jesus's first followers.

apostolic tradition: oral or written materials that are believed to bear a close connection to Jesus, his original disciples, or the missionary Paul, or believed to be congruent with what those people taught.

FOR FURTHER READING: 2 Peter

Callan, Terrance D., and Duane F. Watson. *First and Second Peter*. Paideia. Grand Rapids: Baker Academic, 2012.

Chester, Andrew, and Ralph P. Martin. *The Theology of James, Peter, and Jude*. New Testament Theology. Cambridge: Cambridge University Press, 1994.

González, Catherine Gunsalus. *1 & 2 Peter and Jude: A Theological Commentary*. Belief Series. Louisville: Westminster John Knox, 2014.

Harner, Philip B. *What Are They Saying about the Catholic Epistles?* Mahwah, NJ: Paulist Press, 2004.

Jobes, Karen. *Letters to the Church: A Survey of Hebrews and the General Epistles*. Grand Rapids: Zondervan, 2011.

Puskas, Charles B. *Hebrews, the General Letters, and Revelation: An Introduction*. Eugene, OR: Cascade, 2016.

Reese, Ruth Anne. *2 Peter and Jude*. Two Horizons Commentary. Grand Rapids: Eerdmans, 2007.

Wright, N. T. *The Early Christian Letters for Everyone: James, Peter, John, and Jude*. 2nd ed. Louisville: Westminster John Knox, 2004.

⊙ Go to www .IntroducingNT.com for summaries, videos, and other study tools.

28

The Johannine Letters: 1 John, 2 John, 3 John

"God is love." Just about everyone knows that the Bible teaches this. Some people might think that it's found in every book of the Bible and on practically every page. But only twice does the Bible come right out and say, "God is love," and both occurrences are in the same book: the first of three letters attributed to John (1 John 4:8, 16).

What does it mean to say that God is love? It does not mean that God and love are exactly the same thing, any more than saying "God is light" (1 John 1:5) means that God and light are the same thing. Still, it means something more than just saying "God loves" or "God is loving." Love is not just one of God's behaviors or characteristics; love is a defining attribute of God, an ultimate quality that must always be taken into account. Love is the motive for everything that God says and does, the harsh words as well as the kind ones, the acts of judgment and punishment as well as the acts of salvation and mercy.

At first, the Johannine Letters may seem like an odd setting for such an insight to be developed, for they were written in the midst of conflict and discord. Still, there it is: the fundamental insight that "God is love" stands at the heart of these three letters. It was originally presented as a focal point in a crisis, and for many in the Christian church (which has never lacked for crises), it has remained that ever since.

⊙ EXPLORE 28.0
1 John: Outline of Contents

Overview

1 John

The letter opens with a prologue grounding the "word of life" that it offers in the personal experiences of the author or authors (1:1–4). The message of the letter is introduced with a contrast between walking in darkness and walking in the light of God (1:5–2:2). The love of God is made perfect in those who obey God's commandments, especially the command to love one another (2:3–11). After a poetic oracle to various groups in the community (2:12–14), the letter offers an impassioned plea for its readers not to love the world (2:15–17).

The author distinguishes his readers, who know the truth, from "antichrists" who have left the community (2:18–27). The readers are encouraged to fix their hope on the coming of Jesus (2:28–3:3). A clear delineation is made between children of God and children of the devil (3:4–10), and between people who hate fellow believers and people who have God's love in them (3:11–24). The author proposes two tests for identifying false prophets: they do not confess that Jesus came in the flesh, and they do not heed the tradition preserved from the beginning (4:1–6). Then the author returns to his main point: love is the sign and source of a true relationship with God (4:7–21). He emphasizes that victorious faith accepts various testimonies to Jesus and leads to a life that is lived in him (5:1–13). In conclusion, the author urges the readers to pray confidently for others (5:14–17), and then he offers a series of concluding proclamations (5:18–20) and a final warning against idolatry (5:21).

2 John

A salutation identifies the letter as being from "the elder" to "the elect lady and her children" (vv. 1–2). The elder begins by highlighting faithfulness that has been exhibited by some (v. 4). He urges his readers to love one another and to keep God's commandments (vv. 5–6). Then he warns them to be on guard against deceitful antichrists and urges them not to welcome anyone who fails to keep to the teaching of Christ (vv. 7–11). He expresses hope to visit them soon and sends greetings from their "elect sister" (vv. 12–13).

3 John

⊙ EXPLORE 28.1
2 John: Outline of Contents

⊙ EXPLORE 28.2
3 John: Outline of Contents

The letter opens with a salutation from "the elder" to a beloved man named "Gaius" (v. 1). The elder offers a prayer for Gaius's health (v. 2) and commends him for providing hospitality for missionaries (vv. 3–8). He then censures a church leader, Diotrephes, who has aggressively opposed support for these missionaries, rejecting the elder's authority (vv. 9–10). Finally, he urges Gaius to avoid evil

Accolades for 1 John

The New Testament letter of 1 John has been a favorite book of the Bible for many notable persons throughout history.

- Augustine: "This book is very sweet to every healthy Christian heart that savors the bread of God, and it should constantly be in the mind of God's holy church."
- Martin Luther: "This is an outstanding epistle. It can buoy up afflicted hearts . . . so beautifully and gently does it picture Christ to us."
- John Wesley: "How plain, how full, and how deep a compendium of genuine Christianity!"

and do good, then offers a brief testimony on behalf of a highly regarded man named "Demetrius," and concludes with travel plans and greetings (vv. 11–15).

Historical Background

In English Bibles, these three books are labeled very nicely for us: "The First Letter of John," "The Second Letter of John," and "The Third Letter of John." Thus all three are letters, all three are written by someone named "John," and they are presented in a definite order (first, second, third). Of course, these titles were added much later, for our convenience, and one does not have to look very hard to see that there is little in these books to justify the designations. For one thing, the book called "1 John" does not appear to be a letter: it neither opens nor closes like a letter, nor does it have a sender or a recipient. It appears to be a theological treatise or tract. Beyond this, none of the three "letters" (we will call them that) indicates that it is by John: the first one is anonymous, and the latter two are by someone who calls himself "the elder" (2 John 1; 3 John 1). And, finally, there is virtually nothing in these books to indicate the sequence or order in which they might have been written (except, possibly, for the comment in 3 John 9).

So where do the titles come from? In the early church, the works came to be ascribed to the apostle John, a disciple of Jesus. This may have been based on two considerations: (1) the language, style, and outlook of the three letters are similar to that of our fourth Gospel, leading many to believe that the four books had the same author; and (2) the author of that Gospel had come to be identified with the apostle John on the basis of verses indicating that some of its material had been put into writing by "the disciple whom Jesus loved" (John 21:24) (for discussion of why people thought the beloved disciple might be John, see "Historical Background" in chap. 9). No one knew anything about the order in which these books were written, so the three "letters" were simply arranged and numbered according to length, from longest to shortest.

beloved disciple: an unnamed follower of Jesus whose written testimony is said to be incorporated into the Gospel of John (21:20, 24).

⊙ EXPLORE 28.11
Authorship of the Johannine Letters

Many modern scholars maintain that this construal of the evidence still holds up, but most amend it slightly. For a start, the dominant view today is that John's Gospel was produced in stages: the apostle John may have been responsible for the "first draft" of that Gospel, but others expanded and edited it. Accordingly, the stylistic similarities between the Johannine Letters and the Gospel of John are taken as an indication that the author of the letters may have been one of the later editors of the Gospel rather than the apostle John himself. A popular theory holds that the letters may have been written by a person known to us from church history as "John the Elder."

According to Eusebius, John the Elder was a disciple of the apostle John and a member of his congregation—apparently, the two were often confused in later traditions. Since the author of 2 John and 3 John calls himself "the elder," most scholars think that it makes more sense to identify that author with John the Elder than with the man more commonly known as John the apostle. And, if John the Elder wrote those two letters, then he probably wrote 1 John as well, and also may have served as one of the final authors/editors of John's Gospel.

What seems certain is that the voice behind 1 John, 2 John, and 3 John is steeped in the language and theology of John's Gospel. Furthermore, it is a voice that speaks both pastorally and authoritatively, expecting to be recognized by the readers as providing them with a reliable declaration of the message that has been proclaimed "from the beginning" (1 John 1:1).

Most interpreters think that the three letters were written at about the same time and probably after the Gospel (or at least after a time when the Gospel

⊙ EXPLORE 28.12
Three Persons
Named John?

⊙ EXPLORE 28.13
Only One John: The
Apostle Who Wrote
Five Books

Box 28.2

Similarities between the Johannine Letters and the Gospel of John

- light and darkness (1 John 1:5–7; 2:9–11; cf. John 8:12; 12:46)
- unity of Father and Son (1 John 1:3; 2:22–24; 2 John 9; cf. John 5:20; 10:30, 38; 14:10)
- references to "the truth" (1 John 2:21; 3:19; 2 John 1; 3 John 3, 8; cf. John 8:32; 18:37)
- use of *paraklētos*, "Paraclete" (1 John 2:1; cf. John 14:16, 26; 15:26; 16:7)
- being hated by the world (1 John 3:13; cf. John 15:18–19; 17:13–16)
- God sending Christ into the world out of love (1 John 4:9; cf. John 3:16)
- Jesus coming in the flesh (1 John 4:2; 2 John 7; cf. John 1:14)
- Christ laying down his life for others (1 John 3:16; cf. John 10:11, 15, 17–18; 15:12–13)
- being born of God (1 John 2:29; 3:9; cf. John 1:13; 3:3–8)
- knowing God (1 John 2:3–5, 13–14; 3:1, 6; 4:6–8; cf. John 1:10; 8:55; 14:7; 16:3)
- abiding in God/Christ (1 John 2:6, 27–28; 3:6, 24; 4:13–16; cf. John 6:56; 15:4–10)
- new and old commandments (1 John 2:7; 2 John 5; cf. John 13:34)
- loving one another (1 John 2:27–28; 3:11, 23; 2 John 5; cf. John 13:34; 15:12)
- water and blood (1 John 5:6–8; cf. John 19:34–35)
- that joy may be complete (1 John 1:4; 2 John 12; cf. John 15:11; 16:24; 17:13)

Fig. 28.1. Walk in the light. The world is a dark place, according to the Johannine Letters. Believers are urged to walk in the light of God (1 John 1:5–7). (The Bridgeman Art Library International)

was almost in its final form). By most reckonings, this would place them somewhere in the 90s (for discussion of a likely date for the Gospel of John, see "Historical Background" in chap. 9). In any case, the letters presuppose a setting in which a number of "house churches" in different localities relate to one another through mutual friendship, hospitality, and support. The elder (2 John 1; 3 John 1), Gaius (3 John 1), and Diotrephes (3 John 9) apparently are leaders of churches in neighboring communities.

The occasion for all three letters is the outbreak of conflict and schism in this network of churches. The letters speak of "deceivers" (2 John 7), "liars" (1 John 2:4, 22; 4:20), "false prophets" (1 John 4:1), and "antichrists" (1 John 2:18, 22; 4:3; 2 John 7), at least some of whom are to be identified with former

⊙ EXPLORE 28.8
Analogous Heresies
to the Problem in the
Johannine Letters

church members who have left the dominant community (1 John 2:19) but who continue to seek converts for their position (2 John 7–11). The letters provide no description of what these secessionists believe, but we may gain some clues by noticing what the letters condemn or commend.

On the one hand, these letters speak very negatively of people who

- claim to be without sin (1 John 1:8–10)
- claim to know God but disobey God's commandments (1 John 1:6; 2:4)
- claim to love God but do not love their brothers and sisters (1 John 2:9, 11; 3:10–18; 4:8, 20)
- love the world or things that are worldly (1 John 2:15–16; 4:5; 5:19)
- deny that Jesus is the Christ (1 John 2:22)
- deny that Jesus has come in the flesh (2 John 7)
- deny the Father and the Son (1 John 2:22–23)
- do not confess Jesus (1 John 4:3)
- do not abide in the teaching of Jesus (2 John 9–11)

On the other hand, they speak positively of people who

- confess that Jesus has come in the flesh (1 John 4:2)
- confess that Jesus is the Son of God (1 John 4:15; 5:5, 10, 13)
- affirm that Jesus Christ came with water and blood, not water only (1 John 5:6)

Some of these remarks could be general comments that have nothing to do with the schism that has occurred, but most scholars think that it is logical to assume that the secessionists exhibited some of the condemned tendencies (and failed to exhibit the commended ones).

Many scholars also think that the secessionists believed that they were deriving their ideas from the Gospel of John itself (or at least from the traditions within the community that had been or were being incorporated into that Gospel). This is not hard to imagine. We know, for instance, that the gnostics of the second century prized the Gospel of John, interpreting it somewhat selectively in ways that supported their ideas. John portrays Jesus as a divine figure who comes from heaven to earth and reveals secrets about the divine realm and how to enter it (John 3:1–15); his teaching conveys knowledge that sets people free (John 8:32). These points, at least, were wholly compatible with gnosticism (see "On the Horizon: Gnosticism" in chap. 1). In a similar fashion, the secessionists associated with the Johannine Letters might have tried to justify ideas that are condemned in the three letters on the basis of a rival

gnosticism: a religious movement or perspective that regarded "spirit" as fundamentally good and "matter" as fundamentally evil.

interpretation of the Gospel of John (highlighting certain passages, ignoring others). Perhaps they taught things like these:

- The preexistent Logos and Son of God comes into the world as light (John 1:1–3), not as an actual flesh-and-blood human being (cf. 1 John 4:2; 2 John 7; but see also John 1:14).
- Salvation results from God sending the Son into the world (John 3:16), not by Jesus's earthly life or death (cf. 1 John 4:10; but see also John 1:29).
- People are spared condemnation by believing in the Son (John 3:17), not by keeping commandments (cf. 1 John 1:6; 2:4; but see also John 14:21).

There is some indication that the secessionists thought of themselves as "progressives," pushing the church to "go beyond" the original teaching of Christ to embrace new revelation (2 John 9). The Johannine Letters, by contrast, call their readers back to what they have heard "from the beginning" (1 John 1:1; 2:7, 14; 3:11; 2 John 5–6). Perhaps the secessionists claimed to be inspired by the Spirit, who, according to John's Gospel, would continue to teach people new truth when they were ready to receive it (John 16:12–13); in response to such a claim, 1 John insists that "spirits" need to be tested (1 John 4:1–3), for there is not only a "spirit of truth" (cf. John 14:17; 15:26; 16:13) but also a "spirit of error" (1 John 4:6).

The purpose of all three letters is to deal with some of the repercussions of such conflict and schism in the church. The immediate historical situation for each letter may be described as follows:

- *1 John* offers general advice and encouragement for the benefit of those who have remained in the community, offering them counsel and guidance for the difficult time. They need to pull together now as never before, upholding one another in love.

Box 28.3

Who Is the Elect Lady?

The second of the Johannine Letters is explicitly addressed to "the elect lady and her children" (2 John 1). Who was this person? Was there some prominent woman in the early church to whom this letter was written?

Some interpreters have thought that the "elect lady" might be the leader of a house church, similar to those churches that are apparently led by Gaius (3 John 1) and by Diotrephes (3 John 9) and by the elder himself.

The more common view, however, is that "elect lady" is a metaphorical expression for the church itself: the lady is the church in some particular vicinity, and her children are the members of that church. In support of this interpretation, scholars note that the elder seems to refer to his own church as the lady's "elect sister" (2 John 13).

- *2 John* is addressed to a local church at some distance from the main community, warning the congregation that missionaries from the schismatic group may come to them and advising that no hospitality or audience be granted to such people (2 John 10).
- *3 John* offers a letter of recommendation on behalf of a missionary from the elder's own community, a man named "Demetrius" (3 John 12). The elder wants Gaius, the recipient of the letter, to grant Demetrius hospitality, something he has done for other missionaries in the past (3 John 5–8). This simple request is complicated, however, by the fact that a leader in a nearby church, Diotrephes, is trying to prohibit anyone from doing this.

There is no sure way to know which letter was written first, second, or third. One attractive proposal suggests that 1 John had been developed as a tract to help congregations in the Johannine tradition deal with the aftermath of the schism and that, as such, multiple copies were sent to different congregations. According to this theory, 2 John may be the "cover letter" accompanying this tract (1 John) when it was sent to one particular church, perhaps the one led by Gaius, and 3 John may be a personal note for Gaius that the elder drafted to accompany the other two pieces of correspondence (cf. 3 John 9). What we have in our New Testament, then, is essentially a "three-letter packet" that was received by one church, similar to other packets that might have been sent to other churches. (See Luke Timothy Johnson, *The Writings of the New Testament: An Interpretation*, rev. ed. [Minneapolis: Fortress, 2002], 561–65.)

Major Themes in the Johannine Letters

The Humanity of Christ

The Johannine Letters emphasize the reality and significance of Jesus's humanity. The prologue of 1 John recalls the first words of John's Gospel through its use of the words "in the beginning" (1 John 1:1; cf. John 1:1). But there is a difference: in the Gospel, "the beginning" referred to the beginning of time, before the heavens and earth were created (cf. Gen. 1:1; but see also 1 John 2:13–14); in the letter, it refers to the life and ministry of Jesus, who was an actual person, a man who could be heard and seen and touched (1 John 1:1–3; cf. 2:7, 24; 3:11). This emphasis on the physical reality of Jesus surely sets the stage for the later claim that only spirits that confess "Jesus Christ has come in the flesh" are from God (1 John 4:2–3). In the Gospel of John, some people thought that since Jesus was a human being, he could not really be divine (6:42). Now it appears that the same logic has been applied in reverse: some people

Fig. 28.2. What we have touched. The Johannine Letters insist that Jesus Christ came to earth as a flesh-and-blood human being who could be touched with human hands (1 John 1:1; 4:2–3; 2 John 7). This seventeenth-century painting illustrates a story from the Gospel of John that made a similar point: the disciple Thomas must touch Jesus with his hands to be convinced Jesus is not a spirit or a ghost (20:24–28). (The Bridgeman Art Library International)

think that since Jesus was a divine being, he could not really be human—a view that theologians refer to as docetism. Still, the letters emphasize Jesus's humanity without giving any ground on his divinity: his identification with God remains so close in 1 John that it's often impossible to tell whether pronouns refer to "God" or to "Jesus" (1:9–10; 2:3–6, 27–28; 3:23–24; 4:17). In time, most Christian churches would subscribe to a doctrine of the "two natures of Christ," insisting that Jesus Christ was both "fully divine" and "fully human" in a manner compatible with what is presented in the Johannine writings.

Atonement

One aspect of Christ's humanity emphasized in these letters is the significance of his death for salvation (see 1 John 2:2; 3:16; 4:10; cf. 1:9). One explanation for the curious affirmation that Jesus Christ came by water and blood and not

atonement: an action that makes amends for sins, such that guilty persons may be restored to fellowship with God.

water only (1 John 5:6) is that the author wants to emphasize the significance of Jesus's baptism and crucifixion in the face of some who must have thought that only his baptism was important. Specifically, 1 John refers to Jesus's death as a *hilasmos* (translated as "atoning sacrifice" in the NRSV). The meaning of this word, used in 1 John 2:2; 4:10, is greatly disputed: it might mean either "propitiation" (placating an offended God) or "expiation" (cleansing or removing defilement). For centuries, exegetes have disagreed as to which meaning is intended, and theologians have worked out different conceptions of atonement theory accordingly.

propitiation: a term used in discussions of atonement to describe Christ's death as an act that placates the wrath of a God offended by human sin.

expiation: a cleansing or removal of defilement, used in discussions of atonement to describe the effects of Christ's death as covering or removing human sin.

Sin

In 1 John we perceive an undeniable tension between the reality of sin and an ideal of sinlessness. On the one hand, the person who abides in Christ does not sin (3:6), and those who have been born of God are unable to sin (3:9); on the other hand, those who say that they have no sin deceive themselves and make a liar out of God (1:8, 10). How can both be true? Likewise, 1 John maintains that people who sin do not know God and are from the devil (3:8), but then it also seems to recognize sin as typical of Christian experience, exhorting believers to confess their sins (1:9; cf. 2:1–2; 5:16). Numerous explanations for this paradox have been offered: perhaps the author means to say that those who "willfully continue in sin" do not abide in Christ and are not born of God. Or maybe his point is that a person who sins is not "born of God" or "abiding in Christ" at that moment—that is, in the instance of sinning. More often, scholars assume that the point is rhetorical, not logical: the author wants to motivate his readers to seek a life without sin, while also recognizing pragmatically that what sins are committed should be acknowledged (see 2:1).

In any case, the topic of "sin" in 1 John is complicated by a strange reference to "mortal sin" (NRSV) or "sin that leads to death" (NIV): the readers are instructed not to pray for anyone who commits such a sin (5:16–17). This could mean that it is inappropriate to pray for those who have died in their sins (once they are physically dead), but most interpreters understand the reference as being to sin that leads to spiritual death. Is the reference, then, to sins that are especially serious (e.g., idolatry [cf. 5:21] or denying Christ [cf. 2:22])? Or to sins that are willful and persistent? Or what? Theories abound, with no clear conclusion.

Love

⊙ EXPLORE 28.9
1 John 1:8 in Light of the "Confession of No Sin" in Gnostic Literature

The author of 1 John summarizes the expectation and demands of God with a single two-part commandment: "We should believe in the name of his Son Jesus Christ and love one another" (3:23; cf. Matt. 22:36–40; Mark 12:28–31;

Luke 10:25–28). The exhortation to "love one another" is repeated seven times in these letters (1 John 3:11, 14, 23; 4:7, 11, 12; 2 John 5; see also 1 John 3:10, 18; 4:8, 19, 20–21; 5:2). The letters do not provide a detailed description of what such love entails (as Paul does in 1 Cor. 13:4–8), but three points seem to stand out:

- People love one another when they keep God's commandments (1 John 5:2–3). The commandments specify what it means to love, so people who obey God's commandments are practicing love. This is one reason why the "new commandment" to love one another is really an old commandment (1 John 2:7; 2 John 5).
- People love one another when they imitate God (1 John 4:9–11) and when they imitate Jesus (1 John 3:16). People love like God (1 John 4:11–12)

Fig. 28.3. Love one another. This contemporary painting, *Fields of Forgiveness*, imagines a world in which everyone practices the ethic of 1 John 4:7. (The Bridgeman Art Library International)

when they live like Jesus, walking "as he walked" (1 John 2:6) and laying down their lives for others as he laid down his life for them (1 John 3:16).

- People love one another when they use their material resources to provide for brothers and sisters who are in need (1 John 3:17). This is the only concrete example that the letters offer for what it means to show love to another member of the community; thus it stands out as a matter of special importance.

Beyond this, we should note that this community's love ethic is solidly grounded in its theology: the letters teach that both the possibility and the necessity of loving one another have their origin in God, who *is* love (1 John 4:8, 16) and who takes the initiative *in* love (1 John 4:10, 19). All love is from God (1 John 4:7), and so "knowing God" and "loving one another" go together. No one can love without knowing God (1 John 4:7), and no one can know God without loving (1 John 4:8).

In a slightly different vein, many readers cannot fail to note that the emphasis in these letters is on loving "one another"—that is, "brothers and sisters" or other members of the community of faith. Nothing is ever said about loving one's neighbor, much less about loving one's enemies (cf. Matt. 5:44; Luke 6:27). In fact, 2 John 10 issues a strong prohibition against welcoming (or even greeting!) anyone whose teaching contradicts that of the elder—*that* doesn't seem very loving. Also, community members are instructed not to love the world (1 John 2:15). The usual explanation for this narrow focus on loving "one another" is that these letters reflect only one aspect of a church in the middle of a crisis: the immediate need is for strengthening internal bonds. For this church, right now, containing the current crisis and preventing the spread of a schismatic heresy is deemed a higher priority than maintaining dialogue or even civil relations with the heretics.

Conflict and Schism

Since these letters seem to be the products of a church in crisis, they often are examined for what they reveal about the dynamics of church conflict. In particular, 2 John and 3 John seem to be concerned with

---

Box 28.4

Dualism in 1 John

The fabric of 1 John is imbued with language depicting sharply opposed alternatives; it is always a case of either/or, not both/and.

- light or darkness (1:5–7; 2:8–9)
- truth or falsehood (1:6; 2:4, 21, 27; 4:6)
- church or world (2:15; 3:1, 13; 4:3–5; 5:19)
- life or death (3:14)
- love or hate (4:20)
- children of God or children of the devil (3:8–10)

Ne'er the twain shall meet!

establishing boundaries within a divided community. At the heart of the matter may be a doctrinal dispute, a disagreement over something so serious that the elder is prepared to claim that those who have the wrong teaching do not have God (2 John 9). But apart from the theological issues (as important as those may be), there appear to be power struggles within the church that are coming to a head over issues of hospitality. In 2 John, the elder sets forth a policy that churches are not to provide lodging and meals for visiting representatives of the schismatic faction (v. 10). Those who do provide such hospitality, even if they don't subscribe to the teaching of that group, are participating in the evil deeds of these deceivers (v. 11; cf. v. 7).

Such a policy implies a negation of neutrality, and this is seen further in 3 John, where the elder seems to be receiving a taste of his own medicine: we discover now that there is a church led by Diotrephes that has instituted a "no hospitality" policy with regard to representatives of the elder's community. Significantly, the elder does not identify Diotrephes as one of the secessionists or as someone who holds to any false doctrines himself. Rather, Diotrephes appears to favor a "pox on both your houses" approach to this controversy: his church refuses to welcome representatives from either side. But the elder attributes Diotrephes's actions to personal dysfunctions: he says that Diotrephes likes to put himself first and has problems acknowledging authority (v. 9). Thus, from the elder's perspective, Diotrephes is not maintaining neutrality but rather is exploiting the controversy to enhance his own position as leader of what will now be an independent church. In any case, there can be no neutrality. The elder sees things in line with words of Jesus uttered in the midst of conflict: "Whoever is not with me is against me" (Matt. 12:30). This is a very different perspective from that espoused by Jesus in happier times: "Whoever is not against us is for us" (Mark 9:40).

We might wonder how things could get this bad in a community organized around a Gospel that emphasizes friendship (John 15:13–15), humble service (John 13:14–15), and mutual love (John 13:34; 15:12). Certainly the crisis must have tested their sense of identity, to say nothing of compromising their witness to outsiders (see John 13:35). Given the circumstances, it is somewhat remarkable that 1 John is so free of polemic (cf. Jude; 2 Pet. 2). Despite what has happened, the author is confident and joyful (1 John 3:21; 5:14; 3 John 4). He does not (here) offer any personal attack on the secessionists or even seek to refute their positions. Instead, the focus is on those who remain with the church, affirming them in ways that will reestablish their spiritual self-esteem and calling them to remember what makes them who they are. There is an unusually strong emphasis on the intimacy of their relationship with God, and this is worked out in a reciprocal way: the readers abide in God or Christ (1 John 2:6, 24, 27–28; 3:6, 24; 4:13, 15–16; cf. 2:10; 4:16) and God abides in them (1 John

Affirmation in 1 John

The author of 1 John affirms his readers, assuring them that they are doing well and that they enjoy a positive status before God.

- They have had the word of life revealed to them (1:1–2).
- They have an Advocate with the Father, Jesus Christ (2:1).
- They have assimilated the truth of the new commandment (2:8).
- They have received forgiveness of sins (2:12).
- They know the Father, the one who is from the beginning (2:13–14).
- They have overcome the evil one (2:13–14).
- They are strong, and the word of God abides in them (2:14).
- They have been anointed by the Holy One and know the truth (2:20–21).
- They do not need anyone to teach them (2:27).
- They are children of God already, and they will be like Christ (3:1–2; 5:19).
- They have Christ abiding in them, and he has given them the Spirit (3:24; 4:13).
- They are from God and have conquered spirits of the antichrist (4:3–4, 6).
- They are indwelt by one who is greater than the one who is in the world (4:4).
- They have experienced love being perfected among them (4:17).
- They have faith that conquers the world (5:4).
- They believe in the name of the Son of God (5:13).
- They have eternal life (5:13).
- They have boldness before God in prayer (5:14–15).
- They have been given understanding to know God (5:20).
- They are in the God who is true, through his Son, Jesus Christ (5:20).

3:24; 4:12–13, 15–16; cf. 2:14, 24, 27; 3:9; 2 John 2). Most of all, the readers need to realize how much God loves them (1 John 4:8–11, 16). Then they just need to let God's love be perfected in them (1 John 2:5; 4:12, 17–18) and love one another, not just in word or speech but in truth and action (1 John 3:18). When this happens, the author's joy will be complete (1 John 1:4).

Conclusion

The church historian Eusebius (ca. 311) recounts what he regards as "a memorable tale" regarding the apostle John, a story told also by Irenaeus (ca. 180), who claims to have gotten it from Polycarp (ca. 69–155):

> One day John the apostle went into a bathhouse to take a bath, but when he found out that Cerinthus was inside, he leapt from the spot and ran for the door, as he could not endure to be under the same roof. He urged his companions to do the same, calling out: "Let's get out of here, for fear the place falls in, now

that Cerinthus, the enemy of the truth, is inside." (Eusebius, *Ecclesiastical History* 3.28.6; 4.14.6)

This story probably is not historical, but it did become a popular "urban legend" in the early church. One version has John fleeing the bathhouse naked, like the man who fled Gethsemane in Mark 14:51–52.

The story captures one aspect of the man who probably founded the community with which the Johannine Letters are associated: he was remembered as someone who took heresy or false doctrine very seriously. This is true of the Johannine Letters. But the story also recounts a response motivated by fear, and that does not sound like the author of these letters at all. The position taken in the Johannine Letters is that "perfect love casts out fear" (1 John 4:18). One ought not welcome the deceiver (2 John 10), but there is no need to flee the bathhouse!

Gethsemane: the site of an orchard on the Mount of Olives just outside Jerusalem; the place where Jesus was arrested (Mark 14:32–52; John 18:1–14).

FOR FURTHER READING: **The Johannine Letters**

Donelson, Lewis R. *From Hebrews to Revelation: A Theological Introduction.* Louisville: Westminster John Knox, 2001.

Harner, Philip B. *What Are They Saying about the Catholic Epistles?* Mahwah, NJ: Paulist Press, 2004.

Jobes, Karen. *Letters to the Church: A Survey of Hebrews and the General Epistles.* Grand Rapids: Zondervan, 2011.

Lieu, Judith M. *The Theology of the Johannine Epistles.* New Testament Theology. Cambridge: Cambridge University Press, 1991.

Parsenios, George L. *First, Second, and Third John.* Paideia. Grand Rapids: Baker Academic, 2014.

Puskas, Charles B. *Hebrews, the General Letters, and Revelation: An Introduction.* Eugene, OR: Cascade, 2016.

Rensberger, David. *1 John, 2 John, 3 John.* Abingdon New Testament Commentaries. Nashville: Abingdon, 1997.

Wright, N. T. *The Early Christian Letters for Everyone: James, Peter, John, and Jude.* 2nd ed. Louisville: Westminster John Knox, 2004.

⊙ Go to www
.IntroducingNT.com
for summaries,
videos, and other
study tools.

29

Jude

If Jesus had written his Sermon on the Mount for an English composition class, he probably would have gotten it back marked with red ink. At one point, he tells people to beware of false prophets who are like wolves in sheep's clothing, adding, "You will know them by their fruits" (Matt. 7:15–16). This is what grammarians call a mixed metaphor: wolves do not bear fruit, trees do.

Still, Jesus's point was perfectly clear, and the short Letter of Jude, which may have been written by his baby brother, could be read as a commentary on this exact point. The letter is concerned with warning people about dangerous intruders who have snuck into churches, people who appear to be Christians but are not (v. 4). These intruders probably were people whose doctrines and ideas Jude would have rejected, but the letter offers no clear refutation of what the phony Christians taught or believed. The accent, instead, is on how they lived: their behavior gives them away.

Jude is a difficult letter in many ways. It contains a few obscure passages and some odd references to nonbiblical materials. In a few places, our best Greek manuscripts disagree with one another, so we cannot even be certain what the letter originally said (see, e.g., the footnotes to vv. 5, 12, 22–23 in the NRSV). Still, as with the Sermon on the Mount, the main point that Jude wants to make is clear: watch out for the wolves in sheep's clothing—you will know them by their fruits!

Overview

The letter opens with a salutation and blessing that identifies it as a message from Jude, the brother of James, to those who are "kept safe for Jesus Christ" (vv. 1–2). The author explains that the intrusion of ungodly people who pervert the grace of God into licentiousness has made necessary a letter that champions

Sermon on the Mount: traditional name given to the teaching of Jesus in Matthew 5–7; it includes such well-known material as the Beatitudes, the Lord's Prayer, and the Golden Rule.

⊙ EXPLORE 29.0
Jude: Outline of Contents

523

orthodox faith (vv. 3–4). He recites a list of occasions in which God punished the wicked in the past (vv. 5–7) and promises that the current "dreamers" who "slander the glorious ones" will likewise be destroyed (vv. 8–10). He pronounces a prophetic "woe" or curse upon them in language filled with invective and illustrated by allusions to various Jewish writings (vv. 11–16). The letter concludes with exhortations to faithfulness (vv. 17–23) and a doxology to God, who is able to keep people from falling (vv. 24–25).

Historical Background

The Greek name *Ioudas* is variously translated as "Jude," "Judah," or "Judas" in English Bibles, and we hear of several persons who bore that name. The author of this letter, however, is almost always associated with the Jude who is identified in the Gospels as one of four brothers of Jesus (Matt. 13:55; Mark 6:3). Another of those brothers, James, became the leader of the church in Jerusalem (see Acts 12:17; 15:13–21; 1 Cor. 15:7; Gal. 1:19; 2:9), and we also have a letter in the New

---

Box 29.1

Use of Apocryphal Writings

The Letter of Jude draws on Jewish writings that are not considered to be canonical Scripture by either Jews or Christians.

- Jude alludes to a story found in *1 Enoch*, according to which the angels that mated with earth women to produce a race of giants (reported in Gen. 6:1–4) were imprisoned by God for the day of judgment (v. 6; cf. *1 Enoch* 6–8).
- Jude quotes from *1 Enoch* in a way that indicates he regards the book's prophecies as reliable and true (vv. 14–15; cf. *1 Enoch* 1:9).
- Jude refers to a story in which the archangel Michael had a dispute with the devil over who should take possession of the body of Moses (v. 9).

The book of *1 Enoch* is an apocalyptic Jewish writing from the third century BCE; its contents may also be assumed by 1 Peter 3:18–20. The tale about the body of Moses is not recorded in any literature available to us, but Clement of Alexandria (ca. 150–215) and a number of other early Christian scholars maintain that it was reported in a Jewish work called the *Assumption of Moses*, which was extant in their day. Most contemporary scholars think that this writing was probably part of a Jewish work known to us as the *Testament of Moses*; our manuscripts of the latter work are incomplete, and the story to which Jude refers may have been contained in the portion that is missing.

Neither *1 Enoch* nor the *Assumption of Moses* belongs to the Old Testament, nor are they part of the collection of books that Protestants call the Apocrypha, some of which are regarded as a secondary canon by Roman Catholic and Eastern Orthodox Christians. Today, Jude's reliance on these books usually is viewed as a curious holdover from a time when the concept of canon was still in flux.

Testament attributed to him (see box 25.1). According to the Gospels, the brothers of Jesus did not believe in him during his life on earth (Mark 3:21; John 7:1–5). They did, however, come to faith after the resurrection (Acts 1:14). At least two of them became missionaries, accompanied by their wives in their travels (1 Cor. 9:5). It seems likely that Jude was one of these. At any rate, although Jude did not attain the same level of renown as James, the very existence of this letter indicates that his name carried some weight in certain circles. One historical report indicates that his grandsons were still leaders of churches in Palestine toward the end of the first century (Eusebius, *Ecclesiastical History* 3.19–20).

Still, many scholars would regard all of this as irrelevant. They consider Jude to be a pseudepigraphic letter written by some second-generation Christian who wanted his words to be regarded as part of the legacy of the Holy Family. They claim that the author writes in a sophisticated Hellenistic style and looks back on the apostolic age as a bygone era (v. 17). But a number of factors may also be cited in support of an earlier date, such as the author's belief that he is living in the last days (v. 18) and his use of nonbiblical Jewish traditions (vv. 6, 9, 14–15). The question remains in dispute, but in recent years an increasing number of scholars have been willing to grant the possibility that this letter actually was written by Jude the brother of Jesus (probably with the help of an amanuensis).

The proposed date of the letter often is linked to decisions about authorship: if it is by Jude, it could probably have been written at any time in the second half of the first century; if it is pseudepigraphic, it was probably written sometime between 80 and 120. There is nothing in its contents that allows us to determine this with certainty.

In any case, the Letter of Jude is addressed to a readership that is identified theologically rather than geographically: "To those who are called, who are beloved in God the Father and kept safe for Jesus Christ" (v. 1). Some interpreters take this to mean that the letter was not intended for any particular church or group of churches. Most, however, think that a particular crisis is being addressed: false Christians (called "intruders" in v. 4) are wreaking havoc somewhere in the church (we don't know where), and the Letter of Jude pulls no punches in condemnn such troublemakers.

A good deal of research has been devoted to determining who these troublemakers were and what they did that was so offensive. Although Jude says that they "deny our only Master and Lord, Jesus Christ," the people whom he has in view almost certainly claim to be Christians (see vv. 4, 12). Most likely, the point is that although these troublemakers do not deny Christ overtly, their words and deeds have the effect of doing so. (For a list of attributes that Jude's opponents shared with the persons attacked in 2 Peter, see "Historical Background" in chap. 27.)

The intruders are described with a number of colorful insults:

- "irrational animals" (v. 10)
- "waterless clouds carried along by the winds" (v. 12)
- "wandering stars, for whom the deepest darkness has been reserved forever" (v. 13)
- "autumn trees without fruit, twice dead, uprooted" (v. 12)
- "wild waves of the sea, casting up the foam of their own shame" (v. 13)

We also hear that they are "worldly people" (v. 19) who are "ungodly sinners" (v. 15) and "devoid of the Spirit" (v. 19). They are "malcontents" (v. 16) and "scoffers" (v. 18); they grumble (v. 16) and flatter people (v. 16); and they are self-indulgent with regard to their own lusts (vv. 16, 18). All of this, however, is generalized invective; we easily gather that the troublemakers are bad people who exhibit lots of vices, but we would like to know if there was some particular philosophy or failing that caused them to be this way. Although many proposals have been put forward, none has carried the day.

⊙ EXPLORE 29.9
Which Jude? Jude Confusion in the Bible and in the Church

⊙ EXPLORE 29.8
Authorship of Jude

In any case, the presence of such people in the community has proved divisive (v. 19), which implies that the intruders have garnered support from some members of the church. In fact, most scholars believe that at least some of these troublemakers present themselves as teachers in the church. They might be itinerant prophets who travel from church to church making converts and charging fees for their services (see v. 11; cf. v. 16 with Rom. 16:18). Thus the issue is not simply one of dealing with wayward Christians who fail to live as they should; rather, these people are actively promoting an understanding of the faith that supports their appalling lifestyle. The Letter of Jude seeks to address this crisis. Its purpose is stated clearly: to appeal to the readers to contend for the faith that was delivered to them by the apostles (vv. 3, 17–18).

Box 29.2

Infamous Sinners of the Past

Jude associates the intruders who have stolen into the church with six notorious examples from Jewish tradition:

- Israelites in the wilderness (v. 5; cf. Num. 14; 1 Cor. 10:1–11; Heb. 3:7–19)
- angels who mated with women on earth (v. 6; cf. Gen. 6:1–4; *1 Enoch 6–8*)
- citizens of Sodom and Gomorrah (v. 7; cf. Gen. 19)
- Cain (v. 11; cf. Gen. 4:1–16; Heb. 11:4; 1 John 3:12)
- Balaam (v. 11; cf. Num. 22–24; Rev. 2:14)
- Korah (v. 11; cf. Num. 16)

Major Themes in Jude

The Certainty of Judgment

The first and most prominent thing that Jude wants to say is that the fate of the false believers is sealed: they were designated long ago for condemnation (v. 4). The judgment of God upon them is inevitable (vv. 13–15). In order to drive this point home, he reminds his readers of how God has judged infamous sinners of the past (see box 29.2). The current batch of troublemakers belongs on the same list and is likewise destined for eternal fire (v. 7) or deepest darkness (v. 13). Jude makes no attempt to argue with his opponents. He doesn't even call them to repentance. Like an Old Testament prophet, he simply pronounces a "woe" against them, and that's that. The church should, of course, have a merciful attitude toward all sinners, but in the case of these false believers, such mercy must be exercised with caution; the greater concern is to rescue those who might come under their influence (vv. 22–23).

The Apostolic Faith

The positive affirmation in Jude is for readers to build themselves up in their "most holy faith" (v. 20), which is the faith that has been entrusted to the saints "once for all" (v. 3; cf. Acts 2:42; Rom. 6:17; 1 Tim. 4:6; 2 Tim. 1:13; 4:3; Titus

⊙ EXPLORE 29.10
Who Were the Troublemakers Denounced by Jude?

Fig. 29.2. End of the world. Jesus taught in his Sermon on the Mount that houses lacking a firm foundation will collapse when severe storms arise (Matt. 7:26–27). Jude maintains that the "most holy faith" entrusted to saints and received from apostles offers the only sure foundation to survive divine judgment. (Bridgeman Images)

1:9). Jude believes that the tradition received by the apostles is sufficient and needs no supplementation; his readers simply need to remember those things of which they have already been informed (vv. 5, 17). Thus innovation can be equated with wavering (v. 22) or even with a denial of Christ (v. 4). There is no need for innovation, furthermore, because all things have been taken into account; even the current crisis was predicted by the apostles, who said that troublemakers would appear in the last days (vv. 17–18; cf. Acts 20:29–30; 1 Tim. 4:1; 2 Tim. 3:1–9).

Jude provides no summary or description of the faith tradition that he commends, but we gather from the letter that it involves identification with God as Father and Savior (vv. 1, 25), with Jesus Christ as Master and Lord (v. 4), and with the Holy Spirit (v. 20; cf. v. 19). These relationships are made possible through the grace of God and the mercy of Jesus Christ (vv. 4, 21), but such grace must not be exploited as an excuse for self-indulgence. Indeed, there is a certain synergy assumed for the divine-human relationship: God is able to keep people from falling (v. 24), and God does do this (v. 1), but people must also do things to keep themselves in the love of God (v. 21). Finally, the apostolic faith has a strong eschatological component: believers look forward to eternal life (v. 21) without forgetting the prospect of eternal punishment (vv. 7, 13–15).

eschatology: study or focus on "last things," such as the return of Christ, final judgment, or other phenomena associated with the end times.

⊙ EXPLORE 29.5
Keeping and Being Kept: A Motif in the Letter of Jude

Conclusion

Jude is a polemical letter. It employs harsh rhetoric, laden with threats, insults, and derogatory remarks. If it is unpleasant to read, this may be because it deals with an unpleasant topic: the capacity for religion to do great harm. The author is convinced that his readers are being hurt. They are not simply being convinced to adopt wrong ideas; they are also being duped and exploited by people who are only pretending to have their interests at heart (v. 16). This explains why Jude cannot adopt a tolerant "Let everyone believe what they want to believe" attitude. He writes from necessity (v. 3), driven by a passionate concern to rescue those whom he believes are in danger—to snatch them from the fire, so to speak (v. 23).

The Letter of Jude received something of a second life in the church when apparently it was taken up by the author of 2 Peter and used as a source for the composition of that letter. Indeed, students who have become familiar with Jude and then go on to read 2 Peter inevitably experience a bit of déjà vu, as words, examples, and biblical references from the one letter are employed over and over again in the other one (see box 27.1). This tells us that the problem Jude addressed was no isolated incident: Christians continued to struggle with the question of which voices within the church should be trusted, and with the related question of how to define criteria according to which the validity of diverse faith expressions should be determined.

FOR FURTHER READING: **Jude**

Chester, Andrew, and Ralph P. Martin. *The Theology of James, Peter, and Jude.* New Testament Theology. Cambridge: Cambridge University Press, 1994.

González, Catherine Gunsalus. *1 & 2 Peter and Jude: A Theological Commentary.* Belief Series. Louisville: Westminster John Knox, 2014.

Harner, Philip B. *What Are They Saying about the Catholic Epistles?* Mahwah, NJ: Paulist Press, 2004.

Jobes, Karen. *Letters to the Church: A Survey of Hebrews and the General Epistles.* Grand Rapids: Zondervan, 2011.

Painter, John, and David deSilva. *James and Jude.* Paideia. Grand Rapids: Baker Academic, 2012.

Puskas, Charles B. *Hebrews, the General Letters, and Revelation: An Introduction.* Eugene, OR: Cascade, 2016.

Reese, Ruth Anne. *2 Peter and Jude.* Two Horizons Commentary. Grand Rapids: Eerdmans, 2007.

Wright, N. T. *The Early Christian Letters for Everyone: James, Peter, John, and Jude.* 2nd ed. Louisville: Westminster John Knox, 2004.

⊙ Go to www .IntroducingNT.com for summaries, videos, and other study tools.

30

Revelation

Angels blowing trumpets! Monsters rising from the deep! Lakes of fire and rivers of blood! Ah, yes—the book of Revelation. There is nothing like it anywhere else in the New Testament. It certainly is the only book to feature dragons (12:3–13:10), giant bugs (9:3–11), and airborne horses (6:2–8; 19:11–12).

Revelation is a book to excite the senses. The Bible does not often tell us what color things are, but here everything is red, purple, yellow, blue, green, gold. It is also a noisy book, rumbling with the din of battle and the crash of thunder. Earth echoes with the wailing of the damned; heaven rings with songs and shouts of the saved. And those trumpets! There is hardly a moment's peace. No, wait—there are a thousand years of peace, but that's just three verses (20:4–6), and then all hell breaks loose (literally). The imagery is fantastic: buildings and furniture made of gems, and a menagerie of creatures like something Dr. Seuss might have thought up after a sleepless night reading Stephen King: the locusts wear armor like horses (9:7–9), and the horses have serpents for tails (9:19). And what's this thing that's part leopard, part bear, and part lion but lives in the sea (13:1–2)?

In a sense, to "interpret" this book is to misinterpret it, for often the appeal is to the imagination; it's a book to be experienced, not explained. Could the impact of its visual imagery ever be captured in literal illustrations? Imagine the questions that would arise at some film studio determined to bring Revelation to the big screen: Why do the beasts have ten horns but only seven heads (13:1; 17:3)? How, exactly, does a lion look like a lamb (5:5–6)?

Just as jokes are seldom funny when they have to be explained, so Revelation may lose some of its power when it has to be interpreted. Of course, modern scholarship enables us to understand some things about this book that are missed by readers at large. But it is worth noting that, throughout history, Revelation has proved to be one of the most popular books in the Bible among people who lack formal (much less, theological) education, especially those who belong to lower economic classes and/or marginalized social groups. Why? What do they (these uninstructed readers) get out of this book? Or, to put the question more broadly: Why does Revelation work so well for some people and not at all for others?

Overview

This book opens with an expanded title and a beatitude for its reader (1:1–3). After a salutation similar to those with which many New Testament letters begin (1:4–8), John, on the island of Patmos, reports that he received a revelation while "in the spirit on the Lord's day" and that he was directed to write this in a book and send it to seven churches (1:9–11).

The first thing that he sees is a spectacular image of the Son of Man (1:12–20), who dictates seven letters to him, specific messages for each of the churches (chaps. 2–3).

After recording these letters, John sees a door open in heaven, and he is taken up into the heavenly realm itself. There he beholds the throne of God, angels, and other wondrous creatures (chap. 4). The one seated on the divine throne holds a scroll bound with seven seals, and there is a search to find someone who is worthy to open this scroll. The only one worthy is the Lion of Judah, who, as it turns out, looks not like a lion but rather like a lamb that has been slaughtered (chap. 5).

One by one, this Lamb opens the seals of the scroll, and as he does this, catastrophes strike the earth until, with the sixth seal, stars fall from the sky and the sky itself rolls up like a scroll and disappears (chap. 6). Then angels intervene to ensure the safety of God's faithful ones: 144,000 people of Israel are marked for protection, and John sees an innumerable multitude of people, robed in white, from all nations being brought before the Lamb (chap. 7). The Lamb opens the seventh seal, initiating a half hour of silence in heaven (8:1).

Seven angels appear, each with a trumpet, and as these trumpets are blown, more disasters strike the earth (chaps. 8–9). But following the sixth trumpet, there is a brief interlude: an angel appears with a small scroll, shouting with a sound of seven thunders. John is told to seal up what the seven thunders said and not write it down, and he is given the scroll to eat; it tastes sweet but makes his stomach bitter (chap. 10). He then takes some measurements in heaven and is told about two witnesses who will come to the earth, be martyred, raised from death, and taken up into heaven. Finally, the seventh angel blows the seventh trumpet, and God's temple in heaven is opened amid loud shouts of praise (chap. 11).

▶ EXPLORE 30.0
Revelation: Outline of Contents

Fig. 30.1. The heavenly militia. Revelation tells of angels in combat in heaven and on the earth (e.g., 12:7–9; 14:15–20), here depicted in a painting by the fourteenth-century Italian artist Guariento. (The Bridgeman Art Library International)

Great portents appear in heaven: a cosmic, pregnant woman and a red dragon, which turns out to be Satan. War breaks out as Michael the archangel leads the heavenly forces to defeat Satan (chap. 12). On earth, a series of beasts blaspheme God, oppress the saints, and insist on conformity to idolatrous ways (chap. 13). Angels call for saints to endure this tribulation, and John beholds a vision of the Son of Man reaping the earth with a massive sickle; the wrath of God comes mightily upon the earth, as evidenced by an awful river of blood (chap. 14). Seven angels with seven bowls appear, and each bowl brings a terrible plague upon the earth (chaps. 15–16).

John is invited to witness the judgment of a "great whore," who is identified as the city of Babylon. Her downfall is lamented on earth but celebrated in heaven (chaps. 17–18). Amid great canticles of praise, John then sees heaven opened, and a rider who is called "Faithful and True" comes on a white horse to wage a final victorious war against all the kings of earth. The flesh of those kings is consumed in a grotesque but spectacular banquet, and the beasts responsible for the tribulation mentioned earlier are thrown into a lake of fire (chap. 19). Satan is imprisoned, and those who proved faithful in the previous trials are allowed to reign with Christ on earth for one thousand years. After that time, Satan is released for a final battle and then is thrown into the lake of fire to be tormented forever (chap. 20).

Then John sees a new heaven and a new earth, and a new Jerusalem coming down from heaven. He concludes his book with a thrilling vision of paradise: gates of pearl and streets of gold, and a city in which there is no fear or pain or trouble of any kind (chaps. 21–22).

What Sort of Book Is This?

What are we to make of such a book? Scholars sometimes say that Revelation shares the features of three different types of literature.

First, the book is something like a *letter*. It begins (1:4–8) and ends (22:21) like a letter, and it is supposed to be sent to seven churches (1:11). Perhaps this book was composed as a "circular letter" to be distributed and read in particular congregations, as were some of the letters of Paul (Col. 4:16). If so, then some of the content might apply to specific situations in those churches or be intended to address questions that members of those churches were asking.

Second, the book is presented as a *prophecy* (1:3; 22:7, 10, 18–19). The reader is expected to "keep" the words of this book, implying that the message is something that can be obeyed—a call to repentance, perhaps, or an exhortation to perseverance. In some sense, the book may be compared to writings of certain Old Testament prophets who also claimed to be passing on direct communications from God and who sometimes did so through symbolic language or by recounting visionary experiences (see Ezekiel, Zechariah, and especially Daniel). Prophets often announced what God was about to do and detailed blessings and woes that were to come upon people when God acted (assuming that everything continued on its present course; for one instance in which a change in course allowed the predicted judgment to be averted, see

⊙ EXPLORE 30.6
Prophetic Literature and Apocalyptic Literature

⊙ EXPLORE 30.7
Other Apocalypses

Jonah). To the extent that Revelation is read as a prophecy, its content may be regarded as a series of colorful exhortations or warnings about what will happen when God's purposes are fulfilled.

Third, the book has much in common with a genre of literature known as *apocalypse*. This type of writing is not well known today, but it was popular at the time when Revelation was produced. As a result of archaeological discoveries in the last century, we now have copies of numerous apocalypses that were read by Jews and Christians in the centuries just before and after the time of Jesus. These books are different from Revelation in certain ways, but they do display some marked similarities (see box 30.1). They typically report divine or transcendent visions that are granted to a seer and then interpreted by angels or other spiritual beings. As in Revelation, the seer sometimes is transported to a heavenly or spiritual realm to describe what is seen there. Symbolism is prominent, and the content of the visions often involves bizarre creatures, fantastic spectacles, and mysterious events similar to those found in Revelation. Such books tend to be dualistic in their outlook, which means that they describe a universe where there are clear distinctions between good and evil; the story pits angels against demons or saints against sinners with little allowance for ambiguity. And the themes of such works typically are matters of cosmic significance: the end of the world, the defeat of evil, the vindication of the righteous.

apocalyptic literature: a genre of heavily symbolic literature that displays distinctive literary characteristics and claims to unveil the truth about the world as viewed from a dualistic and deterministic perspective.

dualistic: exhibiting the tendency to separate phenomena into sharply opposed categories.

Box 30.1

Some Common Features of Apocalypses

- pseudonymous
- addressed to persons experiencing suffering and persecution
- seek to motivate faithfulness in a time of crisis
- heavy use of symbolism, including numbers and colors
- engagement with otherworldly beings, such as angels and demons
- bizarre menagerie of fantastic creatures
- spiritual or supernatural visions, often interpreted by otherworldly beings
- portentous dreams that must also be interpreted
- mystical journeys from the earthly plane to a heavenly or spiritual realm
- review of history with ultimate culmination linked to the present era
- secrets revealed about imminent cosmic transformations
- forecast of cosmic catastrophes
- liturgical settings and elements, such as altars, temples, hymns
- unveiling of the true-but-hidden character of present circumstances
- radically dualistic outlook: clear distinction between good and evil with no ambiguity
- deterministic view of history: all proceeds according to a preordained divine plan
- pessimistic forecast for the world as is: things will go from bad to worse
- hope for a favored remnant lies in radical divine intervention

Fig. 30.2. Impressions. The book of Revelation is often compared to abstract or nonrepresentational art, in which colors and shapes create impressions to fire the imagination. The Russian artist Wassily Kandinsky said this painting, *Study for Improvisation V*, was inspired by Revelation. Audiences and critics have often seen specific images in it: on the left side is a cross with a multitude of people gathered beneath it; just behind the cross stands a figure of Christ, viewed from the back (his head, at the top, is blue, he is dressed in red, and he has a white hand); kneeling before Christ is a woman with an orange body and blue hair—she probably represents the church; in the top right, two of the four horsemen of the apocalypse are fleeing the advent of Christ. Whether you see these images or not, the book of Revelation functions in a similar inviting-but-confusing manner: at first a collage of absurd imagery, it may, on further reflection, offer impressions that begin to make sense. (Bridgeman Images)

Many scholars think that some confusing aspects of Revelation can be best understood in light of what the book's original readers would have known about "how to read an apocalypse." For example, some scholars maintain that apocalypses often employed visions in a concurrent rather than consecutive manner, and that readers knew the visions were more kaleidoscopic than chronological. If this is true of Revelation, then it might be a mistake to regard the different visions in the book as laying out scenarios that will occur one after another at the end of time. Rather, different visions might offer repeated depictions of the same events. This would explain how the world could appear to come to an end in chapter 6 and yet be described as still experiencing various cataclysms in chapter 8, or why God's righteous ones appear to be gathered into heaven in chapter 9 only to be described as suffering persecution on earth in chapter 13. The one basic story of judgment and salvation is being told over and over again through visions that use different symbols or images to describe the same occurrences.

How Is This Book to Be Read?

There is probably no other book in the Bible for which the divide between scholarly interpretation and popular reception is as wide as it is with the book of Revelation. Scholars usually focus on determining what the book of Revelation meant to its first-century readers, while at a popular level Revelation is taken as a blueprint for understanding or predicting events taking place in the world today. These tendencies do have their exceptions, but they raise the fundamental question of what the book of Revelation intends to communicate and of what a basic approach to understanding this book should entail.

Over the years, Christians intent on understanding Revelation have taken three approaches.

- *Historical.* The book is understood with reference to the time and place in which it was written. Its main purpose was to disclose the truth about what was happening in the world at that time.
- *Idealist.* The book is understood with reference to universal themes and symbols. Its main purpose was to provide spiritual insight that is meaningful for every time and place.
- *Futurist.* The book is understood with reference to times and places after its composition. Its main purpose was to predict what would come to pass in generations yet to come.

To illustrate how these approaches lead to divergent or competing interpretations, let's apply them to a couple of examples.

Fig. 30.3. A letter for an angel. This tenth-century illustration from Spain depicts John handing a letter to "the angel of the church in Ephesus" (2:1), a letter that had been dictated to him by "one like the Son of Man" (1:12–20). At some point in art history, an inattentive reader gave the illustration an official name that gets this backward: "The Angel Gives John the Letter for the Church of Ephesus." (Bridgeman Images)

Example One: The Seven Letters

Revelation 2–3 presents seven letters dictated by Jesus to the angels or messengers of seven churches. How are these letters to be understood?

A *historical* approach views the letters as actual correspondence addressed to churches that existed in Asia Minor at this time. Archaeologists have excavated some of the cities where these churches were located, and scholars have sought to document and clarify specific problems or incidents mentioned in the letters, such as the martyrdom of Antipas (2:13) and the heresy of the Nicolaitans (2:6, 15).

An *idealist* approach treats the letters as generic advice to seven types of churches that might be found in any age: a "Thyatiran church" is one given to

Box 30.2

Gematria

The practice of "gematria" consists of assigning a numerical value to a word or phrase by adding together the values of the individual letters. This works in Hebrew and in Greek, where the letters of the alphabet can also serve as numerals. In Greek, the marks signifying 6 and 90 were not used as letters in New Testament times.

Hebrew Letters

1 = א	5 = ה	9 = ט	40 = מ	80 = פ	300 = ש
2 = ב	6 = ו	10 = י	50 = נ	90 = צ	400 = ת
3 = ג	7 = ז	20 = כ	60 = ס	100 = ק	
4 = ד	8 = ח	30 = ל	70 = ע	200 = ר	

Greek Letters

A α = 1	F ϝ = 6	K κ = 20	O o = 70	T τ = 300	Ω ω = 800
B β = 2	Z ζ = 7	Λ λ = 30	Π π = 80	Y υ = 400	
Γ γ = 3	H η = 8	M μ = 40	Q ϙ = 90	Φ φ = 500	
Δ δ = 4	Θ θ = 9	N ν = 50	P ρ = 100	X χ = 600	
E ε = 5	I ι = 10	Ξ ξ = 60	Σ σ = 200	Ψ ψ = 700	

In the Roman world, gematria became a basis for riddles, jokes, and games.

- Graffiti on a wall in Pompeii reads, "I love her whose number is 545."
- As a political joke, Suetonius (*Nero* 39) indicates that the name "Nero" (Νέρων) and the phrase "killed his own mother" (ἰδίαν μητέρα ἀπέκτεινε) have the same numerical value (1,005) when written in Greek. This was pertinent because the emperor was rumored to have murdered his mother.

In Christianity and Judaism, gematria could provide a basis for religious symbolism.

- Rabbis noted that "Eliezer" (אליעזר), the name of Abraham's favored servant (Gen. 15:2), has a numerical value of 318, which is the total number of servants mentioned in Genesis 14:14. Thus Eliezer was the equal of all the rest of the servants combined.
- The Hebrew letters in the name "David" (דוד) add up to 14, so that number could be accorded messianic significance: the Messiah was to be the Son of David. This is probably why Matthew's Gospel emphasizes that the genealogy of Jesus can be divided into three sets of fourteen generations (Matt. 1:17).
- The Greek letters in the name "Jesus" (Ἰησοῦς) add up to 888, which some early Christians found significant: eight surpasses seven (the number for perfection) and heralds a "new creation" beyond what God did in the first seven days (Gen. 1:1–2:3).

Many scholars think that gematria holds the clue to resolving the puzzle of 666, the number attributed to the beast in Revelation 13:18. (See box 30.3.)

gross corruption (2:18–29), and a "Laodicean church" is one in which people are lacking in zeal (3:14–22).

A *futurist* approach may take these letters as representing Christ's description of what at the time were still future eras of church history. A scenario

Fig. 30.4 The four horsemen. One of the more memorable images from the book of Revelation is that of the four horsemen unleashed upon the earth: Pestilence (or Conquest), War, Famine, and Death.

popularized by *The Scofield Reference Bible* (1909) identified those eras as: (1) faithful apostolic church (Ephesus); (2) persecuted postapostolic church (Smyrna); (3) worldly Constantinian church (Pergamum); (4) corrupt medieval church (Thyatira); (5) orthodox Reformation church (Sardis); (6) missionary early American church (Philadelphia); and (7) lukewarm modern church (Laodicea).

Example Two: The Number of the Beast

Revelation 13:18 tells us that the beast who oppresses God's faithful ones has "the number of a person," and this number is 666 or, in some Greek manuscripts, 616. What does this mean?

Historical readings usually take the number as a reference to Nero, the Roman emperor famous for persecuting Christians. His name was spelled "Neron Caesar" or, sometimes, "Nero Caesar." In Hebrew, letters of the alphabet also serve as numerals (a system called "gematria"), and when "Neron Caesar" is written in Hebrew, the letters have a numerical value equal to 666, while the Hebrew letters for "Nero Caesar" have a value of 616. Other scholars have noted an alternative connection to a different emperor, Domitian: the numerical value of the Greek letters that appeared on certain coins bearing his inscription also totaled 666. (See box 30.2.)

Idealist readings usually take the number as a symbol for anyone supremely evil. Just as the number "seven" represents what is pure or perfect, the number "six" symbolizes impurity or imperfection. A threefold six is "triple bad" (constantly falling short), and anyone who repeatedly fails or opposes God may be said to have earned this number.

Futurist readings usually assume the number to be a code for some evil person who is to come into the world at the end of time. Such readers sometimes scrutinize the names, addresses, phone numbers, and other data pertaining to potential candidates to determine if anyone in the modern world can be associated with the number of the beast (see box 30.3).

With regard to these three basic approaches to Revelation (historical, idealist, futurist), we should note that the use of one approach some of the time does not rule out preference for a different approach at another time. Many popular

Box 30.3

Who Might Bear the Number 666?

Most Bible scholars think that the number of the beast, given as 666 in Revelation 13:18 (or 616 in some manuscripts), employed the system of gematria (see box 30.2) to designate a hostile Roman emperor:

- A popular spelling for the name of the emperor Nero adds up to 666 when written in Hebrew (נרון קסר = Caesar Neron). An alternative spelling (נרו קסר = Caesar Nero) adds up to 616, a variant reading for the number of the beast found in some manuscripts of Revelation.
- A designation for the emperor Domitian that sometimes appeared on Greek coins also adds up to 666: *A. Kαι. Domet. Seb. Ge.* (an abbreviation for *Autokratōr Kaisar Dometianos Sebastos Germanikos* = Emperor Caesar Domitian Augustus Germanicus).

But Bible readers throughout history have sought to determine if there might be anyone in their contemporary world who bears the number of the beast. In the second century, Bishop Irenaeus warned the church to be wary of anyone named "Evanthas," "Lateinos," or "Teitan," because the letters of those names in Greek equaled the fateful sum. Later, in the thirteenth century, some Franciscans noted that the Greek name of Pope Benedict XI (*benediktos*) made him suspect for the same reason. Some Protestant Christians in the twenty-first century would likewise cast aspersions on Pope Benedict XVI.

But why would the name have to be in Hebrew or Greek? English systems of gematria also exist: it was noted in the 1960s that "Kissinger" (President Richard Nixon's secretary of state) is a name that equals 666 in English gematria.

In recent years, beast hunters have set computers to work on this problem, and the pool of potential beasts now includes phenomena in addition to proper names. Words or phrases whose letters produce the ominous number (in accord with English gematria) include "computer," "New York," "US of America," and "SS Number."

Guesses can also be made without any appeal to gematria. Former US president Ronald Wilson Reagan was once identified as a candidate for the beast simply because he had six letters in each of his three names—and then after he left the presidency he moved to a house located at 666 St. Cloud Road (his wife later had the address changed to 668).

Finally, since an English "w" is equivalent to the Hebrew letter vav, which has a numerical value of six, some pundits have wondered whether "www" is not just another way of writing 666, in which case the beast could be the internet.

readings of Revelation see a shift at 4:1, from "messages for the early church" to "visions for the church at the end of time." Accordingly, such readings might take a historical approach to interpreting the seven letters (which come before 4:1) but adopt a futurist or idealist approach when it comes to figuring out the number of the beast (which comes after 4:1).

In the academic world, biblical scholars have tried to base their conclusions regarding the best approach to Revelation on what they have learned about the book's genre (discussed above). They frequently conclude three things: (1) to the extent that the book of Revelation is like a letter, it should be read as a communication intended primarily for people at the time when it was written (not primarily for people born long after it was written); (2) to the extent that Revelation is prophecy, it also should be understood as addressing the current circumstances of its original readers, since that is what prophecy typically does: like most prophets, the author of Revelation discloses things about the future, not so that people at a later time will have a guide to those events when they happen but rather that the disclosures might affect the attitudes and behavior of people in his own day; and (3) to the extent that Revelation is an apocalypse, it should be read as a book that employs imaginative symbolic language to convey general truth about God and the world, rather than as one that tries to provide detailed predictions regarding specific future events.

Accordingly, there is a clear preference in academic scholarship for historical readings of this book, with some allowance for idealist application. Futurist readings generally are disparaged in academic circles, though they remain very popular in church and society as a whole. To avoid overstatement, however, we should note that most scholars do grant that the book of Revelation intends to portray what will happen at the end of time in a broad and general sense. What they object to is the detailed futurist interpretations that try to line up references in Revelation with specific people or occurrences in the modern world. Most scholars hold that such interpretations are incompatible with the book's intent, based on a premise that we should not understand the book in ways that its original readers would not (and could not) have understood it.

The author of Revelation says that he is going to reveal "what must soon take place" (1:1). Accordingly, most scholars think the author believed the eschaton would arrive during his own lifetime or at least during the lifetime of his readers. This perspective accords with the scholarly preference for situating the book within its original context but raises theological questions concerning the book's continued significance for people who know that its most significant portents did not in fact occur. Simply stated, first-century Christians were assured that many things would take place "soon" that, two thousand years later, have still not happened. For one suggestion as to how Christians might resolve this dilemma, see 2 Peter 3:8.

Fig. 30.5. *St. John on Patmos.* John pens the book of Revelation, as depicted in a late medieval painting by Spanish artist Mates. (Bridgeman Images)

By any reckoning, Revelation can be one of the more confusing or disorienting books of the Bible. Those who try to take it as a fairly literal projection of "things to come" still end up disagreeing over how to construe the eschatological timetable (see box 30.4). And those who understand Revelation as a proclamation to readers of its own day still end up struggling to discover what messages were being conveyed and why the author chose this medium as the means for conveying them. Furthermore, although everyone agrees that the book of Revelation is heavily symbolic, readers do not always agree on *which* elements of the book are symbolic. Did John want his readers to believe that heaven literally has pearly gates and streets of gold (21:21)? And what about that millennial reign with Christ (20:6)? Is this something that John wants his readers to believe will literally happen on earth, or is it instead a figurative way to describe an ultimate triumph of peace and justice?

Box 30.4

Millennium, Tribulation, Rapture

In Revelation 20:1–10 John sees a vision in which Satan is bound and some Christian martyrs are raised from the dead. Faithful saints reign with Christ for one thousand years, and then Satan is released, but only to be cast in the lake of fire following a final battle.

Throughout the centuries Christians have adopted various positions with regard to what this vision of the "millennium" means:

- *Premillennialism*. Christ returns before the millennium: his faithful saints rule with him on earth for one thousand years after the second coming but prior to the final judgment and establishment of the new kingdom.
- *Postmillennialism*. Christ returns after the millennium: his faithful saints will successfully evangelize the world and rule it in peace for one thousand years before Christ's second coming.
- *Amillennialism*. Christ returns without any literal millennium: his faithful saints experience spiritual victory symbolized in Revelation as a triumph equivalent to a thousand-year reign.

Premillennialists take a futurist approach to interpreting Revelation and sometimes try to relate their understanding of the book to two other eschatological events: the "tribulation" (a seven-year period of woes thought to be described in Rev. 6–9 and specifically mentioned in Dan. 9:27; Rev. 11:2–3) and the "rapture" (a miraculous removal of God's faithful from the earth thought to be referenced in Matt. 24:40–41; 1 Thess. 4:15–17; Rev. 4:1). Thus premillennialism yields subcategories:

- *Pretribulationism*. The rapture will come prior to the onset of the tribulation (so the unfaithful who are left behind will receive a wake-up call regarding what is now to come).
- *Midtribulationism*. The rapture will come at some midpoint during the tribulation (so the faithful may regard any onset of terrible woes as a possible sign that the rapture is near).
- *Posttribulationism*. The rapture will come after the tribulation, at the time of Jesus's second coming (so even the faithful should expect to endure suffering prior to Christ's return).

Historical Background

word of God:
proclamation that expresses what God wants to say; in John 1 Jesus Christ is identified as the Word of God made flesh.

Unlike most apocalypses, Revelation does not pretend to be written by some famous religious figure out of the distant past. The person responsible for this book identifies himself as a Christian named "John" who was on the island of Patmos "because of the word of God and the testimony of Jesus" (1:9). The latter reference probably indicates that he has been banished from the mainland for witnessing to his faith and sent into exile on this island. But who is this person? In a popular vein, he often has been identified with the apostle John, who was one of the twelve disciples of Jesus. This view, however, was sharply challenged by authorities in the early church, and most modern scholars do not think that it can be maintained. Most interpreters today simply view the author of Revelation as a Christian prophet named "John" who is otherwise unknown to us.

Nevertheless, scholars do seek to surmise certain facts about the author from the book itself. He is steeped in the Old Testament and familiar with the imagery and style of Jewish apocalypses. Indeed, this John (whoever he was) appears to write Greek as one whose native language was Hebrew or Aramaic. So it is often suggested that (like the apostle) he was a Jewish Christian from Palestine who immigrated to Asia Minor at some point during or after the Jewish war with Rome. Since he seems to assume that the churches in that part of the world will regard him as a prophet (1:3; 22:7, 10, 18–19), he may have served those churches in

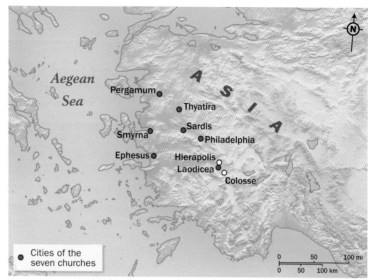

Map 30.1. Asia Minor: Churches addressed in Revelation.

a capacity similar to that of the itinerant prophet Agabus mentioned in Acts 21:10–11. Eventually, he ended up on the island of Patmos, probably banished from the mainland by political authorities.

When was Revelation written? The dominant theory places it during the reign of the Roman emperor Domitian (81–96), most likely toward the end of that period. This was the view of the early church, as reflected in testimony from Irenaeus, Tertullian, Clement of Alexandria, and Origen. The time period also fits concerns addressed in the book: Domitian referred to himself as a god and demanded emperor worship in a manner similar to what is attributed to "the beast" in Revelation (13:4). Domitian, however, is not known to have inflicted the sort of violent persecution on Christians that is prominent in this book (2:10, 13; 6:9; 17:6; 18:24; 20:4). The emperor Nero (54–68) was more famous in that regard, and some scholars think that connections to him can be found as well (such as the interpretation of 666 as a cipher for "Caesar Neron" mentioned above). Do those connections mean that the book might have been written earlier, during Nero's reign? Possibly. Or, perhaps, the book simply means to present Domitian as a "second Nero." Some scholars take a reference to the beast having recovered from a mortal wound (13:3) as a hint that Domitian is "Nero redivivus": everyone thought the beast was gone when Nero died, but now it is back. Discussion continues, but the most common approach today is to date Revelation around 95, during the reign of Domitian. One popular suggestion accepts this date but holds that our version of the book could be a "second edition," an expansion of an earlier work that hailed from the time of Nero.

The visions of Revelation were received by John on the island of Patmos and sent to seven churches in Asia Minor (now western Turkey; see map 30.1):

⊙ EXPLORE 30.14
The Date of Revelation: Clues within the Book Itself?

Ephesus, Smyrna, Pergamum, Thyatira, Sardis, Philadelphia, and Laodicea. Our New Testament also contains a "letter of Paul" to Ephesus and mentions a letter from Paul to Laodicea (see Col. 4:13–16). In the early second century (probably just fifteen years after Revelation), Ignatius of Antioch wrote letters to churches in Philadelphia, Smyrna, and Laodicea. The book of Acts makes mention of Thyatira (16:14) and contains colorful stories about early missionary work in Ephesus (18:18–20:1).

All of these cities were located in the Roman province of Asia, which is to say that all were part of the Roman Empire. They were somewhat distant from the capital city itself, but they remained dependent on that city for stability and prosperity. Loyalty to Rome was intense, as the general populations of these cities competed for Roman attention and favor. For example, Ephesus and Pergamum were rivals for the honor of being named *neōkoros* ("temple warden"), the city responsible for overseeing emperor worship for the entire province. On more than one occasion this official designation was withdrawn from one of these two cities and granted to the other, with attendant changes in fortune and prestige. And, of course, the main claim to fame of Ephesus was its magnificent temple to the Roman goddess Artemis (see Acts 19:23–41).

What was life like for the small (but growing) groups of Christians in these cities? Many Christians no doubt were viewed as disloyal and unpatriotic for despising the very things that most people considered to be emblems of local pride and national honor. They also were considered to be antisocial for shunning the banquets, festivals, and public amusements that were the stuff of ordinary people's lives. And they were thought to be irreligious for refusing even to acknowledge (much less propitiate) the gods whose favor was deemed essential for continued protection and prosperity. In short, there was tension between Christians and the general population, and many believers appear to have suffered as a result. Some were victims of violence, even to the point of death. Others had to deal with the reality of being publicly shamed in a culture in which social disgrace was often regarded as a fate worse than death. And many had to endure penalties and discrimination that led to economic hardship. For example, Christians may have been excluded from joining various trade guilds in which membership was all but essential for success in business or advancement in one's chosen profession.

The book of Revelation reflects that, in addition to having problems with Roman society in general, the Christians in these churches appear to have been on poor terms with the Jews in the local synagogues

Fig. 30.6. The divine Caesar. This Roman coin shows the emperor Domitian enthroned upon the earth with seven stars encircling his open hands. The inscription reads, "To the Divine Caesar." The book of Revelation presents Jesus Christ as the divine ruler of earth and describes him as holding seven stars in his hand (1:16).

(2:9; 3:9). And even within the Christian fold all was not well: some people who called themselves Christians were advocating ideas and practices that the book of Revelation regards as abhorrent. Though we do not know for certain who the so-called followers of Balaam (2:14) or Jezebel (2:20) were, it seems likely that they were Christians who had adopted an accommodating stance toward the Roman environment. Thus some teachers or prophets in these churches apparently were telling the people to just "lighten up" and "go with the flow": cooperate with the powers that be and learn to adapt; figure out how the world works and try to fit in; let the emerging religion of Christianity develop a compatibility with culture that will make it more appealing to society as a whole.

Fig. 30.7. The beast, a saint, and a hypocrite. The one whom Revelation calls "the beast" tramples a devoted believer of Christ while a hypocritical believer pays homage to the beast. (The Bridgeman Art Library International)

The stated purpose of the book of Revelation is to reveal "what must soon take place" (1:1). It attempts to do this in ways that will (1) inspire confidence in those whose obedience to God may prove costly; (2) stir up indignation toward those who defy God and promote injustice; (3) provoke repentance on the part of those who have been overly accommodating; and (4) inspire praise for God from those who realize that the Lord of history is worthy of their trust.

Major Themes in Revelation

Unveiling

The word *apokalypsis* (translated "revelation" in 1:1) literally means "unveiling." The book of Revelation seeks to pull back a veil and show Christians the truth about God and the truth about the world in which they live. Accordingly, the message of the book is both negative and positive, an oracle of doom infused with a promise of hope.

The Corruption of Human Society

Revelation shows believers what their world is really like, and it is not a pretty picture. In chapter 17 John beholds a vision of a woman who is "the great city that rules over the kings of the earth" (17:18). Scholars identify this city as Rome: the woman sits on seven mountains (17:9), just as Rome was built on seven hills, and she is also seated on many waters (17:1), just as Rome was fabled for its control of the seas. She is adorned with jewels and clothed in fine linens (17:4) in a manner emblematic of Rome's great prosperity. But although this woman seems rich and powerful, she is not a figure to be envied; she is, in fact, a drunken whore, supported by a monster, covered with blasphemies, sated with the blood of martyrs and saints (17:1–6). A horrible fate awaits her, and when it comes, she will be getting her just deserts (17:15–16). Thus one prominent message of Revelation is that the powerful and prosperous empire is not what it appears to be: when the empire is unveiled, it is exposed as a corrupt and horrible reality that believers should renounce and abhor.

⊙ EXPLORE 30.15
Church and State: Revelation as an Example of the Ethic of Resistance

Some theologians complain that Revelation's perspective on human society is too pessimistic, and they suggest that this extreme perception be balanced by more positive or neutral takes on the political world elsewhere in Scripture

---

Box 30.5

The Grapes of Wrath

Did you ever wonder about the title of John Steinbeck's 1939 novel *The Grapes of Wrath*? The book focuses on the hardships of tenant farmers during the Great Depression, but what exactly are "grapes of wrath"?

The book's title was inspired by a line from "The Battle Hymn of the Republic," composed by abolitionist Julia Ward Howe in 1861:

> Mine eyes have seen the glory of the coming of the Lord: He is trampling out the vintage where the grapes of wrath are stored.

But that line in itself makes little sense unless one realizes that it is an allusion to Revelation 14:19:

> The angel swung his sickle over the earth and gathered the vintage of the earth, and threw it into the great wine press of the wrath of God.

The biblical verse describes divine judgment meted out on those who have oppressed and exploited others: they will themselves be oppressed by God's avenging angel. The vision of judgment day as an awful, final harvest also recalls the words of Jesus in Matthew 13:24–30, 36–43.

(e.g., Rom. 13:1–7; 1 Pet. 2:13–17). But by the same token, Revelation is highly regarded as a work that takes seriously the power and nature of sin, portraying unrighteousness not just as personal immorality but rather as systemic evil and social injustice (see especially chap. 18). In this regard, Revelation usually is recognized as offering the most sustained political critique of an "anti-God society" anywhere in the New Testament: a society is "anti-God" when it uses its power to enslave others, when it becomes prosperous by making others poor, when it revels in self-adulation, or when it becomes cavalier about justice, ignoring the suffering of the innocent and allowing or perpetrating violence against the righteous. And, in a basic sense, an anti-God society is one that claims for itself the prerogatives of authority and power that belong to God alone.

systemic evil: evil that arises from or manifests itself in structures within human society, assuming a corporate dimension that transcends individual wickedness.

Fig. 30.8. *To God Be the Glory*. This work illustrates the scene described in Revelation 5:1–14. The artist, Peter Attie "Charlie" Besharo, was a Syrian immigrant to the United States whose activity as an artist remained undiscovered until after his death in 1960, when numerous acclaimed works were found in a garage that he had rented in Pennsylvania. (Ricco/Maresca Gallery / Art Resource, NY)

The Judgment of God

Revelation depicts human society as standing under God's judgment, which is imminent, final, and absolute. The readers are assured that whatever trouble comes on those who spurn the corruption of this world will be of minimal consequence compared to this divine judgment; their current experience of temporal tribulation will prove to be nothing compared to what God's angels dole out. This, then, is the real crisis, what requires their full attention. The visions of Revelation alert believers to this true crisis, so that they will not compromise their faithfulness in ways that might spare them minor troubles today, only to guarantee them harsher judgment from God in the near future.

God Controls the Future

Revelation not only exposes the corruption of the world and its power systems but also pulls back the veil of heaven to reveal who truly is in control of history. In so doing, it provides an ultimate proclamation of confidence and hope. God alone is Lord of history, and so the forces of evil will not prevail. Suffering is only temporary, for God is preparing a new world in which all sorrow and injustice will be banished: God will dwell with God's people and "wipe away every tear from their eyes. Death will be no more; mourning and crying and pain will be no more" (21:4). Indeed, Revelation does not just predict that this will happen; it also claims that this victory over evil has already been won through the death and resurrection of Jesus Christ (5:9–10). The truth that this book unveils is that what is currently happening on earth and what will soon take place are but a playing out of events for which the ultimate outcome has already been determined. Those who have been loved by Jesus and freed from their sins by his blood (1:5) are able to witness troubling times unfold without giving in to despair, for they know how the story ends. The church, accordingly, becomes a community of prophets (19:10; 22:9), empowered to speak and live for the one who, they know, is already ruling in heaven.

Worship

Finally, Revelation answers the question, "Who is worthy of adulation?" No earthly power, however grand, but only God and the Lamb are worthy of receiving "power and wealth and wisdom and might and honor and glory and blessing" (5:12; cf. 4:11). For this reason, the entire book of Revelation is threaded with songs of worship and hymns of praise (1:5–6; 4:8, 11; 5:9–14; 7:10–12; 11:15–18; 12:10–12; 15:3–4; 16:5–7; 19:1–8). Despite its bleak portrait of injustice in a corrupt world, Revelation remains an optimistic book. It is, in the final analysis, an ironic invitation to joy.

Conclusion

The book of Revelation often has created problems for theological leaders in the church, who have not always known what to make of it. It was the only book of the New Testament on which John Calvin did not write a commentary. And Martin Luther admitted freely, "My spirit cannot accommodate itself to this book." Still, it has been a boon to artists and poets. Pieter Brueghel, William Blake, Salvador Dali, and countless others have been inspired by its fantastic imagery, and no other book in the New Testament has contributed so generously to the church's hymnody and liturgy. At a crassly popular level, it continues to fuel everything from pulp fiction to Christian rock operas to Hollywood horror movies. Revelation has proved to be a book to fire the imagination, to take readers beyond themselves. It expands our horizons, spatially and temporally: we travel from earth to heaven and from the present to the future, without always knowing exactly what the experience means—except that God, here in the final book of the Bible, as in all things, has the last word.

FOR FURTHER READING: **Revelation**

Bauckham, Richard J. *The Theology of the Book of Revelation*. New Testament Theology. Cambridge: Cambridge University Press, 1993.

Koester, Craig. *Revelation and the End of All Things*. Grand Rapids: Eerdmans, 2001.

Lewis, Scott. *What Are They Saying about New Testament Apocalyptic?* Mahwah, NJ: Paulist Press, 2007.

Michaels, J. Ramsey. *Interpreting the Book of Revelation*. Grand Rapids: Baker Academic, 2015.

Puskas, Charles B. *Hebrews, the General Letters, and Revelation: An Introduction*. Eugene, OR: Cascade, 2016.

Thomas, John Christopher, and Frank D. Macchia. *Revelation*. Two Horizons Commentary. Grand Rapids: Eerdmans, 2016.

Trafton, Joseph. *Reading Revelation: A Literary and Theological Commentary*. Rev. ed. Reading the New Testament. Macon, GA: Smyth & Helwys, 2005.

Walhout, Edwin. *Revelation Down to Earth: Making Sense of the Apocalypse of John*. Grand Rapids: Eerdmans, 2000.

Witherington, Ben, III. *Revelation*. New Cambridge Bible Commentary. Cambridge: Cambridge University Press, 2003.

Wright, N. T. *Revelation for Everyone*. 2nd ed. Louisville: Westminster John Knox, 2004.

⊙ Go to www
.IntroducingNT.com
for summaries,
videos, and other
study tools.

Glossary

Abba the Aramaic word for "Father" used by Jesus, and so employed by some of his followers (Gal. 4:6).

ad hominem attacking an opponent's character rather than addressing his or her arguments.

allegory a type of figurative speech in which the elements or characters that make up a story signify concepts or other entities in the real world; for example, the parable of the sower is an allegory because the seed stands for the word of God and the four types of soil stand for different people who hear the word of God.

amanuensis a secretary or trained scribe who writes letters for other people.

amillennialism the belief or doctrine that Christ will return without any literal millennium: his faithful saints will experience a spiritual victory (symbolized in Revelation as a triumph equivalent to a thousand-year reign).

animism belief in the existence of spirits that can possess people, animals, and other entities (trees, brooks, rocks, etc.).

antichrist in a general sense, anyone opposed to Christ and his followers (1 John 2:18); specifically, an ultimate enemy of Christ to appear at the end of time.

antitheses six statements of Jesus in Matthew 5:21–48 in which he states his own view over and against that which people "have heard said."

apocalyptic ideas ideas influenced by a pessimistic forecast for the world at large, combined with an optimistic outlook for a favored remnant, who will be rescued out of the evil world through some imminent act of divine intervention.

apocalypticism a religious worldview that combines a radical dualistic outlook (clear distinction between good and evil) with a deterministic view of history (the idea that everything is proceeding according to a divine plan).

apocalyptic literature a genre of heavily symbolic literature that displays distinctive literary characteristics and claims to unveil the truth about the world as viewed from a dualistic and deterministic perspective. See "apocalyptic ideas."

Apocrypha books of the Old Testament whose status as Scripture is disputed by Protestant, Roman Catholic, and Eastern Orthodox Christians; for the most part, these are writings that were included in the Septuagint but not the Hebrew Bible.

apostasy the abandonment or renunciation of one's religious faith.

apostle "one who is sent" (*apostolos*); used for certain leaders among the earliest followers of Jesus, especially the twelve disciples and Paul. See "disciple."

apostolic having to do with the earliest followers of Jesus and/or the apostle Paul; apostolic writings are ones produced by people who knew Jesus or Paul (or, at least, writings that are in line with the thinking of such people).

apostolic age the time period between the crucifixion of Jesus and the deaths of his first followers.

apostolic authority in Paul's letters, the claim that the author has the power and responsibility to instruct, exhort, and discipline persons who were brought to faith through his ministry.

apostolic council a meeting of leaders in the early church to discuss acceptance of gentiles into the new faith community (Acts 15); also called "Jerusalem council."

apostolic tradition oral or written materials that are believed to bear a close connection to Jesus, his original disciples, or the missionary Paul, or believed to be congruent with what those people taught.

apprentice authorship a situation in which an author dies and persons who had been previously authorized to speak for that author continue to do so by producing materials in the author's name.

aqueduct an artificial conduit for conveying water from a distance, usually by means of gravity.

Aramaic a Semitic language similar to Hebrew that was the native tongue for Jesus and many other Jews living in Palestine during the New Testament period.

archaeology the study of human history and prehistory through the excavation of sites and the analysis of artifacts and other physical remains.

Areopagus a hill in Athens where Paul preached to pagan philosophers, according to Acts 17:16–34.

ascension the event in which Jesus Christ left the physical earth and went up into heaven, as reported in Luke 24:50–51 and Acts 1:9.

ascetic religiously strict or severe, especially with regard to self-denial or renunciation of worldly pleasures.

atonement an action that makes amends for sins, such that guilty persons may be restored to fellowship with God.

augury a field of science or sorcery devoted to discerning the future, specifically through observation of birds; the term is also used more generally to refer to divination by other means (oracles, mediums, observation of stars, etc.).

authentic in discussions of authorship, "not pseudepigraphic"—that is, written by the person to whom a work is ascribed.

Ave Maria a classic prayer or hymn used in the Roman Catholic Church; its words are based on the acclamation of Mary by Elizabeth in Luke 1:42–45.

baptism a religious rite involving symbolic washing with water; it sometimes signifies repentance, purification, or acceptance into the community of God's people.

BCE an abbreviation meaning "before the common era"; in academic studies BCE is typically used for dates in place of BC ("before Christ").

beatitude any statement of divine blessing (though the term has come to be associated more specifically with the blessings offered by Jesus in Matt. 5:3–12 and Luke 6:20–23).

Beatitudes the blessings offered by Jesus in Matthew 5:3–12 and Luke 6:20–23.

Beelzebul slightly corrupted version of the Hebrew name for a Philistine god (2 Kings 1:2); the term is used as another name for Satan in the New Testament (Matt. 10:25; 12:24).

beloved disciple an unnamed follower of Jesus whose written testimony is said to be incorporated into the Gospel of John (21:20, 24); church tradition has associated this individual with the apostle John, one of Jesus's twelve disciples.

benediction a blessing, often offered at the conclusion of a document or worship service.

Benedictus a hymn in Luke 1:67–79, expressing the words of Zechariah upon hearing that he would be the father of John the Baptist.

benefactor in a patron-client relationship, the powerful party who provides benefits for others and to whom service, loyalty, and gratitude are due.

bind (a law) to discern God's will by determining that a commandment applies to a situation that it does not explicitly address

bishop "overseer" (*episkopos*); a type of leader in the early church, perhaps analogous to a pastor today. See "deacon"; "elder."

Boanerges Aramaic for "sons of thunder"; a nickname that Jesus gave to two of his disciples, the brothers James and John (Mark 3:17).

Book of Glory the second half of John's Gospel (13:1–20:31), so-called because it deals with the last week of Jesus's life when the time for Jesus to be "glorified" had come (17:1).

Book of Signs the first half of John's Gospel (1:19–12:50), so-called because it relates stories of remarkable things Jesus does, which are repeatedly called "signs."

canon literally, "rule" or "standard"; used by religious groups to refer to an authoritative list of books that are officially accepted as Scripture.

Captivity Letters (Epistles) See "Prison Letters (Epistles)."

casting lots a practice akin to "drawing straws," used to select a person for a given task; "lots" were marked stones similar to dice (see Acts 1:26).

catholic "general" or "universal"; in religious studies, the phrase "catholic church" refers not to the Roman Catholic Church but rather to all Christians throughout the world.

Catholic Letters (Epistles) See "General Letters (Epistles)."

CE an abbreviation meaning "common era"; in academic studies CE is typically used for dates in place of AD (*Anno domini*, "in the year of our Lord").

centurion a Roman army officer, typically in charge of one hundred soldiers.

Cephas an Aramaic word meaning "Rock," the Greek form of which is "Peter"; a nickname given by Jesus to Simon, one of his disciples.

chiasm an organizing device for speaking or writing that arranges items in an "a, b, b, a" pattern—for example, "light and darkness, darkness and light."

Christ "anointed one"; the man known as "Jesus the Christ" eventually came to be called simply "Jesus Christ." See "Messiah."

Christ crucified the main focus of Paul's preaching according to 1 Corinthians 1:22–24; 2:1–2; the phrase seems to be shorthand for what theologians call a "theology of the cross" (*theologia crucis*).

Christ Hymn the poetic passage in Philippians 2:6–11 that describes Christ as one who was in the form of God but humbled himself to become human and die on a cross.

Christology a branch of theology that focuses on the person and work of Jesus Christ, often understood as an eternal divine figure. See "Historical Jesus Studies."

circumcision a surgical procedure that removes the foreskin of a penis; in the Jewish tradition, the rite is viewed as a sign of the covenant that God had made with Israel.

clergy leaders who are officially ordained or authorized to perform religious duties.

client in a patron-client relationship, the person lacking power, who is expected to respond to the benefactor with gratitude, loyalty, and service.

collection for Jerusalem a fundraising effort conducted by the apostle Paul among gentile believers on behalf of Jewish believers in Jerusalem (see Acts 11:29–30; 24:17; Rom. 15:25–27; 1 Cor. 16:1–4; 2 Cor. 8–9; Gal. 2:10).

Colossian Hymn the poetic passage in Colossians 1:15–20 that exalts Christ as the image of the invisible God, the ruler of the universe, and the one who reconciles all things in heaven and on earth.

Community Discourse a speech by Jesus in Matthew 18 dealing with life in the church, forgiveness, and discipline.

composition analysis the study of how units are arranged within a particular book—order or placement, sequence, and overall structural layout.

confessional concerns matters of faith pertinent to particular religious groups or denominations.

confessional statements declarations on matters of faith pertinent to particular religious groups or denominations.

cosmic Christ an exalted understanding of the risen Christ as the creator and ruler of the universe.

cosmic powers spiritual beings, perhaps associated with stars and other heavenly bodies (Eph. 6:12).

covenant in the Bible, an agreement or pact between God and human beings that establishes the terms of their ongoing relationship.

creed a confessional statement summarizing key articles of faith.

crucifixion a Roman form of execution by which the condemned person was fastened to a wooden stake and left to die a slow and torturous death.

cultural anthropology an academic discipline that seeks to understand a culture (and its literature) by way of comparison with what is known about other cultures.

Cynicism a philosophical orientation that emphasized radical authenticity, repudiation of shame, simplicity of lifestyle, and a desire to possess only what is obtained naturally and freely.

deacon a type of leader in the early church, the exact duties of which are unclear; the word means "one who serves" (*diakonos*) and sometimes was used of a table waiter. See "bishop"; "elder."

Dead Sea Scrolls a collection of Jewish documents copied and preserved between 250 BCE and 70 CE. See "Essenes"; "Qumran."

deconstruction a method employed by postmodern biblical critics to demonstrate that interpretations of texts are based on subjective criteria and thus possess no intrinsic claim to legitimacy.

delay of the parousia in theological studies, a term used for the problem faced by second-generation Christians who had to grapple with the fact that Jesus had not returned to his (original) followers as expected.

delegated authorship a situation in which an author describes the basic content of an intended writing to an amanuensis, who then produces the writing for the author to approve.

Demiurge in gnosticism, an evil or at least inferior deity responsible for creating the world of matter.

demon an evil (or "unclean") spirit capable of possessing people and incapacitating them with some form of illness or disability. See "exorcism."

denarius a silver Roman coin equal to the typical wage for a day's labor.

deuterocanonical writings a term used primarily by Roman Catholics with reference to eleven of the fifteen books that Protestants call the "Apocrypha"; the books are thus regarded as a "secondary canon," part of Scripture, but distinct from both Old and New Testament writings.

deutero-Pauline letters letters ascribed to Paul that are believed to have been written after Paul's death by persons who felt qualified to address the church in Paul's name; also called the "disputed letters of Paul."

Diaspora Jews living outside Palestine; also, "Dispersion."

Diatessaron a Gospel harmonization produced by the second-century Syrian Christian Tatian; it combined material from the four Gospels into one continuous narrative, eliminating the need for separate Gospels.

diatribe a rhetorical device derived from Greek philosophy in which an author argues with an imaginary opponent by proposing objections and then responding to them.

dictation a situation in which an author dictates a writing almost word for word to an amanuensis.

Diolkos a paved trackway near Corinth in the Roman period by which boats could be moved overland between the Adriatic and Aegean Seas.

disciple "one who learns" (*mathētēs*); used broadly for anyone who follows Jesus and more narrowly for someone who belongs to his hand-picked group of closest followers (the "twelve disciples"). See "apostle."

Dispersion typically, Jews (including Jewish Christians) living outside Palestine (synonymous with "Diaspora"), but 1 Peter seems to apply the term to gentiles.

disputed letters of Paul the six letters ascribed to Paul that many New Testament scholars believe to be pseudepigraphic: Ephesians, Colossians, 2 Thessalonians, 1 Timothy, 2 Timothy, Titus; also called the "deutero-Pauline letters."

divination any practice used to discern the will of divine beings and/or to predict the future.

docetism the belief that Jesus was not actually a human being but only appeared to be one.

doctrine a belief or set of recognized beliefs held and taught by a church.

dominions powerful spiritual beings (Eph. 1:21; Col. 1:16).

doublet in literature, a pair or duplication of references.

doxology a hymn or group of words that expresses praise to God.

dualism the tendency to separate phenomena into sharply opposed categories, with little room for anything in between (e.g., to regard everything as either "good" or "evil").

earthly Jesus in distinction from the "exalted Jesus," this is the man Jesus who lived physically on earth for a period of time. Also called "pre-Easter Jesus."

ecclesiology beliefs and ideas about the nature and function of the church, or of the Christian community in general.

effective righteousness the notion that, because of Christ, God imparts righteousness to sinners, transforming them so that they are able to please God in ways that would not be possible otherwise.

elder a type of leader in the early church, the level of authority and exact duties of which probably varied in different contexts. See "bishop"; "deacon."

elect, the those chosen by God, predestined for salvation or some special purpose

election in theology, the notion or doctrine that people may be chosen by God for salvation or some predetermined destiny.

elemental spirits of the universe a generic term for powerful spiritual beings (Col. 2:8, 20).

emendation analysis the study of alterations that an author probably made to source material—additions, omissions, and other changes that reveal the author's priorities and preferences.

Emmanuel Hebrew name meaning "God with us"; it was first used in Isaiah 7:14 and later applied to Jesus in Matthew 1:23. Sometimes it is written as "Immanuel."

Epicureanism a philosophical orientation that emphasized free will, questioned fate, and encouraged the attainment of true pleasure through avoidance of anxiety, concentration on the present, and enjoyment of all things in moderation.

epiphany a manifestation of divine truth or presence.

Eschatological Discourse a speech by Jesus in Matthew 24–25 dealing with the end times, the second coming, and the final judgment.

eschatology study or focus on "last things," such as the return of Christ, final judgment, or other phenomena associated with the end times.

Essenes ascetic, separatist Jews who lived in private communities; they probably are to be identified with the group that lived at Qumran and preserved a library of manuscripts now known as the Dead Sea Scrolls.

eternal life in biblical terms, life that is endless both qualitatively and quantitatively; life filled with value and meaning that has already begun, will continue after death, and will last forever.

eternal security the idea or doctrine in some Christian traditions that those who find salvation through Jesus Christ can never lose that salvation.

Eucharist from a Greek word meaning "thanksgiving"; the ritual meal observed by Christians in a manner that commemorates Jesus's last supper with his disciples; also called "Lord's Supper" and "Holy Communion."

eunuch a castrated male; often a religious devotee (Matt. 19:12) or an attendant in a royal court (Acts 8:27).

evangelical pertaining to or in keeping with the Christian gospel and its teachings.

evangelist in New Testament studies, an author of any one of the four Gospels; Matthew, Mark, Luke, and John are the four evangelists.

exalted Jesus in distinction from the "earthly Jesus," this is the divine figure who dwells in heaven and interacts spiritually with his followers through faith. Also called "post-Easter Jesus."

excommunication the practice of expelling unrepentant persons from the church, so-called because the excluded person is no longer allowed to commune, to take part in the Lord's Supper.

exegesis scholarly study of the Bible with an emphasis on the explication of texts using various academic approaches (called "exegetical methods").

exiles in Israelite history, the Jewish people who spent fifty years in Babylon after they were deported from their homeland in 587 BCE and before they (or their descendants) were allowed to return in 537 BCE.

exorcism the act of casting a demon out of a person or thing, thereby liberating the possessed entity from the control or influence of the evil or unclean spirit.

expiation a cleansing or removal of defilement, used in discussions of atonement to describe the effects of Christ's death as covering or removing human sin. See "propitiation."

faith (as a verb) sometimes, a strong belief in God or religious doctrines; more often, an orientation of complete trust and confidence in God that transforms one's life and being.

Farewell Discourse in the Gospel of John, a final speech given by Jesus on the night of his arrest (chaps. 13–16).

Farrer Theory a minority solution to the Synoptic Puzzle/Problem that does away with any need to posit a Q source: Mark was written first; Matthew used Mark as a source; and Luke used both Mark and Matthew.

feminist criticism an academic approach that seeks to understand texts from a feminist perspective.

fertility the ability to produce offspring; used of humans able to conceive children, or of fields able to produce crops.

fictive fiction-like; the Gospels are said to be "fictive narratives" because even when they report historical events, they do so in a literary style more closely associated with fiction.

firstfruits an agricultural term for crops collected at the beginning of the harvest season; Jesus is called the "firstfruits of the resurrection" because his resurrection is thought to precede and anticipate the general resurrection of all.

foot-washing the act of washing another person's feet, which, in the early Christian church, became a ritual practice symbolizing service.

forgery a situation in which authors produce writings in the name of a prominent individual in order to present that person as a supporter of their own ideas.

form criticism an academic approach that attempts to classify literary materials by type or genre and identify the purposes for which such materials were usually intended.

Four-Source Hypothesis a variation on the Two-Source Hypothesis, suggesting that Matthew and Luke not only each made use of Mark and Q but also drew separately on source material called "M" and "L."

fruit of the Spirit nine moral characteristics that Paul lists in Galatians 5:22–23, maintaining that they are produced in believers by the Spirit of God: love, joy, peace, patience, kindness, generosity, faithfulness, gentleness, and self-control.

fulfillment citation a form-critical category for a declaration that something has happened in order to fulfill what was prophesied in the Scriptures (e.g., Matt. 2:15).

gematria the practice of assigning a numerical value to a word or phrase by adding together the values of the individual letters; this works in Hebrew and in Greek, where the letters of the alphabet can also serve as numerals.

General Letters (Epistles) seven letters traditionally thought to have been written to the church "at large" rather than to specific individual congregations: James, 1 Peter, 2 Peter, 1 John, 2 John, 3 John, Jude. Also called "Catholic Letters (Epistles)."

genre a type or form of literature (e.g., poetry, letter, narrative).

gentile a person who is not Jewish.

gentile mission the intentional effort of Paul and other Jewish followers of Jesus to evangelize non-Jews, proclaiming the gospel of Christ to pagans and converting them to what would become known as the Christian religion.

Gethsemane the site of an orchard on the Mount of Olives just outside Jerusalem; the place where Jesus was arrested (Mark 14:32–52; John 18:1–14).

Gloria in Excelsis a liturgical hymn used in many churches, based on the angel's song in Luke 2:14.

glorification an understanding of God's saving activity according to which, through Christ, people share in the glory of God (Rom. 8:18, 21, 30; 1 Thess. 2:12).

glossolalia See "speaking in tongues."

gnosticism a religious movement or perspective that regarded "spirit" as fundamentally good and "matter" as fundamentally evil.

God-fearers gentiles who were sympathetic to Jewish theology and morality, participating somewhat in the culture and worship but without full conversion.

Golden Rule a traditional name given to the words of Jesus in Matthew 7:12: "In everything do to others as you would have them do to you."

Golgotha An Aramaic word meaning "skull"; the name of the place where Jesus was crucified.

gospel literally, "good news" (*euangelion*); the word was first used to describe the essential content of Christian proclamation and later was applied to books that present semibiographical accounts of Jesus ("the Gospels").

grace the free and unmerited favor of God, as manifested in the salvation of sinners and the bestowal of undeserved blessings.

Great Commission a traditional name given to concluding words of Matthew's Gospel, where Jesus tells his followers to go and make disciples of all nations and promises to be with them always (Matt. 28:18–20).

Great Omission in Lukan studies, a reference to Mark 6:45–8:20, none of which is paralleled in Luke's Gospel. See "Little Omission."

Greco-Roman world the lands and culture around the Mediterranean Sea during the period from Alexander the Great through Constantine (roughly 300 BCE to 300 CE).

Griesbach Hypothesis See "Two-Gospel Hypothesis."

Hades the underworld, or place where the dead dwell; in the New Testament, it sometimes appears to be synonymous with hell.

Hanukkah an eight-day Jewish festival commemorating the rededication of the Jewish temple in 164 BCE after it had been defiled by Antiochus Epiphanes; also called "Feast of Dedication" and "Feast of Lights."

Hasmonean the family name of the Jewish rebels who led a successful revolt against the Syrians in 167 BCE. See "Maccabees."

Haustafel a German term (plural, *Haustafeln*) often used in biblical studies for a "household table" of family responsibilities (see Eph. 5:21–6:9; Col. 3:18–4:1; 1 Tim. 2:8–15; 5:1–2; 6:1–2; Titus 2:1–10; 1 Pet. 2:13–3:7).

heavenly intercession the concept or doctrine that the risen Jesus (now in heaven) prays to God for human beings.

Hellenism a set of ideals that characterized Greek and Roman culture, customs, philosophy, and modes of thought.

Hellenistic affected by Hellenism—that is, the influence of Greek and Roman culture, customs, philosophy, and modes of thought. For example, Jewish people were said to be "Hellenized" when they adopted Greco-Roman customs or came to believe propositions derived from Greek philosophy.

heresy false teaching, or teaching that does not conform to the official standards of a religious community.

hermeneutics philosophical reflection on the process of biblical interpretation, including consideration of what the goal of interpretation should be, of different ways in which biblical passages might be regarded as meaningful, and of the ways in which authority is ascribed to biblical texts.

Herodians supporters of Herod; in the New Testament, the term probably refers to a Jewish party that favored the Roman ruler.

historical criticism broadly, academic study that deals with matters pertinent to the historical composition of a writing (author, date, and place of writing, intended audience, etc.); increasingly the term is used more precisely to refer to investigations concerning what can be verified as authentic historical data in accord with accepted criteria of such analysis.

historical Jesus the figure of Jesus who emerges from an analysis of sources in accord with generally accepted principles of historical science.

Historical Jesus Studies a branch of historical research that focuses on the life and work of the man Jesus, to the extent that this can be reconstructed from the available sources. See "Christology."

historical present in grammar, the use of a present tense verb to describe an action that occurred in the past; a common phenomenon in the Gospel of Mark.

historiography "the writing of history"; a written work that offers a particular representation of history.

Holy Communion the ritual meal observed by Christians in a manner that commemorates Jesus's last supper with his disciples; also called "Eucharist" and "Lord's Supper."

holy kiss a ritual greeting practiced in early Christian liturgies in which men and women kissed not only same-gendered persons on the lips (as was common) but also other-gendered persons, on the premise that all believers were brothers and sisters in Christ.

homosexual acts a term that when used precisely refers to sexual acts engaged in by homosexuals, but when used imprecisely may refer to sexual acts engaged in by persons of the same sex regardless of whether they are homosexuals. See "same-sex acts."

honor the positive status that one has in the eyes of those whom one considers to be significant. See "shame."

honorable pseudepigraphy a situation in which people produce writings in the name of a (probably deceased) prominent person as a tribute to that person's influence on their thinking.

humility the quality of consciously seeking what is best for others rather than what is best for oneself.

"I am" Sayings passages in John's Gospel in which Jesus describes himself with metaphors (6:35, 51; 8:12; 9:5; 10:7, 9, 11, 14; 11:25; 14:6; 15:1, 5).

ideological criticism a field of academic study that explores how texts are understood when they are read from particular ideological perspectives (e.g., feminist, evangelical, Jungian, Marxist).

idol food food available for consumption that had been used in a sacrifice to a pagan god or idol; in Roman society, this included most meat sold in the marketplace.

Immanuel See "Emmanuel."

immortality of the soul the idea from Greek philosophy that each person has a soul that continues to live after his or her body dies.

imputed righteousness the notion that, because of Christ, God reckons people as righteous: people are counted as righteous even though they continue to struggle and fail to live as God wishes.

incarnation the Christian doctrine that God became a human being in the person of Jesus Christ.

inclusio a literary device in which parallel expressions are used at the beginning and the ending of a literary unit.

infancy narrative the first two chapters of either Matthew or Luke that relate events associated with the birth and upbringing of Jesus.

insula a building common in Roman cities in which the top floor consisted of living quarters and the bottom floor of shops that opened out onto the street.

intercalation a literary device in which one story or narrative is inserted into the middle of another.

Jerusalem council a meeting of leaders in the early church to discuss acceptance of gentiles into the new faith community (Acts 15); also called "apostolic council."

Journey to Jerusalem a long section of Luke's Gospel (9:51–19:40) that presents stories and teaching of Jesus as he and his disciples travel from Galilee to Jerusalem.

Judaism a general term for the religious systems and beliefs of the Jewish people; in Jesus's day, there were varieties of Judaism, though all of these had certain fundamental ideas and practices in common.

Judaizer a term sometimes used by scholars to describe Christians who insisted that gentile Christians be circumcised and observe other practices that had traditionally identified Jews as the covenant people of God.

justification the act of being put into a right relationship with God.

justification by faith a term used interchangeably with "justification by grace" (depending on whether one wishes to emphasize the grace of the giver or the faith through which the gift is received).

justification by grace the idea or doctrine that God has acted graciously through Jesus Christ in a manner that allows people to be put right with God through faith (i.e., by trusting in God's gracious, unmerited favor).

kingdom of God / kingdom of heaven phrases used to describe the phenomenon of God ruling, wherever and whenever that might be; sometimes the phrases refer to a more precise manifestation of God's reign—for example "in heaven" or "at the end of time."

Last Supper a final Passover meal that Jesus ate with his disciples on the night he was arrested; the context that gave rise to Christian celebrations of the Lord's Supper (Eucharist, Holy Communion).

law, the "the law of Moses" or any regulations the Jewish people understood as delineating faithfulness to God in terms of the covenant God had made with Israel.

lawless one according to 2 Thessalonians, an ultimate enemy of Christ to appear at the end of time (2:3–12), possibly to be identified with the antichrist of 1 John 2:18 (cf. 1 John 2:22; 4:3; 2 John 7) or with the beast of Revelation 11:7; 13:1–18.

legion a unit of three thousand to six thousand soldiers in the Roman army.

liberation theology a movement in Christian theology, developed mainly by twentieth-century Latin American Roman Catholics, that emphasizes liberation from social, political, and economic oppression as an anticipation of ultimate salvation.

limited good in economics, the belief that money and things that money can buy are finite, such that acquisition of wealth or resources by some necessitates depletion of wealth or resources for others.

literal authorship a situation in which an author produces a document by literally writing it in his or her own hand.

Little Omission in Lukan studies, a reference to Mark 9:41–10:12, none of which is paralleled in Luke's Gospel. See "Great Omission."

L material material found only in Luke's Gospel, meaning that Luke did not derive it from Mark's Gospel or from the Q source but rather from a variety of other, unknown sources.

Logos in Greek philosophy, a word referring to ultimate truth or reason; in John's Gospel, the term is used for the eternal divine entity that takes on flesh to become the human being Jesus Christ (see John 1:1–4, 14; most English Bibles translate *logos* as "Word").

loose (a law) to discern God's will by determining that a commandment, while valid, does not apply to a particular situation.

Lord's Supper the ritual meal observed by Christians in a manner that commemorates Jesus's last supper with his disciples; also called "Eucharist" and "Holy Communion."

lots See "casting lots."

love feast a term used for the Lord's Supper in the early church. See Jude 12.

Maccabees literally, "hammers"; the nickname given to the Jewish rebels who led a successful revolt against the Syrians in 167 BCE. See "Hasmonean."

magi astrologers or sorcerers associated with Persian religion.

Magnificat a hymn in Luke 1:46–55, expressing the words of Mary on hearing that she would give birth to Jesus.

mammon money and things that money can buy.

manuscript in biblical studies, an ancient handwritten document containing a book or portion of the Bible.

Markan priority the theory that Mark's Gospel was written first and was used as a source for both Matthew and Luke.

Messiah an Aramaic word meaning "anointed one"; it designated a promised and expected deliverer of the Jewish people. See "Christ."

messianic secret in biblical studies, a term employed to describe the motif in Mark's Gospel according to which Jesus's identity appears to be intentionally shrouded in mystery.

midtribulationism a subset of premillennialism, according to which a rapture will come at some midpoint during the tribulation (so the faithful may regard any onset of terrible woes as a possible sign that the rapture is near).

millennium a thousand-year period; Revelation 20:1–8 speaks of a millennium during which Christ will rule after Satan is defeated.

Mishnah a collection of rabbinic discussions regarding interpretation of the law of Moses; the Mishnah forms one major part of the Jewish Talmud.

Missionary Discourse a speech by Jesus in Matthew 10 dealing with mission, persecution, and radical faithfulness.

misunderstanding a literary motif, prominent in John's Gospel, according to which characters miss the point because they take literally words that are intended to be understood symbolically.

M material material found only in Matthew's Gospel, meaning that Matthew did not derive it from Mark's Gospel or from the Q source, but rather from a variety of other, unknown sources.

monotheism the belief that there is only one God; compare "polytheism."

mujerista criticism an academic approach that seeks to understand texts from the perspective of Hispanic women.

Muratorian Fragment a document from the latter half of the second century that lists which New Testament writings were considered to be Scripture at that time.

mystery in the biblical world, something hidden that can be known only if and when it is revealed by God.

mystery religions popular religious cults that flourished during the Hellenistic era and tended to keep their doctrines and practices secret from outsiders.

mystics practitioners of mysticism, a Christian tradition in which believers seek union with God through prayer and contemplation in a manner that transcends intellectual explanation.

narrative criticism an academic approach that draws on modern literary analysis to determine the effects that biblical stories are expected to have on their readers.

neōkoros "temple warden"; the city appointed to serve as an official headquarters for the imperial cult, in charge of festivities and rituals honoring and worshiping the emperor.

new creation an understanding of God's saving activity according to which, through Christ, people are given a new life in a new age that has already begun (see 2 Cor. 5:17; Gal. 2:20; 6:15).

new perspective on Paul an academic position that maintains that the point of Paul's emphasis on "justification by grace apart from works of the laws" was to claim that people are put right with God through divine grace rather than by observing the legal codes that marked Israel as God's chosen people.

Northern Galatian Theory the theory that Paul wrote his letter to the Galatians to churches founded on his second missionary journey in north-central Asia Minor. See "Southern Galatian Theory."

Nunc Dimittis a liturgical hymn used in many churches, based on the song of Simeon in Luke 2:29–32.

obedience of faith a concept in Paul's theology (Rom. 1:5) indicating that people not only are accepted by God as righteous because of their faith but also are transformed through faith so that they are able to please God in ways that would not be possible otherwise.

oracle a person, usually female, capable of receiving messages from the gods in response to particular queries, including questions about the future; the term is also used for the place where such messages are given, and for the message itself.

oral tradition material passed on by word of mouth; early Christians relied on oral tradition as well as on written sources when writing the Gospels.

original sin the concept or doctrine that all humanity is lost in sin because of an inherent sinful nature bequeathed to all on account of Adam's trespass.

orthodoxy "right thinking" or correct doctrine.

orthopraxis "right practice" or correct behavior.

ostraca shards of pottery, sometimes used as small tablets for writing.

pagan Greco-Roman religion and culture as viewed from the perspective of Jews and Christians, who tended to associate what was "pagan" with erratic religious beliefs and an immoral lifestyle.

pagan images images associated with the people who Jews and Christians regarded as pagans (nonconverted gentiles).

pagans nonconverted gentiles, often associated by Jews and Christians with idolatry, polytheism, erratic religious beliefs, and an immoral lifestyle.

Palm Sunday the day one week before Easter when Jesus entered Jerusalem mounted on a donkey, to the acclaim of crowds waving palm branches (see John 12:12–15).

papyrus a cheap but brittle type of writing material made from plant fibers (plural, "papyri").

parable a figurative story or saying that conveys spiritual truth through reference to mundane and earthly phenomena.

Parables Discourse a speech by Jesus in Matthew 13 consisting primarily of parables and dealing with mysteries of the kingdom of heaven.

Paraclete a term for the Holy Spirit used in the Gospel of John and in 1 John, often translated in English Bibles as "Comforter," "Counselor," "Advocate," or "Helper."

parenesis a type of teaching that seeks to motivate or persuade.

parenetic containing advice, counsel, or exhortations intended to motivate or persuade.

parousia the second coming of Christ.

participation an understanding of justification according to which people of faith are united with Christ through baptism, participating in his death and ultimately in his resurrection.

passion in Christian theology, a term for the suffering and death of Jesus Christ.

pastoral concern concern for the physical, emotional, and spiritual well-being of persons for whom one feels responsible.

pastoral exhortation advice motivated by concern for the physical, emotional, and spiritual well-being of persons for whom one feels responsible.

Pastoral Letters (Epistles) the three letters addressed to colleagues of Paul entrusted with pastoral leadership of churches: 1 Timothy, 2 Timothy, Titus.

patron the benefactor in a patron-client relationship; the powerful party who provides benefits for others.

patron-client relationship a social system according to which people with power serve as benefactors to those lacking power, who are expected to respond with gratitude, service, and loyalty.

Pax Romana Latin phrase meaning "Roman peace"; a three-hundred-year period (including the New Testament era) during which the Roman Empire exercised such dominance within its geographical area that warfare with other nations was limited.

Pentateuch the first five books of the Bible: Genesis, Exodus, Leviticus, Numbers, Deuteronomy.

Pentecost a Jewish harvest festival at which, according to Acts 2, the Holy Spirit came upon 120 early followers of Jesus, empowering them for mission and causing them to speak in tongues.

persecution a program or campaign to exterminate, drive away, or subjugate people based on their membership in a religious, ethnic, or social group.

Pharisees one of the major Jewish groups active during the Second Temple period; the Pharisees were largely associated with synagogues and placed high value on faithfulness to Torah; most rabbis and many scribes were Pharisees.

phylactery a small case containing texts of Scripture worn on the forehead or left arm by pious Jews in obedience to Exodus 13:9, 16; Deuteronomy 6:8; 11:18.

Platonism a philosophical orientation that emphasized the reality of a transcendent world of "ideals" standing behind everything physical or earthly.

polytheism the belief that there are multiple gods. Compare "monotheism."

polyvalence multiple meanings; the capacity for a text to mean different things to different people or in different contexts.

postapostolic age the time period related to the first or second generation after the deaths of Jesus's first followers

postcolonial criticism a field of academic study that seeks to read texts from the perspective of marginalized and oppressed people.

post-Easter Jesus the exalted Jesus, who dwells in heaven and interacts spiritually with his followers through faith. Also called "exalted Jesus."

posthumous authorship a situation in which an author finishes or produces a composition that a mentor had intended to write, sending it posthumously in the mentor's name.

postmillennialism the belief or doctrine that Christ will return after the millennium: his faithful saints will successfully evangelize the world and rule it in peace for one thousand years before Christ's second coming.

postmodern philosophy a relativistic approach to life and thought that denies absolutes and objectivity.

posttribulationism a subset of premillennialism according to which the rapture will come after the tribulation, at the time of Jesus's second coming (so, even the faithful should expect to endure suffering prior to Christ's return).

praetorium a Roman governor's or general's headquarters

predestination the concept or doctrine that some or all events are predetermined by God, or that the destinies of individuals and nations may likewise be predetermined.

pre-Easter Jesus the earthly Jesus, who lived physically on earth for a period of time. Also called "earthly Jesus."

preexistence the Christian doctrine that the person now known as Jesus Christ existed (as the Son of God) before he became the man Jesus who lived and died on earth.

prefect in the Roman Empire, a magistrate or high official whose duties and level of authority varied in different contexts.

premillennialism the belief or doctrine that Christ will return before the millennium: his faithful saints will rule with him on earth for one thousand years after the second coming but prior to the final judgment and the establishment of the new kingdom.

pretribulationism a subset of premillennialism according to which a rapture will come prior to the onset of the tribulation (so, the unfaithful who are left behind will receive a wake-up call regarding what is now to come).

priests in Second Temple Judaism, people authorized to oversee the sacrificial system in the Jerusalem temple; closely associated with the Sadducees.

principalities powerful spiritual beings that exercise their influence in a dimension not perceptible to human senses.

Prison Letters (Epistles) the five letters attributed to Paul that are said to have been written from prison: Ephesians, Philippians, Colossians, 2 Timothy, Philemon. Also called "Captivity Letters (Epistles)."

proconsul a governor appointed by the Roman senate to administer a province for one year.

procurator a governor appointed by the Roman emperor to administer a province for an indefinite period of time.

proleptically anachronistic but anticipatory; one speaks proleptically when one speaks in a manner that has little meaning for present circumstances but will become more relevant in another time and place.

pronouncement story in the Gospels, an anecdote that is crafted to preserve the memory of something Jesus said.

prophetic acts unconventional public displays intended to reveal something that God wishes to communicate.

propitiation a term used in discussions of atonement to describe Christ's death as an act that placates the wrath of a God offended by human sin. See "expiation."

Protestant Reformation the religious movement of the sixteenth century that sought to reform the Roman Catholic Church and that led to the establishment of the Protestant churches.

pseudepigraphy "false ascription"; in New Testament studies, the practice of ancient authors attributing their own writings to other people, such as a revered teacher or prominent church leader who had influenced their thinking.

pseudonym a fictitious name used by an author instead of his or her real name; the author of a pseudepigraphic writing may be said to use a name such as "Paul," "Peter," or "James" as a pseudonym.

pseudonymous author an author who uses a pseudonym (fictitious name); the author of a pseudepigraphic writing.

Ptolemies Egyptian dynastic family that ruled Palestine during the years 320–198 BCE. See "Seleucids."

purity codes regulations derived from Torah that specified what was "clean" or "unclean" for the Jewish people, enabling them to live in ways that would mark them as distinct from the general population.

Pythagoreanism a philosophical orientation that emphasized the value of intelligent reasoning, memory, and radical honesty, all in service of a quest to attain harmony of ideas and of body and soul.

Q source according to the Two-Source Hypothesis, a now lost collection of Jesus's sayings that was used as a source for the Gospels of Matthew and Luke.

Qumran a site in Palestine near the Dead Sea where it is believed the Essenes had their monastic community; the Dead Sea Scrolls were found here.

rabbis Jewish teachers, many of whom had disciples or followers; closely associated with the Pharisees.

ransom the redemption of a prisoner or slave for a price; or, in Judaism, the offering of a substitute sacrifice.

rapture a miraculous removal of God's faithful from the earth, thought to be referenced in Matthew 24:40–41; 1 Thessalonians 4:15–17; Revelation 4:1.

reader-response criticism an academic approach that focuses on how texts might be understood by readers who engage them in different contexts.

realized eschatology the belief that blessings and benefits typically associated with the end times can be experienced as a present reality.

reconciliation an understanding of God's saving activity according to which, through Christ, people are placed in a right relationship with God and one another (Rom. 5:10–11; 2 Cor. 5:18–19).

redaction criticism an academic approach that tries to discern the intentions of authors by analyzing how they arranged and edited their source materials.

redemption a theological term derived from commerce (where it means "purchase" or "buying back"); associated with the concept that human salvation was costly to God, requiring the death of Jesus.

Reformation See "Protestant Reformation."

resurrection generally, life after death; more specifically, the post-death entrance of Jesus Christ or his followers into a new, transformed existence in which they will live forever.

revelation in theology, the disclosure (usually by God) of things that could not be known otherwise. See "mystery."

rhetorical criticism an academic approach that focuses on strategies employed by biblical authors to achieve particular purposes.

righteousness of God in Paul's writings, the essential quality of God comprising justice, faithfulness, love, and generosity, which God graciously imparts to others through faith, while also regarding them as already righteous in Christ.

Sabbath a day of the week set aside for worship and for rest from normal endeavors; for Jews, the Sabbath is the last day of the week (Saturday); for most Christians, it is the first (Sunday).

sacrament a ritual action (such as baptism or Holy Communion) through which God is believed to deliver divine benefits.

sacrifice in Second Temple Judaism, the offering of something valuable (e.g., crops from a field or an animal from one's flock) as an expression of worship.

Sadducees one of the major Jewish groups during the Second Temple period; the Sadducees were closely associated with the temple in Jerusalem and were concerned with maintaining the sacrificial system; most priests appear to have been Sadducees.

saints people who are holy; some New Testament writers use the word as a virtual synonym for "Christians," referring to those who through faith have been made holy in the eyes of God.

salutation a more-or-less formulaic phrase used to open a letter ("greetings" or "grace and peace"); often identifies the author and intended recipients.

salvation an act of God through which human beings are delivered from the power and consequences of sin.

Samaritans Semitic people who lived in Samaria at the time of Jesus and claimed to be the true Israel; descendants of the tribes taken into captivity by the Assyrians.

same-sex acts an ambiguous term that may refer to sexual acts engaged in by homosexuals, or to sexual acts engaged in by persons of the same sex regardless of whether they are homosexuals.

sanctification the act or process of being made holy or sinless.

Sanhedrin a ruling body of the Jewish people during the time of Roman occupation; composed of the high priest, chief priests, and other powerful Jewish leaders, the Sanhedrin was granted authority for matters of legislation that did not require direct Roman involvement.

scribes Jewish professionals skilled in teaching, copying, and interpreting Jewish law; closely associated with the Pharisees.

Scripture the sacred writings of a religion, believed to be inspired by God and viewed as authoritative for faith and practice.

second-career theory in Pauline studies, the notion that the apostle was released from captivity in Rome and went on to do things not reported in the New Testament before being recaptured and executed later than has traditionally been thought.

Second Temple Judaism a general term for the diverse culture, practices, and beliefs of Jewish people during the Second Temple period (515 BCE–70 CE).

Second Temple period the era in Jewish history between the dedication of the second Jerusalem temple in 515 BCE and its destruction in 70 CE.

Seleucids Syrian dynastic family that ruled Palestine during the years 198–167 BCE. See "Ptolemies."

Septuagint a Greek translation of the Old Testament produced during the last three centuries BCE. The Septuagint (abbreviated as "LXX") includes fifteen extra books that Protestants call the "Apocrypha" (eleven of these are classed as "deutero-canonical writings" by Roman Catholics).

Sermon on the Mount traditional name given to the teaching of Jesus in Matthew 5–7; it includes such well-known material as the Beatitudes, the Lord's Prayer, and the Golden Rule.

Sermon on the Plain traditional name given to the teaching of Jesus in Luke 6:20–49; it offers parallels to some of the material found in the better-known Sermon on the Mount (Matt. 5–7).

shame negative status, implying disgrace and unworthiness. See "honor."

Shema the central affirmation of Jewish faith. Based on Deuteronomy 6:4–9; 11:13–21; Numbers 15:37–41, it was recited daily. *Shema* is the Hebrew word for "Hear!"

signs in the New Testament, often a term for miracles, because they demonstrate a manifestation of supernatural power and sometimes reveal some truth about God; used especially in the Gospel of John.

signs and wonders spectacular acts (miracles) performed by people who access either divine or demonic supernatural power.

Signs Gospel according to some theories, a now lost book containing numbered miracle stories that may have served as a source for the Gospel of John.

sin any act, thought, word, or state of being contrary to the will of God.

Sitz im Leben German for "setting in life"; in biblical studies, the situation in which a biblical text would have been meaningful for the early church (e.g., liturgical worship, catechetical instruction).

Social Gospel movement a movement among American Protestant Christians in the latter half of the nineteenth century and early twentieth century claiming that faithfulness to the gospel of Jesus Christ necessitates work in the area of social reform, particularly with regard to living conditions among the urban working class.

social location a person's social identity in terms of factors such as age, gender, race, nationality, social class, and marital status.

sociological criticism academic approaches that draw on the social sciences to analyze New Testament documents in light of phenomena that characterized the social world in which they were produced.

source criticism an academic approach that tries to identify and sometimes reconstruct materials that the biblical authors used in composing their documents.

Southern Galatian Theory the theory that Paul wrote his letter to the Galatians to churches in southern Asia Minor prior to the Jerusalem council. See "Northern Galatian Theory."

speaking in tongues the phenomenon by which the Spirit enables a person to speak in known languages that the speaker has never learned (e.g., Acts 2:4–8) or in ecstatic languages unintelligible to any who do not possess the gift of interpretation (e.g., 1 Cor. 14:26–28). Also called "glossolalia."

spiritual gifts manifestations of the Holy Spirit activated by God in the lives of individuals for the common good.

steward a person who takes care of things that belong to someone else; theologically, human beings are stewards of all that belongs to God. See "stewardship."

stewardship caring for that which belongs to another; in Christianity, the term often applies to care of the earth, or to use of one's time, talents, or possessions. See "steward."

Stoicism a philosophical orientation that emphasized the attainment of virtue through acceptance of fate, based on the notion that all things are predetermined and that there is logic to all that transpires.

subsistence level a standard of living that enables one to survive, albeit with no surplus and with little margin.

substitution an understanding of atonement or justification according to which Jesus died on the cross to take the penalty for sin that humans rightly deserved.

super-apostles opponents of Paul in Corinth, discussed in 2 Corinthians; they apparently were rhetorically gifted and claimed that their abilities and successes marked them as more commendable leaders than Paul.

supersessionism the idea or teaching that Christians have replaced Jews as the chosen people of God.

synagogue a congregation of Jews who gather for worship, prayer, and Bible study, or the place where they gather for these purposes.

syncretism the combination or fusion of different religious or cultural beliefs and perspectives

Synoptic Gospels the Gospels of Matthew, Mark, and Luke, so-called because their overlapping content allows them to be viewed as books that offer parallel accounts.

Synoptic Puzzle / Synoptic Problem the question of the literary relationship between the Synoptic Gospels—for example, which ones used one or more of the others as a source.

systemic evil evil that arises from or manifests itself in structures within human society, assuming a corporate dimension that transcends individual wickedness.

tabernacle portable tent-shrine that housed the ark of the covenant and was used as the central place of worship for the Israelites prior to the construction of the temple in Jerusalem.

Talmud a collection of sixty-three books (including the Mishnah) that contain Jewish civil and canonical law based on interpretations of Scripture.

Targums Aramaic paraphrases of Scripture, widely used in Palestine among Jews who no longer knew Hebrew.

testament (1) a written account of a covenant—it is in this sense that parts of the Bible are called the "Old Testament" and the "New Testament"; (2) a genre of literature that provides a fictitious but pious account of a famous person's dying words, presented in a manner pertinent to present circumstances.

tetrarch a ruler of a quarter of a province or region.

text criticism academic study of available manuscripts that attempts to determine the most reliable reading of a document for which no original has been preserved.

theios anēr "divine man"; a person believed to have an especially close link to the spiritual realm and, typically, one to whom miracles are attributed.

theologia crucis See "theology of the cross."

theologia gloriae See "theology of glory."

theology of glory a way of understanding the gospel that views faith in Christ as a means to self-betterment, success, and the attainment of power. See "theology of the cross."

theology of the cross a way of understanding the gospel that views faith in Christ as an immersion into a life of service and sacrifice, marked by vulnerability and recognition of one's failings. See "theology of glory."

tongues, speaking in See "speaking in tongues."

Torah the law of Moses, as contained in the Pentateuch; or, frequently, a synonym for "Pentateuch" (referring, then, to the first five books of the Hebrew Bible).

transfiguration an event narrated in the Synoptic Gospels in which the physical appearance of Jesus is momentarily altered to allow his disciples a glimpse of his heavenly glory (Matt. 17:1–8; Mark 9:2–8; Luke 9:28–36).

transformation an understanding of God's saving activity according to which, through Christ, people are changed so that they evince or embody the image of God (Rom. 12:2; 2 Cor. 3:18).

triad a set of three.

tribulation a seven-year period of woes thought to be described in Revelation 6–9 and specifically mentioned in Daniel 9:27.

Trinity the Christian doctrine that God is "three in one," existing as only one God but also as three persons: Father, Son, and Holy Spirit.

Two-Gospel Hypothesis a minority solution to the Synoptic Puzzle/Problem, suggesting that Matthew was written first, Luke used Matthew, and Mark used both Matthew and Luke (eliminating need for the Q source). Also called the "Griesbach Hypothesis."

two natures of Christ the Christian doctrine that Jesus Christ was simultaneously fully divine and fully human.

Two-Source Hypothesis the dominant proposal that offers a solution to the Synoptic Puzzle/Problem: Mark was written first; Matthew and Luke each made use of a copy of Mark, and also each made use of a now lost source, called "Q." See "Four-Source Hypothesis."

unclean spirit a demon; a spiritual being that inhabits people and causes them to become sick or disabled.

undisputed letters the seven letters ascribed to Paul that almost all New Testament scholars affirm were actually written by him: Romans, 1 Corinthians, 2 Corinthians, Galatians, Philippians, 1 Thessalonians, Philemon.

variant in text criticism, an alternative reading of a text, supported by some manuscripts.

Via Egnatia a road constructed by the Romans in the second century BCE; it crossed the Roman provinces of Illyricum, Macedonia, and Thrace, running through territory that is now part of modern-day Albania, the Republic of Macedonia, Greece, and European Turkey.

Vulgate a Latin translation of the Bible produced by Jerome in the fourth century; it was virtually the only Bible used in western Christianity for over a thousand years.

"We Passages" texts in the book of Acts in which the author uses the first-person plural in his narration, indicating that he was with Paul and others at the time.

widow a woman whose husband has died; also, an office in the church that honored aged women who had no spouse or family by providing them with care in exchange for their prayers and spiritual counsel.

Wirkungsgeschichte German for "history of influence"; an academic discipline that documents and explains how texts have been read throughout history.

wisdom literature / wisdom tradition biblical and other ancient materials that focus on commonsense observations about life; examples include the books of Proverbs, Job, and Ecclesiastes.

womanist criticism an academic approach that seeks to understand texts from the perspective of African American women.

word of God proclamation that expresses what God wants to say; sometimes the Scriptures (a written record of what God wants to say); in John 1, Jesus Christ is identified as the Word of God made flesh.

words from the cross seven sayings of Jesus spoken during his crucifixion; see Mark 15:34 (Matt. 27:46); Luke 23:34, 43, 46; John 19:26–27, 28, 30.

works of the law (1) meritorious acts of human achievement (keeping command-ments, performing good works, etc.); or (2) covenant markers that identify Jews as belonging to God's chosen nation (circumcision, Sabbath observance, dietary restrictions, etc.).

Zealots radical anti-Roman Jews who advocated armed rebellion against the Roman forces.

Art Credits

Preface: Frontispiece *Cross 2* (2012) by Kume Bryant. **Chapter 1: Frontispiece** *Entry of Herod the Great* (c. 1470). Illumination by Jean Bourdicho. Photo © Tallandier. Bridgeman Images. **1.1** *Herod Orders the Slaughter of the Innocents* (5th c.). A. Dagli Orti. Bridgeman Images. **1.2** *Salome* (1974) by Romare Howard Bearden. Morris Museum of Art. Purchase made possible by The Passailaigue Acquisitions Fund. Bridgeman Images. **1.3** *Christ before Pontius Pilate* (1985) by Tamas Galambos. Hungarian National Gallery. Bridgeman Images. **1.4** *The Triumph of Truth* (1848) by Luigi Mussini. Mondadori Portfolio. Art Resource, NY. **1.6** *Archaic God of Bushes and Small Trees* (2009) by Gerhard Gronefeld. Private Collection. Bridgeman Images. **Chapter 2: Frontispiece** *Entry into Jerusalem* (1964–68) by Marc Chagall. © 2017 Artists Rights Society (ARS), New York. Chagall State Hall, Knesset. Lauros. Giraudon. The Bridgeman Art Library Nationality. **2.4** *Madonna of the Harvest* (2010) by John Swanson. **2.5** *Christ the Student* by Mickey McGrath. **2.6** *Ecstasy* by Randy Zucker. **Chapter 3: Frontispiece** Holy Bible depicted on stained glass. Photo by Godong/UIG. Bridgeman Images. **3.1** *Brother Isnardo of Vicenza* (1325) by Tommaso da Modena. Episcopal Seminary, the Chapter House of the Dominicans, Treviso. Bridgeman Images. **3.3** Rabbi Teaching Two Children (20th c.) by Dora Holzhandler. RONA Gallery. Bridgeman Images. **3.4** *Reading the Bible* (1859) by Hugues Merle. By kind permission of the Trustees of the Wallace Collection. Art Resource, NY. **Chapter 4: 4.2** *Músicos Tarahumaras* by Lalo Garcia. **4.3a** *African Madonna* by Rose Walton. **4.3b** Annunciation basilica. Photo by Godong/UIG. Bridgeman Images. **4.3c** *Madonna and Child*. Anonymous. National Trust Photo Library. Art Resource, NY. **4.5** *Christ in Glory*. De Agostini Picture Library. G. Dagli Orti. Bridgeman Images. **Chapter 5: Frontispiece** *The Evangelists' Symbols* (1997) by Manolis Grigoreas. Malvagallery.com. **5.1** *Jesus Driving Out the Unclean Spirit* (10th c.). Hessisches Landesmuseum Darmstadt. The Bridgeman Art Library International. **5.2** "Fol.70r." from *Codex de Predis* (15th c.) by the Italian School. Biblioteca Reale di Torino. Alinari. The Bridgeman Art Library International. **5.3** *Crucifixion* (1970) by Sadao Watanabe. Private Collection. Photo © Boltin Picture Library. The Bridgeman Art Library International. **5.5** "Image of St. Luke and St. John the Evangelists" from *Octateuch, Four Gospels and Synodicion* (17th c.) by the Ethiopian School. © British Library Board. Bridgeman Images. **Chapter 6: Frontispiece** *St. Matthew*. Osterreichische Nationalbibliothek Vienna. The Bridgeman Art Library International. **6.1** *The Three Magi*. The Keur Moussa abbey church, Thies, Senegal. Photo by Godong/UIG. Bridgeman Images. **6.2** *Flight into Egypt* by Nalini Jayasuriya. **6.3** *St. Peter, Storno* (16th c.) by the Hungarian School. Magyar Nemzeti Galeria. The Bridgeman Art Library International. **6.5** *St. Matthew* (1473) by Carlo Crivelli. Sant'Emidio, Ascoli Picena, Italy. The Bridgeman Art Library International. **6.6** *We the Peoples* (1984) by Ron Waddams. Private Collection. Bridgeman Images. **Chapter 7: Frontispiece** "1 fol.60v" from the *Ebbo Gospels* (816–835) by the French School. Bibliotheque Municipale Epernay. Giraudon. The Bridgeman Art Library International. **7.1** "The Paralytic of Capharnaum Is Lowered from the Roof" from *Scenes from the Life of Christ* (6th c.) by the Byzantine School. Sant'Apollinare Nuovo. Bridgeman Images. **7.2** Icon depicting Christ's entry into Jerusalem (17th c.) by the Russian School. Arkhangelsk Museum. The Bridgeman Art Library International. **7.3** *The Last*

Supper (19th c.). Alsace. Musee des Civilisations de l'Europe et de la Méditerranée. Photo by Jean-Gilles Berizzi. © RMN-Grand Palais. Art Resource, NY. **7.4** *Judas' Kiss* by Tamas Galambos. Private Collection. The Bridgeman Art Library International. **7.5** "Fol.149va" from *Codex de Predis* (15th c.) by the Italian School. Biblioteca Reale di Torino. Alinari. Bridgeman Images. **7.6** *Golgotha* (1900) by Edvard Munch. © 2017 Artists Rights Society (ARS), New York. Munch-museet, Oslo. Bridgeman Images. **7.7** *Women Arriving at the Tomb* by He Qi. He Qi Gallery. **Chapter 8: Frontispiece** "Ms 4 fol.101v St. Luke" from the *Gospel of St. Riquier* (9th c.) by the French School. Bibliotheque Municipale, Abbeville. The Bridgeman Art Library International. **8.1** Ecumenical community of Taizate in France. Photo by Godong/UIG. Bridgeman Images. **8.2** *Christ in the Stable* (20th c.) by C. Pal Molnar. Magyar Nemzeti Galeria. The Bridgeman Art Library International. **8.4** *The Solitude of Christ* (1918) by Maurice Denis. Private Collection. Bridgeman Images. **8.5** *Walk in the Park* (1989) by Laila Shawa. Private Collection. The Bridgeman Art Library International. **8.6** *Lazarus and the Rich Man* (15th c.) by the German School. The Barnes Foundation. Bridgeman Images. **8.7** *The Entombment* (20th c.) by Charles Filiger. Galerie Daniel Malingue. The Bridgeman Art Library International. **Chapter 9: Frontispiece** *Saint John the Apostle* by Mickey McGrath. **9.1** *The Miracle at Cana*, painting in a church. Photo by Godong/UIG. Bridgeman Images. **9.2** *Jesus and the Samaritan Woman* by He Qi. He Qi Gallery. **9.3** *Servant of All* by J. Kirk Richards. **9.4** *Christ of St. John of the Cross* (1951) by Salvador Dali. Art Gallery and Museum, Kelvingrove, Glasgow. © Glasgow City Council. The Bridgeman Art Library International. **9.5** *The Raising of Lazarus* (1970) by Sadao Watanabe. Private Collection. Photo © Boltin Picture Library. The Bridgeman Art Library International. **9.6** *Christ and Mary Magdalene (Noli Me Tangere)* (14th c.) by an unknown artist from the Byzantine-influenced Coptic school. De Agostini Picture Library. G. Dagli Orti. Bridgeman Images. **Chapter 10: Frontispiece** *The Awakening* (1996) by Peter Davidson. Private Collection. Bridgeman Images. **10.1** Mary and the apostles. Photo by Godong/UIG. Bridgeman Images. **10.2** *The Vision of St. Peter* (1913) by Margaret Gere. Private Collection. Photo © The Fine Art Society, London. Bridgeman Images. **10.3** *Calling St. Paul* by He Qi. He Qi Gallery. **10.5** *Paul, Silas and Timothy* (19th c.) by the French School. Private Collection. © Look and Learn. Bridgeman Images. **Chapter 11: Frontispiece** *St. Paul the Apostle* (17th c.) by Claude Vignon. Galleria Sabauda. Alinari. The Bridgeman Art Library International. **11.2** Fresco of a girl reading (1st c). Museo Archeologico Nazionale. Ken Welsh. Bridgeman Images. **Chapter 12:**

Frontispiece *St. Paul* (2001) by Manolis Grigoreas. Malva Gallery. **12.1** Carved ivory tablet of Thecla and Paul (11th c). Erich Lessing. Art Resource, NY. **12.3** "Ms 558 f.21v," detail from a missal (1430s) by Fra Angelico. Museo di San Marco dell'Angelico. The Bridgeman Art Library International. **12.5** *St Paul* (1468) by Marco Zoppo. Ashmolean Museum, University of Oxford. Bridgeman Images. **Chapter 13: Frontispiece** "The Crucifixion," a detail from *The Easter Painting* (1994) by Laura James. Private Collection. The Bridgeman Art Library International. **13.2** *Eve and Jesus* (1990) by Albert Herbert. Private Collection. England & Co. Gallery, London. The Bridgeman Art Library International. **Chapter 14: Frontispiece** *The Risen Lord* by He Qi. He Qi Gallery. **14.3** *Jordan's Quaker Meeting 2* (1993) by Ron Waddams. Private Collection. The Bridgeman Art Library International. **14.5** *Praising the Most High* (1992) Bernard Stanley Hoyes. Private Collection. Bridgeman Images. **Chapter 15: Frontispiece** *Crucifixion* (1999) by Craigie Aitchison. Private Collection. The Bridgeman Art Library International. **15.3** St. Paul escapes Damascus in a basket (12th/13th c.) mosaic. Ancient Art and Architecture Collection Ltd. The Bridgeman Art Library International. **Chapter 16: Frontispiece** *St. Paul the Apostle* (14th c.) by Martino de Bartolomeo. © York Museums Trust. The Bridgeman Art Library International. **16.1** Papyrus depicting circumcision, reconstructed relief from private funerary mastaba of Ankh-ma-Hor. De Agostini Picture Library. Bridgeman Images. **16.2** *SS. Peter and Paul Embracing* (12th c.) by the Byzantine School. The Bridgeman Art Library International. **16.3** *Loquats* (20th c.) by Qi Baishi. Private Collection. Bridgeman Images. **Chapter 17: Frontispiece** *Above the Village* (1999) by Peter Davidson. Private Collection. Bridgeman Images. **Chapter 18: Frontispiece** *The Crucifixion* (1910) by Odilon Redon. Musee d'Orsay. Giraudon. The Bridgeman Art Library International. **18.4** Panathenaic black figure depicting a foot race (5th c.). Musee Municipal Antoine Vivenel. Giraudon. The Bridgeman Art Library International. **Chapter 19: Frontispiece** *Tree, Sun and Rising Bird* (1989) by Peter Davidson. Private Collection. Bridgeman Images. **19.1** *Adam and Eve* (1962) by Suad Al-Attar. Private Collection. **19.3** *Resurrection Icon* (20th c.) by Sophie Hacker. Cotgrave Church. The Bridgeman Art Library International. **19.4** "Fol.44v" from *Codex de Predis* (15th c.) by the Italian School. Biblioteca Reale di Torino. Alinari. The Bridgeman Art Library International. **Chapter 20: Frontispiece** Resurrection icon. Photo by Godong/UIG. Bridgeman Images. **20.3** *The Painter of Uruapan* (1930) by Alfredo Ramos Martinez. © The Alfredo Ramos Martínez Research Project, reproduced by permission. Photo © Christie's Images. Bridgeman Images. **20.4** "Fol.120r" from

Codex de Predis (15th c.) by the Italian School. Biblioteca Reale di Torino. Alinari. The Bridgeman Art Library International. **Chapter 21: Frontispiece** *Ascension* (2000) by Laila Shawa. Private Collection. The Bridgeman Art Library International. **21.1** *Christ in Glory with the Saints* (1660) by Mattia Preti. Museo Nacional Del Prado. The Bridgeman Art Library International. **21.2** "Fol.154r" from *Codex de Predis* (15th c.) by the Italian School. Biblioteca Reale di Torino. Alinari. The Bridgeman Art Library International. **21.3** "The Preaching of the Antichrist," detail of *Christ and the Devil*, from the Chapel of the Madonna di San Brizio (1499–1504) by Luca Signorelli. Duomo di Orvieto. The Bridgeman Art Library International. **Chapter 22: 22.1** Timothy with his mother and grandmother. Photo by Bill Forbes. St. Mildred's Church. HIP. Art Resource, NY. **22.2** *No Tengan Miedo* (1999) by Xavier Cortada. Private Collection. Bridgeman Images. **22.3** Stained glass. Photo by Godong/UIG. Bridgeman Images. **Chapter 23: Frontispiece** *Jesus Dies on the Cross–Station 12* (2005) by Penny Warden. Blackburn Cathedral. The Bridgeman Art Library International. **23.2** "Joseph sold by his brothers" from a book of Bible Pictures (1250) by William de Brailes. Musee Marmottan Monet. Bridgeman Images. **23.3** Spartans bound, chained, and captured by the Athenians on Sphacteria in 425 BC during the Peloponnesian War (3rd c.). © Ashmolean Museum. The Bridgeman Art Library International. **Chapter 24: Frontispiece** *Christ Blessing* (10th–11th c.). Museo Lazaro Galdiano. Giraudon. The Bridgeman Art Library International. **24.1** *Christ and the Angels* (20th c.) by A. Bazile. Collection Manu Sassoonian. Art Resource, NY. **24.2** *The Sacrifice of Melchizedek* (1181) by Nicholas of Verdun. Erich Lessing. Art Resource, NY. **24.3** *Jesus Christ is our High Priest who unites earth with Heaven* (1993) by Elizabeth Wang. Private Collection. © Radiant Light. Bridgeman Images. **Chapter 25: 25.1** Bas relief of a hairdresser (2nd c.). Rheinisches Landesmuseum. The Bridgeman Art Library International. **25.2** *Head of Christ* (1993) by Sophie Hacker. Private Collection. The Bridgeman Art Library International. **25.3** Tapestry in Saint-Pierre of Solesmes Abbey. Photo by Godong/UIG. Bridgeman Images. **25.4** *Jesus Healing the Crippled and the Blind* (12th c.) by the Byzantine School. Monreale Duomo. Giraudon. The Bridgeman Art Library International. **Chapter 26: Frontispiece** *St. Peter*, side panel from the altar of the Church of San Pere, Oros (13th c.) by the Spanish School. Museu Nacional d'Art de Catalunya. Giraudon. The Bridgeman Art Library International. **26.1** *St. Peter*, from

the crypt of St. Peter (8th c.) by the Byzantine School. St. Peter's Basilica. The Bridgeman Art Library International. **26.2** Catacombs of the Good Shepherd. Photo by Godong/UIG. Bridgeman Images. **26.3** "The Harrowing of Hell," a detail from *The Easter Painting* (1994) by Laura James. Private Collection. The Bridgeman Art Library International. **Chapter 27: 27.1** "St. Peter," detail from the *Sant'Emidio polyptych* (1473) by Carlo Crivelli. Ascoli Piceno Cathedral. The Bridgeman Art Library International. **27.2** *Hell* (15th c.) by Hieronymus Bosch. Hermitage, St. Petersburg. The Bridgeman Art Library International. **Chapter 28: Frontispiece** *Christ Enthroned* (12th c.) by the Russian School. Private Collection. Photo © Boltin Picture Library. Bridgeman Images. **28.1** *The Posillipo Cave at Naples* (18th c.) by Hubert Robert. Musee Jeanne d'Aboville. Lauros. Giraudon. The Bridgeman Art Library International. **28.2** *The Incredulity of St. Thomas* (17th c.) by Giovanni Francesco Barbieri. Vatican Museums and Galleries. The Bridgeman Art Library International. **28.3** *Fields of Forgiveness* (20th c.) by Fred Yates. Private Collection. The Bridgeman Art Library International. **Chapter 29: Frontispiece** *Judgement* (13th c.) by the Master of Soriguel. Catalan art. De Agostini Picture Library. G. Dagli Orti. Bridgeman Images. **29.1** "The Last Judgement," detail of *The Damned in Hell* (11th–12th c.) by the Veneto-Byzantine School. Cathedral of Santa Maria Assunta. Cameraphoto Arte Venezia. The Bridgeman Art Library International. **29.2** The end of the world and the Last Judgment. All houses and villages be destroyed. 6th time. (1476) by Cristoforo de Predis. Biblioteca Reale di Torino. Photo © Tarker. Bridgeman Images. **Chapter 30: 30.1** *The Heavenly Militia* (14th c.) by Ridolfo di Arpo Guariento. Museo Civico, Padua. Alinari. The Bridgeman Art Library International. **30.2** *Study for Improvisation V* (1910) by Wassily Kandinsky. Minneapolis Institute of Arts. Gift of Bruce B. Dayton. Bridgeman Images. **30.3** Spain: The Angel gives John the letter for the Church of Ephesus. Apocalypse II. From the Escatorial Beatus version of the Apocalypse (10th c.). Pictures from History. Bridgeman Images. **30.5** *St. John on Patmos* (14th or 15th c.) by Juan Mates. Musee Goya, Castres. Bridgeman Images. **30.7** "Ms 870 Fol.8" from *La Somme le Roy* (13th c.) by Frere Laurent, illuminated by Maitre Honore. Bibliotheque Mazarine. Archives Charmet. The Bridgeman Art Library International. **30.8** *To God Be the Glory. Rev. 5:1-14* (1950) by Peter Attie "Charlie" Besharo. Ricco/Maresca Gallery. Art Resource, NY. **Art Credits: Frontispiece** *Heavenly Cross* (2007) by Lee Davis.

Index

Paul and, 151–52, 213, 254, 296–97
  salvation and, 178–80, 372
  theology of, 320–21
  words from, 164, 192
cultural anthropology, 67
culture
  biblical scholarship and, 67, 70
  Christians and, 423, 488–89, 492–93
  corruption in, 488–89
  Jesus and, 85
  Roman, 31–34
Cybele, 374
Cynicism, 25

date, authorship and, 244–45
day of the Lord. *See* parousia, the
deacon, 359, 420–21
Dead Sea Scrolls, 25
death, 281–82, 295, 397–400, 516
deconstruction, 72
defense, letters of, 236
delay of the parousia, 177–78, 405–7, 408–9,
  502–3. *See also* parousia, the
delegated authorship, 240
delivery, epistolic, 234
Demas, 432
Demiurge, the, 29
demons, 84, 103, 104
deuterocanonical writings, 52–53
deutero-Pauline letters, 238–39
Diaspora, 50. *See also* Dispersion
Diatessaron, 116. *See also* distinctive, Gospels as
diatribe, 25, 464
dictation, 240
Didache, 461, 477
didactic letters, 236
Diolkos, 292
Diotrephes, 519
disadvantaged, ministry to the, 174–75, 222
disciples, the
  failure of, 156–57
  in John's Gospel, 186–89, 202
  in Luke and Acts, 169, 180, 227
  in Mark's Gospel, 156–57
  in Matthew's Gospel, 127, 135–36
discipleship, 132, 135–36, 155, 156–59
discussions, topical, 237
Dispersion, 466, 484, 490. *See also* Diaspora
disputed letters of Paul, 238–41, 250, 346, 347–
  48. *See also individual letters*
distinctive, Gospels as, 116, 125–29, 147–50,
  166–72, 191–94
dividing wall, 350

divination, 28
divine, Jesus as. *See* two natures of Christ
divine men, 28–29
divisions, church. *See* conflict, church; schism;
  unity, church
divorce, 155, 302
docetism, 514–15
doctrine, 421–24
dominions, 349
Domitian, 541, 545
double-minded, 461, 471, 474–75
doublet, 119
doubt, faith and, 135–36
doxology, 237
dualism, 29–31, 53, 518, 535–37

earthly Jesus, the, 78–89, 150–51, 452–53, 514–15
Easter, 80. *See also* resurrection, the
ecclesiology, 351. *See also* church, the
ecology, 384
economy, Roman, 31–32
effective righteousness, 280
elder, office of, 420–21
elder, the, 508–9, 510, 511
election, 157
elemental spirits of the universe. *See* demons
emendation analysis, 69
emperor worship, 27
encouragement, letters of, 236
ending, Mark's, 148–49
Enoch, Book of, 524
environment, the, 384
Epaphras, 375, 432
Epaphroditus, 362, 365
Ephesians, 339–55
Ephesus, city of, 341–42
Epicureanism, 25
Erastus, 293, 318
Eschatological Discourse, the, 131
eschatology
  the future and, 155–56, 550
  Paul's, 254, 297–99, 333–34, 397–400
  realized, 177–78, 353–55, 380–81
  See also judgment; parousia, the
Essenes, 25, 44–46
ethics, 300–303, 352, 353, 354, 396–97
Eucharist, the, 265, 299–300
Euodia, 368
euphemism, Paul's use of, 438
evangelism, 99, 380
evil, systemic, 548–49
exalted Jesus, the, 78–80, 90–92, 150–51, 196–
  97, 378–80

excluded, ministry to the, 174–75, 222
excommunication, 300–301
excuse, letters of, 236
exegesis, 72–74
exhortation, 236, 467
exiles, 491
exodus, the, 122
exorcism, 84, 103, 104
expiation, 265, 516
eyesight, Paul's, 328

faith
  apostolic, 527–28
  as basic teaching, 447
  doubt and, 135
  justification by, 278–79, 332–36
  love, hope, and, 393
  obedience and, 279–80, 284–85
  patronage and, 33
  works and, 471–73
family, Jesus's, 169
family, the church as, 394
Farewell Discourse, 189
Farrer Theory, 113, 115–16
fear, faith and, 135–36
Felix, procurator, 23
fellowship, 367–68
feminist criticism, 70–71, 72
fertility, 27
Festus, procurator, 23
fig tree, barren, 503
fire, judgment by, 503
five speeches of Jesus, 128, 131–32
food, 173, 303–4
footrace, faith as, 366
foot-washing, 194
forgery, 241, 242
forgiveness, 81, 372
format, epistolic, 234–38
form criticism, 69
Four-Source Hypothesis, 110–15
freedom, 265, 299
friendship, 236, 362–63, 367
fruit of the Spirit, 336
fulfillment, 147, 216–17
fulfillment citation, 128
functions, epistolic, 236–37
fundraising, Paul's, 258, 275–76, 315
futurist reading, Revelation and, 537, 539–40,
  541, 542–43, 544

Gaius, 293
Galatians, 323–27

gaps in the record theory, 418, 420
gematria, 539, 541
gender
  in Ephesians, 354
  in Luke's Gospel, 174–75
  ministry and, 420–21, 424, 425
  in Romans, 276, 277
  work and, 48
General or Catholic Letters (Epistles), 61, 232
generosity, Lukan, 222
genre
  apocalyptic, 535–37, 542
  biographical, 214–15
  epistolic, 234–38, 534, 542
  friendship letter, 362–63
  Gospel, 96–99
  historiographical, 212–14
  parenetic, 419, 485
  prophetic, 534–35, 542
  sermon, 445–46
  testament, 499–500
  treatise, 344–47, 465–66, 509
  See also individual writings
gentiles
  Judaism and, 49–50, 254
  mission to the, 219–20, 333, 350
gifts, spiritual, 226, 305–6, 336
giving. See fundraising, Paul's
Gloria in Excelsis, the, 170
glorification, 196–97, 265
glory, 186, 320–21
glossolalia, 305–6
gnosticism, 29–31, 64–65, 374, 512–13
God
  as father, 131
  history and, 216
  Israel and, 282–83
  in James, 468
  Jesus and, 91–92, 128, 129, 194–96, 451–52
  judgment and, 548, 550
  as love, 507, 518
  ministry and, 314, 319–20
  mystery and, 349–51
  righteousness of, 277–78
God-fearers, 49
godliness, 503–4
Golden Rule, 89
Gomorrah, 527
gospel, 264–67
Gospel of Thomas, 463
Gospels, the
  characteristics of, 60
  genre of, 96–99

Paul, the apostle
  in Acts, 207–9, 250–52, 254–55, 258–61,
    326–27
  age of, 437
  authority of, 312, 316–19, 329–32
  authorship and, 233–34, 238–41
  gentiles and, 49
  James and, 471–72
  journeys of, 258–59, 263, 326–27, 342, 374–75
  Judaism and, 249–52, 260, 266, 275–76, 392
  life of, 249–63
  ministry of, 314, 319–20
  as missionary, 255–61, 275, 317
  theology of, 254, 264–67
  wit of, 438
  See also individual Pauline letters
Pax Romana, 34, 35
pens, writing, 232
Pentateuch, the, 138
perfection, Hebrews on, 453
persecution
  in Bithynia-Pontus, 494
  discipleship and, 158–59, 411, 546–47
  Paul and, 249, 252, 254, 258, 260–61
Persian period, 40
persuasion, use of, 438
Peter, First Letter of, 479–94
Peter, Second Letter of, 497–505
Peter, the apostle
  in Acts, 227
  authorship and, 480–81, 493–94
  in the Gospels, 123, 125, 144, 202
  Paul and, 295, 329–32
Petrine perspective, 482–83
Pharisees, 42–43, 44, 249. *See also* leaders,
  religious
Philemon, 375, 431–41
Philippi, city of, 359–60
Philippians, 357–69, 378
Philo, 449
philosophy, 24–26
Phoebe, 277
phylactery, 17
Pilate, Pontius, 23
pilgrims, Christians as, 456–57, 459
Platonism, 25, 449
Pliny the Younger, 436
Plutarch, 319
polemic, 329
polyvalence, 70
Pontius Pilate, 23
poor, the. *See* poverty
postcolonial criticism, 71–72

post-Easter Jesus, 80. *See also* exalted Jesus
posthumous authorship, 240
postmillennialism, 544
postmodern philosophy, 72
posttribulationism, 544
posture, body, 355
poverty
  in James, 473–76
  the Lord's Supper and, 299–300
  in Luke and Acts, 174–75, 222
  in the Roman era, 31–32, 34–35
power, 296, 492
praise, letters of, 236
prayer, 172, 236, 237, 355, 400
preaching, 81–83, 155–56
pre-Easter Jesus, 80. *See also* earthly Jesus, the
preexistence, 195, 451
prefect, 23
premillennialism, 544
presence, authorial, 245
presence, God's, 128, 129–31, 222–23
present, historical, 147–48
pretribulationism, 544
priests, 43–44, 490
Prisca, 277
Priscilla, 293, 448
Prison Letters or Captivity Letters (Epistles),
  232, 263
probability, intrinsic, 242–43
Problem, Synoptic, 109–16
process, epistolic, 232–34
proclamation. *See* preaching
procurator, 23
promises, God's, 216–17
pronouncement stories, 104–6
prophecy, genre of, 534–35, 542
prophetic acts, 84
prophets, Jesus and the, 83
propitiation, 516
Protestant Reformation, 271, 286–87, 336
provision miracles, 103
pseudepigraphic composition theory, 419, 420
pseudepigraphy, 238–45, 499–500
Ptolemies, 40
pun, Paul's use of, 438
purity codes, 54–57, 155
Puzzle, Synoptic, 109–16
Pythagoreanism, 25, 374

Q source, 111–15
Qumran community, 134, 202

rabbis, 43
ransom, 152

rapture, the, 398, 544
reader-response criticism, 70
realized eschatology, 177–78, 353–55, 380–81.
    See also eschatology
recommendation, letters of, 236
reconciliation, 265, 279
redaction criticism, 69, 188–89
redemption, 265, 279
Reformation. *See* Protestant Reformation
religion, Roman era, 26–31
reminders, evangelical, 388, 393
repentance, 447
report, letters of, 236
respectability, social, 423, 488–89
response, letters of, 236
rest, salvation as, 455–56
restrainer, the, 409
resurrection, the
    bodily, 297–99
    death and, 281–82, 447
    of Jesus, 80, 107–8
resuscitation miracles, 103
revelation, 194–96, 252–53
Revelation, book of, 61, 531–51
rhetorical criticism, 70, 284
rich, the, 31–32, 175, 473–75. *See also* inequality,
    economic
righteousness
    effective, 280, 281
    faith and, 280
    God's, 277–78
    imputed, 280, 281
    lived, 503–4
Roman Empire, the
    period of, 17–35, 41
    in Revelation, 546–47, 548
    slavery in, 34–35, 432–37
Romans, letter to the, 271–87, 378
rubbish, Christ and, 366
rule, Roman. *See* government, Roman
rulers, 349
running, faith as, 366
rural, Jesus's ministry as, 81

sacrifice, 454–55
Sadducees, 43–44. *See also* leaders, religious
salutation, epistolic, 235
salvation
    atonement and, 515–16
    Jesus and, 223–24, 265
    present, 177–80, 197–98
    as rest, 455–56
    universal, 280–81, 333, 335, 337, 350

Samaritans, 46–49
same-sex acts. *See* homosexual acts
sanctification, 265, 280
sandwich, literary, 148
Sanhedrin, 44
Satan, dualism and, 53
Saul, Paul as, 251. *See also* Paul, the apostle
sayings, individual, 106–7, 115, 464–65
schism, 511–14, 518–20
scholarship, biblical, 66–72, 242–44
scribes, 43. *See also* amanuensis
Scripture, 63, 132–38
seated, believers as, 355
secessionists, Johannine, 511–14, 518–20
second-career theory, 244, 262, 263, 418–20
second coming, the. *See* eschatology; parousia,
    the
Second Temple period, 249
secrecy, Mark's, 149–50, 152–55
secretary. *See* amanuensis
sectarianism, John's Gospel and, 202–3
Seleucids, 40
self-commendation, 319–20
Septuagint, 52–53, 445
Sermon on the Mount, 131–32
Sermon on the Plain, 171
seven letters, the, 538–40
sexual morality, 276, 300–303, 396–97. *See also*
    ethics; marriage
shame, 33–34, 395–96, 424–25, 457
sharing, friendship and, 367
sheep, the church as, 490
Shema, 43
sicarii, 46
signs, 227, 260. *See also* miracles
Signs Gospel, 190, 191
Silas, 208, 293, 486
Silvanus. *See* Silas
Simon ben Kosiba, 35
sin
    grace and, 285, 337
    judgment and, 81, 527
    paradox of, 516
    temptation and, 467–69
slavery, 34–35, 383, 432–37, 439–40
Social Gospel movement, 476
society
    biblical scholarship and, 66–67
    Christians and, 423, 488–89, 492–93
    corruption in, 548–49
    Jesus and, 85
    location in, 70
    Roman, 31–34

weak, the, 284–85, 296, 303–4, 314, 319–20
wealth, 31–32, 175, 473–75. *See also* inequality, economic
We Passages, 163–64, 209
widow, office of, 420–21, 425
Wirkungsgeschichte, 70
wisdom
  the cross and, 296
  in James, 469–71
  literature, 464, 465
  theology, 53
  tradition, 83, 196, 452, 464–65
wit, Paul's, 438
wives, 492–93. *See also* marriage
woman, the church as a, 490
womanist criticism, 70–71, 72

women
  as disadvantaged, 174–75
  household codes and, 354, 492–93
  ministry and, 277, 368, 420–21, 424, 425
  work and, 48
wonders, 227, 260. *See also* miracles
word count, epistolic, 237–38
wordplay, Paul's use of, 438
words from the cross, 164
work, 48, 397, 409–10
works of the law, 332–37, 447, 471–73
world, the, 129–31, 199–201
worship, 60, 121, 135–36, 172, 550
wrath, God's, 392, 548. *See also* judgment

Zealots, 35, 46